MODERN THINGS ON TRIAL

Islam's Global and Material Reformation in the Age of Rida, 1865–1935

LEOR HALEVI

Columbia University Press
New York

Columbia University Press
Publishers Since 1893
New York   Chichester, West Sussex
cup .columbia .edu

Library of Congress Cataloging-in-Publication Data
Names: Halevi, Leor, author.
Title: Modern things on trial : Islam's global and material reformation in the age of Rida, 1865–1935 / Leor Halevi.
Description: New York, NY : Columbia University Press, [2019] | Includes bibliographical references and index.
Identifiers: LCCN 2018056100 | ISBN 9780231188661 (cloth) | ISBN 9780231547970 (e-book)
Subjects: LCSH: Islamic modernism. | Islamic countries—Civilization. | Muslims—Intellectual life. | Islam and science. | Muḥammad Rashīd Riḍā.
Classification: LCC BP166.14.M63 H356 2019 | DDC 909/.09767—dc23
LC record available at https: //lccn .loc .gov /2018056100

Cover design: Elliott S. Cairns

CONTENTS

MAPS AND FIGURES

ACKNOWLEDGMENTS

To write this global history of modern Islam, I have ventured far from the period and regions on which I focused in my first book, *Muḥammad's Grave: Death Rites and the Making of Islamic Society*, after years of training as a medievalist. In that book, I concentrated on the rise of Islamic death rites in the Arabian Peninsula, Mesopotamia, and the Eastern Mediterranean in the seventh and eighth centuries. The present book deals with modern Muslim perceptions of consumption, technology, and trade not only in these regions but far beyond them, too, in countries as remote as Argentina, Russia, and China. To learn about times and places that I knew nothing about when I began researching for this book took many more years than I originally anticipated, and I would never have completed this historical journey without a tremendous amount of support from multiple sources.

In particular, I would like to acknowledge the fellowships that I received from the National Endowment for the Humanities; the American Council of Learned Societies; L'Institut d'études avancées de Paris (IEA); and the Wissenschaftskolleg zu Berlin (WIKO). These institutes and agencies allowed me to research, write, and wander far afield in optimal conditions. They provided essential funding and, in Paris and Berlin, the stimulating company of fellows from many different countries and disciplines. I especially enjoyed my year in Paris, where the director of the IEA at the time, the wonderful Gretty Mirdal, took pity on me for occupying a small office next to a construction site and allowed me for a few months to use Baudelaire's apartments in the Hôtel de Lauzun, overlooking the Seine. It was also a privilege to spend a year at the WIKO, whose librarians enjoyed fulfilling my requests for rare books.

Conversations and exchanges with many colleagues shaped this book in different ways. In 2009 I presented to the Vanderbilt History Seminar a paper on the fatwas of Rashīd Riḍā about toilet paper, gramophones, and few other things. At the time, I thought that this paper would become a single chapter of a monograph that would survey fatwas about technological objects from the origins of Islam to the present day. My colleagues' unanswered questions motivated me to dig deeper; eventually the chapter turned into a book. Fellows at IEA and WIKO offered me excellent reading suggestions. Discussants on panels and participants in workshops challenged my interpretations and spurred me to revisit my sources. I often had to turn to experts on various regions for advice, especially when I needed assistance in identifying an individual fatwa seeker or understanding the historical context behind a local religious dispute. The list of scholars who helped me along the way is long. I have made an effort to acknowledge specific contributions in the notes, but I would like to mention here my thanks to Gabriel Abend, Doris Behrens-Abouseif, Jane Burbank, Nicholas Cronk, Barry Flood, Michael Gordin, Gudrun Krämer, Frédéric Lagrange, Jonathan Lipman, Muhammad Khalid Masud, Matsumoto Masumi, Roger Owen, A. J. Racy, Gregg Starrett, Tony Stewart, David Wasserstein, and Kosugi Yasushi.

Two research assistants, Lu Sun and Chin-Ting Huang, interpreted for me a few Chinese texts, including translations of Arabic fatwas. The fruits of this research appear in a recent article on which I draw in this book: "Is China a House of Islam? Chinese Questions, Arabic Answers, and the Translation of Salafism from Cairo to Canton, 1930–1932," *Die Welt des Islams* 59 (2009).

Several people assisted me with the illustrations and maps. Erin Greb, a freelance cartographer, designed the map of fatwa seekers. Ola Seif, the curator of the American University of Cairo's photograph collection, shared her knowledge of Cairo postcards with me, and she helped me to obtain reproductions. Spink & Sons allowed me to reproduce the image of the banknote that graces the cover. Chris Strasbaugh and Shelby Merritt of Vanderbilt University photographed and scanned dozens of images for me.

The anonymous, learned readers of this manuscript for Columbia University Press made incredibly helpful and insightful suggestions for revision. Mary Bridges, a graduate student in U.S. history in my department, line edited the entire manuscript and explained to me how to make the text more accessible. Patti Bower copyedited my revised submission with outstanding diligence and meticulous attention to inconsistencies. Robert Swanson and his colleagues at Arc Indexing compiled the index. Wendy Lochner, my editor at Columbia University Press, and her team were a pleasure to work with.

I am grateful to my mentors, Michael Cook and Roy Mottahedeh, for supporting this project and my career and for their patience and encouragement.

I hope they will recognize traces of medievalism in this book, however modern its subject.

My family accompanied me to Paris and Berlin for the sabbaticals when I worked on this book. Together we overcame many challenges and had great adventures abroad. I am so thankful to my children, Naomi, Nathaniel, and Joshua, for accompanying me on these journeys, for their understanding, and for their love. All too often I have had to work long days and strange hours to finish this book, and I am extremely grateful to my wife, Lauren Clay, for allowing me to do that. She has been generous with her time and talents, and I have been fortunate to have her support.

Through their own personal stories, my parents, Bracha Gams-Shauli and Peter Halevi, made me curious about cultures other than my own, and they always encouraged me and my sisters to discover new worlds through reading and traveling. I am happy to dedicate this book to them.

MODERN THINGS ON TRIAL

Prologue

The Parable of the *Montgolfière* and the Translation of Haleby's Corpse

It happened but a few hours before the great dog massacre that a crowd gathered around Birkat al-Azbakiyya, a large pond in Cairo, to see a marvelous new French invention. The French had just ordered the evacuation of houses in the neighborhood to build their own separate quarter. They had seized precious household possessions, gem-encrusted daggers, and other weapons from the homes of Mamluk officials; and at nighttime, according to a rumor that circulated in the city, a rabble of soldiers had broken into the shops by one of Cairo's historic gates to pilfer processed sugar.[1] For weeks the city had been in great turmoil. To put down a jihadi rebellion, French soldiers had stormed into al-Azhar Mosque without bothering to remove their shoes. While they plundered from the mosque every material object that they considered valuable, they trampled upon copies of the Qur'an and other Muslim books—or so alleged an Azhari *shaykh*—as if these sacred things had no value at all. Previously, ʿAbd al-Raḥmān al-Jabartī, the scholar who chronicled this event, had dismissed with incredulity Napoleon Bonaparte's claim that the French were faithful Muslims. Now he concluded that they were "the religion's enemies."[2]

To relieve the tense atmosphere and lift subdued spirits, the French decided to impress their new subjects with a demonstration of the latest technology. They placed printed posters in the city's marketplaces announcing that on the tenth day of Frimaire, year 7 of the Republican era, they would make "a craft fly . . . in the air by means of a strategic device that belongs to the French nation." On that Friday afternoon, which coincided with November 30, 1798 CE, and Jumāda II, AH 1213, al-Jabartī headed toward the pond together with the masses, whose enthusiasm for this "wondrous thing" he found beneath him. Then he beheld the object. He noticed first a woven fabric suspended from a pole and bearing the colors of the French Republic. He noticed, too, precisely how this pole fit into a cylindrical vessel that also housed a bowl with a wick soaking in oil. Soldiers—surely members of the Compagnie d'aérostiers, the first air force in the history of the world—perched themselves on surrounding rooftops to hold the ropes that were tied to the vessel in order to assist and control its ascent upon ignition. It was of course a hot air balloon, a *machine aérostatique.*

Soon the machine swelled up and it began to fly—without a pilot on board. This happened, according to al-Jabartī's conception, because the smoke that filled the balloon wanted to rise higher but found no way to escape, propelling the vehicle skyward. Unfortunately, the balloon soared for only a short while. With the wind blowing, a hoop that probably served to fasten the net of ropes knocked the wick down and the balloon collapsed, crashing like Icarus to the ground. "The French were ashamed at its fall," gloated al-Jabartī. They were unable to prove their claim that this was a craft upon which troops could sit to travel to various countries so as to gather intelligence or investigate reports. Instead, their machines turned out to be "like the kites that carpet-spreaders manufacture for festivals and celebrations."[3] Dejected, deflated, the French soldiers patrolling the streets that night grew irritated at all the barking dogs and gave them poisoned bread; the next morning Cairenes woke up to find scores of canine carcasses in the marketplace.

French troops had deeper reasons to be disappointed in the performance. Before the invasion of Egypt, the Compagnie d'aérostiers had experimented and trained with hydrogen balloons (known as *charlières*) as vehicles for military reconnaissance. To observe and intimidate the enemy, their plan had been to move tethered balloons, directed by earth-bound pilots, toward the battlefield. Maybe they had entertained visions of a beautiful ascension and an orderly march upon Cairo: a triumphant parade resembling the 1796 movement of the aircraft *L'Entreprenant* toward Augsburg during the Revolutionary Wars.

But the translation of things rarely works out overseas in accordance with the schemes laid at home. No sooner had Napoleon's troops disembarked in Alexandria than *le Patriote*, the ship that transported scientific instruments, iron filings for producing hydrogen, and other balloon-making tools, foundered after striking a rock. A month later, set on curbing their rival's ambitions for overseas expansion, the British Royal Navy attacked the French fleet anchored at Abū Qīr Bay; the warship *l'Orient*, which carried the rest of the air force's supplies, exploded sensationally after catching fire. Once they installed themselves in Cairo under the direction of Nicolas-Jacques Conté, the celebrated inventor of the aerostatic telegraph and an expert craftsman in the art of balloon making, French engineers were forced to improvise, to tinker like bricoleurs with the materials at hand.[4] At Birkat al-Azbakiyya that day, as well as on maybe two

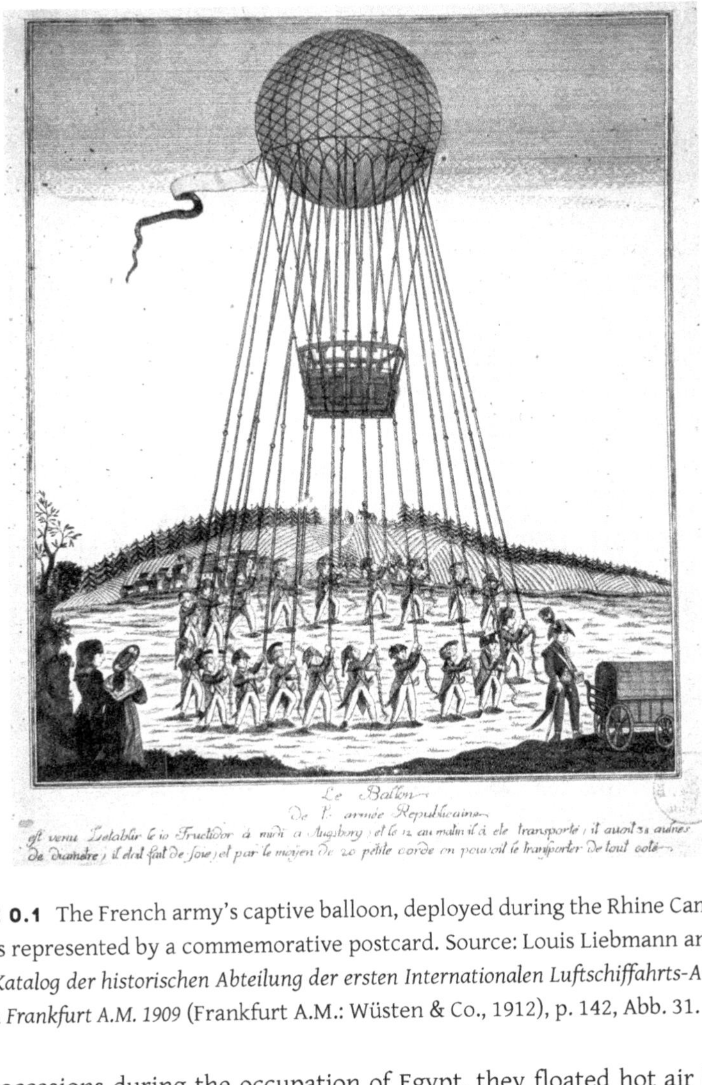

FIGURE 0.1 The French army's captive balloon, deployed during the Rhine Campaign of 1796, as represented by a commemorative postcard. Source: Louis Liebmann and Gustav Wahl, *Katalog der historischen Abteilung der ersten Internationalen Luftschiffahrts-Ausstellung (ILA) zu Frankfurt A.M. 1909* (Frankfurt A.M.: Wüsten & Co., 1912), p. 142, Abb. 31.

other occasions during the occupation of Egypt, they floated hot air balloons (known as *montgolfières*) merely for show during festivals and parades. They never succeeded in launching a hydrogen balloon in Egypt. On his return to France, no longer so excited by the dream of this military technology's potential, Napoleon disbanded the balloon corps.[5]

Masking their own disappointment with signs of hubris, the French began to reflect on local perceptions of their modern invention. A week after the event in their official newspaper, the *Courier de l'Égypte*, they related that the local inhabitants had gazed at the vehicle with incredulity, refusing to "believe in the possibility" of flight, until French engineers produced a spectacle that filled them with admiration. Made of paper, this tricolor balloon caught fire, and as it started to descend in flames the Egyptian spectators grew terrified. Fleeing from the scene, they concluded that it was a new "instrument of war, which we would know how to direct at will and which we use to burn our enemies' cities."[6] A few weeks later, in commemoration of a key battle, the French celebrated by inflating a large canvas *montgolfière*, which flew successfully and landed gently. But the *Courier de l'Égypte* now found striking that "the natives" appeared absolutely incurious. To find examples of such "extraordinary indifference," the newspaper's editor indulged in a bit of cross-cultural anthropology. He compared apathetic Egyptians to the Chinese fishermen and the Maori tribesmen who showed no reaction whatsoever—perplexingly—upon first encountering the things that European explorers considered so very impressive: the sight of Lord Anson's flagship, the sound of Capt. James Cook's firing cannon.[7] The image of terrified Egyptians, desperate to escape from the French machine, became the standard description of the event.[8]

Other members of the expedition also contributed their own hazy remembrances. From the confines of Saint Helena, Napoleon reminisced about the flight of Conté's balloon, launched to celebrate the New Year of the Republic with muftis and shaykhs. Forgetting to mention that the festival had been postponed by many weeks due to material difficulties, Napoleon described how the aircraft flew toward Libya's desert and disappeared. He then mused about a popular rumor, which held that the balloon functioned as a medium for the Sultan El-Kébir (Bonaparte himself) to communicate with Mahomet.[9] The army's chief surgeon, Dominique-Jean Larrey, claimed that Muslims imagined a causal link between the balloon's ascension and the dog massacre. Too many dogs, he explained, disturbed the French cavalry as it tried to march through the city's streets. Yet, because these beasts were "the object of the inhabitants' veneration," the French decided to feed them meat laced with poison nut, under the cover of night. When the townspeople woke up to the sight of dead dogs, they did not complain. They believed that, by God's will, the flammable gas that they had observed entering the balloon as it sailed westward had caused the death of the revered creatures.[10]

The famous Egyptologist Edme-François Jomard devoted a few pages of his biography of Conté to Cairo's balloons. "We are familiar," he reflected, "with the astonishing apathy of Oriental men." Never have they shown any surprise at witnessing mechanical miracles. When the most learned Muslim scholars observed the physical and chemical experiments that French scientists conducted in Egypt—the metamorphosis of things, chemical changes in color, the effects of electricity—they argued that "all of that," even the methods for manufacturing cannons and gunpowder, had already been written in the Qurʾan. Hence, every local resident, from grave scholars to common subjects, greeted the "majestic ascension" of Conté's second montgolfière "with absolute insouciance."[11] If it surprised the expedition's savants that ordinary Egyptians had not lingered, with breathless curiosity, to witness the astonishing spectacle of a balloon taking off, it bothered them even more that their counterparts, the *ʿulamāʾ*, affected the greatest indifference. Even after successful flights, learned Muslim scholars reportedly remained phlegmatic, impassive.[12] It was as if the French expected al-Jabartī and other Egyptian intellectuals to dream enthusiastically about the grand possibilities of flight, like Benjamin Franklin in the Bois de Boulogne, and to join that fin-de-siècle craze, *la ballomanie*, when as a matter of fact they encountered balloons amid a foreign invasion and a military occupation as strange, new, menacing things that flew the colors of the Republican flag.[13]

Perhaps a faint echo of this story of France's failed experiment in Egypt sounded in the grand amphitheater of the Sorbonne in 1883—a year after a French flotilla desisted from participating in the fateful British bombardment of Alexandria. The famous Semiticist Ernest Renan delivered in this venue an infamous lecture, where he argued that Islam had turned Arabs into the enemies of scientific innovation. By way of illustration, he presented Rifāʿa al-Ṭahṭāwī, an Egyptian shaykh who had written a book "full of the most curious observations about French society" based on his sojourn in Paris between 1826 and 1831. This shaykh had the "fixed idea that European science, with its principle about the immutability of nature's laws, was from one end to another a heresy."[14]

Yet the book—an early and critical contribution to the discourse on reforming Egypt and Islam in the era of European dominance—was more of a testament to the enlightened wonderment that al-Ṭahṭāwī learned to express about strange new things.[15] With more cultured astonishment than jealous scorn, he remarked on everything that struck him as different and foreign and meaningful: from the paid advertisements for useful commodities of "outstanding craftsmanship" that shopkeepers placed in newspapers to the experiments that scientists performed to discover "the secrets of machines." Through such illustrations, the Egyptian traveler showed how French merchants were devising ingenious methods to pursue wealth, and how French scientists were acquiring the fundamental knowledge to further technological progress.[16]

Still, on display in the Gallery of Comparative Anatomy of the Jardin des Plantes, surrounding the skulls of Asian elephants, by the buttocks of the Hottentot Venus and the hunchbacked skeleton of Bébé the court dwarf, al-Ṭahṭāwī observed the embalmed cadaver of a French general's assassin. Still bearing signs of physical torture, for his dagger-wielding hand had been burnt to the bone before his punishment onto death, Haleby's corpse was exported from Egypt to France by surgeon Larrey, the very man who narrated that story about the balloon and the dogs. Al-Ṭahṭāwī's contemporary Alexandre Dumas remarked that the stake on which Haleby had been impaled broke two thoracic vertebrae; the taxidermist replaced them with wooden ones that imitated perfectly, or almost perfectly, the natural kinds. For science's sake, phrenologists could there inspect the cranial protuberances of what an English guidebook to Paris's "most remarkable objects" would simply label "the Mussulman fanatic." This and other exhibits of lifelike exotic animals, including the artfully mounted skins of orangutans and chimpanzees misidentified as "species of monkeys," were shown in cabinets of curiosities that al-Ṭahṭāwī called "storerooms of strange things." However scandalous and irreligious he found the transformation of an Islamic corpse into a scientific object, he nevertheless maintained a broader perspective. For he explained to his Arabic readers one advantage that French natural scientists had over their Muslim counterparts: they could now directly examine things that in the past scholars could encounter only in books.[17]

This book analyzes representations of modern things made by a journal that a Syrian mufti, an expert on Islamic law, established in Cairo a hundred years after the flight of the *montgolfière*. Most of these things were manufactured abroad, in Europe and North America, but they did not seem altogether foreign. Nor did they seem as dangerous as an aerostatic machine or as disturbing as Haleby's corpse. By and large, they were things that some Muslims already possessed or wanted to possess, but that provoked, for one or another reason, the deepest religious and legal questions.

Introduction

Good Things Made Lawful: Euro-Muslim Objects and Laissez-Faire Fatwas

Around 1940 Muḥammad Shafīʿ, an interpreter of Islamic law from a seminary in British India, wrote a fatwa to persuade his followers to resist a new foreign commodity—the synthetic toothbrush. He wanted Muslims to brush their teeth with a *miswāk*, a type of tooth-cleaning twig used by those who wanted to imitate the practice of the Prophet Muḥammad, rather than with a toothbrush, "nowadays usually made of pig-hair."[1] A Japanese company had recently introduced the synthetic alternative into the colony. It had the grand ambition to sell its pork-free product in what multinational corporations would eventually call "the global Islamic market." Competition soon followed from an American firm that began to advertise Dr. West's Miracle-Tufts, equipped with the now familiar nylon bristles, at home and abroad.[2] Under different brands, the product quickly spread across the world. Its early adoption by Muslim consumers in India is what inspired a circle of wary disciples in the seminary to inquire about its legality.

Their attitude is easy to understand historically when we consider that they belonged to a revivalist movement that arose in the wake of the rebellion of 1857. This was the great uprising that began with that "mutiny" of the East India Company's Muslim and Hindu soldiers, who were spurred to action by the rumor that the paper cartridges for their new Enfield rifle-muskets had been lubricated with the fat of forbidden animals. Since the military drill required biting the cartridges to extract the bullet, this was all the more upsetting.[3] Within a decade of their momentous rebellion, disenchanted religious scholars established the first of many Deobandi madrasas: retreats where seminarians spurned the metropolitan English curriculum and colonial British culture to concentrate instead on the cultivation of Islamic orthodoxy and orthopraxy.[4]

Since this discipline required purging foreign corruptions from everyday life, Muḥammad Shafīʿ had every reason to reject boar-bristle if not synthetic toothbrushes and to recommend instead the genuine Islamic article.

This is a book about the trials of modern goods—from the toothbrush to the telegraph—under Islam's sacred law. It focuses closely on many strange and wonderful new things: gramophone records, brimmed hats, tailored trousers, lottery tickets, paper money, gigantic gongs, and even toilet paper. These things provoked religious conundrums as they crossed cultural and political frontiers in a transitional period at the end of the imperial era. Scattered in diverse colonies, protectorates, mandates, and rising nations, Muslim societies under European hegemony nevertheless shared one powerful experience: they all encountered an astonishing array of novelties fabricated overseas. With early adoption and rising consumption came riveting communal debates. Pious actors at times demanded the banishment of foreign products to the other side of that invisible boundary that separated the lawful from the forbidden. But the day's most pressing discussions were not about technological innovation in the abstract, the imperial ideology of free trade, or the meaning of modernity. They were far more concrete. Muslims specifically wanted to know if their divine scriptures sanctioned particular interactions with particular goods. They turned to arbiters of the sacred law, who responded with ad hoc fatwas: casuistic sentences that pronounced the objects and actions on trial economically advantageous or socially harmful, conducive to piety or suggestive of infidelity, and—in the final analysis—admirable or abominable.

The fatwas that this book focuses on were published by *al-Manār*, or *The Lighthouse*, a magazine that promised, by its very name, an Enlightenment. Printed in Cairo by an Arabic press, this monthly magazine grew famous during its run in the early twentieth century. Despite its modest circulation, it earned a global readership. The Ottoman Syrian cleric who founded it in 1898, shortly after he immigrated to Egypt under British suzerainty, was the entrepreneurial religious reformer Muḥammad Rashīd Riḍā, a critical figure in modern Islam's history. He edited *al-Manār* and issued its "enlightening" fatwas until his death in 1935. An admirer of modern inventions, he would never have asked his urbane Muslim readers to surrender their artificial toothbrushes and take up *Salvadora persica* twigs.

His fatwas matter because they show how advocates for Islam's reform as well as their opponents responded to a changing material and technological environment. Modern things of foreign origin had a profound impact on Muslim societies in the late imperial and early nationalist periods, stimulating religious reflections on the new world of goods. Rather than taking everything for granted, laypersons pondered things discriminately. They wondered about the role and place of new objects in an ideal Islamic society. With their everyday questions about novelties, they breathed new life into a moribund legal genre; they helped to turn the fatwa, in the age of print, into an exciting vehicle for trans-imperial Islamic communications.

Pressed to judge European commodities and technologies that had become objects of controversy, Riḍā repeatedly argued that Islam's law presented few, if any, barriers to trade, consumption, and adoption. His liberalizing rulings were justified by a method of legal interpretation that privileged scriptural precedents (verses from the Qurʾan, narratives from the Ḥadīth) and ancestral paragons (idealized accounts of early Islamic heroes known as the Salaf). I call this method "laissez-faire Salafism." By this technical term, I basically want to describe Riḍā's prosperity gospel: the good tidings, which he spread far and wide, that adherence to the shariʿa's original spirit would empower modern Muslims to overcome hardship and rise to affluence. This was the ethos of the economically liberal movement of Islamic reform that arose under the aegis of the Empire of Free Trade. It manifested itself in an incipient form in Cairo around 1900, at a booming time in the city's history, and then developed over time as its adherents, including Riḍā, elaborated upon its inchoate propositions under changing material, social, and political conditions. Emerging before the elaboration of "Islamic economics" as a postcolonial discipline for Muslim nation-states, it had one central goal: to interpret and invoke scriptures, the Qurʾan and the Ḥadīth, as well as the principles of the Salaf, the exemplars of a golden age, in order to bless "the good things" (*al-ṭayyibāt*) that came from factories abroad.[5]

Islamic Law's Abstractions: A Disciplinary Bias Against Material Evidence

The practice of Islam has always had a material dimension, embodied by objects such as the Kaʿba, prayer mats, prayer beads, patched frocks, amulets with Qurʾanic verses, shrines for the dead, and lodges designed for spiritual retreat. Yet scholarship on Islam has traditionally paid little attention to tangible things. Perhaps this disregard stems from a post-Enlightenment Protestant influence on the academic study of religion: the conception of true faith as consisting of interiorized belief and personal spirituality, mental states that seemed far removed from the fetishism of commodities and the worship of icons.[6] In recent years, however, scholars have turned to study "material religion" systematically. Joining art historians and cultural anthropologists, specialists on Islam, too, have made strides to develop our understanding of the materiality of various Muslim practices in many different contexts.[7] Critical areas of inquiry into

Islam's history nevertheless remain virtually untouched by the material turn. The history of Islamic law in the early twentieth century, which is absolutely crucial for understanding the rise of Salafism and the globalization of Riḍā's brand of reform, is one of these areas, and it to this area that I hope to contribute with the present book.

Pioneers in the study of "material religion" have argued that the Protestant Reformation's bias against icons and idols predisposed scholars of modern religion "to overlook the importance of things."[8] But the neglect of material culture in the historiography of Islamic law and society may be explained without considering such a bias.[9] Legal historians have frequently discussed property, yet in generic terms, so that we learn about the thief's possessions or the son's inheritance shares but without really grasping what were the specific objects in question.[10] This disregard for concrete things, with their individual characteristics and distinct histories, reflects and magnifies a standard way of reasoning by Muslim jurists who searched for abstract rules of broad applicability. With a predilection for categorization, they routinely subsumed things on trial, however unique, under classes of objects.

In addition, we must recognize the discipline's bias against material evidence. Cultivating a disdainful attitude toward this type of evidence, medieval Muslim theorists of law privileged oral testimony over physical clues in their evidentiary rules. In the absence of eyewitnesses, some determined an expert witness's representation of material evidence admissible in a shariʿa court, as a circumstantial indicator of a crime. But they held this evidentiary mechanism in low regard. Ideally, they wanted judgments to be based on the testimony of just humans; they doubted the probity of mute things.[11] By establishing a parallel legal system where Islamic laws of evidence had no priority, modern Muslim states found effective ways to skirt, not overcome, this bias.[12] Traditional evidentiary rules have continued to inform, though not always to determine, proceedings in modern shariʿa courts.[13] In spite of all of this, Muslim legal sources actually offer a wealth of incidental and original evidence: unique representations of real things, projected like shadows on the walls of a cave. The challenge in this book has been to write a history of such things on the basis of *The Lighthouse*'s projections.

Europe's Civilizing Commerce, London's Enlightened Bourse, Orientalists' Mecca

Driving this book is my fascination with the movement of commodities from one culture to another. I grew up in a provincial city in Mexico at a time when foreign things—from Kentucky Fried Chicken to Van Halen tapes—could easily be found in the new ritzy mall, La Plaza Dorada. If my friends denounced Yankee imperialism, they also marveled at the Ford Taurus and the Big Mac. Like the villagers of Gabriel García Márquez's Macondo, who discovered ice, the burning power of a magnifying glass, and the magic of magnets, we stood in awe before the latest inventions. It did bother us a little that so many of these things came from the United States. But quickly we overcame our qualms. The story of technology and modernity was for us mostly about the belated arrival of American products in our mall. Later on, still as a teenager, I lived for a year in a kibbutz in Israel. There I encountered pride in local industry, an antimaterialistic ethic, and communal limits on household consumption. Long before I conceived of writing this book, these experiences led me to think about ways in which cultures can distinctly shape our attitudes and behaviors toward internal and external goods. But if it is true that commodities from distant lands can have a life of their own—it is just a matter of "awakening their spirit," as Melquíades the gypsy exclaimed when he brought to Macondo all sorts of inventions—then there is also a question about these commodities' magical, transformative power.[14]

This is a controversial topic, I know, because the cross-cultural transfer of technological objects has often taken place in modern times by means of trading relations between developing countries and highly industrialized, capitalist nations. Classical economic orthodoxy has long held that free trade between unequal partners leads not only to mutual material benefits, as a result of comparative advantage, but also to spiritual benefits. John Stuart Mill, who spent three decades working for the East India Company, stated this opinion baldly. After explaining with mathematical precision foreign trade's economic advantages, he turned to moral justifications. "A people may be in a quiescent, indolent, uncultivated state," he explained, "for want of any sufficient object of desire." By tempting them with new objects, however, foreign commerce "sometimes works a sort of industrial revolution" in an "undeveloped" country. When they venture into such a country, the empire's "commercial adventurers" expose its inhabitants to advanced "modes of thought and action." They effectively operate as "the first civilizers of barbarians." In Mill's eyes, international commerce was more than a civilizing force; it was "the principal guarantee" of world peace.[15]

Even before Mill published his liberal treatise on political economy, British free traders began describing Muslims as intractable foes to the pursuit of capital. An influential pamphleteer, Richard Cobden, explained why the Turks held trade in contempt: they dogmatically opposed "receiving interest for money" and held fast to the Quran, which supposedly declared: "There is but one law, and that forbids all communication with infidels."[16] He thus anticipated the notorious argument that Islam's sacred law inhibited capitalism.[17] Lord Cromer, Egypt's most powerful politician during Riḍā's first decade in Cairo, mostly agreed with Cobden and Mill. However, as an unabashed British imperialist, he found unbearably naïve the internationalist notion that "trade, with its handmaids the railway and the telegraph," would bind nations together in peace and harmony. He was a passionate advocate of "free" trade when it served the interests of the British Empire, and his critiques of Islam in Egypt had everything to do with this advocacy.[18]

What was the imperialism of free trade for Cromer and why was he convinced that Islamic ideology opposed it? It meant a great deal more to him than promoting capitalist policies to reduce tariffs and encourage investments with interest. His loftier goal was to establish a legal system that would end discrimination in the commercial field on the basis of religion or nationality. Accordingly, he celebrated the signing of the 1899 convention that turned the Sudan into an Anglo-Egyptian condominium and placed "the German, the Frenchman, the Italian and others . . . on a precisely similar commercial footing to that enjoyed by a subject of the Queen of England." By "others" he did not mean to gesture vaguely toward Sudanese and Egyptian merchants. His argument was that the British Empire afforded equal opportunity to European merchants.[19] His liberalism, though based on universalistic claims, depended on a strategy of exclusion: the systematic disregard of colonial subjects' interests in the establishment of conventions that granted European Powers commercial privileges in de facto colonies.[20]

Enlightenment philosophes had shaped one of the ideals that inspired Lord Cromer to separate economic from religious pursuits conceptually. They held that—in rational capitalist transactions—religion must be set aside. As Voltaire famously remarked about the London Bourse in his letter on the Presbyterians: "Take a View of the Royal-Exchange in London, a place more venerable than many courts of justice, where the representatives of all nations meet for the benefit of mankind. There the Jew, the Mahometan and the Christian transact together, as tho' they all profess'd the same religion, and give the name of Infidel to none but bankrupts." Voltaire proceeded to comment on London's religious pluralism. "At the breaking up of this pacific and free assembly," the merchants of different sects retire to the synagogue, the church, or the pub, to engage freely in their strange communal rituals. One merchant "goes and is baptiz'd in a great tub, in the name of the Father, Son, and Holy Ghost," another has "his son's foreskin cut off."[21] Yet in the Stock Exchange, they were all equal. Religion there was irrelevant.

Islamic law worked against this ideal, in Lord Cromer's view, because it brought religion to bear on financial and commercial matters. By condemning usury, it "discouraged the outlay of capital." The deeper problem was that religious and civil laws appeared "inextricably woven" in Muslim states, and it was difficult to imagine how the legal strands could ever be separated and rearranged to fit the pattern of "civilized" European states.[22] (The Ottoman Empire had in principle committed itself to the abolition of all impediments to commerce in the famous *firman* of 1856, which had also promised equality to Christian and other non-Muslim subjects.) At any rate, the ideology that Cromer called "Islamism" worked against free trade for another reason, too. Instead of preaching love and charity, it preached contempt toward disbelievers and warfare against infidels, engendering "the idea that revenge and hatred . . . should form the basis of the relations between man and man."[23]

Lord Cromer knew that Muḥammad had been a merchant before he became a prophet. This was common knowledge. Every nineteenth-century Orientalist recounted tales of Arabia Felix's commerce. The article on "Mohammedanism" in the ninth edition of the *Encyclopaedia Britannica* related that Mecca's pre-Islamic inhabitants "practiced piety essentially as a trade" and engaged in a "lively trade in idols with the Bedouins." Of course, it featured Muḥammad—before he received his first revelation—as a merchant undertaking commercial journeys on behalf of a wealthy widow, his future wife Khadīja.[24] *The Speeches & Table-Talk of the Prophet Mohammad* by Stanley Lane-Poole, one of Lord Cromer's key informants about Islam, described pre-Islamic Mecca as the "little republic of commerce" that supported Muḥammad's "adventurous trade" as a "camel-driver."[25] These biographical sketches have a long history. They can be traced back to the earliest medieval European biographies of Muḥammad, which represented the Prophet as a greedy usurer who wandered the earth for business and to indulge in carnal pursuits.[26]

But Orientalists had a special interest in the intertwinement of religious and commercial interests at the origins of Islam.[27] Aloys Sprenger, an Austrian who worked as an official government interpreter in Calcutta under Company rule, related in *The Life of Mohammad* the story about the pagan boycott of the first Muslims. Their archenemy, Abū Jahl, had declared to the earliest merchants converted by the Prophet: "We shall ruin thy commerce and thy property." When discussing the taming of savage Arabia through religion and commerce, he disclosed that Muḥammad had given "permission to trade even during the pilgrimage." In antiquity, "the Arabs were undoubtedly much more civilized than they are now. Commerce encouraged industry, and furnished wealth, the source of civilization." Yet Mecca, and Arabia as a whole, "had much declined at the time of Mohammad," when there existed "limited opportunities, and little desire, profitably to invest capital."[28]

Islamic Opposition to Western Technology: An Obsolete Dichotomy

During the Cold War, when it seemed intellectually appealing to divide the world into ideological blocs, a renowned historian of the Ottoman Empire's decline returned to the question that had preoccupied and entertained Orientalists since the disappointing flight of the *montgolfière*: Why did Islamic civilization reject technological innovation? In response, Bernard Lewis offered a powerful and influential indictment: religious conservatives, this civilization's spokesmen, are bound to "the Muslim tradition," which rejects innovation as if it were heresy. In *The Muslim Discovery of Europe*, he explained that this tradition made them see "adopting or imitating practices characteristic of the infidel" as in itself amounting "to an act of infidelity and consequently a betrayal of Islam." Therefore, they rejected public clocks, printing machines, and all sorts of other European inventions. They made only one exception readily; they had no difficulty declaring licit the commercial acquisition of European guns, telescopes, and other instruments that seemed useful for holy war.[29]

Lewis's dichotomy had its counterpart in nationalistic Muslim grievances against Western hegemony. The worry, prevalent in the postwar period, was that globalization would cause cultural differences to vanish. Nobody, in my opinion, expressed this worry more effectively than the Iranian intellectual Jalāl Āl-i Aḥmad in his book *Plagued by the West*. Nearly two decades before the Iranian revolution, he denounced the mandatory exchange of goods that followed the dictates of Western companies. Lamenting the loss of Iran's personality, he diagnosed the "effeminate" and "faithful" consumption of mechanical products—the transformation of the home into a space for the display of the television, the electric washing machine, and worthless kitchen gadgets—as a symptom of the malaise. For political reasons, he conceptualized imported products as imbued with an overbearing masculine power that would overwhelm a fragile feminine culture. While Europeans had given rise to "an industrial resurrection," Persians had "passed into the slumber of the Seven Sleepers." In this state, they were seduced by the West and turned into "gentle and tractable consumers" of face powder and lipstick, the feminine signs of cultural extinction.[30]

Euro-Muslim Goods: Moving Beyond the "Westernizing Innovations" Paradigm

Foreign goods have not presented "Islamic civilization," whatever this abstraction might mean, with a single challenge over the course of centuries since at least (from Bernard Lewis's perspective) the Ottoman Empire's alleged decline.[31] They certainly cannot be reduced, all together, to modernity's defining challenge. Rather, given their varied material qualities and diverse functions, they have either provoked multiple questions or none at all. The fact of the matter is that countless machines and products have crossed political borders and geographical barriers to enter zones inhabited by Muslim communities without ever becoming the subjects of theological or legal reflection. They have never worked to separate, symbolically or imaginatively, one religion from another. This is a critical point. Because we live in a world where material objects move with astonishing speed in spectacular quantities across the globe, it is essential not to inject all foreign products with artificial cultural meaning. Doing so risks making world cultures—not to mention humankind—appear more divergent than they have been in the past. Nevertheless, select foreign objects have ended up bearing a special cultural burden at particular historical junctures. This book concerns such cross-cultural objects.

Against the impression that Muslim scholars have reacted against "Westernizing innovations" due to their commitment to a sacred tradition, I would make two arguments. The first has to do with Muslim jurists' pragmatic tendency to interpret legal commandments flexibly in order to sanction current developments. Their tradition was not, like the cosmological constant, a fixed force that prevented them from moving forward in time but a quintessence that allowed them to make sense of dynamic changes in their universe. The second argument is against the technologically deterministic presumption that European goods operate as agents of Westernization or modernization. How exactly did Muslim individuals or societies become "Westernized" or "modernized" (no longer so medieval, nor quite so Oriental) by using these goods? Imports were not equipped with an awesome mechanism for acculturation. If Muslim cultural critics ever pretended that this was the case in their jeremiads against foreign influence, then they turned a blind eye to the many ways in which Muslim consumers appropriated these goods, disregarding the country of origin and manufacturers' intentions to find their own uses and purposes.

Goods originating in Europe or North America that made the passage into Muslim societies in Riḍā's lifetime cannot be adequately described as "Western" goods.

When Muslim consumers gave meaning to both their European origin and their Islamic utility, I would describe them as "Euro-Muslim" goods. Moving beyond the cultural disjunctions of Lewis and Āl-i Aḥmad, this book presents commodities and technologies originating in Europe and the United States that Muslims deliberately appropriated as the material agents behind an Islamic awakening.

Cross-Cultural Entanglements: Historical-Anthropological Views of Globalization

My approach to the cross-cultural passage of objects under the New Imperialism of the late nineteenth and early twentieth century builds on historical-anthropological conceptions of the globalization of trade. To understand better the impact of foreign artifacts on indigenous societies, Nicholas Thomas introduced the flexible concept of entanglement. In early encounters with European or American adventurers, islanders in the Pacific responded in different ways to invitations to trade. They appropriated goods—things such as guns, tobacco, knives, and scrimshawed whale teeth—selectively. The symbolic meanings, ceremonial functions, and pragmatic uses that they initially assigned to these goods depended as much on their native cosmology as on specific historical circumstances at the time of acquisition. Insofar as they remained resilient and able to accommodate change, Pacific islanders' cultures did not suffer a critical transformation at the beginning of this process of material entanglement.[32]

Yet this focus on first encounters brings up an essential question about the adaptability of a culture in places such as fin de siècle Cairo that had been subject to intense and prolonged cross-cultural interactions. In a colonial-indigenous "middle ground" evoked by a historian as well as in a postcolonial bazaar observed by an anthropologist, cross-cultural brokers devised a shared culture, with its own rules and conventions for barter, even though they remained invested in maintaining religious and social barriers in other spaces.[33] Similarly, in towns or regions where local actors repurposed technological objects that originated abroad or manufactured what purists would perceive as "syncretic" or "hybrid" artifacts, there emerged a dynamic material subculture, if not a broader culture, that flourished by mixing elements until it was no longer clear what was "foreign" and what was "indigenous."[34] There is no need to treat such places as if they were auguries of what a transnationalist called, with too much enthusiasm, "the global ecumene."[35] Nor is there a reason to regard manifestations of cultural continuity there, or reactionary assertions of ancestral identity, as vestiges of a vanishing era. Nevertheless, their transcultural products suggest quite an extraordinary and meaningful process of historical change.

Another historical anthropologist, Marshall Sahlins, established what remains, for me, the principal goal: a "sustained analysis of how local peoples" made sense of entanglements with new European or American goods "in their own cultural terms." He joined the "anthropological chorus of protest against the idea that the global expansion of Western capitalism" had turned colonized peoples into "passive objects of their own history." In the history of world capitalism, local cultural systems have always mediated, he insisted, the "specific effects" of global-material forces.[36] I agree. Led by Rudolf Mrázek's *Engineers of Happy Land*, histories of the flow of technology to the ends of empires have begun to reveal new aspects of the astonishing variety of local responses.[37] Concentrating on mobility and materiality, recent collections of essays by multiple authors, including *Global Muslims in the Age of Steam and Print*, have shown how in the late nineteenth and early twentieth centuries networks of Muslims adopted and adapted technologies that originated in Europe to their own diverse ends.[38] Along these lines, too, On Barak's *On Time* has analyzed the unique contretemps of Egypt's passage into technological modernity, highlighting how Egyptians themselves creatively engaged with the colonial systems and machines that promised but did not always deliver efficiency.[39] It is an important historiographical turn, since a generation ago world history's pioneers, researching almost exclusively European sources and perspectives, thought of these technologies as tools of European dominance whose diffusion overseas required overcoming all sorts of endemic obstacles.[40]

My book contributes to this broad historical and anthropological research program by introducing the prism of Islamic law. Like historical anthropology, Islamic law refracts white light. It certainly does not permit us to look at the entrance of modern objects into Muslim societies as if through a pane of transparent glass. It offers instead its own set of judgments, distortions, in a spectrum of colors. This system for distinguishing right from wrong behavior as well as good from bad innovations transcended provincial and imperial boundaries in the early twentieth century. It gave Muslims, although they were scattered around the world, the impression that they possessed a common ethical framework: a seemingly universal code of rules by which to judge their local entanglements with modern things.

Strains of Salafism: A Review of Riḍā's Role as a "Modernist" and a "Fundamentalist"

At stake in this book is how we think of modern Islam, whose spirit Riḍā tried to realize in *The Lighthouse*, in connection with the world of goods around the end of Europe's imperial era. It is best, I believe, to rehearse the standard narrative of Riḍā's place in history, then to proceed and explain how this history will revise it. Historians have conventionally represented Riḍā as the third in a line of famous intellectuals who led an Islamic "movement" of sorts—or at least wrote and propagated a series of ideas and ideals to inspire Muslims far and wide to think about religion in new ways while agitating for cultural, political, social, and economic reforms. Independently and collaboratively, this trio of reformers—Jamāl al-Dīn al-Afghānī (1839–1897), Muḥammad ʿAbduh (1849–1905), and their younger successor, Riḍā—elaborated some of the most influential responses to European dominance. Reacting to Orientalist critiques of their religion as the reason for backwardness, they contended that Islam itself must not be blamed for Muslims' modern misfortunes. In a renovated form, it could even inspire Muslims to make the passage into modernity.

In the interwar period, European historians of Islam began to call the movement or ideology that these reformers putatively founded "Salafism." The conceit behind this intergenerational movement or ideology, insofar as it existed, was that antiquity's virtuous Muslims, the Salaf, had been the vanguard of modern Islam. While harking back to the time of the Salaf, ʿAbduh and Riḍā in particular criticized what they viewed as stultifying, parochial, or scholastic interpretations of the sacred law by establishment clerics. To support their ideas for change, they turned directly to the Qurʾan and the Ḥadīth, where they found inspiration and justification. They pretended to locate the original meaning or intent of scriptural rules. Riḍā devoted himself to this task systematically, with conviction and zeal, which is why I would characterize his perspective on religion and law as "originalist" and "scripturalist" in certain respects. Through the hermeneutic and rhetorical techniques that he developed to make authoritative arguments for the primacy of canonical laws and ancestral opinions, he contributed—far more than ʿAbduh—to the eventual rise of a "Salafist" methodology.[41]

Unlike eighteenth-century Islamic revivalists who owed nothing to Europe, Muslim reformers in the era of European dominance readily recognized Europe's commercial and technological superiority, and they agreed that Muslims had much to learn from Europe in order to thrive.[42] Their broad goal was to modernize medieval educational systems and legal institutions and to encourage the global Islamic community to rise—upon overcoming religious disunity—toward political independence and world power. Who stood in the way of this goal? Reformers' principal enemies (real and imagined) changed over time during the late nineteenth and early twentieth century. They would include members of the *ʿulamāʾ* who defended obsolete methods and vanishing privileges; a despotic sultan who suspended the constitution and restricted civil liberties;

secularists and feminists, who dared to flaunt their freedom from religious strictures; the sects and orders that followed "heterodox" beliefs or "schismatic" rituals instead of the sacred law; and colonialists, who thwarted dreams of unity and sovereignty.

When he returned to Egypt, ʿAbduh adopted a conciliatory stance toward de facto British rule and commenced a rapid ascent to the pinnacle of Egypt's legal and religious hierarchy. He rose by the end of the century to the office of Grand Mufti, the chief, official interpreter of Islamic law. He developed at this time a mode of reconciling Islamic rules with Protectorate designs. In addition, he started to emphasize the enlightened virtues of a few extraordinary ancestors, the Salaf. His model ancestors were not the multitude of pious Muslims from the first and second centuries of Islamic history but a few medieval theologians who reflected independently on the principles underlying divine laws. ʿAbduh invoked many spirits, in addition to these premodern exemplars, as paragons of modernity.[43]

It was in this period that Riḍā, seeking ʿAbduh's patronage, moved from the environs of Tripoli, in Ottoman Syria, to Cairo. An admirer of the pan-Islamic, anticolonial journal that ʿAbduh and al-Afghānī had collaborated on during their exile in Paris in 1884, *al-ʿUrwa al-Wuthqa* ("The Firmest Bond"), Riḍā persuaded ʿAbduh to support his own plan to publish an "enlightening" Islamic journal. The pair of reformers interacted for around eight years, until the end of ʿAbduh's life. They collaborated on an edition of ʿAbduh's lectures on the Qurʾan, which Riḍā serialized in *al-Manār*. During public controversies, Riḍā came to ʿAbduh's defense.

With more loyalty than originality, according to his intellectual critics, Riḍā continued expounding the principles of "Islamic modernism" after ʿAbduh's death. He did so until at least World War I, by their reckoning. Thus, he systematically developed a utilitarian approach to the sacred law: he legalized all sorts of modern innovations through readings of the Qurʾan and the Ḥadīth that ultimately rested on progressive appeals for Muslims to change—for the public interest—their outdated perceptions of Islam. What changed after the world war? Unsettled by the scramble for the Ottoman Empire, frustrated by the League of Nations, and shaken by the abolition of the caliphate, he turned with a vengeance toward Arab-Islamic nationalism.[44] His inclination toward political activism and social conservatism, muted under ʿAbduh's influence and restrained by wartime censorship, broke into the open.

During the awakening of the interwar period, he assumed a key role in the Syrian struggle for independence and in Egypt's culture wars. Excited by the Saudi-Wahhabi conquest of the Ḥijāz, Islam's birthplace in Arabia, he also became a leading supporter of Ibn Saʿūd's sovereign ambitions and a controversial defender of Wahhabi clerics' historical campaigns to return to the pristine monotheism of Islam's founders.[45] He published sympathetic portraits of Ibn ʿAbd al-Wahhāb (d. 1792) and his descendants, the zealous clerics of a remote central Arabian region, Najd, where Saudis and Wahhabis formed their fateful alliance. With Saudi financing, he issued the first printed editions of their obscure theological and legal verdicts in several thick tomes.[46] In addition, he helped organize and promote a Saudi agenda at the 1926 Muslim World Congress.[47]

For these and other reasons, scholars have asserted that he abandoned the "modernist" Salafism of his mentor to embrace, with dire consequences, the reactionary strain of Salafism associated (rightly or wrongly) with Najd's Wahhabi clerics.[48] They have cited his "deviation" from al-Afghānī's and ʿAbduh's philosophy as one of the causes behind the transformation of Salafism into a "backward-looking ideology ill-prepared to confront the challenges of the modern world."[49] This allegation of an ideological shift, of a move toward radicalization, matters not because it affects Riḍā's legacy but because of the impression that he worked, effectively and influentially, to spread first one and then the second major strain of Salafism around the Muslim world.[50]

Although there has been a surge of interest since September 11, 2001, in the historic role that he played during the interwar period to affirm the "fundamentalist" strain of Salafism, postcolonial assessments of Riḍā mainly focused on his contributions to "modernist" Salafism—on the ways in which he extended, modified, and propagated the progressive philosophy and methodology developed by ʿAbduh. Some intellectual historians and political scientists judged their joint project—which seemed neither purely "Islamic" nor sufficiently "European" but a discomfiting mixture of the two—a failure borne out of duplicity. Others declared their attempt "to reform and revive the sharīʿa on the basis of a utilitarian methodology" doomed from the start because Islamic law seemed to them fundamentally irreconcilable with this secular system of principles.[51] Muslim utilitarianists paid "no more than lip service to Islamic values," explained Wael Hallaq in his sweeping history of Islamic legal hermeneutics; they "drastically manipulated" the pragmatic medieval principle that the sacred law should serve the common good.[52]

Similarly, one of modern Islam's leading historians, Reinhard Schulze, argued that under European imperialism, "Muslims were not even allowed to create modernism on their own." They were subjected to something "much worse than economic colonialism," a wave of cultural propaganda that implied that "all progress" was Europe's "inalienable property." While the entire "cultural framework of progress was to be put at the Orient's disposal as a loan," things like telegraphs and railways were "all marked as imports, as made in Europe." At this conjuncture, Muslim reformers failed to develop an independent, alternative modernity; they merely managed to give rise to the derivative, defiant reaction to Eurocentric modernity known as Salafism.[53]

My historical investigations have led me to conclude that the history of Salafism in the early twentieth century has been greatly distorted by anachronistic projections, teleological distortions, and an elitist, overly intellectual approach to the generation of religious ideas. The problem stems in part from an exaggerated view of historical continuity in the multigenerational effort to reform Islam.[54] Riḍā has been so closely associated with his predecessors, al-Afghānī and ʿAbduh, that historians have often treated him and at times even categorized him as a nineteenth-century reformer, all but forgetting the fact that his life's work as *al-Manār*'s editor began in 1898 and ended in 1935. Judgmental descriptions of his early doctrines as "modernist" and of his late doctrines as "fundamentalist" are misleading. There is little or no correspondence between these words, overloaded with meaning, and the terms that he himself used to describe his identity. He did not identify first with European modernity and then with Islamic antiquity. Throughout his career, he identified with aspects of both ages simultaneously. This history will show that Riḍā worked, together with a vast network of fatwa seekers and international partners, to devise new ways to use the symbolic capital of the Salaf as well as scriptural laws to reflect on matters of the day. Before World War I, they jointly developed many of the core Salafist stances and principles that *al-Manār* continued to defend, with relatively few changes, after World War I. My revisionist argument, in other words, is for discontinuity between the nineteenth- and twentieth-century projects of reform and for a high level of continuity in the religious and legal doctrines preached by *al-Manār* during its long run.

Islamic Consumers' Reformation

The present history is not a search for a pure and pristine Islamic "reformation." I use this term to describe the manifold changes to Muslim practices that occurred during Riḍā's lifetime, not merely the programs of reform advocated by Riḍā and his allies. This history deals with a period of intense cross-cultural interactions, when Muslims who identified as "reformers" encountered European persons and European goods on a daily basis in their neighborhoods. Although these reformers dreamed about freedom from colonialism in the past and in the future, they nevertheless had to focus intensely on the issues of the present: precisely the everyday entanglements and encounters that blurred the line between "European" and "Muslim," making it seem artificial or arbitrary.[55]

Reformers made many efforts to reimagine and redraw this line to make it correspond to their vision of Islam and the realities of the time. Their efforts were not, for the most part, covert responses to European ideas or values. Chiefly, they were overt responses—made in the language of Islamic law—to material goods of European origin that had already lost some of their strangeness.

My "history from below" approach to fatwas, which begins with microhistorical investigations of particular religious or legal questions in a local context and ends with reflections on broader global patterns, has led me to defend two arguments that challenge the historiography of Islamic reform under the imperialism of the late nineteenth and early twentieth centuries. First, whereas historians of this movement have dwelt on the intellectual appropriation of European ideas, I would dwell on the consumer appropriation of foreign commodities. Second, instead of representing Salafism as a movement that intellectual elites elaborated in their ivory towers, I present various social actors, especially fatwa seekers, as active participants in the making of this ideology.

Intellectual historians and political scientists frequently explained Muslim debates over the appropriation of modern European ideas and values as stemming from the indelible foreignness of secular "Western" concepts. A similar explanation for the reasons behind Muslim debates over the appropriation of "European" commodities would be inadequate in most cases. Only rarely did Muslim activists politicize the act of consuming imperial or metropolitan commodities. This happened during anticolonial boycotts, when both Muslim and non-Muslim boycotters targeted products and services that they associated symbolically with imperial interests. In general, however, Euro-Muslim commodities became objects of controversy—as this book shows—when their use had some impact on practices that Muslims perceived as Islamic. Ritualized salvation goods actually posed a deeper religious and legal quandary than profane commodities. The use of the gramophone to play records of the Qurʾan presented, as we shall see, a greater theological-juridical puzzle than the use of the gramophone to play secular classical music. In addition, it provoked popular debates that involved a wide range of religious actors, not just an intellectual elite. My impression is that products designed for "Islamic" consumers, such as Odeon's "Arabian Celebrity" gramophone records, mattered far more to the making of Islam's reformation than did Arabic translations of European literature.

My emphasis on the Islamic consumption of imported goods complements histories that have explored different aspects of colonial production and consumption. Written in part to counter imperialistic narratives that had boasted about the gifts of empire, these histories have showcased instead domestic and nationalistic initiatives. In the historiography of Egypt, they have featured among other things the foundation of a national finance company, Banque Miṣr, the emergence of an indigenous tobacco industry, and the anticolonial politics of urban consumption.[56] Other histories, while acknowledging the significance of European and American capital investments and technological diffusions in the Middle East, have similarly emphasized the extent to which Arab entrepreneurs succeeded in developing industries and products for regional consumption more or less independently. These entrepreneurs engaged a German record-pressing factory to establish their own label, Baidaphon; they adapted printing presses; and they invested in instruments such as Singer sewing machines and Kodak cameras. On this basis, they produced for the market Arabic newspapers, Arabic disc records, Arab garments, and Arab photographs.[57]

How does the present history contribute to this historiography? It contributes to it by concentrating on the engaged, reflective, and at times inventive use of European and American products by Islamic actors in Egypt and the world, and by featuring an Arab-Islamic commodity, *al-Manār* magazine, mass-produced by a Cairo publisher for consumers at home and abroad.

Scripture and the Salaf as Flexible Tools for Laissez-Faire Islam

My other contribution to the historiography of Islamic reform also flows from my interest in writing a history of Islamic law from below. Rather than conceiving of Salafism in one or another strain as an ideology consisting of a fairly coherent system of beliefs, methods, and norms that Riḍā propagated from the lofty heights of his lighthouse to Muslims far and wide, I have come to realize that the Salaf in the early twentieth century functioned above all as a flexible tool of reform. Experts on religion and law such as Riḍā learned to put this tool to diverse uses to meet laypersons' demands and their own goals.

Salafism arose gradually, later than historians had until recently assumed, and as a result of multiple exchanges between clerics and society at large.[58] The ascription of a Salafist identity or orientation to nineteenth-century thinkers is problematic, as the historian Henri Lauzière has recently argued, given that individuals and societies did not identify themselves as Salafist then. According to him, a conceptual understanding of Salafism as an ideology or movement emerged only in the interwar period—and as an academic French invention.[59]

During the first decade of the twentieth century, however, Riḍā and his associates began to employ configurations of the term "Salaf," which had a long and varied history in Islamic thought, in new ways: as a commercial banner for a bookstore, as an ideological slogan to awaken Muslims politically and economically, and as a name for an alternative Sunni denomination or branch. These "latter-day Salafis" started to articulate a shared identity and common interests; they formed relationships and imagined an association. Furthermore, they started to elaborate ideals and cultivate dispositions in accordance with their emerging interpretations of scriptural rules and ancestral norms as well as their conceptual distinctions between religious and secular matters. They were present, in other words, in the making of "Salafism" before the coining of the term.

This book's analysis of *al-Manār*'s fatwas offers a new perspective on the reasons for the rise of Salafism as a religious movement with a penchant for scriptural authority and ancestral models. To defend his laissez-faire rulings in an authoritative manner, Riḍā routinely curated memories of the Salaf and proof-texts that he culled from the canons of Islam. If we relinquish a top-down, center–periphery model to explain the origin and appeal of these rulings, then we should arrive at a new understanding of the rise of Salafism, too. Indeed, I argue in this book that Riḍā made arguments for freer trade and technological adoption on the basis of the Qurʾan, the Ḥadīth, and the Salaf because fatwa seekers pressed him to do that. They wanted him to give them this kind of authentic justification for their actions. His responsive rulings reflected in some respects a more secular and in other respects a more religious outlook on modern life, but the key is to recognize that the inspiration for them came from below.[60]

Fatwas from Below: Historical and Methodological Considerations

It may strike readers as somewhat ironic that I have chosen to base this history of reformist Islam's facility for modernity on fatwas. Fatwas are not exactly known as instruments of accommodation. They make the news when they ban familiar things (chess, yoga pants, snowmen, Mickey Mouse, Valentine's Day roses, photos with cats) or when they try to solve an ordinary problem in an extraordinary way. I first heard the word "fatwa" in 1989, when Ayatollah Khomeini made his edict against *The Satanic Verses*. Iranian clerics used the novel to pose as the defenders of the Islamic republic in a battle against "a filthy thing" that issued from the loins of "global infidelity." With his inimitable style, Khomeini himself spoke of "world devourers" bent on eradicating, like white grubs, the roots of Islam. He also evoked Muslim jurists' excruciating cultural battles, "nobler than the blood of the martyrs," to protect all that is sacred from foreign attacks.[61]

Reactionary fatwas such as these could serve every historian to tell sensational stories about the constraints that the sacred law has placed on the consumption of strange new things. Maybe they would serve to confirm, too, what the aerostatic corps of the Napoleonic expedition discovered long ago: that Muslims find technological innovation terrifying. Yet the sacred law is not a rigid ideological superstructure that has worked to restrict the free flow of goods because it was revealed ages ago in ancient Arabia. It is better to conceive of it as an amorphous and malleable body of archaic rules that legal experts have manipulated to either criticize or condone various embodiments of modernity, including things such as synthetic toothbrushes and provocative novels.

Featured in this book are the fatwas of a religious authority who used his legal toolkit to argue against contemporaries' suspicious, negative judgments. With guarded enthusiasm, Riḍā endlessly excavated Islam's foundational sources in a tremendous effort to discover traces and fragments that would support his rulings, which sanctioned the Muslim appropriation of European fabrications. He contributed in this manner to the making of "laissez-faire Salafism." His fatwas reveal a concerted effort to resolve for the sake of a future generation the tension that had run through the whole history of Islamic law between commercial and devotional pursuits. He tried to reconcile economic and religious interests not in a vague sense, by peddling platitudes, but by struggling to relate scriptural models to particular objects. He worked very hard, for years on end, to arm his readers with fatwas that sounded persuasive precisely because they pretended to revive the original spirit of the first Muslim age, when the ancient paragons (the Salaf) had realized Islam's potential to bring *yusr*, prosperity.

The extent to which he devoted himself to this thesis was exceptional. By no means, however, was he the only jurist in history to write accommodating fatwas that encouraged Muslims to adopt technological imports or conduct international trade. Partly under Riḍā's influence, many twentieth-century jurists would make efforts to adapt Islamic law to changing material circumstances. His signature solutions to legal problems can be easily detected in pragmatic fatwas that legalized the radio, fiat currency following the abolition of the gold standard, and the sale of canned pork in non-Muslim countries. Economically progressive jurists such as the Syrian notable Muṣṭafā al-Zarqā (d. 1999) and Egypt's Grand Mufti at the end of a period of neoliberal reforms, ʿAlī Gomʿa, definitely appropriated some of his techniques.[62] Scholars who made critical contributions to Saudi Salafism, including ʿAbd al-Razzāq ʿAfīfī (d. 1994) and Muḥammad Nāṣir al-Dīn al-Albānī (d. 1999), admired his principles and methods too.[63] Among his direct disciples were the founders of influential Islamic organizations in the late 1920s: Muḥammad Ḥāmid al-Fiqī (d. 1959), the Salafist who founded Anṣār al-Sunna al-Muḥammadiyya; and Ḥasan al-Bannāʾ (d. 1949), the founder of the Muslim Brotherhood.[64]

But it is striking that before Riḍā's time, too, Muslim jurists wrote legal opinions in favor of goods produced by non-Muslims—and they did so in a religious and legal idiom grounded in Muslim tradition. In the early fifteenth century, to give one striking example, the North African jurist Ibn Marzūq (d. 1438) issued a fatwa justifying the use of Italian paper decorated with watermarks of the cross. By no means did he judge this innovation as if it were inevitably a "Christianizing" instrument. On the contrary, in his view Muslims could appropriate this paper—physically and symbolically they could convert it from a Christian into an Islamic good—by blotting out the symbols of another god with the ink of Qurʾanic verses.

Ibn Marzūq justified this original ruling by a religious utilitarianism that was firmly grounded in Muslim tradition and scripture. He knew that the Prophet had permitted his wife ʿĀʾisha to turn a curtain woven on foreign looms, which displayed scandalous ornaments associated with the esthetic taste of infidels, into cushions. This precedent helped him to approach the sacred law pragmatically. There existed no commandment to burn controversial foreign things. Believers were rather urged not to squander material resources: to alter or refashion, not destroy, troubling goods. Steeped in a medieval scholastic tradition, Ibn Marzūq recalled that early Muslim jurists had sanctioned consuming cheese made by Zoroastrians and wearing clothes made by Christians. Nobody lost his religion through these practices. How far should any Muslim take the cult of authenticity when the Prophet of Arabia himself, remembered the jurist, had worn a Syrian cloak? Everything that Muslims had to adopt out of need or necessity was lawful if it benefited society, unless God had revealed to the Prophet a specific interdiction on its consumption.[65]

Clearly, pragmatic considerations swayed Islamic legal reasoning long before the Muslim discovery of European utilitarian doctrines.[66] So how, then, did Riḍā move beyond the medieval juridical tradition? Contrasting him with Ibn Marzūq is instructive. First, whereas Ibn Marzūq wrote as a loyal follower of precedents set by earlier Maliki jurists, Riḍā belonged to a new generation of reformers who forswore allegiance to any one school of law. To justify his rulings, he turned directly to the Qurʾan and the Ḥadīth. He used medieval juridical opinions selectively, expediently, and noncommittally, whenever he required additional justification.[67] Second, Ibn Marzūq composed his fatwa in a technical, recondite manner as a legal thinker communicating with other legal thinkers. By contrast, as a journalist with a special interest in preaching to a broad audience of Arabic readers at a time of rising literacy, Riḍā crafted his fatwas in an accessible style. He wanted to instruct and persuade readers who knew Arabic but had not been schooled as experts in Islamic law. Third, whereas Ibn Marzūq made a ruling to resolve a dispute in his own city, Riḍā frequently intervened in disputes abroad. Benefiting from the ease of communications by way of steamships and telegraphs, and from the affordability of Arabic printing presses in the early twentieth century, he established a publishing business that permitted him to dispatch fatwas to correspondents scattered worldwide—from Brazil to China.[68]

Both muftis justified the Muslim use of European goods but in radically different political and economic contexts. Ibn Marzūq penned his fatwa before European hegemony, and he had to sanction but one controversial import. Riḍā launched his career in Egypt halfway through the period of British rule that a colonial official baptized "the veiled protectorate," and he felt obliged to condone hundreds of European objects. Egypt had an agricultural economy shaped by British interests, and it dedicated itself to the cultivation of a single crop for export. In exchange for long-staple cotton, it obtained the most incredible variety of imported goods—delivered by steamships—in a historically unprecedented volume. This lopsided exchange was characteristic of colonial economies administered by free traders: officials like the Earl of Cromer, who did little to encourage the development of diverse factory industries and who actively opposed proposals to protect fledgling enterprises, by means of tariffs, from international competition.[69] Under this British regime, when Egyptian factories produced little for export besides hand-rolled cigarettes and cottonseed oilcakes, all sorts of novel machines fabricated overseas entered the country. Cairo became a city of tramways and boutiques, where European tourists and cosmopolitan residents competed with one another to display trendy things. Never did "the modern" seem so nearly synonymous with "the foreign" as it did then and there.

As a Muslim modern, Riḍā strove to convince the readers of his fatwas that this semantic association was arbitrary and temporary. But the fact that he had no jurisdiction anywhere in the world, not even in Cairo, raises a question about his authority and efficacy as a global mufti. Fatwas are generally represented as nonbinding, advisory rulings that play a role in the process of applying the sacred law to a society.[70] Even if delivered with forceful rhetoric, they lack an automatic mechanism for coercion. However authoritative and persuasive, they count—in legal theory—as nothing more than opinions or interpretations, which judges, rulers, or private individuals may choose to disregard, comply with voluntarily, or enforce.[71] For this reason, historical analyses of fatwas often focus on their potential effect on judicial proceedings, executive actions, and popular opinions. Along these lines, a history of official governmental fatwas, Skovgaard-Peterson's *Defining Islam for the Egyptian State*, argued that Grand Muftis' communiqués had a tremendous influence in twentieth-century

Egypt—not so much politically but socially and religiously—because they countered secularization and promoted Islamization as they shaped public viewpoints. Such an approach seems justifiable only in those rare cases when there is concrete evidence of fatwas' use, reception, impact, or causal role.[72]

My approach to fatwas is different, however. Riḍā published around 1,060 of them in *al-Manār* between 1903 and 1935, enough to fill six volumes once they were collected after his death. I would not rush to represent them as effective decrees that came from the upper echelons of the Islamic legal order or as influential directives that emanated from Riḍā's press, after the mufti's independent contemplations of the divine law, to affect the beliefs and behavior of a community of readers, God willing. Like most fatwas, *al-Manār*'s fatwas emerged from below—in response to fatwa seekers' questions and consumer demand for Islamic answers to everyday problems.

Since fatwas generally arise in the middle or at the end of a chain of causation, historians should in the first place treat them as effects, not as causes. Every fatwa begins with a question or demand. The layperson, the judge, or the ruler who solicits the fatwa initiates the process. In *al-Manār*, the solicitor appears as the first author, identified by name and location. This is the person who frames the problem, motivating and affecting the mufti's response. As a historian of social practices and material culture, I insist on going back even further in time in order to understand better agency and causation, for the fatwa solicitor often reveals the existence of a social conflict or a religious dispute, which is what prompts the appeal to the mufti as an informal arbiter. In addition, in the fatwas under analysis in this book, the conflicts and disputes revolve around new products, technologies, and enterprises. Material objects, however inanimate by legal standards, certainly animate the process. They set in motion the chain of events that leads in the end to the fatwa. In most cases, when a fatwa condones a material entanglement, there is little reason to contemplate its economic effect. It simply sanctions, with the inevitable caveats, what is already in existence. It works as a kind of blessing that one group of social actors might brandish to show its rivals that its way of interacting with the object on trial is lawful.

These evidentiary and methodological considerations should make it clear why I will not advance a Weberian argument about the impact of religious beliefs on economic behavior.[73] The demand for a legal opinion, which plays a central role in this book, suggests in some cases that pious considerations had an effect on the financial decisions of a portion of the population for a period of time. In 1901 and 1902, for example, qualms about usury inspired a few Egyptians—only 10 percent of those who deposited their money in a government bank—to opt out of earning interest. This issue prompted policymakers to press the Grand Mufti, Muḥammad ʿAbduh, to intervene with a juridical response. In addition, a demand for a legal opinion can reveal how Muslim consumers responded positively or negatively to the appearance of new "Islamic" commodities: products such as records of the Qurʾan that multinational companies manufactured and marketed in an effort to cultivate and profit from an "Islamic" taste. As for fatwas, they reveal little more than a mufti's religious ideals. In and of themselves, they shed no light on the economic effects of his counsel. Therefore, my focus in this book is not on the question that new institutional economists would ask about the effects of fatwas, understood as informal constraints, on economic performance or modernization plans.[74] As a historian of Islam, I am rather more interested in the modern entanglement of religious ideals with economic goods.

The Qurʾan's Mysterious Signs

Every Muslim knows that Islam has always been about sharing spiritual goods, not accumulating material possessions.[75] But to what extent did the Qurʾan inspire believers to enjoy the world of goods? At the turn of the twentieth century, in Muslim societies under European dominance, few ideas generated as much passionate debate as the charge that the Qurʾan placed insurmountable obstacles on the way to the market. In a period when the world's religions were measured and compared with an economic yardstick, no Muslim scholar did more than Riḍā to challenge this charge. Through great exegetical exertions, he tried to magnify scriptural principles that supported the impression that Islam was an easygoing religion that favored freer trade. But his opponents did not always appreciate his desperate struggle to minimize taboos and explain away inconvenient precedents. They made the point that the scriptures of Muslims did impose significant restrictions on economic behavior and the pursuit of profit.

Besides the famous prohibition on usury, which Lord Cromer fixated on, there were other prohibitions. The Qurʾan outlawed, for one, the use of divining arrows and sacrificial stones—made by Satan himself, no less (Q. 5:90)—while the Ḥadīth imposed a prophetic ban on the sale of wine, carrion, pork, and material idols, cursing the Jews who turned a profit from forbidden fat.[76] Yet the Qurʾan also included verses, which Riḍā and his allies never failed to highlight, that suggested a freer approach to commerce and consumption. Beyond a doubt, the most inspiring one of them was the fifth verse of the fifth chapter. It gave Muslims permission to consume the food made by the People of the Book. "On this day," it announced, "the good things are made lawful for you."

This liberating verse, Qurʾan 5:5, was a critical scriptural proof-text for Riḍā. He often turned to it to support his laissez-faire approach to cross-cultural consumption. Thus, for example, he made use of it in 1922, when he published a permissive ruling in a battle of fatwas against a restrictive ruling by a mufti from British India. The mufti, Mawlawi Shafīq al-Raḥmān, had outlawed all uses of alcohol: not just drinking beer, wine, or spirits but also medical and industrial applications. Among other things, he warned Bombay Muslims against painting the doors and walls of their mosques with paints, varnishes, or lacquers that contained ethanol. Alcohol in every form symbolized danger and impurity in his eyes.

Riḍā reacted, as a laissez-faire Salafist and as a Muslim reformer, against the Bombay mufti's compulsive wariness. He praised many modern uses of alcohol, highlighting among other things the benefits of antiseptic solutions such as tincture of iodine. He argued that European supremacy was in great measure due to scientific, industrial, and pharmacological breakthroughs with the chemical compound. He suggested that there was a good reason to extend the scriptural prohibition on fermented grape juice to all intoxicating beverages but considered the blanket ban on alcohol ridiculous and unjustified. The future of Islam depended, as he saw it, on challenging the mentality of unreformed religious authorities such as Shafīq al-Raḥmān. Their advice, if heeded, would frustrate the plan to establish a powerful Islamic state, and it would drive progressive Muslims to lose their religion.[77]

To support his fatwa, Riḍā invoked the Qurʾan and the Salaf. He discussed the challenge that Muḥammad's Companions faced when they first traveled to lands populated by People of the Book. To eat and drink, they had to use the dishes and kettles of non-Muslims who indulged in wine and pork. Worried about consuming forbidden things, a few of these Muslims started to wash the cooking and eating utensils obsessively. But this "exaggerated" regime of "cleanliness" made it difficult for them to display their sociability and preach their beliefs. Upon their return to Medina, they asked the Prophet for guidance. In response, he obtained a divine revelation, Qurʾan 5:5, that gave Muslims the freedom to enjoy "the good things" of Christians and Jews. Hence, the Salaf learned that, to win converts to Islam and prosper in the world, it was essential not to treat non-Muslims' material possessions with suspicion or disgust. Muḥammad himself showed posterity the right way to behave when he performed a rite of purity with water from a pagan woman's leather canteen. Thus, he showed, in Riḍā's view, that the goods of infidels could play an instrumental role in the religious life of Muslims and even work, like rubbing alcohol, as agents of purity.[78]

1

The Toilet Paper Fatwa

Hygienic Innovation and the Sacred Law in the Late Imperial Era

In 1909 in the Anglo-Egyptian Sudan, a coy Muslim who identified himself as "Ṣ-M from Karmūs" removed his oversized shoes before he entered an assembly room with his band of brothers, apparently military officers. He had inserted a cardboard pad into the shoes "because there was too much room in them." Noticing the shoes by the assembly's entrance, a man in his company could not resist quipping, "Using paper for that purpose goes against religion." Somehow or other the reprimand devolved into a discussion, more humorous than learned, about the status of toilet paper before the shariʿa, Islam's sacred law. Even after a lengthy debate, however, the question remained unresolved, and the gathering was adjourned without the soldiers determining if toilet paper was a pure and lawful product or, like the *montgolfière*, a dangerous foreign thing. To conclude the debate, they needed a fatwa.[1]

If they followed prophetic norms, then Muslims in the Sudan used stones and water to cleanse themselves, always with the left hand, after defecation. The oral tradition, a body of scripture known as the Ḥadīth, recorded that the Prophet had favored a minimum of three stones for this purpose.[2] In one of these canonical traditions, Muḥammad's wife ʿĀʾisha revealed that the Prophet never failed to clean himself with water upon visiting the latrine.[3] A narrator of vignettes about the beginning of Islam, Anas ibn Mālik (d. ca. 709), remembered that he and a nameless lad, maybe a slave, had the honor of carrying a waterskin for Muḥammad to use for the removal of impurities from the body whenever he had the need to relieve himself.[4]

By cultural conventions or legal norms, the circle of Muslims that debated paper wipes in 1909 knew that the combination of water and stones was preferable. Still, they wondered whether using toilet paper was permissible in certain pressing circumstances: out of necessity when, for example, a captain intent on enforcing British rules of hygiene would prohibit Muslims traveling on his steamship "from transporting water to the toilet."[5] Would toilet paper defile their bodies? If they prayed after using it, would their prayers count as valid and meritorious? Or must they repeat their prayers after disembarking from the ship, when they would have the opportunity to wash all impurities away? The officer who had been accused of violating his religion failed to find "a clear scriptural text" to resolve his conundrums. After much hesitation, he decided to send a letter to an expert on Islamic law, Cairo's renowned Syrian reformer, seeking his advice.

A few years earlier, in 1903, Rashīd Riḍā had inaugurated in his journal a section dedicated to fatwas. Solicited by correspondents such as Ṣ-M from the unidentifiable town of Karmūs, these were authoritative yet nonbinding rulings.[6] Since they were issued outside of the official framework of competent courts exerting jurisdiction, and without any institutional connection to executive powers in any state, Riḍā's fatwas were not automatically enforceable. They were effective and influential insofar as they shaped perceptions and provoked discussions or persuaded individuals and communities to follow a course of action. There exists little evidence, however, to establish the impact and reception of most of his fatwas.[7]

Many of Riḍā's fatwas dealt with local religious controversies over the passage of modern commodities into Muslim societies, the adoption of foreign technologies, and the exploitation of new commercial opportunities at the end of the era of free-trade imperialism. Published in his journal as responses to petitioners from many corners of the world, these fatwas form the present book's backbone. Before turning to Riḍā's fatwa on toilet paper, however, it is critical to try to determine what exactly was the object in question and why it provoked a culturally meaningful debate: a debate about new things that served, like border crossing signs, to mark the line between religious conformity and religious deviance, and to establish the difference, if any, between being Muslim and becoming modern.

The Thing on Trial

A most modern invention, factory-made toilet paper arrived in the Sudan with the compliments of the British Empire following a period of tremendous innovation in the history of this everyday product. Located in New York, Diamond Mills Paper Company won a medal at the Paris World's Fair of 1878 for its entry, Bromo Paper. On every package of this "perfectly pure article for the water closet," it boasted that it had earned "the highest prize" at the universal exposition. Scientific experiments with disinfectants and curatives, mixtures of bromine, aluminum chloride, and carbolic acid had eventually yielded the medicated product, ideal for relieving that widespread condition: the piles. But the American company that made it declared that in several countries, though nowhere more so than in India under the British Raj, pharmacists had started to offer a counterfeit version in an imitation package. Customers could distinguish the "genuine Bromo" article by the watermark in every single sheet.[8] Not long after the makers of this product received kudos for their innovation from the exposition's judges, British and American manufacturers began developing, then marketing, the first perforated rolls. As this commodity spread, it began to replace earlier alternatives: rags, maize husks, newspapers, catalogs, old almanacs. Engineers rushed to invent new, specialized machines to satisfy growing consumer demand. Their patented inventions would range from Bradford Babbitt's "coin-operated machine for furnishing toilet-paper" to Arthur H. Scott's machine for mass-producing the tightest rolls.[9]

The relentless capitalist quest to profit exclusively from the creation of new personal hygiene products became so intense and so intriguing that in 1894 the U.S. Supreme Court decided to interfere in a relevant dispute over what exactly makes a patentable invention. Legendary entrepreneur Seth Wheeler, founder of the Albany Perforated Wrapping Paper Company, had conducted himself reprehensibly—according to Justice Brown—in filing an application for a patent in England for an apparatus (the "Oval King" fixture) that he had not invented himself but merely purchased in the market and dispatched across the Atlantic. The question before the Court, however, was different: whether the original inventor of the thing, Oliver H. Hicks, could legally extend his domestic monopoly over the novel mechanism to cover the exclusive production of a band of oval-shaped toilet paper. The Court ruled that Wheeler's enterprise did not, in the end, infringe upon Hicks's patent to the innovative fixture because the paper rolls in question, though designed to fit Hicks's protected innovation, were nothing but "perishable" things.[10]

Marketers and moralists urged Americans and Europeans to hurry and get the innovation. "Toilet paper is now a staple product," explained the *Pharmaceutical Era*, an American druggists' journal, in 1894.[11] Soon after its legal victory, Wheeler's company began to advertise in newspapers and catalogs that it would ship a case of its celebrated "A.P.W. Brand" satin-tissue rolls (a year's supply for "the average" family) to any post office in the United States, for one dollar.[12] By 1901 a manual on military hygiene recommended the appointment of "a reasonable quantity of toilet paper" as part of every soldier's allowance. "The use of such material is largely conducive to both comfort and cleanliness," and definitely preferable to "objects like sticks, grass, or leaves," which could well aggravate the rectum. Already the British Army had made this provision for its troops. "At present under trial," toilet paper ought to be readily available in latrine stalls, argued the American captain who wrote the book.[13]

In no time—under a regime of moral imperatives—the British came to see dedicated toilet paper as an indispensable hygienic product, a civilized convenience that they just absolutely needed to have in all corners of their empire. By the new century's dawn in the cosmopolitan city of Cairo under British influence, foreign and local elites could purchase the most elegant toilet paper fixtures at the showroom of Steinauer & Company, the khedive's sanitary engineers. At Stephenson's, Egypt's first English pharmacy, they could buy sundry drugs, a variety of imports, and—no doubt—the necessary rolls.[14]

But what specific paper product did the officers encounter in the Sudan? And what exactly did Riḍā envision, in Cairo, when he thought about toilet

FIGURE 1.1 Toilet appliances and fixtures in Max Steinaeur's showroom. Source: Arnold Wright, chief editor, and H. A. Cartwright, assistant editor, *Twentieth Century Impressions of Egypt: Its History, People, Commerce, Industries, and Resources* (London: Lloyd's Greater Britain, 1909), 361.

paper? It is unfortunately unclear. There is a lack of reliable data on the export of sanitary tissues to Egypt and the Sudan before World War I. American consular reports indicate that in this period British, American, French, and German toilet paper brands (Bronco, Sanico, Ideal Sanitaire, Lune, Jodler, etc.) competed with each other in European markets. Japanese brands were popular as well. The 1907 catalogue for the Army & Navy Co-Operative store reveals that various brands were available at the time in London. For three shillings and ten pence, customers could choose between a dozen packets of Victoria toilet paper, sanitized with the disinfectant Jeyes Fluid, and a dozen rolls of Mikado, nonperforated Japanese crêpe paper. (Surprisingly, these goods were located on the first floor in the stationery department, on a shelf near paper goods for the office, rather than on the ground floor, next to toiletry soaps or medical drugs.) Perhaps the same national products were available in the capital cities of Egypt and the Sudan, but that was not necessarily the case. There is no way to determine which company from which power had the dominant market share there around 1909, although it is worth recording that later, in the interwar period, the United States would emerge as the product's chief exporter. All the evidence nevertheless shows that the commodity crossed into Egypt and the Sudan as a foreign good. Local factories did not make it. Employing German, American, and French machines, Alexandria's lone papermaking mill had the capacity to transform rags and straw into cigarette boxes. But it did not yet possess the technology to make ultra-soft, pliable tissues. Eventually an Egyptian mill did acquire American machinery for cutting and rewinding soft tissues, thus embarking on the domestic manufacture of paper rolls. But this development still lay in the future. In 1909 there did not yet exist a national Egyptian brand.[15]

Still novel enough not to have a specialized name in Arabic, the article in question was called *al-waraq al-nashshāf fī al-istinjā*ʾ, which literally refers either to blotting paper or to absorbent wipes for the removal of excreta. It is impossible to locate contemporary statistics on Sudan's trade in this good. Yet the country's commerce was intertwined with Egypt's, and this fact could in theory help to indicate the object of trade. Possibly what reached privies in the Sudan was actually blotting paper, a product that writers normally used to absorb excess ink, which Egypt imported from diverse European countries including Hungary. But it is just as likely that it was an article made expressly for the toilet.

Whatever it was, whether dedicated toilet paper or blotting paper used as toilet paper, one thing is sure: the article reached the Sudan with British imperialism. Near the end of the nineteenth century, the empire's administrators turned the country into a condominium, which meant that it fell in theory under joint Anglo-Egyptian rule. With this arrangement came the garrisoning of British as well as Egyptian forces throughout the shared dominion. This fact helps to elucidate the political and social context underlying the religious debate about the legal status of toilet paper. Given the heavy presence of the Egyptian Army in the Sudan, given the difficulties that the British experienced when trying to recruit locals into the military that served to support foreign rule, and given the extraterritorial appeal to a jurist in Cairo, the original discussion that sparked the fatwa probably took place among Egyptian, rather than native Sudanese, soldiers.[16]

The Regime of Hygiene in Tropical Sudan and the Valley of the Nile

Toilet paper captured, in a convenient package, a Victorian and Edwardian zeal for modern manners and personal hygiene, which inspired new technologies and codes of conduct throughout the British realm.[17] The rules of this seaborne empire extended from Buckingham Palace to everyman's ship. A revised edition of the era's epitome, R. H. Notter and J. Lane Firth's *The Theory and Practice of Hygiene*, conveyed the pertinent norms and acts in stunning detail. With more than 300,000 British nationals, Lascar sailors, and other foreigners employed by the Mercantile Marine and the Royal Navy during King Edward's reign, authorities were gravely worried about the spread of exotic illnesses such as yellow fever through human and nonhuman vectors.

Notter and Firth's book included an entire chapter on the topic of marine hygiene. Readers learned that the Public Health Act of 1885 applied to ships the regulations originally designed to combat contagious diseases in hospitals. There were many strict rules. Adopted by the Board of Trade, the 1894 Merchant Shipping Act held in its eleventh schedule that "every passenger or emigrant ship must be provided with at least two privies on deck for every 100 passengers." Meanwhile, article 1154 of the Admiralty Instructions of 1904 specified the necessary physical qualities for seamen in His Majesty's Navy. In theory, an anal fistula, symptoms of hemorrhoids, or any kind of bowel disease automatically disqualified sailors from the royal service.[18]

Notter and Firth addressed systematically the problem of the "removal of excreta" from ships. Although they complained that pails were "the only form of convenience" on outdated cargo boats, they applauded modern steamships' efficient water-flushing systems. Latrine floors "should be impermeable, the surface being finished with a good fall outwards." Ventilation was essential. They recommended the installation of a short galvanized-iron hopper. They had sensible suggestions, too, for the design of the toilet: "If the seat be made to lift up, the closet may be used as a urinal, thus obviating the necessity for what is always a source of trouble on ships."[19]

In the Sudan, as in other colonies, the British were extremely preoccupied with hygiene. A teacher at a medical school that the British had established there reminisced that doctors were first of all concerned with "the establishment of elementary principles of cleanliness and sanitation in larger towns."[20] William Byam, an army doctor stationed in the Sudan in 1909, described in detail his "crusade for cleanliness." Fearing infected meat, he targeted butchers whose "clothing was far from clean" and who had in some cases "open sores upon their hands." (In quite a memorable reaction, one angry butcher, defensive about his own methods of slaughter, charged at the colonial doctor with his blade.) Increased communications between Egypt and the Sudan gravely worried Byam. So did plans for Egyptian workers to build a dam on the Blue Nile. He feared the spread of an infectious disease, bilharzia, from Egypt. Those bathing or drinking in water where "human beings pass excreta" would be exposed to parasitic worms, which would cause anemia and fatigue. Byam's concern eventually led to the establishment of a quarantine station, which allowed disinfected Egyptian workers to travel to the Sudan in "improved health and vigour," having become "more useful members of society."[21]

In this vein, too, Dr. Andrew Balfour, leader of the hygiene campaign in the Sudan, lectured on "Some Aspects of Tropical Sanitation." "Nothing is more progressive," he declared, "than sanitary science." The British faced "enemies of sanitation in tropical countries." These enemies included mosquitoes, the absence of water, "native customs and prejudices," and "the cultured but ignorant fanatic." Consequently, "tropical sanitation meant war, ceaseless, exhausting war," with the ultimate goal of eradicating diseases in order to enable "the swarms of black, merry, pot-bellied children on the shores of Omdurman" to "grow up with some hope for the future." Rather predictably, Balfour described the British sanitary inspector as the bearer of "that White Man's burden which, of all burdens, was perhaps the noblest to bear."[22]

In their criticisms of colonial habits, British writers often juxtaposed relatively new hygienic practices against native rites. To them, traditional rites appeared mired in a primitive, superstitious view of the world—whereas new practices and their devices (soaps, toilet paper, sewer systems, disinfectants, quarantine stations, and so on) appeared entirely rational, derived from a modern scientific understanding of the causes of infectious disease.

The British were very keen on sanitation in Egypt too. Beginning in the late nineteenth century, colonial authorities waged a battle for hygiene on multiple fronts, targeting disorderly city streets and dirty village customs.[23] The Sanitary

Department required Egyptian medical students to take a course in hygiene, a key subject in their final examination.[24] It also did "much good," Lord Cromer reported, "in the way of improving the sanitary condition of the mosques."[25] Apparent on the pages of the *Sanitary Record*, an English journal devoted to the science of hygiene, is British imperial pride in bringing modern sanitation to Egypt. One article tells of the extensive efforts involved in building drainage pipes in Cairo as part of an ambitious project to deliver a "complete sewage scheme" to the city.[26]

A scientific approach to cleanliness had broad cultural and commercial appeal in turn-of-the-century Cairo. Steinauer & Company did not fail to tell prospective customers that it had hired British plumbers to supervise the installation of sanitary appliances imported from Britain. Rattcliffe's engineering store boasted that it had a monopoly on the sale of Hall's sanitary distemper. An "excellent wall-covering" for Egypt's extreme climate, this colorful line of paints contained a "percentage of cresylic acid," which worked as an "efficacious germicide." Established in Shubra by a merchant from Edinburgh, the Hygienic Dairy advertised the production of pasteurized milk in hermetically sealed, refrigerated bottles. However dissimilar their products, these three firms decided to capitalize on one and the same value: hygiene.[27]

Another article in the *Sanitary Record* reveals how British sanitarians regarded Muslims as dirty, unhygienic subjects. It recounts an outbreak of cholera in the country, which caused the deaths of a number of British troops. "The introduction of the disease" it attributes "to the returning pilgrims from Mecca." According to a story first published by another journal, "one of the devout brought back with him a skin of holy water for the use of his friends, but finding it insufficient, he emptied it into the village wells, so that it might reach the greatest number! And it did. When the wells of the place were examined they were found to be teeming with cholera germs." One woman died in Cairo's "densest and filthiest quarters." But the disease killed more foreigners than natives, and this fact galled the English correspondent: "It is one of the eccentricities of the epidemic that Europeans of the cleanliest habits have died, and not one of the 300 scavengers of Alexandria has even been attacked."[28]

A governmental initiative to combat the spread of cholera, whose main symptom is severe diarrhea, preceded the rise of British rule over Egypt. It dated from the modernizing reign of Muḥammad ʿAlī. A British guide to Egypt claimed that this inadequately funded initiative failed "on account of the ignorance and fanaticism of the people, who looked on such measures as contrary to divine law and against the precepts of religion." Real progress came only when Britain took over the administration of public health in the country, generously funding an engineering department and a hygienic research laboratory. The sanitary engineers employed by these institutions were specifically charged with the sanitation of mosques and the diagnosis of pilgrims' feces samples.[29]

Long before the invention of toilet paper as a patented commodity, European authors exhibited an anthropological interest in Muslims' toilet etiquette. Once François Rabelais broke every literary taboo with his story about Gargantua's inventive experiments with the transformation of everyday objects into *torcheculs*, the comparative analysis of anal cleansing tools and methods became almost respectable. Scholars published "singular and curious treatments" of the customs and manners of nations and kingdoms. The topic was definitely not off limits in early modern times. In the seventeenth century Jean-Baptiste Tavernier, a French merchant who had twice visited Constantinople, remarked: "The Turks and all Muslims in general do not at all avail themselves of paper for vile usages." He then revealed the supposed reason for this: Muslims worried about the potential sacrilege of soiling disposable pieces of paper with writing on them since there was the risk that hallowed words would be present—in a carnal sense—in those texts. In addition, explained Tavernier, they did not believe that paper could properly purify the body for the performance of prayer. Therefore Easterners, *les Orientaux*, favored the use of water.[30] The ablutions of Turks, Arabs, and other Muslim peoples continued to receive scholarly attention, culminating in the oddest of cross-cultural studies: a bizarre nineteenth-century dissertation on the religious origin of the "excrementitious" rites of all nations.[31]

Colonialism changed the nature of this interest. A bawdy ethnographic curiosity about the routines of others gave way, by the turn of the twentieth century, to a slightly hysterical scientific crusade aimed at sanitizing the rites of native subjects. Suspected of presenting a risk to the health of European settlers, Muslim religious practices (especially the assembly of Muslims at "unsanitary" mosques and the flow of "infectious" pilgrims to Mecca) drew the attention of Egypt's British engineers. As in the Sudan, in this historical context, too, the decision by Muslims to adopt or reject toilet paper was laden with cultural and religious significance.

Riḍā's Easygoing Fatwa

"Using the paper found in steamships' lavatories," ruled Riḍā in his toilet paper fatwa, is permissible regardless of the availability of water there. Legal permission to use this article does not depend on necessity: Muslims are entitled to wipe themselves with toilet paper even when they are not stuck on a British steamship. It is better, opined the jurist, to use toilet paper than to use stones. Early Islamic traditions—the scriptures that turned episodes or memories from the life and times of the Prophet into rules, which all together constituted a behavioral code—had plainly granted Muslims permission to wipe themselves with stones, in imitation of Muḥammad.[32] This precedent served Riḍā to make, by extension, the case for toilet paper. Nothing was required here but a straightforward substitution of a natural object, the smooth stone, for an artifact designed to carry out the same basic function, anal cleaning, in an ostensibly superior way.

A reactionary jurist, disposed to entertain other relevant precedents set by the sacred law in order to cast doubts on the legality of the modern thing, could have taken a very different approach. He might first have recalled the Prophet's rejection of dung and bone as bumfodder, thereby demonstrating that Islamic law had placed restrictions on Muslims' choices.[33] He might then have contended that Muḥammad's recommendation had been quite specific: the messenger had favored an odd number of stones, which are patently incommensurable in every respect with an unspecified number of pliable, degradable tissues. On this basis, he could have ruled that, though not strictly forbidden, toilet paper was nevertheless a dubious article that wary, god-fearing Muslims must not rush to adopt. Finally, by relying on the doctrine that Muslims must not imitate the mores of Christians, he might have denounced the practice on principle. All of this is not just disciplined speculation. Aḥmad Raẓā Khān Barēlwī (d. 1921), a South Asian mufti who abhorred toilet paper, actually made the last argument when he considered the challenge of defecating in a passenger train.[34] Riḍā despised such arguments. He resented the fact that they made things so difficult. At the end of his fatwa he added a personal note to fortify the man with the excessively large pair of shoes: "Your friend erred in telling you that placing a paper pad in shoes is a taboo. To prohibit strictly what God himself did not forbid is an insolence against religion."[35]

It is nearly impossible today to think about toilet paper in relation to the shariʿa without reflecting on an anthropological classic, Mary Douglas's *Purity and Danger*. This is not because Douglas commented in passing on an old Brahmin rule against the use of paper after defecation but because she paid close attention to the construction of "matter out of place" by biblical lawmakers and because she compared modern and primitive as well as religious and secular notions of impurity. The attitude of one of the soldiers in the Sudan, the scandalized provocateur, is easy to grasp with her framework.

Human waste is universally or nearly universally regarded as an impure thing, whose offensive traces must be removed from the body. Toilet paper in the Anglo-Egyptian condominium was immediately linked, however, to a foreigner in a position of power (the imperial ship's captain) who symbolized, like all pork-eating, wine-drinking Europeans, the threat of ritual pollution. Not only did the commodity appear inadequate to the soldier as a tool for restoring the body to a state of purity in the absence of water. It apparently also figured in his eyes as a symbol of the material invasion by foreigners who worshipped another god. With the expansion of the British Empire into the Sudan, the entire social and political system came under pressure. So a foreign commodity that a Muslim subject might have heedlessly incorporated into his toilet routine in a more relaxed setting became, in such trying circumstances, a contested object: precisely the kind of strange new thing that might foster—as a marker of external danger—an impression of internal solidarity.[36]

Although never conveyed by the fatwa's solicitor, the imperial British attitude might be putatively grasped through Douglas's framework as well. A secular obsession with bodily hygiene, sharpened by scientific anxiety over the infectious habits of the empire's subjects, produced a set of modern rules to combat pollution within the captain's domain. It behooved the ship's commander to follow and enforce regulations. Upon approaching any English port, the sanitary authority depended on him to signal, with black and yellow flags, the presence of an infected ship. In the Royal Navy, captains received instructions from the Admiralty making it clear that seamen's personal cleanliness was their moral responsibility.[37] Nowhere did this obligation appear more critical than in the tropics, where naval hygiene was the bulwark between the civilized crew and savage diseases.[38] "The master of the ship," held the 1894 Merchant Shipping Act, "shall alone be liable to a fine for breach of the regulations as to privies." Imposing standards for the maintenance of these installations "in a serviceable and cleanly condition throughout the voyage" was one of the captain's duties.[39] Had Mary Douglas analyzed this modern, secular system of sanitation, she would have argued that it differed from its archaic counterparts in superficial, even trivial, ways. She found something universal, fundamentally human, in all the bizarre rules that diverse cultures had enacted to reduce anxiety about disgusting things.[40]

One problem with Douglas's universalizing approach to impurity is that it fails to explain very well cross-cultural encounters in a colonial context, where, in addition to different purity norms, there was also a power discrepancy. Although there were limits on his ability to force compliance, the captain had the authority to promulgate a single set of rules for everyone on board. Confined to the steamship, his realm was small and therefore manageable. Achieving success there was easier than elsewhere in the vastness of the tropics, where imperial sanitizers' dreams of hygienic modernity were endlessly frustrated—as postcolonial historians have suggested—by recalcitrant defecators.[41] In theory, though this is nearly inconceivable, subaltern passengers could rebel against the ship's rules in the privacy of the latrine. But the captain had the means to impose one rule effectively (the prohibition on carrying water to the toilet) upon passengers who were unable to wait until disembarking to defecate. In these circumstances, nobody cared about any structural similarities between Islamic rules of purity and Victorian rules of hygiene. What mattered from the perspective of Sudanese soldiers on board was the captain's power to enforce a British code.

However well it may explain why one soldier in the Sudan suspected that the imperial commodity was dangerous and impure, Douglas's model in no way serves to explain the varied social and cultural responses that actually took place in 1909. Instead of producing a unified communal front against the commodity, as a product signifying the divide between Muslims and infidels, toilet paper provoked an internal Islamic debate, dissension within the ranks. Riḍā's relaxed attitude was drastically different, too, from the censorious attitude of the soldier who had charged that using toilet paper was "against religion."

Riḍā's insistence on the hygienic article's superior virtue may reflect a "modernist" dismissal of medieval norms concerning purity and pollution. But his fatwa did not exactly break with the past. He found it necessary to cite a premodern precedent (the scriptural model granting Muslims permission to use stones for *istinjāʾ*, deliverance from bodily wastes) in order to justify his legal opinion. As a result, it is not clear whether to consider him a modernizer or a medievalizer. If a materialist reading of the fatwa would disregard the symbolic dimension of his argument to concentrate on the physical reality, the inevitable replacement of a natural object by a factory-made good, an idealist reading of it would insist on the fundamental value of the simile. It is the comparison between a scriptural emblem and a modern thing that allowed Riḍā to argue in favor of incorporating the commodity into Muslim practice. This semantic play entailed, in turn, the dissociation of the modern commodity from its foreign origin. Never did Riḍā refer to it as a "European" product. This elision made it easier for him to argue for Muslim appropriation.

Arguably, this ruling in favor of toilet paper derived from Riḍā's conviction that Islam imposed on the believer only reasonable, moderate obligations. In his mature defense of this view, he wrote that the stipulations of the Qurʾan must remain in force in the modern period, determining what a believer can and cannot do. These ancient requirements and prohibitions formed an easy path. As interpreters of the divine law, jurists had to insist on adherence to this path, but they were not entitled to throw new obstacles in the way of believers. Instead, they were morally obliged, in Riḍā's view, to help Muslims move forward. The notion that God made Islam an easy, convenient religion constituted such a basic principle of his thought that he would refer to it in the title of his work on legal hermeneutics, "The Prosperity of Islam and the Principles of General Legislation." The keyword that he used to evoke "prosperity," *yusr*, derived from the sacred law. It had long served theologians to argue that, as the balanced and sensible "religion of ease," Islam had liberated Muslims from the extreme rules of Judaism and Christianity, whose laws allegedly caused privation and hardship.[42]

In that book, serialized in *al-Manār* beginning in 1928, he made a surprising distinction between specifically "religious laws," where intransigence is justifiable, and civil, political, or military matters, where flexibility is desirable for society's benefit. God brought to perfection all directives pertaining to dogmatic beliefs and rites of worship. Every Muslim throughout history needs to follow these divine, immutable directives, based on unambiguous revelations, for they lead to happiness in the hereafter. Prescriptions concerning "worldly matters," by contrast, may change over time and vary from one place to the next. As an example, Riḍā mentions oral traditions relating to customs, such as medical usages and eating habits. To follow these traditions is commendable. Yet some variety in local practices is admissible. Despite the quest for a universal Islamic standard, those in power should not endeavor to change forcibly local practices that do not expressly contradict the revealed law or that cause no harm to the commonweal. When jurists confront cases that have nothing to do with ritual or doctrine, and on which the shariʿa sheds no direct light, then they ought to step aside, humbly, and grant Muslims the discretion to choose their own course of action. Thus empowered, human beings will make choices based on personal interest, communal benefit, and economic necessity—choices that will conform readily to Islam's progressive spirit.[43]

Paving an easy path, laissez-faire Islam seemed perfectly compatible with modern European civilization, nearly all of its technological advances, and many of its conveniences, including toilet paper. It was, in other words, a religion for freer trade: not, of course, an individualistic religion whose laws would grant each and every import duty-free passage into Muslim countries but certainly a religion whose laws placed minimal restrictions, for the sake of social progress, on the passage of foreign goods.

An expert on Islamic legal thought through the ages, Wael Hallaq, has argued that Riḍā's doctrine amounted to a "total negation of traditional legal theory." In addition to privileging interest, advantage, and necessity to an unprecedented degree as factors to consider when making judgments for Muslim moderns, Riḍā began to prepare the ground, argued Hallaq, "for a total dissociation of religion from strictly non-religious, mundane matters."[44] Whether or not

Riḍā's hermeneutic marked such a modern turn in the history of legal theories, it is difficult to agree with this teleological characterization of Riḍā's program as one tending toward a clear partition between religious and secular affairs. The theoretical division that Riḍā proposed between fixed religious norms and changeable social conventions was never quite so obvious in his legal opinions, where he dealt with cases that arose when religious principles became entangled willy-nilly with mundane things.

The fact that soldiers in the Sudan voluntarily appealed to Riḍā for an Islamic ruling suggests a willingness on their part to extend the sacred law to cover a novel thing. It is easy to envision how a multiplicity of such appeals for legal advice could add up, fatwa by fatwa, to give Muslims the impression that the shariʿa was in effect a total system of judgments: a system that could be applied in theory to everything—even to something as far removed from spiritual worship as toilet paper. Arguably, by responding to one after another request for fatwas, Riḍā contributed to this understanding of God's revealed laws as always relevant—no matter the object or practice on trial.[45] In this respect, *al-Manār*'s fatwa requests and fatwas did not reflect the retreat of the shariʿa in the era of European dominance or growing secularism; they rather reflected the shariʿa's advances into new areas of religious interest.[46]

In the toilet paper fatwa, Riḍā shined the light of Islam on the most banal of things, all but enchanting the steamship's latrine. The commodity came first, however; the religious debate among laypersons followed it; the reformer's expert legal ruling arrived at the end. This is an important sequence to mark if we want to understand the chain of causes that led, in this instance, to the trial of a modern object before the sacred law. The same basic sequence also appears, as the coming chapters make clear, in many other instances. More than merely the existence of a standard pattern, a microhistorical investigation of multiple fatwas may reveal the unfolding of a broader process: the making, case by case, of Islam's reformation. For more than a century this reformation has been presented as if it had been inspired and directed by a select group of intellectual elites: a coterie of illustrious divines such as Rashīd Riḍā. But if their interventions in social disputes and religious conflicts occurred late in the day, after the objects of debate and the parameters of debate had been fixed, then their historical agency has been greatly exaggerated. Perhaps things such as toilet paper, zealots such as the soldier who commanded the right and prohibited the wrong at that gathering in the Sudan, and fatwa seekers such as Ṣ-M from Karmūs, the aggrieved fellow who framed the legal questions after conducting his own scriptural investigations, deserve more credit. They were the makers of this history.

2

Fatwas for the Partners' Club

A Global Mufti's Enterprise

Al-Manār became the most successful Islamic journal of its era by serving a globalized, trans-imperial community of Muslims readers, and this success was in some measure due to Riḍā's international focus on religion. The very first issue, published in February of 1898, included a news report about Germany's fateful dispatch of cruisers to China after the killing of two Catholic missionaries.[1] At the end of that year the periodical published an article thanking "the sons of our nation," Syrian migrants to Brazil, for subscribing to an Islamic magazine though they were Christian.[2] A decade later readers did not need even to open the journal to sense its reach. The cover announced that an annual subscription cost 60 piastres in Egypt and the Sudan, 3.5 riyals in the Ottoman Empire, 18 franks abroad, 15 shillings in India, and 7 rubles in Russia.[3] Clearly, Riḍā envisioned an international readership that would pay, in diverse currencies, for his publication. He included the journal's addresses on the cover, too, as an invitation for international correspondents. Readers could simply address letters to al-Manār's office—located, together with the printing press, on Darb al-Jamāmīz Street—or telegrams to "al-Manār in Cairo."

Over the years, Arabic readers from all over the world—from Canton, Ohio, to Canton, China—wrote to Riḍā as an authority on Islamic matters. They approached him for legal and religious advice from Beirut, Bombay, Batavia, Bangkok, and Berlin as well as Montenegro, Paris, and Lausanne. They wrote to him from Dongola in the Sudan, Qāʾenāt in Khurasan, Kazan in Tatarstan, and from the islands of Borneo, Ceylon, and Zanzibar. Most of his international communications took place with fatwa seekers across the Indian Ocean and around the Mediterranean Sea. Now and then correspondents sent him letters from the other side of the Atlantic Ocean: in 1909 he heard from a certain Ilyās Laṭifullāh,

المنار
١٣١٥
مجلة شهرية تبحث في فلسفة الدين وشؤون الاجتماع والعمران
« تصدر في كل شهر عربي مرة »
لمنشئها
السيد محمد رشيد رضا
عنوانها (مصر — ادارة مجلة المنار) والتلغرافي « المنار بمصر »
المجلد الاول
سنة ١٣١٥ وسنة ١٣١٦
قيمة الاشتراك عن سنة ستون قرشاً صاغاً في مصر والسودان
وفي المملكة العثمانية ثلاثة ريالات ونصف وفي الخارج ١٨ فرنكاً
و١٥ شلناً في الهند و٧ روابل في روسيا والدفع سلفاً
﴿ حقوق إعادة الطبع والترجمة للكل أو البعض محفوظة لمنشيء المجلة ﴾
الطبعة الثانية سنة ١٣٢٧
طبع بمطبعة المنار بشارع درب الجماميز بمصر

FIGURE 2.1 Covers of *al-Manār* such as this one indicated an international circulation.

who somehow or other had ended up in Tinogasta, Argentina, and who wanted very much to know why non-Muslims were barred from entering the Ḥijāz, the Ottoman Empire's province in western Arabia.[4] Indeed, the globalization of Islamic legal communications took off in the late nineteenth and early twentieth centuries, and no written medium reflected and promoted this development as much as Riḍā's far-flung enterprise.

In its long history, Islamic law offers many examples of the movement of legal knowledge from one to another place. This process began at the origins of Islam with the transmission of oral traditions from Mecca and Medina to nearby cities such as Ṣanʿāʾ in the Yemen. It continued with the transfer of rulings to cities as far as Cordoba. Many of the earliest, foundational Muslim texts, from ʿAbd al-Razzāq al-Ṣanʿānī's *Muṣannaf* to Yaḥyā al-Andalusī's edition of Mālik ibn Anas's *Muwaṭṭaʾ*, are themselves products of legal knowledge in motion. The most famous compendium of "Indian" fatwas, the great digest that Emperor Aurangzeb commissioned in the seventeenth century, was basically a reconfiguration of eighth- and ninth-century Iraqi rulings, adjusted to fit a different place and time. By the late nineteenth century, as colonial steamships made it easier for Muslim pilgrims to travel to the Ḥijāz, the flow of legal communications across vast distances increased too. These were precisely the historical circumstances that gave rise, by 1892, to a bilingual, Arabic–Malay edition of fatwas, which conveyed Meccan jurists' opinions to Southeast Asia's Muslims.[5]

A more efficient mailing system made legal consultations across vast distances less extraordinary than in the past. Prominent religious authorities such as Riḍā's mentors began to hear more and more from correspondents overseas. Around 1899 one of his teachers, the Ottoman Syrian educator Ḥusayn al-Jisr (d. 1909), received a request for a juridical opinion from an Arab-Javanese scholar, Sayyid ʿUthmān (d. 1914), who had traveled throughout the Middle East before he settled back down in Batavia. The Batavian scholar wanted the Syrian jurist's support in a battle over the legal status of the gramophone that he was poised to wage—in the peripheries of the Islamic world—against a rival authority from Singapore.[6] As Cairo's Grand Mufti, Muḥammad ʿAbduh heard from places such as the Transvaal in 1903 and the Punjab in 1904. His Transvaal fatwa gave rise to fierce debates, eagerly amplified by the Cairo weeklies.[7] Trafficking in speedy and controversial communications, newspapers greatly contributed to the quicker dissemination of fatwas to the public within and across geographic borders and legal jurisdictions.

Coming of age in this world, where printing presses, railroads, and steamships facilitated the flow of religious communications, Riḍā realized early on in his career that fatwas were newsworthy and marketable items. This realization unfolded on the pages of *al-Manār* over the course of a year between the summer of 1903 and the fall of 1904. Like many previous issues, the June 1903 issue included a section on juridical responses to readers' questions, unassumingly titled "Questions and Answers." The same issue discussed the replies of a prominent Azhari judge, Muḥammad Bakhīt al-Muṭīʿī (d. 1935), to a set of questions that Muslims from the Transvaal mailed to an Egyptian newspaper. On his own initiative, Riḍā decided to criticize the judge's opinion and publish his own dissenting verdict.[8] Such exchanges made him realize that Muslim readers wanted responsa, and that new possibilities existed for transmitting Islamic advice through printed journals. Later that same year, he rebranded his responses, more boldly, as "fatwas." After a few months of experimenting with this column, he decided to turn the demand for fatwas by consumers of newspapers into a moneymaking venture. In June 1904 he began specifying in "The Section on Questions and the Fatwa" that he would publish legal responses only for readers who had paid for his magazine. A few months later he gave this feature a more marketable title, "The Fatwas of the Lighthouse," and posted the same advertisement: a notice disclosing that the privilege of obtaining legal advice would be restricted to the exclusive circle of paying subscribers.[9]

Readers' demands for religious and legal advice motivated Riḍā to pursue a career as an independent mufti. In 1902 a Najdi merchant from Bahrain wrote to him to ask for a ruling on banknotes. He received only an "answer." A year later, when the same merchant asked a new question, he received a "fatwa."[10] Both replies were legal responsa. The formal difference between them was that the first bore a generic title, whereas the second carried the aura of an authoritative interpretation of the sacred law. Encouraged by a steady trickle of religious and legal questions from correspondents domestic and foreign, Riḍā made the transition from one to the other genre smoothly.

Riḍā's career as a writer of fatwas was, from the very beginning, a globalized one. He wrote his ninth fatwa, in 1903, for Ḥ-Ḥ of Montenegro; his twentieth, for the Singaporean Anjī Ambūgh ibn Aḥmad; his twenty-third, for a teacher and preacher in Russia, ʿAbdul Kabīr Efendi al-Muṣṭaffawī; his forty-eighth, for a medical student in America, Najīb Efendi Qunāwī; his sixty-eighth, in 1904, for an Egyptian traveler, Aḥmad Zakī, who had written a famous account of the Paris World Fair; and his ninety-eighth for Nūr al-Dīn of the Punjab. Basking in this international attention, Riḍā titled the last two exchanges "Parisian Questions" and "Indian Questions," respectively.[11] In this manner, he suggested his journal's worldwide fame as well as his capacity to act as an Islamic legal authority for Muslims overseas. Due to his unprecedented success in reaching a trans-imperial audience, Riḍā perhaps deserves to be called "The First Global Mufti." No fatwa-giving authority before him had received such a high volume of questions from so many disparate parts of the world. His feat in communications, unparalleled at the time, rivals the accomplishment of Yūsuf al-Qaraḍāwi, who years later would use satellite television and the internet to cultivate a global audience.[12]

Riḍā did not fashion for himself an identity as an official mufti, however. On the contrary, he made every effort to distinguish himself professionally from contemporary muftis in Cairo such as Muḥammad Bakhīt: accommodating justices in the government's employ whose scholastic juridical discipline, honed at al-Azhar, struck Riḍā as hopelessly provincial and inadequate for resolving modern dilemmas.[13] He certainly did not aspire to become a mufti in this mold.

He presented himself instead as an Islamic reformer, as the founder and owner of the Lighthouse Press, and as the editor of an enlightening Arabic journal, *al-Manār*.[14] In these capacities, he published fatwas, scriptural commentaries, book reviews, news roundups, editorials, and a variety of other kinds of articles. He issued fatwas not as an official Islamic authority encumbered by a state's legal system but as the free, entrepreneurial publisher of an Islamic magazine. This was a new kind of venture. As a journalistic mufti, he wanted his fatwas to edify and entertain as well as attract a general readership. Insofar as he succeeded in these aims, he made a significant contribution to the history of Islamic law in connection with modern media.[15]

Channels and Barriers: The Global Circulation of *al-Manār*

Al-Manār offers historians one measure of the globalization of the project to reform Islam in the early twentieth century.[16] To what extent did the journal circulate globally? What channels facilitated its diffusion overseas? What barriers prevented it from reaching a wider readership at home and abroad? *Al-Manār* did not flow freely to Muslims worldwide. Its core readership consisted of relatively affluent, highly educated, and religiously devoted Sunni Muslim men with competence in Arabic. It had female readers and Christian correspondents, including a women's literary club in Beirut and a Danish pastor in Damascus.[17] But their numbers were small.

Although it circulated widely in the Middle East, the Arabic periodical did not establish itself successfully in areas where the population spoke mainly Turkish or Persian. Despite the fact that he lived for more than a year of his life in Istanbul, Riḍā received only one request for a fatwa from the Ottoman Empire's capital.[18] Legal communications with Persian territories under the Qajar shahs were minimal, too. Tellingly, besides one solicitation from Qāʾenāt in South Khurasan, he received only one other demand for a fatwa from a city under Iranian sovereignty, and it came from Linja, a multiethnic though largely Sunni port on the Persian Gulf, in a region that was very much under British dominance.[19]

Imperial spheres also limited the journal's reach. The Dutch Empire favored local, rather than universal, expressions of Islam. Finding trans-imperial connections between Muslims a threat to their colonial enterprise, Dutch authorities restricted the journal's circulation. Copies of *al-Manār* had to be smuggled into Javanese ports by international traders and by pilgrims on their return from Mecca. Enforcing the ban effectively—in an archipelago with countless ports—was of course impossible. At least one Dutch censor in charge of Arabic communications decided to permit deliveries to a Sudanese scholar who had moved to Batavia. Still, the existence of a ban meant that potential subscribers had to consider whether they wanted to risk spending money on a serial product that could be confiscated at the border.[20]

The Ottoman Empire also banned the publication. Its regime of censorship, by turns strict and capricious and quite burdensome until the Young Turk Revolution, focused with some anxiety on the writings of Syrian expatriates. Code words such as "reform" (*iṣlāḥ*) and "nation" (*waṭan*) that sounded relatively innocuous when printed by local newspapers carried an ominous sense, tinged with dissidence, when they were published by exiles such as Riḍā. By the summer of 1898 Syrian readers began to cancel their subscriptions on account of confiscations, and Riḍā had to ask the post office to return to him undelivered issues. The censor of the *vilayet* of Beirut gave *al-Manār* a warning in 1901 for printing forbidden words in violation of the fundamental principles of the law of the press. In 1906 a nearby court went so far as to order Riḍā's arrest for printing "traitorous" and "seditious" propaganda.[21] This barrier to trans-imperial legal communications was significant. Riḍā published more than 170 fatwas in response to questions sent to him from Beirut or Damascus, yet he wrote every single one of them after the restoration of the constitution, once lawmakers secured the freedom of the press.[22]

The cultivation of Arabic by Muslim subjects of the British, Dutch, Russian, and French Empires enabled Riḍā to spread his ideas broadly. Realizing the power of Arabic to bring together the world's *umma*, as an imagined global community, he himself preached the virtues of Arabic whenever he had the chance. He did so, for example, in his fatwas against translating and transliterating the Qurʾan. He argued that Europe's political and civil jihad against Islam had sown division among Muslims of different ethnicities who should rather rally behind the original, inimitable scripture.[23] When he visited India in 1912, he promoted the study of Arabic for true knowledge of Islam. *Al-Manār* found scores of readers outside of the Middle East and North Africa thanks to a range of new Islamic schools that shared this vision and taught their students Arabic as the language of theology and law.[24] In addition, among the subscribers to Riḍā's journal were members of highly mobile communities of native Arabic speakers, such as the Syro-Lebanese diaspora in the Americas and the Ḥaḍramī or South Arabian diaspora in Southeast Asia.

But a low level of literacy in Arabic at the time limited Riḍā's active readership to an intellectual elite, even in Arabic-speaking countries such as Egypt. The 1897 census classified 8 percent of sedentary male Egyptians and 0.2 percent of sedentary female Egyptians over seven years old as possessing the ability to read and write. Literacy rates climbed steadily over the next twenty years, when

Egypt's Ministry of Finance held another census. Statisticians then classified more than 85 percent of the male population and more than 97 percent of the female population as illiterate.[25] Riḍā cultivated an accessible journalistic style of writing that made technical juristic concepts intelligible to readers without specialized training in Islamic law. In an era of rapidly expanding print production and consumption, he made every effort to attract laypersons. Through oral diffusion, his more controversial arguments could certainly reach a broad audience with at least functional literacy. Still, nothing limited the purchase of his journal as much as the rare ability to read Arabic expertly.

Muslims with little or no Arabic were able to access some of Riḍā's writings indirectly. Tatar, Urdu, Malay, and Chinese readers encountered select articles in translation through a number of new Islamic journals in these languages. The bilingual editors of *Shūrā* ("Council") in Orenburg, *al-Hilāl* ("The Crescent") in Calcutta, *al-Munīr* ("The Enlightener") in Padang, and *Tianfang Xueli Yuekan* ("Arabic Theology Monthly") in Guangdong, to give a few examples, drew inspiration from *al-Manār* in their own calls for revival and reform. Beyond simply translating its articles, several editors modeled the content and format of their journals after *al-Manār*.[26]

Riḍā's widespread network of communications relied heavily on personal connections. In an age of high mobility, he met with many foreign students who visited Cairo and enrolled at al-Azhar in order to improve their knowledge of Arabic and Islamic law. During his own missions abroad to cities such as Istanbul, Mecca, Damascus, Lucknow, and Geneva, he established multiple connections with a new generation of Muslim leaders who cared deeply about educational reform and agitated for political change, seeking national liberation.[27] Riḍā's circle of influential acquaintances included figures such as Ali Kayaev, an educator from the North Caucasus who studied in Cairo and then returned to Dagestan to found a school where Muslims could study both chemistry and Islam; Abul Kalam Azad, a polyglot journalist and a prominent leader of the movement for India's independence; and Ahmad Dahlan, the founder of Muhammadiyah, a massive Southeast Asian organization dedicated to modern schooling for Muslims, the eradication of local syncretism, and a nonviolent struggle against Dutch colonialism.[28] Readers of *al-Manār* who had not met Riḍā personally felt connected to him through the section on fatwas, where they received answers to their most pressing questions about Islam. A Javanese subscriber, Basyūnī ʿImrān (d. 1953), was so moved by Riḍā's "pure knowledge of religion" that he traveled to Cairo, where he stayed in an apartment owned by Riḍā's family and enrolled in a school established by Riḍā.[29]

The journal's viability and commercial success depended on these personal links and on the connections that Riḍā established with readers from afar through the section on fatwas, where he responded to individual subscribers' questions. These readers' loyalty, their continued patronage, enabled him to continue publishing the journal until his death in 1935—and slightly beyond that because a devoted reader, the Muslim Brotherhood's founder, produced a few issues posthumously.

The Business of *al-Manār*: Circulation, Subscriptions, Profits

Devout Sunni reformers intensely committed to the search for a modern Islam formed *al-Manār*'s target audience, but very few of them could afford to subscribe to the journal. An annual subscription to Riḍā's monthly cost less than an annual subscription to Egypt's high-circulation dailies.[30] Still, the magazine was a bourgeois extravagance. How did the expense compare to other urbane luxuries? In 1905, when a year's subscription to *al-Manār* cost fifty piastres, Cairo consumers could buy a new gramophone, which came with five "free" discs, for just two hundred piastres.[31] Five years later, when *al-Manār*'s cost had risen by twenty piastres, an Englishman remarked that all cafés supplied "a cup of Turkish coffee and five Egyptian cigarettes for one piastre."[32] A subscription to the journal cost as much, then, as seventy indulgent pauses for coffee and tobacco.

Which professionals considered *al-Manār* affordable? Low-income workers in Egypt who earned as little as five piastres a day would have had to toil for ten days in order to buy an annual subscription at the beginning of the twentieth century. The Islamic monthly probably also seemed prohibitively expensive to muezzins and imams, even after the 1904 salary raises. Their monthly salary ranged from 1 to 2.5 Egyptian pounds, and this was but two to five times the sum of money needed for a yearlong subscription. Painters, electricians, mechanics, and sanitary engineers would have reckoned that the cost amounted to three or so days' wages. Translators, reporters, teachers, and clerics earned on average three to four times more than muezzins and imams, and many of them had a compelling professional reason to consider subscribing to *al-Manār*. But the expense would not have seemed trivial to them. *Al-Manār* was more affordable, however, for district doctors, police inspectors, the corps of High ʿUlamāʾ at al-Azhar, and professors at the college of law. An annual subscription cost them no more than half a day's earnings.[33] As for notables from merchant families, they paid for it with ease. Among its loyal subscribers, the journal counted rich and influential men such as ʿUmar Bey al-Dāʿūq, Beirut's former mayor; Shaykh Muqbil al-Dhakīr, a pearl magnate who made his fortune in Bahrain; and the Singaporean trader Muḥammad ibn ʿAqīl ibn Yaḥyā.[34]

Riḍā did not reach these readers by chance. In addition to leveraging personal connections, he experimented with different business approaches to attract customers. Originally, when the paper was formatted as an eight-page weekly broadsheet, he printed 1,500 copies and mailed them to potential customers in Egypt and Syria. Most of the Egyptians returned the product to him. The Syrians who expressed an interest soon discovered, to Riḍā's frustration, the Ottoman government's ban on deliveries. He reduced the print run to 1,000 copies, converted the journal to a monthly magazine, and offered students of religion a 20 percent discount. Still, he managed to attract only a third as many subscribers. These committed customers, around 330 in number, provided him with a steady revenue of around 165 pounds per year at the beginning of the twentieth century. This was a significant sum if the total cost of production added up to 40 pounds per year, which corresponds to his own estimate.[35] Most of his income came from these subscriptions because mechanisms for distributing single issues were limited and a commercial clientele was unattainable. Egypt's high-circulation dailies published classifieds, but *al-Manār* had too small and scattered a readership to secure funding from this source. It never published advertisements.

The initial lack of success troubled him.[36] He contemplated liquidating the business and selling unsold magazines as material for kindling or as wrapping paper for merchants' wares. But he decided to persevere. He continued publishing *al-Manār* even after burglars broke into his print shop in 1900, stealing equipment and the stock of paper. With a fifty-pound loan, he restarted the operation.[37] Five years after he inaugurated the printing press, around the time that he launched the feature on fatwas, the number of subscribers began to rise. He started to earn enough money to pay off his debts, and his confidence in the viability of his enterprise grew.[38]

To succeed as an international Islamic entrepreneur, Riḍā had to experiment often with foreign subscription rates and zones. He kept the price of *al-Manār* fairly stable for domestic subscribers, raising it ten piastres at a time between the financial crisis of 1907 and the Great Depression.[39] It was harder for him to determine the optimal price for overseas sales. In 1900 he declared that a subscription to his magazine would cost 16 francs in all foreign countries except for India, where it would cost 12 shillings. In 1904, he increased the standard price by 2 francs, while specifying separate rates for India (10 rupees) and Russia (7 rubles). Two years later he incorporated the Sudan into the Egyptian subscription zone and changed the price for India once more. He first listed the Ottoman Empire as a market for his journal in 1909, following the restoration of constitutional liberties. At this point, he determined that Ottoman subjects would need to pay 3.5 riyals for a subscription. But in 1917 he dropped the Ottoman Empire from this list of international markets and rather offered *al-Manār*—in a gesture of nationalism—to "Egypt, the Sudan, and the rest of the Arab countries" for the single price of 80 piastres, as if a single currency zone united them all. By 1929 the Saudi kingdom of the Ḥijāz replaced Russia and India on the cover of *al-Manār*. Despite the extra shipping costs, he decided to charge subscribers in Mecca the exact same amount as subscribers in Cairo: one Egyptian pound.

All these currencies and price changes hint at the faltering character of Riḍā's venture into foreign markets. They suggest his global aspirations; they do not, however, give a sense of the scale of the enterprise. Al-Manār Press remained quite a small business, despite Riḍā's international marketing designs. It is telling that, two years after he began specifying the cost of his magazine in rubles, he had succeeded in attracting no more than two dozen subscribers in Russia.[40]

Like many other globalized businesses, Riḍā's enterprise, too, apparently fell on hard times during and after World War I.[41] He lost Russian and Indian customers; the total number of subscribers requesting fatwas from him dropped significantly, by nearly half, in the interwar period; and he died with a thousand-pound mortgage on his house.[42] Whether his business as a magazine publisher suffered from the contraction of world trade or from the changing tastes of Muslim readers, Riḍā nevertheless found new ways to make a profit out of his publishing house. Notably, he secured Ibn Saᶜūd's patronage in the 1920s. The Saudi sultan and king paid him a fortune—four thousand pounds sterling, or so Riḍā confessed in a private letter—to edit and print the writings of Muḥammad ibn ᶜAbd al-Wahhāb and his descendants.[43]

In addition, Riḍā's press published a fair number of monographs, books that had originally appeared in a serialized form in *al-Manār* as well as editions of medieval and modern texts. This production, limited in scope before World War I, increased in volume after 1922.[44] Every historian of Islam's reform knows that Riḍā promoted the works of Muḥammad ᶜAbduh; and every historian of Salafism knows that Riḍā edited and published books by Ibn Taymiyya (d. 1328) and Ibn ᶜAbd al-Wahhāb. Whatever these activities reveal about his political persuasion or religious inclination, it is important to keep in mind that his livelihood depended on printing and selling magazines and books. In 1927 he advertised a list of fifty titles published by his press. Customers could order by telephone the fifth edition of ᶜAbduh's *Theology of Unity* for eight piastres; *The Reformer and the Imitator*, *The Wahhabis and the Ḥijāz*, and *The Caliphate and the Grand Imamate* for five piastres each; *New Epistles and Fatwas* for ten piastres; *Fatwas on the Reform of the Woman* for two piastres; or the full collection of past issues of *al-Manār* magazine in twenty-eight volumes for twenty-eight pounds. This information derives from the back cover to a book that al-Manār Press published as well: the first Arabic translation of Gandhi's *Guide to Health*.[45]

Fatwas for Money: The Contract with Invested Readers

As an independent author whose income derived mainly from selling his own magazine, Riḍā made a critical distinction among his readers between subscribers and free riders. His "partners," the readers who spent money on an annual subscription, were entitled to a special benefit: fatwas. Since this was a new kind of venture, Riḍā decided to define the expectations clearly. In 1904 he published a contract of sorts, frequently reprinted, between himself as the journal's mufti and future fatwa petitioners:

> We have opened this section to answer the questions of our partners exclusively; it does not extend to people in general. We make it a condition for the enquirer to specify for us his first name, his family name, his country, and his work (his profession). After doing so, it is then up to him to indicate if he wishes for his name to appear [in print] by its initials only. Although in most cases we publish the questions in succession, sometimes we advance a later [question] for a reason, such as people's pressing need for an elucidation of the topic. On occasion, for this kind of reason, too, we respond to a non-subscriber. Whoever has to wait for two or three months with a question [that has not been resolved in print] should send a single reminder. If we do not report it, we have a legitimate excuse for omitting it.[46]

The announcement is interesting for many reasons, beginning with the fact that it placed fatwas in a capitalistic framework. Riḍā basically granted fatwas for money. It is not that his fatwas were commodities in the marketplace, where each product had a price tag, but they were privileged communications whose publication required buying a membership in the select club of *al-Manār*'s partners.

The historiography of the "popular" press has long emphasized the democratic idea that a relatively small number of printed copies of journals could circulate widely in society. Multiple readers could indeed enjoy a single newspaper or magazine; the number of subscribers represented only a fraction of the number of readers and listeners.[47] Nevertheless, Riḍā made an important moral and economic distinction between paying and nonpaying readers. He realized, as a businessman, that his enterprise depended on readers buying his journal. Profits were not his sole interest as a publisher; he gave many copies of his commentary on the Qurʾan away for free, as donations to Indian mosques. Yet he needed to sell magazine subscriptions in order to finance these gifts and carry on the business of reform.[48] On the cover of his magazine, he regularly specified that partners would need to pay in advance for the delivery of future goods. What he introduced in 1904 was a modification to the benefits of a subscription to persuade more readers to join the partners' club.

The announcement reveals a great deal, too, about Riḍā's expectations. His referring to the potential subscriber as a man (*his* name, *his* country, *his* profession) was not simply a linguistic convention. Although women read his magazine, his sponsors—the subscribers who had the right to demand fatwas—were overwhelmingly if not exclusively men. His request for male subscribers to identify their line of work or their position in society shows his interest in highlighting, in print, their professional identity or social status. At the same time, he recognized that some of these subscribers would want to remain anonymous. If they asked politically controversial, socially contentious, or personally compromising questions, they would require protection from public exposure. This is why he permitted them to use only their initials, and a fair number of *mustaftis*, or fatwa seekers, took advantage of this option. Riḍā alluded as well to the possibility of censorship. He could not promise that he would publish a response to every subscriber's question.

Al-Manār's contract between the mufti and his fatwa seekers also established expectations about timing. Riḍā had to deal with impatient and demanding subscribers who complained when they did not receive fatwas promptly, within a month. His fatwas—often long and learned—would normally be published within two months based on a first-come, first-served procedure unless they concerned a truly urgent matter. In 1908 he added one proviso: subscribers who wanted answers within the two-month period had to send him their demands for fatwas on separate sheets of paper, with multiple questions displayed according to a specific format. If they tucked these requests in a book or mixed their juridical and administrative correspondence in a single envelope, then they might need to wait a long time for his answer.[49]

Finally, Riḍā made clear that he would occasionally compose fatwas for nonpaying readers as a public service, especially if there existed a pressing social need for his legal expertise. But his policy was to reject in most circumstances demands for free fatwas by nonsubscribers. This and the other disclosures were necessary to explain to all readers the rules of a new game. Unlike the Grand Mufti, who received a handsome salary directly from the government, Riḍā was under no obligation to grant the state and its citizens his religious and legal counsel. Nor was he employed as a clerical judge or teacher by the legal system or an educational institution. Unlike them, Riḍā had to find a way to earn his living independently while serving Islam and society. His entrepreneurial proposal, to require a journal subscription in exchange for fatwas, was his creative solution to this dilemma.

Before and After 1919: Fatwa Seekers from British Singapore to Mandatory Lebanon

Given its dispersed circulation, *al-Manār* is an especially important publication for historians interested in the globalization of Islamic communications in the late imperial and early national periods. It is not possible to determine how far its fatwas traveled, but it is possible to analyze the origins of the legal questions. Were fatwa generators mostly from the great capitals of the world? Which country or empire produced the greatest number of requests? How did communication patterns change over time? These are answerable questions.

All in all, between 1903 and 1935, Riḍā issued roughly 1,060 fatwas to around 430 petitioners.[50] Nearly two-fifths of them resided in Egypt; the rest, overseas.[51] They came not only from capital cities but also—to a surprising extent—from a wide range of towns. Many of the Egyptian correspondents lived in Cairo or Alexandria. Yet Riḍā received fatwa requests from nearly forty cities and towns in Egypt alone. Correspondents from the neighboring country of Sudan came from eleven different cities, including Khartoum, Dongola, Suakin, ʿAṭbara, and Korti. At least four fatwa seekers wrote to him from Batavia, the capital of the Dutch East Indies. Others sent him letters from Padang, in Sumatra; Surabaya, Surakarta, Banjarnegara, and Purworejo, in Java; Sambas, in Borneo; Kupang, in Timor; and a few other obscure cities on these far-away islands. With a few countries, then, Riḍā had quite a dispersed correspondence.

For comparative purposes, the fatwas that *al-Manār* published can be divided into two sixteen-year segments—with the year 1919 serving as a partitioning line.[52] Riḍā did not publish a single fatwa that year, perhaps because he was extraordinarily busy with political activities related to the foundation of Syria.[53] There is a good historical reason, too, for grouping the fatwas into two segments: the first from 1903 to 1918 and the second from 1920 to 1935. Drastic political events that occurred after the world war (the fall of the Ottoman Empire, the establishment of new European mandates, and the declaration of Egypt's independence) affected the circulation of the journal overseas.

Analyzing comparatively the segmented sets of fatwas reveals a few unusual trends and patterns. Because he identified as a Syrian and had many professional and personal contacts in Tripoli and Damascus, one might expect that most of his foreign correspondents were Syrian too. This was not at all the case,

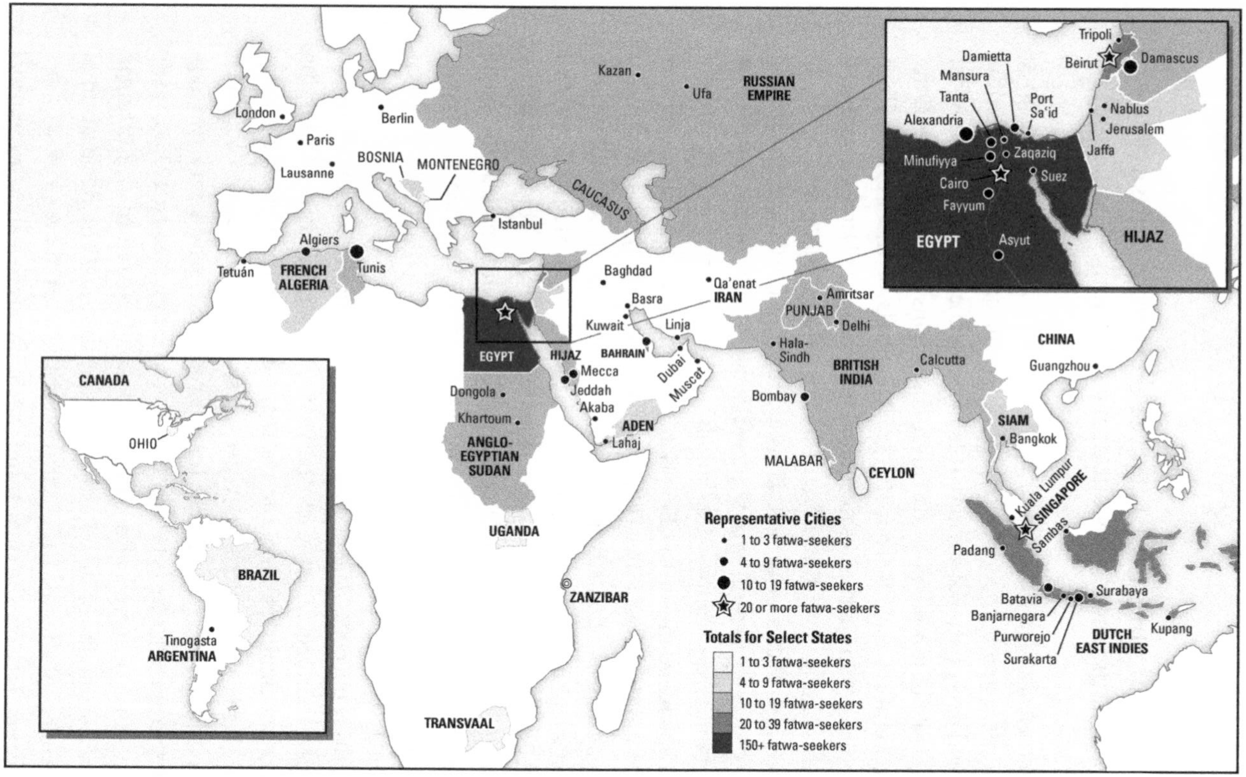

MAP 1 A geographic impression of *al-Manār*'s fatwa seekers, 1903–1935. The map represents their cumulative distribution and concentration at a glance, but it distorts history in some ways. Political borders changed drastically during this period, as new states and mandates came into being. Ideally, the map would focus exclusively on fatwa seekers' cities. But Riḍā often mentioned only their countries of origin. Therefore, the map represents these countries in different shades of gray, using names or indicating borders that correspond to the situation at the time of the legal correspondence. This means that countries that did not exist simultaneously appear on the map. Credit: Designed for this book by the cartographer Erin Greb.

however, before 1919. *Al-Manār*'s legal communications with the Ottoman Empire's Arab provinces were few and infrequent. Between 1903 and 1918, Riḍā heard from as many fatwa seekers from a single Southeast Asian island, Singapore, as from all of the Ottoman Empire's Syrian, Lebanese, Palestinian, and Iraqi provinces put together. In each case, there were twenty-six *mustaftis* total.[54] It is interesting, too, that there were significantly more fatwa seekers from Singapore than from the Dutch East Indies in this period, despite the miniscule number of Arabs in Singapore and the relatively small Muslim population there. Singapore therefore offers a wonderful example of the warps of globalization in this period. Islamic legal communications did not flow smoothly, along perfectly straight and uniform lines: rather, they flowed in unexpected if not random patterns, like lines along a distressed wood plank, with unexpected concentrations, strange twists and knots.[55]

What explains Singapore's surprising prominence? Non-Muslims of Chinese origin made up the vast majority of the population of around three hundred thousand inhabitants. Most of the Malay and many of the Indian residents practiced Islam, but they spoke little or no Arabic. Those fluent in Arabic were migrants or descendants of migrants from the Arabian Peninsula, by and large members of the Ḥaḍramī diaspora. Their total number added up to 708 men and 518 women according to the 1911 census.[56] Many of them were successful merchants who had little trouble buying copies of *al-Manār* for their personal libraries and mosques. Moreover, they had a special cultural and religious interest—as members of a diasporic community—in maintaining and deepening ties to Arab Muslims across the Indian Ocean.[57] These reasons explain why they appreciated Riḍā's Arabic appeals for transregional Islamic unity.

Within this community, a single rich merchant, Muḥammad ibn ʿAqīl ibn Yaḥyā, dramatically affected the circulation of *al-Manār*'s ideas. He decided to use the fortune that he had made trading in Java to promote the cause of reform. He founded a reformist academy as well a reformist magazine, *al-Imām* ("The Prayer Leader"), published between 1906 and 1908. Patterned after Riḍā's publication, this magazine translated reformist concepts into Malay for Southeast Asian readers. Furthermore, he worked assiduously to circulate copies of *al-Manār* to Arabic readers in Singapore and elsewhere in that corner of the world. Apparently, he also set in motion a smuggling operation to introduce *al-Manār* into the Dutch East Indies.[58]

But why was Singapore, a remote city on an island with very few Arabic readers, a more active center for the generation of *al-Manār*'s fatwas of 1903 to 1918 than all of Syria? Communications between Cairo and Singapore took place within an empire, while communications between Cairo and Syria took place across an imperial border. Singapore was part of the Straits Settlements, a British

Crown colony; Egypt was under de facto British rule; and Syria was under Ottoman rule. The Ottoman Empire placed strict bans on the circulation of foreign periodicals before the lifting of censorship. Meanwhile, the British Empire censored the Arabic press relatively lightly. As a result, several Syrian journalists besides Riḍā migrated to Cairo around the end of the nineteenth century, and they contributed to turning the city into the world's capital of the Arabic press.[59]

In addition, the British Empire facilitated communications through institutions such as the postal system. By 1908 it cost only half a piastre to send a letter to any destination in the British Empire with the exception of Newfoundland. It cost twice as much to send a letter to an address in the Ottoman Empire. Communicating with Damascus was therefore twice as expensive as communicating with Singapore for Riḍā. A higher postage rate did not, of course, deter him from mailing copies of his magazine. The important point is that the British Empire established mechanisms to make internal communications ever more efficient. The lower cost of correspondence is but one of many indicators of the increased circulation of goods and ideas within this empire.[60] As a consequence, Singapore suddenly appeared closer to Egypt than ever before in history—closer than Syria in several respects.

To what extent did *al-Manār* circulate within and beyond the British Empire? Only two Muslims wrote to Riḍā from England with demands for fatwas. Yet 60 percent of fatwa generators before 1919 were Muslim subjects of Her Majesty's dominions, colonies, and de jure or de facto protectorates.[61] Only 13 percent were from the Ottoman Empire: nearly all of them from the Arab provinces, mainly Syria and the vilayet of the Ḥijāz; 7 percent were from the Dutch East Indies; close to 5 percent were from the French colonies in North Africa; and 4 percent were from the Russian Empire.

Many things changed for *al-Manār* in the aftermath of World War I. The total number of fatwa seekers declined sharply, by approximately half, from the first to the second sixteen-year period.[62] Following the Egyptian Revolution of 1919, fewer and fewer Egyptians turned to the Syro-Lebanese mufti for fatwas.[63] The British Empire ceased to be a crucial zone for the generation and circulation of Riḍā's fatwas; Singapore and the Sudan more or less vanished from the map of fatwa seekers. Muslims from the Russian Empire stopped demanding fatwas as early as 1912, around the time that the Tsarist regime and its secret police started making heavy use of propaganda and surveillance techniques to curb the supposed threat of pan-Islamic communications.[64] This precipitous drop in the number of Russian, Singaporean, and Sudanese correspondents reflects quite a significant contraction in the volume of international communications between Riḍā and others.[65] If *al-Manār* is a good source by which to assess the globalization of Islam in the early twentieth century, then it reflects a profound historical shift: the breakdown around World War I of an important trans-imperial network of Muslim reformers.

Only Lebanon, as it made the transition from Ottoman to French rule, saw a significant rise in demand for *al-Manār*'s fatwas during the interwar period. There was a fourfold increase in the number of fatwa seekers from this country, and all together they asked for fifteen times as many fatwas as their predecessors.[66] Beirut in particular became quite an active center for Riḍā's legal communications. The statistics therefore suggest that, with the fall of the Ottoman Empire and the rise of a nationalist movement in Greater Syria, new opportunities emerged for him—as a mufti, as the editor of a journal, and as the owner of a publishing business—in the country of his birth. In addition, Syro-Lebanese migrants and exiles who recognized him as their diaspora's leading Islamic authority and as a prominent activist for their homeland's liberation from French colonialism wrote to him from countries as far as Switzerland and Brazil.[67] Yes, many doors closed for him around the world—in Egypt, the Sudan, Russia, and Singapore—with the transition to a new world order. Yet new doors opened for him, especially in and around Beirut and in Syro-Lebanese circles worldwide.

Fatwa Generators: *Mustaftis* as Authors

Al-Manār's subscribers consisted of highly educated and relatively wealthy Muslim men, and their interests had a direct effect on coverage in the section on fatwas. In the aftermath of the 1905 revolution, while revolutionary socialists agitated against world capitalism, the journal's Russian readers cogitated upon the religious benefits of their imported gramophones. Riḍā did not receive queries from the proletariat, fulminating over the price of bread, factory conditions, and unjust wages. He heard from the bourgeoisie. And his editorial policy of publishing their questions together with his answers allowed them to shape the very product of their consumption.

Their requests for fatwas provide a new vantage point on authority and agency in the history of Islamic law and the "movement" of religious reform in Riḍā's age. The paradigm in Islamic legal studies has long centered on a top-down approach to the interpretation of the shariʿa. Focusing first and foremost on the role of legal experts, the goal has been to establish muftis' influence on court judgments, polities, individuals, or societies. Everyone recognizes that muftis found ways to adapt Islamic law to different social, political, and economic circumstances. But innovation in Islamic legal thought continues to be studied as a relatively independent process, with the critical aim to determine how one jurist's theories differed from other jurists' theories.[68] Whether they have emphasized the success or the failure of shining lights such as ʿAbduh and Riḍā to inspire followers around the world, intellectual histories of Islam's reform have similarly favored a top-down approach to religious change.

Yet the fatwa literature offers historians evidence of quite a different dynamic in play. It shows that diverse social actors, many of them laypersons, formulated basic ideas that served as springboards for muftis. Rarely neutral or naïve, their inquiries usually suggested their own perspective on a legal dispute or religious conflict. Sometimes they went so far as to propose, politely or pretentiously, their preferred way to resolve the problem. Of course, *mustaftis*' questions always appeared, in *al-Manār* as in other journals and books, before the fatwas themselves. However authoritative or charismatic, muftis in the era of print worked as legal counselors whose rulings—judgmental or forgiving, thoughtful or dismissive—had to respond, by the genre's conventions, to these questions. Accordingly, the fatwa generators who wrote to Riḍā should be considered as more than simply attentive, expectant readers; they were the authors of the legal questions.

A similar point might be made about most of the fatwas that were promulgated, years later, through the radio, satellite television, or the internet: except in cases where muftis invented petitioners and fabricated questions, fatwa seekers determined the agenda and framed the discussion. With their demands for fatwas, laypersons and judges, citizens and monarchs, effectively urged muftis to interpret and reinterpret the sacred law to suit new circumstances. They drove the discourse forward. In this respect, the fatwas arose from below—not from the highest rung of the legal hierarchy. *Mustaftis* could easily outrank muftis by some measures of social distinction; they could possess great wealth, extensive political power, or a high level of education in fields such as medicine or engineering. They could also possess force in numbers, when they acted in concert to advance a popular cause. Although they ranked below muftis in legal theory, these historical actors played an essential role in legal practice by inspiring, motivating, and pressuring muftis to extend the shariʿa as an ideological superstructure to cover new modes of behavior.

Within this general framework for understanding fatwas as legal communications that originated from below, with *mustaftis*' demands, one thing makes *al-Manār*'s printed fatwas most intriguing: Riḍā's audacious insistence on obtaining money, the price of an annual subscription, for his juridical advice. His fatwas were capitalistic commodities, printed by a machine for profit. Riḍā was perfectly willing to compose them for his readers, but they had to pay him a goodly sum in advance. To remain effective as an independent reformer, he had to consider these readers' likes and dislikes, their religious and political orientation, and their specific goals whenever they sought his legal advice. They were the consumers of *al-Manār*, and he depended on them financially. They not only determined the topics of his fatwas; they also affected his perception of what issues were of burning interest to his international readership and therefore worth incorporating into the program of Islamic reform.

Originalism from Singapore to Cairo: Qurʾan 5:5, the Prophetic Era, and the Salaf

The authors of *al-Manār*'s demands for fatwas challenged Riḍā to develop his religious and legal philosophy in response to specific issues. Thus, for instance, Muḥammad ibn ʿAqīl ibn Yaḥyā, *al-Manār*'s rich patron in Singapore and a pioneering leader in the Southeast Asian movement for the revival of Islam, asked Riḍā to explain how precisely Christians and Jews had slaughtered animals in "the age of the Prophet" and whether their method of butchering had not changed over the years.[69] A half-page long, his question displayed a learned familiarity with ʿAbduh's Transvaal fatwa, which had authorized the consumption of Christian butchers' meats on the world's fringes. He had also read a fatwa on the same topic by a Ḥaḍramī mufti, Sālim ibn Aḥmad al-ʿAṭṭās al-ʿAlawī. What made the question significant was its originalist perspective on scripture: its historicist aim to determine and fix the holy text's original intent or meaning. Riḍā recognized this goal immediately, for he titled the exchange "The Slaughter of the People of the Book in the Epoch of the Revelation."

In the 1905 fatwa that he wrote in response, Riḍā argued for the right of Muslims to consume the meat of animals slaughtered by non-Muslims. He drew attention to an early Islamic ruling supporting this right given by an unnamed "imam of the Salaf." This imam, the Prophet's Companion Abū al-Dardāʾ (d. 652), had allowed Muslims to consume mutton butchered by Christians, even if the ram had been slaughtered for the church of Saint George. The permissive opinion of the Salafi exemplar seemed justified to Riḍā, given the revelation of the Qurʾan in the fifth chapter, fifth verse, through which God made lawful "the good things" as well as "the food of those who were given the Book," meaning Christians and Jews.[70]

To emphasize the openness of Islamic law to interfaith commerce, Riḍā presented a contrasting ruling too: a Muslim butcher's meats were lawful for consumption only if he followed orthodox conventions. If, instead of slaughtering "in the name of God," the butcher slaughtered "in the name of the Prophet or the Kaʿba," then his meat became a forbidden food. Heterodox or heretical blessings in effect transformed the flesh into an illicit good. The sacred barrier to consumption was higher, in other words, when the producer was a Muslim who failed to express the monotheistic creed than when the producer was a Christian, who had the freedom to bless God or not to bless God in a particular way while working.

In this legal correspondence, the fatwa seeker from Singapore was the first to suggest the value of finding an originalist, scripturalist solution to the problem of consuming the goods of non-Muslim butchers. His priority matters because it calls into question the standard historical account of the transmission of Salafism to Southeast Asia. Following a top-down, center–periphery model, historians have cast ʿAbduh and Riḍā as the elite reformers from the Middle East whose writings inspired Salafist awakenings abroad. The exchange under analysis suggests, however, that even on the outskirts of the Islamic world, Muslims independently generated ideals and proposals for reviving scriptural laws in accordance with the historical conditions that existed during Islam's foundational era—precisely the sort of ideals and proposals that historians have attributed not to the vitality of Islam in locations outside of the Middle East, such as Singapore, but to the global spread of Salafism as a foreign ideology. Indeed, Muḥammad ibn ʿAqīl was far more than a recipient and transmitter of wisdom from *The Lighthouse* of Cairo. He challenged Riḍā to develop a scripturalist response and thus participated in the making of the Salafism of *al-Manār*. He clearly thought that the Syro-Egyptian reformer ought to consider conditions at the origins of Islam. According to his logic, God's indulgent rule for Muslim consumption, encapsulated in Qurʾan 5:5, remained in force only if Jewish and Christian moderns slaughtered animals exactly as Jewish and Christian ancients had slaughtered animals in seventh-century Arabia.

Riḍā balked at this approach to religion and law; he viewed it as overly restrictive and intellectually incoherent. He did believe that moderns should turn to Islam's origins for inspiration. But the Salafism that he espoused did not mean shackling Muslims to the past. It meant combing through ancient texts to locate liberalizing models.

After presenting the most permissive Salafi opinion imaginable, he proceeded to mock what may be called "piecemeal fundamentalism." Why did troublemakers, as he labeled those who disputed ʿAbduh's fatwa, invoke the early Islamic past selectively? Even they must realize that it would be ludicrous, an "oppressive restriction," to fetter Muslims to every single custom from that day and age. In approaching the past as a model, distinctions had to be made between what truly pertained to religion and what did not. Muslim moderns had no reason to worry about the precise method by which Christians or Jews had slaughtered animals in the era of divine revelation, for the question about *their* food did not present a "devotional" problem in Riḍā's eyes. Nor was it tied in any way to "the sprit and essence of religion." In this stripped-down sense of religion, a *religious* issue would arise in connection with non-Muslim food only in one case, when it originated in a cultic offering to a pagan divinity.[71] Evidently, like the fatwa about toilet paper on a captain's ship, the fatwa about Christian butchers' meat became an occasion for reflection about the meaning of religion and, in particular, the boundary between the religious and the secular.

Readers of *al-Manār* from Singapore to Brazil asked Riḍā for fatwas because they valued his integrity, recognized his expertise, and appreciated his convictions. Moreover, they anticipated that, in exchange for their rubles or francs or pounds, he would give them what they wanted: an enlightening Islamic ruling. Nobody could really know how exactly he would defend such a ruling, but his economically liberal inclination to let modern things pass into Muslim societies became predictable after a while. He gathered the seeds of this laissez-faire legal philosophy in the Mediterranean port of Tripoli under Ottoman rule, where he spent his formative years. But it took relocating to Cairo, where British officials preached the virtues of free trade and Arabic journalists found auspicious conditions for their industry, for him to bring this philosophy into fruition. In Cairo, he worked not as the keeper of a lonely lighthouse but as the owner of a small, independent Islamic business that aimed to fulfill the wants of a global network of privileged subscribers who shared his commitment to the reform of Islam. These men, collaborators in the generation of fatwas, encouraged him to think about the things that mattered to them, and they expected him to take their side in the religious struggles of their times.

3

In a Material World

European Expansion from Tripoli to Cairo

Muḥammad Rashīd Riḍā was born in 1865, as a subject of the Ottoman Empire in its Syrian provinces, in the Mediterranean village of Qalamūn—a short walk to the city of Tripoli and very close to Mount Lebanon's northern frontier. The year of his birth was not a prosperous one. A devastating outbreak of cholera, a plague of locusts, and a financial crisis that culminated in hundreds of bankruptcies, since local merchants had been borrowing money at exorbitant rates, took their toll on the local economy.[1] Tripoli then lay just beyond a new political border. Following the violent sectarian conflicts of 1860 between the Druze and Maronite communities, France intervened on behalf of the Christians. Together with other European powers, it persuaded the Ottoman Empire to subdivide the region and to appoint over Mount Lebanon a foreign Christian governor (*mutasarrif*) with plenipotentiary authority.[2] Tripoli remained part of the Ottoman Empire in the reconfigured province of Syria.[3] In contrast to Mount Lebanon's towns, it was considered a Sunni bastion. But its population was in fact rather mixed. In 1865 one-fourth of its twenty thousand residents were Christian. Most of the non-Muslims, over four thousand residents, followed Greek Orthodoxy, but six hundred Catholics, fifteen Protestants, and eighty Jews also remained in the city after the partition.[4] Entanglements with European persons and things multiplied in this multiconfessional harbor in the years that followed the tumultuous events of 1860.[5]

For centuries before the rise of European hegemony, Tripoli had been open for business.[6] But its exposure to trade changed significantly with the expansion of global capitalism and the development of steam power. One generation before Riḍā's birth, during the brief Egyptian occupation of Syria, the government had planted tens of thousands of mulberry trees in the district, and it had exported a French olive-pressing machine to produce oil more efficiently. Given the harbor's small size and the difficulties of anchoring there in winter, only thirty to forty foreign merchants' ships reached the port each year in the 1830s. All together they arrived with fewer than 5,000 tons of merchandise annually and departed with far lighter cargoes of around 2,000 tons.[7] By 1870, despite the outbreak of the Franco-Prussian war, which greatly affected Tripoli's commerce given French dominance, over 1,100 sailboats and nearly 200 steamships reached the port—with cargoes of around 27,000 and 139,000 tons, respectively.[8] By 1897, Riḍā's last year in Tripoli, over 1,500 sailboats and nearly 400 steamships made it to the harbor; collectively they conveyed goods weighing approximately 21,000 and 460,000 tons, respectively.[9] These figures indicate that with steam power there came roughly a tenfold increase in the number of ships and a hundredfold increase in freight.

The French, British, Russian, and Austrian steamships that led in this commerce unloaded at the port sugar, coffee, copper, iron, broadcloth, leather, furniture, and sundry European luxuries. In exchange, they took cargoes that weighed more or less the same but had a much higher monetary value. These consisted not only of silk and olive oil but also of tobacco, wool, oranges, lemons, sesame seeds, wheat, barley, oak marble galls (used to make inks and dyes), and natural sponges. Harvested by divers along the coast, these sponges were Tripoli's most lucrative export after tobacco and silk; they were in high demand in France, where women relied on them for menstruation and contraception, and where surgeons indicated them to stop the flow of blood after an amputation. Tripoli's merchants and financiers profited tremendously from this trade—as the middlemen who collected sponges and other domestic products for shipment to Europe, as the buyers of the European commodities that they in turn dispatched to various cities in Syria and beyond it to different destinations along the Mediterranean coast, and as moneylenders.[10]

All of this is critical to understanding Riḍā's worldview and especially his economic outlook. He grew up in a world of goods that was intimately tied to European trade rather than, as the intellectual historian Albert Hourani remarked long ago, "in a self-sufficient Islamic world of thought" far removed from Europe.[11] Already during Riḍā's childhood, European steamships and Ottoman sailboats regularly flowed in and out of the harbor, al-Mīnāʾ. Guided to the port by the lighthouse on the island of Ramkīn, their arrivals and departures were part and parcel of the rhythm of daily life, especially during the summer months. Like other Tripolitanians of his age, Riḍā saw foreign exchange as normal, desirable, and absolutely essential to economic vitality. It inspired him to dedicate much of his life to shining a light, as the keeper of an Islamic lighthouse, on European–Muslim exchanges.

This chapter deals, in the first place, with the formative values and dominant structures that Riḍā encountered in Tripoli and Cairo. It gives a sense of the educational training that he received in Tripoli and then turns to developments in Cairo. A description of the transformation of his street and neighborhood in the decade after his move to this city leads to a discussion of the globalization of commerce and consumption in a broader urban framework. To illustrate British dominance, the chapter dwells on a British guidebook's representations of Cairo's colonial cosmopolitanism. It also clarifies Egypt's political and legal status under British rule, and it recounts the official British rationale for continuing the country's military occupation and financial management. The chapter ends with an analysis of few fatwas by Egypt's Grand Mufti, Muḥammad ʿAbduh, and by his Syrian protégé, Rashīd Riḍā, that illustrate how they dealt with some of the cultural effects of European hegemony.

Riḍā's Education in Tripoli

The good fortune of the city where Riḍā was schooled depended on trade with Europe. So did many new developments around town—from the building of a road and railway in 1876, which linked the port city better to landlocked Homs, to the foundation of a Lasallian Brothers' Christian school in 1886, where the brethren vowed to teach merchants' sons accounting and other practical subjects.[12] Louis Lortet, a French savant who visited Tripoli twice in the course of five years, between 1875 and 1880, lamented the rapid pace of development: among other things the replacement of picturesque donkeys driven by colorful riders with the installation, "just as in Europe, of a tramway whose vulgar cars are pulled by pathetic old horses." Soon, Lortet knew, a steam train would supersede this tram, for Syria's governor had plans to make the transportation of imports and exports ever more efficient.[13] Indeed, nowhere did the relationship between foreign trade and domestic growth seem quite as obvious as in Tripoli. Throughout his life, Riḍā retained a Tripolitanian openness to international trade. Even as he became increasingly resentful of European hegemony, he continued to defend foreign exchange as necessary for the economic development of Muslim societies.

But it was the education that Riḍā received in Tripoli that most influenced the manner in which he would express this openness to trade. Not long after graduating from the local village school, he joined the Patriotic Islamic School (al-Madrasa al-Waṭaniyya al-Islāmiyya), founded in 1879. Here he interacted with the school's founder and director, Ḥusayn al-Jisr, who developed innovative techniques for reconciling ancient scriptural revelations and modern

FIGURE 3.1 Tripoli's mule-drawn tramcar ca. 1900, a sign of modernity in the Ottoman city where Riḍā studied Islamic law. This selection from a pair of nearly identical stereographs forms part of the G. Eric and Edith Matson Photograph Collection of the Library of Congress in Washington, D.C.

scientific theories. At times this tendency meant defending the Darwinian model of evolution as not necessarily incompatible with Qurʾanic notions of creation. At other times it meant defending standard Muslim dogmas about the resurrection of the dead from the assaults of materialists (*māddiyyūn*), who trusted only sense perception and experiential reason. Within the curriculum, al-Jisr's philosophy manifested itself in a wide range of courses beginning with engineering and ending with exegesis. The course in jurisprudence, *fiqh*, would have favored a progressive reading of standard texts from the Ottoman Empire's official school of law. It was perhaps in this context, if not later at the Religious School (al-Madrasa al-Dīniyya), where he continued studying under al-Jisr's direction, that Riḍā must have first read works by Ḥanafi jurists, such as Ibn ʿAbidīn's *Marginalia in Response to "The Chosen Pearl's" Perplexed Reader*, that argued for the legality of trafficking in forbidden goods in non-Muslim lands.[14] These works had a profound impact on his thought. Years later, during his long career as a mufti, he would often turn to their doctrines, presenting a reformist Ḥanafi perspective on international trade without, however, ever professing adherence to the Ḥanafi school of law.

In 1897, after working for a few years as a journalist and finally earning the official title of *ʿālim*, doctor of divinity and law, Riḍā left Syria for Egypt. In his early thirties, he wanted to advance the cause of reform as Muḥammad ʿAbduh's disciple. During his exile from Egypt in the 1880s, ʿAbduh had made a powerful impression on Syrian reformists, partly through his activities as a teacher at a college in Beirut directed by al-Jisr and partly through his publications.[15] Riḍā himself found deeply inspiring the magazine that ʿAbduh had published together with al-Afghānī during their sojourn in Paris. Reminiscing about the impact that "The Unbreakable Bond" (*al-ʿUrwa al-Wuthqa*) had on him in his twenties, he emphasized its call for liberation from European subjection; its appeal for Muslim peoples to overcome political and linguistic barriers in order to realize their one and only citizenship (*jinsiyya*)—in their common religion; its appreciation of the operation of God's natural laws (*sunan Allāh*) in determining the order of societies and the fate of nations; its argument that Islam was a sovereign religion whose military power would serve—in the Muslim ideal state—not to convert subjects by force but to protect the sacred law; and its defense of Islam as a powerful religion that must guide believers not only in their spiritual quest but also in their social, civil, and military affairs. Riḍā found appealing, too, the method that al-Afghānī and ʿAbduh had followed in seeking proof for their judgments in Qurʾanic verses.[16]

Around and About Sycamore Lane in Cairo

As in Tripoli, in Cairo, too, Riḍā witnessed a city on the brink of an incredible transformation, where the boundaries between the medieval and the modern—visibly shifting through creative and destructive reconfigurations of the townscape—seemed apparent but impermanent. He set up a publishing house on Sycamore Lane, Shāriʿ Darb al-Jamāmīz, a sinewy road at the edge of the southwestern district that tourists treasured for its "medieval Islamic" esthetic. Throughout the neighborhood Riḍā could see old three-story houses with their intricately carved wooden lattice windows, which seemed so very different—a world apart—from the city's newer, nineteenth-century residences with their large, rectangular iron-framed windows.[17] Long ago, reflecting on such differences, the British Orientalist Stanley Lane-Poole told the story of Cairo as a tale of two cities. There was the medieval Islamic city with its crowded streets, exotic sounds, pungent odors, and "sweet sticky" tastes; and there was the

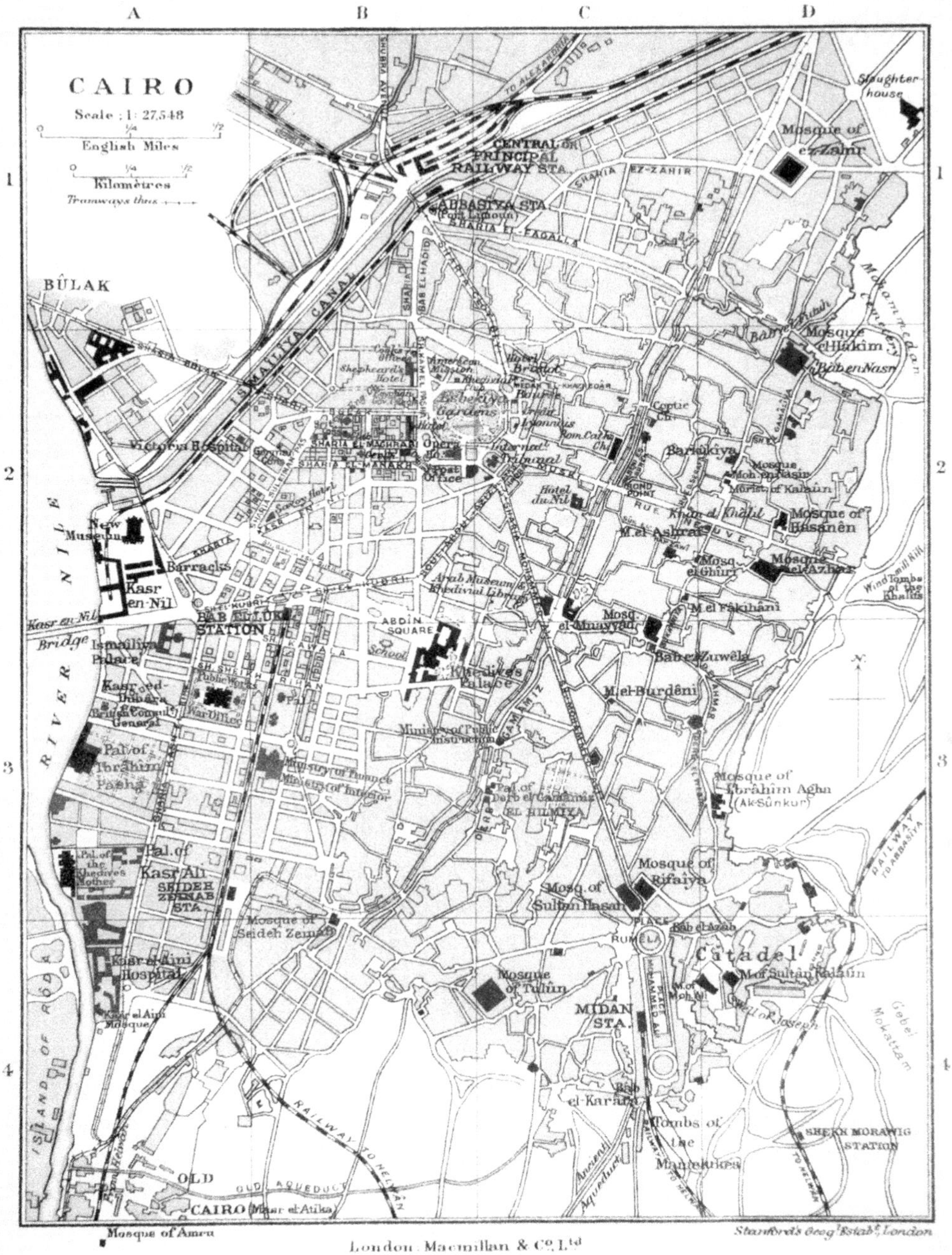

MAP 2 Cairo around 1905. Riḍā's publishing house was located on Derb El Gamamiz (Darb al-Jamāmīz), the diagonal street in row 3, columns B & C. Source: Macmillan & Co., *Guide to Egypt and the Sûdân, Including a Description of the Route Through Uganda to Mombasa* (London: Macmillan, 1905), between pp. 48–49.

FIGURE 3.2 Sycamore Lane, Riḍā's winding street in "medieval" Cairo, as depicted in a watercolor, with a view of the minaret of the Mamluk mosque Qarāqujā al-Ḥasanī in the background. Source: David Samuel Margoliouth, *Cairo, Jerusalem, & Damascus: Three Chief Cities of the Egyptian Sultans*, with illus. in color by W. S. S. Tyrwhitt, and additional plates by Reginald Barratt (London: Chatto and Windus, 1907), 164.

modern European city with its straight boulevards, magnificent villas, and "breezy balconies." The contrast between these districts was, of course, not so stark. Lane-Poole recognized that only a short distance—easily traversed by carriages and drums—separated the "two cities," and he described one quarter as a "medley of East and West." But he exaggerated, as his critics have pointed out, the differences.[18]

There were, in fact, many recent developments around Sycamore Lane. Three decades before Riḍā's arrival, Egypt's minister of schools—on his return to Cairo after an inspiring trip to Paris—took over a disfavored Ottoman prince's palace on this street. There he established a whole number of new professional schools as well as a scholarly library—placed under the direction of German librarians—that included tens of thousands of rare Arabic, Persian, and Turkish books. The street became known for these new educational institutions.[19]

Riḍā's Cairo was a historically layered city where new and old structures competed for space in the urban landscape and where, on the very façade of buildings, foreign and native styles mixed together to produce either an experimental fusion or an incongruous pastiche. From his printing shop, which was also his home, he could briskly walk south in a zigzag course to reach Ibn Ṭūlūn Mosque, Cairo's oldest and grandest Islamic monument, whose famous minaret architectural historians have described as a thirteenth-century Mamluk reconstruction of the original ninth-century structure, which had followed the "Samarran" style.[20] Alternatively, he could head in a northeastern direction to reach, within minutes, ʿĀbidīn Palace. Built by an Italian architect for Ismāʿīl Pasha as the ruler's official residence, this sumptuous neoclassical building represented the most luxurious nineteenth-century effort to transplant into Egypt the finest European taste.[21]

There were other exciting changes, too, in the vicinity of Sycamore Lane. Khalīj Canal, a mile or so to the west of the Nile, ran roughly parallel to it. In the nineteenth century, governmental concerns over health and hygiene came to concentrate on the canal, where residents habitually dumped rubbish, urine, and excrement. A nauseating stench rose from it. Alarmed, the pasha's chief physician, the Frenchman Clot Bey, warned about the risk of epidemic outbreaks.[22] Finally, in 1897, the year that Riḍā immigrated to Cairo, Egyptian authorities signed a concession that would lead to the draining of the canal and the construction of a wide boulevard to serve for the passage of an electric tram. A Belgian industrialist and financier with global ambitions, Baron Empain, won the concession and raised the capital from Europe. In 1900 his company inaugurated the new tramway line on the newly filled, level boulevard. Alongside rickety donkey carts and elegant horse-drawn carriages, trams began to transport passengers to the city's peripheries.[23]

Both Sycamore Lane and the Khalīj tramway line led directly to Bāb al-Khalq square, where at the turn of the century construction began on a new home for the Museum of Arab Antiquities. (Eventually, in the revolutionary fervor of 1952, the president of the Free Officers movement would change its name to the Museum of Islamic Art.) Islamic artifacts deposited by European preservationists in a Fatimid mosque's overflowing rooms were transferred to this new building for its inauguration in 1903. So was the collection of rare manuscripts in the Ottoman palace on Sycamore Lane, which became the new Royal Library, on the upper floors. This building, so close to Riḍā's new home, serves in some respects as a wonderful metaphor for Riḍā's enterprise. Designed by the Italian architect Alfonso Manescalo, its neo-Mamluk façade marked a radical departure from Ottoman styles. It made manifest to the public the rising value of Islamic antiquities, precious things such as gilded, enameled mosque lamps, now housed decorously in a modern revivalist structure. This "Islamic architectural revival began," according to Donald Reid, "less as a locally inspired renaissance than as another fashionable European import."[24] Like Max Herz (d. 1919), the

FIGURE 3.3 The Khedivial Library and Museum of Arab Antiquities at the edge of Riḍā's neighborhood, by the last stop of the new tramway line. Postcard by Max H. Rudmann. Rare Books and Special Collections Library, American University in Cairo. Reproduced with permission.

Austro-Hungarian architect who served as the Museum of Arab Antiquities' director in its new location, Riḍā came to devote his career to preserving and restoring fragments of the Islamic past.[25]

Even more than in the coastal city of Ottoman Syria where Riḍā grew up, in Cairo the presence of Europeans was felt everywhere. De facto British rule, together with the legal and commercial protections established by the Mixed Courts system, motivated many Europeans to migrate to the city. German librarians, Italian architects, and Belgian industrialists represented a tiny fraction of what was a broad movement of peoples. In her sociological history of Cairo, Janet Abu-Lughod described Riḍā's first decade in the county as a "unique period of Egyptian history," characterized by the influx of a "surprisingly large number of foreign immigrants." Between 1897 and 1907 Cairo's population of foreigners more than doubled to reach over seventy-five thousand persons. At the same time the general population increased, too, on account of rural migration and a decline in the rate of deaths from cholera and smallpox. But by 1907, the year that the flow of overseas migration subsided as a result of the global financial crash, eleven out of every hundred residents had been born outside of Egypt.[26] Many of these foreign-born residents came from the Ottoman Empire, yet the number of Europeans was significant too. In 1907 the census counted 19,395 Greek, 13,307 Italian, 8,571 British, and 6,478 French nationals in Cairo.[27] In the building industry, these foreigners worked not only as architects and contractors but also as masons, marbleworkers, painters, carpenters, electricians, mechanics, and sanitary engineers.[28] In addition, three decades after the opening of the Suez Canal, hundreds of thousands of passengers started to cruise down the Nile every year.[29] More and more tourists visited Cairo annually; thousands of them made it to the Museum of Arab Antiquities.[30]

Riḍā saw Europeans in his neighborhood on a regular basis, and he interacted with them in a range of ways in different places. His biography reveals the indignity that he suffered on an occasion at a restaurant when an Englishman rudely demanded that the shaykh leave "his" table. It shows, too, that he enjoyed the company and manners of first-class English passengers on the Royal Mail steamship, which he boarded in 1912 on a voyage to India.[31] But these were extraordinary events in his life. What his biography does not reveal are the everyday sightings that he took for granted, such as the bustle of European tramway engineers and construction workers moving in and out of Bāb al-Khalq square.

He formed a close relationship with one British official, Alfred Mitchell Innes, whom he taught Arabic.[32] An economic thinker of the highest caliber, Innes served as undersecretary of state for finance during the 1907 financial crisis. Against Adam Smith's "metallic theory," the "old idea that gold and silver are the only real money and that all other forms of money are mere substitutes," Innes would advance "the credit theory" of money. For him the official value of money was arbitrary; it had no relation to the intrinsic value of precious metal coins. All forms of money, including banknotes, were currencies that served by social convention to discharge debts. It was high time, he argued, for economists to overcome their attachment to the gold sovereign and embrace, in its place, an "abstract, intangible standard."[33] Did Riḍā hear an early version of Innes's theory in the course of their Arabic lessons? It is impossible to tell, although they shared an interest—as the next chapter shows—in revising concepts of money.[34]

Snapshots of Global Trade and Cosmopolitan Consumption Before World War I

Capitalism made strides during Riḍā's first few years in Egypt. Foreign capital poured at a fast rate into the country. Between 1897 and 1907, the shares sold and the bonds held by internationally funded companies, including the Suez Canal Company, rose from 30.9 to 94.2 million Egyptian pounds. If we exclude the Suez Canal Company's shares and take a longer perspective, then we can record a mindboggling fourteenfold increase of these assets between 1892 and 1914. In concrete terms, this meant an exponential rise in the number of new companies there. Between the foundation of the Suez Canal Company in the 1850s and the beginning of the British Occupation, one, two, or three new companies were established with foreign capital each year. In the boom before the 1907 crisis, forty or so new companies of this kind emerged each year. By and large the infusion of European capital went into mortgage firms, led by Crédit Foncier Égyptien. Founded in 1880, this understudied institution had by 1907 accumulated more paid-up capital and debentures than the Suez Canal Company.[35] But there was also significant movement in other sectors of the economy. Industrial, mining, and commercial companies registered more than a tenfold increase in capital between 1892 and 1907. Miscellaneous enterprises—from the Compagnie frigorifique d'Égypte to British Beer Breweries—embodied this development. Never in Egypt's history did the country seem as great a haven for European capitalists as it did then.[36]

Riḍā's first decade in Egypt coincided, too, with an impressive rise in the volume and value of imports. From 1897 to 1907, traffic at Port of Suez rose from 110 steamers carrying around eighty thousand tons to 277 steamers carrying around three hundred thousand tons. As in Tripoli, this development was part of a longer and broader trend that preceded Riḍā's migration, and it reflected the growing capacity of steamships to transport goods across the world. In 1870 approximately five hundred vessels passed through the Suez Canal bearing, altogether, 436,609 tons of cargo; in 1907 more than four thousand vessels took this passage yet they bore, all together, the astonishing freight of 14.7 million tons.[37] Most of these ships were bound for foreign shores. It is important to recognize, nevertheless, that imports to Egypt more than doubled in value between 1897 and 1907: from around 13.5 million to nearly 33.9 million Egyptian pounds. Over a longer period, between the imposition of Anglo-French control and the economic upheaval of World War I, imports grew by nearly 350 percent.[38]

World War I greatly disrupted international commerce. Cotton prices plummeted, and foreign capital began to flow back to Europe. A recovery from the depression started in the middle of the war, with a sharp rise in cotton prices. Egypt's economy as a whole grew steadily during the next decade. But high population growth in this period meant little change in per capita domestic output. In the late 1920s and early 1930s, the Great Depression would take a serious toll as well.[39] These developments happened in Riḍā's lifetime, during the second half of his career, and they stimulated the rise of a nationalistic approach to consumption and trade.

What balanced the unprecedented expansion of imports before World War I was an even more astonishing increase in the export of raw long-staple cotton, the single crop that allowed Egypt under British Occupation to achieve a favorable trade balance. In 1907 cotton, cottonseed, and cottonseed oil cake—one of Egypt's most successful industrial products—made up nearly all (around 94 percent in value) of the articles shipped overseas. (In competition with the American seed-crushing industry, a handful of Egyptian mills made the oil cakes, which sold very well in Britain as feed for cattle.) Besides cotton and its byproducts, Egypt exported cigarettes, onions, hides, rice, eggs, raw wool, gum arabic, sugarcane, ostrich feathers, henna, tomatoes, and live quail.[40] The mills of Lancashire were its chief customer, followed by Germany and the United States, which in 1907 happened to outrank France as a destination for the country's exports. With a booming agricultural economy came a significant increase in purchasing power, and this turn of fortune explains in large part the dramatic rise in the value of foreign goods.[41]

These imports consisted of just about everything: factory machines and railway locomotives; high-end luxury products for affluent residents and tourists; cheap commodities and basic foodstuffs. Slow and uneven industrial development often meant a lack of competitive domestic alternatives. But the British regime's insistence on low tariffs—in this era of free-trade imperialism—contributed to the wide availability of imports of all sorts. With its broad brushstroke, the Customs Department registered textiles, thread, ready-made clothes, underclothes, leather goods (English saddles, Moroccan slippers, Swiss boots), and indigo among the main imports. Iron, steel, coal, Swedish timber and Turkish firewood, British and Belgian machinery, Russian petrol, ironmongery, and haberdashery also made it to the list of key foreign goods. Tobacco and cigars, American maize, French flour, Syrian livestock, fresh fruit, dried fruit, rice, butter and cheese, rough and refined sugar, Brazilian coffee, and smoked fish were significant too. Jute-fiber sacks, made in India and used to pack cotton, competed with Italian paper, Austrian stationery, and French books in importance, if measured by cost. In terms of value, more than a third of the 1907 imports came from Great Britain and its possessions; the Ottoman and French Empires each supplied slightly more than 10 percent; the rest came from the Austro-Hungarian Empire, Germany, and a host of other nations. Amazingly, with cotton and its byproducts alone, Egypt paid for all of these imports together, totaling more than 26 million Egyptian pounds in 1907. Like every profitable British colony, it ran a slight surplus.[42]

Material signs of this great movement of goods abounded in Egypt. In Alexandria, the Karam brothers, Greek-Orthodox Syrian immigrants from Riḍā's hometown, Tripoli, established a timber-importing corporation with branches in several cities, including Cairo. Wood for the construction boom, railways, and boat building no longer reached the port of Alexandria mainly from the coasts and hills of Anatolia: hewn balks now came from Swedish and Finnish planing mills; white fir planks and scantlings from Austria, Romania, and Galicia; and pitch pine from Florida.[43] Another example of this translation of goods and persons into Egypt is the machine-importing business of an association of British engineers, Allen, Alderson & Co., who settled down in the vicinity of Alexandria. Like the Karam brothers' Commercial and Estates Company, this was a well-established, second-generation company with deep ties to government and society. Remarkably, in 1903 one of the firm's founders, George Beeton Alderson, erected at Abū Qīr a mosque, "which he presented to the natives of that village." According to Arnold Wright's 1909 merchants' almanac and travelers' guidebook, *Twentieth Century Impressions of Egypt*, this was "the only instance on record of the acceptance of such a gift by Mahomedans from the hands of a Christian." The company specialized in importing and installing irrigation pumps and cotton-ginning machines, with English and American firms supplying the engines and accessories.[44]

Something of a mecca of consumption, turn-of-the-century Cairo offered endless temptations to its affluent denizens. Located in Shepheard's Hotel on Shāriʿ Kāmil, Diemer's bookstore, managed by a Prussian, stocked literature in twelve different languages.[45] Fred Phillips & Co., the "colonial outfitters" on Shāriʿ Qaṣr al-Nīl, boasted of "English cloths of the best manufacture and latest design." Unbearably elitist and chauvinistic, the owner advertised that only Europeans working under his direct supervision tailored breeches and trained gowns. Then there was Joseph Cohen of Smyrna who vouched that his carpets were authentic Persian manufactures—and not, as in some tourist establishments, Birmingham imitations. Hugo Hackh, a native of Württemberg, imported musical instruments. An officer in the Germany army reserve, he specialized in fixing the instruments of the military bands of the British forces in Egypt. "Thoroughly abreast of the times," his shop by the Suarès roundabout displayed the latest marvel: an electric Welte-Mignon piano that could reproduce, all by itself, the finest performances. As for Alfred Moring, he all but gave up on his father's business back in London, the manufacture of surgical tools, to sell instead in Cairo accessories for cars and—what was more exciting—Hudson, Singer, Raleigh, and Norton motorcycles.[46]

At the Grands Magasins des Nouveautés on Shāriʿ al-Bawākī, a side street east of Azbakiyya Garden, a Frenchmen sold—among other things—lingerie, while Raff's boutique, located nearby on Place ʿAtaba al-Khaḍrāʾ, displayed hosiery and millinery as well as a stunning array of ready-made clothes in "ever-changing European fashions." The opening of this boutique in 1905 suggests how much Cairo had become—for many a foreigner—a land of opportunity. Orphaned as a child, H. Raff—a Romanian Jewish immigrant—began to

FIGURE 3.4 H. Raff's "cosmopolitan" boutique in Cairo. Source: Wright and Cartwright, *Impressions of Egypt*, 374.

work as teenager in Stein's famous department store. He rose to the top of this enterprise, eventually becoming the manager of a branch in Constantinople before resigning to establish his own boutique in Cairo.[47]

Arnold Wright's *Twentieth Century Impressions of Egypt*, on which I have based these sketches of Cairo's globalized trade and consumption, emphasized the city's "cosmopolitan" character. This book was not a nostalgic romance. It was published in 1909, before historians and others began to write about Cairo's cosmopolitanism with a sense of loss.[48] But it was an imperialist romance—written for British readers, residents or tourists, to appreciate the British Empire's accomplishments in the veiled protectorate.[49] It celebrated Cairo's polyglot and multiethnic offerings. The "mixture of races" as well as the variety of architectural styles made the city appear "cosmopolitan to an extent unequaled elsewhere."[50]

Wright's *Impressions* recommended for tourists to sit on the terrace of one of the grand hotels and "watch the cosmopolitan crowd" surging along Shāriᶜ Kāmil, "the point of contact between the East and the West." From this lookout, tourists could behold the beautiful spectacle, in the right season, of Indian jugglers, Sudanese vendors, effendi styles, the bewitching eyes of veiled Egyptian damsels, the shiny anklets and sparkling teeth of fellah-girls, and Parisian hats and gowns.[51] The city's linguistic diversity was astonishing too. Tourists could revel in cosmopolitanism by engaging with new media: every telephone operator spoke four or five languages; the Continental Hotel's gramophone shop furnished records in seven different languages. Journals were available in multiple languages, too. The editor of the *Egyptian Morning News*, who wrote the article on the country's multilingual press, praised the Greek newspaper *Kaïpon* for venturing into "cosmopolitan journalism" by publishing advertisements from diverse European firms that catered to an international readership.[52]

Wright described an exclusive venue, the Khedivial Sporting Club, as cosmopolitan due to its mixed British and Egyptian membership. Patronized by the city's political and military elites, this was the club where high society gathered to play croquet, watch polo tournaments, and enjoy a mild winter's day of Arabian horse races. What Wright turned a blind eye to was the role that ordinary Egyptians played to facilitate Cairo's Englishness. He described a hardware store located near the Central Railway Station as one of the oldest "local English firms" in this sector. The owner, Mr. Ratcliffe, imported many things from

FIGURE 3.5 Cosmopolitanism's other side: Egyptian workers promoting Hall's sanitary paint in front of an Englishman's hardware store in Cairo. Source: Wright and Cartwright, *Impressions of Egypt*, 366.

England. He prided himself in being the sole supplier of Hall's sanitary distemper, an oil-bound, water-soluble paint (available in more than seventy colors) manufactured by a factory that shipped its products from the port of Hull, East Yorkshire, "to all quarters of the globe."[53] In his presentation of Cairo's English ironmonger, Wright did not point out that the store depended on Egyptian workers. But a photograph reveals what the book failed to discuss: the presence of a pair of barefoot employees wearing a uniform to promote in English the English good.[54] This, too, was an aspect of "colonial cosmopolitanism."[55]

Most of the merchants featured in Wright's *Impressions* were immigrants, like Riḍā, searching for fortune in Cairo or Alexandria. Wright paid little attention to Arab businesses, such as Riḍā's *al-Manār*, that did not cater to Europeans. But a semblance of affinity can be found between Riḍā's enterprise and one enterprise celebrated by Wright's book: a furniture and souvenir shop founded by an Italian named Giuseppe Parvis that lay "somewhat hidden" just past the entrance to the Muski bazaar. The finest of carpenters, Signor Parvis had the honor of exhibiting his "Oriental" cabinets in the Paris World Expositions of 1867 and 1878. When he retired, the business passed into the hands of his eldest son, Pompeo. With "wonderful fidelity," according to Wright, the workshop under Pompeo's ownership reproduced originals from the Egyptian Museum. Integrating pharaonic designs and medieval Arabesques into modern furniture was its prized specialty. Like Pompeo, Riḍā came to traffic, too, in the modernization of antiquities.[56]

Egypt's Political Status in the Era of British Dominance, 1882–1936

During Riḍā's career in Cairo, which stretched from his immigration in 1897 to his death in 1935, Egypt's legal status changed more than once—mostly on the surface but significantly in 1922. He reached the country three decades after the Ottoman Empire agreed to recognize it as a khedivate, or viceroyalty, which meant that the khedive could rule with greater autonomy while remaining in theory under the Sublime Porte's suzerainty. On the books, this political configuration lasted until World War I. In reality, neither the Egyptian khedive nor the Ottoman sultan ruled autonomously. Militarily and politically the British assumed control of the levers of power well before the world war. They did so between 1882, when British forces entered Egypt, and 1936, when a treaty set limits on the territories to remain under British military protection.

In 1882 Great Britain effectively extended its informal empire into Egypt without bothering to proclaim it an imperial protectorate. Doing so would have required a legitimate declaration defining the purpose and the extent of this form of guardianship. It would also have entailed political justifications at home and diplomatic negotiations abroad. Instead Egypt became what a colonial administrator, Alfred Milner, famously described as a "veiled Protectorate."[57] In 1914, as a direct consequence of World War I alignments, the British Empire finally wrested suzerainty from the Ottoman Empire. It deposed the khedive, instated a sultan in his place, and formally declared Egypt a protectorate. This legal status lasted but a few years.

In 1922 the British government announced that Egypt would become an "independent sovereign state," and it promised to lift martial law. On a symbolic level, this unilateral proclamation marked Egypt's momentous transition into a nation-state. But it was made with the provision that the status quo would continue in some respects: the security of imperial communications, the military defense of Egypt, and the protection of "foreign interests" as well as minority rights would stay in British hands. In addition, Egypt's economic policy remained subject to foreign constraints. Until 1930 the government did not have the authority to impose tariffs, and British advisers continued to exercise their influence. With the country's independence thus limited, even as the last of the sultans assumed the title of monarch, still, the state remained something of a cross between a sovereign nation and an imperial protectorate. Yet another significant sign of change in Egypt's international legal status came a year after Riḍā's death, with the 1936 treaty that confirmed Egypt's path toward nationhood and also recognized, in article 13, that the "capitulatory régime now existing in Egypt is no longer in accordance with the spirit of the times."[58]

Protectorate Capitalism: The Official British Narrative

Financial and commercial interests motivated Great Britain to occupy Egypt militarily. Advanced by British and French imperialists, these economic interests were powerfully evident a decade before the invasion; the ʿUrabi revolt, which served as an excuse for British mobilization, was itself a reaction to their manifestation. In 1875, a few years after the opening of the Suez Canal, the burden of Egypt's foreign debts became unbearable. This forced the khedive, Ismāʿīl Pasha, to sell Egypt's shares in the Suez Canal Company—mostly owned by French capitalists—to the British government, which had to secure funding from a Rothschild banker. British and French financial interests were also behind the establishment, in the late 1870s, of a novel system of debt collection. With Egypt effectively in bankruptcy, European creditors pressed their governments to interfere to protect their capital investments. Responding to bondholders' demands, France and Britain imposed on Egypt the "dual control" system: a joint takeover of the state's finances, which entailed the imposition of direct Franco-British administration of the government's revenue for the satisfaction of foreign moneylenders.[59]

Dual control was but a prelude to the development of an elaborate supervisory structure following the 1882 occupation. The British Empire's expeditious, expansionist policy, which John Gallagher and Ronald Robinson described in a classic article as "the imperialism of free trade," may adequately explain why British troops invaded Egypt and why British officials remained stationed there for decades.[60] But since Egypt was not formally incorporated into the empire as a colony, British administrators came under pressure to justify the informal and supposedly impermanent arrangement as ultimately beneficial for both England and Egypt. In response, they developed the official ethos of the veiled protectorate: the reluctant paternalism cultivated by British officials, who represented themselves as technocratic instructors with expertise in handling the complex "machinery" of government in a state that needed an infusion of foreign capital for agricultural and industrial development. The result was a system of values and policies that is best described as "protectorate capitalism."

In his 1892 book *England in Egypt*, Undersecretary of State for Finance Alfred Milner traced what became the standard imperial narrative—often criticized in nationalistic and postcolonial histories—of the veiled protectorate's financial administration. He celebrated, of course, Britain's role in leading the country from bankruptcy to prosperity.[61] Capitalism figured first as the villain, who had run amok in the country, and then as the hesitant hero and eventual savior, coming back after a retreat overseas. It changed from a destructive to a constructive force, with the imposition of control by good government—once "the cult of laissez faire" no longer seemed tenable "even to its most faithful votaries." "European usury," as he put it, had "gone near to ruin the country" in the period before British protection; now "European capital," judiciously directed toward key areas of the economy, would save it. Foreign capital remained "shy of Egypt" one decade after the invasion, since there was still fear abroad about the return of "uncontrolled native administration." Investors, however, had reason for confidence. Great Britain had vowed to place upon Egypt not an invisible hand but "a controlling hand," so international investments could proceed with security and protection. Already "wisely expended" capital had formed "the basis of all the material improvement of the past ten years."[62]

Egyptian peasants, a large majority of the population, had been subjected to a "crushing tyranny" until 1882. "Rapid, unsound development" under Ismāʿīl Pasha had enabled "the small foreign capitalist without a conscience" to exploit the peasantry—already taxed heavily and arbitrarily by the inept khedivial government. "Industrious after their own fashion," these peasants nevertheless lacked "the strenuousness and the progressive spirit which would characterize any equally intelligent race" conditioned by a "more bracing" environment. "Such a race will not of itself develop great men or new ideas, or take a leading part in the progress of mankind," without proper (British) guidance. Nothing would stimulate their lot as much as increasing the agricultural yield by means of new irrigation projects. Through "training in a better school," Egyptians in general would eventually attain all the skills required for independence: political stability and fiscal responsibility.[63]

Meanwhile, opportunities abounded for capitalists to make investments that would yield both private and public advantages: "Egypt is a country which cries aloud for the application of capital to elicit its great latent wealth." "It will never be a great manufacturing country," Milner warned, "but there is room for industrial enterprise in many directions." Contemplating the work of "British engineers" backed by "British capital," he remarked on the veiled protectorate's success in enticing "capitalists to look at schemes equally beneficial to the country and to the investing public."[64]

Turning to the topic of international trade, Milner took pains to justify Britain's "material interest" in Egypt's Occupation. He first acknowledged the flow of goods. Britain purchased more than three-quarters of Egypt's exports, and it supplied nearly two-fifths of its imports. Rising prosperity and the revival of commerce meant that ordinary Britons, manufacturers and workmen, had a direct interest in Egyptians' growing buying power. But it was a grave mistake, he emphasized, to imagine that material gains for Britain would mean losses for Egypt and its other major trading partners, France and Austria. On the contrary, British administrators did not "unduly" favor British merchants. They worked hard for impartiality. They gained "not at the expense of others, but along with others." Every trading nation's profits grew, he insisted, as a consequence of Britain's guardianship. To describe the veiled protectorate as "honorable and praiseworthy from the point of view of humanity" was a gross exaggeration, but Milner's point was that there was nothing shameful in Britain obtaining a "recompense" for its good works in Egypt.[65]

England in Egypt had all the basic elements of the triumphalist narrative that British officials, high and low, told themselves and others—especially before the crash of 1907—to justify their reluctant "guardianship" of Egypt. Sound financial policy had everything to do with Britain's political success in Egypt. After serving in Egypt for thirty years as controller-general and as consul-general, the Earl of Cromer dedicated a chapter of his 1908 oeuvre, *Modern Egypt*, to "the repellent subject" of finance. Details aside, all that mattered was recognition of the difference between the "magic words" deficit and surplus.

Rescued from disastrous financial mismanagement, the country would not be permitted to slide back into the "slough of bankruptcy." When the Treasury finally posted a surplus, every government official had asked for funds. This reversal of fortunes came with the promise that "all the paraphernalia" of European civilization—its legal institutions, hospitals, schools, and reformatories—would eventually make it to Egypt. In the short term, the administration would control expenditures with discipline. But since revenues grew at an astonishing pace, rising from 8.9 to 15.3 million Egyptian pounds between 1883 and 1906, the administration was able to finance the construction of canals and railways as well as public buildings on an unprecedented scale. This period of growth and largesse coincided with a systematic effort at taxation reform, which involved measures of relief (the abolition and reduction of diverse taxes, tariffs, and tolls) as well as an elimination of privileged exemptions defended by capitulatory powers. In its fiscal policy Cromer's regime insisted on the "principle of equality" between Europeans and Egyptians. These and other changes elevated the country's creditworthiness, and they brought financial relief to the population. Thanks to British financiers, tens of millions of Egyptians could begin climbing "the ladder of moral and material improvement."[66]

Why could Egyptians not manage their own country's finances and assume themselves the reins of government? By Cromer's own admission, Egypt's economic problems were not intractable. Nor were they so challenging theoretically to require consulting political economists from Thomas Malthus to David Ricardo and from John Stuart Mill to Frédéric Bastiat. Dealing with the "cumbersome system of accounts which was the main offspring of internationalism" was perhaps the finance minister's greatest challenge. Until a 1904 reform of the system, he had to make convoluted financial calculations in coordination with the commissioners who represented English, French, Austrian, Italian, German, and Russian bondholders.[67] Yet there were deeper, structural challenges too. The influx of European capital, the "heterogeneous and cosmopolitan" population, and the persistence of capitulatory rights and privileges, turned Egypt into a quasi-European state with "exotic institutions." Whereas British "ingenuity and technical knowledge" remained instrumental to resolving complex administrative problems, corrupt pashas and rude shaykhs still lacked the skills to operate such a "complicated machine." Only "sentimental politicians" could entertain the notion that Egyptians were ready to manage their own nation-state independently.[68]

Strict adherence to the Qurʾan by the country's zealous and sincere Muslims was one of the principal reasons that Cromer gave to justify continued British guardianship. He saw Islam as a belligerent, hierarchical faith that clashed (as discussed in this book's introduction) with the imperial British value of free trade. It was impossible, in his view, for devout Muslims to accept honestly the enlightened virtue of indifference to religion in the market since they were bound to a sacred law that classified Christians as either foreign enemies or tributary subjects. Cromer knew that Islamic states could find ways to circumvent this medieval classification scheme, but history taught him to be wary of these states' secular bypasses. In his historical understanding, a legislative stratagem to avoid Islamic law had given birth to the system of capitulations: the set of privileges that the Ottoman Empire had granted to the European powers. "A legal fiction had to be created," he explained "in order to afford justification to strict Moslems, who were guided solely by Koranic principles, for dealing with Christians on the basis of equality."[69] The regime of capitulations that emerged as a result of this circumvention was extremely inefficient. It spawned the "incubus of internationalism" that had paralyzed Egypt's governmental machine until the arrival of British engineers and financiers.[70] To overcome the legal obstacles to free trade that remained, due to difficulties of dismantling piece by piece the cumbersome system of Islamic concessions to European nations, Egypt still needed skillful British guidance.

Cromer was convinced that Egyptian Muslims under British rule would eventually assimilate the West's "exotic secular ideas and forms of government" and earn the right to rule their country independently. But they would perhaps lose their religion. "It has yet to be proved," he quipped, "that Islam can assimilate civilisation without succumbing in the process."[71] Driven by self-interest, the lax Egyptian Muslim seemed ready to betray his own beliefs. He was "obliged to have recourse to all sorts of subterfuges" in order to transact with European moneylenders and not violate the letter of the sacred law: "The presence of the Christian usurer, with whom it is at times possible for the Muslim to form an unnatural alliance based on a community of interest, facilitates subterfuges of this sort."[72]

Still, Cromer found a glimmer of hope in the "agnostic" modernism of the veiled protectorate's Grand Mufti. He described the late ʿAbduh as an enlightened, broadminded reformer, suspected of heterodoxy because he would apply the spirit—rather than the letter—of seventh-century laws to the demands of the twentieth century. In his 1906 annual report to His Majesty's government, he mentioned that Pan-Islamism as a worldwide movement "to defy and to resist the Christian Powers" had to some extent infected the Egyptian national movement. Then he devoted a few sentences to the deceased mufti's patriotic followers: "Their fundamental idea is to reform various Moslem institutions without shaking the main pillars on which the faith of Islam rests." Untainted by Pan-Islamism, their "nationalist" program "involves not opposition to, but co-operation with Europeans in the introduction of Western civilization into the country." These patriots were Britain's "natural" allies. Their vision for "a truly autonomous Egypt" appeared compatible with the goals of the imperialism of free trade.[73] As a Syrian expatriate living in Cairo, Riḍā did not belong to this patriotic Egyptian camp. But he certainly grasped the argument that the struggle for independence from European imperialism depended on the degree to which Islamic law could be reformed to support the liberalization of trade.

The Transvaal Fatwa: European Hats and Christian Meat

ʿAbduh's liberalism was not boundless. But it extended far beyond his inclination to support capitalist institutions and investments for it also covered various social and cultural entanglements that resulted from European hegemony. This is evident in an infamous fatwa that he dispatched from Egypt to the Transvaal in 1903. The Transvaal fatwa dealt with the assimilation or acculturation of Muslims—specifically with the adoption of a European fashion accessory and with the consumption of meat associated with Christian butchers. Instead of prohibiting these things, ʿAbduh determined that their permissibility depended on various circumstances such as local Christian norms and subjective Muslim convictions.

With the end of the Boer War a year earlier, the South African republic that lay north of the Vaal River had lost its independence to become a colony of the British crown. Various groups represented Islam in the Transvaal: Cape Muslims, who descended in part from slaves brought to the region by the Dutch East India Company and who often identified as Malay despite their diverse ethnic origins, and recent immigrants from India's western shores.[74] The Indians, who numbered approximately ten thousand according to a census conducted in 1904, were principally from Gujarat and Konkan, but some stemmed from Madras on the Coromandel Coast. They worked in various professions, as indentured laborers in sugarcane fields and gold mines, as greengrocers and peddlers, and as prosperous international traders. They dressed in various outfits; they spoke different languages.[75] Even more than in Egypt or India, hats in this part of the world functioned as liminal markers of social, racial, and professional identity. Gandhi experienced this firsthand a few years earlier when, after enduring discriminatory blows during his travels in the region, he finally reached the Supreme Court of the British colony of Natal wearing faultless English dress. After swearing him in as a barrister, the Supreme Court's chief justice told him: "You must now take off your turban, Mr. Gandhi."[76]

In this Babel of dialects, customs, and economic occupations, it was only natural for Muslims to reflect on the things that could potentially distinguish them from others. Thinking along these lines, al-Ḥājj Muṣṭafā the Transvaalian wrote to ʿAbduh: "Individuals can be found in the Transvaal who wear [European] hats for the gratification of their wellbeing and for their accretion of profits. Is this permitted?" Perhaps the object in question was a large, wide-brimmed, soft felt hat that soldiers used during the Second Boer War in order to shield their eyes. But just as easily it might have referred to a derby or a panama, maybe even a top hat, articles of dress that Indian workers and traders frequently observed and occasionally wore either for practical reasons or to pass for Europeans.[77] Maybe a trader himself, al-Ḥājj Muṣṭafā presented a second question that also pertains to the subject of religious identity. Are Muslims in the Transvaal authorized to buy meat butchered by a "transgressor" (*mukhālif*), a man who strikes cattle with an axe and never offers a religious invocation?

A turban wearer himself, ʿAbduh knew that a brimmed hat was culturally meaningful as the last article of European dress that Muslim men who had embraced a European style still generally eschewed. Only dandies dared to wear it. An early twentieth-century edition of *The Encyclopaedia Britannica* sketched a picture of contemporary Egyptian dress. It was "increasingly common" for "men of the upper and middle classes" to wear long cotton shirts and drawers underneath a silken vest, the kaftan, that was "confined by the girdle." A red felt fez, which could still be perched on top of a turban in the old-fashioned style, was the standard headdress; "men who have otherwise adopted European costume retain the tarbush."[78] That was indeed the case. Even in professions where uniform dress and style were normative, headdress usually remained distinct. A photograph of the justices of the Mixed Tribunal of Alexandria demonstrates this attachment to the brimless cap wonderfully. Justices with names such as Mohamed, Aly, and Ragheb were virtually indistinguishable from justices with names such as Béla, Ernest, and Giovanni. Even their moustaches were the same. The one thing that made them look slightly different from their hatless peers was the headgear. European lawyers in Egypt wore anything from white wigs to top hats when they dressed up for court; their Muslim counterparts uniformly donned a truncated cone for a cap.[79]

Even so, ʿAbduh had the opinion that, so long as a Muslim gentleman did not wear a European hat (*burnayṭa*) to signal his intent to leave Islam for a different religion, there was no question of infidelity.[80] Furthermore, if this gentleman wore the hat to fulfill a need—to shade his visage, ward off what was loathsome, or attain some advantage—rather than to imitate foreign manners, then there was no reason to declare his act repugnant. The hat, in this semiology, did not necessarily represent European hegemony or Christian dominance. It signified just as easily a practical, upwardly mobile attitude to dress. As a modernist interpreter of the law, ʿAbduh considered the individual's intent and, in the

FIGURE 3.6 The hatted and hatless justices of Alexandria's Mixed Tribunal. Source: Wright and Cartwright, *Impressions of Egypt*, 96.

absence of details about the state of his mind, he developed a rationale to render the object licit by imbuing it with positive meanings.

His opinion about Transvaalian meat was also a liberal one. He held that Muslims living on the fringes of the world (*al-aṭrāf*) may lawfully consume the flesh of animals slaughtered by a Christian butcher. It is not at all clear why he assumed that the term *mukhālif*, used to describe the butcher, referred to a Christian rather than to an animist or, as is perhaps more likely, a Cape Muslim whose failure to adhere to orthopraxy troubled a reform-minded immigrant from India.[81] Local habits of consumption, rather than methods of production, determined for ʿAbduh what counted as lawful. However Christians slaughtered cows, sheep, and goats seemed irrelevant to him; the only criterion that really mattered in his view was the meat's status in Christian eyes. If Christians ate the meat, then Muslims could do the same. To justify this ruling, ʿAbduh cited the opinion of a medieval Andalusian scholar, Abū Bakr ibn al-ʿArabī. He also referred to the famous Qurʾanic revelation of chapter 5, verse 5, that gave Muslims permission to eat the food of Christians and Jews. But what most reveals ʿAbduh's frame of mind is the last phrase of the last sentence of his fatwa, which specifies that the meat of Transvaalian Christians is lawful for Muslims in order "to stave off any restriction of social intercourse and commercial relations with them."[82] Cosmopolitan sociability and free trade were clearly the mufti's reigning goals.[83]

Fiercely debated by Egyptian newspapers, the fatwa that rendered Christian meat lawful deepened the divide between reformers and their foes. Those who opposed ʿAbduh's liberalism argued against it on technical grounds, holding that it was forbidden for Muslims to consume the flesh of animals knocked down violently by the blow of an axe. They also placed some stress on the importance of pronouncing God's name before the act of slaughter. At the deepest level, they worried about Muslim imitation (*tashabbuh*)—whether cultural or religious, the line between the two was not so clearly drawn—of Christian customs. Thus, as well as banking with interest, food and clothes linked to European cultural hegemony became integral components of a symbolic code that conservatives would use to assert a distinct Islamic identity.

ʿAbduh, who was dying of cancer, was probably too ill to defend his fatwas and too old to change his juridical style. His practice had been to write very brief fatwas, sometimes no longer than a sentence or two, that were meant to reflect his authoritative, learned judgment. He made little effort to expose his rationale; and he never tried to persuade readers that he was right by offering to them extensive proofs from the Islamic tradition. Riḍā, by contrast, would take it upon himself to defend ʿAbduh's rulings by furnishing such proofs. Moreover, since he was just beginning his career as a writer of fatwas, he learned a valuable lesson from the brouhaha: he learned that fatwa readers had a taste for an ingredient that was missing from ʿAbduh's liberal fatwas, the spice of authenticity.

Beneficial or Harmful Imitation? The Critical Legal and Theological Question

Within months of migrating to Egypt under British rule, Riḍā addressed the problem of "imitating and emulating" the Europeans. He made a rough utilitarian distinction between adopting advantageous things, which he considered as good as mandatory, and adopting either useless or harmful things. There was absolutely no reason to approach European sciences, technologies, and industrial principles cautiously. In the case of battleships and other instruments of war that offered a political advantage, Muslim states needed to move beyond passive importation and toward active production. As for European goods that offered no strategic benefits, these were best avoided—even if their consumption was technically lawful. A mild or strict prohibition applied only to strange new objects and manners that would presumably or assuredly cause "damage to us." The chief difficulty lay in determining how exactly to categorize European inventions whose useful or harmful qualities were not yet apparent. Foreign innovations had no fixed status before the sacred law. Judgments depended on multiple factors, and they differed from place to place and time to time.

Riḍā's legal relativism is best illustrated by his equivocal views about the adoption of non-Muslim clothes. He recommended abstaining from European habits that would yield no advantage for Muslims. But he did not go so far as to ban European clothes as if they were irreligious articles. Instead, he told a story about a letter that caliph ʿUmar I sent to one of his generals, ʿUtba ibn Farqad, criticizing Arab troops for wearing "the attire of the polytheists and garments of silk." Glossing the tradition, Riḍā explained that the caliph wanted to ensure that Arab warriors would not grow weaker in the pursuit of jihad. Adopting fancy foreign clothes would lead them to a life of comfort and leisure, with tragic political consequences. Riḍā's yardstick, when he published this 1898 reflection on the ideal Muslim way to relate to Europe's material advantages, was clearly a martial one. It measured the virtue of Arab austerity in the framework of a holy war. This was not Riḍā's sole standard, however, for he rushed to reassure Muslim moderns that wearing European clothes was not blameworthy in all circumstances. In Arabia, the Prophet and his companions had worn a cross-cultural garment that apparently resembled a fringed Jewish shawl made in a sumptuous Persian style. In that place at that time, indulging in luxury had been just fine.[84]

But when does Arab or Muslim conformity to foreign tastes become legally inexcusable? Where exactly did Riḍā draw the line, as an expert on the sacred law, between cultural and religious imitation? It was the easiest matter for him to judge goods that symbolized the worship of other gods. When he was asked to rule on an interfaith entanglement, a Muslim calligrapher's work on behalf of Christian missionaries in North Africa, Riḍā minced no words. He declared the calligrapher an apostate who should be denied last rites. Similarly, in one of his very last fatwas, published a month before his death, he had no trouble prohibiting Muslim printers from engraving crosses on zinc or copper plates or embossing gold crosses on book covers: "The cross is a sign of a religion other than Islam, and it is unseemly for a Muslim" to help Christians display it.[85] Riḍā felt no ambivalence about Muslim participation in this production. His ruling against it was straightforward and blunt. The real difficulty for him, as for other reformers, lay in sentencing secular goods that had originated abroad and that symbolized not Christianity but European culture. A brimmed hat presented, for this exact reason, a greater conundrum than did an engraved cross.

When Riḍā confronted the problem of cultural assimilation, he thought about rituals as well as objects. To what extent should Muslims under European rule participate in Christian ceremonies? In 1904 a correspondent from Montenegro specifically asked if it was okay for him to honor a Christian acquaintance who had visited him during a Muslim festival with a reciprocal visit at Christmas or Easter. At the time, Montenegro reckoned itself a principality rather than, as in the first half of the nineteenth century, a Serbian Orthodox theocracy. But the fellow who wrote to Riḍā did not perceive the Balkan nation in secular terms; he wrote to *al-Manār* that Montenegrin Muslims, who constituted a sizable multiethnic minority, lived "under the administration of a Christian government." Visits to Christians during their holidays formed part of an experiment in coexistence, an endeavor to put the past behind rather than to nurse the distant memory of the Montenegrin Vespers, when Muslims had been given the legendary choice, on Christmas Eve, between martyrdom and the grace of baptism. Still, when he deliberated whether to accept or decline the Christian invitation, it seemed significant to the fatwa seeker that the ruler of the state was a Christian prince.[86]

In 1904 a correspondent from the Egyptian city of Asyut also sought the jurist's advice about Muslim involvement in Christian festivities. Every year American missionaries, likely Presbyterians, organized public events in their schools that would commence with an invocation of Christ as "the son of God and the redeemer of humankind."[87] Could Asyut's Muslims lawfully attend these events and, if so, heed the summons to pray to Christ as if he were their savior, too? Four years later an anonymous fatwa seeker from Cairo who identified himself by the initials J.A. wanted to know what Muslims should do when, as citizens of a Christian country such as Russia, they were expected to participate in religious or national ceremonies that involved breaking a Muslim taboo by toasting the Romanov czar with wine.[88] An Egyptian postman had raised a related question in 1907: If Muslims died while fighting for the Russian army in the course of the Russo-Japanese War, would their sacrifice count as an act of disobedience to God? Although it dealt with military activities rather than ritual ceremonies, this question similarly probed the extent to which Muslims could loyally serve a non-Muslim state.[89]

However much they varied in tone, Riḍā's responses consistently stressed the value of interfaith sociability—within religious limits. They emphasized the importance of national unity in every state, regardless of its religious composition. When Muslims wield judicial power over non-Muslims, they ought to show them noble manners, "the basis of our religion." When they lack such power, they should behave amicably just the same because in that circumstance their welfare depends on the civility of others. By visiting non-Muslims in their homes and joining them at public events, Muslims could become better integrated into predominantly non-Muslim nations. Yet there are boundaries that must never be crossed in the quest for integration. To drink wine in honor of a king or an emperor, pray to Christ, glorify religious icons, and partake in forbidden rites—all these acts were utterly unacceptable. If private or public events threatened to spur the process of cultural and religious assimilation, then the Muslim in attendance should become a bystander and refrain from participating actively.[90] Similar considerations, where there was a need to distinguish between autonomous and subordinate conformity, would apply to the consumption of foreign goods that seemed harmless but not all that useful.

Beyond Shariʿa Courts: Fatwas in a Pluralistic Legal System

Riḍā wrote his fatwa for Montenegrin Muslims and ʿAbduh wrote his fatwa for Transvaalian Muslims on the margins of a pluralistic legal system that had confined the application of Islamic law in their country of residence. As Egypt grew more integrated into world trade in the late nineteenth century, pressure built up to reform the legal system in order to deal effectively with cases involving both native and foreign parties. Consular courts, established by capitulation treaties, had the privilege of extraterritorial jurisdiction. But they could neither easily adjudicate cases nor effectively enforce judgments against the khedivial government or against foreigners represented by other consulates. European financiers wanted legal institutions to protect their investments and loans, which ranged from government bonds to interest-bearing mortgages. Egyptian reformers recognized the need for a new judicial system, too, in order to attract foreign investment with legal guarantees and represent khedivial subjects, who of course lacked capitulatory privileges, more equitably in litigation with foreigners.

All of this gave rise, by 1875, to the Mixed Courts—a remarkable development in legal history. Significant changes to the Egyptian legal system had begun earlier, in the middle of the nineteenth century, leading to what Rudolph Peters called "the development of a secular judiciary."[91] But the Mixed Courts would rule on civil and commercial cases on the basis of codes that were primarily based on French models. These codes marked another significant step toward secular codification in an astonishingly pluralistic legal system, where European and Islamic laws as well as Ottoman and Egyptian decrees had different roles to play in different spheres. In the Mixed Courts, as if in homage to the enduring prestige of the Napoleonic Code, French was the official language. Appointed by the government, tribunals of native and foreign judges resolved all kinds of new commercial disputes between native and foreign litigants. They diminished capitulatory powers' legal prerogatives too: although consular courts continued to operate for more than half a century after the inauguration of the Mixed Courts, their jurisdiction was increasingly confined to criminal cases and personal-status disputes.[92]

Through a series of subsequent reforms that unfolded between 1875 and 1897, Egypt reestablished or reconfigured a great multiplicity of courts whose jurisdiction would depend on the personal status of the parties to a lawsuit and on the nature of the legal case. It founded, notably, the Native Tribunals (Tribunaux indigènes). Modeled after the Mixed Courts, these tribunals had competence in civil, criminal, and commercial cases devoid of foreign involvement. The Native Civil Code resembled so closely the Napoleonic Code that a legal historian described it as "break with all legal tradition in Egypt," marking "the adoption—or imposition—of a totally foreign legal system in that country."[93]

Then there were the shariʿa courts, whose jurisdiction was now all but relegated to Egyptian Muslims' marriage, divorce, and inheritance cases, as well as their counterparts for Egyptian Jews and Christians, the religious minorities' councils. Like consular courts, confessional councils were institutions with long histories—in a country whose religious diversity as well as its commercial pacts with foreign nations had meant the coexistence of a range of legal systems with distinct yet overlapping areas of competence. The series of reforms that began in 1875 thus expanded what had already been a pluralistic legal structure.

Under this reformed political and legal system, fewer and fewer cases fell within the shariʿa courts' delimited area of competence. In a state where the legitimacy of power was directly linked to effective oversight of the economy, Islam's sacred law had a vanishingly small role to play in economically significant cases, which typically involved a "mixed" foreign interest. Whether or not this framework signified the progress of "secularization" in Egypt, an extended political process whose beginning historians have dated to the piecemeal reforms initiated by Muḥammad ʿAlī (r. 1805–1848), it clearly reflected the diminishing capacity of Islamic law to influence financial and commercial affairs. However frustrated by this turn of fortune, judges hired to interpret the shariʿa neither rebelled nor resigned; they found ways to continue functioning, if grudgingly, in a marginalized legal position.[94]

Sitting at the top of the Islamic legal hierarchy, ʿAbduh had no reason to feel frustrated or marginalized. But his office obliged him to think about Islamic law with institutional legal constraints, always recognizing that it was neither universally enforceable nor automatically applicable. His fatwa in favor of Lady Nafīsa's right to control independently her Suez Canal shares, to which the next chapter turns, was, for example, an argument for the application of "Islamic" law rather than "French" codes in what would otherwise be tried as a "mixed" interest case. Perhaps it is in this light, too, that we should understand his fatwa to the Transvaal. In this new British colony, as in Egypt, the shariʿa was institutionally confined and narrowly enforceable. It made sense for ʿAbduh to conceive of it—under British influence—as a personal system of law to which individual Muslims could adhere voluntarily based on their own subjective convictions. Accordingly, he ruled that it was up to each Muslim in the Transvaal to decide when material entanglements with Christian colonizers put his or her soul at risk.

Boldly, Riḍā chose a different path. He decided to strike out on his own and work outside the system. Founding an Arabic press to publish an Islamic magazine, he ventured into a unique career that would allow him to profit from his theological and legal training without needing to rely on the government and its institutions, from al-Azhar university to the shariʿa courts, for his livelihood. This independence freed him to return to the sacred law with an expansive agenda: to disregard institutional constraints, which had practically reduced the shariʿa's scope to the resolution of family disputes, and to contemplate instead the theoretical applicability of divine revelations, prophetic rules, and foundational acts, to every sphere of life. Financial and commercial cases that stemmed from novel exchanges between Muslims and non-Muslims certainly fell within his boundless purview. Liberated from Egypt's judicial system, he became the opposite of a bureaucratic justice in the employ of the state, turning instead into a legal counselor to individuals and communities anywhere in the world of Islam. Like a mufti advising a judge, he made judgments known as fatwas. But his judgments had no connection to any enforcement mechanism; they were basically advisory rulings that Muslim moderns were free to heed or dismiss when they tried to settle informally disputes that took place outside of the courtroom.

By orienting his judgments toward a pious reading public, he contributed—perhaps more than any other scholar in history—to the reinvention of the fatwa genre for modern times. Pithy or convoluted, the fatwas of the past had often served as instruments for communication among legal experts, who possessed the rare privilege of literacy as well as a technical education in jurisprudence. Shorn of jargon, Riḍā's accessible fatwas were designed, instead, for laypersons in a period of expanding literacy. These lay readers shaped his agenda. With only incidental or occasional references to the legal systems of the states where they lived, they wanted to know how to apply Islamic law in their own societies. They were profoundly invested in figuring out how to respond as Muslims to new material objects, such as national banknotes, that were not receiving a hearing in the shariʿa courts.

4

Paper Money and Consummate Men

Capitalism and the Rise of Laissez-Faire Salafism

It is strange but true that Egypt's first national banknote was a foreign fabrication.[1] With a few months to spare before the new century's dawn, one of London's richest merchant bankers, Sir Ernest Joseph Cassel, joined forces with a family of Jewish financiers in Cairo and a cotton baron in Alexandria to establish the National Bank of Egypt, and they received, by a khedivial decree, the sole privilege to make paper money. The currency was fabricated overseas by the London designer, printer and engraver Bradbury, Wilkinson & Co. The least valuable note this company manufactured proclaimed in Arabic and English, in words artfully arrayed around an image of the sphinx, the national bank's "Promise to pay the bearer on demand the sum of FIFTY piastres." Promising to pay higher and higher sums, up to one hundred pounds, other notes displayed pyramids, pharaonic temples, or feluccas.

The most striking image of all appeared on the one-pound banknote. It displayed a dromedary standing incongruously by a kneeling Bactrian camel, whose natural habitat lay so very far from Egypt—in the steppes of Central Asia. Nothing other than Bradbury, Wilkinson's Orientalist fantasy, the image illustrates marvelously that the "national" banknote was quite a foreign artifact.

It took a while for Anglo-Egyptian banknotes to become familiar things. Twice a year from the end of the century to World War I, the National Bank of Egypt shipped paper money from London to Alexandria, and the total value of these notes rose gradually from sixty thousand to nearly three million Egyptian pounds. Meanwhile, in the same period, British gold sovereigns remained in such high demand that, depending on the cotton harvest, Egypt imported every year between four and thirteen million pounds sterling. Egyptians preferred

FIGURE 4.1 The National Bank of Egypt's banknote, an Orientalist representation of Arabian and Central Asian species of camels. Spink & Son. Reproduced with permission.

precious metal coins; and they retained this preference until the outbreak of the world war, when Britain suddenly turned banknotes into legal tender, effectively ending their automatic convertibility into gold.[2]

This chapter deals with the relationship between the reform of Islam and a few embodiments of capitalism, including colonial banknotes. It concentrates on the perspectives of three famous reformers on paper money, banking with interest, life insurance plans, Suez Canal Company shares, and philanthropic Muslim millionaires. These reformers—Riḍā, ʿAbduh, and the éminence grise of Islamic modernism from Russia, the Crimean Tatar Ismail Gasprinski—helped to turn Cairo into a global center for Islam's reform in the first decade of the twentieth century. At different points between the foundation of Egypt's national bank at the end of the century and the financial crash of 1907, these reformers thought seriously about the benefits of capitalism for Muslims. This was a remarkable period of financial speculation and economic growth in Egypt. At no point in the long history of Islam's reform did capitalism seem as attractive as it did then and there.

This period coincided with the rise of "Salafism" in Egypt, too, which raises a series of historical questions about the effects of the spirit of capitalism upon the emerging Salafist ethic. How did Salafi reformers meet the challenge of capitalism? Did they envision an alternative moral economy? Or did they strive to justify financial innovations and the individual pursuit of money? Did they see the Qurʾan and the Ḥadīth as compatible with free enterprise or as a bulwark to protect Muslims from greedy, godless bankers? How necessary was capital for reforming Islam? And what made the perfect man, possessing the spirit of reform or spending a fortune on Islamic causes? This chapter shows how, while entertaining a few scruples and qualms, Riḍā devised ways to use the tools of Salafism (direct and independent interpretations of scriptural rules as well as exhortations for moderns to emulate the heroes of a golden age) to support embodiments of capitalism.

Of Men and Money in 1900: Industrious Reformers and the Capital of the Salaf

During the first decade of *al-Manār*, the modern system of ideas, values, and attitudes that historians have come to call "Salafism" was neither an all-encompassing ideology nor a strict discipline. There was no behavioral code for adherents to follow or any institutions to verify compliance with a set of programmatic rules. In its period of formation, Salafism was above all a bold plea for religious reform: an originalist critique of contemporary clerical structures as dusty medieval accretions that had covered, like layers of dirt at an archaeological site, the glorious foundations of the first Muslims. This project of excavation and recovery had a political dimension, which Riḍā made manifest through frequent evocations of the rightly guided caliphs. These were the Prophet's successors, celebrated for their accomplishments as conquerors and lawmakers. Military strength and legal reform were indeed key priorities for the Muslim moderns who wanted to return to the heroic path of the ancients. Riḍā considered it a virtue, too, for modern religious authorities to emulate their forefathers' engagement with the world; thus, they had to be ready and willing to admonish sultans and criticize heretics.[3] This suggests that Salafism had a political and doctrinal orientation, but what was its economic orientation? In an era when wealth and power seemed inextricably linked, how did Riḍā relate the pious ancestors, the exemplary Salaf, to the pursuit of capital?

A fine place to begin the search for an answer is the front-page article "Of Men and Money" that Riḍā published in *The Lighthouse* on October 5, 1900. Reformers were divided on what should be the principal engine of reform: consummate men or capital? Some argued that money should be the first and foremost means for restoring the Muslim community to prosperity. Riḍā disagreed, offering instead a humanistic vision. He argued that the community needed leaders who would place the "existence of persons" on a higher plane than the "existence of possessions." Martin Luther, Booker T. Washington, Jamāl al-Dīn al-Afghānī, and Sayyid Aḥmad Khān were the models that he presented as examples of the indispensability of upright men. Was Luther wealthy, he asked rhetorically? Did he advertise his path or rite by means of money? As for Booker Washington, did he not pawn his pocket watch in order to pay for a brick kiln to build a school for impoverished black students, who then learned, by making and selling bricks, the virtue of industry? Did the founder of Aligarh's Muhammadan Anglo-Oriental College belong to the affluent or destitute ranks of society? (A nobleman's son, Sir Syed was actually born into privilege; he faced some financial difficulties after his father's death.) As for al-Afghānī, did he spread purses of cash or the spirit of reform?

All of this did not exactly make an anticapitalistic argument. The article was a call for investing in human capital—in the inspiring reformers who would work to improve Muslims' welfare. It expressed indignation at the squandering of the Salaf's wealth by incompetent managers, tyrannical commanders, and unjust rulers who had indulged in "bestial desires and sensual pleasures" and wasted Muslims' rightful inheritance. Was anything left, then, of the legacy of the Salaf? "What remains of the capital that the pious Salaf left behind is a tool," held Riḍā, and to work every tool, instrument, or machine needs a factor, an agent, a worker: a human being with motive power. But who possessed the skills to operate this Salafi tool? Consummate men: the accomplished reformers who would lovingly nurture their community with spiritual rather than materialistic values, even when they needed money to realize their aims.[4]

Capitalist values and metaphors thus began to pervade the spirit of Salafism from the very beginning of the twentieth century. Historians have not recognized this fact, but Salafism emerged as an ideological tool for the reform of Islam in a world where capital was so deeply appreciated that the Salaf themselves had to be resurrected from their graves to work in capitalistic terms. Indeed, the perfect reformer in Riḍā's eyes was the man who could skillfully put the symbolic capital of the forefathers to work, managing the instrument or running the machinery that they had bequeathed to future generations.

Riḍā's article was part and parcel of a broader reformist discourse that tried to stir contemporary Muslim intellectuals to conceive of money, industry, and trade in new ways—without lapsing into a trite critique of materialism. It was a commonplace of religious thought in colonial times to juxtapose the East's spiritual advantages with the West's material advantages. The radical Egyptian reformer Qāsim Amīn (d. 1908) wrote in *The New Woman* that every Muslim witnessed the "material proofs" of the superiority of Westerners in industry and science. These proofs were apparent everywhere, in the home and on the street, in household devices and electric machines. It was too easy, he argued, for Muslim scholars to seek refuge from shame in the claim of superiority in the invisible field of spirituality. He challenged them to wake up from the lull of this unverifiable claim, examine with a progressive mindset the original sources of Islam, and embark on a liberal reform of religion and society.[5]

Reformers who leveraged the symbolic capital of the Salaf preached, among other things, the virtue of industry. In his fictional account of a conference in Mecca, ʿAbd al-Raḥmān al-Kawākibī (d. 1902), Riḍā's associate in Cairo and a fellow Syrian exile, blamed an ascetic inclination to avoid "exertion, work, and the ornament of life," together with a lack of vocation for industry, as reasons for the lassitude of Muslim societies. On the same list of "the causes of languor," he criticized the rigidity of jurists who adhered zealously to their schools of law. To achieve a religious resurgence and an industrial revolution, Muslims needed to return to scripture and the Salafi path.[6]

As well as trade, scripture seemed like a necessary key for unlocking the door to power and prosperity. Riḍā affirmed this conviction in an unexpected way—with a couple of quotations attributed to the missionary queen of the Empire of Free Trade. On one occasion, Queen Victoria had supposedly remarked to a West African chief, "The secret to England's greatness is the Holy Book." In addition, a missive sent in her name to the Yoruba nation had pronounced international trade "blessed" if it dealt not in slaves, and then explained: "Commerce alone will not make a nation great and happy, like England. England has become great and happy by the knowledge of the true God and Jesus Christ." *Al-Manār*'s obituary of Queen Victoria omitted the last three words, "and Jesus Christ," as well as any references to slavery and imperial British missions to African chiefs. Shorn of context, the Arabic translations effectively communicated one basic idea: the notion that a commitment to both scripture and commerce had propelled England to greatness.[7]

The challenge was to find in Islam's Holy Books and in the acts of the Salaf secrets for economic success. These sources could in theory afford edifying examples of the rewards of industry and commerce as well as admonitions not to engage in illicit or immoral moneymaking activities. But reformers charged with issuing fatwas had to move beyond administering vague inspirational sermons. They had to offer legal counsel about contested practices, and this was a risky endeavor. Egypt's senior reformer, Muḥammad ʿAbduh, found himself in a fraught situation, for example, when he was asked to give an official ruling—as the country's Grand Mufti—about the legality of banking with interest. He got caught between the veiled protectorate's British authorities, who wanted him to liberalize Islamic law, and the pious Egyptian Muslims who did not want the state's leading legal authority to make light of the Qurʾanic ban on usury. He decided to sanction the new way to earn money, but the mere rumor of his fatwa caused a great uproar.

The Grand Mufti in the Service of Capitalism: ʿAbduh's Fatwas

In *Modern Egypt*, after alluding to legalistic ruses by ʿAbduh and other jurists to work around the taboo on usury, Cromer remarked: "Moslem depositors in the Government Savings Bank often decline to accept interest on their deposits."[8] He exaggerated the extent of their principled rejection to banking with interest. Only a minority of Egyptian depositors (362 out of 4,197 in 1901 and 721 out of 8,663 in 1902) refused to accept interest payments on their deposits in the khedive's brand-new Postal Savings Bank.

A few figures can give a more concrete sense of the depth and breadth of their protest against usury. Included in the total number of Egyptian depositors were Copts and Jews. This makes it impossible to calculate the exact percentage of objectors out of the total number of Muslim depositors; roughly 10 percent would be a good estimate. The vast majority of depositors at this time were officials, government servants, commercial employees, and factory manufacturers, followed by artisans, journeymen, and students. Professional religious scholars also opened bank accounts; the number of shaykhs and members of the *ʿulamāʾ* who patronized the Postal Savings Bank grew from eighteen to forty-two between 1901 and 1902. No doubt several of them refused interest payments, yet the number of scrupulous objectors—Muslims who were willing to sacrifice a financial profit due to their qualms over usury—was roughly twenty times higher than the number of clerics. If the majority of Muslims who opened a bank account had no problem with the opportunity to earn money from money, a significant minority harbored intense pious doubts about the financial scheme. Inspired by scriptural prohibitions against usury, this minority willingly chose an Islamic over a capitalistic interest. Their choice disturbed powerful figures in Egypt, who wanted to remove all religious obstacles from the path toward capitalism.[9]

In his response to this tense situation, Egypt's Grand Mufti declined to declare the bank's interest on loans simply lawful. Instead, ʿAbduh privately drafted a fatwa, which he shared with Lord Cromer, where he sketched a method to legalize earnings. Rather than loaning money to the bank usuriously, at a fixed interest rate, depositors qua speculators—risking, in theory, the loss of principal—might invest their capital with the bank, which would act as their commercial agent. Thus, they would enter into a type of profit-sharing venture (*muḍāraba*) sanctioned by Islamic law. Never officially published, this capitalist fatwa stirred a great deal of controversy. Defensively the khedive, ʿAbbās Ḥilmī Pasha, accused ʿAbduh of surreptitiously sanctioning usury (*ribā*) for devout

Muslims, while critics for the popular press began to excoriate the mufti for devising schemes to turn pious money over to the empire of capitalism.[10]

Since the fatwa was never published, questions remain about the degree of ʿAbduh's economic liberalism. To condone interest, did he simply indulge in a naming game, redefining the standard relationship between depositor and banker as a profit-sharing venture? Or did he demand specific modifications to the business of banks, placing restrictive conditions on the investments that a banker could undertake on behalf of a pious Muslim? A suggestive answer to these questions can be found in a pair of fatwas—official, published fatwas that have received little or no scholarly attention—where ʿAbduh developed his Islamic legal perspective on capitalist finance.

Dating from 1902, the first fatwa concerns the legality—by Islamic standards—of an American insurance company's business:

> The honorable director of the American company Mutual Life asked about a man who agrees with the company's association to give them a fixed sum of money within a fixed period of time, by scheduled installments, for trading in whatever they think promises fortune and advantage (*maṣlaḥa*). Now, if the defined period of time passes and the man is still alive, he obtains from them the sum of money [that he presented to them] together with his [share of the] profit from the trades during this period of time. But if he dies in the middle of this period, either his heirs or those to whom he assigned guardianship (*wilāya*) get that sum, together with the profit that ensued from his payments. Is this in harmony with the sacred law?[11]

At this point in history, multinational life insurance companies were moving aggressively into Egypt. One sign of this expansion can be found in litigation before the Mixed Courts. In a memorable case, a life insurance company, Le Kosmos, moved to nullify the policy of a certain Angelo Spoletti for falsely declaring that his mother had died of typhus when she had apparently died of tuberculosis.[12] As many as sixty-two firms provided insurance coverage of various kinds in the country, with several specializing in life insurance. Mutual Life of New York competed in this market against Mutual Life Assurance of Australasia, not to mention other American, British, French, Swiss, Austrian, and Canadian establishments.[13] Posed by Mutual Life's director, the question under consideration stemmed from the rapidly expanding business of risk management in the country. It is an early and precious example of capitalism's cultural flexibility, revealing how an American financier tried to figure out the best way to represent his services to Egypt's Grand Mufti so as to obtain his backing: a ruling declaring that the company's life insurance policy conformed to Islamic law.

In response, ʿAbduh decreed: "The man's agreement with the association, for him to give that sum in the way that was mentioned, is a kind of commercial partnership, which is permissible." It is not forbidden for the man, for his heirs, or for their guardians, to take the capital (*māl*), together with the profits earned from the labor of trading. It did not matter to ʿAbduh that the man purchasing this instrument did not place his principal at risk, as required by a standard Islamic venture-sharing partnership (*muḍāraba*). Nor did it matter to him that Mutual Life's business was all about speculating on the length of investors' lives.[14]

The second fatwa, dating from 1903, is worth quoting in full. Dealing with the redemption of Suez Canal Company shares, it reveals how a wealthy woman—operating deftly within the structure of legal pluralism—made a claim for the competence of Islamic rather than French law.

> Lady Nafīsa Ḥamdī, daughter of the deceased Pasha Ismāʿīl Ḥamdī, asked about 100 shares that she owns in the Suez Canal Company. These shares are safeguarded in the Company's central office, with the voucher under her authority. Now, she wanted to withdraw them, but the company contended that wives are not permitted to dispose of their properties, except with their husbands' permission, as established by the French legal code (*al-qānūn*). Nevertheless, since both she and her husband are Muslim, French law has no jurisdiction (*sulṭa*) over them, because they do not have [foreign] protection (*ḥimāya*). So does the Islamic sacred law grant her permission to redeem those shares by herself, without her husband's mediation, or not?[15]

Pasha Ismāʿīl Ḥamdī had been the governor of Port Saʿid when the ʿUrabi revolt broke out. He was famous for taking refuge on an English ship for several weeks until his reinstatement into office. He left Nafīsa a fortune. By 1903 each share of the Suez Canal Company—with the original, nominal value of 500 francs—was trading at approximately 3,800 francs. One hundred shares were worth roughly 380,000 francs or, at the current exchange rate, 14,660 Egyptian pounds. This was a staggering sum. (British officials estimated that the public residence of the director-general of the Antiquities Department, the French Egyptologist Gaston Maspero, would cost E£4,400. The Port Saʿid governorate's municipal mansion must not have cost much more than E£13,000, based on an estimate made soon before its completion. As for Cairo's model workshop, accommodating a hundred artisans' shops for carpentry, leatherwork, metalwork, and other building specialties, it cost approximately E£15,000.) With her vast sum of money, Lady Nafīsa could have purchased a lavish mansion or endowed an impressive public building.[16]

Lady Nafīsa's claim was that the Egyptian version of the Napoleonic Code had no jurisdiction in her case. The Mixed Courts, whose legislation mostly derived from French civil law, had competence in commercial cases that involved foreign and native persons.[17] Given the predominance of French and English shareholders in the Suez Canal Company, disputes about its shares typically fell under adjudication by the Mixed Courts. The Napoleonic Code did indeed prevent wives from managing their property freely. In the standard marriage (by *communauté*), "the husband administers alone the goods of the community." Even in cases where a couple opted to marry without the default "community" of property, still the husband retained the prerogative "to administer the wife's movable and immovable possessions." An apposite exception to this patriarchal order was made for any woman who entered into a contract as a public trader (*marchande publique*); she had the right, by article 1426, to engage in business without her husband's consent.[18] Nevertheless, it is true that the French code confined women's usufruct to an extreme degree—a surprising fact given its reputation as a progressive force in world history.

By contrast, under liberal interpretations of Islamic law, women had the right to own, manage, and freely dispose of their own property. Although there is no reason to imagine that Muslim women everywhere actually enjoyed this theoretical right, it is the case that wealthy Muslim women in urban communities succeeded in exercising it legally in several respects.[19] Given Lord Cromer's conviction that "Islam keeps women in a position of marked inferiority," in a position of degradation that differs radically from the high status attained by European women, it is worth highlighting this unexpected point of contrast between Islamic law and the French code.[20] Attuned to this difference, Lady Nafīsa wanted to enjoy the freedom that Islamic law would grant her to redeem her shares without needing to obtain her husband's consent. She argued, therefore, that French law did not apply to her in this instance because there existed no "mixed" interest: both she and her husband were Muslim.[21]

In response, ʿAbduh ruled: "The sacred judgment that the sacred law demands is that, since these shares are Lady Nafīsa Ḥamdī's exclusive property, they are owned by her. She has the right to seize them and take possession of them by herself. This does not depend on her husband's permission."[22] The fact that she held shares in a joint-stock company—a type of incorporation that had no basis in the shariʿa, which emphasized transactions among legal persons rather than within socially constructed organizations—did not bother ʿAbduh in the least.[23] Nor did he find troubling the fact that the daily value of the shares, traded in Paris and London, depended mostly on financial speculation—arguably forbidden by Islamic law as a form of gambling.[24] At no point did he warn that there were licit and illicit ways to make money. Instead, in a legal opinion that demonstrated not only economic but also social liberalism, ʿAbduh supported Lady Nafīsa's right to transact shares independently.

Concentrating on removing rather than erecting legal obstacles, these fatwas demonstrate how much the Grand Mufti worked to grease the wheels of capitalism. But it would be a mistake to cast ʿAbduh as Islam's laissez-faire ideologue without qualification, for he harbored some resentment toward imperial capitalism. In his commentary on the Qurʾanic verse that threatens "devourers of usury (*ribā*)" with dire punishments in Hell (2:275), ʿAbduh made clear his indignation at the exploitative financiers who made money out of money (*istighlāl al-māl bi-l-māl*). He argued that in an economic system where profit comes from capital invested in banks rather than from labor, the value of what workers produce diminishes while the poor classes are led to ruination. In this exegetical gloss, he developed a theme that he had broached earlier, in a series of articles published around 1880, where he responded indirectly to the Franco-British establishment of dual control. He also railed against bankers and traders, "the greatest supporters of tyranny," and against foreign moneylenders who had saddled the country's poor farmers with unbearable debts. With great sympathy for impoverished farmers, he advocated the adoption of mechanical methods to increase production and diminish the burden of labor.[25] But if his Qurʾanic interpretation, written two decades later, sounds rather like a Russian critique of capitalism, it is because that is exactly what it was. ʿAbduh concluded this passage on the social problem generated by usury with praise for the Russian philosopher Tolstoy, who revealed to ʿAbduh that Europe was turning human beings into "slaves to capital."[26]

Translated in the 1880s into French, Tolstoy's book *What Is to Be Done?*, which ʿAbduh read, is an anticapitalist manifesto. It argues, indeed, that, with the spread of coins and credit, money, *l'argent*, had become the means by which a man could sell his future work. Due to the existence of violence in social relations, it represented "nothing but the possibility of a new kind of impersonal slavery."[27] *What Is to Be Done?* idealizes classless communes: workmen's associations that would "conscientiously recognize the communism of the land," where farmers would either own their own simple tools or borrow those of others "without interest."[28] Tolstoy resented the social gap between workers, on the one hand, and capitalists and government elites, on the other hand. He blamed money and engineers for deepening this gap. "An engineer builds a railway for the government, to facilitate wars, or for the capitalists for financial purposes. . . . His most skillful inventions are either directly harmful to the people, as guns, torpedoes, solitary prisons, and so on; or they are not only useless, but quite inaccessible to them, as electric light, telephones, and the innumerable improvements of comfort."[29] Money caused endless troubles. Coined and stamped by governments, it reduced subjects into a new kind of slavery. It was not a harmless medium for exchange but an all-too-convenient mechanism for states to force workers, who lacked land and capital, to pay impossible taxes and inexhaustible debts at fluctuating rates.[30]

Fiji's passage into colonial history served Tolstoy as an allegory into the "true meaning of money in our time." These Polynesian islands had been free and prosperous, blissful with their barter economy, until the mid-nineteenth century when the United States—in an exercise of gunboat diplomacy—demanded $45,000 as indemnification for harm done to Protestant missionaries and American prospectors. (In response to damages made by the "cannibals" of Rewa to the American consul's house and the Methodist mission-station, the commander of the sloop *John Adams* initially demanded only "$1,200 in pigs, gum, and fish," rebuilding of the American consul's house, and repossession of two small islands.) But the size of the claim grew quickly, with compounded interest. Bewildered by the notion of credit, the Fijian chief signed a treaty with a joint-stock corporation, the Polynesian Company of Melbourne, which assumed the debt in exchange for more than a hundred thousand acres of land, various capitulatory privileges, and the exclusive right to print banknotes. Natives were soon subjected to a crushing regime of taxation. (In this period, the majority of white settlers were British, and interest grew in growing cotton and raising capital to make sugar, which a planter called "the most money-making of tropical crops.") By 1874 Britain resolved to incorporate Fiji into its empire as a colony, which meant the imposition of taxes in kind. For Tolstoy, the islands' rapid transition—from precarious independence under the threat of America's "loaded guns" to the "slavery of money" under the British Empire—showed everything that was wrong with the lethal mixture of capitalism and imperialism in his era.[31]

ʿAbduh was so captivated by Tolstoy that he wrote an embarrassing letter to him, empathizing with his excommunication, praising him for removing the "veils of the traditions" (*ḥujub al-taqālīd*) to perceive clearly the ultimate reality of God's oneness (*ḥaqīqat al-tawḥīd*) and celebrating his very existence as God's rebuke to the rich.[32]

Tolstoy and Cromer were on opposite ends of the spectrum ideologically, so how did ʿAbduh manage to write fatwas that pleased the free-trade imperialist if he found more appealing, deep down, the anarchist's philosophy of poverty? One possibility is that he cultivated artificially—against his spiritual inclinations—an economically liberal interpretation of Islamic law as a way to make the case for Egyptian independence before British judges. Another possibility is that he approached economic matters in different ways in different genres. In his fatwas he focused on specific cases and issued succinct rulings, whereas in his Qurʾanic exegesis he allowed himself to wax poetic on profound principles of social justice. If these principles made him uneasy about his rulings, they were—like giant mallets—too unwieldy to serve effectively as juridical tools to nail down precise financial practices. Since he wrote his fatwas long before the emergence of "Islamic economics" as a discipline that would position itself as an alternative to capitalism and communism, a third possibility is that he did not feel torn asunder when incorporating elements from contradictory ideologies.

Regardless, the slightness of scriptural justification for ʿAbduh's economic philosophy is striking in light of later developments in Islamic thought. Sanction for the commercial partnerships (*muḍāraba* contracts) that he favored came not from the Qurʾan but from the medieval juridical tradition whose authority he called into question. A leap of faith was needed to legalize banking with interest on the basis of the proof-text that referred to believers "journeying in the land" (*yaḍribūna fī al-arḍ*) seeking God's bounty (Q. 73:20).[33] In the absence of a clear scriptural precedent, ʿAbduh might have sought inspiration for the modern Muslim pursuit of money in stories about the richest early Muslim ancestors, astonishingly wealthy merchants such as Muḥammad's companion ʿAbd al-Raḥmān ibn ʿAwf (d. 652). But the construct of the Salaf did not play a legitimating role in his capitalist fatwas, as it would in Riḍā's, and his efforts to revive the sacred law were negligible.

Usury, Paper Money, and the New Spirit of the Sacred Law

Riḍā strove to think more systematically and concretely about ways to apply Islam's sacred law to modern financial instruments, but he did not venture down this path on his own. Readers of *al-Manār* repeatedly stimulated and encouraged him to reform legal traditions and review scriptural canons; they wanted rulings that would bear upon their religious and economic interests. His effectiveness as a religious reformer and his success as the editor of an Islamic journal depended on satisfying these readers. He made great efforts, therefore, to craft fatwas that would fulfill their demands.

One of these readers, an advisor to Bahrain's ruler, wrote to Riḍā in 1902 to ask for *al-Manār*'s doctrine concerning national banknotes, an object whose newness drew out an elaborate description: "the papers that are called 'the notes' (*al-anwāṭ*) which some states invented for trading as a substitute for silver coins such as rupees."[34] This correspondent, Shaykh Muqbil ʿAbd al-Raḥmān al-Dhakīr, came from a family of Najdi merchants who had migrated to Manama and made a fortune in the international pearl business.[35] He raised a series of complicated questions that compelled Riḍā to revisit Islamic laws regarding usury and currency. To understand the questions and answers, it is necessary first to review briefly the traditional ban on usury as well as medieval juridical debates about currency.[36]

One critical problem for Muslims wary of engaging in usury was the specification in a famous canonical tradition that "gold for gold, silver for silver, wheat for wheat, barley for barley, dates for dates, salt for salt" could only be exchanged "hand to hand" in equal amounts.[37] Jurists generally understood this tradition to mean that commodities belonging to the same category could *not* be traded in unequal amounts, as determined by weight or volume. Such a trade would count as "the usury of excess." Technically, this ban meant—as caliph ʿUmar I interpreted it on one occasion, when he explained it to a distraught jeweler who wanted to charge money for his craftsmanship—that jewelry made entirely of gold had to be sold for exactly its weight in gold.[38] Barter across commodity categories (silver for barley, salt for gold) was obviously not subject to such a restriction, but jurists held on the basis of the same oral tradition that the exchange needed to take place immediately, "hand to hand," rather than on credit. They described a time-delayed transaction as constituting "the usury of deferral." Why God imposed these prohibitions on believers is a mystery that nobody has unraveled. A Japanese historian has recently argued that the prohibitions resulted from a combination of Umayyad monetary policies and from the commercial losses endured by merchants of dried fruits, spices, and grains. Whatever the reasons and causes behind the scriptural proscriptions, our present concern lies with the ensuing juridical conundrums.[39]

Over the centuries Muslim jurists would debate how far to extend these restrictions, by analogy, to other kinds of commodities not directly mentioned by scripture. Should the proscriptions on silver also apply to copper? What about raisins and grapes? Jurists simply could not agree on an answer. Even when they agreed to divide the six classes of things mentioned in the oral tradition into two broad groups, metals and foodstuffs, it was not at all clear how far to extend and by what criterion to define each group. Did gold and silver mean cash, precious metals, or any good whose value was measured by weight? Did the other group refer only to foods that did not spoil quickly or also to fresh foods such as meat and eggs? Schools of jurists diverged in particular in their view of gold and silver currency: whereas some regarded coins domestic or foreign as nothing but metal of a certain type, weight, and fineness whose value could be determined by metrology, others assigned minted coins the status of money, a medium of exchange issued by governments with the consent of societies.[40]

The first perspective came closer to capturing the conditions that inspired caliph ʿUmar I's interpretation of the ban. Neither the Prophet nor any of the Rightly Guided Caliphs struck coins, but the Arab conquests enriched the coffers of the caliphate with precious metals in various forms. Perhaps it made little sense, when assessing the value of booty and tribute, to make fine distinctions between jewels and coins made of the same material. In these circumstances, the Byzantine solidus basically corresponded to a certain amount of pure gold. Once caliphs began to mint gold dinars in the late seventh century, each of their dinars contained, like the solidus, a fixed amount of gold. There was still no compelling reason to distinguish legally between gold coins of whatever origin, Byzantine or Islamic, and gold jewels or bullion.[41]

Given this legacy, paper money presented a great juridical challenge. As currency, it seemed comparable to gold coins. But the value of these coins for trade had rested—from a medieval juridical perspective—on their standard precious metal content. The value of national banknotes depended, on the other hand, not on the raw material out of which they were made but rather on the sovereign promise of liquidity through the offices of the national bank. This made their international circulation, as representative money that was backed by a territorial promise of conversion, seem radically different from the international circulation of standard gold coins. Indeed, national banknotes were instruments of exchange that crossed political boundaries; they ended up circulating in countries where their convertibility into silver or gold could not be taken for granted.

This was precisely the situation that Shaykh Muqbil had to face in Bahrain. Putatively governed by the House of Khalīfa, Bahrain was, like Egypt at the time, part of Britain's informal empire: a protectorate of sorts. In an effort to clarify its legal status, British officials argued that it was a country "under the suzerainty" of the British Crown "exercised through the Governor-General of India."[42] It enjoyed, in theory, the same relation to the British government as any other native state in India. To elucidate its unusual political status, a historian has aptly described it as the British Raj's Arabian frontier.[43]

Under British India's sphere of influence, Bahrain did not have its own sovereign currency. Merchants there easily exchanged pearls and dates for things like Enfield rifles and silver rupees.[44] But paper rupees also circulated in this market. What was Shaykh Muqbil to make of these paper notes circulating in Bahrain, which the government of India pledged to redeem for their decreed value? The liquidity of these notes could not be taken for granted, even in India. The notes that he encountered were not yet backed by a universal guarantee. To minimize the production and circulation of forgeries, the British Raj had introduced a set of banknotes equipped with all sorts of security safeguards, including manufacturer's watermarks and guilloche engravings. In addition, it had established a system of currency circles, which meant that the government made a vow to convert paper notes into metal coins only in the zone of issue. "Beyond this the law imposed no obligation to pay," as the economist John Keynes

FIGURE 4.2 Paper money issued by the government of India circulated in Bahrain, which did not have its own banknotes, as a quasi-official currency. The ten-rupee banknote's value was indicated in English, Urdu, Hindi, Gujarati, and Bengali but not in Bahrain's principal language, Arabic. Spink & Son. Reproduced with permission.

explained in his first book, *Indian Currency and Finance*. A year after Shaykh Muqbil wrote to Riḍā, the government began to reform this system, by making five-rupee banknotes legal tender across currency circles. Yet "there must have been many occasions under the old system," mused Keynes, "on which ignorant persons suffered inconvenience through having notes of foreign circles passed off on them; and a long time may pass before distrust of the notes, as things not readily convertible, bred out of the memories of these occasions, entirely disappears."[45] Nevertheless, despite the inconveniences and uncertainties, Indian banknotes certainly flowed outside of their currency circles, even reaching—as the 1902 request for a fatwa proves—Manama on the Gulf. As a Muslim, Shaykh Muqbil wanted to know if these notes could circulate in his country as if they were merchandise. Or should they be reckoned as if they were cash?

The distinction between goods and money mattered, especially in Bahrain, where paper money had migrated without a government guarantee. Even in countries where this type of money represented the pledge of instant redemption in silver or gold, it was a puzzling problem for interpreters of the sacred law to establish equivalence between media of exchange. If a single five-rupee paper note belonged to the same commodity category as ten silver half-rupee coins, could these things be exchanged given the proscription on trading "like for like" in unequal weights? Evidently for this reason, Shaykh Muqbil suggested that it would be absurd—by the standards of reason, revelation and tradition—to place paper in the same legal class as silver or gold.[46]

Shaykh Muqbil was bothered, too, by another problem of convertibility. The Islamic legal tradition had established incredibly precise rules and regulations for paying alms taxes, *zakāt*, on different kinds of possessions. The rate varied for precious metals, livestock, and agricultural products. But no duties applied to certain assets, and copper and paper were among these assets, tax-free goods. Were banknotes analogous to gold, silver, or copper coins, although they were made of paper? It was pressing, revealed Shaykh Muqbil, to review and revise Islamic rules concerning alms taxes, money-changing, debt, the transference of bills, and cash sales. Rational Islamic laws were needed to deal with the new currency.

To answer these questions, Riḍā might have turned first to medieval juridical rulings on alternatives to silver and gold coins. Over the centuries jurists had discussed the legality of various types of money. Despite a strong bias in favor of precious metal coins, they had recognized the reality that copper coins circulated in societies by convention. Al-Shaybānī (d. 805) had argued that these coins should be considered legal tender, despite their lack of intrinsic worth and their unstable value, so long as they remained in circulation.[47] Ibn Ḥazm (d. 1064) held that every lawful commodity could stand for a "sound" currency. He criticized the juridical tradition for distinguishing arbitrarily, without scriptural justification, gold and silver from wheat, barley, dates, and salt. Instead, he proposed that the Qurʾan and the Ḥadīth had envisioned a system of trade where any licit good, even a sachet of barley, could serve as the medium of payment.[48] Riḍā might have relied on these opinions to claim that paper banknotes were, like copper coins, perfectly lawful tokens of currency that could be easily converted into commodity money. Alternatively, he might have turned to mildly censorious opinions about credit instruments, such as the long-distance merchant's bill of exchange, to argue that the juridical tradition had not prohibited promissory notes strictly.[49] But Riḍā did not dwell on medieval perspectives on money. In his eyes, the banknote was a novel thing that had to be tried in accordance with the sacred law. Judging it required reassessing the original proscriptions against usury.

Paper money presented a unique dilemma for him. As a religious reformer dedicated to economic development, he aimed, on the one hand, to give the ancient canons of Islam a renewed life in modern times and, on the other hand, to reduce barriers to free trade. The Qurʾan and the Ḥadīth had laid down no rules for paper money, but to declare the sacred law irrelevant was anathema in this instance given the continued centrality of scriptural regulations concerning usury and charity. By an extremely literalist reading of the oral tradition that banned certain "gold for gold" and "barley for barley" exchanges, Riḍā might just have claimed that the original restrictions on usurious transactions did not apply to paper money because it was neither a precious metal nor a kind of food. Such an interpretation, while economically liberating, would have turned the scriptural restriction into a dead letter. Riḍā did not want such an outcome, however. So how did he rise to this challenge?

Arguing against legal literalism, he maintained that Muslims should rather interpret scriptural laws according to their original intent. "Paper is not capital susceptible to usury in juridical thought," he explained. For this reason, Shafiᶜite scholars have declared outright that usury cannot circulate through the banknote, since it is made out of paper, as it can through gold or silver coins and various foods. As for Ḥanafis, they traditionally permitted exchanges within a category only if the objects had the exact same weight. But this way of relating to the problem of usury struck Riḍā as ridiculous if applied to paper money, since a one-hundred-rupee note weighed exactly the same as a one-thousand-rupee note. Everyone needed to recognize "that capitalist papers are worthless as paper yet are backed by a sum of money in coins." Consequently, it was crucial to contemplate "the objectives of the sacred law" rather than to follow blindly jurists whose representations would hinder almsgiving and facilitate "the damaging usury tabooed by God."[50]

Instead of rushing headlong to abolish a sacred text through an overabundance of literalism, modern jurists should strive, in Riḍā's opinion, to reason independently in order to determine the underlying wisdom and lasting significance of scriptural injunctions. Doing so led him to the conclusion that, for all their complexity, usury laws were originally revealed to curb the exploitation of fellowman: unjust enrichment at another's expense. Unlawful or deceptive transactions of this sort could take place as easily with paper money as with coined money, and it was important, for the benefit of the entire community, to continue censuring them. Similarly, Riḍā upheld alms-tax rules, arguing for their applicability to banknotes while conceding that the rate of dues would differ depending on their classification as articles of trade or as a form of currency. Given the conundrums that the novel financial instrument still posed, he argued that "the man of religion" is free to follow any jurist's advice, provided that he neither enable usury nor disable almsgiving.

At the same time, Riḍā fulminated against muftis who resorted to legal stratagems to dismantle sacred laws pertaining to economic behavior. He even admonished them for worshipping God in the most superficial manner imaginable, by focusing only on the letter rather than the spirit of scriptural expressions. But how could merchants know, then, which legal advice to follow? They should listen to their hearts instead of following fatwas that will make them feel uneasy. If they heed the spirit of the law, they will comprehend that "the heart leans toward treating [banknotes] as currencies," somehow or other equivalent to silver or gold coins.

This ruling on paper money seemed crucial to Riḍā for communicating his fundamental goals as a religious reformer. Indeed, he declared grandly: "I advise the brother who asked the question as well as other Muslim merchants preoccupied by the matter of religion to bear in mind this real jurisprudence and to make it the fundamental principle of their commercial transactions, because it is the spirit of the religion and the secret behind the heart's reformation and the soul's purification."

But it is critical to recognize that Riḍā presented his allegorical reading of scriptural rules and taboos in a material context: what inspired him to preach about the spirit of religion and secret of reform was, undeniably, money in a new form. The tentative quality of his response, the freedom that he gave merchants to follow any jurist who would work to preserve the ban on usury and the duty to give alms, suggests a lack of resolution. He lacked a ready-made answer at the time. Although intellectual and legal historians have invariably represented his rulings as determined by his legal principles, it is clear that challenging questions about new material realities raised by readers of *al-Manār* such as Shaykh Muqbil prompted him to reflect about the significance of the sacred law, to develop his philosophy, and to give concrete shape and meaning to a project of religious reform that was still in formation. Puzzling things like paper money were, in other words, indispensable components of the papier-mâché of Islam's reformation.

Banking in India and the Bankers' Panic of 1907

Five years later, in a time of financial crises, a fatwa seeker from Calcutta named Aḥmad Mūsā asked Riḍā to reflect on the problem of banking with interest. After praising him as "the great reformer and the famous philosopher," he raised the following dilemma: A Muslim merchant residing in Calcutta receives financial drafts for deposit in a bank whose owners are European Christians. If he agrees to leave his money with the bank for at least half a year, he would earn rupees at the rate of 2 percent per year. Meanwhile, the foreign bankers would make a handsome profit by lending his money at a higher interest rate. If the "lords of the bank" take the money freely and unconditionally, is it acceptable for the Muslim merchant to earn money in this way?

Riḍā justified this type of financial exchange, but only after taking the trouble to explore in detail arguments against it. He realized, of course, that doubt and suspicion about ill-gotten gains had provoked the question in the first place. He readily disclosed that jurists from the Ḥanafi school of law, to which most Indians belonged, might place all sorts of restrictions on loans with interest and contracts with stipulations. In addition, he discussed several canonical traditions that opponents of banking relied upon to discourage Muslims from accepting returns on deposits. According to one of these traditions, when a traditionist from Kufa, Abū Burda al-Ashʿarī (d. 723), visited Medina, the Prophet's Companion ʿAbdallāh ibn Salām (d. 663) warned him not accept any presents, such as bundles of barley, because usury was rife in the city of the Prophet.[51] Riḍā called into question the reliability of this tradition on historicist grounds. He found the allegation of widespread usury in Medina strange, contending that it could only have been made after the death of the Prophet and the expulsion of the Jews. Eventually, after dispensing with several other objections to banking, Riḍā explained his perspective. God prohibited usury to prevent coercion and exploitation. He did not, however, impose on Muslims a "religious interdiction" that would keep them from acting freely with their monies, at their own pleasure, provided they steered clear of vile, abominable, and tabooed transactions.[52]

Neither the fatwa seeker nor the mufti discussed the financial turmoil afflicting their countries, but Indians and Egyptians were living in interesting times. In India, inflation was running rampant. Prices of food grains rose by as much as 50 percent between 1905 and 1907. Poor harvests and an overabundance of rupees had created conditions of scarcity. An unusual flow of capital in and out of India made a bad situation worse, by altering the amount of money in circulation. The government of India had sold an excess of council drafts, which could be cashed in Calcutta, to investors in London, and the minting of coins for the redemption of these drafts had contributed to the inflationary trend.[53] In a country where there was still a preference for metallic currency, this situation led to increasing demand for the security of gold sovereigns and silver rupees.[54] There was probably no worse time than 1907 for Calcutta's Muslim merchants to deposit their drafts in banks for a specified term at a fixed interest rate.

Conditions in Egypt, though radically different, were equally conducive to thoughts about banking, for the economy had been powerfully shaken by the Panic of 1907. This was a serious financial crisis, and it had international repercussions. A cotton boom had led to speculation in land and stocks, which increased the demand for credit and cash. When the financial bubble burst, shares dropped in value, prudent banks refused to continue extending advances, and anxiety spread, leading to bank runs. In Cairo and Alexandria, bearers of bank accounts and promissory notes demanded gold coins. A relatively minor bank, Cassa di Sconto, had to close its doors and suspend payments, deepening the bankers' panic.[55] At a shareholders meeting in London, representatives of the Bank of Egypt explained that great prosperity had stimulated cotton farmers and speculators to gamble madly on land and shares, which caused the financial crisis that affected all "business undertakings" in the country.[56]

Due to limited gold reserves and the globalization of the capitalist system, this event triggered financial crises elsewhere in the world too. Everywhere that the crisis struck, it raised questions about the elasticity of the supply of money.[57] What compounded the problem of liquidity in Egypt was the fact that the national bank's shares, traded on the Royal Stock Exchange, were bound in investments overseas. A new supply of banknotes, which would need to be covered by reserves of gold for up to 50 percent of their value, could in theory be printed in London and shipped to the country. Yet, in this moment of crisis, the national bank lacked the capacity to inject liquidity into the market instantaneously, and Egyptians wanted immediately the assurance of gold.[58] Reflecting on the Panic of 1907, an American economist who served the Treasury Department blamed Egypt's cotton producers for hoarding a commodity needed by the rest of the world. He claimed that "no paper representative of the yellow metal" was acceptable to them. "All of the arts of modern finance have failed to counteract" what he described as the "Oriental habit" of gold hording.[59] Similarly, the *Economist* fantasized about gold buried in Egyptian cellars, and remarked: "It is to be feared that Egypt will prove to be about as much of a sinkhole for the gold of the world as India has been."[60]

The Panic of 1907 is what made Egyptian nationalists realize that the National Bank of Egypt was, despite its name, too foreign an institution. Two months before Riḍā published his fatwa, an editorial by the country's daily newspaper, *al-Ahrām*, complained that this bank had invested a million pounds in London, rather than in the nation, deepening the crisis of liquidity.[61] Nationalists began to draft plans to establish a truly Egyptian bank. It was at this juncture in Egyptian history that Aḥmad Mūsā of Calcutta asked Riḍā for his opinion about Muslims entrusting their money to European-Christian banks. Remarkably, instead of railing against foreign capitalism, Riḍā ruled that Muslims were not religiously barred from trusting these banks.

Gasprinski's Pan-Islamic Appeal and Riḍā's Salafi Denomination

The Bankers' Panic of 1907 motivated Riḍā, as well as other Muslim reformers, to think more systematically about money's religious advantages. This financial crisis certainly had much to do with the enthusiastic Egyptian reception of a

Russian Muslim's capitalist model for pan-Islamic reform. Two years after the October Revolution liberated him to pursue stormier political activities abroad, Russia's leading Muslim modernizer, Ismail Gasprinski, visited Cairo.[62] He hoped to organize a trans-imperial Muslim congress in the city, which he described as Islam's second center, following Constantinople. Learned clerics and illustrious intellectuals should assemble in it to sanction (as the London *Times* put it in October 1907) "the unavoidably necessary reforms and innovations" without fearing "the European clamour of Pan-Islamism." He focused especially on the problem of economic backwardness in a comparative religious framework. It troubled him that the Algerian Jew had surpassed the Algerian Arab. He found it "astonishing and quite inexplicable that the poor and devout Buddhist should get ahead of the once energetic Moslem."[63] In a speech at the Continental Hotel the following month, he exclaimed that it was "rare to find a Muslim merchant in America or Europe, and if by chance one encountered an Oriental merchant there, he would be Armenian, Greek, Buddhist, Hindu, or Chinese." He urged the Islamic world's leaders to encourage Muslims to become capitalists, stakeholders in steamship companies and banks in order to earn their freedom from European financial domination.[64]

For inspiration, Gasprinski told his audience in Cairo stories about the successes of Muslims in Russia. First he delivered a brief history of the incorporation of Muslims of diverse ethnicities into the Russian Empire. He spoke also about the rule of Islamic law in marriage, divorce, and inheritance cases; significant advances in the education of girls in Islamic schools; diverse curricular reforms; and the foundation of Islamic presses. Then he turned to his main topic: the economic situation for Russian Muslims. He mentioned that in Kazan and its environs, many Muslims worked in the soap and leather industries. Thousands of Muslims also worked in a textile factory that supplied broadcloth to the Russian army.

More impressive, however, was the fact that a Muslim industrialist owned such a factory. This was the Rockefeller of Baku: the Azeri oil magnate Zeyn al-ʿĀbdīn Taghiyev (d. 1924), whose diversified acquisitions included the Caspian Steamship Company. The director of this company "used to be an Englishman," remarked Gasprinski—immediately capturing the attention of an audience that lived under British rule. Then he added, in his most electrifying line: "But there is no longer a need for the English today, since its owner now manages it by himself."[65]

A major philanthropist, Baku's oil baron sponsored many *jadidi*—that is, Muslim modern—initiatives in the field of education not only in and around Baku and elsewhere in Russia but also in Qajar Iran and Ottoman Iraq. He partially funded, too, Gasprinski's Russian-Turkish journal, *Tercümān* ("*The*

Interpreter"), which first published the appeal for the international Islamic conference. Taghiyev endowed mosques as well, and he gave money generously for poor relief. For all of his humanitarian contributions, Gasprinski asked the men in the audience to join him in a prayer for the Russian Muslim millionaire.[66] With this example, he showed dramatically why it was a fine idea for Islam's reformers to promote moneymaking activities. If they preached the virtues of capitalism, there would be more Muslim philanthropists like Taghiyev, who would give their material support to their causes and ultimately bring about their countries' independence—as of that cloth-making factory—from European financial control.

Gasprinski's appeal for clerics to support the pursuit of profit for Islam's sake came at an opportune moment in history. Capitalism was on everyone's mind in 1907, the year of the bankers' panic, when excessive speculation had contributed to the stock market's crash. The political repercussions in Egypt were profound. Politicians representing different parties joined together to demand greater oversight of foreign capital. The financial crisis was a critical turning point for nationalists like Muḥammad Ṭalʿat Ḥarb (d. 1941), the eventual founder of Banque Miṣr, who after 1907 dedicated himself to solving economic problems.[67] Ḥarb's teacher and ally, ʿUmar Bey Luṭfī, a member of the conference's organizing committee, would soon establish credit cooperatives to finance agricultural development.[68] A provocative newspaper editor, Shaykh ʿAbd al-ʿAzīz Shāwīsh (d. 1929), proposed the foundation of a bank to finance Ottoman projects and Islamic causes. With an interest in the religious politics of consumption, he envisioned the establishment of committees to boycott the corporations of colonial states that oppressed their Muslim subjects and the launching of a "Buy Muslim" campaign of import substitution.[69]

Riḍā's response to Gasprinski's initiative was also shaped by the Bankers' Panic of 1907. In the August issue of *al-Manār*, he had published an article on the financial crisis in Egypt where he had expressed grave concern about the exploitation of poor Muslims by European financiers, whom he described—with uncharacteristic resentment—as blood-sucking usurers with a carnivorous appetite. He made clear that gambling and usury were the most forbidden things. Yet he perceived these sacred prohibitions as the reason for the bewilderment of Muslims, who "do not know how to live with these European nations" and have no experience with competing in fortune's path. Disengagement from capitalism was not an option. What, then, was the solution? Riḍā thought that Muslims needed first to overcome an impulsive, reactionary approach to banks as "houses of usury." They needed to grasp that "most of the banks' transactions have no iniquity in them." Bankers, rather, should show some compassion for those engaging in business, and at times they should assist disabled persons, helping them to profit from an inheritance. Everybody wins, the bank and the depositor, when the enterprise is designed to satisfy mutual interests.[70]

Gasprinski's plan for a pan-Islamic congress generated considerable enthusiasm for the possibility of a pan-Islamic solution to the problem of underdevelopment. The plan came to naught, as a result of internal rivalries among Cairo's religious authorities.[71] Nevertheless, it was amply covered by the press. As well as publishing an Arabic translation of Gasprinski's speech, Riḍā dedicated an entire article to it.

He favored the proposal for a pan-Islamic conference and he appreciated the focus on economic challenges. But he did not think that the idea to hold such a conference was altogether original. Jealous of Gasprinski's reception and sidelined by Gasprinski's promoters in Cairo, Riḍā highlighted earlier proposals to unite the global community of Muslims. In particular, he gave credit to his friend and compatriot, al-Kawākibī, for imagining, years earlier, a fictional conference in Mecca.[72] Despite his resentments, Riḍā found Gasprinski's agenda attractive. Why, he asked, have Muslims lagged behind other nations economically? "We assert that Muslims, like other human beings, are ready," he held, "for every step toward progress and civilization." Political despotism and rigid traditionalism, the mindless imitation of the religion of the past, prevented them from moving forward. He blamed especially ultraconservatives from al-Azhar, who wasted their energy condemning trivial things such as black boots, and narrow-minded judges in shariʿa courts, who spent their time opposing the efficient use of electric bells to page bailiffs and attendants.[73]

Riḍā did not think that it would be easy to persuade such backward scholars to support capitalist corporations, which he described as "the highest pillars of wealth in our day and age." To illustrate, he recounted a precious anecdote of a gathering of Muslim notables, which he attended, before former Prime Minister Riyāḍ Pasha (d. 1911). Debating the permissibility of owning shares of the Suez Canal Company, a prominent Azhari scholar had argued that this investment was unlawful for two reasons: because water, a communal resource, cannot be privately owned and because "paper shares had no value in and of themselves." On that occasion, Riḍā contended that these shares were comparable to perfectly lawful instruments, such as contracts and deeds, which were also recorded on paper to document the purchase of property or the loan of money. His defense of financial papers must have impressed the movers and shakers at the gathering, or so Riḍā boasted, for one of them—a great supporter of Gasprinski's plan—had begun to work actively to establish a national bank.[74] His point was that he had embarked before Gasprinski's arrival on the arduous task of convincing influential Muslims of the compatibility between Islamic law and capitalist enterprises.

Commenting on Gasprinski's convocation as a Salafist, Riḍā specified that the conference should represent the totality of Muslims: "the Salafi Sunni as well as the non-Salafi Sunni, the Shiʿi and the Ibaḍi." God's book and the normative practices that were associated with the Prophet would unite, he hoped, the disparate groups.[75] But these groups often disagreed vigorously about the correct interpretation of scriptural rules and prophetic practices. What else would bring them together? Money, or the want of money, for after the crash of 1907 reformers swayed by Gasprinski put raising capital for Islam at the top of the agenda.

The Salafist Discovery of Physiocracy: The Industrious Salaf as Economic Models

In the wake of the bankers' crisis, Riḍā contributed—as a Salafist—to the Arabic discovery of a European academic discipline: political economy. Through his journal, he promoted the publication of a new textbook, Muḥammad Fahmī Ḥusayn's *Principles of Political Economy* (Mabādiʾ al-iqtiṣād al-siyāsī), which presented, in 1908, the fundamentals of the dismal science.[76] Among other political economists, Riḍā profiled François Quesnay, one of the originators of the doctrine of the liberty of labor and commerce from government interference. Quesnay, the author of *Physiocracy, or, The Natural Constitution of the Most Advantageous Government for Humankind*, coined the slogan *laissez faire, laissez passer* to criticize protectionist customs; he made an early contribution to the intellectual discourse of free trade. Riḍā focused, however, on the standard critique of the physiocrat's emphasis on fertile land, rather than industry or labor, as the primary generator of national wealth. This was a meaningful point for discussion in Egypt, an agricultural economy whose industrial development its managers, as free-trade ideologues devoted in the first place to Britain's economic interests, refused to protect from foreign competition.[77]

Ḥusayn's textbook of political economy concentrated on French authors, as did in general contributors to *al-Manār* when they focused on European thought. In his book review, Riḍā referred only once to Adam Smith, and this was an exceptional reference to one of the founders of the discipline.[78] The first Arabic translation of *The Wealth of Nations* would appear, in an abridged form, long after Riḍā's death. Virtually absent from the journal were the names of John Stuart Mill and Karl Marx.[79] By contrast, eighteenth-century French authors loomed large in the pages of *The Lighthouse*. ʿAbduh and a few other contributors to the journal sprinkled their discourse with casual references to Rousseau, Voltaire, and Diderot.[80] Reflecting on basic questions of political economy on such varied matters as the causes of economic crises or the reasons for the fall of kingdoms, they would comfortably turn to Montesquieu's *The Spirit of the Laws*.[81] They knew, if not the originals, the translations of key works of comparative national psychology or racial sociology by Gustave Le Bon and Edmond Demolins.[82] Overwhelmingly they favored, as these lists suggest, French rather than English or German works.

Eighteenth-century French concepts were more inspiring than useful for solving the economic realities of the early twentieth century. The article on coins in *L'Encyclopédie* argued that princes did not give money its value. They just stamped the coins whose value came from the silver or gold content. Interested in durable wealth, the rich chevalier who wrote the article, Louis de Jaucourt, mocked the fanciful philosophical idea that "men of different nations" could assign an "imaginary value" to money.[83] The new theory of money proposed by Riḍā's Arabic student, Alfred Innes, explained far better how paper money actually functioned in society.

Riḍā seldom cited European authors as models, perhaps because doing so would have conflicted with his mission for Islamic authenticity. But he owed to the French Enlightenment the ideal of freeing international commerce from religious burdens. In one instance, a critique of his ignorance of French writings spurred him to remonstrate that already in Tripoli he had gained some familiarity with Arabic translations of key works. He indicated that he had studied closely what European philosophers had written about codification.[84] In addition, he declared political economy, which basically meant physiocracy, an extremely useful branch of knowledge that helped to explain why some nations were wealthy and others poor and what mechanisms existed for societies to progress from hunting and gathering to agriculture and eventually industrialization.

In "Work," his 1908 review of Ḥusayn's textbook of political economy, Riḍā turned to the Salaf as models for an industrious revival. Immediately before alluding to the labor and skills of the pious Muslim ancestors, he offered what can only be described as a colonialist history of Australia. Due to the indolence of the aborigines, the country had languished in a primitive stage of development. Once settlers who realized the advantages to civilization reached the continent, they set to work in the land and in the sea, and they began to mine profitably the treasures that had remained trapped inside the earth. The country's astonishing economic transformation proved that development depended mainly on human industry and knowledge, not on the presence of natural wealth. As for Arabia in early Islamic times, it had been—unlike aboriginal Australia—an urbane rest stop for caravans, a cradle of knowledge, a source of prosperity. Unfortunately, Riḍā lamented, the wealth generated by the industrious Salaf was squandered by successive generations, "until they grew old in the new world." Like the Seven Sleepers, the Salaf had lapsed into a dormant state, awaiting an awakening.[85]

The Rise of Salafism: Ancients versus Moderns in *The Lighthouse*

Riḍā began as early as 1900 to cultivate the idea of the Salaf as rich models for men of religion: bequeathers of a symbolic capital that was more precious than money. He saw them as spiritual animators who could help Muslims attain economic salvation. Using the Salaf as an essential, though not the sole, tool in the toolkit of legal reform, he invoked the memory of the pious ancestors in liberal judgments that favored cross-cultural commerce and consumption. Following the Bankers' Panic of 1907, he began using the Salafi tool in new contexts. Not only did he mention "the Salaf" in his review of an Arabic textbook of political economy; he also referred to "Salafi Sunnis" as an existing denomination whose representatives would attend the ecumenical assembly of Muslims proposed by Gasprinski. Remarkably, by then he imagined Salafis as a collectivity in the present, and he represented this collectivity as one of Sunni Islam's two major denominations. In effect, he viewed the Islamic world as divided into three main branches (the Sunni, the Shiʿi, and the Ibaḍi branches) but perceived the first as a bifurcation that kept the Salafi and the non-Salafi apart.

But who were these contemporary Salafis in his eyes? Were they his close associates in Cairo and Damascus? Were they a loose and informal network of international allies, including subscribers to *al-Manār*, who seemed to share the same ideals? In 1907, would he have classified or recognized Wahhabi clerics from Najd and the Partisans of Ḥadīth from Bhopal as fellow members of the Salafi delegation? Perhaps. In the 1920s he would certainly emphasize the theological and legal affinities between these groups.[86] It is not clear, however, how he related to them around the time that Gasprinski visited Cairo. What is clear is that, in his imagination, the "Salafi Sunnis" were already numerous enough or significant enough to merit representation in the pan-Islamic congress.

Through articles and fatwas, Riḍā gradually developed a Salafist doctrine and ethic: a set of principles that unfolded, year by year, on the pages of *al-Manār* with the intention of guiding the beliefs and conduct of the latter-day Salaf. He made no mention of the early Islamic exemplars, the Salaf, in the introduction to the very first issue of *al-Manār*, where he proclaimed his journal's mission.[87] By March of 1898, in his very first answer to a correspondent's question, he did establish what would eventually become a standard Salafist hermeneutic: he evoked "the pious ancestors" to determine the right way to recite the Qur'an for the dead.[88] This only shows that, like many Sunni jurists before him, he considered "the Salaf" a useful legal instrument. Eventually, however, the Muslim forefathers would appear in every corner of *The Lighthouse*. They would make a significant appearance, even where they were least expected, to resolve a crisis: in Riḍā's review of Ḥusayn's physiocratic textbook, for example, they suddenly popped up, like a deus ex machina, as models for an industrious Muslim revolution.

Why did Riḍā turn so often to the Muslims of antiquity? Why did he represent them as tools for reformers? What virtues, besides industriousness and an "enlightened" attitude to commercial exchange, did they exemplify? In 1901 he introduced a series of articles that he subtitled "Acts of the Ancestors: A Lesson for the Successors." This was, in one sense, a unique intervention in the famous philosophical quarrel of the ancients and the moderns. Like Giambattista Vico, a philosopher who had treasured ancient methods and traditions, Riḍā ventured into this quarrel as a pious humanist bearing a powerful message from a faithful age. Through biographical vignettes, he made it clear how much he thought that twentieth-century Muslims could learn from seventh-century Muslims. He celebrated in particular the foundational works of the first two caliphs, Abū Bakr and ʿUmar ibn al-Khaṭṭāb, and the exploits of conquerors. These were men of action who pursued their political, religious, and legal aims with vigor and glory.[89] In a serialized fictional dialogue that also dates from this time, Riḍā mocked a crusty old cleric for clinging to the teachings of medieval scholars, the successors, instead of drawing inspiration from the original paragons, the Salaf. This fictionalized cleric, a defender of the religious establishment, had to be persuaded by a youthful interlocutor to leave the Middle Ages behind. On this basis, turn-of-the-century Salafism may simply be characterized as a literary or philosophical movement spearheaded by reformers who sought enlightenment in Islamic antiquity but wanted to form the vanguard of Islamic modernity.[90]

Exchanges with correspondents were a critical factor in the elaboration of Salafism by *The Lighthouse*. In 1901, for example, an Egyptian shaykh from the town of Tūkh al-Qarāmūṣ, Aḥmad Muḥammad al-Alfī, asked whether jurists inspired by the Salaf, in particular the medieval theologian Ibn Taymiyya and the editor of *al-Manār*, subscribed to the same doctrine of mediation between humans and the divine as did the Wahhabis of Arabia, who insisted on worshipping God alone and reacted against the veneration of prophets and saints. In addition, he enquired out of ignorance or peevishness: Why would an adherent of a new creed from the Kharijite, Wahhabi, or Bábist sect not make use of the Qur'an and the prophetic tradition to support his principles covertly?

These questions forced Riḍā to deal with a bewildering mélange of sects, religions, and movements and to clarify his theological views. He explained, for example, that the Bábis could not be classified as heterodox Muslims because they had formed a new religion, whereas the Wahhabis—firm believers in the creed of the Salaf—upheld the orthodox doctrine of prophetic mediation. Furthermore, the questions gave him an opportunity to recommend Ibn Taymiyya enthusiastically for his devotion, centuries earlier, to the school of the Salaf. Concretely, this meant for him the duty to command right and forbid wrong as well as the need to combat heretical innovations.[91]

The capital of the Salaf could be invested in risky projects to agitate for political and legal transformation in the name of Islam, and Riḍā and his allies looked for opportunities to spend it on subversive campaigns. A few years after two Syrian reformers, ʿAbd al-Razzāq al-Bīṭār and Jamāl al-Dīn al-Qāsimī, visited ʿAbduh and Riḍā in Cairo, they joined a revolutionary movement to check the absolute power of the sultan of the Ottoman Empire and restore constitutional rule. To this end, they evoked "the pious ancestors" as if they had been pioneer constitutionalists. When Riḍā visited them and their associates in Damascus in 1908, in a tumultuous month right before parliamentary elections, he was all but assaulted by a furious crowd who drove him to flee from the city. His opponents in Syria alleged that he supported the Ottoman Empire's enemies in Arabia, the Wahhabis.[92]

Through their relentless emphasis on the construct of "the righteous Salaf," Riḍā and his comrades in arms made an unparalleled contribution to Salafism. It is important to appreciate historically how much this construct rose to prominence in the early twentieth century because the history of "modernist Salafism" has described two nineteenth-century intellectuals, al-Afghānī and ʿAbduh, as the Salafist pioneers, and Riḍā as little more than the earnest follower and developer of their original ideas.

A genealogical approach to the rise and global spread of Salafism emerged long ago. Soon after World War I, the French Islamicist Louis Massignon projected the intellectual movement of the Salafiyya, "partisans of primitive Islam," back in time. According to his sources and informants, the seeds of Wahhabism (adherence to a strict version of Ḥanbalism, the idealization of primitive Islam, a democratic impulse, cultic austerity, sumptuary laws, and an intolerance for innovations) spread from Arabia to India, where they were cultivated by the prince consort of the tributary state of Bhopal, Ṣiddīq Ḥasan Khān (d. 1890). Under the influence of a Yemeni reformer and reviver, Muḥammad al-Shawkānī, he composed multiple books, printed in Constantinople and Bhopal, and promoted a revivalist movement known as Ahl-i Ḥadīth, Partisans of the Prophetic Tradition, that turned directly to the scriptures of Islam for inspiration. According to Massignon, the princely reformer from Bhopal disseminated a cultured or printed version of Wahhabism, which al-Afghānī and ʿAbduh took up as the avant-garde program that he all but labeled "Islamic primitivism." They proceeded to spread this intellectual movement throughout the Muslim world, from the Maghreb to Java, and inspired a series of monumental publications, including the review *al-Manār*.[93] Different genealogical narratives of Salafism, such as this one, have circulated over the years, giving a false impression of intergenerational continuity in projects of revival and reform. This makes it necessary to emphasize that Salafism was not in vogue in the late nineteenth century and that the agendas of early twentieth-century Salafists were filled with matters of the day.

Too many articles and books have identified al-Afghānī and ʿAbduh as the founders of an intellectual movement posthumously named "Salafism."[94] Surprisingly, however, not a single article in *The Unbreakable Bond*, the journal that they collaborated on in the mid-1880s, even includes the word "al-Salaf" in its title. If they preached Salafism during their exile in Paris, they did so covertly.[95] Moreover, al-Afghānī espoused a progressivist philosophy that seems incompatible with the conceit of Salafism: the notion that Muslims were at their best and finest in the age of the pious ancestors.

This inclination is evident in his response to Renan's lecture at the Sorbonne on "Islamism and Science." Renan had argued that all races of Muslims with the exception of Persians consecrated themselves to a fanatical hatred of scientific innovation and that Islamists had "always persecuted science and philosophy," crushing "vast portions of our globe" with their dogmas.[96] Al-Afghānī conceded that "the Muslim religion tried to suffocate science and arrest its progress." But he countered: "All religions are intolerant, each in its own way." Christianity also had its history of antiscientific bans: "By whatever name one calls them, religions resemble each other." Al-Afghānī disagreed, too, with Renan's bleak view of the prospects for Arab Muslims, "many hundreds of millions of men." He thought that "through a religious education" all races could ascend to a higher plane, and he took courage from the achievements of Muslims who flourished after the ʿAbbasid revolution and the passing of the third generation of forefathers.[97]

ʿAbduh did far more than al-Afghānī to cultivate "the Salaf" as models for moderns.[98] However, his famous *Theology of Unity*, published in 1897, was anything but a Salafist manifesto. It referred somewhat dismissively to the religious orientation of the Muslims who flourished in the era of the first two caliphs for looking no further than the plain, literal meaning of scripture and for debating nothing deeper than the application of legal rules. By contrast, it celebrated the theologian Ḥasan al-Baṣrī (d. 728) for his rational quest to understand "the fundamental principles behind doctrines and laws." Critically, he singled him out, instead of praising collectively the pious women and men of his generation.[99] Subsequently, the *Theology of Unity* highlighted the historic role that those who clung to "the school of the ancients" played in checking the exuberant, undisciplined rationalism that had taken flight under the early ʿAbbasids. ʿAbduh associated these authorities, the partisans of Ibn Ḥanbal (d. 855), with excessive literalism, zealotry, and a persecuting mentality. He admired rather more the theologically unifying Sunni synthesis that emerged—with al-Ashʿarī (d. 935) and his successors—as a result of these tensions. Hence, ʿAbduh was certainly not a Salafist in any ideological sense of the word, and he rejected a violent approach to heterodoxy. He merely celebrated a few choice ancestors who had searched for the truth beyond the letter of the law or who had liberated their minds to soar in a theological ether that burned religious discord away.[100] These were the ancestors who inspired him to reflect, in an autobiographical passage, on his quest to understand religion "according to the way of the Salaf."[101]

"Inattention to the Traces of the Salaf," the title of a chapter in ʿAbduh's *Islam and Christianity Between Science and Civilization*, sounds promising as a source for determining what else "the ancestors" meant for the modern theologian. *Al-Manār* serialized this book beginning in 1902, *after* Riḍā had published his short biographies of a few seventh-century heroes. Who were ʿAbduh's Salaf? They were several of the finest theologians and exegetes who flourished between the tenth and the thirteenth centuries. He recommended their books, chastising modern readers for disregarding the medieval Sunni canon. If these ancestors embodied Salafism for ʿAbduh, then his Salafism was essentially bookish medievalism.[102]

In form if not substance, Riḍā's judgments on modern things owed little to ʿAbduh. It is critical to appreciate one major methodological difference: ʿAbduh preferred to contemplate general concepts abstractly, whereas Riḍā tended to deal specifically with specific objects. When, as Egypt's Grand Mufti, ʿAbduh was asked to judge particular transactions or things, from the Postal Savings Bank's interest to Transvaal hats, he issued brief and vague responses that lacked, in his critics' eyes, an authentic Islamic referent. He dictated these succinct solutions with faith in the force of his charismatic authority and high office. In his fatwas, he aimed to reveal his conclusions about the divine law, not the process of interpretation by which he arrived at these conclusions. Riḍā developed an altogether different style. He wrote expansively, seeking to persuade readers, who made it clear that they had some familiarity with the shariʿa, of the validity of his own laborious deductions. In his fatwas, he delved into scripture, locating a multiplicity of Qurʾanic verses, oral traditions, and ancestral acts that struck him as relevant precedents for judging the commodities on trial. His art was the art of analogical juxtapositions. It involved the creation of imaginative and at times arresting comparisons between sacred laws and modern things.

This matters, although not because there is a pressing need to give Riḍā credit for his original contributions to the style of the fatwa. It matters because Riḍā began his career when ʿAbduh reached the end of his: at a time when Cairo, like many other cities in a world of empires, experienced a stunning material transformation. Around the turn of the twentieth century, markets worldwide witnessed an unprecedented expansion in the volume and variety of imports and exports: the explosion of world trade that economic historians have baptized "the first globalization." In Muslim societies under European dominance, new types of consumer goods stimulated a religious awakening: an awakening that focused not on European products indiscriminately but rather specifically on innovations that made it difficult to follow Islamic law to the letter. Paper money is a perfect example of this dynamic: an instrument whose adoption gave rise to legal questions precisely because it was difficult to apply to it literally, as Shaykh Muqbil of Bahrain made painfully clear, the sacred laws that had been designed for silver and gold bullion.

ʿAbduh's sweeping legal approach was ill suited to answer such questions in a satisfying way. Truth be told, he had little to offer besides the platitude that Islam was compatible with capitalism and modernity. Something else was needed at the beginning of the twentieth century: a jurisprudence that would meet the demands of readers who knew their Qurʾan and their Ḥadīth and wanted specific advice. Like Ṣ-M, the officer who asked Riḍā for a fatwa about toilet paper, these readers wanted scriptural judgments. The shockingly modern and at times startling application of Muslim scriptures to new goods, which became one of the hallmarks of Salafism, originated with such demands.

Laissez-faire Salafism, which Riḍā developed in concert with his readers, was not about letting all foreign things cross the border freely, dismantling each and every Islamic barrier to commerce and consumption. The taboos of the shariʿa had to be respected and maintained. Nor was laissez-faire Salafism a movement against tariffs and taxes; Riḍā thought it was essential, after all, for jurists to find some way to apply rules concerning usury and alms taxes to the strange new currency that was made of paper.

But laissez-faire Salafism was very much about minimizing, in the name of scripture and the Salaf, religious and legal barriers toward individual prosperity and communal welfare. Of course, the Salaf of the seventh and eighth centuries were an assemblage of heterogeneous individuals with divergent inclinations, and they bequeathed to their successors diverse behavioral examples and endless variety of opinion. Moderns could turn to one of the Prophet's Companions, ʿAbdallāh ibn Salām, to argue against buying anything in an economy where usury had spread extensively and there existed overwhelming doubts about everything on the market. Or they could turn to another Companion of the Prophet, the renowned ascetic Abū al-Dardāʾ, to argue for consuming Christian things. Riḍā knew and acknowledged both opinions, but he cast doubts on the validity of the first one, and he decided, when he dealt with the second one, to substitute the name of the early Islamic authority with a prestigious, generic title, "an imam of the Salaf." This was laissez-faire Salafism in a nutshell: a system that in theory allowed Muslims to spend the capital of the Salaf freely but in practice introduced a symbolic currency to let things pass and let things be, even though these things were, like Egypt's first "national" banknotes, made abroad.

Interwar Developments: Currency Depreciation and Nationalist Banks

Banks and banknotes returned to the forefront of Islamic economic deliberations in the interwar period. Financial instability, the demise of the caliphate, and the rise of economic nationalism motivated Riḍā to think anew about the sacred law and the quest for prosperity. Like activists for Egypt's independence, he began to ponder financial matters in nationalistic terms. He reflected as a jurist on the causes of European wealth and Muslim poverty. He also elaborated on a geopolitical dichotomy that distinguished the pursuit of usury in a House of War from the pursuit of usury in a House of Islam. This perspective allowed him to sanction, as the last chapter of this book explains in detail, Muslim participation in all sorts of financial schemes and capitalist ventures under colonial rule.

Inflation rose significantly with the outbreak of World War I, as many nations suspended or abandoned the gold standard and central banks took to issuing paper notes at their discretion.[103] Monetary instability continued after the war. Wreaking havoc on currency exchanges, the instability encouraged speculation about the future value of coins and banknotes. Such circumstances led a correspondent from Sambas, Borneo, to present to Riḍā, in 1921, several financial puzzles. He wanted to know, first, if it was legal for one man to extend to another a loan of ten Dutch rupees made of silver for the return of fifteen Dutch rupees made of paper. He alleged that a Javanese scholar who had studied in Mecca had justified such a transaction by maintaining that the ban on "silver for silver" transactions did not apply to "silver for paper" transactions. The Javanese correspondent also wanted to understand if it was permissible to sell 1 silver rupee for 120 copper coins when the nominal exchange rate in the Dutch colony was set at 1 for 100. In the third place, much like the merchant from Calcutta, he wanted Riḍā to issue a fatwa on the permissibility of keeping interest payments made on deposits by Posts Paarbank, a colonial Dutch bank.

There is no need to relate all of Riḍā's answers since they reprise earlier themes. Of course, he rejected, as in the past, the argument that silver for paper exchanges could never count as usurious because they involved different sorts of material currencies. What is worth relating, however, is his attempt to deal with the depreciation of banknotes. He declared that Austrian, German, and French banknotes at times sold in the market for a fraction (half, a fifth, and even a seventh) of their nominal value. Paper money in such cases effectively became one of the market's commodities—an object rather than a medium of exchange. This transformation took place, as he understood it, due to the ebb and flow of international relations. The governments that printed the money, he held, were not responsible for the decrease in their currency's value. However, in foreign trade, trust between countries can rise and fall. In an economic crisis, when one nation fails to pay its debts, merchants in other countries worry about insolvency and therefore rush to sell their stock of banknotes at a loss.[104]

He made a clear distinction between countries under Muslim rule and countries under non-Muslim rule when he reflected on the original reason for the divine ban on usury. Thus, in a fatwa where he responded to another correspondent from Java, he explained that the Qur'anic ban arose to prevent iniquity and the wrongful consumption of capital. Based on a rational rather than a devotional calculus, it had the goal of ending "exploitation of the plight of the poor man," desperate for a loan. Given this rationale, Riḍā could never simply "make usury lawful under any circumstances." He appreciated God's wisdom in protecting vulnerable Muslims from predatory moneylenders in the House of Islam. He understood how loans with compounded interest could easily ruin a poor family. Nevertheless, he saw nothing wrong with a non-Muslim banker lending his money to a Muslim borrower, especially in the House of War, if the transaction benefitted both parties.[105] Mutually advantageous fixed-term loans at an invariable interest rate did not seem to him usurious; they differed from the scripturally forbidden loans whose liquidation could be deferred by a crippling agreement to make additional payments.

The collapse of the Ottoman Empire at the end of the world war spurred Riḍā to think about the failure of Islamic legal institutions to support the accumulation of capital, which in his view states and societies needed to prosper and thrive in modern times. He analyzed the problem in his 1922 treatise, *The Caliphate and the Grand Imamate*. The chapter of this book on "canonical legislation" dealt mainly with the urgent need to restore the sacred law in order to contend effectively with the challenge of capitalism. He argued that, while Muslim jurists in the centuries following the period of divine revelations had introduced many restrictions to limit the rules that governed financial contracts, the non-Muslim nations that traded with Islamic polities had developed new kinds of contracts and commercial associations, and they had perfected economic sciences and financial practices.

This pair of historical developments was the deep cause of the disparity between the wealth of the European powers and the poverty of Muslim communities. The rise of capitalism in Europe and a restrictive legal regime in Islamic states were the fundamental reasons for "the long divergence."[106]

> Capital has always been always the foundation of the life of communities and states. But in our time, it has assumed a significance that it did not have in the past, especially in the era of the Prophet, when the community had few needs and did not depend for its life on trading with other nations. . . . Is it conceivable that the canonical law of this religion has sentenced its people to be poor? Or demanded that what is essential for their subsistence and the power of their community and their state be placed in the hands of the covetous men in their midst who belong to other nations?[107]

The sacred law's clerical interpreters, "the most ignorant people in their countries in the arts of finance," had created the grave problem. By forbidding interest in Islamic states, they had left the business of moneylending to Jewish and Christian subjects and to foreign allies and enemies, who took advantage of the system of capitulations.[108]

There was one way to move forward: Muslim jurists could stop objecting to capitalist institutions and start giving their blessings to nationalist banks. The rousing nationalist rhetoric that had led to the foundation of Banque Miṣr in 1920 was a great inspiration to Riḍā. This bank, established by Ṭalʿat Ḥarb and his associates, had one central mission that was directly tied to the revolutionary struggle for independence: to benefit a free Egyptian nation with Egyptian capital.[109] Swayed by this political turn, Riḍā decided that the time had come to practice what he preached. He joined forces to found a bank with Ḥabīb Luṭfallāh, a Syrian Christian financier who had made a fortune as a moneylender in the Sudan before he relocated to Cairo, and a few other notables. They tried and failed to win a concession first from the sharif of Mecca, then from the Saudi king of the Ḥijāz, to establish a national bank in Islam's holy land.[110] Had they succeeded, Riḍā's resume as a Salafist reformer would have included an extraordinary turn as the Saudi kingdom's banker.[111]

5

The Qurʾan in the Gramophone

Sounds of Islamic Modernity from Cairo to Kazan

American entrepreneurs were busy selling Victrolas around the world when Abū Adīb Ḥāfiẓ Ḥilmī wrote to Riḍā from Kazan, Russia, to ask him if Islamic law prohibited using "the cabinet of the phonograph" to listen to records of the Qurʾan. The turn of the century was a period of dizzying technological innovations in sound technology, especially in the United States. Inventors developed and marketed many models of phonographs and gramophones, which played either wax cylinders or flat discs, for consumers worldwide. By 1910 one of the machines that played disc records—if not a Victor Talking Machine then a competing model designed to conceal the horn inside a fine, boxy piece of furniture—had reached a circle of Tatars in Kazan, and they were using it, remarkably, to hear the voices of Arabs reciting Qurʾanic suras.[1]

Like toilet paper, the mass-produced gramophone was a perfect embodiment of industrial capitalism in this era. In the late nineteenth century, inventors still had only a vague idea about the future of the instrument. At the Franklin Institute in Philadelphia in 1888, Emile Berliner, a German immigrant to the United States who would play a key role in the technology's development, dreamed of possibilities. "Supposing his Holiness, the Pope," should desire, mused the Jewish inventor, to "broadcast a pontifical blessing to his millions of believers," he could simply speak into a recorder. The pope's words would be etched upon a plate. Within a few hours, a printer could produce "thousands of phonautograms on translucent tracing paper" for dispatch to "the principal cities in the world," where they would be reproduced, ad infinitum, through a standardized process of factory production. On the same occasion, Berliner also entertained an alternative process of production where individuals could visit local gramophone offices to make their own personal recordings. He grasped readily not only the religious but also the commercial potential of mass-producing gramophones and musical records. He gathered inventors in the United States, and with their backing he founded in 1895 the Berliner Gramophone Company.

Berliner asked his audience to imagine a technology that would allow Catholics, however dispersed they were on the earth, to hear the pope speaking as if he were in their presence. Once his dream became a reality, critics around the world found reasons to criticize it. Manufacturing imperfections distorted the human voice, and early records failed to reproduce sound at certain frequencies. They emitted a hissing noise, caused by friction between the gramophone's steel stylus and the record's groove. To promote wax cylinders, which were played on the instrument that he invented, Thomas Alva Edison criticized flat discs for their "rotten scratchy" sound.[2] Around 1904 the Egyptian composer and musicologist Muḥammad Kāmil al-Khulaʿī emphasized the artificiality of the medium. He compared listening to music through a phonograph to "eating with dentures."[3] In 1906 the American composer John Philip Sousa penned a famous traditionalist attack. Resentful of the record industry, which made and sold unauthorized reproductions of his marches, he lobbied Congress to recognize composers' right to profit from their own compositions. He castigated the purveyors of "canned music" and railed against the "tireless mechanisms" that repeated the same "story day by day, without variation, without soul."[4]

While Berliner and his partners recited rhapsodies of praise about the gramophone's ability to make the absent sound present, intellectuals emphasized ways by which the instruments accentuated feelings of absence. Franz Kafka, who found "the confounded din" raised by the Parlophon factory a personal threat, described mediating machines (the telegraph, the telephone, the radiograph) as ghosts that fed off emotions, rendering long-distance relationships all the more poignant—and artificial. He preferred trains, cars, and airplanes: inventions that facilitated "natural communications."[5] Similarly, Walter Benjamin, a German Jewish cultural critic, emphasized the depreciation of the "quality of presence" that happened with mechanical reproduction. Authenticity derived, according to him, from the presence of the original artwork or performance in time and space.[6]

In his historical-materialist approach to new media, Benjamin argued that art "originated in the service of a ritual—first the magical, then the religious kind." Until the Renaissance, works of art had derived their aura from magical or religious performances. Gradually, with the development of secular aesthetics, they began to lose their "ritualistic basis." Capitalism supposedly brought this process of secularization, the "shattering of tradition," to its expected culmination: "for the first time in world history, mechanical reproduction emancipates the work of art from its parasitical dependence on ritual."[7] Benjamin's formulation depended here on a Weberian conviction about the secularizing effects of capitalism. Elsewhere, in a fragment of an essay titled "Capitalism as Religion," he played with the idea that capitalism had the structure of a religious cult devoted to the global spread of despair.[8] Capitalism appeared to him as a soulless system of industrial production that would eradicate the last traces of mystical enchantment and medieval spirituality from the modern world.

Ritual was also central category of analysis for the Muslims who debated the irreligious sale and the religious utility of the gramophone at the beginning of the twentieth century. Some of them greeted the mass-produced Qur᾽anic records with suspicion, seeing them as a challenge to the traditional art of Qur᾽anic recitation. Others saw the same records as a boon to the modern worshipper.

This chapter explores the rationale of each camp. It dwells on the opinions expressed by self-styled reformers and their foes in Kazan, Singapore, and Cairo, between the turn of the century and World War I. How did they relate to the commodification of Qur᾽anic discs? Did they think of them as inviolable ceremonial objects that had to be handled with respect? Or did they think of them as goods that could play a religious role but did not require the reverential treatment accorded to Qur᾽anic manuscripts? How, in other words, did they relate to Qur᾽anic discs materially? In addition to answering these questions, insofar as the sources allow, this chapter also exposes the system of values behind the casuistry that moved Riḍā to permit the gramophone reluctantly but ban the gong readily. Before turning to any theological and legal subtleties, it is critical, however, to appreciate a few salient features of the system of production and marketing that brought Qur᾽anic discs and gramophones to Cairo and Kazan.

Capitalism for Ethno-Religious Markets: The Realization of Islamic Consumers' Dreams

The production of sound technology emerged as a fiercely competitive international business. Entrepreneurs raced to profit exclusively from the inventions of others; advertisers hurried to market models under rivals' brand names; and lawyers rushed to represent clients in patent infringement and exclusive sales rights cases.[9] In the United States, the quest to invent new things for individual profit in this field was intense, and it had such social depth and breadth that it marks a key moment in the history of capitalism. So many tinkerers participated in this quest that a sourcebook details 2,118 phonograph-related patents by 1,013 inventors in the span of three and a half decades, beginning in 1877. Acting upon their global commercial ambitions, several of these inventors began competing with each other to establish factories and shops internationally.

Russia proved to be a thriving market for this technology. Victor Talking Machines sold beyond all expectations in the country. By 1900, according to a historian of the phonograph, "there were gramophone shops in every large Russian city."[10] A merchant who owned one of these shops on St. Petersburg's main avenue, Nevsky Prospekt, played a role in marketing Victor's new line of luxury discs by proposing that they be stamped with distinctive red labels.[11] Multinational corporations hurried to extend branches to the enthusiastic Russian market. Between 1902 and 1907 Zonophone International, Deutsche Grammophon, and Pathé Frères, joint-stock companies incorporated in London, Berlin, and Paris, respectively, established record-making factories in Riga and Moscow, where they began to press as many as 12,000 records every day.[12] On their new gramophones, Russians in Kazan, as in other cities, could enjoy unique recordings by Enrico Caruso and Medea Mei-Figner. But they were not obliged to listen to Italian opera; they could use the same machine to enjoy Russian and Turkish music—perhaps even Tatar folksongs. By 1901 the Russian subsidiary of the Anglo-American company that owned Emile Berliner's patents had recorded Tatar as well as Armenian and Georgian artists in the Caucasus at the Oriental Hotel in the city of Tiflis. Within a few years, as indicated by catalogues, the multiethnic subjects of the Russian Empire could listen to a very wide range of records in a multiplicity of native and foreign languages, including Arabic.[13]

The instrument's incredible versatility is what allowed a circle of Volga Tatars to hear recordings in the language of the Qur᾿an. A remarkable quality of the gramophone is that it could serve just as well—without requiring a single adjustment to turntable, stylus, or horn—to play records in Arabic, Russian, or Tatar. To listen to Arabic with a gramophone in Kazan, the only thing needed was a sound recording in that language pressed on a compatible disc. And to profit from this technological flexibility, companies such as Gramophone decided to exploit the great variety of ethnic tastes. Already in the fin de siècle, they began systematically to record discs in diverse languages for sale in diverse cultures.[14] Contemplating the diffusion of the innovation across borders, they treated linguistic and cultural differences as a market opportunity, not as a market problem. Their multilingual production facilitated the rapid adoption of the instrument worldwide.

In Cairo, as in Kazan, record shops competed to sell records in multiple languages to the city's cosmopolitan population. The British firm Gramophone Company Limited established its shop in the Continental Hotel buildings in 1905. Within three years it was selling records in what Wright's *Impressions of*

Egypt described as "seven different languages and dialects—English, French, Italian, Greek, Turkish, and Egyptian, Syrian and Arabic." The guidebook gave credit to K. F. Vogel, a representative of the company, for realizing the importance of producing Arabic records, and it remarked: "The Oriental has a great love of music, and, though the long-drawn notes and apparently monotonous cadences of the native songs do not appeal to Western ears, the Arabs themselves hold their artistes in high esteem, and no social function is complete without the services of one or more of them."[15]

Led by American and European entrepreneurs with ambitions that transcended national and imperial boundaries, the business of making ethnic records for ethnic consumers required an intuitive strategy of what corporations would call, decades later, "global market segmentation." This was the categorization of societies around the world into overlapping groups of potential consumers based on models, impressions, or stereotypes of the general or average taste. Success depended on a delicate balance between anticipating and creating wants as well as on the flexibility of the industrial enterprise to respond quickly to local trends. This orientation to foreign markets entailed the theoretical construction of new social types, including "the Islamic consumer" in Cairo and Kazan.[16]

This multicultural facet of industrial capitalism has been overshadowed by critical and historical retellings of the rise of an American system of automated, undifferentiated factory production. In this phase of capitalism's history, machines and semiskilled workers were organized from the top-down (as in a Ford automobile factory) for the assembly-line production of standardized consumer goods, including durable machines (such as Ford's "universal car," the Model T), for sale to the masses within and across national boundaries.[17] "Fordism," the name that the neo-Marxist Italian critic Antonio Gramsci gave to this hegemonic system, supposedly reigned in the world until an economic crisis in the postwar period forced corporations to devise flexible production strategies and cross-cultural advertising techniques.[18] Strikingly, however, already in the first decade of the twentieth century, Emile Berliner and his allies and rivals in the record industry developed such strategies and techniques in a global contest for ethnic consumers.

Their competition for Muslim customers in the Russian Empire paved the way for the grand entrance, by 1910, of Arabic and Islamic records into the markets of Kazan. One of these records was likely a German-Egyptian product. The Kazani fellow who wrote to Riḍā offered a clue about the object in question when he identified (or rather misidentified) one of the performers by name as Abū Salāma al-Ḥijāzī, an Egyptian singer. The recording of Arabic songs for commercial purposes took off early in Egypt. Entering the country first, in 1903, the Gramophone Company alone made more than a thousand recordings there during the first decade of the century. A Lebanese company, Baidaphon, soon followed it, with considerable success. So did Berlin's record label, Odeon.[19]

Capitalist competition for Arab and Muslim consumers was fiercer in Cairo than in Kazan. In 1907 a pair of rival shops repeatedly targeted the thousands of readers of one of Cairo's prominent dailies, *al-Muʾayyad*, with classified advertisements. Whereas most advertisements in the newspaper consisted of a few lines of text, the columns advertising their products captured readers' attention with a black-and-white image. Jack Zaki Sedaka managed or owned the National Odeon Store. His rival's store was called the Francis Shop. Both were located in a commercial area, near a famous Egyptian department store, ʿUmar Effendi, on or off ʿAbd al-ʿAzīz Street, and both advertised records by "the famous" singer Shaykh Salāma Ḥijāzī (1852–1917) as well as other things. The Francis Shop, which could be reached by telephone, had a commercial banner suspended from the entrance to attract passersby. It boasted that it was "The Biggest and Most Famous Shop in All of Egypt Selling Phonographs and Records."

But Sedaka's National Odeon Store offered customers a variety of services. Not only did it sell phonographs and records, it also operated as a repair shop for these instruments, for timepieces, and for sewing machines. The phonographs on sale had the most beautiful shapes. There were all sorts of new models made by a "famous" American company whose trademark was synonymous with fidelity. (Evidently, the shop stocked Victor Talking Machines, whose logo showed Nipper the dog listening to his master's voice.) For just three hundred piastres, customers could purchase one of these machines, which would come with a three-year service guarantee, and five double-sided records. The selection of discs was extensive, too. The advertisement mentioned a number of popular Egyptian artists by name. In addition, it referred to male and female singers and various genres: comedy, bagpipe music, and Egyptian military bands. Not mentioned in the advertisement, alas, were any records of Qurʾanic recitation.[20]

Ḥijāzī, the Egyptian artist featured in every advertisement, had signed an exclusive and lucrative recording contract with Odeon, and his early training included the art of reciting the Qurʾan. The company's 1913 catalog of Arab songs featured him first. By this date, he had recorded forty-four double-sided discs, most measuring twenty-seven centimeters in diameter. He was one of the musicians whose voice graced a high-quality line of discs: Arabian Celebrity Odeon Records, distinctively stamped with a red and white label.[21] In addition to Ḥijāzī's discs, an Odeon catalog listed many other artists and musical genres as well twelve discs of Qurʾanic recitation by three relatively unknown performers: Ḥasan Khaḍr, ʿAlī al-Fallāḥ, and Muḥammad Salīm.[22]

المحل الوطني

اديون

جاك زكى سيدا كاه

بأول شارع بين النهدين نمرة ٩ بالقرب
من محلات عمر أفندي على الشمال

محلنا المذكور مستعد لخدمة الجميع على حد
سواء ويوجد به جميع أصناف الساعات
والفونوغرافات من أحسن شكل وطرز جديد
وارد برسمنا خاصة من أكبر فوريقة بأمريكا
مشهورة بنطق الصوت الحقيق والفونوغراف
الذي عندنا بالشكل الموضح أعلاه وتابع له ٥
اصطوانات ذات وجهين هو يباع بمحلنا المذكور
بمبلغ زهيد جدا للغاية وهو مبلغ (٣٠٠) قرش
صاغ . كما وان المحل يضمنه لمدة ٣ سنوات
وأيضا يوجد عندنا اسطوانات ذات وجهين اديون
حضرت برسمنا خاصة في هذه الايام بأدوار
مستجدة لحضرة المطرب الشهير الشيخ سلامه
حجازي وعبد الحي أفندي حلمي على نحت ابراهيم
أفندي سهلون والمرحوم أحمد أفندي حسنين
وحضرة محمد أفندي السبع والشيخ سيد الصفتي
والشيخ محمد سليم وحضرة محمد أفندي سالم وسليمان
أفندي أبو داود وغيرهم من المغنين والمغنيات
الشهيرات وبخلاف ذلك واسطوانات مضحكة
وموسيقات وخصوصاً موسيقة القرب وموسيقة
البيادة المصرية كما وان المحل يوجد به ورشة
كبيرة لتصليح جميع الساعات والفونوغرافات
ومكينات الخياطة بكل دقة وكل ضبط وجميع
الطلبات التي ترد لنا من جميع الجهات ترسل بكل
سرعة لمن يطلبها والاثمان متهاودة جدا لا يمكن
لغير التجاسر عليها ومن يشرف محلنا المذكور
يرا ما يسر خاطره وعلى الله الاتكال

FIGURE 5.1 Jack Zaki Sedaka's advertisement for the National Odeon Store ran repeatedly in a Cairo newspaper in 1907. Sedaka's store competed for customers with the Francis phonograph shop. The column reproduced here, taken from a microfilm, was originally printed in the November 28, 1907, issue of *al-Mu'ayyad*. Source: General Research Division, New York Public Library, Astor, Lenox and Tilden Foundations.

Perhaps, then, it was a German company's disc records of Egyptian artists' recitations of the Qur'an that turned around and around on an American gramophone in Kazan. Another possibility is that the Gramophone Company, based in the United Kingdom, pressed the Qur'anic records.[23] One way or the other, this "object of translation" did not have a single origin.[24] It was a multicultural product of capitalism's turn-of-the-century experimentation with the promise of ethnic consumption: a fascinating artifact that transcended cultural, national, religious, and even—as a modern rendition of scripture—temporal boundaries. Indeed, however novel were methods of chanting, techniques of recording, and experiences of listening, the recited texts dated from the seventh century. The scriptural record was an Islamic realization of the shellac dream, a commercial Muslim version of the papal phonautogram that Berliner had envisioned in 1888. But why, if this new embodiment of the Qur'an was so perfectly designed for Islamic consumers, did a religious or legal case against it ever arise in the city at the confluence of the Volga and Kazanka Rivers?

FIGURE 5.2 Odeon's "Arabian Celebrity Records" line featured the famous singer Shaykh Salāma Ḥijāzī as well as several other Egyptian musicians. Ḥafiẓ Ḥilmī's request for a fatwa reveals that his records had reached Kazan, Russia, by 1910. Source: Scan of a record in the author's possession.

The Sound of Religious Discord: Modernists Versus Conservatives in Kazan

In Ḥāfiẓ Ḥilmī's view, the case arose because one of Kazan's Muslim factions saw religious innovations as if they were transgressions. Tensions in the community had led to a split, manifested in the formation of two antagonistic camps. Ḥilmī did not identify these camps by name, but his reference is clear, for Russia's Muslims felt torn asunder by a struggle between *jadidis*, partisans of the new, and their opponents. Those who favored change liked to imagine that different cultural attitudes had given rise to a social barrier, even though a strict partition did not actually exist in Kazan. They mockingly labeled their rivals, the conservatives who worried about radical change and defended traditions, *qadimis*, partisans of the old. What set *jadidis*, or Muslim moderns, apart was their enthusiasm for educational innovation, the pursuit of commerce, and modern technology.[25]

Ismail Gasprinski, the Europeanized Tatar who urged an audience in Cairo to pray for his oil baron, was Russia's leading Muslim modern. Among other things, he advocated the reform of Muslim schools. Those who embraced his method tried to change the curriculum, to introduce secular subjects and new textbooks that would serve better to train a new generation of Tatars. They wanted to transform the way religious subjects were taught too. Criticizing a pedagogy that stressed rote memorization of a scripture that God had sent down in Arabic, they proposed that students read a Tatar translation of the Qur'an instead. They founded many new schools for Russia's Muslims. Then they began to clamor not only for educational but also for cultural, social, and political reforms. The 1905 Russian Revolution gave them an opportunity to demonstrate their commitment to challenge old ways: a *jadidi* school in Kazan established the Reform Party, al-Iṣlāḥ, whose members participated in protests against the Tsarist regime, behind barricades.[26] In the aftermath of the revolution, Muslim moderns grew more successful, particularly in the field of education. More and more confessional schools adopted their method.[27]

The *qadimi* agenda is best understood, in the simplest terms, as developing in opposition to the *jadidi* one. Conservatives attacked innovations such as the introduction of desks and blackboards into schools, the use of new textbooks in the Tatar vernacular, and the fashion of wearing European clothes.[28] They did not simply aim to turn the clock back; they romanticized vanishing traditions. Part and parcel of the modern world, their religious conservatism made sense only in light of new historical conditions.

Ḥāfiẓ Ḥilmī responded enthusiastically to the possibility of modernizing a religious practice through the adoption of a new device, and this sentiment makes obvious his allegiance to the *jadidi* faction.[29] Central Asia's moderns tended to be very enthusiastic about technological innovations. Those who traveled abroad to gather European goods wrote wide-eyed chronicles of the wonders of European civilization.[30] Moreover, strong personal links began to develop between Tatar and Egyptian reformers around the turn of the century. So many Tatar students traveled to Cairo to study Islam that they formed their own ethnic fraternity.[31] Gasprinski's visits to Cairo in 1907 and 1908 deepened ties. Tatar reformers considered *al-Manār* an exemplary publication: they translated its articles and imitated its style. Ḥāfiẓ Ḥilmī himself formed part of this network of Muslim moderns who worked to establish deeper ties through the medium of print. At one point, he translated for *al-Manār*'s Arabic readers a fatwa request concerning a local dispute over the prudence of a prayer, which had originally been published in the new Volga Tatar magazine *Shūrā* (Council).[32] Printed in Orenburg and devoted to the *jadidi* cause, this magazine modeled itself after *al-Manār*. The Kazani appeal for a fatwa about the gramophone's religious utility was part of these broader exchanges.

Signaling his affiliation with the moderns in town, Ḥāfiẓ Ḥilmī revealed to Riḍā that one faction eagerly embraced the phonograph "because the people of Kazan need a reform [of the practice] of reciting the Qur᾽an."[33] Locals, he lamented, recited Muslim scripture with a horrible Tatar accent. They failed to convey the sound of the Arabic letters, the language of the divine revelation, in high fidelity. "Yet it is not easy for everyone" in Kazan, continued Ḥāfiẓ Ḥilmī, "to travel to Egypt or the Ḥijāz so as to listen to the voices of the shaykhs there." Arguing that records of the Qur᾽an could play an important role in confessional education, he defended the phonograph as a lawful instrument that enabled Muslims outside of the Middle East to grasp "melodious Arabic intonations" and "marvelous voices." He had "no doubt that using [the machine] with this intention was an act of worship" which would merit religious rewards.

The gramophone was thus trumpeted in Kazan by one of its fans as the perfect instrument for the consummation of Islam in a land where Arabic was not the native tongue. From his point of view, the machine reduced the distance that separated Russia from Egypt and the Ḥijāz wondrously; it made the faraway voices of Arab reciters sound nearby, virtually present in Kazan. It is a striking sentiment, especially if juxtaposed to the intellectual critique of mechanical reproductions as works of industrial disenchantment that lacked the aura of authentic performances and pulled modernity further away from religiosity. Ḥāfiẓ Ḥilmī certainly noted the vast distance that separated the audience in Kazan from the original performance in Cairo or Mecca; he knew the difference between a sound record and a live recitation. But instead of dwelling on what was lost, on specters and ghosts, he focused on what was gained as a consequence of mechanical transmission. Odeon's discs gave him and likeminded Tatars a taste of Arab authenticity. They felt closer than before to the heartlands of Islam when the semblance of an "Arabian" celebrity finally reached Kazan.

But why did conservatives react to the mechanical reproduction of the Qur᾽an in Kazan? According to Ḥāfiẓ Ḥilmī, they perceived the phonograph as an instrument for "amusement and play" that was in no way suitable for worship. Playing the Qur᾽an on a machine designed for entertainment seemed to them irreverent. They preferred to continue listening to the Qur᾽an as they had in the past, through live recitations. On that basis, they declared the modern practice "strictly prohibited." Due to his evident enthusiasm for Qur᾽anic records, Ḥāfiẓ Ḥilmī explained the *qadimi* reaction to the new technology in a superficial, dismissive way. But conservatives likely reacted to the new medium for several different reasons.

Conservative Reasons Reconstructed

Objections to the use of the gramophone to play music, rather than Qurʾanic recitations, likely played a role in the Kazani reaction to the instrument. To explain their opposition, religious conservatives in Kazan could easily have drawn on a wealth of puritanical traditions that decried musical instruments, sensual pleasure, and mixed-gender performances. In addition, the use of a machine to play Qurʾanic verses made it difficult to follow the rites that customarily took place during recitations of scripture by live performers. Finally, the local authorities whose respect and livelihood depended on performing recitations at communal events had reasons to feel slighted by the *jadidi* enthusiasts who praised Arabic discs and scorned Tatar accents.

The popular use of the gramophone to play music records instead of plain speech or measured recitation could well have troubled some *qadimis*. With a new design that enhanced the quality of the sound, Victor Talking Machines were marketed as musical instruments, and most of the discs that were designed for these instruments were records of music.[34] Only 12 of Odeon's 460 Arab records (fewer than 3 percent) were dedicated to verses of the Qurʾan. Part and parcel of the era's Arabic awakening, al-Nahḍā, many of the rest consisted of modern musical interpretations of early Islamic poems and medieval Sufi hymns. The lyrics were generally pious, but the repertory included a few strikingly profane songs.[35] Although it headlined singers, Odeon's catalog granted a few pages at the end to "Arab orchestration," where it featured *ʿūd* players, Egyptian bagpipers, military bands, and one famous violinist. Evidence has not surfaced to determine which of these varied musical discs made it to Kazan. However, since Shaykh Salāma Ḥijāzī recorded exclusively for Odeon, and since neither the company's catalog nor the artist's discography suggests that he ever recorded a Qurʾanic disc despite his training in this art, it is all but certain that the circle of *jadidis* that listened to him in Kazan heard him singing, not reciting, in Arabic.[36] Ḥāfiẓ Ḥilmī asked Riḍā to sanction the phonograph for devotional purposes, but his faction was using the instrument for secular entertainment too.

Conservatives in Kazan could easily have turned to Islamic traditions to justify their opposition to music. Medieval Islamic authorities did not present them with a uniform front against music and its instruments. With some leniency, some had devised arguments to legitimize playing select types of instruments on particular occasions and listening to musical remembrances of God. Al-Ghazālī (d. 1111) thought it permissible to listen to a beautiful voice; Ibn Taymiyya had no objection to solemn scriptural chants that conformed to his high monotheistic standards.[37] They were circumspect in their authorizations, however, because the Islamic tradition included sharp statements against certain instruments and against musical enjoyment, which can stir up the devil. According to one narrative, God sent Muḥammad on a mission "to annihilate string instruments and musical pipes."[38] Now and then ascetics who considered music a forbidden pleasure not only denounced musical performances; they also smashed musical instruments.[39] Little wonder that, after conquering the Ḥijāz, Wahhabi vigilantes seized gramophone needles.[40]

In Central Asia, in a muted expression of this spirit, *qadimis* reacted against *jadidis* for "wasting money on all sorts of music and useless things." They condemned them for indulging themselves at events where "forbidden [elements] such as musical instruments, singers, gambling, and women" mixed together.[41] This reaction came in the wake of earlier disputes over worshipping with music. Mystical chanting, drumming, and dancing, the devotional practices of remembering God, had deep foundations in the religious life of one Sufi order, the Qādiriyya, which had spread in this region. A competing Sufi brotherhood, the Naqshabandiyya, had opposed this musical exuberance. It had recommended silent worship. Ironically, Sufis who had been initiated into this order of silence figured among the founders of the movement that eventually embraced the gramophone as a devotional instrument.[42] *Jadidis* came to enjoy folk music, live and recorded, for which they were criticized by *qadimis*.[43] The factional Kazani debate over recorded recitations of the Qur᾿an cannot therefore be isolated from this broader, longer struggle over the practice of Islam in relation to music.

Musical recitations of the Qur᾿an were especially disconcerting to those who preferred staid or silent readings of scripture. Muslims through the centuries have appreciated oral and liturgical performances of the Qur᾿an.[44] Performed by gifted voices, these recitations could sound rather musical. But in modern as in medieval times, jurists liked to uphold a theoretical distinction between Qur᾿anic recitation and musical performance. They contended that any recitation should focus the listener's attention on the sacred text, not on the vain beauty of a human voice. A recitation that violated this distinction by indulging in rhythmic variations or melodic flourishes risked censure.[45] Eventually, in the era of radio transmissions and cassette recordings, a preoccupation with the propagation of alleged "errors" would lead to the establishment of institutions designed to enforce orthodox conventions.[46] In the gramophone's heyday, however, Egyptian artists found plenty of room for experimentation. Reciting the holy book in an ornate, melismatic style, they made it more difficult than ever to sustain the distinction between reciting and singing.[47] They blurred the line by singing across genres too. Salāma Ḥijāzī's training as a Qur᾿an reciter affected his style as a singer—in particular his ability to shift abruptly from one to another octave.[48] Shaykh Muḥammad Salīm recorded for Odeon love songs and melodic poems as well as recitations of the Qurʾan. Played on a musical "talking machine," these unconventional turn-of-the-century recitations moved in an ambiguous space between the realm of scripture and the realm of music. Their undeniably musical quality made them all the more dubious.

Qurʾanic discs were vexing and perplexing objects, too, because they made it difficult to observe the social and religious conventions that audiences had customarily observed when listening to recitations. Traditionally, ritual gestures accompanied these recitations. During key passages, upon receiving a signal from the reciter, the audience would engage in synchronic prostrations.[49] Sūrat Maryam, recorded by Zonophone, Gramophone, and Odeon, included one of these special verses. Precisely when the reciter narrated that, on hearing God's revelations, Abraham's descendants prostrated themselves in tears (Q. 19:58), listeners were collectively expected to perform the same act.[50]

The mechanical reproduction of Qurʾanic discs shattered this tradition. Instead of facing a live reciter, Muslims hearing a record of the Qurʾan confronted a machine that was not designed to prompt ritual action. The gramophone was simply not built to script this kind of behavior effectively.[51] Nor was it desirable to interrupt the flow of a recorded recitation with stage directions, oral instructions, or a series of beeps to substitute for the physical cues that a live reciter could give speechlessly. Whereas a mechanical reciter would spin heedlessly, moving on to the next verse without giving the audience the chance to complete its prostrations, a human reciter could easily time the speech act and resume the liturgical service after a variable pause. As a "scriptive" machine, the gramophone was a failure; as a consequence, Muslim audiences occasionally found themselves at a complete loss—in desperate need of a ritual expert. Indeed, *al-Manār* received several queries from perplexed individuals from different corners of the world, including one from a Russian subscriber, wondering whether it was a religious requirement for them to execute the normative prostrations before the machine.[52]

Qurʾan-playing phonographs had an unsettling effect on the local religious hierarchy too. In Kazan, before the arrival of the instrument, Tatars who had attended religious schools and memorized the Qurʾan performed recitations. The official religious establishment disliked the fact that unlicensed clerics, patronized by laypersons, thrived in this business, which the historian Robert Crews has described as "a gray religious underground."[53] Phonographs enabled laypersons to assume greater control over scripture. The proud owner of a phonograph, armed with a record of the Qurʾan, could bypass Kazan reciters and Kazan imams in order to present the word of God himself to an audience of Muslims. This presentation made him into a religious authority of sorts: an authority attained not through years of learning but simply through the acquisition of a new instrument, which cost, depending on the model, eighty to six hundred rubles. *Qadimi* reciters had a professional reason, therefore, to resent the instrument that *jadidis* touted as wondrously modern while criticizing their traditional services as lackluster, parochial, and obsolete.[54]

However, there was no risk of their imminent replacement by machines. Turning at around seventy-eight revolutions per minute, disc records in this period lasted only two or three minutes; and the repertory of Qurʾanic verses recorded by Odeon was still limited to a dozen extracts from select chapters. Competing companies offered relatively few supplementary titles since the record industry concentrated on many of the same narratives: generally brief, dramatic stories.[55] Consequently, at funerals and on other occasions when assemblies expected extended recitations of the Qurʾan lasting several hours, human reciters remained in demand—even if they had a Tatar accent.

The Jurist's Sanction: An Appropriable Instrument for Orthodoxy's Sake

With a few caveats, Riḍā sided with Kazan's moderns. First, he acknowledged that a reason did exist for considering a ban. It had nothing to do with the mechanics of the phonograph. To consign the Qurʾan to the planks of the sound box or the grooves of a disc record was acceptable; so, too, was the fact that the disc made revolutions in order to produce sound. But conservatives had a legitimate concern in worrying that Muslims would play records of the Qurʾan for "amusement and play," displaying an attitude at odds with the grave reverence due to the sacred text. There was little cause for concern, however, if Muslims used the phonograph with pious intentions for devotional purposes.

Riḍā tried to reassure wary and scrupulous believers who worried that the instrument would give its users "an excuse for insulting the sacred book." "What is forbidden to avoid" the possibility of dishonorable treatment "becomes permitted on account of need." Using a phonograph to listen to a record of the Qurʾan is not strictly forbidden, unless there occurs "a breach of good manners." Customary law to a large extent determines what counts as proper etiquette in a given place. Even so, as a mufti charged to give universal advice, Riḍā ruled that listening to a recorded recitation was "commendable" if the purpose was to derive from it moral advice or right pronunciation and "imperative" if there was no other way for a believer to memorize the sound of the essential prayers of the holy book's opening chapter, Sūrat al-fātiḥa.

Although he issued this permissive ruling, Riḍā was aware that the phonograph was already challenging traditional standards of behavior. "I do not deny," he conceded, "that in Egypt some fail to comply with the requisite etiquette." Because of this expectation, he found it tempting to impose certain restrictions and thus ensure that Muslims would abide by the shariʿa while using the phonograph. Nevertheless, he resolved not to ban a thing, adhering instead to a key principle of his jurisprudence. Advancing a strict prohibition should be "no easy matter, because it would count as new legislation." The modern jurist had to refrain from manufacturing novel prohibitions. His role was to uphold the canonical rules that God and his Prophet had established long ago. Upon encountering new objects and practices that did not clearly fall under classical proscriptions, it was his responsibility to apply the default ruling in their favor: to presume that things and actions not banned by the sacred law are lawful.[56]

However much this juridical code kept him from inventing prohibitions, Riḍā felt free to remind Muslims to observe caution when making use of the new technology. He warned Kazan's Muslims specifically against listening to melodious interpretations of the sacred text. The style of chanting developed by some Egyptian reciters has been interdicted, he alerted his readers, due to its incompatibility with the humble state of reverence required during acts of worship. Instead of distracting audiences with singing, reciters ought to help listeners attend to the sacred text. As for Shaykh Salāma Ḥijāzī, the famous Egyptian artist whose records had reached Kazan, "he is not one of the reciters, but one of the singers."[57] Thus, on the one hand the 1910 fatwa made a strong case for Qurʾanic discs, as it suggested that in certain contexts they could fulfill a religious need, and on the other hand it warned against the musical recitations and nonreverential attitudes that followed the adoption of the gramophone.

The fatwa to Kazan, which tried to resolve the case of "the Qurʾan in the phonograph," was neither the first nor the last fatwa on the topic. Already in 1899, a mufti from the Dutch East Indies, Sayyid ʿUthmān, had written a pair of fatwas about this topic—after consulting by mail with Riḍā's old teacher, Ḥusayn al-Jisr, the director of Tripoli's Patriotic Islamic Madrasa. He saw that the phonograph as a frivolous instrument and opined that listeners could reap no religious reward from it. He assumed a combative stance as he responded to a range of related issues: a question about profiting from operating a gramophone, a concern about the ritual status of Qurʾanic wax cylinders or shellac discs, and the problem of audience prostrations during recorded performances. Riḍā, who would develop a bitter long-distance rivalry with Sayyid ʿUthmān, might not have read these Indonesian fatwas.[58]

But he was certainly aware of a range of clerical opinions at home and abroad. In 1906 he responded to a tract about the phonograph by one of Egypt's leading legal experts, the Azhari judge Muḥammad Bakhīt. Bakhīt decided that listening to records of the Qurʾan was permissible if the recitation was flawless and if the audience had pious intentions. He placed some restrictions on usage to defend orthopraxy, but Riḍā considered these restrictions insufficient. He criticized Bakhīt for making a "statement in absolute favor" of the phonograph without knowing anything about the "science of its invention."[59]

Riḍā liked to present himself as advocating knowledgeably, like Daedalus, the middle course between endless confinement and reckless flight. His qualified ruling in support of the *jadidis* of Kazan was far more liberal than Sayyid ʿUthmān's fin-de-siècle rulings. The best historical explanation for this departure is that, by 1910, the mass production and consumption of Islamic records had taken off. This trend alone meant that the technology's religious users, petitioners such as Ḥāfiẓ Ḥilmī, exerted great pressure upon clerics to sanction their new, reformed way of listening to the Qurʾan. However, Riḍā's ruling was not as permissive as Bakhīt's, and the differences were deliberate. He stated his reservations about the gramophone carefully, having criticized his rival's blanket authorization. To flourish as an independent mufti, he had to compete against other muftis and earn prestige and recognition. Riḍā's brand of reluctant modernism, his laissez-faire Salafism, was part of a prolonged and ambitious effort, which lasted throughout his career, to gain prominence by cultivating a style of judging things that would strike readers as fairly liberal but true to Islam.

The Invisible Qurʾan: Impurity, Materiality, and Capitalism

The set of fatwas about the gramophone and its discs that *al-Manār* published over the years concentrated on different matters in accordance with correspondents' interests. The fatwa for the subscriber from Kazan mainly dealt with the gramophone's promise as an instrument for Islamic worship. An earlier fatwa, written in 1907, replied to a question posed by a pair of Singaporean Arabs who prompted Riḍā to reflect on Qurʾanic discs in a different way: as commercial objects and as material objects whose grooves stored the words of God.

The fatwa seekers from Singapore inquired about "an articulating machine" that was capable of reproducing the sounds of letters, poems, and songs. In Singapore, as in Kazan, the central concern revolved around the instrument's religious applications: its ability to replay Qurʾanic recitations and the call to prayer, which Odeon offered in two versions by different artists. What specifically preoccupied some Arabs in the Southeast Asian entrepôt was the defilement of religious things through their commodification. The consignment of Islamic blessings to shellac discs basically symbolized for them the deepening alienation of a consumer society from live reciters and muezzins, whose labor of worship could now be reproduced industrially and then sold in impersonal markets by merchants of any faith, who traded in the sacred as if it were the profane.

A certain ʿAwn Allāh al-Ḥaḍramī, one of the Arabs who had settled down in the British Crown colony, fervently expressed his dismay at this commerce in records of the Qurʾan. One could buy them "in every shop," and not just from Muslims but also from shopkeepers of "any religion." He worried that the rules of purity and impurity that pertain to the handling of the Qurʾan applied as well to its acoustical recording. If people in a state of ritual impurity were strictly forbidden from touching the glorious book, as Qurʾan 56:79 implies, should the shariʿa not prohibit the passing around of records of the Qurʾan from the hands of the infidels to the hands of the tyrants in every coffee shop, party tent, and alley? "The Muslim community," he lamented, "had deviated [from the path of tradition] because of these technologies, as if struck by madness, and we no longer know what will come to pass." Did the sacred law permit this innovation or not?[60]

With greater discipline and dispassion, the Ḥaḍramī reformer Ḥasan ibn ʿAlawī ibn Shihāb exposed the more technical questions implicit in ʿAwn Allāh's dualistic query: "What is the ruling about disc records in which the voice of the reciter of the Qurʾan has been lodged? Are they like a Qurʾanic manuscript in connection with the rules about transportation, handling, and inviolability or not? The intellects here have divergent views, and I have the conviction that no ruling applies to it, for it is rather like other inanimate, inorganic solids."[61]

Evidently, then, not every member of the diasporic community of Singapore Arabs, dominated by business-oriented migrants from Ḥaḍramawt, worried about the fate of Islam under free trade. There was some debate. Unable to reach a resolution, two contenders agreed to appeal to an external authority, a mufti whose international fame was growing, for arbitration.

As a remote mediator in that local dispute, Riḍā explained that the purpose of the user determined the legality or illegality of the instrument. If contemplation and edification were the goals, then there was no reason for banning it. "Whenever the intention is entertainment, however, and this is what the masses seek whenever they listen to the phonograph, then there is absolutely no way to deem it lawful. And I am afraid that the operator [of the phonograph] will become one of those people who take their religion for mockery and fun."[62]

To make the gravity of this leisurely pursuit painfully obvious, Riḍā cited several Qurʾanic verses that promised grievous, hellish tortures would await those who took their religion lightly, as if it were a divertissement, and "purchased frivolous new tales" (6:70, 7:51, 31:6).

Then the mufti turned to the more technical question about scriptural mediation: whether or not the Qurʾan on a disc was analogous to the Qurʾan on a page in relation to the laws of purity. Jurists would have reasons to disagree. Some might hold that the phonographic cylinder or disc that generated the sound of words with the bouncing of the needle was categorically distinct from "a written Qur᾿an, since the observer of it can see neither the words nor the letters of the holy book."[63] On this basis, they could declare irrelevant the divine warning, "Only the purified may touch it," which medieval scholars had applied to handwritten copies of the heavenly book (56:79). The invisibility of the words on the disc record obviated, from this perspective, the risk of transmitting a material impurity to the book's hallowed letters.

Alternatively, if jurists could appreciate the wisdom behind the warning against defiling scripture, they would be able to make a universal ruling to cover transcriptions and transmissions of the Qur᾿an through different media. With the philosopher's gaze, they would recognize that the record's thin grooves deserve to be called words or speech more than do "written inscriptions" because they are a form of "natural writing." Created by an etching needle, which responds to the vibrations of air made by sound waves, the series of miniscule engravings in the spiral groove store without error the original words articulated by a reader. Conventional writing, by contrast, can be riddled with mistakes since it does not record information naturally. A thought experiment served to establish the sound technology's superiority: "Had there been a phonograph in [the prophet's] age to store his recitation, we would certainly have decided in its favor."[64] Hence, even a fragment of a Qur᾿anic recitation stored on a flat disc ought to be treated with the same level of reverence that is due to the holy book.

Much of this may sound as a particularly Islamic discussion that stemmed from particular Islamic concerns about the Qur᾿an. But it is striking that one of the key legal questions driving this discussion, the question about the comparability of printed and sound media, was under debate at the very same time in the legislative branch of the American government. Was the talking machine's disc record a form of "writing" or not? The question was essential for determining whether to extend copyright protections, which had been secured by authors, to the composers of music reproduced (without permission and without royalties) by the record industry. Those supporting the amendment of the old copyright law argued for an expansive definition of "writing" to cover the notation of sound in the grooves of discs. When it became clear that the argument would persuade the government's committee on patents, a representative of the Victor Talking Machine Company contrived the strangest definition of "writing" ever penned: "The talking machine is a writing upon a record tablet—not to be read visually, but audibly to be read through the medium of a vibrating pencil engaging in the record groove. This reproduces the thing that is uttered."

Property rights should therefore extend, Victor argued, to the manufacturers of actuating machines.[65]

As a defender of the philosophical perspective, Riḍā encouraged the cultivation of a metaphysical, not a ritualistic, attitude to material embodiments of God's words. Whether printed on paper or engraved on shellac, the Qurʾan deserved honor and respect. To appreciate it intellectually or emotionally, however, readers or listeners did not need to observe a medieval code of behavior: they could stop obsessing over rituals and taboos designed to protect temporal manifestations of the eternal Qurʾan from the dangerous touch of infidels. No, according to Riḍā, many juridical restrictions on handling a Qurʾanic codex had no clear basis in the sacred law.

Just as in the toilet paper fatwa, in this fatwa, too, Riḍā argued for overcoming anxieties about impurity that had been triggered by the introduction of modern things. In both instances he made a case in favor of adoption, representing the new product as an improvement—in terms of hygiene or fidelity—on the old models.

Sanctioning adoption meant condoning tacitly what ʿAwn Allāh al-Ḥaḍramī had found scandalous: the irreligious commerce in the sacred good. The Qurʾan had warned monotheists not to sell God's verses for a trifling price (3:199, 5:44), so opponents of the gramophone could point to this and other authoritative sources to deplore the devaluation of scripture by capitalism. In premodern times, jurists had often discussed whether it was permissible to buy or sell a manuscript of the Qurʾan or, in a similar vein, to charge money for teaching scripture. Many jurists had allowed such transactions, seeing them as necessary for the dissemination of religion.[66] Although some authorities had opposed the commodification of divine things, others had found creative accounting schemes to work around proscriptions: if a good Muslim could not purchase the Qurʾan outright, he could certainly buy parchment or vellum and pay a scribe not for the final good but for the labor of copying verses.[67] Still, phonographs could enable a man without a single religious qualification to profit from Muslim demand for the sound of the Qurʾan. The business in Singapore, a hub for the record industry in Asia, was certainly dominated by non-Muslim corporations. Stamford Raffles Robinson, an Englishman whose department store stocked everything from bicycles to typewriters, and Wilhelm Heinrich Diethelm, a Swiss magnate whose industrial ventures ranged from matches to chemical dyes, led the companies that acquired the exclusive rights to sell Odeon's and Gramophone's diverse ethnic records in the city.[68] ʿAwn Allāh's concern about the handling of Qurʾanic records by infidels and tyrants stemmed from this commercial reality.

In his fatwa to Singapore's Arabs, Riḍā passed over in silence the delicate issue of non-Muslims selling records of verses of the Qur᾽an to Muslims. But his ruling that persons whose bodies had been compromised by minor ritual impurities could nevertheless treat the Qur᾽an with respect supported, implicitly, the case for freer trade. Certainly, he held back from placing restrictions on the cross-cultural commerce, which would have violated the principles of laissez-faire and his own easygoing approach to the quest for profit. Indeed, in 1911 a Javanese fellow, Ḥājjī ʿAbdallāh Aḥmad (d. 1933), asked him if it was forbidden for a professional to make money by operating the phonograph—work that involved, among other things, the labor of winding the crank of a spring-motor machine. As shown long ago by the Dutch Orientalist Christiaan Snouck Hurgronje, a pioneer in the recording of Arabic recitations and songs on wax cylinders, muftis in Southeast Asia had been debating this and other phonographic questions since the end of the century.[69] How did Riḍā contribute to their debate? Finding no precedent and no reason to prohibit this new way to earn capital, he ruled that it was perfectly fine to make a livelihood from the technology. Tellingly, he refrained from voicing reservations about the audience's composition or the selection of records. He fell back, instead, on the most liberal juridical principle about modern inventions or unprecedented objects: "The basic status with regard to things is legitimacy."[70]

The Gong in the Javanese Mosque: An Excursus on an Archaic Instrument

Riḍā's flexible, philosophical, and seemingly imperturbable attitude to the gramophone did not extend to all musical instruments that played a role in the ritual life of Muslims everywhere in the world. The idea that Javanese mosques were using an instrument known as a *nāqūs* made him break out in a rash of judgmental reactions. ʿAbd al-Ḥāfiẓ, a Javanese residing in Mecca, wrote to him that in some towns—located in Southeast Asia, it later became clear—Muslims had begun to strike the *nāqūs* to alert prospective worshippers of compulsory prayer times. The sounds made by this instrument had not replaced *adhān* and *iqāma*, the traditional calls to prayer by the human voice. They served as an additional mechanism to rouse Muslims to worship. The problem was that, at some level, they reminded Muslims of church bells. In certain places where Christians had renounced striking bells the association with Christianity had grown weaker; Muslims resorting to the same or a very similar practice did so without intending "to imitate Christians."[71] Still, worry persisted. Were mosque bells lawful devices or signs of infidelity?

The modern meaning of the word "*nāqūs*" was a bit of mystery. The Arabic term derived from a Classical Syriac word. In early Arabic texts, it referred to a gonglike instrument, the *semantron*, which Eastern Christian used to call the faithful to prayer.[72] A percussion instrument, it emitted a sonorous sound when a short piece of wood struck an oblong piece of brass, copper, or wood. Islamic legal texts used the word "*nāqūs*" to denote a gong or a bell often encased in a church tower that served to strike the hours of prayer. In modern times, it might have come also to signify, metonymically, a public clock—a mechanical device with a striking mechanism, such as a bell or a gong, that Christians elevated to the top of lofty clock towers in order to alert worshippers far and wide of the canonical hours.[73] It may seem strange that the word "*nāqūs*" might have referred to either a bell or a clock. But in Europe, too, where clockmakers devised an escapement to drive and control a pendulum, thus creating a timekeeping machine, bells were intimately associated with clocks. In Middle Dutch, the word "*clocke*" referred either to a bell or to the new bell-ringing apparatus.[74] Both before and after the invention of the mechanical clock, Muslim jurists opposed the *nāqūs*. Whether it signified a bell, a wooden gong, or a striking clock, they denounced it. Frequently, they tried to muffle the instrument and even to ban it outright in Muslim towns because loud pounding forced the public to pay attention to Christian worship.[75] To ring bells or strike clocks in mosques, emulating the tradition of churches, was out of the question. These devices belonged only within the ambit of the church, if anywhere.[76]

Muslims in the Dutch East Indies might have used the word "*nāqūs*" to designate a clock that the colonial administration placed in Banda Aceh's famous mosque. After a major uprising in the late nineteenth century the Dutch rebuilt the Grand Mosque, known today as Masjid Baiturraḥman, in an effort to win over the subject population. At the front of the central dome they placed a public clock with a striking mechanism. There is some possibility that Muslims, grounded in the language of Islamic law and strongly opposed to the Dutch venture into Islamic architecture, called the timekeeping machine by a despised name, *nāqūs*, to indicate opprobrium, to mock what one historian has called "a great symbol of modernity."[77] Indeed, that was precisely the sort of naming game that they played to express opposition to Dutch colonial culture when they described an article of European dress, the tie, by the medieval Arabic term for a monkish girdle, *zunnār*.

There is a more likely meaning, however, for the word. The Javanese used many kinds of drums and gongs in the gamelan ensemble. Among reform-minded Muslims eager to uproot local practices that had no basis in scripture, the word "*nāqūs*" might well have served to criticize one of these instruments. That, at least, was the interpretation of the Orientalist who made the earliest ethnomusicological recordings of Mecca. In 1911, after summarizing the fatwa published by *al-Manār*, a learned French journal asked the Dutch scholar Snouck Hurgronje to comment on the "linguistic reviviscence" of the word "*nāqūs*" and to illustrate how Javanese Muslims used the *cloche*. He explained that the technical Arabic term of Syriac origin referred to an instrument known in the language of Java by the word "*bĕdoug*." He revealed that mosques in the Indian archipelago lacked minarets but for a few exceptions, and in a country overwhelmed by tropical vegetation, the voices of the muezzins did not carry far. To overcome architectural limitations and the challenges of the natural environment, Muslims in the East Indies had developed a new practice: the practice of striking from their mosques, in conjunction with the standard call to prayer, an immense, resonant gong. Apparently of Chinese origin, the instrument consisted of a hollowed tree trunk wrapped on one or both ends by buffalo hide. Suspended horizontally, it was pounded with a wooden mallet. Javanese Muslims used it on several different religious occasions—not just to mark the five daily prayers but also to celebrate the annual festival of Muḥammad's birthday. Hurgronje, who was eager as ever to promote colorful local rather than universal Muslim practices, argued that wise and orthodox "Arabs" considered the *bĕdoug* "lawful" and even "commendable."[78]

Several Javanese jurists had issued fatwas in response to the installment of huge gongs or striking clocks in mosques, and their responses were less uniform and more conflicted than suggested by the Dutchman. The man who wrote to Riḍā from Mecca excerpted their fatwas, which revealed a range of attitudes. Not one of them saw the development through Dutch glasses, but the shades that they wore varied in darkness. At one extreme, they described gongs or clocks in mosques as reprehensible but allowable if they served to gather people rather than to mark the hour of prayer. At the other extreme, they described the placement of bells in mosque towers as an imitation of Christian practice—a strictly forbidden innovation whose perpetrators had committed an unforgivable sin and turned infidels. Those in power were urged to bring an end to the practice, so that "common people" might not begin to mix up licit things with confounding novelties.

Running through the Javanese fatwas was a fascinating tension between Muslim universalism and local syncretism. One of the Javanese scholars cited a Shafiʿite authority from Cairo, ʿAlī al-Shabrāmallisī (d. ca. 1677), who had written an esteemed commentary on a key manual of Islamic law, al-Nawawī's *Minhāj al-ṭālibīn*, "The Path of the Seekers." Written after the invention of mechanical clocks, al-Shabrāmallisī's seventeenth-century gloss focused in one section on the *nāqūs* in relation to Christian worship. It invoked a Muslim tradition concerning the origins of the Islamic call to prayer. According to this tradition, an emancipated slave of Abyssinian origin, Bilāl ibn Rabāḥ (d. ca. 640), was the first Muslim to call believers to prayer, shortly after the migration to Medina, at Muḥammad's urging. The story mattered because it helped to establish a Muslim way of gathering believers for worship—in contrast to Zoroastrian, Jewish, and Christian ways, which involved the use of fire, a ram's horn, or a gong of sorts.[79] When Javanese muezzins called Muslims to prayer, they established a universal connection with Islam as it was practiced, or as they believed that it was practiced, in the lifetime of the Prophet. At the same time, they developed a local custom which owed more to Javanese culture than to any Arabo-Islamic tradition. Percussion instruments in general, and gongs in particular, played an essential role in Javanese rituals and ceremonies. In some cities of Java, according to the most accommodating of the muftis quoted in *al-Manār*, muezzins struck a big drum (*ṭabl*) to gather Muslims for prayer. The Javanese had apparently "grown habituated" to this local practice, which the sympathetic mufti did not find problematic because he considered the drum a lawful instrument when it was used for religious purposes rather than for entertainment.

That a Javanese student residing in Mecca would send his request for a legal viewpoint to Cairo instead of presenting it to a local Ḥijāzī mufti shows the centrality of Riḍā's *al-Manār* in the Muslim landscape.[80] Perhaps he expected that Riḍā would issue a liberal opinion, following the legal philosophy of ʿAbduh. Just as hats in ʿAbduh's semiology were not Christianity's permanent and inseparable emblems but things that Muslims could use without losing their religion, so, too, bells could appear as temporary signifiers of Christian worship that mosques could incorporate without becoming churches. In this vein, the symbolic link between bells and Christianity would seem not universal but arbitrarily constructed and valid only in a particular context at a particular time. But in a different culture at a new conjuncture, the bell could mean something else altogether. Alienated from its original context and appropriated for the mosque, it could even become a symbol of Muslim worship. Why not? If the Javanese inquirer expected a fatwa along these lines, he must have been sorely disappointed.

"O Lord!" lamented Riḍā, "What is this contrariety in doctrines, acts of worship, and manners, that afflicts Muslims when they digress from the gift of your mighty book and from the tradition of your noble prophet." He found it bewilderingly subjective that, in their quest for cultural independence, Javanese scholars rejected certain European products but "then adopted church bells for their mosques." Technological progress and economic development might come from purchasing hats, phonographs, or commodity futures, but what benefit could possibly come from taking up an element of Christian worship? However open he was to European innovations, Riḍā drew the line when these things seemed to threaten Islamic rituals. He reminded his readers that God revealed to Muslims a religion perfect and complete. To exchange the rites of Muslims for the rites of others was a crude attempt, in his eyes, to turn Islam into another religion. Striking drums or ringing bells to call believers to the mosque counted, in his view, as a heretical "innovation in religion—and in every innovation," he warned, "there lies an error" that will lead believers astray. Merging infidelity with belief was strictly forbidden. He concluded by urging Javanese Muslims to disavow in the strongest terms the imitation of Christian rites through the appropriation of objects associated with the church.[81]

It is unlikely that he knew when he outlawed the Javanese gongs exactly what was the object in question. He had little knowledge of ceremonial gamelan drums. He associated the instrument, incorrectly, with an ancient Christian instrument—by fixating on a familiar word, "*nāqūs*," that revivalists in Java had deliberately chosen to cast aspersions on a local Muslim rite. Nor did he have any appreciation of the environmental circumstances that made it challenging in parts of Southeast Asia for the call to prayer to travel far and wide. This was the risk in sentencing things from afar. Riḍā's acerbic reaction to the notion of Muslim mosques adopting gongs nevertheless reveals the fault line that separated in his mind the archaic Christian artifact from the modern Euro-Islamic commodity.

Echoes of the Gramophone in *al-Manār*

Over the next two decades, as the phonograph became more affordable and the diffusion of sound technology accelerated, musical recordings reached mass audiences in Egypt and elsewhere.[82] In spite of this trend, Riḍā remained anchored to his refusal to issue a blanket authorization, and the restrained enthusiasm that he had felt for the instrument's Islamic uses waned over the years. By the late twenties and early thirties, the novelty of Qurʾanic records had worn off, and Riḍā had reached an age—over sixty years old—of cynicism and despondency over the behavior of music fanatics. His affects changed, yet his rulings stayed the same.

In 1927 a student of religion from Dongola in the Sudan wrote to him that workers in town would gather in a salon or café to seek spiritual diversion from their laboring pains. The phonograph brought joy to their hearts. He clarified that family and friends, as well as laborers, enjoyed gathering to listen to songs and recitations in a wholesome venue where alcohol was not served and where nobody felt pressured to skip the day's prayers. Was this leisure activity acceptable?

Riḍā adopted quite a critical tone in response.[83] He referred to the pertinent opinions that he had published long before the issue arose in Dongola. Like a broken record, he rehearsed word for word an argument that he had made two decades earlier, in the fatwa for Singapore, when he had warned about the conflation of leisure and religion by the masses. "I am unhappy," he confessed, "by the use of the phonograph for the recitation of the Qurʾan." He wished that Muslims would pay greater honor to the "discs on which the verses of the Qurʾan are recorded." Decades earlier as well, in response to a Russian subscriber's question, he had recommended the continuation of the ritual of prostrations at key verses without, however, making its observation strictly obligatory. By 1927 he did no more than lament the phonograph's deteriorating influence on this tradition. Despite his discontent, he did not rescind his earlier judgment. He resisted the temptation to either legalize or outlaw anything in its entirety.[84]

In 1933 he published his last meaningful fatwa about the phonograph. A correspondent residing in India's Malabar Coast wanted to know if it was acceptable to enjoy songs played at weddings on the phonograph or radio. Once more the mufti put a hedge around his authorization. He permitted Muslims to use their talking machines to hear reproductions of music and speech but with social safeguards in place. "Listening to the instrument," he ruled, "is just like listening to people." Like live music, recorded music was not tabooed in and of itself, yet epicurean listening could easily lead to sexual infatuation. Muslims therefore had to remain on guard.[85]

In this regard, the phonograph was exactly like the piano. When ʿAbd al-Qādir al-Baʿalbakī of Beirut wondered, in 1929, whether it was permissible for women to obtain piano lessons, Riḍā had argued that a man could teach his wife or a close female relative to play a musical instrument, provided that the objective was spiritual diversion in a domestic setting. Nevertheless, it was strictly forbidden to provide musical instruction to a woman who intended to entertain, publicly and lewdly, drunk and dissolute men. As an example, Riḍā referred not to Umm Kulthūm, whose fame as a singer was growing, but to "the foreign woman" who exhibited her body while singing for strange men.[86] Yes, Cairo had jazz. European and American artists performed at what *The Spectator* called the "one or two cabarets of repute."[87] By the roaring twenties, however, singing was becoming a "respectable" profession for Egyptian women too. They could perform in concert halls and at wedding parties for mixed audiences and without always hiding behind veils. The popularity of their voices soared, and records of their songs could be heard in every trendy coffeehouse.[88] Rather than the music itself, it was the new social dynamics that came with popular music in the era of mechanical reproduction that troubled Riḍā. Whatever disc played on the gramophone, he wanted Muslims to maintain traditional gender roles.

The Qurʾan in New and Old Media

Thinking in general about Riḍā's gramophone fatwas over the span of his career, they appear progressive economically, conservative socially, and ambivalent religiously. He had no problem with the cross-cultural trade in records of the Qurʾan, and he expressed no qualms about the new profession of gramophone operator. He did scoff at the frivolous desires of the masses. Instead of criticizing mass production and popular consumption, however, he dwelled on the advantages to adopting the modern invention, which he regarded as instrumental for the orthodox, missionary goal of disseminating the Qurʾan (in perfect Arabic) to remote places. In his ideal world, the machine would be used mainly for religious edification. In the real world, it was mainly used, as he recognized, for musical entertainment. What disturbed him in particular—because he had an old-fashioned, patriarchal view of gender roles—was the fact that the technology's affordances made it exciting for Muslim communities to gather for mixed social events devoted to sensual enjoyment. Despite this concern, his commitment to the idea that Islam was an easy, convenient religion, coupled with his opposition to restrictive legislation against "modern" commodities, translated into judicial restraint: a disciplined effort to refrain from imposing a ban on an instrument whose social uses troubled him.

The gramophone's most enthusiastic Muslim users, the *jadidis* of Kazan, had an irrepressibly sanguine attitude toward the future of religious practice in concert with new technology. They tried to dissolve whatever tension existed between old and new media for recording and transmitting the word of God. This point brings us to Friedrich A. Kittler's landmark study of modern media, *Gramophone, Film, Typewriter*, which presents the Qurʾan as the epitome of writing that celebrates "the storage monopoly of the God who invented it." By this expression, Kittler alludes to the Qurʾan's self-reflexive messages and refers to the way that texts preserved for posterity the establishment of Islam as a religion of the book. He recounts the process by which a "miraculously alphabetized" prophet figured out "all too soon" how to decipher the divine pen's revelations, brought down from the seventh heaven. He mentions as well the traditional account of the preservation of these revelations on "primitive surfaces," such as leather and bones, before their collection in a recension. In Kittler's view, the Qurʾan is, like other holy books, the emblem of an era when mediated communications, dominated by cultures of readers, happened exclusively through the "homogenous medium of writing." This homogeneity started to break down at the end of the nineteenth century—with the historic rise of the gramophone, which signaled "the demise of writing's storage monopoly" and the beginning of a media revolution. Since the gramophone communicated invisible, vanishing sounds, it heralded a shift away from the "sacredness" that authors and readers had attached to the visibility and materiality of words on a page. It competed with the book, in Kittler's conception, as an alternative medium designed to store and transmit not texts but sounds.[89]

But the battle in Kazan did not pit the profane instrument against the sacred book as if they were contestants in a struggle between media new and old. The contest rather turned on the difference between live and recorded recitations, both of which involved the oral transmission of "the book," *al-kitāb*, whose everlasting primacy nobody called into question. The gramophone did not transform readers into listeners of the Qur᾿an, for oral performances of the text had been part and parcel of the culture of Kazan long before the instrument's invention. Its ardent advocates certainly did not perceive the gramophone records in question, which reproduced the recitations of native Arabic speakers, as somehow or other competing with printed copies of the Qur᾿an; they perceived them as competing with local Tatar reciters.

Qur᾿anic discs stimulated Muslim audiences to think about rites of purity and rites of prostration. From reluctant adopters to resolute reactionaries, a wide range of actors worried about the effect of these records on the customary code of behavior during recitations and about the possible defilement of a sacred object: the secular commerce and casual handling of shellac discs that contained miraculous signs in their grooves. Riḍā wanted Muslims to preserve the tradition of prostrations at key verses, which commemorated, with the most humble of gestures, gratitude to God for his bestowal of the revelations. But he had no problem with the global capitalist system that brought the records to the markets of Muslims, and he dismissed concerns about material impurity.

Indeed, he found no reason to defend the practice of restoring the body to a pure, prayerful state in anticipation of handling the incarnation of divine words. Perhaps, under the influence of a regime that gloried in the "modern" virtue of hygiene while mocking "primitive" notions of purity, he came to dismiss the importance of this rite. Or perhaps, with his foray into metaphysics, he wanted Muslims to move beyond a carnal, superstitious affection for scripture, the surrounding of mechanical reproductions with an aura of taboo, and to behold instead the spirit and meaning of the book's injunctions. One way or the other, when he thought about the problem of ritual impurity in relation to the cross-cultural commerce in scriptural discs, he expressed no reluctance to break with the rules of the past.

If his conservative temperament made him waver for a moment from the concessions that he had made as a reluctant modernist, he nonetheless remained steadfast in his commitment to a single goal: the appropriation of a modern technology for Islamic ends, for the propagation of Arabic and the Qur'an. The significance of his verdict lies in his recognition of the gramophone as a flexible medium for communication that could be used—from his moralistic perspective—for good or bad. Therefore, when placed on trial, the instrument could not be subjected, in all fairness, to a single sentence. A righteous judge could legitimately criticize a society's impious uses, yet he had no ground for banning the machine altogether, given the potential for pious uses. This discriminating relation to controversial machines would eventually become, after some growing pains, the hallmark approach of "Islamists" to new media: an approach embraced in the late twentieth century by both Muslim Brotherhood propagandists and global Salafist missionaries.

But Riḍā did not reach this conclusion about the gramophone's promise for the future of Islam by reflecting in the abstract. The very idea derived from a new material reality: the recording of Qur'anic reciters by companies like Odeon. Furthermore, instead of addressing this development independently, he did so in response to questions that originated in social debates. From Kazan to Singapore, fatwa seekers prompted him to examine the matter as an expert jurist and as an external arbitrator. Of course, Riḍā made intellectual contributions to Islam's material reformation. But it is essential to recognize the critical role that many other actors—beginning with Emile Berliner, the Muslim moderns who first adopted Odeon's discs, and the authors of legal questions—played in the process of realigning religion toward modernity's new sounds.

6

Telegraphs, Photographs, Railways, Law Codes

Tools of Empire, Tools of Islam

In 1904 a Punjabi physician, scholar, and mufti named Nūr al-Dīn sent Egypt's Grand Mufti his own version of Samuel Morse's famous electromagnetic message, "What hath God wrought?" He had been pondering the admissibility of testimony delivered by telegraph, which he linked in a cryptic and indefinite way to Christians and Magians. By "Magians" the Punjabi doctor likely meant to designate Parsis as well as Hindus and Sikhs, who jointly formed around half of the population of Punjab Province under the British Raj.[1] Was he uncertain about the trustworthiness of a telegram transmitted by non-Muslim operators who purported to convey a Muslim's testimony? Or was he uncertain about the probity of testimony given by a non-Muslim witness not orally but telegraphically? He did not make the specific reason for his question clear. Regardless, he asked for a ruling on the evidentiary value of telegraphic testimony that he associated in some capacity with non-Muslims.[2]

The Punjabi personage—whose name, titles, location, command of Arabic, and knowledge of Islamic law suggest a unique identity—also posed to ʿAbduh a significant question about Muslim participation in a colonial legal system.[3] Presumably, the Punjabi doctor was none other than Mawlawi Ḥakīm Nūr al-Dīn (d. 1914), a high-ranking member of a messianic Islamic group, the Aḥmadiyya Muslim Community: the very man who would become, in 1908, the community's caliph. Four years earlier, around the time that Nūr al-Dīn wrote to ʿAbduh for fatwas, a lawyer for the Aḥmadiyya community had to defend the messiah, Mīrzā Ghulām Aḥmad, from criminal charges; the messiah had been sued for defamation in a district court.[4]

Perhaps this experience led Nūr al-Dīn to ask the Grand Mufti for a ruling on the involvement of Muslim justices in the colony's secular legal system: "May the Muslim employed by the English make a judgment in accordance with the English codes (*bi-l-qawānīn*), although they contain laws that conflict with the divine revelations?"[5] More likely, however, what inspired the question was the Aḥmadiyya's conciliatory relationship to British rule. Ghulām Aḥmad took pride in the education and respectability of the movement's members, boasting that some held "high office under government."[6] His lawyer, a graduate of Forman Christian College, came from a family that knew much about accommodation; his grandfather had served as Lahore's chief Muslim judge under Sikh rule. At the same time, the question definitely suggested reservations: the feeling, articulated by internal or external voices, that in an ideal world Muslim justices would judge according to the shariʿa.[7]

This chapter addresses various questions that Muslims in *al-Manār*'s network had about instruments that embodied the expanding capacities of the imperial state. Principally, it focuses on their religious and legal concerns about the utility of the Ottoman, British, and French telegraphic systems. Could Muslims use these systems of communication, especially if they were controlled by Christian operators, to transmit legal evidence that conformed to the evidentiary guidelines of the shariʿa or news about the timing of Muslim rituals? In addition, this chapter pays some attention to the Ottoman construction of the Ḥijāz railway, which served to transport pilgrims from Damascus to Medina; the Russian Empire's initiative to take photographs of imams for identification and surveillance purposes; and constitutions and legal codes. What binds together this odd assortment of instruments? All of them entangled Muslim subjects in the growing webs of the imperial state in the late nineteenth and early twentieth centuries.[8]

When Riḍā responded to these questions, he did it with an enthusiasm for the technological and legal instruments of empires that was practically boundless. The analysis of his fatwas about these instruments should lead to a reassessment of his political perspective before World War I. A reassessment is needed because, although historians have studied Riḍā's politics extensively, they have done so in a technological vacuum, without grasping his appreciation of the material affordances that empires introduced into the environment.

Riḍā's political thought has received considerable scholarly attention because of his high-profile campaigns for the restoration of the caliphate, for Syrian independence, and for the liberation of the Arabian Peninsula. The main focus has been on the interwar period, when Arab movements of self-determination gathered momentum. But historians have also examined Riḍā's political ideas and initiatives before World War I, partly to assess changes and continuities in his thought. Thus, one historian analyzed his fin-de-siècle proposal for a unified

Muslim front "against European encroachments" as well as his expression, around 1900, of a sentiment described as "Arab religious nationalism."[9] Another historian devoted an article to Riḍā's foundation of "the first and perhaps the only society in the period before the outbreak of World War I" that strove to establish a single, independent state in the Ottoman Empire's Arab provinces. This was the Society of the Arab Federation, a secret society formed in 1911 to unify the lands of the Arabs in a struggle for freedom from Ottoman imperialism.[10]

Riḍā's nationalistic pronouncements and activities had some importance in their time, but their historical significance has been magnified by a teleology that has been oriented toward the rise of nation-states.[11] It is essential to remember, however, that for most of his life he lived in a world of empires. This world gave him the opportunity to examine critically diverse "imperial repertories," to compare and contrast the different strategies that empires chose for incorporating Arab or Muslim peoples and for including or excluding Islamic law.[12] His political horizons were vast and distant; they were above all shaped by his experiences as an Arab-Muslim subject of the Ottoman and British Empires, by his resentment of French colonialism, and by his impressions of Dutch and Russian imperialism. In fact, until his participation in the making of the Arab Kingdom of Syria and his representation of the Syrian right to self-determination before the League of Nations, Riḍā had had neither a reason nor an opportunity to formulate concrete, pragmatic thoughts about the ideal arrangement of religious and political authority in the constitution of an Arab nation-state.[13] Before this Wilsonian turn, he dreamed not so much about the foundation of an Arab-Muslim nation-state as about the foundation of an Arab-Muslim empire. His political and religious vision was an imperialistic vision.

The telegraph, a technology that characterized imperial power in the late nineteenth and early twentieth centuries, ushered a revolution in communications not only for the state but also for Riḍā's own industry: the newspaper industry.[14] *Al-Manār*'s global reach depended in part on the ability to receive messages from all corners of the networked world with dispatch. Telegraph wires and stations allowed his journal to gather news and urgent fatwa requests from far-flung places. By publishing responses swiftly, his journal made every effort to remain current and valuable to foreign subscribers. The telegraph was thus an extremely useful technology for pan-Islamic communications, enabling believers to exchange views swiftly across political and geographical boundaries. Riḍā himself hinted at its significance for his journalistic enterprise by frequently publishing his telegraphic address (as well as his postal address) on the cover of *al-Manār*. Early issues of his magazine included a roundup called "The

Telegraphic News." But he had another reason, too, for favoring telecommunications: he was a great advocate of what Daniel Hedrick called "the tools of empire."

The Ḥijāz Railway: An Imperial Islamic Dream

Before we return to telegraphs, which have a complex history as Islamic legal objects, it is worth illustrating Riḍā's sunny attitude to the nexus of religion, technology, and empire with the very simple case of the Ḥijāz Railway. In 1900 Sultan ʿAbdülḥamīd II issued an order for the construction of a railroad to connect the Ottoman Empire to the holy cities of Arabia. The train would enable pilgrims boarding at the terminal in Damascus to reach Mecca more quickly and safely than ever before. The sultan depicted the initiative as an imperial Islamic enterprise through and through: not only because the final goal was to connect the capital of the Ottoman Empire's Syrian vilayet to Islam's birthplace in the Ḥijāzī vilayet but also because of the developmental plan to rely only on Muslims to construct it. In the late nineteenth century, the Ottoman Empire had been forced to depend heavily on European experts to build its network of train tracks and telegraph lines. By contrast, the plan in this case was for Muslim laborers and engineers to carry out the work by themselves, without any assistance from foreigners or Christians. What is more, if Muslim pilgrims had chafed at the mistreatment that they had endured on European steamships led by non-Muslim captains, those boarding the Ḥijāz train would be able to travel and visit Medina and Mecca with pride, enchanted by the idea that a Muslim conductor would be driving the engine. In addition to a religious advantage, the Ḥijāz train also offered an obvious political advantage. It would facilitate the Ottoman Empire's locomotion, allowing it to extend more effectively its administrative power and military control into the Arabian provinces along the Red Sea. The only problem was that to fulfill this wonderful and expensive project, new compulsory taxes did not suffice; the empire wanted Muslim donors to contribute money voluntarily too.

This grand enterprise captivated Riḍā. He encouraged his magazine's readers to make charitable contributions to bring it to fruition. The love of God and his prophet, he entreated, should inspire generosity. Muslims should receive a reward in the afterlife for financing the railway to the Kaʿba. Poetically, he transformed the train tracks into God's path. He argued that defensive jihad—which he defined as striving in the path of God by spending money for Islam's sake—was worthier than offensive jihad. Inspired, he pronounced almsgiving to build "this iron railroad" a venerable sunna, or tradition, "created by our Lord Protector, the Caliph, the Grand Sultan," whose enterprise Muslims should assist monetarily in order to earn a divine recompense.[15]

Believers gave alms and workers laid down tracks, but the ideal of self-sufficiency—the drive to rely exclusively on Ottoman goods and Muslim workers—gave way to pragmatic accommodations. To expedite the project, Ottoman officials contracted with a German railroad engineer, Heinrich Meissner, who in turn relied on an experienced staff of German and Belgian as well as Ottoman engineers. Hundreds of skilled Italian, Greek, Montenegrin, and Egyptian builders were hired to reinforce the Ottoman Army's workforce. The naval arsenal in Istanbul succeeded in making a mosque car and several first-class passenger cars independently. However, it quickly became apparent that purchasing rails abroad would be less expensive and more expeditious. In the end, most of the manufactured goods required were shipped from Germany, Belgium, and the United States. These adjustments were made, as William Ochsenwald has shown in *The Hijaz Railroad*, in the interests of efficiency and lower costs.[16]

A key religious accommodation was maintained, however, to honor Muslim sensibilities about sacred space: only Muslim workers were permitted to work on the long southern track, the 540 kilometers from the station in al-Akhḍar to the terminal in the Ḥijāz. The train, as things turned out, never quite reached God's house in Mecca. But the tracks did connect Damascus to Medina by rail; and the engine made its inaugural voyage in the summer of 1908. The train continued to run, with inevitable interruptions, until the great disruptions of World War I, in spite of the fact that Arab rebels against the extension of the Ottoman state repeatedly attacked the imperial infrastructure.[17] Dreams of restoration and completion continued, however, after the fall of the Ottoman Empire. Unifying scholars from Palestine to India, the Ḥijāz Railway would figure as a topic of discussion during the international Islamic congresses, which Riḍā of course championed, that convened in Mecca and Jerusalem in 1926 and 1931.[18]

The sultan never had to summon clerics to bless this project with fatwas. Given the scrupulous care taken to mobilize an all-Muslim workforce in the forbidden zones of Arabia, the project never became religiously controversial. Quite the contrary, it stimulated admiration for the Ottoman Empire in the Syrian and Ḥijāzī provinces and in the Egyptian khedivate, where newspapers campaigned for voluntary contributions.[19] In the eyes of Arab reformers like Riḍā, heirs to the Tanẓimāt mentality, the passage toward modernity very much depended on investments by the state in costly infrastructures such as steam trains. The Ḥijāz Railway stood, in their eyes, for the technological realization of an imperial Islamic dream.

The Ottoman Empire's Capitulations to European Corporations

Other railway and tramway projects in the Ottoman Empire's Arab provinces did generate some religious and political controversy. The problem, as a fatwa seeker from Damascus explained it in 1912, lay with the nature of the capitulations that the caliph had offered "foreign companies." Were these European companies safeguarded corporations, protected by a treaty, or were they enemies? If their owners entered "our territory" and demanded concessions from "our government" by coercive methods, did the shariʿa guarantee "their rights" of possession? The man who asked Riḍā these questions, a certain Muḥammad Jamāl Efendī Sibṭ al-Qawādrī, enclosed a pamphlet by a local shaykh who had urged his followers to dispossess the corporate European invaders.

"The goods of the foreigners in our lands are permitted to the Muslims," the Syrian shaykh had declared. Briefly, Riḍā explained that the "charlatan of a shaykh" had given swindlers the license to seize as much as they could of the property of the tramway and railway companies. He associated his position with the dangerous politics of "derogating the Christians" and provoking their estrangement.[20]

The radical shaykh's idea was to deprive European corporations of security of protection. Their goods had, in his view, the same legal status as the goods of infidels that warriors for the faith could justifiably seize in the pursuit of jihad. Yes, European companies conducted their business in a Muslim territory under the cover of "diplomatic" agreements, but the fiercest opponents of the capitulations distinguished between the legitimate safe conduct traditionally granted to individual foreign merchants and the rash of privileged concessions that European Powers had wrested from the Sublime Porte in the throes of reform. Opposition to these treaties broke out into the open in 1908 with the restoration of constitutional rule and the abolition of censorship, and the press would cover the issue intensely until the abrogation of the capitulations in 1914.[21] The belligerent rhetoric of the 1912 fatwa request was part and parcel of this rebellion against European dominance.

The concessions granted by the Ottoman Empire to railroad companies were extraordinary, and their financial and material consequences were profound. The sultan essentially "mortgaged his empire" to German and French bankers when he signed the Baghdad Railway convention, which included provisions to extend branches to Syrian cities.[22] One article of the convention permitted the company to acquire iron and coal as well as "engines, carriages, and wagons" without paying taxes or tariffs. Other articles granted the company permission to transform the landscape. They granted it the right to dig quarries and "gravel-pits for ballast" wherever it seemed necessary and to acquire wood and timber from the empire's forests. Since the enterprise was defined as a "public utility," the treaty also gave the company the authority to take over the lands of "private persons . . . in accordance with the law of expropriation." Destruction and expropriation were critical aspects of this European-Ottoman enterprise.[23]

As a result of these and other developments, Damascus become an imperial construction zone. In 1903 Belgian and French capitalists funded a company, worth six million francs, to develop an electrical tramway system in the city.[24] Streets were widened for the new tramlines, and wires were attached to connect lampposts to the power station that lay beyond Victoria Bridge. In 1907 its three generators illuminated 1,442 Edison lamps, and Damascus entered into the era of electric light.[25] In addition, the company installed more than ten thousand fixtures for private customers, and it placed on the streets of the city nineteen trolleys and six trailers.[26] These were some of the things that Damascenes thought about when they debated the merits of the shaykh's expropriation proposal.

Damascenes had another reason, too, for contemplating the proposal from a unique vantage point. No provincial capital experienced the difference between two approaches to development as sharply as did Damascus.[27] It was the terminal for two rival train systems: the Ḥijāz Railway, which was an independent Ottoman project, and a competing French concession.[28] In addition to pilgrims, the Ḥijāz Railway carried tons of wheat, salt, and sugar, within Syria, and it charged a lower, preferential rate for shipping these commodities than did the French line. Commercial competition between the two systems, with their parallel train tracks, was nearly a zero-sum game. The French company pressed the Ottomans to pay compensation for the loss of business that resulted from the availability of an alternative track. And in 1911 it decided to form the "Committee for the Defense of French Interests in the Orient," which dedicated itself to the expansion of France's empire in the region.[29]

The radical shaykh's fatwa authorizing Muslim rebels to usurp the goods of the European train and tram companies emerged in this political environment and in relation to these material developments. It was not necessarily a nationalistic Syrian response to European dominance. Arguably, it was a defiant Ottoman Muslim response to foreign capitulations, which came at a time when there was already concrete evidence, thanks to the shiny train tracks that linked Damascus to Medina, of the virtues of imperial Islamic protectionism.[30]

As an enlightened free trader and as a defender of the rule of law, Riḍā of course decried the shaykh's "baseless" interpretation of the capitulations. "There is no doubt," he said, "about [the validity] of these pacts, even if [the signatories] are our enemies." The Muslim world was not at war with any

European country, he clarified, with the exception of Italy, which had recently occupied the Ottoman provinces of Tripolitania, Fezzan, and Cyrenaica in North Africa as well as the Dodecanese Islands in the Aegean Sea. But treaties must be honored whether they are signed with an enemy or a friend. If a caliph, a ruler, or even, according to some jurists, a laborer or a slave, grants foreign enemies the right to enter safely into a Muslim polity, then other Muslims in that state need to respect the agreement. The benefits to society of making and honoring such pacts with foreign traders seemed clear and self-evident to him. Only the sovereign ruler or the leading executive authority had the prerogative to nullify them: "Were it not so, the [entire legal] order would collapse," dealing the commonweal a staggering blow. "Were our just, sacred law to permit" the easy abolition of treaties, "no country on earth would trust our [commercial] contracts and our assurances of protection." Reneging on international obligations would furthermore present the European Powers with an excuse "to unite for our extirpation." Without a doubt, they would conquer and partition the Ottoman Empire's Arab provinces.[31]

The political logic behind Riḍā's defense of the capitulations regime was not uncommon. The leader of the Egyptian National Party at this time, Muḥammad Farīd (d. 1919), had similarly declared in 1908, while lobbying in Paris: "The English, in order to gain the support of the Europeans of Egypt, shock them by raising the specter of fanaticism and xenophobia . . . Yet our program includes respect for capitulations and treaties . . . The capitulations prevent the total absorption of Egypt by England." In this respect the capitulations, by maintaining internal competition among the Great Powers, appeared as the legal bulwark that stood between limited sovereignty and outright colonialism.[32] Making the same political calculation, Riḍā defended the Sublime Porte's suzerainty: its power to make and break treaties that granted foreign corporations extraterritorial privileges and generated electric sparks.

An Imperial Technology for Muslim Moderns: A Very Short History of Telegraphs

Like steam trains, telegraphs were not a technological novelty at the beginning of the twentieth century, when the Punjabi doctor wrote to Egypt's Grand Mufti. The East India Company had completed its first telegraph line in 1855, linking military cantonments. Within two years, during the Sepoy Rebellion, a telegram would play a heroic role, according to an English major, in "the salvation of the Punjab."[33] Also in 1855, under Saʿīd Pasha of Egypt, a British firm, the Eastern Telegraph Company, received a concession to erect posts, string wires, and lay down submarine cables to link Alexandria to Cairo, Crete, and Istanbul. Eventually, according to the plan, the network would extend all the way to Bombay.[34] The Ottoman Empire made an early commitment to telegraphy as well. During the Crimean War, it approved a French plan for the construction of a line that linked Istanbul to Şumnu via Edirne, and the first telegram through this line was sent in 1855 as well.

But inter-imperial agreements had to be reached and wires had to be extended, post by post, so the process of expanding the telegraph network to fulfill both Ottoman and British imperial ambitions took some time. In the wake of the Indian rebellion of 1857, the British government urgently pressed the Sublime Porte to sign concessions with a British company that would allow it to establish a line of communications between England and India. The Ottoman state had its own priorities, however, and it wanted to control the development. Eventually, it decided to hire teams of British geographers and engineers to build a network.[35]

In 1864 the British and Ottoman Empires ratified a convention that defined the workings of a parallel telegraph system. Negotiations specified the number of English persons (no more than fifty) who could staff a telegraph office "on Ottoman territory," albeit under the "exclusive orders of a British stationmaster." "Desirous that the expeditious transit of the Indo-European messages over its territory should be rendered still more satisfactory," the Ottoman government promised to inaugurate an office in Constantinople devoted exclusively to Indian telegrams and to employ there "officials who are thoroughly conversant with the English language." Meanwhile, the government of India agreed "to lay down, at its own expense, a submarine telegraphic cable" that would connect with the Ottoman land line at Shaṭṭ al-ʿArab. At this confluence of rivers there would be a joint station with separate but proximate British and Ottoman compartments. An elaborate legal and diplomatic framework thus arose to facilitate, in the interests of each sprawling empire, rapid long-distance communications.[36]

By the mid-sixties, as a result of this and other examples of inter-imperial cooperation, the British were able to send telegrams from London to Karachi.[37] Among other things, to secure submarine cables in the Gulf, they had to negotiate with the sultan of Muscat and Oman, which led to the establishment of Telegraph Island—a lonely outpost guarded by a gunboat in the Strait of Hormuz.[38]

Expansions of the Ottoman grid took place over several decades. Tripoli, where Riḍā conducted his studies, became a central node in the system, and the road from his birthplace, Qalamūn, to Tripoli actually followed the coastal wires for a long stretch. By the turn of the century, the Ottoman network had grown to 755 stations, which were used to dispatch annually more than two million telegrams to destinations within the empire and nearly half-a-million telegrams abroad.[39] There was no rush, however, to extend wires to the Ottoman provinces in the Arabian Peninsula. Medina joined the Ottoman network forty years after Damascus, in 1901.[40] As for Riyadh, a remote desert city in a region that defied Ottoman plans for expansion, it had to wait still three more decades, until 1932, for its first telegraph station: a wireless tower for radio transmissions.[41]

Even though the British-Ottoman conventions placed limits on the presence of foreigners in the name of imperial sovereignty, telegraphy became a "unique space for inter-cultural experimentation." By the 1870s, at the busiest telegraph offices in the Ottoman Empire, French, British, Greek, Turkish, Arab, and Armenian experts interacted with each other and with a varied clientele of local residents and foreign travelers in order to realize an enterprise that required diverse linguistic and technical skills.[42]

The medium's linguistic flexibility facilitated its adoption by state and society. French was the original language of official telegraphic communications in the Ottoman Empire. But authorities eventually admitted thirty-seven languages, including Turkish and Arabic, which required no technical adjustment other than adapting the Morse code.[43] Cities like Damascus had two stations: one for internal Ottoman communications in Arabic or Turkish, the other for international communications in what Thomas Cook's *Handbook* called "any of the principal modern languages, particularly English, French, and German."[44] Similarly, under the auspices of the Railways Department, Egypt operated two telegraph systems, which separated domestic from foreign transmissions. By the beginning of the twentieth century, the internal system boasted over three hundred stations. Demand for its use was high enough to justify installing quadruplex wires, which allowed operators to transmit four signals simultaneously between the principal stations. These wires were used to send telegrams day and night in every European language. By 1907 the system was so firmly established that the state used it to send nearly 3.5 million "public service" communications, while citizens used it to send nearly 2.5 million commercial or personal messages—mostly in Arabic.[45]

As the utility and popularity of this new medium became apparent, Muslim adopters pressed muftis directly or indirectly to justify the European invention and legalize diverse uses. It mattered to some clerics, especially in the late nineteenth century, that God had chosen non-Muslims for the invention of the technology. Furthermore, the degree to which Europeans participated in the extension and maintenance of the infrastructure in the twentieth century (through decades-long concessions, the importation of wires and machines, and the provision of surveyors, engineers, directors, and foreign-language operators) remained a thorn in the side of apologists, exclusivists, and protectionists.[46]

Nevertheless, jurists—even early respondents—recognized that the technology did not belong inextricably to its non-Muslim inventors. A Malay publisher who studied Islamic law in both Mecca and Cairo, Aḥmad al-Faṭānī (d. 1908), praised the telegraph, the submarine, and the hot air balloon as examples of "wondrous things" that God had bestowed upon humanity.[47] Along these lines, too, an anonymous Ottoman author penned a theodicy of sorts to explain why God had chosen to make steamships, industrial factories, and telegraphs manifest to infidels first. Regarding these innovations as the products of God's omnipotence, he argued that telegraphs were miraculous inventions that God had "brought to light through sinners and unbelievers." This theological construct allowed him to recognize the telegram as an admissible document in a legal court, a document given the same evidentiary weight as an ordinary letter.[48] His openness to telegraphy was due, of course, to the manifest adoption of the medium by Muslim legal actors.

Telegraphic Evidence and Islamic Law Under the British Raj

Early twentieth-century fatwas focused not on the legality of telegraphy in a general sense but on more technical questions about the dependability of the medium for Islamic ritual and legal communications.[49] This point brings us back to Nūr al-Dīn's confounding question about the admissibility of telegraphic testimony, which he related in an ill-defined way to Magians and Christians.

The Islamic legal tradition established, as Nūr al-Dīn must have known, a hierarchy of evidence. In theory, courts of law operating according to sharīʿa rules had to privilege oral testimony by reliable witnesses over any other type of evidence. These courts could also admit written documents as well as expert interpretations of material clues in many cases. But oral rather than written evidence set the gold standard.[50] The social status of witnesses was a crucial factor, too, for determining the admissibility and the veracity of the evidence in accordance with traditional Islamic rules. Upright male Muslims were considered the ideal witnesses, possessing full personhood unless they were slaves. Free Muslim women's testimony, when admissible, was considered exactly half as reliable as that of free Muslim men. Non-Muslims could testify against each other, but they lacked the legal right to testify against Muslims.[51]

The Punjabi doctor specified neither the religion nor the gender of the witness, but he wrapped two questions about legal evidence into one: first, a question about the admissibility of testimony submitted in the form of a telegram, and, second, a question about the trustworthiness of Christian or Magian telegraph clerks. While conflating the two questions, however, he was specifically interested in the problem of technological mediation across a confessional boundary. Perhaps, therefore, he assumed that a telegram purportedly dictated by a Muslim witness and transmitted by Muslim telegraphers was admissible as written evidence in an Islamic court; he apparently wanted to know if testimony dictated by a Muslim witness but transmitted by non-Muslim telegraphers was admissible too.

To appreciate fully Nūr al-Dīn's question about telegraphic evidence as well as his question about Muslims judging in accordance with English codes, it is critical to review briefly a few aspects of the history of religion and law in British India. The most important thing to bear in mind is that British rule gave a sharp edge to the distinction, which had existed in some form under the Mughal emperors, between imperial and divine law. Under British rule, Muslim subjects had reason to view these bodies of law as incompatible, rather than complementary, in many respects, for the colonial state contrasted secular with religious legislation, and it emphasized the need for codification as well as the inferiority of indigenous testimony.

The history of this contrast between Islamic law and English law originated in the distinction, introduced during Company rule and continued by the British Raj, between "personal" and "public" law. On the public side, the British government introduced several reforms that would have some bearing on Nūr al-Dīn's questions. Beginning in the early nineteenth century, muftis assisting British judges as "law officers" in criminal cases were instructed to issue fatwas on the supposition that the testimony of non-Muslims was equivalent to the testimony of Muslims.[52] Similarly, if justices who happened to be Muslim heard criminal cases under Crown rule, they had to rule—exactly as did their Christian or Hindu counterparts—on the basis of the Criminal Procedure Code of 1861.

The shariʿa, which India's first governor-general had called "the laws of the Koran with respect to the Mahomedans," could be applied only to the "personal" realm of communal religion and family tradition.[53] On the basis of "Anglo-Mahomedan" translations of Islamic law, British judges adjudicated Muslims' inheritance disputes and divorce proceedings. As judges, or *qazis*, Muslim experts on the sacred law participated officially, too, in the interpretation and application of "personal" law in India both before the 1864 abolition of the office and after its partial reinstatement in 1880. Whitley Stokes, a barrister who participated in the drafting of codes for India, described the haphazard procedure that had existed in the provincial, *mofussil* courts, where the customary law drawn from Charles Hamilton's 1791 translation of a great twelfth-century compendium, Burhān al- Dīn al-Marghīnānī's *Hedaya*, competed with English textbooks and English barristers' arguments during debates about the admissibility of evidence.[54] The authors of the Indian Evidence Act of 1872 aimed to bring such deliberations to an end.

Governing both public and personal law, this act sidelined Anglo-Muslim as well as Anglo-Hindu evidentiary rules and norms. It maintained the admissibility of oral evidence to prove facts, but it affirmed the superiority of written evidence. An entire chapter of the act was devoted to "the exclusion of oral by documentary evidence." One article made it clear that oral testimonials that served simply to corroborate commercial contracts were superfluous and therefore inadmissible, and it excluded oral interpretations of "ambiguous or defective" documents.[55] This system differed greatly from previous ones, and not by accident. British lawmakers deliberately shaped their evidentiary standards in opposition to their construction of Muslim and Hindu judicial procedures after years of endless suspicions about the alleged mendacity of indigenous witnesses.[56]

Enthusiastic arguments for the admissibility and reliability of material evidence—new things like forensic photographs and criminal fingerprints—arose in this very context, as Christopher Pinney has shown in *Camera Indica*. Victorian scientists and colonial magistrates described native subjects as "illiterate, disputatious, wily, deceitful," and prone to advance "slippery facts." Through such negative characterizations, they hoped to persuade ministers and enforcers of the law to adopt these technologies systematically.[57]

This historical context also inspired the confidence and trust that British lawmakers placed in telegraphic communications. The Indian Evidence Act of 1872 instructed courts to presume that a telegram corresponds with the message "delivered for transmission at the office from which the message purports to be sent." Judges had to presume that the text of the telegram was genuine, an authentic declaration as opposed to a forged or fraudulent message fabricated by the telegraph company's clerks.[58] The irony is that the technology was fallible: communications depended on the decipherment of signals and codes and the interpretation of ciphers and abbreviations. Errors were common.[59] Perhaps for this reason, a Punjabi judge refused to heed a telegram that had authorized a public prosecutor to withdraw from a 1902 criminal case against a certain Haidar. The telegram had misspelled the name of the accused, Sadar, and the judge decided that a telegraphic communication did not deserve to be called a "written instruction." An appellate court disagreed with the judge's reservation, however. It held that "definite instructions" could be obtained by telegram; there was no reason to wait for a signed, handwritten letter.[60]

The Indian Evidence Act of 1872 had nevertheless distinguished between original documents and mechanical reproductions, and it considered photographs and placards admissible, though only as a form of "secondary evidence."[61] A comparative encyclopedia of American and English law implied that the bar for admitting telegraphic evidence was equally high. It explained that wired communications were ordinarily but not necessarily identical to the original handwritten message given to the telegraph operator at the originating station. For this reason, it concluded: "A telegram is not admissible as evidence in the absence of proof of its authenticity, either by proof of the handwriting where the original message is offered, or by other evidence of its genuineness." If the original text had been lost or destroyed, then the court could admit the message—without, however, valuing it as if it were the best form of evidence.[62] The Indian Evidence Act did not address this specific issue. But if its framers thought of telegrams as mechanical reproductions comparable to photographs and placards, then the same rules of evidence applied to them too.

All of this means that Islamic rules of evidence had little or no effect in Indian courts of law after 1872. Justice Syed Mahmood (d. 1903), a London-trained barrister who served on the High Court of Allahabad and translated the Indian Evidence Act into Urdu, often needed to explain to the chief justice "the facts of native life" to help him "appreciate the weight of the evidence of native witnesses" and the importance of "vernacular documents." However, Justice Mahmood was the first to recognize the abrogation of Islamic evidentiary laws: "At the present time, the criminal and civil courts are bound to administer the law of evidence promulgated by the English government when making rulings in every kind of matter whether it relates to inheritance or marriage or any other kind of property dispute or any other right."[63]

Given this historical context, the answer to Nūr al-Dīn's question about telegraphy could have no influence on the outcome of any formal legal procedure under the British Raj. The Punjabi doctor might have raised it to acquire theoretical knowledge rather than practicable advice. Government-appointed Muslim judges presiding over personal suits had been empowered by the Kazis Act of 1880 to officiate at marriages, confirm divorces, attest to deeds of transfer, and perform diverse rites and ceremonies. These judges likely evaluated wired testimony in various circumstances. Although they needed to comply with the Indian Evidence Act, they were expected to discuss Islamic rules of evidence knowledgeably. Alternatively, Nūr al-Dīn wanted guidance for extraofficial Muslim arbitrators, who had the freedom to judge informally—in accordance with Islamic rather than colonial law. As a mufti in his own right, Nūr al-Dīn himself was in a position to offer such legal advice.[64] After all, he belonged to a generation of Punjabi scholars who championed a return to the shariʿa.

Preoccupied by other matters and too busy to answer, Egypt's Grand Mufti asked his young Syrian colleague to reply on his behalf. Riḍā did so, publishing his answers to the "Indian Questions" in a 1904 issue of *al-Manār*. He informed the Punjabi mufti that jurists do not use the term "*shahāda*," which suggests oral testimony, to refer to a telegraphic report (*khabar*). He then advised judges or arbitrators to treat telegrams as if they were a type of written evidence. He did not address explicitly any concern about mediation by non-Muslim telegraph clerks in communications between Muslims. But he did clarify that a telegraphic confession, an admission of guilt (*iqrār*) by a Christian or a Magian, was admissible in court. He also clarified that this kind of legal actor may testify against a person like him, thereby alluding to the formal exclusion of non-Muslims from testifying against Muslims.

The fatwa encouraged Muslim judges to allow "everything that might serve to clarify the truth" into their courts and, thus, to admit telegrams into evidence. This flexible approach to rules of evidence stemmed, Riḍā held, from the Qurʾan and the Muslim tradition. Nevertheless, judges had the duty to ponder the authenticity of reports sent through the wire; they needed to protect the integrity of their sentences, to guard against forgery and deceit. Riḍā acknowledged that at times they would have reasons to suspect that the purported author of a telegram did not, in fact, write or dictate the text submitted as evidence. He advised judges to learn from the government and merchants, who placed their trust in certified telegraphic communications.[65]

Newspapers and Telegrams for the Fast of Ramaḍān

Another question about new media, especially telegraphs and journals, sprung from doubts about their dependability for determining the timing of religious holidays. By tradition, a lunar calendar set the key dates. The oral tradition specifically instructed Muslims to begin and end the month of fasting, Ramaḍān, by sightings of the new moon. This advice worked fairly well without instruments or calculations—except under dark, cloudy skies that made the crescent invisible. To solve this problem and to help the Muslim community plan its celebrations, scheduled in advance, medieval astronomers developed methods to calculate the earliest appearance of the new crescent moon. These innovations inspired debates—long before the invention of new media—between those who preferred to rely on the astronomer and his instruments to predict the moon's cycles and those who preferred to rely on the muezzin and his naked eye, following scriptural injunctions.[66]

A new twist to that old story took place at the turn of the twentieth century, with increasing reliance by state and society on newspapers, telegraphs, and telephones to mark the beginning and the end of the annual fast. Eighteen days into the month of Ramaḍān of the year AH 1320, which coincided with December 19, 1902 CE, a deputy judge in a small Syrian town showed more "faith in lunar sightings than electronics," as Eugene Rogan put it, when he wrote to officials in Damascus to ask for "confirmation *by post* of the official end of Ramaḍān." The judge had already received a telegram to that effect. But al-Salṭ, the town where he lived, had only recently inaugurated its telegraph office—a station along the new electrical wire that connected Medina to Damascus. His response suggested the depth of local distrust in the medium and perhaps also a touch of hesitancy in accepting a directive from the central government prognosticating a future event.[67]

In this vein, too, Muqbil al-Dhakīr, the shaykh from the British protectorate of Bahrain who had requested a ruling on banknotes, wrote to Riḍā once more to ask whether Muslims should depend on newspapers to mark the first day of the month of abnegations. The shaykh reported that newspapers published abroad had notified the public that Ramaḍān would commence on a Friday, November 20, 1903. *Al-Manār* itself, printed in Cairo, had stamped this date on the cover of an earlier issue. Yet observers in "remote" regions, such as Iraq and the Persian Gulf, had sighted the new crescent moon the next evening, and they began counting the days of prescribed fasting from that point onward. When the next month's crescent moon is not visible, Muslim authorities simply declare the end of Ramaḍān after thirty days of fasting. The entire community then gathers to celebrate, in unity, a paramount feast: *ʿīd al-fiṭr*, the breaking of the fast. If believers begin fasting on different days, however, and atmospheric conditions make it impossible to see the waxing crescent at the expected time, then members of the community would end up celebrating the holiday on different days, in disunity and disarray. Could Riḍā solve the calendrical puzzle?

At stake was the authority of the press, whose announcements traversed the borders of states, to dictate the timing of one of Islam's most meaningful celebrations—in absolute disregard of the authority of local observers. Riḍā's solution, published two months after Ramaḍān, was for Muslim communities to defer to authorities in their own district. Bahrainis would thereby begin and end the fast together. Under no circumstances should they follow the schedule established in Basra, despite its proximity to Bahrain, because that city belongs to an Ottoman province. Nor should they follow the dictates of the Indian or

Egyptian press.[68] Riḍā did not urge his readers to forget about subjective moon sightings and embrace objective scientific methods. He thought it was ridiculous for citizens and officials to depend on complicated astronomical calculations and convoluted channels of communication. Islam was supposed to be an easy and accessible religion. Nevertheless, for the sake of social unity and religious uniformity, he thought that citizens should grant the state the power to decide the timing of feasts and fasts.[69]

A related question about the uneven impact of telecommunications on communal holidays arose in a colonial context in the Maghreb. A fatwa seeker from Tunis revealed to Riḍā the havoc that occurred in Tunisia when Muslims in several towns, acting upon news that reached them by telegraph and telephone, rushed to celebrate the end of Ramaḍān of 1909, while other Muslims waited for official confirmation from the capital's chief judge. As a result, some Tunisians began to feast whereas others continued to fast.

The fatwa seeker, one of the government's chief comptrollers at the time, had professional reasons to trust telecommunications. Highly competent in both French and Arabic, Muḥammad ibn al-Khawjah, better known as Belkhōja (d. 1943), began his administrative career as an interpreter and translator. Years after writing to *al-Manār*, he would gain some renown in Tunisia as a provincial governor and as a man of letters. But by 1910 he had already contributed many articles to a modernist Arabic newspaper, *al-Ḥāḍira* ("The Capital"), that tried to harmonize contemporary European and Islamic ideals; in addition, he had gained some distinction as a trusted mediator between French authorities and Tunisian elites. Flourishing as a bilingual bureaucrat who collaborated effectively with the colonial regime, he ended up having a remarkable career full of political and intellectual achievements.[70] Like other Young Tunisians at the time, Belkhōja was convinced that the old religious establishment lay at the root of many problems. Thus, in his fatwa request to Riḍā, he complained that the country's judges clung to "sacred principles." They rejected the telegraph because it was "in the hand of non-Muslims." And they rejected the telephone because callers' voices resembled each other, making it difficult to separate reliable from deceitful communications. He advocated, instead, the telegraph's adoption. The instrument, he argued, would facilitate communications between the central government and the fringes of the country, thus ushering religious festivals into modernity.[71]

Distrust of telecommunications in Tunisia stemmed not from an irrational fear of machines but from historical resentment of French technological dominance and exploitation. France had obtained a concession from the Bey of Tunis to lay down telegraph lines before 1860. Over the next few decades it would defend a monopoly over this technology, rebuffing British and Italian overtures to build a wider network in the region. The protectorate that it established in 1881 charged a bankrupt Tunisia for developing an infrastructure to send wires across land and sea, although the principal goal of this project was to link the metropole to its imperial outposts in order to facilitate French—rather than Tunisian—military, administrative, and commercial communications.[72] This helps to explain Tunisian resistance to the telegraph in certain quarters. Nomads rebelled against the process of colonial centralization by sabotaging telegraph lines. The *ʿulamāʾ* found the new communication systems useful.[73] But they suspected the privileged *colons* of technological manipulation, as the fatwa seeker suggests, in part because telephone and telegraph operations in the French protectorate were in the hands of Catholics.

Technological mediation by French Catholics meant that operators who had no intention to fast played an essential role in spreading the news of the new moon's appearance to a networked town. They were outsiders, suddenly empowered to play a role in an Islamic ritual process; in effect, they functioned as colonial messengers charged with the task of delivering the official signal to ceremonial heralds. No wonder that opponents of telegraphic announcements of the breaking of the fast of Ramaḍān spoke about the messages' transmission through "infidel" hands.

Riḍā's response broke with his tendencies to write his own fatwas and preach, as a Salafist, the virtue of freedom from loyalty to a school of law. Perhaps this departure from his inclinations had to do with his circumstances at the time, for he entertained the Tunisian request for a fatwa, originally mailed to Cairo, in Constantinople, where he was staying for an extended sojourn in an effort to procure Ottoman support to establish a progressive Islamic college. At any rate, he remained true to his values in one way: he lamented, as free-trade Salafist, that "most Muslims had come to dislike the ease and convenience of the religion" in contravention of Islam's fundamentals, the Qurʾan and the prophetic tradition known as the Sunna, which encouraged openness to new media. After this preamble, he quoted a lengthy fatwa on the subject of telegraphy by al-Azhar's Grand Shaykh at the time, Salīm al-Bishrī (d. 1917), who belonged, "like the majority of Tunisians," to the Maliki school of law. The implication was that Malikis should be able to listen to a legal authority from their own school of law. Years later, in 1922 and 1930, he would make a similar accommodation for Indian and Chinese petitioners, publishing for their benefit Ḥanafi fatwas written by him. In these three cases, his proclivity to tailor fatwas to local audiences clearly overpowered his insistence on the need to overcome the tradition of loyal affiliation (*taqlīd*) with a single school of law.

Al-Azhar's rector had issued the original fatwa for the benefit of the Malikis of the Sudan, an Anglo-Egyptian condominium with an impressive history of telegraphic developments. In the 1870s the state's British and Egyptian sovereigns had worked jointly to establish telegraph stations and secure lines to facilitate long-distance trade and military communications. Then the Mahdists, in their rebellion against foreign control, took to cutting the wires so as to disrupt the network.[74] In the Sudan as in Tunisia, religious and legal concerns about using the telegraph came in the wake of episodes of violent resistance to one of the new instruments of power.

Writing in defense of the imperial technology, Salīm al-Bishrī argued that "in our age," transmitting "news by telegraphic wire" is the superior way. If the Just Ruler authorizes a wire specifying that the new crescent moon has been sighted, then everyone in the nation or empire must follow his directive. Failure to do so implied rebellion "from what is right and proper."[75]

What did Sudanese and Tunisian scholars make of his edict? It is difficult to determine factually. But Sudanese subjects who perceived Egypt's khedive as a legitimate ruler would have understood the fatwa to mean that they had a duty to obey orders—fired by cannon and telegraph from the seat of government in Cairo—to end the fast and begin the feast. In contrast, *al-Manār*'s readers in Tunisia must have found the fatwa irrelevant to their state. The Tunisian clerics and judges who resented France's monopoly over the telegraph and the telephone would likely have bristled at the notion that their colonial overlords might qualify as just rulers. Meanwhile, their critic, the Tunisian fatwa seeker who favored the dictation of ritual events by a telecommunications hub, may well have found the fatwa useless and disappointing, for it did nothing to allay the suspicion of technology that existed in his country as a result of French mastery.

The exchanges on the telegraph between muftis and petitioners from the Punjab to the Maghreb reveal a critical feature of Muslim entanglements with imperial modernity at the beginning of the twentieth century. Through telegraph lines and telegraph stations, this telecommunications technology physically embodied the extension of state power. It gave rise to theological dilemmas not because of its secular capabilities but because of its religious adaptabilities.

Telegraphy itself did not present muftis with a singular or general problem that demanded resolution. Most messages sent through the cable had nothing to do with the practice of Islam; they were irrelevant from an Islamic legal perspective. This telecommunications medium gave rise to conundrums, stimulating religious reflection and contention, only when it was used to transmit information that affected Islamic rituals and judgments. Ramaḍān telegrams in particular diminished the agency of local authorities, such as muezzins, to determine and announce communal events; they brought to the foreground questions about who had the right to decide, by what mechanisms, when to feast and when to fast. It is for this reason that they became, like Qurʾanic discs, objects of legal controversy. They differed from the shellac discs, however, in one important respect: they were transmitted by a system of communications that formed part of the modernizing state's infrastructure.

In addition, the telegraph provoked judges and arbitrators to reflect on rules of evidence once witnesses tried to introduce telegrams into court. Around the turn of the twentieth century, both Muslim and non-Muslim jurists had to think carefully about the production of telegrams: whether to admit and trust the representations of clerks as if they were the original written letters of the alleged authors. The fundamental difference between these jurists is that only the Muslim ones needed to consider the low status of written evidence in Islamic law and the partial ban on non-Muslim witnesses.

Riḍā did not admire each and every instrument that Muslims could use to facilitate ritual communications; he had a special bias in favor of instruments that embodied modernization. Prayer gongs, like telegraphs, were useful instruments for conveying religious information (the hours of prayer) to large, dispersed audiences in Java. But Riḍā despised them, as we have seen. He argued for their rejection as forcefully and as passionately as he argued for the telegraph's appropriation. He assigned to gongs a ritualistic significance, spurning them as if they were the satanic tools of an alien cult, when he might have ruled, with philosophical detachment, that they were neutral things that could be used, like telegraphs, for Islamic communications. The disparity between one and the other judgment has something to do with the way that he distinguished the adoption of European technologies from the imitation of Christian devotions. But his judgment was also influenced by the fact that gongs were, for him, archaic, handmade artifacts that had no place in the toolkit of modern empires.

Photographs and the Technological Expansion of the Modern State

Riḍā's bias in favor of technologies that served the modern state to exercise power in novel ways is also evident in his rulings about governmental uses of photography. In 1903 a preacher and teacher from Russia, ʿAbdul Kabīr al-Muṣṭafawī, disclosed to *al-Manār* that some of the empire's Muslim subjects opposed a new mandatory program for photographic identification. A technique for "taking images with a specialized instrument has spread in our age. We are compelled by our government, Russia, to be photographed by that instrument in various circumstances, so as to establish our personal identities."[76] A man who wanted to become a mosque preacher was required first to take his picture and then to send the photograph to the Legislative Assembly (al-Jamʿiyya al-Sharʿiyya) in Ufa, Bashkiria, which certified his identity. The reference here was to one of many steps that Bashkiri, Volga Tatar, and other Muslims needed to take in order to register officially as imams with the Orenburg Spiritual Assembly, an institution that Empress Catherine II had founded in 1788 in order to exercise greater state control over Muslims.[77] With the development of chemical photography in the nineteenth century, the Russian Empire, like other states, seized upon the technology to create daguerreotypes and photographs of its subjects to identify them more effectively. Suspicious of the novel extension of state power, the fatwa seeker who wrote to Riḍā wondered if the sacred law permitted photography. In light of the new technology, how should Muslims interpret oral traditions that had prohibited image-making?

An iconoclastic mufti evaluating the Orenburg Spiritual Assembly's photographic requirements would have ruled that Muslim traditions forbidding figural representation remained in force. Riḍā was familiar with such an approach to photographs. In a fatwa, he recalled the shock that he experienced, presumably during his childhood in Syria, when he witnessed an iconoclast's discipline: "I used to see one scrupulous shaykh, whenever he was given a piece of paper with a photographic image on it and it fulfilled a want, as is often the case with paper and non-paper commodities from Europe, he would take a razor in his hand and cut out the head of the image from the paper. Then he would say, 'Now its likeness lives no more!' I wondered endlessly about this action."[78]

Riḍā chose to approach scriptural rules about the representation of humans or animals in a different mode. He argued, as a historicist, that the divine revelations against images had emerged in an environment where the Arabs, indulging in heathenism, had decorated the Kaʿba with figures. A monotheistic principle lay behind the original prohibitions, aimed at eradicating the glorification of pagan icons and graves. But in the twentieth century, in a radically different environment where it would never occur to a Muslim to worship idols, the seventh-century proscriptions mattered no more. Yes, they continued to influence perceptions of right and wrong, which is why Muslims had been slow to adopt photography. But the polytheistic superstitions that had given rise to the scriptural taboos had vanished, so a reassessment was in order.

What remained in force—as a moral economic principle—was an oral tradition about Muḥammad's response to ʿĀʾisha's curtains. The Prophet had condoned the transformation of these curtains—embroidered with designs that he had at first found offensive—into cushions.[79] Overcoming his initial, impulsive reaction to the designs, he decided to tolerate or accept his wife's aesthetic taste. (The typical, slightly confusing juridical inference was that the cushions could not become objects of worship because of their debased position on the floor, whereas the curtains, raised high above the ground, would distract

Muslims at prayer and entice them to glorify not God but representations of natural or supernatural beings.) By following the example of ʿĀʾisha or Muḥammad, Muslim moderns could cultivate a relaxed attitude toward nondevotional photographs. Since the risk of idolatry had vanished, and since the Russian government forced subjects to undergo this harmless process of identification to gain an advantage, Riḍā ruled that identification photographs were lawful things.[80]

Local Muslim debates about photographs, which stretched from Mecca to Minangkabau, led to more requests for fatwas. The most significant of these requests dated from 1911, and it came from a West Sumatran reformer who, inspired by *al-Manār*, had launched the journal *al-Munīr*, "The Enlightener," a few months earlier. Ḥājjī ʿAbdallāh Aḥmad of Padang had a question about the legality of hanging photos of animals on the wall. His question is historically meaningful because he proceeded to make use of photographs and statues in a controversial campaign to reform Muslim educational institutions.[81]

In his reply to this and other related questions, Riḍā preached the advantages of photography, which he saw as a science and practice that caused no religious harm. Photography could even have a positive effect on Islam, he argued. It could enable wary believers to identify strange animals and therefore to distinguish lawful from forbidden meat. Images in dictionaries and encyclopedias were becoming indispensable for the acquisition of precise, technical knowledge. In natural science and in medicine, as aids to anatomy and surgery, illustrations were absolutely necessary. The technology benefited state and society as well, for how could the military identify spies and how could the police identify criminals without photographs?

To understand Riḍā's multifaceted response in a local Egyptian context, it is essential to remember that Cairo, where he lived, had a long and multifaceted exposure to photography. It was, for one, a city where photographs could seem at once familiarly foreign and strangely local, as much a European construct as an Egyptian reality. They rarely appeared scandalous. It is true that a year before Riḍā received the question about imperial Russian photographs, a muckraker in Egypt had published a sensational photograph of his mentor, ʿAbduh, posing for a photograph in the company of Europeans, including unveiled women with bare arms. That photograph became controversial, however, not because it violated a taboo by turning a human being into a forbidden icon but because it served as visual evidence that the Grand Mufti had enjoyed consorting with Lord Cromer's wife.[82]

By the turn of the century Cairo had already been, for many decades, one of the world's premier destinations for photographers. In the 1840s, as Gérard de Nerval reported, a French artist set up a studio in a hotel in Cairo where he made a series of daguerreotypes of Egypt's "principal races" by persuading sugarcane vendors, who rarely agreed to remove their veils, to model for him.[83] By 1850 Cairo had its first professional studio, catering to tourists in search of souvenirs. If this trade began to decline in the late nineteenth century, with the adoption of Kodak cameras, tourists visiting Cairo at the fin de siècle could still easily find, at the Pyramids of Giza, a Hungarian photographer offering his services on site.[84] European tourists on "photographic expeditions" pointed their devices at the Ayyubid citadel, Mamluk tombs, winding roads such as Riḍā's Sycamore Lane, and "the picturesque street characters which abound, but are averse, as a rule, to being photographed."[85]

Egypt was also a leading destination for scientific photography in the late nineteenth and early twentieth centuries. Pharaonic monuments and racial differences drew Europeans' attention. By taking pictures of "the innumerable sculptures of foreign races," a famous English archaeologist, Flinders Petrie, found a way to combine both interests in single photographs.[86] In a series of studies conducted in 1901 and 1902, an anthropologist specializing in anthropometry, Charles S. Myers, used "descriptive, metric, and photographic methods" to try to determine racial differences between Muslims and Copts, the original inhabitants of Upper and Lower Egypt, and "the ancient and the modern Egyptians." Through the offices of the sirdar, Reginald Wingate, Myers obtained access to Egyptian and Sudanese soldiers. He took around seventeen thousand measurements of their anatomy and around two hundred photographs of their bodies, keeping subjects' heads at "a constant distance from the camera, so that the negatives may be of use for composite portraiture."[87] He then compared cranial measurements of "prehistoric" and "modern" skeletons, and finally concluded that "new anthropometric data" did not support the hypothesis that at least two races populated Egypt. It suggested, instead, that the Egyptians had always been a "homogenous people who have varied now towards Caucasian, now towards negroid characteristics," with the differences between them ascribed to environmental factors.[88]

These examples may give the impression of photography as an oppressively Orientalist, racist, or pseudo-scientific European pursuit. So why, in that case, did Riḍā sing its praises? The fact is that his responses followed a bourgeois trend. Expatriate studios such as the one opened in Cairo by Istanbul's famous Catholic photographer, Pascal Sébah, catered not only to tourists but also to local notables who posed for formal portraits and visiting cards. A social history of Arab portraiture has recently described the photographs as hybridized transnational productions, involving partnerships between indigenous and foreign photographers. Reformers had no objection to these dignified portraits; they posed for the cameras themselves, with conventional formality. They grew

FIGURE 6.1 Riḍā's portrait as a young man. Source: Shakīb Arslān, *al-Sayyid Rashīd Riḍā: aw, Akhāʾ arbaʿīn sana* (Damascus: Maṭbaʿat Ibn Zaydūn, 1937).

interested, too, in photographic records of Islamic monuments and ceremonial processions. ʿAbduh himself apparently encouraged one photographer to take pictures of pilgrims and holy sites on the road from Cairo to Mecca during the *ḥajj* as a way to chronicle the journey and as a means to improve conditions. The photographer would do so, even though he felt compelled to conceal his camera and adopt a disguise when he ventured into the Prophet's Mosque in Medina.[89]

Riḍā's defense of photography was not a futurological argument for the adoption of "French" methods or "American" instruments that had not yet made their debut in his society; it followed countless uses of albumen prints and Kodak cameras, for religious and nonreligious purposes, by Muslims in Egypt and elsewhere. His efforts to sanction a great variety of secular applications of photography, as opposed to merely incidental "Islamic" applications, reveals much about the utilitarian philosophy that fueled his agenda for progress through the pursuit of science and technology. During the trials of photography, the genre of the fatwa basically served him and his readers to condone religiously things that did not strike them as entirely religious.

Thus, Riḍā used the fatwa as a broad platform to legalize multiple uses of the camera, including the employment of photography by law enforcement agencies. It is not clear when Cairo's police forces started to take photographs of arrested persons and crime scenes systematically. There is some evidence that the state, in Egypt as elsewhere, invested photography with an immense power to identify criminals and resolve crimes.[90] In the late 1870s the Ministry of Interior ordered that photographs of European convicts be posted at passport control offices in order to identify them before granting them entry into the country.[91] A decade later, police forces began to use photos to register prisoners and locate suspects.[92] In the early 1890s Lord Cromer recounted an episode where, as a result of inefficient communications between departments, a corpse that had lain too long in wait for a forensic photographer's ministrations had decomposed badly. The anecdote indicates his expectation, frustrated in this instance, in the production of photographic evidence at the crime scene.[93] More significantly, the commandant of the Cairo police, pasha George Harvey, established an anthropometric bureau in 1895. At that time police departments in major cities around the world were opening such departments to implement a new Parisian method for identifying repeat criminals, *bertillonage*. Precise photographic techniques—accompanied at first by cephalic measurements, then mainly by fingerprint records—were an integral part of this method.[94] Criminal identification processes greatly changed around the end of the century, and so did the use of photographs by Cairo police.

The British regime also experimented with the use of photographs for deterrence. On one memorable occasion in 1906 it permitted photographers to witness and newspapers to publish evidence of the executions of villagers who had been convicted of murdering British officers. An Irish member of the House of Commons described the hangings and floggings as "judicial murders" that had "marred and blurred" Lord Cromer's administration, which had authorized the photographs "to educate the public mind." Appearing under the caption "Retribution," one infamous image shows the condemned man mounting the scaffolding with the assistance of the hangman and the police.[95]

However useful in police investigations and governmental identifications, photography spread into colonial societies without the assistance of the state. Cameras had little in common with trains and telegraphs, which depended on massive monopolistic investments in infrastructures that physically transformed the landscape. Given the dispensability of the state for most uses of photography, it is striking that Riḍā chose to highlight its advantages to the state. He argued in favor of governmental photographs not only when a petitioner asked him to assess the subjection of prospective imams to the bureaucratic demands of the Russian Empire; he did so as well in the fatwa that he wrote in response to the Sumatran reformer's question about hanging animal posters on the wall. Tellingly, instead of confining himself to resolving the problem of putting the likeness of an animal on a pedestal of sorts, he decided on his own to indulge in a wide-ranging defense of photography that culminated in a remark about its usefulness for identifying criminals and spies. Almost like enthusiasts of the *montgolfière* a century earlier, he viewed the utility of the technology for the surveillance of suspects as a good reason for approving its diffusion. But he had other reasons for sanctioning it, too, including the photographic identification of forbidden animals.

English Codes, the Ottoman Constitution, and the Arab Empire's Organic Law

In his fatwas on telegraphy and photography, Riḍā distinguished specifically "religious" from diverse "secular" utilities. This distinction brings us back to the Punjabi doctor's question about Muslim participation in the implementation of English codes that contained rules that conflicted with Islamic law. The codes of the British Raj definitely differed from Islamic and Hindu rules of proof and punishment. Written in English—the sole, binding language—these codes were a tool for the realization of British ideals of imperial government and imperial justice. In Nūr al-Dīn's eyes, they manifested the difference between the judgments of the English government and the judgments that God revealed to the Prophet. Muslims employed by this government could perhaps resist these codes in small ways, but mainly they faced a choice between resignation and reconciliation.

The fatwa that Riḍā wrote in response shows how much his approach to British imperial rule was pragmatic and conciliatory at this point of history. He immediately recognized the question as one of the hardest of the age, for it related to Muslim involvement in projects of codification and to the distinction between life and work in a "House of Islam" and life and work in "House of War." He then explained that devout Muslims who opposed the collaboration of Muslim justices with Native Tribunals, which followed French codes, based their reservations on a Qurʾanic verse. This verse, Qurʾan 5:44, specified that "those who judge not by what God revealed, they are the disbelievers." Challenging what he described as a Kharijite or sectarian interpretation of this verse, he held that Sunni exegetes had traditionally conceived of the disbelieving judges as Jews or Christians who failed to follow Allāh's revelations.

In his eyes, England had brought to the world the most lenient and tolerant form of government, which realized best the ideal of justice. "Let it be known," he declared, "that the laws of this state come closer to the Islamic shariʿa than the laws of other states." He affirmed this in part because the English system "entrusts many cases to judges' individual discretion." In addition, he agreed for all practical purposes with the distinction that the British Raj made between "personal" religious laws and secular "public" laws. He conceived of rules of worship, marriage, divorce, and inheritance as linked to "the religion itself" and universally applicable to Muslims in every time and place. By contrast, he conceived of rules of criminal and civil procedures as changeable because they governed the affairs of this world. Muslims under a non-Muslim regime had every right to obey the second set of rules; they could even justifiably disregard the ban on usury that applied to financial transactions in an Islamic territory.[96]

The distinction between laws of religion and laws of the world, which Riḍā made in the fatwa for India, differed significantly from the medieval distinction between rules of worship (*ʿibādāt*) and rules of social exchange (*muʿāmalāt*). The first category covered not only "personal" acts, such as the confession of faith, but also "public" regulations concerning the leading of prayers and the collection of alms taxes. Similarly, the second category encompassed "public" rules related to commercial transactions and criminal punishments as well as a wide range of "personal" rules made to recognize and guide familial relationships. Moreover, all of these rules fell, in theory, under the purview of Islam's sacred law. Sweeping aside these medieval categories and conceptions, Riḍā embraced a "modern" way of thinking about religion's scope within an imperial legal system that happened to coincide in its broad outlines with the colonial British model.

This coincidence made it easier for him to rule that it was lawful under the present circumstances for a Muslim to work as a judge in an enemy state. Such a judge would need to follow the legal codes of that state, rather than the shariʿa. But he could work to "strengthen the rules of Islam to the best of his ability." This situation, though not ideal, was bearable and permissible since it increased the welfare of the Muslim community. Muslims who lived in a state that caused them harm had the obligation to emigrate to a country that would allow them to practice their religion. But Muslims had no reason to flee from India, for this British colony had a pluralistic legal system that allowed its subjects to maintain their personal law in a reconfigured form. His appreciation of the employment of Muslim judges by the British Raj was so deep, in fact, that he described it as a "sublime service."[97]

Although it sanctioned, as did other fatwas, the Muslim use of an imperial tool, this 1904 fatwa is surprising because it shows that Riḍā supported India's legal system despite the fact that it had sidelined the shariʿa. Based on other sources, a recent history of the revival of Islamic law has represented Riḍā in a different way—as the early twentieth century's principal opponent of the marginalization of the sacred law. It is true that Riḍā resented the outcome of the process of codification in Egypt, which resulted in the promotion of "Frankish" laws and the demotion of divine laws. Regretting it as a missed opportunity, he wished that nineteenth-century Muslim authorities had possessed the vision to codify God's revelations.[98] But he approached the challenges of the present as a realist, which meant endorsing Muslim collaborations with a colonial legal system and hoping for the gradual invigoration of Islamic rules. Furthermore, he clearly thought that India's Muslims had the good fortune to live in a colony that sustained the branches of Islamic law that really mattered religiously.

A few years later, the political debates that took place in the aftermath of the Young Turk Revolution gave Riḍā the chance to present his views about religion and imperial law in a different context. In 1908, Sultan ʿAbdülḥamīd II capitulated to the revolutionary demands against his autocracy. He agreed to restore the constitution of 1876, which had been based on French, Belgian, and Prussian models. Shortly afterward, a countercoup stirred up more turmoil. Then, in April 1909, during the heady days that would lead to the sultan's deposition, clerics from Istanbul to Beirut started to discuss with great passion the shape of things to come. Some worried about a growing political divide between Turks and Arabs; others hoped for ambitious reforms that would culminate in the drafting of a new constitution.

Pondering a proposal in the air, Riḍā decided to warn against the possible codification of laws derived from the books of the Ottoman Empire's official school of law. This would be an oppressive development, he told a public assembly in Beirut, because Muslims should not be compelled to follow a single juridical tradition. Were he to draft these legal codes himself, he would base them not on Ḥanafi rulings but solely on the Qurʾan and the prophetic tradition. Nevertheless, he welcomed the opportunity to interpret these scriptures in a way that would support the goals of a modern state: "There is nothing in our religion, I would say, that opposes modern civilization, including everything that is regarded as beneficial by developed nations with the exception of a few questions concerning usury." So "I feel inclined," he continued, "to reconcile true Islam with everything that the Ottomans need to develop their state on the basis of what the Europeans tried before them."[99]

Riḍā's excitement about the Young Turk Revolution was deep enough that it motivated him to leave Cairo for several months and visit revolutionaries abroad. In Damascus, he formed ties with the Committee of Union and Progress, one of the political forces behind the revolution. Like other members of this committee, he opposed Arab separatism. He then traveled to Constantinople in October 1909, where he remained for a full year to work for better Arab-Turkish relations and obtain funding from the state for him to establish a missionary college. He came close to fulfilling his second goal, but the government's insistence on placing the school under the supervision of the *şeyhülislam*, the chief Ottoman mufti, and on making Turkish the institution's official language embittered him. Disillusioned with the empire's policy of Turkification, he returned to Cairo, where he began to undertake secret missions for the cause of Arab independence.[100]

Empires rather than nation-states nevertheless continued to mold his political aspirations. He would express his imperial ideals fully in "The General Organic Law of the Arab Empire," a kind of preamble to an undrafted constitution that he submitted to British authorities in the middle of the world war.[101] This document was certainly not an expression of "Arab nationalism."[102] As the title indicated, it was an expression of Arab imperialism. Riḍā's empire would cover "the Arabian Peninsula, the Provinces of Syria and Iraq and the territory between them."[103] Its boundaries would stretch from the Arabian Sea to the eastern Mediterranean coast and from the Tigris River to the Red Sea. It would begin with the Arabian Peninsula's principalities and provinces (the vilayet of the Ḥijāz, the Saudi emirate of Najd and al-Aḥsāʾ, the Rashidi emirate of Ḥāʾil, the Aden Protectorate, the Trucial sheikhdoms, and so on) but extend to the Iraqi vilayets and the Syrian *mutasarrifates*. With the notable exception of Najd and Ḥāʾil, these territories were formally or informally under either Ottoman or British paramountcy.

His imperial vision made room for provinces that possessed a degree of administrative independence and governmental autonomy. The decentralized federation that he envisioned reflected in many ways the political landscape that was familiar to him as a longtime subject of states that lacked sovereignty. Thus, every province in his Arab Empire would "be subject to the Central Government in its general policy and in matters of common interest to all the Empire."[104] The official language would be Arabic, and the official religion Islam. Geographically dispersed, this polity would have two main centers of government: Damascus and Mecca. The caliph's headquarters would lie in Mecca; the president's, in Damascus.

The choice of two seats of imperial authority, Damascus and Mecca, reflected Riḍā's design to separate the administration of "civil and political affairs" from the administration of "religious affairs." This arrangement did not indicate the disestablishment of the caliphate from the state, however. The Arab Empire's caliph would possess political and legal prerogatives as well as symbolic and ceremonial power. He had the privilege of selecting the president from one of three democratically elected deputies, and he had the authority to review treaties and judgments proposed by the deputies' council before their ratification or execution. In addition, to celebrate his authority over the faithful, his name would be hailed "in religious sermons, and stamped on coins."[105]

Perhaps the thorniest set of issues that the organic law needed to address concerned the rights of non-Muslims in the Arab-Muslim empire. Would Christians and Jews enjoy the same religious freedoms and political opportunities as

Muslims? Would they be able to serve as judges, alongside Muslims, in courts that would follow secular rather than religious codes? The second question was essentially the same question that Nūr al-Dīn of Punjab had posed to ʿAbduh, but in an inverted form. In this instance, Riḍā had to try to answer it to the satisfaction of colonial British officials—for whom he wrote, in confidence, his draft of a constitution. Two clauses addressed this set of issues:

> All the peoples of the Arab Empire are free in their religious beliefs, personal rights and financial operations, unless they go beyond the limits of religion, law and general morality. The non-Muslims have the same rights as the Muslims in the privileges and official posts of the Kingdom with the corresponding duties save in affairs of religion.
>
> A non-Muslim can be a Minister but he cannot be a judge in Muslim Courts. Non-Muslim questions of personal status among non-Muslims [will] be decided before their religious authorities.[106]

It is not clear what exactly would constitute a transgression of religious and legal boundaries or an offense to public morals. What is clear is that Jews and Christians would be able to serve as ministers in Damascus. They would be excluded from Meccan affairs.

The Arab Empire's legal system would have much in common with the pluralistic legal systems that Riḍā knew intimately. As in Syria and Egypt following the reforms of the last quarter of the nineteenth century, there would exist, for one, a separation between personal religious courts and other courts. Each religious community would have the autonomy to try its own personal cases in its own courts. Christian and Jewish judges were barred from serving on Muslim courts, but perhaps they would have the right to sit alongside Muslims on mixed tribunals that would hear commercial and criminal cases. The constitution made no provision, however, for establishing such tribunals. Nor did it specify that codes would be enacted to guide nonreligious courts. Perhaps Riḍā took the future existence of these institutions for granted. One way or the other, he clarified that the caliph would be the ultimate legal authority. Advised by a chief mufti who would bear a grand title, the caliph would have the power to "settle any dispute, litigation or disagreement brought before him by any of the authorities of the Empire."[107]

A historian of Islamic currents of reform has argued that Riḍā was among the first Muslim intellectuals to provide "Islamic legitimation for each and every institution of the modern, European nation-state." By formulating "religious" ideas in the service of a "secular" state that tolerated no "plurality of laws," Riḍā supposedly contributed to the eventual rise of an "Islamist" ideology that would encompass "all aspects of life."[108] One problem with this teleological argument is that empires were Riḍā's political reality as well as his political models until the end of World War I. Legal pluralism was the order of the day. In Egypt's legal system, there were native, mixed, and consular courts as well as personal Jewish, Coptic, and Islamic courts that all followed different gods and codes. When Riḍā permitted Muslim judges to rule based on India's English laws, wrote in favor of the restoration of the Ottoman constitution, and drafted his blueprint for the Arab Empire of his fantasies, he clearly conceived of present and future polities as multiconfessional empires that accommodated a plurality of religious and secular legal systems.

Riḍā's fatwas provided legitimacy to the new tools of state and society, but his arguments in favor of these tools were not solely religious. He justified photography in part because it enabled institutions dedicated to law and order, from Cairo's Anthropometric Bureau to Ufa's Legislative Assembly, to increase their capacities for surveying suspects and investigating crimes. In addition, he highlighted a few scientific and at least one religious benefit: the use of photographs to identify animals whose consumption was forbidden to Muslims. In effect, Riḍā's fatwas distinguished Islamic from non-Islamic applications of photography, and they offered a combination of religious and secular judgments. By contrast, al-*Manār*'s fatwas about telegraphy concentrated not on diverse governmental benefits but on technical Islamic questions about rites and legal procedures. Should Muslim communities in remote locations fast and feast in accordance with telegraphic directives sent by a central state institution? Should telegrams be admitted as probative evidence in an Islamic legal process? What difference does it make if colonial Christian clerks work as mediators between Muslims attempting to communicate information through the wire? The fatwas that responded to these questions focused on legitimizing the tool's Islamic, not secular, utilities.

How far Riḍā or other muftis stretched Islamic law to cover multiple aspects of modern life very much depended on the known interests of fatwa seekers and the anticipated interests of fatwa readers. Riḍā's fatwas were not independent edicts issued in a vacuum. Rather, they were responses to petitions made by correspondents such as Nūr al-Dīn of Punjab, ʿAbdallāh Aḥmad of Padang, Muqbil al-Dhakīr of Bahrain, Muḥammad Belkhōja of Tunis, and ʿAbdul Kabīr al-Muṣṭafawī of Russia. Although these men lived far apart and worked in different professions, they had much in common: notables in their own societies, all of them were also relatively knowledgeable about Islamic law and contemporary affairs. They steered the legal discussion, directing Riḍā to reflect as a reformer on all sorts of new things.

Their aspirations for Islamic reform emerged in a world where telegraphs in Christian hands transmitted directives concerning the end of Ramaḍān, where railways transported Ottoman pilgrims from Damascus to Medina, where police departments took photographs of criminals while legislative assemblies took photographs of imams, where Indo-Muslim judges followed English codes, and where, for all the hopes for change before World War I, empires rather than nation-states delimited the boundaries of the political imaginary.

7

Arabian Slippers

The Turn to Nationalistic Consumption

Riḍā was already a crusty old mufti in 1928 when a correspondent from Beirut, Ibrāhīm al-Lādiqī, asked him to put sexy French trousers on trial. These trousers were the new craze in the French Mandate's capital city. They fit tightly, revealing the bulk of a man's privates as well as the shape of his buttocks. Al-Lādiqī exaggerated their constrictiveness. A looser, more relaxed cut was in vogue in the interwar period, especially among the young men who cultivated a casual, athletic style.[1] Regardless, al-Lādiqī described form-fitting pants that left little to the imagination. Pants thus tailored might provoke sexual desire, he teased, but was wearing them actually unlawful? Yes, responded Riḍā. These trousers are medically reprehensible because they harm the body and religiously reprehensible because they prevent Muslims from praying. Prostrations to the ground characterize the Muslim rite of worship, and these gestures of submission to God are best done with loose-fitting garments. If French trousers present Muslim dandies, worried about ripping the expensive fabric, with an excuse against prayer, then they should be strictly tabooed.

To wear such clothes seemed terribly crude to Riḍā. He advised Muslims to heed caliph ʿUmar I's interdiction. "It may not be sheer," the caliph had said about a garment made by Coptic weavers. Nevertheless, "it traces" the shape of the body. (Riḍā's legal reasoning in this case is striking for one reason: not because of the presumption that physically revealing French clothes are analogous to physically revealing Coptic clothes but because of the deliberate blurring of a gender line. The caliph's ban had originally applied to women. Riḍā omitted this fact, eliding a gender-specific pronoun when he extended the prohibition to cover men.) He concluded the fatwa by railing against "today's madmen" who follow the latest fashions—to which he refers by both an Arabic term (*ṭuruz*) and by an Italian or French borrowing (*mōdāt*). These prisoners of desire, slaves of style, heed invitations to "apostasy and licentiousness." Advertisements persuade them to crave new things—to prefer the new precisely because it represents "depravity and profligacy."[2]

Two years later, a Javanese correspondent gave Riḍā an opportunity to tone down his legal ruling. Would the mufti actually assign the rank of infidels to Muslims who wear *pantalons* and *cravates*? Even in constricting clothes, such men remain Muslims, ruled Riḍā. By adopting foreign "customs that are not religious," they do not really forsake Islam. Nor do they sin against God. Nevertheless, their willingness to cast away traditional attire in favor of modern European clothes is abominable for religious, political, and national reasons.[3]

Of all the types of goods that Muslims associated with Europeanization in the years of *al-Manār*, none stirred quite as much trouble as clothes. Clothes mattered economically since they were one of the principal articles of international trade. Egypt under British rule spent more money on textiles, which could be tailored to fit any style, than on any other class of imports: maize and wheat flour, coal, builders' wood, iron and steel, tobacco and cigars, machinery, livestock and frozen meat, refined sugar, dried and fresh fruit, rice, and petrol. Year after year, customs officers counted cotton and other textiles as well as ready-made clothes and underclothes among the top classes of imports.[4] Clothes mattered culturally, too, since they served as markers of poverty and wealth, social status, professional identity, confessional affiliation, and, of course, gender.

Al-Manār's readership mainly consisted of elite Muslim men, and they were mainly interested in the changing fashions of upwardly mobile Muslim men. Of course, they debated the question of the veil. Riḍā himself contributed to this debate in 1899, when he made an apologetic rejoinder to a famous feminist publication, Qāsim Amīn's *The Liberation of Women.* He argued for respecting women's choice to wear the *ḥijāb*, by which he meant a face veil, but also contended that the sacred law permitted women to expose their faces at the mosque and during the *ḥajj*.[5] Women's consumption habits changed considerably in the late imperial and early national contexts. In Egypt, they drove many of the most significant debates, which is why historians of gender, politics, and consumption have focused on them.[6] Nevertheless, because of their gender, *al-Manār*'s fatwa seekers had a reason to obsess rather more about male consumption. They wrote about men's fashions with nuance and discernment, as pious men who had the financial means to strike the right balance between tradition and modernity. They knew how much could be said, without words, by the magnificent combination of an Edwardian suit and a red tarbush. What they lacked were fatwas to defend their choices.

Unlike most other imported goods, imported clothes were explicitly identified as foreign in juridical discussions about the problem of "imitating" or "resembling" others. Fatwa seekers did not identify most of the things profiled in this book in this manner. They debated the use of phonographs and telegraphs, not of "American" phonographs and "British" telegraphs, and it was rare for them to associate technologies and commodities made abroad with that vague geopolitical construct known as "the West." Their disregard of imported novelties' foreign origin arguably reflected a low cultural barrier to adoption. It certainly made it easier for an economically liberal mufti such as Riḍā to make an Islamic case for appropriation and legalization. But foreign fashions, luxuries such as French couture and French perfume, were a different matter. When imperial Muslims debated wearing them, they resorted to adjectives such as "Frankish" or "European" (*ifranjī*) to describe them. Such formulations were not necessarily prejudicial. In certain cases, they could reflect a positive bias or a degree of ambivalence. A fatwa about wearing "French" perfume in mosques was predicated, for example, on the premise that the fragrance was irresistible, so desirable that it drove Muslim worshippers mad with distraction.[7] Yet the description of the essence as "French" made it difficult to counter that it could be fully converted into an "Islamic" good. It carried with it an indelible whiff of foreignness.

From black boots to top hats, European clothes had special significance in Islamic legal cultures for another reason too. As caliph ʿUmar's denunciation of Coptic linens suggests, there was a long juridical tradition of Islamic responses to non-Arab dress. When Riḍā and other muftis judged toilet paper and banknotes and many other modern inventions, they had to take a deep look into the sacred law's recesses in order to find sentences that they could present as relevant precedents. This was a necessary step for the construction of legal cases that had to be based on analogical arguments. When they turned to modern clothes, however, they faced no difficulty whatsoever finding apposite canonical precedents; they could easily identify a wealth of foundational cases that had already dealt extensively with the clothes of strangers. Their interpretative work was limited to selecting and marshaling their favorite pieces of evidence.

Riḍā's fatwas about articles of European dress, issued from the beginning to the end of his career, are historically valuable sources because they reveal how a Muslim legal expert's judgments changed in the course of a long transition from a culture that accommodated foreign dominance to a culture that celebrated national independence. They reveal why a political turn in the interwar period finally affected his attitude to consumption. Before World War I, he largely adhered to the basic values and principles that had inspired ʿAbduh's concession to hat wearers in the Transvaal. But he did not remain so open to cultural borrowings throughout his tenure as *al-Manār*'s mufti. His fatwa against sexy French pants, published a quarter of a century after the Transvaal fatwa, suggests a shift to the economics of an anti-imperialist awakening. It makes Riḍā sound far more like Mahatma Gandhi than ʿAbduh. To understand the changes is the purpose of this chapter, and this requires paying attention not only to multiple fatwas but also to diverse writings by Riḍā, including an 1898 article about cultural imitation, a secret 1915 plan for an Arab state, a 1926 edition of a book by Gandhi, and a 1930 lecture about the renewal of Islam.

Riḍā's economic ethic would appear remarkably consistent had his fatwas not taken this turn. His openness to cross-cultural trade and his receptivity to technological innovations changed relatively little over the years. Even as he started to take a stronger stance against British and French imperialism, when it became easier to campaign publicly for Arab independence, his economic outlook remained quite stable. During and after World War I, metropoles enacted protectionist policies to promote domestic industries or intra-imperial trade, while campaigners for home rule in the colonies trumpeted anti-imperial boycotts. Riḍā generally continued advocating open markets. The fatwas that he wrote against buying foreign clothes in the late twenties and early thirties count as the most striking exception to his general tendency toward economic liberalism. They show how his legal interpretations eventually yielded to the ideological currents and material changes of the twenties, when imperial conformism gave way to the politics of nationalistic production and consumption.[8]

The laissez-faire Islam that *al-Manār* represented allowed a fairly free exchange of goods between Muslims and others. The shariʿa, as Riḍā interpreted it, placed only minimal restrictions on financial transactions and the consumption of "harmful" products that might undermine the faith. He made endless concessions to freer trade, banning almost nothing other than thievery and fraud. Eliminating parochial Islamic barriers to commerce and consumption seemed greatly beneficial to him. Doing so would in theory lead to what free-trade imperialists had promised: not only economic development but also sovereignty and modernity. Yet this proposition came with a religious risk, for the unfettered consumption of European commodities threatened to erase everything that distinguished Muslims from others externally. Riḍā had personal reasons to feel relaxed about this risk. Before he assumed the dignified habits of a member of the *ʿulamāʾ*, he had occasionally worn European clothes. There happens to be a photograph of him as an adolescent where he appears wearing a gray suit, fez and tie, solemnly posing besides his older brother, who had put on a similar outfit.[9] Yet over time he grew to worry about the adoption of things that came to symbolize Europe's cultural hegemony and Muslims' religious alienation.

Upper-Class Neckties and Soldiers' Apparel: Fatwas for Adoption Before World War I

Riḍā maintained a distinction between specifically "religious" and broadly "cultural" imitation while assessing the Muslim imitation of European fashions. He conceptualized this distinction in relation to the worship of God. The first critical issue for him to determine was whether the Muslim appropriation of a European style was devotionally relevant or not. If it had no devotional relevance, then the practice could be declared either permissible or reprehensible; otherwise, it would be placed under the strictest of bans. The second issue that Riḍā deliberated was the utility of the practice. Was the Euro-Muslim fashion beneficial or harmful to individuals and the community at large? Responses to this question varied in tone depending not only on the object and the practice but also on his sense of the priorities of the time. The legal relativism that characterized his utilitarian approach to the Europeanized consumption of clothes was predicated on early Muslim traditions, which offered him conflicting and ambiguous standards. Depending on his interests, he could turn to the letter that caliph ʿUmar I had sent to his general, ʿUtba ibn Farqad, which criticized silken garments and polytheistic habits, or to the canonical narratives that suggested that the Prophet himself had worn fine Persian clothes.[10]

Before World War I, he typically found reasons to sanction the acculturation of Muslims to European fashions and styles. He issued relatively permissive rulings in relation to hats, neckties, and hooded cloaks—as well as hairstyles and furnishings, which were similarly associated with Europeanization. Repeatedly, he declared that Islam neither bans nor prescribes a specific type of attire "for the people" in the course of everyday life. Pilgrimage rites, which require distinct clothing, were the main exception to this mundane order.[11] Mainly, Riḍā's fatwas focused on menswear, and he explicitly argued—before the nationalist awakening of the interwar period—against regulating it on the basis of the sacred law. Instead, he emphasized Muslims' freedom of choice: "Every individual and every branch of society may wear whatever he wants and chooses."[12]

Penned in 1904 by a Qurʾan reciter from Algeria, the question that elicited the dictum quoted was inspired by a concern over indigenous mobility under French colonialism. The reciter was curious about the adoption of official uniforms by native prefects. Was it lawful for Muslim subjects to wear ceremonial suits that signaled social distinction? He specifically mentioned *le burnous rouge*, a fascinating cross-cultural object and symbol of collaboration. This was the colonial version of a unisex Berber mantle, appropriated by the French army in the color red for the investiture of its elite Algerian cavalry. Disregarding the

French colonial context, Riḍā turned to the relationship between Islamic law and class distinctions in an Ottoman context. He conceded that the shariʿa discouraged the use of opulent dress that marked differences in rank as well as immodest clothes designed for notoriety. But he disclosed that the Ottoman Empire derived its ostentatious, ceremonial style from the conspicuous excesses of Greek Orthodox patriarchs and priests. He also mocked high-ranking Ottoman *ʿulamāʾ* for the corruption and hypocrisy that they showed by, on the one hand, condoning this hierarchical imperial style, with its flagrant display of forbidden elements on festivals and holidays, and, on the other hand, banning European hats as if they were the embodiments of infidelity. In his view, Muslim men were free to wear any article of clothing not embellished by silver, gold, or silk accoutrements. The Franco-Algerian *burnous*, he concluded, was better than the sumptuous Greco-Ottoman robes.[13]

The Prophet Muḥammad's sartorial example was the critical precedent for moderns to reflect on when judging the Europeanization of male appearance. Riḍā explained to another Algerian correspondent, Muṣtafā Abājī, that Muḥammad had worn clothes manufactured by Rumi and Magian weavers and imported from the Byzantine and Sasanian Empires. By doing so, he had not intended to signal Arab subservience. The key in considering the adoption of foreign things or foreign manners was to determine intent in the framework of power relations between Muslims and others. The dimwitted Muslim who would coif his hair with the intent of subordinating himself to French style should be scoffed at. However, if subservience was not the aim, then there was no problem with the appropriation of French coiffure. The "pious forbears" did not turn their back on all the cultural charms or beautification practices that existed before Islam's rise (*maḥāsin dīn al-fiṭra*): they perfumed their hair, groomed their beard, and engaged in other forms of "cultural" restoration that brought them back to a "natural" state. Furthermore, with the expansion of Islam's realm through conquest, Arab Muslims started to dress in different fashions in the East and the West. Caliphs and commanders, exercising personal discretion to reach a legal decision, went so far as to wear "the attire of the Franks." These historical examples showed that adaptability was one of the qualities of Islam's golden age. Riḍā therefore paid no heed to "the ignorant men who disdain anyone who does anything in harmony with the French."[14]

North Africa was not the only region in the wide world of Islam that generated sharp questions about the external transformation of Muslim men under a colonial regime. The islands of Southeast Asia that formed part of the Dutch Empire also generated boiling debates about menswear, reflected in multiple requests for fatwas that spilled over into *al-Manār*.[15] A man from Sambas, West Borneo, worried about a trend that was spreading to "the high class" around

1910. Wealthy Muslims were beginning to balance a European hat on top of "the kaffiyeh that was customary to them." They had also adopted the necktie. Instead of coining a new word or borrowing a foreign term to describe this accent of formal dress, critics of the trend started to call the cravat a "*zunnār*." This was the very word used to designate a kind of sash that monks and vicars had worn around the waist. Medieval Muslim lawmakers had considered it a distinctive and mandatory part of Christian dress, so much so that they had insisted on Christians wearing it. The Pact of ʿUmar established it as a key marker of differentiation. In a Syrian version of this code for non-Muslim subjects, Christians had to pledge not to imitate a Muslim style of dress and to wear instead the distinctive girdle.[16] Word games aside, elegant cravats and fashionable hats elided cultural distinctions. They were the very things that made well-heeled Muslim men look more and more like Dutchmen. Resistance to European fashions devolved into acrimony by 1911. A Javanese subscriber to *al-Manār*, the editor of *al-Munīr*, wrote to Riḍā that the majority of scholars in his town—he lived at the time in Padang, West Sumatra, a major trading city under Dutch rule—had issued a fatwa denouncing the Muslim who wears a neckerchief as a man who has fallen "outside of the religion" (*khārijan ʿan al-dīn*). In this inquisition, the sign of apostasy was not a heretical idea—it was an ascot tie.[17]

The Muslim reaction to European attire was particularly sharp in the East Indies for several reasons. It was a response, in the first place, to the vigorous policy of acculturation that the Dutch imposed on their colony. The Dutch aimed at making natives comply with Dutch rule by encouraging their "association" with Dutch culture. The flow of steamships to Arabia, which indicated a desire to associate with Arab-Muslim culture instead, therefore concerned them. A stronger "pan-Islamic" identity, forged through visits to the holy sites, could help Muslim rebels mount an effective resistance to Dutch colonialism. Pilgrims' ties to Mecca, expressed by the adoption of articles of "Arab" dress, made Dutch officials uneasy, especially during the Aceh War. They saw these clothes as harboring the sinister seeds of anticolonial rebellion. Their "fear of turbans" was so intense that the native affairs advisor, the Orientalist Christiaan Snouck Hurgronje, pleaded with them for moderation, maintaining that a colonial ban would backfire and make Muslims more fanatical.[18]

Once the Dutch began to relax the dress code that they had designed to preserve superficial distinctions between Europeans, native inhabitants, and foreign Orientals (Chinese or Arab), individuals quickly adopted elements of foreign style. The uniformity that had been imposed with mixed success on each class of the population gave way, around 1900, to exuberant experiments in cross-dressing: Javanese *ḥajjis* in Arab headdress; Eurasian men in impeccable tennis outfits; disciples at the School for Native Civil Servants in sarongs, tailored jackets, and bow ties; sensible Dutch housewives in Indies' clothes; Chinese vendors in patent leather shoes; and, of course, Muslim moderns in European hats. All of this seemed passing strange. It bothered many privileged conservatives—from self-righteous Dutch women such as Mrs. J. M. J. Catenius van der Meijden, who in 1908 published *Our House in Indies*, a book of manners that included many supercilious prescriptions on dress, to the princely Javanese theosophist Soetatmo Soeriokoesoemo, who haughtily dismissed the imitation of Parisian fashions.[19] It similarly bothered conservative Muslim scholars, who resented the Muslim trendsetters who appeared so suddenly to pass, in their cross-cultural garments, for Dutch.[20]

Cultural variegation characterized Islam in this cluster of islands. The sheer variety of local forms, which the Dutch exploited to create a multiplicity of customary laws (*ʿādāt* codes) differentiated by province, clashed with other impulses: a vision of Islam as a scriptural religion, universally applicable in Java as in Mecca, and a colonial desire to control the population through laws that accentuated ethnic and religious differences.[21] Reformers who aligned themselves with *al-Manār* would acquire a reputation—with the passage of time—as "scripturalists" or "fundamentalists," the very ideologues who gained notoriety by insisting on uniform Islamic garb. But around 1910 some members of Riḍā's vast network actually undertook the defense of a new trend that was spreading in cities like Padang that had been transformed by Dutch trade: the adoption of European habits of dress by forward-looking Muslims of means. These Indonesian reformers were among the spokesmen for "the New Generation" (Kaum Muda). Their opponents, derogatively called "the Old Generation" (Kaum Tua), were the combustible characters who accused cross-dressing Muslims of infidelity.[22] Ḥājjī ʿAbdallāh Aḥmad, the editor of *The Enlightener* who wrote to the editor of *The Lighthouse*, belonged to the first camp. He wanted to use Riḍā's fatwas, whose "enlightened" Islamic judgments he of course expected, as legal weapons to defeat local foes.[23]

Setting aside the egalitarian argument that Islam opposes class distinctions, Riḍā passed over in silence the fact that European hats and ties served to distinguish prosperous Muslims from the rest. Instead, he developed further one central argument: that Islamic law needed to address the behavior of Muslim consumers pragmatically. The early Islamic jurist Mālik ibn Anas (d. 795) first sketched the argument, not as a general principle but as an ad hoc ruling, in his response to a question about the purchase of new clothes made by Christian weavers. He declared the Muslim consumption of these clothes—whose threads had been dyed with forbidden wine—unproblematic from a legal standpoint because it seemed to him inevitable.[24] Without citing this precedent, Riḍā exhibited the exact same tendency toward pragmatism. He explained that millions of

Turks, Tatars, Arabs, Egyptians, and Syrians had already acquired the habit of wearing European dress. Unenlightened Javanese scholars had turned Islam into a laughingstock by charging Muslims who dressed like them with infidelity. They had given the impression that a few customs formed "the essence of the religion" of Muḥammad.[25] Muslims have a right to adopt European "clothes and customs," he argued, provided that the foreign fashions do not violate any explicit scriptural rule.[26] Underlying this accommodation to European things was Riḍā's fear that Islam would slide into obsolescence if interpreters of the sacred law opposed inexorable trends.

Riḍā's tendency to defend legal pragmatism with a Eurocentric vision culminated in a lengthy fatwa, published in 1911, that answered a question from a Meccan scholar about the adoption of "Judeo-Christian" furnishings and clothes. This scholar, Muḥammad ʿAlawī, likely had a personal connection to participants in the Southeast Asian debates, for the Meccan branch of the ʿAlawī clan had powerful ties to the Ḥaḍramī Arab diasporas of the Indian Ocean. Riḍā himself knew or sensed the connection since he immediately related the Meccan question to the debate raging in Java and the Malay Archipelago. In an external, literal sense, this question pointed to specific concerns with the purchase and use of "Jewish" and "Christian" products. "And I do not know," he stated, "that this should be a subject for legal disputation" since Muslims from ancient to modern times have never stopped "buying what they need from the products of People of the Book and others, whether [directly] from their traders or through [the mediation of] other parties."[27]

This pragmatic ruling technically hinged on a discretionary assessment of the concepts of communal imitation (*tashabbuh*) and social well-being (*maṣlaḥa*). Anti-imperialists justified their resistance to European outfits by citing a tradition that basically defined kinship as a function of external appearance and social mores: "The one who imitates a people, he becomes one of them." Riḍā argued that this canonical tradition could not refer to non-Muslim products in general. He wanted to restrict its application to things like a presbyter's cincture or a cardinal's hat that signified confessional identity. His rationale for minimizing the restriction was progressive, flexible, and utilitarian. The ever-changing goods of strangers will offer many benefits that cannot be anticipated or predicted. Openness to foreign innovations therefore made sense. "Every time has its own advantages and circumstances," he concluded, immediately after recommending Ibn Taymiyya's book *The Exigency of the Straight Path in Opposition to the People of Hell* as a fine meditation on the topic of cross-cultural resemblance.

To persuade reluctant readers to relax their reflexive antagonism to cross-cultural adoption, Riḍā decided to teach a lesson from war. He mentioned the historic victories of European armies: their success in conquering "many

Muslim kingdoms" that had failed to adopt European military innovations and the astonishing speed of their recent capture—in a short week's campaign—of the capital city of one of the Ottoman Empire's provinces. To adopt "new weapons and novel military methods" was essential for political survival. Rebuking the Muslims who had made a religious issue out of the adoption of novel European clothes, Riḍā explained why it was far more important to focus on the sociopolitical advantages. The attire of European soldiers had contributed to their "mastery of military movements and actions" and counted as one of the most important reasons for their supremacy over the Islamic world.[28]

The fatwa came in the wake of battles that highlighted European technological dominance. Three years earlier, the Ottoman Empire had lost Bosnia to the Austro-Hungarian Empire and Eastern Rumelia to Bulgaria. But Riḍā's response took place in the aftermath of the Italian invasion of Libya. Italy's scramble for North Africa was not yet over in December of 1911, when he published the fatwa. But one provincial capital, Tripoli of the West, fell on October 5, just days after the declaration of war on September 29. In November, an Italian pilot made history by dropping a hand grenade on an oasis, the garrison of ʿAyn Zāra. This was one of the most significant developments in aerial warfare since the launching of the *montgolfière* for surveillance and intimidation. In another technological breakthrough, the inventor Guglielmo Marconi succeeded in equipping an airplane with a radio receiver, allowing a pilot to receive instructions from a telegraph station erected on a battleship.[29] The airplane did not entirely displace the technology that Napoleon's aerostatic corps took to Cairo. Armed with a telescope and telegraph, reconnoiters made use of tethered hot air balloons and dirigible blimps in this war too.[30] Meanwhile, the Italian pilots flew on French and German airplanes (Blériot, Nieuport, Farman, and Taube models) that were too small to carry passengers; pilots had to hold the control wheel with one hand and remove the grenade's safety pin with the other hand. They needed to fly low, too, which exposed them to bullets from below. Therefore, they decided to scale back this dangerous pursuit. Instead of dropping bombs, they began to drop leaflets, written in Arabic, that called on "the Arabs" to surrender.[31] Italian troops ultimately encountered fierce and unexpected resistance. Victory was in no way ensured. Yet by October of 1912, due to variety of circumstances, the Ottomans were compelled to cede to Italy the provinces of Cyrenaica and Tripolitania.[32]

Instead of paying attention to aerial bombs and radiotelegraphy, Riḍā focused on military clothes. His emphasis on the advantages of the enemy's apparel is odd for two reasons. First, Ottoman military uniforms resembled Italian ones in functionality; they were not evidently disadvantageous at this time. Headgear was the item of greatest distinction. Ottoman cavalry and artillery units sported an unassuming astrakhan fez, whereas the Italian Army's light infantry corps, the Bersaglieri, wore a brimmed helmet decorated with the impressively long black feathers of the cock of the wood.[33] Those who lacked standard equipment in this war were the irregular fighters: the Sanusi troops and other local militias. Second, Muḥammad ʿAlawī's question referred to home furnishings and clothes generically, not battlefield gear. Riḍā made the unexpected foray into military history entirely on his own. It reveals his disposition to think of reform in a moment of crisis in nineteenth-century Ottoman terms. To critics of the Porte's policy of modernization, nothing symbolized its superficiality as much as the fixation on altering military uniforms to keep up with the times. Resurfacing in the fatwa was that old obsession, ridiculed by Count Alexander Pisani already in 1832, with fezzes and epaulettes.[34]

Even though he made it licit for Muslims to adopt European garb for pragmatic reasons, Riḍā harbored reservations. He resented the loss of pride in Arab things that came with the glorification of French styles.[35] His Meccan fatwa

FIGURE 7.1 Mustafa Kemal, long before he passed Turkey's hat law, with irregular Sanusi troops that tried but failed to defend Libya from an Italian invasion. Italy deployed new military technologies in this war, including aerial bombs, but Riḍā was primarily concerned about the inadequacies of Ottoman military uniforms. Unattributed 1912 photograph in the public domain.

denounced Muslims from Cairo to Istanbul for slavishly imitating European habits. He considered cultural subservience a heinous corruption that would enfeeble the global Muslim community, slacken its faithful covenant, weaken its morals, and sweep away its rich patrimony. He understood how traveling to Britain or France and learning European languages might lead to industrial and commercial benefits. But he railed against men who abandoned their "national dress" (*ziyy al-waṭanī*) and then deepened their cultural assimilation in brothels and bars. Afflicted by the disease of Europeanization, these Muslims squandered thousands of dinars on gambling and all manner of depravity, and they refused to spend a single cent for the good of society.[36]

In the legal opinions that he gave before World War I, Riḍā developed ʿAbduh's flexible, utilitarian approach. Drawing a lesson from the virulent reaction to the Transvaal fatwa, he came to define himself as the forger of a middle path. This entailed criticizing both those who embraced frivolously and those who rejected zealously all things European. If the first group threatened the fabric of Islam, the second chilled the prospect of development. Symbols of secularism, the modern trappings of a Europeanized identity, bothered him insofar as they indicated the slippage of Arab prestige. They motivated him to express patriotic misgivings. Despite this cultural concern, his judicial priority in this period was to convince Muslims to recognize the legality of useful European products. So many things, even ascot ties, struck him as potentially advantageous and therefore licit. He justified in particular the appropriation of articles of dress that suggested either upward mobility or military strength. The tenor and thrust of the fatwas that he issued before World War I were thus significantly different from the tenor and thrust of the fatwas of the late twenties, where he argued passionately against the trendy consumption of European pants and cravats. How can we understand this change? To what extent was it part and parcel of a broader anti-imperial movement for nationalistic production and consumption? The search for an answer will take us first to the Egyptian boycotts of British clothes and then to the first Arabic translations of Gandhi's economic philosophy.

Anti-British Boycotts and Nationalist Economics in Egypt

The Egyptian campaign for independence that began with the 1919 revolution took a new turn, in 1922, toward the politics of economic resistance. Egyptian women launched a consumer boycott of British goods. Historians of this boycott have wondered if participants were familiar with the corresponding Indian model. In an era when persons and news traveled with ease from India to Egypt, they were surely aware of it. As early as 1910 a confidential British report on

"Secret Societies" in Egypt mentioned that a suspended society, the Society for Life (Jamʿiyyat al-Ḥayāh), had "one or two Indians who used to plead the necessity of adopting the Indian system of fighting the occupation." Headed by ʿUmar Bey Luṭfī, another society profiled in the same report was providing "its members with necessary provisions and domestic supplies, with the view of boycotting foreign, and especially English goods in the future."[37] Long in the making, the 1922 Egyptian boycotts were definitely informed by Indian precedents.

Spearheading this effort, a committee of leading women—representing both Muslims and Copts—joined together to take a common "religious oath," an ecumenical vow to struggle steadfastly until victory: "We swear by God . . . to boycott the British aggressor, to deny to ourselves and to the people close to us everything that those usurpers have manufactured. By God, their shops are forbidden to us. By God, their factories are forbidden to us. By God, all that is connected to them is forbidden to us."[38] They protested first the continuation of the protectorate and then, after its abolition on February 28, 1922, the sham of Britain's unilateral declaration of independence. They rallied Egyptians to stop patronizing English bankers, haberdashers, shopkeepers, pharmacists, dentists, and doctors. So long as martial law and censorship of the press continued, and so long as their colleagues remained confined to exile or jail, they pledged to maintain this form of pressure on the government.[39]

Widely publicized and moderately successful, their consumer movement had profound reverberations. Suddenly, it endowed economic behavior with urgent political meaning. The principles of self-abnegation and self-sufficiency, which Gandhi had cultivated, did not motivate Cairo's boycotters to action. Cairo had no *swadeshi* stores. Lacking diversification, indigenous industries offered a limited selection of substitute goods. Symbolic action mattered more than economic purity. Even though they celebrated "national" industry, Cairo's bourgeois boycotters were not opposed to the substitution of British imports with other European alternatives. To resist British imperialism by buying French or Italian—rather than English—clothes was, for them, a political virtue.[40]

Boycotters in Cairo mainly targeted ready-made clothes. Before, during, and after the boycotts of 1922 to 1924, textiles and apparel figured as Britain's most valuable export to Egypt. Overall the leading import in these years, they accounted for more than a third of the total value of imported goods from all nations. Britain's other main exports (coal, machinery, and metals) paled in significance. Between 1922 and 1924 the value of British cloth exported to Egypt declined, however, from approximately 9 million to 7.7 million Egyptian pounds. This decline was part of a long-term trend in the interwar period, when the British cloth-making industry faced depressed demand, lower profits, and higher competition worldwide as well as anti-imperial consumer boycotts. While the value of British textiles imported to Egypt began to decrease, Egyptian expenditures on foreign textiles rose slightly. These trends suggest that the boycott had at least a modest effect on trade.[41]

Despite the dearth of Egyptian alternatives, the boycott nevertheless had a significant impact on the nationalist movement's ethos. In January of 1922, students established boycott committees to urge Egyptians who had opened savings accounts in British banks to entrust their money instead to the new nationalist venture, Banque Miṣr, founded in April of 1920. Here and there in Upper Egypt and the Nile Delta, they persuaded farmers to stop selling cotton and cottonseed at the official concessions of the Egyptian Markets Company. They convinced the fellaheen of Shandawil and a few other villages to instead patronize what an official British report called "unauthorised markets," where they happily avoided the standard dues.[42] In Cairo, student activists urged consumers to patronize "national department stores" (*al-maḥallāt al-tijāriyya al-waṭaniyya*) such as Cicurel, owned by a prosperous Jewish family, and al-Mawardi. Shopkeepers hurried to respond to the novel demand. They advertised the sale of articles such as "national soap" and "Egyptian clothes," and they announced the opening of a boutique for patriotic weavings. Thus, the boycott stimulated merchants and customers to redefine "what it meant to be Egyptian," as Nancy Reynolds explains in *A City Consumed*.[43]

Injecting political meaning into the act of buying imperial goods, boycotters advocated discrimination in the marketplace. Whether or not they held every British citizen (from Manchester magnates to Cairo doctors) responsible for the injustices of colonialism, they justified their agenda on the basis of a consequentialist moral code. On the spectrum of attitudes to trade, anti-imperial consumer boycotters stood at one end; free-trade imperialists at the other. Whereas anti-British boycotters expressed a bias against the empire's goods, British free-trade advocates remained studiously opposed to Imperial Preference, a series of protectionist proposals for privileging, through a new set of tariffs, British over American or German products.

Economic nationalism was on the rise, however, in British circles in Egypt too. The 1922 *Report on the Economic and Financial Situation of Egypt*, submitted to the Department of Overseas Trade, dealt at length with the problem of German competition. It argued that German agencies were "vastly more profitable than British ones," which explained why German "safety razors and nail scissors" were more attractive to the Egyptian consumer than the British alternatives. "German trade propaganda in Egypt," it continued, "is widely spread in many languages, particularly Italian." Counterfeit and contraband steel products presented the greatest challenge. German firms had caused "an epidemic of infringements of trademarks" to spread into Egypt. Through the brokerage of Egyptian and Levantine merchants, they had smuggled into the country German razors whose blades fraudulently displayed the words "Real English," spelled in Arabic letters. As much as he worried about the German steel industry, the British commercial agent for Egypt who submitted this report, a certain Mr. Mulock, lost no sleep over the Egyptian boycott. He described it as "impracticable, except in isolated and relatively insignificant instances."[44]

A Syrian Expatriate's Dilemma: To Champion Egyptian Boycotts or Free Trade?

What did Riḍā make of the Egyptian consumer boycott? Did political events in his adopted country stir him to abandon or modify his commitment to freer trade? His journal offered few hints as to his views on anti-imperial boycotts before the nationalist awakening that followed World War I. In November of 1908 *al-Manār* published an article on the wave of boycotts triggered by the Austro-Hungarian Empire's formal annexation of the provinces of Bosnia and Herzegovina. The article related the Ottomans' resolution "to relinquish purchasing their commodities, and this economic war (*al-ḥarb al-iqtiṣādiyya*)—as they call it—is one of the most beautiful ways by which a nation can fight against its enemy, especially when this enemy is, like Austria, solely a trading nation." On reaching the ports of Beirut, Jaffa, and Latakia, Austrian ships found themselves blocked from conducting trade. Sensationally, some protesters tore their "Austrian clothes" to pieces, shredding "their own possessions." Enthusiasm for the boycott spread even to Egypt. When all the acts of boycotting (*muqāṭaʿa*) were added up, they amounted to a "powerful effect on Austrian factories and mills." The article's enthusiasm for this new method to contend against the expansion of a European empire into the lands of Muslims is clear. Yet it was written not by Rashīd Riḍā but by his brother, Ḥusayn Waṣfī Riḍā.[45] If Rashīd Riḍā agreed, he was not obliged to make an exception to his longstanding opposition to the imposition of new religious barriers to international trade.[46]

As a Syrian expatriate, Riḍā could do little more than witness the Egyptian struggle for independence as a sympathetic outsider. His journal reported at length on "the Egyptian question." But his article on this question in the January 1922 issue made only a fleeting reference to the activities of an unnamed female patriot, Hudā Shaʿarāwī. It simply remarked that she had addressed the members of the nationalist delegation, al-Wafd, "behind a veil" and then organized a reunion of women for "resistance of the adversary by boycotting his merchandise."[47] Two months later, in an article that he published after Britain's declaration of Egypt's independence, Riḍā returned to developments in the country. Instead of representing the boycott as a peaceful instrument of passive resistance, he placed the boycott on a slippery slope toward violence. If the nationalist campaign had begun with the appeal to resist "all English things and persons," it had ended in the assassination of officials and soldiers.[48]

Egypt's boycotting movement did coincide with a rise in acts of political violence. In one instance, a mob of boycotters rushed to loot the goods of an official market, and the police had to interfere to protect its English inspector. At the height of the boycott, confidential British documents reported on several "shooting outrages" in Cairo, resulting in two cases in fatal gunshot wounds. Egyptian newspapers condemned these acts with indignation. So did the Wafd High Command. It denounced "unlawful" tactics as unjustifiable, no matter the motive.[49] But the main suspects were Wafdist radicals who had formed underground cells.[50] As a result of these events, the nationalist movement effectively split up into three camps: liberal politicians who favored conciliatory negotiations with the British, Wafdists who advocated consumer boycotts and more generally a nonviolent policy of noncooperation, and extremists who joined secret insurgent cells. As the vice president of the Syrian-Palestinian Congress, formed to present a demand for independence to the League of Nations, Riḍā had most in common with the moderate Egyptian nationalists who championed a diplomatic solution to the crisis.

Widely covered by the popular press, the boycott was the most exciting and newsworthy issue of the day. What accounts for Riḍā's reticence? Why did he not urge his readers in the dominions of the British Empire to join the Egyptian boycotting campaign? Censorship is one possibility. Field Marshal Edmund Allenby suspended the publication of all newspapers that had printed the Wafdist manifesto, ordered the arrest of its signatories, and banned its republication. British authorities perceived the manifesto's vehement "plea for the cessation of all social and commercial intercourse between English and Egyptians" as an incitement to the insubordination of "all Egyptian Government employees, including officers and men of the army and police, who found themselves charged with the suppression of rioting and disorder of political origin."[51] Under the circumstances, it would have been risky for Riḍā to support the boycott with rousing rhetoric.

Another possibility is that, as a scholar committed to enlightened commercial ideals, he felt little affinity for this popular movement to restrict international exchange. The Cairo boycott of British goods was nearly the perfect inversion of the Enlightenment construct of the London Bourse: the unique place that Voltaire had idealized (as the introduction to this book mentioned) because it served merchants from all nations to trade rationally with one another, in deliberate blindness to confessional distinctions. In the early twenties, Cairo's boycotters were anything but sectarian. An alliance of Coptic and

Muslim boycotters had no problem with Egyptians shopping at department stores such as Cicurel, owned by a Jew, that supported the boycott. But their nationalistic opposition to commercial intercourse with the British Empire's symbolic representatives was very far removed, historically and philosophically, from the eighteenth-century spirit of the Enlightenment.

Furthermore, there was the risk, which Riḍā in particular had reasons to appreciate, that the Egyptian boycott would backfire as a political strategy. Free-trade imperialists could have easily used the calls for consumer action to argue that Egyptians were far from ready for independence; they saw any threat to British economic interests as a powerful argument for extending British rule. Riḍā had special insight into this imperial British perspective as a result of his secret diplomatic negotiations with British officials over the future status of the Ottoman Empire's Arab provinces. He came to realize, as a result of these wartime negotiations, that British officials demanded a political commitment to free trade before they would even consider the question of home rule.

In 1915, following the Battle of Baṣra, he learned that Britain would officially promise nothing more than "free trade to the Arabs in the Arab country which will become possessed by the English government." This was disappointing news to him. British authorities had assured him earlier that they had no designs on Arab territories. But when he tried to publish their "impressive proclamation" in his journal, British censors struck the reassurance out. They replaced the promise of sovereignty with the promise of free trade.[52] In an effort to persuade British officials to reconsider, Riḍā warned that the Arabs were fiercely independent and that calls for a jihad against the English would multiply with the loss of political independence. Discontent would spread to "all the Mohammedans in India" and elsewhere. The resigned bitterness that Egyptian Muslims felt upon hearing the news that Britain had decided to alter their country's de jure status from an Ottoman khedivate to a British protectorate paled in comparison to the righteous enmity that would break out if England decided to extend its rule to the heartlands of the Arabs. On top of these veiled warnings, Riḍā disclosed that he had dined several times with the German director of Oriental Affairs, Baron Max von Oppenheim, who had tried to convince him, "as a man of certain religious influence," to align himself with Germany and warn the Muslim world "against England."[53]

Riḍā delivered these warnings with diplomatic finesse—in a secret memorandum that he decorated with declarations of loyalty, friendship, and admiration for Britain. His stated goal was to explain "the feelings of the Arabs" and the "desires of the Mohammedans" privately, with the understanding that he would "refrain from making these ideas public in such eventful times." He remembered a speech that he had given in India three years earlier, during his visit to Nadwat al-ʿUlamāʾ in Lucknow, where he had openly celebrated "the justice of England and the freedom she gives to religion." His praise of England "produced a very bad effect amongst the Egyptians," who began to mock his conciliatory approach to British power. This "resulted in a great material loss to my religious prestige and the circulation of my religious magazine." Writing as a "real friend and admirer of the English," Riḍā dared to explain to British officials the political aspirations of Arab Muslims because he still hoped—following the bombardment of the Arabian coasts, the military occupation of al-Faw and Baṣra, and the "suspicious" hoisting of the British flag over "the most promising countries in the dominions of the Arabs—that they would relent and support the cause of independence.[54]

Two convictions sustained his naïve wartime hope that Britain would cede territories captured from the Ottomans during the Mesopotamian campaign to a sovereign Arab state. He believed that British rule was relatively benevolent, and he believed that Britain's sole interest in Arab lands was economic. For these reasons, he approached British officials diplomatically and never failed to show his devotion to free trade. Tellingly, the draft of a constitution for an Arab-Islamic Empire, which he submitted to the British during the world war, guaranteed not only freedom of "religious beliefs" but also freedom of "financial operations."[55]

All of this goes a long way toward explaining why Riḍā declined to support the Egyptian boycott of English goods. But the fact of the matter is that their fight for nationhood was not his fight. As a Syrian Muslim, he cared principally about Muslim unity and Syrian independence, not Egyptian sovereignty. He never attached to Egypt the highest level of religious and patriotic significance. On the contrary, when he pressed the British to support "the complete independence of Islam in its cradle," he made it clear that Greater Syria and the Arabian Peninsula "should not be placed on the same level with Egypt and other places in Africa."[56] Although he expressed fondness for Egypt as an adopted fatherland (*waṭan*), he continued to feel like a foreigner there. In the eyes of Egyptian nationalists, he complained, the nonnative Muslim Arab belonged to the country no more than did "a Chinese idol worshipper."[57]

Riḍā did eventually turn into an open critic of the British Empire. By late 1922, a few days after the occupation of Constantinople by Allied troops and the ensuing abolition of the Ottoman Empire, he felt free to describe British imperialism as a crusade directed at eliminating "whatever weak Islamic power remains in the world."[58] There is no reason to dwell on this post-Wilsonian turn in Riḍā's political expression since several historians have focused on it already. Suffice it to say that it had a great deal to do with mounting frustration over British and French rebuffs to diverse Syrian delegations seeking self-determination, not to mention their lack of support for his dream to revive the caliphate in a unified Islamic state.[59]

A Clash of Modernities: A Nationalist-Salafist Reaction to Ataturk's Hat Law

Riḍā's scandalized reaction to Muslims adopting European fashions, apparent in the 1928 fatwa against sexy French trousers, reveals how much his attitudes to European cultural hegemony hardened in the wake of the Egyptian boycotts of British goods. What accounts for this hardening? Why did he alter his relatively relaxed approach to the consumption of European clothes? One course of action that placed him under duress was the policy of secularization initiated by the new Republic of Turkey. In 1925, shortly after dismantling the caliphate, the nation's first president, Mustafa Kemal Ataturk, banned the fez. Criticizing it as a symbol of backwardness, he promoted in its place the fedora. His mandate crystallized opposition to "secular" dress. Religious leaders balked, protesting that the hat's brim prevented believers from performing the ritual of prayer, which involved bringing the forehead to the ground.[60] Riḍā admired Ataturk in some respects. He described him as "a great man" who "unfortunately knew nothing about Islam."[61] But he resented deeply the Turkish leader's view that the fez, which the mufti still wore, stood in modernity's way. Even before Turkey's parliament passed the infamous Hat Law, Riḍā began to publish fatwas against European dress that were motivated by Ataturk's sartorial campaign.[62]

At play was clash of modernities.[63] Throughout his life, Riḍā had dreamed of an Islamic modernity. He had envisioned an age when Muslim moderns would thrive with open markets and prosper, no matter their habit of dress, by remaining true to their religion's original ideals. He maintained this broad perspective, which accommodated a plurality of tastes and trends, for much of his career. As late as 1922, he wrote a fatwa for a petitioner from Canada, Ḥusayn ʿAbd al-Raḥmān Dassūqī, justifying Sultan Maḥmūd II's reforms of 1826, which had obliged Ottoman soldiers to march and fight in Europeanized uniforms. He explained that this strategic change of one military costume for another had nothing to do with religion: Islamic law and the Prophet's example had afforded believers the freedom to dress in motley styles.[64] In contrast to Riḍā, Ataturk intended to realize in his nation an *étatiste* program of cultural reform that derived from a hegemonic and monolithic approach to modernization. His insistence on a stark opposition between religion and modernity, represented symbolically by the battle between the fez and the fedora, profoundly threatened Riḍā brand of Salafism. It forced Riḍā to react.

Accordingly, he struck a defiant, conservative tone in a fatwa about Muslims wearing European suits and hats that he published in two parts, at the end of 1925 and the beginning of 1926. Extolling the religious advantages of "national dress," he argued that traditional robes and turbans facilitated the Muslim rite of prayer. By contrast, tight-fitting pants and brimmed hats made it difficult to perform the mandatory prostrations. They led Muslims to lose their religion and sit in bars. Reflecting more broadly on Ataturk's program of "Westernization," which he preferred to label "Frankization," he warned that Turkey would fail to progress as a nation if it turned its back on its Islamic heritage. The plan to Romanize the Turkish alphabet, and therefore forsake the Perso-Arabic script that had been used by the Ottoman Turks for centuries, bothered him. It confirmed his impression that Ataturk and his heretical vanguard were bent on destroying, like infidels, all signs of Turkish adherence to Islam. He was convinced this was the wrong way forward because the nation needed a strong confessional bond to advance toward modernity. Through their customs and deeds, the first Muslims, the Salaf, had shown the superior way for a civilization to thrive. Had the Turks truly understood Islam, they would have realized that "its basis is military power, wealth, and law and order," qualities needed to build a new empire in the East and the West.[65]

Illustrated Advertisements for the Roaring Twenties: Flappers in Egypt and China

The aesthetic revolution of the Roaring Twenties, embodied by Ataturk and his stylish wife, propelled Riḍā to the vanguard of a countercultural Islamic campaign against Western fashion. Scandalized by brimmed hats and bobbed hair, Muslim conservatives from Egypt to China joined forces to oppose the trends sweeping through their nations. They used a new visual and physical culture—whose ideals consumer magazines worked to spread from Paris, London, and New York to Cairo and Canton—as a counterpoint to their own appeals for the revival of Islamic law. The more they felt out of step with the times, the more they idealized the golden past. Printed fatwas, published in different languages in regional journals, served them to communicate strict interpretations of the shariʿa across vast distances. Through this medium they established a semblance of unity and common purpose: the impression that they belonged to a transnational Islamic community that shared ancestral values and norms, which they needed to defend from the provocative assaults of coercive secularists and conspicuous feminists.

Consumer magazines that had little in common with *al-Manār* were one vector for the transmission of the culture of the Roaring Twenties. In Egypt the magazine of the moment was *al-Muṣawwar* (The Illustrated). Unlike *al-Manār*, this weekly published countless black-and-white photographs of the rich and famous as well as illustrated advertisements. Meanwhile, *al-Manār* still confined its promotional activities to the publication of subscription notices. It never published advertisements. A niche journal, its style was too decorous, its circulation too modest, and its readership too dispersed to attract corporate attention. *Al-Muṣawwar*, on the other hand, was expertly designed for mass circulation. Shortly after its foundation in 1924 it became the premier venue for alluring advertisements. Agencies in this field, led by the Société Orientale de Publicité, turned to it to encourage the consumption of imported luxuries: everything from cars to cosmetics on sale in Egypt's urbane dealerships and drugstores.

Countless advertisements for American, French, and British products exposed the magazine's readers to Western models of beauty, health, and vigor. Many of the illustrations were nothing but reproductions, published anew to seduce Egyptian consumers. In 1926, Holeproof Hosiery reproduced in *al-Muṣawwar* one of the iconic advertisements of the age: an exquisite design made five years earlier by the celebrated illustrator Coles Phillips. It exhibited a beautiful woman with short curls, high-heeled shoes, and a translucent gown inspired by a spider's web. The Arabic text below the illustration differed from the original English text by not drawing the viewer's gaze to the woman's "trim ankles, demurely alluring." Instead, it emphasized that the American stockings, expertly manufactured after decades of experimentation, combined the splendidness of Egyptian cotton and the strength of pure silk.[66] Kolynos placed advertisements for its "scientific dental cream" in newspapers and magazines all over the world. With *al-Muṣawwar*'s readers it shared a voyeuristic fantasy of a woman in a *négligé*, who dared to hold the viewer's gaze. On her vanity counter she placed her boar-bristle or horsehair toothbrush and a tube of Kolynos toothpaste. This was the secret behind her snow-white smile. The text suggested using the product twice a day to prevent tooth decay. The oddest of advertisements for a cosmetic product exploited the cachet of Paris to a ridiculous extent. It consisted of a montage of heads, with distinct coiffures, ascending the Eiffel tower.

Images of perfectly modern men were used as well to sell foreign commodities in Egypt. An advertisement for Quaker Oats that circulated in the press in both Egypt and China showed a ballplayer famished and forlorn, exhausted after playing a strenuous sport. It encouraged a regular diet of oatmeal—charged with vitamins, proteins, and mineral salts—for power and vitality. Unlike William Penn, the Quaker depicted in the logo, the modern American model wore

FIGURE 7.2 Advertisements such as this one for Kolynos toothpaste tried to seduce Egyptian consumers with new ideals of beauty. Source: *al-Muṣawwar* 116 (December 31, 1926): 15.

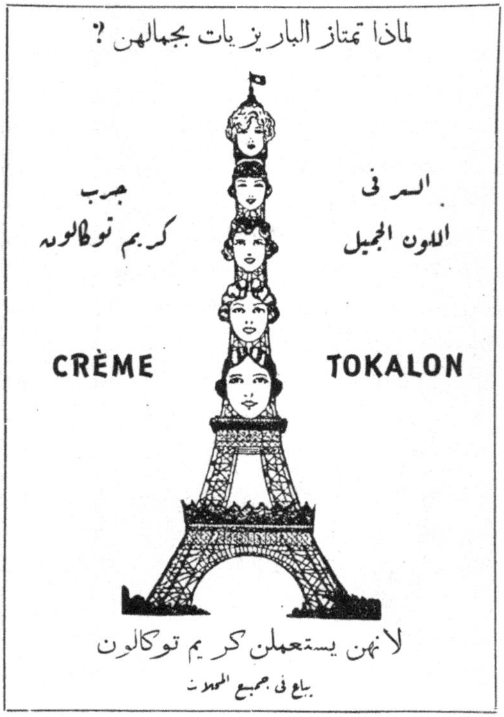

FIGURE 7.3 Why are Parisian women so beautiful? Their secret is Tokalon's vanishing cream. Source: *al-Muṣawwar* 132 (April 22, 1927): 11.

FIGURE 7.4 A dispirited ballplayer in need of a bowl of oatmeal. Quaker Oats used the exact same image in advertisements that it published in China in the late twenties. Source: *al-Muṣawwar* 113 (December 1, 1926): 11.

no hat.[67] Perrier similarly hinted at "vitality, youth, and strength." The paragon of a man illustrated in the advertisement with a raised glass of mineral water and rolled-up sleeves sported loose pants, fit for tennis. He did not wear the constricting "French" trousers that supposedly prevented Muslim men from exercising their body in prayer.[68]

Some British advertisements were essentially experiments in cross-cultural marketing; they explicitly reflected symbols of class status and impressions of religious or ethnic preferences. They differed in this respect from other advertisements (French, American, or British) that circulated the exact same illustrations in Egypt and China. Thus, Anzora, a London perfumery, fabricated a cream for a gentleman to master his hair for an evening about town. Needless to say, the high-class gentleman with impeccable hair, depicted savoring an after-dinner liqueur, wore no hat. Hovering in the background was an attentive waiter wearing a rather unfashionable tarbush.[69] Wincarnis, the brand name of a restorative beverage, probably used the same designer for its advertisement. It showed a bureaucrat reclining in his chair to enjoy a late-morning break, as suggested by the fan on his desk and the clock on the filing cabinet. In his hand, he held a goblet of Wincarnis, a fortified wine further strengthened with malt and meat extracts, a combination of ingredients made to restore a man's body and soul after hours of drudgery. Waiting by his side was an Egyptian boy holding an empty serving tray. The contrast between the male figures represented the advertiser's vision of the benefits of growing up in Egypt: the passage from the humbleness of a lad, wearing a traditional robe and cap, to the hard-earned sophistication of an adult indulging in a drink of Wincarnis. Like Wincarnis, the branch of Horlick's that exported "the original malted milk" for infants and invalids from England to Egypt experimented in cross-cultural marketing, too. One of its advertisements showed a British explorer sporting a pith helmet and explaining the virtues of Horlick's milk to a tarbush-wearer in a suit.[70] Another iconographically striking advertisement captured the moment when an Egyptian family, dwarfed by Horlick's packages, hailed a glass of malted milk shining on the horizon like the rising sun.

The global spread of Western codes and styles, illustrated by *al-Muṣawwar*, provoked the *ʿulamāʾ* of many nations to react. In Turkey, Iran, and Afghanistan, where rulers' secularization projects targeted turbans and veils, clerical reactions were desperate and sharp. But Muslim scholars adopted defensive postures even in states that were not directly affected by the reforms of Ataturk, Reza Shah, and Amanullah Khan, and the dramatic unveiling of their wives.[71] The broader issue in their eyes was the voluntary embrace of Western fashions by Muslim consumers, male and female, although they found especially offensive the flagrant violation of "Islamic" norms by liberated Muslim women. This trend was not just a problem for them; it was also an opportunity. It gave them a good reason to communicate their grievances across national divides and rally for a countercultural cause.

Indeed, the dramatic debuts of the flappers in Muslim societies was one reason behind the most extraordinary correspondence between Egypt and China. This correspondence began in 1930 with an unprecedented request for a fatwa. Ma Ruitu, the Chinese fatwa seeker, was scandalized by Muslim women's self-fashioning around the end of the Roaring Twenties. He was the founder and editor of a new Sino-Muslim journal, "Arabic Theology Monthly" (*Tianfang xueli yuekan*), which served in part as a vehicle for the translation of articles from *al-Manār* into Chinese. He wanted Riḍā to ban the daring trend that he had witnessed in the markets of Guangzhou. Some Muslim women had cut their locks off, in a brash display of the new hairstyle, and they had removed their face veils. How wrong was this?

Making a gesture toward legal relativism, Riḍā explained that the degree of immorality depends on the country's traditional customs and norms. At the same time, he claimed that women's misbehavior would weaken and break the global Islamic community's political and social bonds. Quoting an unnamed Salafi ancestor, he added that women's disobedience was the "harbinger of

FIGURE 7.5 An advertisement for Wincarnis, a fortified wine, that deliberately represents age and class differences to exploit effendis' aspirations. Source: *al-Muṣawwar* 170 (January 13, 1928): 27.

FIGURE 7.6 Like Wincarnis, Horlick's also experimented in cross-cultural advertising, depicting in this instance an Egyptian family hailing a glass of malted milk. Source: *al-Muṣawwar* 157 (October 14, 1927): 17.

infidelity." He concluded—with deliberate vagueness—that different aspects of their Westernization could be described as reprehensible, forbidden, or totally taboo. This as well as other Arabic fatwas, which Ma Ruitu translated into Chinese, exposed Sino-Muslim readers to Riḍā's brand of Salafism. Because in this instance he represented the unveiled Muslim woman's peccadilloes as a threat to "the bonds of the community" (*rawābiṭ al-umma*), it revealed to them, too, his peculiar resort to antifeminist rhetoric to plead urgently for supranational Islamic unity.[72]

Arabian Slippers and the Turn to Gandhi

The arrival of the Roaring Twenties in Muslim societies along with Ataturk's program for Turkey to shed the trappings of Islam spurred Riḍā to react negatively to the consumption of European clothes, with heightened anxiety about cultural assimilation. But it did not motivate him to express his political-economic ideals in a new way. What did inspire him to reframe these ideals was the example of Mahatma Gandhi. Riḍā praised Gandhi for treading "the straight path of his religion" and following "its lofty ideals with all sincerity." In contradistinction to Ataturk and "our cultured intellectuals," who consider religion "antagonistic to enlightened and progressive thoughts," Gandhi "never practiced politics in isolation from religion and ethics." Riḍā wrote effusively about Gandhi. He had some of his writings translated, and he defended his noncooperation movement against Egyptian and Indian critics.[73] His admiration did not cause him to embrace all of Gandhi's beliefs. He never came, under Gandhi's influence, to denounce imperial machines as sinful things. Nor did he ever preach the politics of passive resistance, abnegation, and self-reliance.[74] Instead, he remained until the end of his life committed to the passage of foreign technology into the Muslim world, and he continued to sing the praises of free, or nearly free, commerce between Muslims and others.

Yet Riḍā found tremendously attractive Gandhi's principle of *swadeshi*, an economic philosophy that exalted local production and scorned foreign consumption. This philosophy aimed in part at making consumers aware of the ways in which they supported the British Empire. In practice, Gandhi and other leaders of the independence movement did not expect Indians to boycott all British goods. They targeted symbolic goods: alcohol, because it represented dissipation and dissolution, and machine-made cloth, because it represented the triumph of imperial taste, a loss of communal identity, and the success of English factories at the expense of Indian weavers.[75] In 1922 Riḍā rejected Bombay Muslims' rationale for boycotting all alcoholic products. He felt it was absurd for

Muslims to forgo the best and most useful things that modernity put on offer.[76] But he did not consider garments fabricated in a European style, with the exception of military uniforms, as indispensable for Muslims in modern times. Swayed by Gandhi's writings and aware of the enthusiasm generated by the Egyptian boycotts, he began to assess the Muslim consumption of European luxury goods in a strategic political framework, where the ultimate goal was to achieve freedom from colonialism.

This is why he described the *pantalon* and the *cravat* as reprehensible not just from a religious vantage point but also from a nationalistic vantage point, and why he referred to Muslims who adopted such articles of clothing for no other reason than to imitate the Franks as infidels.[77] It is remarkable to find such value judgments, though commonplace at the time, in an Islamic legal register. Riḍā's decision to incorporate them into his fatwas, beginning around 1925, reflects quite a turnabout in his juridical aims since he had concentrated earlier on convincing Muslims that wearing European clothes was licit. This development shows that fatwas were adaptable instruments in his hands, instruments that could be manipulated by him to rule for and against the same thing depending on the politics of the time. The change in his goals during the mandatory era matters historically, for it reveals how an Arab nationalist agenda came to affect judgments about right and wrong in the sacred law.

It dawned gradually on Riḍā that Gandhi's principles transcended national and religious boundaries. In 1923, in the book where he famously argued for the caliphate's restoration, he mentioned Gandhi as an example of a man who was moved to lead his community by his noble convictions. Yet he presented him specifically as a leader of India's Hindu subjects; he named other men as the leaders of India's Muslim subjects.[78] By the early thirties, Gandhi's fame soared to such a height in the world that every Muslim nationalist in the Middle East, including Riḍā, saw him as an interreligious model. When Gandhi's ship stopped at the Suez Canal in 1931 during a voyage from Bombay to London, the Egyptian press praised him with an enthusiasm bordering on devotional fervor.[79] Within a few months, Riḍā published an article, "Gandhi Testifies to Islam and Muḥammad," where he gave a taste of the affection that Egyptians and Syrians felt for the Mahatma.[80]

But Riḍā began championing Gandhi's model of resistance before this turn of events. In 1930 he referred to Gandhi as a man "venerated by the pagans" and "honored by the Muslims." He gave Gandhi credit for developing the revolutionary strategy of civil disobedience against imperialism. As examples of Gandhi's tactics, Riḍā stressed tax resistance, the boycott of English commodities and alcoholic substances, and the withdrawal of "national" savings from English banks.[81] However familiar today, these novel methods of economic resistance excited Riḍā and other imperial subjects who were still struggling to win independence. It is fair to say that by 1930, they found it pointless to wait any longer for deliverance by the League of Nations. "The Wilsonian moment" had passed into history, giving way to what might be called "the Gandhian moment."[82]

As an editor, Riḍā actually played an essential role in presenting Gandhi in greater depth to Arabic readers before 1930. He published in installments, beginning in 1926, a translation of Gandhi's 1913 *Guide to Health* (*Kitāb al-Ṣiḥḥa*).[83] This was the first translation into Arabic of a book by Gandhi.[84] Riḍā read this work with the utmost care. In the preface to the book, which he printed independently, he explained that he would comment—through glosses on the margins—on whatever struck him as meaningful. It is worth dwelling for a short while on these glosses because so little is known about the Arab discovery of Gandhi.

Much was lost in translation. On the first page, Gandhi had quoted Lucifer's famous line from Milton's *Paradise Lost*, "The mind is its own place, and in itself Can make a Heav'n of Hell, a Hell of Heav'n." Heaven, therefore, "is not somewhere above the clouds," deduced Gandhi, "and hell somewhere underneath the earth." Since Gandhi did not disclose it, Riḍā had no way of knowing that the quotation from Milton's epic poem came from the banished archangel's speech. But he sensed that things were amiss theologically. In a footnote, he commented that Milton was right in one respect: mental perceptions have some effect on pleasures and tortures on earth. Then he added for good measure: "As for the pleasures of the Garden and the tortures of Hell, they are part of the invisible world, which lies beyond Milton's intellect and cognition, so he has no right to pass judgment on it."[85]

Riḍā's edition of Gandhi's *Guide to Health* is a testament to the limits of cultural understanding in other respects too. Gandhi wrote about the evils of drinking tea, coffee, and cacao, whose production depended on indentured labor and whose consumption led to all sorts of harm. Somehow or other, this moved Riḍā to reminisce about his experimentation with tobacco and his tea-drinking habits. When, after praising the virtues of nakedness, Gandhi joked that women wear so many heavy anklets that they can barely move, Riḍā, ever so earnest and pompous, remarked: "India's women really have exceeded all proper bounds in wearing multiple pieces of ugly jewelry. This is harmful and far beneath the tastes of high-class people." Reflecting on the spread of disease, Gandhi counseled his readers to avoid doctors and their drugs. Riḍā agreed that some ignorant physicians cause illnesses, but he advised his readers to trust doctors and their prescriptions. At the beginning of the chapter on sexual relations, before Gandhi had the chance to explain why everyone should strive to escape from "the snares of carnal desire," Riḍā warned his readers that the author had an exaggeratedly abstemious attitude to the prerogatives of married life.[86] Evidently Riḍā found many of Gandhi's values strange, and he assessed them critically. Yet he expressed his dissenting opinions with admiration and respect.

What matters for this history is that Gandhi's book offered Riḍā a philosophical justification for struggling economically for nationalist liberation. Gandhi appealed for "the consummate reform" of habits of dress as an advocate of self-sufficiency. He urged Hindus as well as Muslims to free themselves from the submissive notion that black European suits, if suitable for cold countries, were necessary for decorum and prestige in a tropical country. Riḍā found this line of reasoning so compelling that he decided to make it his own. At the end of the chapter on dress, Gandhi argued that it was healthier to walk barefoot or, if necessary, to wear Indian sandals than to suffer from headaches with European shoes. Getting into the spirit of national competition, Riḍā contended that Ḥijāzī slippers would serve the inhabitants of hot countries better than Indian clogs.[87]

Tellingly, Riḍā explicitly invoked the wide range of Indian models for resisting colonialism in a 1930 appeal that he made for everyone in "the Islamic world" to join together as a single, unified community for a "general economic boycott" of France. It is striking that he did not make a similar appeal eight years earlier, during the Egyptian boycott of English goods and services. What explains the change besides the discovery of Gandhi? He resented French imperialism far more than he ever resented British imperialism. Whereas in his view British imperialists made no concerted effort to alter the religion and culture of Muslims, French imperialists seemed to entertain, again and again, ways to destroy Islam. At the turn of century, his journal had exposed a scandalous proposal for European armies to invade Mecca and Medina, exhume Muḥammad's grave, and translate his cadaver—as a trophy of war—to the Louvre. His resentment of French imperialism intensified in the interwar period, with the establishment of the mandates in Syria and Lebanon. By the fall of 1930, when he published the article, he had long been convinced that France's civilizing mission aimed at forcing Muslims to abandon their religion. France's centennial parades to commemorate the conquest of Algiers, which took place earlier that year, celebrated the successes of *francisation*, and they provoked a wave of anticolonial discontent. Riḍā ventured so far as to compare this cultural program to the Spanish Reconquista, which had forced the Muslims of al-Andalus to renounce their faith. Notwithstanding his longstanding grievances against France, his call for a global Muslim boycott of French goods and services was a new turn in his thought as well as a contribution to the formation of an Islamic politics of consumption, which owed something to the example of Gandhi and his spinning wheel.[88]

Nationalistic Economics and the Rise of Salafist Protectionism

The world powers' slide toward protectionism during the Great Depression must have contributed to the transnational appeal of Gandhi's tributes to domestic manufacturing and domestic consumption. In the United States, Congress passed a series of protectionist measures that culminated in the Tariff Act of 1930. Meanwhile, Japan established some of the highest tariffs to protect its imperial interests.[89] Other industrialized powers followed suit, adopting policies to give an advantage to national or imperial goods and taxing foreign alternatives. In Great Britain, policymakers had for decades fiercely defended the liberal idea of free trade. But in the aftermath of the Great War, the tide began to turn there as well. Parliament passed the Safeguarding of Industries Act to shield nine categories of products, including synthetic chemicals and wireless valves, from external competition, and the government revived and extended duties on artificial silk and other foreign commodities.[90] A stalwart opponent of free trade, the secretary of state for the colonies, Leo Amery, secured funds to establish a new institution, the Empire Marketing Board, designed to persuade British citizens to buy British things. This development heralded, if not quite the end of free-trade imperialism, a cultural turn toward imperial protectionism. By the end of 1931, in response to the economic crisis, the country abandoned both the gold standard and its signature policy of free trade.[91]

How did Riḍā respond to the rise of nationalistic economics abroad? He reflected on it in 1930, with passion and conviction, in a lecture that he gave on a Ramaḍān night at the royal clubhouse of the learned Society of the Oriental League to a mixed audience of Azhari students and European Arabists. Titled "Renovation, Renovating, and Renovators" (Al-Tajdīd wa-l-tajaddud wa-l-mujaddidūn), this was his boldest attempt to present himself as the Islamic renewer of the century.[92] The lecture staked a claim to religious leadership in a new culture war.

Sounding like a prophet for the Muslim Brotherhood, he first spent some time firing a volley at feminists, atheists, and materialists. These revolutionaries were bent on destroying social mores. Everything from the past seemed ugly to them. They wanted to compel men to wear hats and shave their beards. They wanted to liberate Muslim women from the confinement of the house, which they "called a prison even though it is like a palace with a garden." Clamoring for women's rights (*ḥuqūq li-l-marʾa*) and legal equality, they wanted to reform the sacred laws of inheritance and divorce. Libertines, they condoned cavorting with women! Swimming and dancing in mixed company! Troubled by this wave of ideas favoring secular modernization and sexual liberation, Riḍā blamed

Muslim liberals, Coptic intellectuals, and Turkish heretics for the dangerous turn. With a striking commercial metaphor, he criticized "the rabble of apostates in this great country" for peddling foreign doctrines in the nation's market.[93]

Instead of all this, he wanted Egypt and other developing countries of the East to follow the Japanese model: a Meiji Renovation of sorts that would bring forth economic advancement without rending the social fabric.[94] He advocated both a religious and a secular renewal. The first type of renewal meant restoring Islam—through Arabic literacy campaigns and Muslim missionary activities—to its righteous place, the place that it had occupied in "the first period" (*al-ṣadr al-awwal*). The second type of renewal would require social welfare legislation as well as an ambitious, multifaceted program of modernization. He envisioned hospitals, orphanages, and schools as well as a broad slate of economic reforms that would make the state and the Islamic community more powerful: scientific, technological, and industrial developments; financial, administrative, and military restructurings; and investments in infrastructures for transportation by land, sea, and air.[95]

Speaking as an apologist for Salafism in the grip of a nationalist awakening, he decided to address directly the widespread worry in Egypt and abroad that the global spread of Salafism would generate social discord and political fragmentation. To this end, he read a letter from an Indian reformer who was torn between his ardent goal to liberate India from British rule by joining a broad alliance of anticolonial parties and his pious desire "to propagate among the Muslims excellent virtues and Salafi doctrines." The problem was that he hated the Materialist Party. Was it justifiable under these conditions for the religionists (*al-dīniyyūn*) to join forces with the materialists (*māddiyyūn*)? Riḍā proposed a return to Islam's original spirit of convenience and right guidance, which would enable modern Muslims to recapture that elusive sense of primeval unity and cohesion that had supposedly existed among the first Muslims. Upon publication of the lecture, he added a footnote to clarify that he encouraged both parties to reach a compromise and unite in accordance with the method espoused by *al-Manār*.[96]

It was at this historical juncture, when the body politic seemed on the verge of ideological dismemberment, that Riḍā addressed the question of national preference. Only moribund cultures lack the drive "to favor what is national or ethnic over the foreign." As so often in the past when he wanted to defend a novel argument, he drew a parallel between modern European and early Islamic models. For all their rhetoric about free trade, the British were scandalized by the circulation of cheap German manufactures in their country, and they rushed to research and redress the problem. Conversely, during his travels in Germany he personally witnessed pharmacists in Berlin and Munich recoil when he asked for a French medicine that he needed: "That is Latin! That is Latin!" Having illustrated British protectionism and German chauvinism, Riḍā reflected on the patriotic preferences of "the peoples of the West" for their own industrial, commercial, and legislative goods.[97]

But the first Muslims invented the doctrine of national preference, he boasted: "Our ancestors anticipated the Europeans in taking pride in the legislation (*tashrīʿ*) and in other things from Islam's origins." Caliph ʿUmar I had insisted on wearing his old tunic in Syria, and as postprophetic lawmaker he had prohibited his governor in Persia from adopting the Persian garb. Moreover, he had ordered Arab conquerors to preserve their "Arab customs." Thus, Riḍā concluded that the Europeans, and above all the English, "imitated our forefathers."[98]

A few years earlier he had essentially argued the opposite—that the Prophet Muḥammad himself had worn a Persian shawl, indicating to Muslims an openness toward foreign clothes. How did he justify the flip-flop? Was he not bothered by the manipulability of Islamic law, by the fact that it offered so many diverse and contradictory precedents that a jurist could rely on it to justify one course and its opposite? Did the malleability of his models, which could be readily contorted to support both free trade and Arab protectionism, not perturb him?

He never addressed the reasons for his turnabout, but this chapter has offered several explanations. The boycotts for Egyptian independence, Ataturk's Hat Law, the discovery of *swadeshi* economics, the expansion of the French Empire into Lebanon and Syria, and the exaggerated fear that Islamic culture would vanish if secular liberalism continued its relentless advance stimulated him to elaborate on different occasions in the late twenties and early thirties a nationalistic Arab and Salafist approach to consumption. Fatwa seekers motivated him to alter his original rulings, too, by accentuating their religious preoccupation with Europeanization. The 1925 fatwa against the new Turkish program for Westernization was sparked, for example, by a Beiruti petitioner who invited Riḍā to imagine imams leading Friday prayers and annual holidays while dressed in European suits.[99]

There was one more reason—a critical condition—behind the change in his attitude to consumption. This reason, suggested by Riḍā himself in his 1930 lecture on renewing Islam, had to do with material circumstances and consumer choices. Nationalistic taste depended on the presence in the market of nationalistic products: "Had an Egyptian or Arab cure been available" when he visited the Munich and Berlin drugstores, he would have favored it.[100] Commercial realities delimited his horizons as a political consumer; they also delimited his horizons as a religious and legal thinker.

In Egypt, the press began advertising select commodities as "Made in Egypt" during the Great Depression.[101] This was the time when the Society of Muslim

Brothers, swayed by economic nationalism, imposed an Islamo-Egyptian dress code on its first class of schoolboys.[102] By the mid-thirties, during the economic recovery, signs of a patriotic approach to consumption as well as production were reproduced—in great abundance—by the press. In 1935 a new literary and artistic magazine, *Majallatī*, "My Journal," ran a populist advertisement for workers to invest four guineas to buy a single share in a domestic tobacco company and thus participate in building capitalism in the nation.[103] An entrepreneurial seamstress, Layla Shukra, published an appeal for apprentices to join her school for modern tailoring: "The first and only Egyptian institute for instruction in the technique of tailoring cloth in the Arabic language."[104] On a larger scale, the Piastre Plan which was launched by a grassroots movement to encourage industrialization, promoted its culturally significant brimless hats with nationalistic advertisements. Suspended on the roof of a factory appeared a gigantic representation of an old ten-*millième* coin, the piastre with a hole that the sultanate of Egypt had issued during World War I. A new tarbush hovered over the smokestack, like a cloud of steam, and a map of the Nile Delta served as the backdrop for the patriotic illustration of industrial capitalism. The text boasted about the magnificence of the national tarbushes and urged Egyptians

FIGURE 7.7 Advertisements for "made in Egypt" products, such as this one for the Piastre Plan's tarbushes, celebrated nationalistic industrialization initiatives in the thirties. Source: *Majallatī* 1, no. 11 (1935): 1326.

to keep foreign factories from winning the competition.[105] These three advertisements were published in 1935. In 1930, when Riḍā gave his lecture on renewing Islam, all of this was still the stuff of dreams.

At an earlier time, when "Arab" and "Egyptian" products and brands were virtually absent from the market, protectionism had hardly appealed to Riḍā. Actually, it made no economic sense. British management of Egypt's cotton economy before independence meant that there were few domestic industries to protect in the twenties. The "Buy Arab, Buy Egyptian" spirit of the times arose late in his life. His fatwas against *pantalons* and *cravates* encouraged readers to appreciate their own national attire, not to rush to the market to buy Arab or Egyptian substitutes. More than anti-imperial boycotts and the discipline of self-abnegation, it would take the emergence of new factory products to make patriotic shopping seem a viable activity or sensible aspiration. The realization of nationalistic dreams in at least a few tangible products is exactly what was needed to inspire at least a modest refashioning of consumption's sacred law.

8

Lottery Tickets, Luxury Hotels, and Christian Experts

Economic Liberalism Versus Islamic Exclusivism in a Territorial Framework

In 1930 a Sino-Muslim reformer wrote to Riḍā to ask if he might reclassify China as a "House of Islam." Ma Ruitu of Yunnan, the reformer, was the founder and editor of Guangzhou's first Islamic journal, "Arabic Theology Monthly" (*Tianfang xueli yuekan*), which offered Chinese readers a selection of articles from *al-Manār* in Chinese translation. He explained to Riḍā, whose journal he compared to the sun, that Muslims born and raised in China had earned the freedom to manifest "their piety" and follow "canonical acts." Was this not a sufficient reason for renouncing the standard juridical categorization of China as one of the realms of the infidels? If Riḍā were to accept this rationale, then all the rules and regulations that pertained to states under Islamic rule would pertain to China, too.[1]

The question was a meaningful one for Sino-Muslims at this time. Nationalists, celebrating China's political unification after years of war, held that Muslims were one of the new republic's essential constituencies. This meant that they enjoyed legal equality and all the rights of citizenship. Furthermore, the question suggested a willingness to move beyond the divisiveness of late imperial times, when uprisings and massacres had shattered the impression of unity in China. But what if Riḍā decided that China remained, despite its transition to republicanism, a House of War? Ma Ruitu suggested that, in such a case, Muslims would be legally allowed to sell alcohol on Chinese territory.

Ma Ruitu's question betrayed his assumption that Islamic law was not universally applicable to Muslims everywhere in the world. Certain taxes, such as a tithe levied on agricultural produce or imported merchandise, and certain prohibitions, such as the ban on Muslims selling wine, seemed enforceable in a House of Islam but possibly dispensable in a House of War. To earn the more respectable political and religious rank, would China need to comply with such taxes and prohibitions and in general adhere to an Islamic legal regime?

Outside of China, too, Muslims in the early twentieth century often asked themselves about the religious and legal implications of belonging to a state defined as "Islamic" or "non-Islamic." Their deliberations generally focused on financial and commercial practices for two reasons. First, there was a long juridical tradition of treating the goods of enemies captured in holy war, as well as the contracts of Muslims trading in a House of War, differently than in a House of Islam. Second, the expansion of banking institutions, the appearance of money in new forms, and the spread of "Euro-Islamic" consumer goods such as records of the Qurʾan, stimulated lively discussions and heated debates about the economic and religious behavior of Muslim societies in every type of polity. No mechanism existed for Islamic law to govern financial or commercial affairs in the colonies, protectorates, and mandates inhabited by Muslim majorities but ruled by European powers, nor in countries, such as China, inhabited by Muslim minorities. Where secular commercial codes had been enacted, pious individuals wondered more and more about their own religious responsibilities in the absence of state regulations. *Al-Manār* offered some of them answers.

As an independent fatwa-issuing enterprise, *al-Manār* provided personal legal advice across jurisdictions. Its mufti based his rulings on the Qurʾan and the Ḥadīth rather than on the commercial codes that justices had to follow in their countries' tribunals and courts. In theory, he could completely disregard the political systems in existence and issue universal advice for an ideal world where the shariʿa would reign even in China. In practice, however, not all of *al-Manār*'s rulings were universal. Some of its financial and commercial rulings had a territorial dimension. Different, laxer rules were available for the Muslims who lived in a House of War, especially if they chose to heed—as Riḍā recommended—a special Ḥanafi dispensation. Besides, the economic liberalism that fueled many of Riḍā's fatwas to the world did not automatically extend to the Ḥijāz, the region of Islam's birth, which a succession of rulers tried to preserve as an exclusive Islamic space: the opposite of a free-trade zone.

Riḍā made such territorial distinctions before World War I, but momentous political shifts in the interwar period gave new prominence to divisive, binary conceptions of the world. The Ottoman Empire collapsed, the League of Nations granted France a mandate over Syria and Lebanon, and, following the triumphal march of Wahhabi warriors into Mecca, the sultan of Najd proclaimed himself the king of the Ḥijāz. These events shook the status quo, and they motivated Riḍā to elaborate a series of territorial rulings.

Soon after the Ottoman Empire's fall, investors in Beirut started to speculate about new economic opportunities that they might lawfully pursue if their country had become, as a consequence of French rule, a realm of infidelity and war. As a stalwart defender of developmental economics, did Riḍā justify their risky ventures? Or did he argue that the shariʿa prohibited Muslim businessmen from risking their money to build tourist hotels that would traffic in wine? And, as Riḍā became embroiled in Saudi state-building initiatives, what did he have to say about the hiring of Christian experts to establish a modern infrastructure in the Kingdom of the Ḥijāz? Did he defend the principle of free trade, upholding it even for the land of the two holy mosques, or did he revive ancient taboos on the presence of non-Muslims in the vicinity of Mecca? These are the specific questions driving this chapter, and they will lead us to consider how, as an enlightened Islamic journal, *al-Manār* dealt with the problem of territoriality.

Freedom of Religion in Russia: House of Islam, House of War?

The medieval distinction between "the House of Islam" and "the House of War" informed Muslims' understanding of citizenship and religious identity in the early twentieth century. But modern developments made it difficult to identify states as simply belonging to one or the other side of this ideological boundary. In the globalized world of overseas empires, where many states formerly ruled by Muslim leaders retained sovereignty only in theory, the number of countries under "Islamic" rule seemed smaller than ever before World War I and on the brink of further retraction afterward. At the same time, wherever states granted subjects or citizens the right to worship freely, the premodern notion of a boundary between Muslim and non-Muslims lands made less and less sense. Several of *al-Manār*'s international correspondents sensed its inadequacy. They began to boldly imagine a new world, a beautiful map for humankind, where their countries would no longer appear on the wrong side of the border between Islam and infidelity. This was the dream that Ma Ruitu revealed when he wrote to Riḍā to ask if China might count, after all, as a House of Islam. Russia's Muslim citizens had had the same dream years earlier.

In 1905 a Russian fatwa seeker, A.T. from Kazan, informed Riḍā that Muslims in his town were debating whether to consider Russia "an abode of Islam" or "an abode of war." Riḍā responded in rather old-fashioned terms. Some scholars, he explained, may regard the United States and many European countries as abodes of Islam. There, as in Russia, Muslims had the right to practice their religion openly, without fearing internal opposition or civil discord. By the same token, these scholars would consider countries ruled by Muslims as "abodes of war" if they censored their Muslim subjects' duty "to command right and prohibit wrong." In Riḍā's view, a country should count as "an abode of Islam" when the laws pertaining to Muslims belonged to them and when believers had the right to express their religion publicly and the means to execute the sacred law effectively. By this reckoning, Russia remained in his eyes "a realm of infidelity and war."

In June 1905, when Riḍā issued this fatwa, Russia was in the middle of a revolution. Protesting against the Tsarist state, socialists and others had started calling for profound political reforms, including freedom of the press and freedom of religion. Bolsheviks, Mensheviks, and Marxists would play a key role in stirring workers to strike. Non-Orthodox denominations, which in the previous century had been labeled "foreign faiths," had started pressuring Nicholas II to grant his subjects "freedom of conscience." Muslims in the Caucasus demanded "equality of religious rights" and "the appropriate respect" for Islam, which the tsar could signal by legalizing conversion from the Russian Orthodox Church to their faith. The tsar would do so (four months after Riḍā published his fatwa) in the October Manifesto, new legislation that led baptized Tatars to petition official recognition of their conversion to Islam.[2] How well apprised Riḍā was of unfolding events and the ideological turmoil is unclear.[3] But he described "the Russians" in an indifferent manner as People of the Book whose doctrines and works had been tarnished by paganism and idolatry.[4]

In Riḍā's vocabulary, there was nothing very offensive to labeling a place an "abode of war." Even though it derived from a violent, monotheistic vision of the world, it did not appear to him as a call to arms. He favored a defensive interpretation of jihad, and Russia had not declared war on its Muslims. On the contrary, the empire had made many meaningful gestures to maintain good relations with its Muslim subjects, beginning with the printing and gifting of the Qurʾan by Catherine the Great.[5] Riḍā based his conceptions of the foreign state on a martial, religious lexicon because for him, as for other scholars trained in Islamic law, this was the terminology of international relations.[6]

Ironically, this categorization of Russia as enemy territory was an odd diplomatic maneuver that enabled Riḍā to affirm a positive relationship between the non-Muslim empire and its Muslim subjects. A 1906 fatwa made the repercussions clear. It concerned the use of state funds to finance the building of elementary schools in rural areas. The inquirer, Muḥammad Najīb al-Tūntārī, was perhaps Riḍā's most valuable informant about Russian affairs.[7] He explained that the state taxed Muslim peasants just as it taxed non-Muslim peasants, and used the revenue to build schools, hospitals and libraries. For years, rural Muslim had paid taxes without receiving anything from the government. "Muslims had never benefitted from this money," he explained, "not because they were deprived, but because they [had neglected] to ask for it."[8] However, with "ignorance and illiteracy" prevailing in poor villages, they desperately needed funding for schools. To remedy the situation, reformers had petitioned the Royal Court for funding, and the government had granted their request. But "fanatics" refused the money. They argued that the imperial administration had failed to follow Islamic law when it collected taxes from poor Muslims, and that the Royal Treasury had mixed the money collected from Muslim and non-Muslims subjects. Since this made it impossible to separate dirty from pure money, they advised Muslims to decline the empire's funds.

Predictably, Riḍā sided with the reformers. He denounced the zealotry of their opponents, who were "turning crazy with their religion." Recasting the debate in technical terms, he explained that it pitted advocates of social welfare against idealists pursuing the lawful circulation of money according to Islamic standards. The latter concern he quickly dismissed "because a non-Muslim ruler is not required to follow the rules of the shariʿa." "He has full control over the collection [of taxes]. If he agrees to return the money, why should we not take it? In lands beyond the house of Islam, the assets of the non-Muslim are permissible to Muslims as long as they are not taken by treachery or cheating."[9]

To consider Russia "a house of war" thus meant, for Riḍā, to liberate Russia's Muslims from the impossible expectation that the government follow Islam's sacred law in its approach to taxation and education. Rather than urging Muslims to fight against the Russian Empire, he encouraged them to become normal subjects and enjoy in peace the benefits of paying taxes.[10]

Anything Goes in a House of War: Here and There in the Indian Ocean

The "abode of war" designation had repercussions beyond Russia too. It mattered for the assessment of commercial exchanges at Indian Ocean ports that had fallen under the dominion of the British and Dutch Empires, which generated many questions about financial instruments and capitalistic pursuits. In 1905 a group of merchants residing in Aden, an entrepôt under British administration, began to wonder if it was lawful for them or their rivals to benefit financially from a series of current dealings with "the Europeans." Declared a "free" port in 1850, Aden had become one of the British Empire's great transshipment hubs. With duties charged only on salt, arms, spirits, wine, and opium, goods flowed in and out of the port on the thousands of merchant vessels that docked there each year to transport to Bombay things like ivory, ostrich feathers, mother-of-pearl shells, skins, hides, gum arabic, dates, coffee, and vast quantities of salt.[11]

In Aden, Europeans offered Muslims new deals, which sparked questions about the Islamic law of finance. After paying freight charges, a Muslim merchant who wanted to send any of these goods abroad could obtain from the steamship's captain a receipt specifying the measure and value of the cargo. "If one of the Europeans was present," the Muslim merchant could show him the shipmaster's slip of paper and, by paying him five for every hundred rupees of the estimated value, receive a document guaranteeing with his seal, "in the language of the Europeans," the safety of the goods. The insurance agent on site thus offered a security against shipwreck. He promised to indemnify the merchant for a total loss, and "they call this transaction a '*beymah*,' or payment." For a 5 percent premium, then, the insurer assumed the risk of financial loss in case of a shipping accident. But the merchant obtained more than peace of mind, for the security was a liquid asset. If he wanted "cash for his goods," he could locate another European, present to him the insurance documents, and obtain money before concluding any sales abroad.[12]

All of this meant that Muslim merchants in Aden were investing in hedges and speculating on future transactions. The unnamed locals who found this confounding specified that a European agent certified the security in a European language. As if to convey the foreignness of the exchanges as well as British, French, and Italian supremacy around the Gulf of Aden, the Arabic legal discussion was full of fascinating Italian, French, or English loan words: *qubṭān al-wābūr* for *capitano del vapore*, the steamship's captain; *sīkārtū* for *sicurtà* or security; and *beymah* for *paiement* or payment.[13] No "sacred legal expressions" existed to describe this commerce. But would it make a difference, the fatwa seekers asked, if the exchanges on trial took place among believers, which would avoid the entanglement with enemies of the faith?

A mufti residing in Singapore, ʿAlawī ibn Aḥmad al-Saqqāf (d. 1916), replied to the question before Riḍā. This mufti, who was born in Mecca, had joined the Ḥaḍramī diaspora on the British island. He had ties to the Ḥaḍramī community that had settled around the Gulf of Aden, whose mercantile activities included smuggling guns and exporting coffee.[14] It is likely, given his involvement, that members of this community posed the original question. An anonymous reader who found al-Saqqāf's fatwa confusing or wanting appealed to Riḍā for a second opinion. As a result, Muslims in three cities that "belonged" to the Empire of Free Trade—Cairo, Aden, and Singapore—participated in deliberations about the sacred law, the liquidity of securities, and commercial interactions with foreigners in a British colony.

In a learned but convoluted fatwa, al-Saqqāf concentrated on divergences between two Sunni schools of law regarding defective contracts based on future contingencies. He explained that Ḥanafi jurists allowed such contracts if

Muslims signed them in a House of War. However, the Shafiᶜite school of law, to which he belonged, did not offer this accommodation. He realized that the transaction entangled a believer with an unbeliever in territory under British rule, but he refused to describe the settlement of Aden as part of the House of War. His school of law considered conquered Muslim lands "abodes of infidelity" only in appearance.[15] In an ambiguous sense, Aden remained—from this perspective—a House of Islam. Even so, al-Saqqāf found a reason to justify the transaction with reservations and caveats. Generally, he considered voluntary and consensual transactions licit, although he hesitated in this instance because he perceived the risk taken by the insurance agent as analogous to gambling, which was definitely illicit.

In this case the territorial distinctions seemed irrelevant to Riḍā for all intents and purposes. His rationale for legalizing the commercial exchanges and financial schemes made the dilemma of Aden's religious and political status inconsequential. He admitted that jurists qualified commercial insurance contracts as "defective" because there was too much uncertainty about the future value of the asset. But he elaborated a legal maneuver to represent the exchange as a shariᶜa-compliant transaction. If a Muslim merchant in effect "hired" a European insurance agency to "protect" the cargo, then the document that certified their arrangement, the security, was conceivably both lawful and transferable. Doubts about its legality remained, however. Riḍā therefore assured his readers that, licit or not, the contract on trial had nothing to do with the worship of God.

Eventually, *al-Manār*'s legal communications about cross-cultural trade moved beyond this commercial orbit to reach farther destinations around the Gulf of Siam and the South China Sea. In 1922 Bangkok, as in 1930 Guangzhou, Muslims wondered about the relevance or irrelevance of old religious restrictions to the pursuit of profit in their nation-state. Gambling and games of chance were beyond a doubt forbidden in Mecca and Medina. But could Muslims not play the state lottery in Bangkok, a city that represented—in Riḍā's eyes—the quintessence of infidelity?

ᶜAbdallāh ibn Muḥammad al-Masᶜūdī, the director of a madrasa in Bangkok who wrote to Cairo for a fatwa, specified that the government used the profits that it made from the game to buy firearms and aircrafts. Earlier in the century, Thailand had outlawed all forms of gambling except horse betting. But the monarchy lifted the restriction during the world war, under British pressure, to permit the Red Cross to establish a lottery to fund its relief services. Fiscal problems led the government further to relax its opposition to the revenue-raising device. In 1921 the king's paramilitary force, the Wild Tiger Corps, issued the first of a series of state lotteries, printing close to a million tickets, to raise the capital to buy ammunition and guns. This was precisely the historical context behind the Thai question. It had to do with the rush of Muslim citizens to participate in a national financial scheme that ultimately aimed at arming a Buddhist monarchy.[16]

In one of his most economically liberal rulings, Riḍā held Muslim subjects might as well follow the financial and commercial laws of their host countries. "When in Siam," he might as well have said, "trade as the Siamese do." In the House of War, Muslims should feel free to engage in dubious enterprises. Every Muslim knew that the sacred law prohibited usury and gambling. But non-Muslim polities paid no attention to these Islamic prohibitions. Why should their Muslim denizens voluntarily impose upon themselves an extrajurisdictional code of religious disadvantages? They should be able to stand on the same footing as others.

Thus, in Bangkok in 1922, Thai Muslims were as free as their Buddhist compatriots, or so Riḍā held, to play the national lottery. To be sure, the game seemed like an evil European invention that bore some resemblance to a loathsome game of chance. The Qurʾan had placed the pre-Islamic version of lottery tickets, divining arrows, in the same category as idolatrous altars and wine. These were abominable things, the filthy products of Satan's work, that believers had to avoid if they wanted to prosper (Q. 5:90). Moreover, Riḍā realized that the proceeds would benefit a "non-Muslim government in the realm of infidelity." Nevertheless, he declared the lottery lawful because the shariʿa was not enforceable in Thailand, where this form of gambling had been legalized.[17]

Furthermore, Riḍā could not bear the thought of relying on the sacred law to discourage Muslims from turning a profit in a country such as China, where Muslims were a minority and the republic's laws allowed all citizens to earn money from the sale of alcohol. There was a world of difference, he reasoned, between Muslims consuming and Muslims selling the forbidden drink, and between the pursuit of this business in a House of Islam and in a House of War.

When he turned to the query from Guangzhou, he ruled that China had been "a house of infidelity and war from its origin," and its status had not changed with the rise of the republic. As a result, Chinese Muslims were still entitled to profit from a number of forbidden things. Since they belonged to the Ḥanafi school of law, which had cultivated a permissive position on cross-cultural entanglements overseas, they had no reason to mind the old usury taboo. They have the right, instead, to enjoy usury, *ribā*, guiltlessly. But what about selling wine? Riḍā thought that it would be wrong for a Muslim to open a tavern in China because doing so would promote a vile habit. But the Sino-Muslim businessman could lawfully obtain "the value of wine owed to him in a debt" and earn money from the sale of alcohol "to them, not to the Muslims." He expected that, by making their fortune grow "in the contemporary methods made lawful by their school of law," Chinese Muslims would flourish financially and, as a consequence, eventually succeed in converting China into a House of Islam.[18]

The allowances that Riḍā made for Muslim investors in non-Muslim territories were provocative. Some revivalists in the Dutch East Indies who had seen Riḍā as an ally greeted them with disbelief. They resented the implication that believers under colonial rule could give up—with the mufti's approval—the aspiration to follow God's law to the fullest extent.[19] Thus, in 1927 a Meccan immigrant to Buitenzorg, West Java, the editor of the newspaper *al-Wifāq*, "The Concord," approached Riḍā with a sense of grievance. He asked him to defend a fatwa that had made it permissible for Muslims to engage freely in transactions with "the assets of the people of war," even if these assets had been corrupted by usury. Barring only theft and deception, the fatwa had allegedly authorized Muslims to trade with enemies with their consent and in accordance with their laws. Would such a fatwa not transgress against all that God had forbidden? Was permitting usurious transactions with the enemy not comparable to allowing Muslims to consume pork and carrion or neglect acts of worship? *Al-Wifāq*'s bilingual editor, a translator of Arabic pamphlets for Malay readers, dared Riḍā to defend this position and rationale.

In response, Riḍā published a fatwa where he alluded to the laws of holy war, insisting that the shariʿa had given believers permission to take possession of the goods of the enemy. In addition, he defended both a territorial and a universal conception of the prohibition on usury. Throughout the world, he argued, the sacred law proscribed Muslims from exploiting fellow Muslims with the kind of usury banned by God: predatory lending at ruinous interest rates. But it seemed unjustified, in his view, to extend the strictest of bans to all types of "usury" and to transactions across a religious divide. Specifically, he argued that it was fair to grant a concession to Muslims dwelling in a non-Islamic abode under a regime whose codes had legalized usurious capital.[20]

As word of Riḍā's rulings spread, members of the Ḥaḍramī diaspora started to reproach him with growing exasperation. A "sincere student" from Banjarnegara, Central Java, Abū Bakr ibn Saʿīd Bāsalāma, wrote to him accusingly:

> Usury has spread far and wide in the land of Java in our age, so much so that teachers who used to command good and prohibit evil in the past, opposing usury, have left the schools to become today's leading usurers. If they are asked to defend this, they respond in a single voice that the owner of *al-Manār* gave a fatwa legalizing usury amidst the Europeans. And whenever we see one of them lending usuriously to the nationalists, they reply to us that they are government employees, not religious actors (*dīniyyūn*), that we are in a house of war, and that the owner of *al-Manār* has already made usury licit in a house

> of war. Is this true, what has been revealed about your *Manār*? If you say "yes," all of the shops will be shuttered, and the wheels of Arab trade in Java will come to a stop, since they [the Dutch East Indies' Arab merchants] will turn to usury, relying on your fatwa.

A month before he died, in July 1935, Riḍā published a feisty fatwa in his own defense. He criticized the fatwa seeker's objectionable tone and offered once more the explanations that he had given to the editor from Buitenzorg.[21]

Beyond Ḥanbalism: A Brief Note on the Ḥanafi Solution and Laissez-Faire Salafism

To justify the lifting of religious restrictions on the business activities of Muslims in China, Riḍā relied on an exceptional and controversial territorial doctrine traced to the jurist Abū Ḥanīfa (d. 767), the founder of a Sunni school of law. This was the doctrine that liberated Muslims traveling or residing in a House of War from observing Islamic prohibitions on usury and the sale of alcohol. Relatively few Sunni jurists embraced it: most non-Ḥanafi jurists rejected it, and many Ḥanafi jurists dissented from it, beginning with Abū Ḥanīfa's disciple Abū Yūsuf (d. 798).[22] Shafiᶜite jurists, such as the mufti who wrote the fatwa about the use of cargo insurance in the port of Aden, dismissed the doctrine out of hand.[23] Ḥanbalis, who had a tradition of clashing with Ḥanafis, criticized it firmly too.

Why did Riḍā embrace it? He was not a member of the Ḥanafi school of law. As a Salafi reformer, he forswore loyalty to Shafiᶜism, which his ancestors had followed for generations.[24] He professed to follow the Salafi path and placed his trust in his own capacity for independent legal reasoning. In theory, this gave him the freedom to adopt Abū Ḥanīfa's doctrines whenever they seemed reasonable or persuasive. In practice, he did so rarely. Historians have argued that he developed a penchant for Ḥanbalism during the interwar period—yet this was the period when he published the Ḥanafi fatwas that made all manner of forbidden dealings permissible in a House of War. Ḥanbali jurists permitted Muslims to visit and dwell in a non-Muslim territory that granted them the freedom to practice their religion, but they had no tolerance for the territorial remissions and exemptions granted by their Ḥanafi rivals. They favored the universal application of Islamic law.[25] This divergence between the Sunni schools of law makes Riḍā's turn to Abū Ḥanīfa's doctrine intriguing.

Riḍā's favorable view of the doctrine owed much to its reconfiguration by a nineteenth-century Ottoman jurist, Ibn ᶜĀbidīn (d. 1836). The Ḥanafi Syrian jurist's texts formed part of the curriculum of the Ottoman madrasa where Riḍā received his legal training. Ibn ʿĀbidīn discussed Abū Ḥanīfa's ruling in depth, and he made its relevance apparent to international commerce in the modern period. His subject was the Muslim who obtained a visa to enter the House of War in peace. Known as a *mustaʾmin*, such a Muslim had a right to sign a contract with Christians that would be considered flawed under Islamic rule. He also had the right to acquire the money or property of Christians "with their consent, even if it [derived from] usury or gambling," provided he refrained from acts of "perfidy, which are strictly forbidden." In effect, Ibn ʿĀbidīn excused Muslims from the Ottoman Empire, where Ḥanafism reigned, from following Islamic financial and commercial rules when they ventured to trade in Europe. Conversely, he insisted on the obligation that foreign Christians had to accept Islamic rules in the dominion of the sultan. Accordingly, the shariʿa was supposed to affect financial and commercial entanglements only in a territory over which Muslims possessed sovereignty.[26]

When Riḍā wrote to China's Muslims, he relied explicitly on Abū Ḥanīfa. When he wrote to Java's Muslims, he made use of the Ḥanafi ruling as well but without invoking Abū Ḥanīfa's name; instead, he alluded vaguely to juridical precedents. The difference stemmed from his association of Chinese Muslims with the Ḥanafi tradition and Javanese Muslims with the Shafiʿite tradition. In these fatwas, as well as in several others, Riḍā considered regional preferences for one or another Sunni path and showed a savvy sensitivity to legal regionalism. Strikingly, he adapted his rulings to flourish in different climes.

This adaptability, his readiness to grant a Ḥanafi fatwa to Ḥanafi petitioners, cannot be reconciled with the standard narrative that has emerged about his ideological turn to Ḥanbalism after World War I. Historians have repeatedly argued that, in the 1920s, Riḍā fell under the spell of the strictest jurist of the Ḥanbali school, Ibn Taymiyya, and that he became the chief apologist for the Wahhabi clerics of Najd, who followed the same school of law with utmost rigor. Grave disillusions, caused by the caliphate's abolition and by the acts of the League of Nations, and new hopes that arose with the Saudi-Wahhabi conquest of the Ḥijāz supposedly inspired this turn. This reductive narrative has served as the foundation for a broader argument about Islamic radicalization that has featured Riḍā as the pivotal scholar who turned his back on his liberal, modernist roots to foster fundamentalism.[27] There is more than a grain of truth to the story. Riḍā defended the Saudi monarch who established Ḥanbalism as the official school of the Ḥijāz; he celebrated the monotheistic spirit of Muḥammad ibn ʿAbd al-Wahhāb and his descendants; and between 1922 and 1935 his press published their fatwas as well as works by their favorite medieval theologian, Ibn Taymiyya.[28]

As an editor and publisher, Riḍā made a few eclectic choices that call into question the notion that after World War I he became an admirer of Ibn Taymiyya, a "strict Ḥanbali fundamentalist," and a Wahhabi devotee.[29] Actually, he discovered Ibn Taymiyya long before Ibn Saʿūd's forces marched into the Ḥijāz. He endorsed Ibn Taymiyya as early as 1901, when he corresponded with a reader about Wahhabism, heterodoxy, and the Salaf.[30] Before World War I, al-Manār Press published theological and polemical tracts by a few contemporary Muslim reformers from Egypt, Syria, and India.[31] In addition, it published Ibn Taymiyya's fatwa on Sufism and poverty, his book on intercessory prayers, and a treatise by his most famous disciple concerning divorce.[32] Meanwhile, it paid little or no attention to non-Ḥanbali medieval jurists.[33] After World War I al-Manār Press continued and deepened its special interest in medieval Ḥanbali literature. It printed several tomes of Ibn Taymiyya's works. With Saudi financing, it also edited and published a series of Wahhabi letters and tracts. These publications were historically significant, but they did not represent a new and exclusive dedication to Ḥanbalism and Wahhabism. In the interwar period, al-Manār Press also published Gandhi's *Guide to Health* as well as a collection of poetry by Riḍā's friend and ally in Geneva, the Druze prince Shakīb Arslān. These odd ventures did not transform al-Manār Press into a nonsectarian, interfaith operation. Yet clearly the enterprise was not just an organ of Ḥanbali and Wahhabi propaganda.

If Riḍā became a Ḥanbali with Wahhabi sympathies, why did he not offer a Ḥanbali or Wahhabi solution to the conundrums of Muslims in China? Ibn Taymiyya permitted the sale of clothes and food to the Mongol invaders, but he warned Muslims not to help the enemy gain a military advantage. He also approved, with limitations, commercial voyages to states under Christian rule.[34] Likewise, Ibn ʿAbd al-Wahhāb's grandson, Sulaymān ibn ʿAbdallāh (d. 1818), sanctioned trading excursions to the land of "the unbelievers." He found justification for this ruling in Ibn Ḥanbal's collection of oral traditions.[35] But Ibn Taymiyya and Wahhabi clerics incorporated all sorts of restrictions into their allowances; they prohibited many social and material entanglements with others. ʿAbd al-Raḥmān ibn Ḥasan (d. 1869) went so far as to argue that only "religious necessity" could justify traveling to the infidels' abode for trade. ʿAbd al-Laṭīf al-Azharī (d. 1876) denounced the sale of goods, provisions, horses, and saddles to "the enemy infidel."[36] These clerics often concentrated on what was forbidden. Under no circumstances did they allow Muslims to profit from usury and wine in a House of War.

Few twentieth-century jurists knew these obscure rulings. Riḍā was exceptionally familiar with them, however, because he himself edited the Wahhabi fatwas, which had previously existed only in manuscript form. He printed them in Cairo, with al-Manār's seal of approval, in 1927 and 1928. His decision to grant a Ḥanafi ruling to the Chinese question was thus a fully informed one. In light of this evidence, the thesis that Riḍā became a Wahhabi enthusiast and a Ḥanbali doctrinaire no longer seems tenable. He adopted in the interwar period a Ḥanafi approach to cross-cultural trade under non-Muslim rule, and the repercussions were profound, as we shall see, because in his eyes the House of War began to encroach upon the House of Islam.

But why, if he was a Salafist, did Riḍā offer Chinese Muslims a Ḥanafi solution? Salafism has long seemed compatible with Ḥanbalism but incompatible with Ḥanafism, for two reasons: first, because Wahhabi clerics traditionally maintained a commitment to both the school of Ibn Ḥanbal and the doctrines or practices of the Salaf; and, second, because of historical tensions that first arose in the Ottoman Empire's Arab provinces, between Salafi radicals and the Ḥanafi clerical establishment.[37] Riḍā's perspective was in some respects different, however. In one of his fatwas to China, he defended the orientation of the Partisans of the Prophetic Tradition (Ahl-i Ḥadīth) in India. He argued that this and other revivalist movements were right to follow "the four imams," Abū Ḥanīfa, Mālik ibn Anas, al-Shāfiʿī and Ibn Ḥanbal, "and other imams of the Salaf, who strictly prohibited the blind imitation of them and of others." These pious ancestors had stressed, instead, the essential duty to follow the Qurʾan and the normative tradition known as the Sunna. Thus, on the one hand, Riḍā granted Sino-Muslims a Ḥanafi fatwa; on the other hand, he advised them not to conform dogmatically to any school of law.[38]

He explained what this would mean in practice in yet another fatwa where he responded to Ma Ruitu's "Questions from Guangzhou." This fatwa addressed the controversial use of gold in artificial teeth and crowns. Riḍā understood why the dental prosthetics troubled Muslim men who felt bound by their religious tradition to shun gold ornaments. But he did not oppose use of the precious metal in dentistry. To explain his own religious and legal philosophy, he quoted Ibn Taymiyya: "The ancestors never tabooed anything except by definitive proof."[39] Only the Qurʾan or an authentic tradition could furnish such a proof. In this instance, Riḍā invoked the medieval Ḥanbali jurist—in a rather surprising way given his reputation as a hardliner—as model of religious moderation and judicial restraint. His commitment to these values explains in part why he chose, as a Salafist, a Ḥanafi approach to commerce in a House of War. After concluding that the non-Ḥanafi restrictions were based on debatable juridical interpretations, as opposed to definitive scriptural rules, he felt free to support the Ḥanafi approach, which served best to liberate Muslims under Chinese rule from voluntarily observing unnecessary taboos in the economic sphere. Therefore, his Ḥanafi ruling was a fine example of "laissez-faire Salafism" at work.

A New House of War: Lebanon Under the French Mandate

The transformation of the imperial order by the League of Nations led Riḍā to redraw the imaginary boundary between the House of Islam and the House of War. In his fatwas about imperial Russia and republican China, he insisted on the fixity of these states' identity as "abodes of infidelity and war." He made his contentions against the reservations of Russia's and China's Muslim citizens who felt so religiously free and so politically loyal that they began imagining that their states had become "abodes of Islam." By contrast, Riḍā argued in the late twenties that Syria and Lebanon were no longer abodes of Islam: the French Mandate had turned the states of the Levant, where he had grown up, into abodes of war. The fatwa that made this case shows how the anti-imperial politics of the interwar period affected his value judgments. It reveals that his political rhetoric changed significantly in this period, while his economic stance remained more or less the same. He continued to defend a laissez-faire approach to Muslim investments.

Riḍā wrote the fatwa in the bitter time that followed the League of Nations' refusal to grant Arabs a sovereign state in the lands of the defunct Ottoman Empire. Instead, Britain and France divided these lands between themselves. Turkey's abolition of the caliphate only added salt to the wound. More than the demise of a venerable institution, this event signaled the retreat of Islamic power from the world stage. It spurred Riḍā and others to orchestrate a pair of conferences in 1926, in Mecca and Cairo, which explored different options for restoring God's vice-regency on earth.

France's imperial extension into Syria was, for Riḍā, an especially significant development. He had begun worrying about French designs to colonize Arab lands, including the sacred territory of the Ḥijāz, as early as 1900. A dozen years later, when he heard reports of an Anglo-French entente to partition Syria and other Arab provinces, he sounded the alarm.[40] Agitating for Syrian autonomy, he joined the Ottoman Party for Administrative Decentralization. After the world war, he became a Syrian government official. In May 1920, weeks after the coronation of Fayṣal ibn al-Ḥusayn as king of Greater Syria and days after the San Remo conference confirmed France as Syria's Mandatory Power, the Syrian Congress selected Riḍā as its president. His tenure was short. By the end of July of that year, French troops occupied Damascus. Riḍā became the vice president of the Syro-Palestinian Congress, which presented its demands for independence to the League of Nations.[41]

It was in this crucible that ʿUmar Bey al-Dāʿūq, a notable from a merchant family, asked Riḍā a question about the propriety of Muslims investing in Lebanese luxury hotels. The notable had had been Beirut's mayor during the upheaval that led to French rule. A pragmatic critic of the mandate, he collaborated frequently with Maronite and French authorities.[42] Writing as a member of a benevolent Islamic society, he wanted to know if it was permissible to build in Beirut a grand hotel "in the modern style," like those of Egypt. The society would make an investment in the business of renting rooms, and it would give its profits to a charitable cause such as the education of poor Muslim children. The only problem was that this hotel would lodge non-Muslim tourists in a state under non-Muslim rule. The question arose a few years after the Mandate had created a special department to promote travel to "the Nice of the Orient," as part of an initiative to spur economic development. To attract foreign visitors, it published advertisements in Egyptian newspapers, sent brochures to travel agencies, and solicited the publication of a French guidebook, the first *Guide Bleu* to Syria and Palestine. A wave of seaside construction followed, culminating in the opening of the legendary Hôtel Saint-Georges.[43]

Responding to this dilemma, Riḍā first entertained possible reasons for opposing the building of hotels: foreigners staying there might drink alcohol, which the management would of course supply, and they would use the premises to traffic in sinful things and strike corrupt deals. No jurist would advise believers to break religious taboos in the quest for profit. Yet Riḍā, relaxed as ever about money matters, tried to allay Muslim worries. By juridical consensus, he argued, it was acceptable to rent a property to non-Muslims and to licentious Muslims. In Egypt, the ministry that supervised estates in mortmain leased houses without inquiring into the beliefs of prospective tenants, and the country's hotels opened their doors to visitors from foreign lands regardless of religion. Landlords and hotel owners must not expect non-Muslims lodging in the House of Islam to comply with the shariʿa in all respects. Like jurists, they should make accommodations for others.

Muslim developers in Egypt had a right to build hotels that would serve usurers, alcoholics, and strangers, among others, but their counterparts in the French Mandate possessed a special entitlement, for "you know that Beirut and the rest of Syria do not today count as a house of Islam." The country's civil laws were not based on the shariʿa, and power of sovereignty had been wrested from Muslim hands. Riḍā's implication that Beirut had become a city in "an abode of war" had immediate juridical consequences. It gave Muslims there access to a more lenient code of business conduct. "Judges have already issued fatwas making permissible all of the assets of the people of war with the exception [of things obtained by] theft, deception, and such. What comes into circulation with their consent or with their contracts is lawful for us no matter its origin, even if it is plain usury. According to reports that have reached us, Muslims in different quarters [of the world], in China and in some of the states of India, already behave in this way."[44]

In Beirut, he continued, most of the population did not follow the Islamic faith. Adultery, female exhibitionism, wantonness, and the habit of drinking wine had spread from the city's Christians to the Muslim minority there. In a place overwhelmed by immorality, by forbidden capital, and by corrupt social and economic relations, all things become, by exigency, permissible. The wary and devout Muslim investor should still think twice before opening a bar or a brothel, before building a temple for another god, or before profiting directly from sinful trades. Otherwise, anything goes.[45]

Rule by Frenchmen had its silver lining. Mandatory Syria became, exactly like China, a land where Muslims were suddenly empowered to pursue economic opportunities without minding the sacred law. What is remarkable is that, no matter the political context, Riḍā exerted himself to defend steadfastly, for Islam's sake, freer trade. While his public political stances varied over time with the relaxation of censorship rules, military events, regime changes, diplomatic opportunities, and the gradual shift from an imperialistic to a nationalistic conceptual framework, his economic attitudes remained liberal. Arguably, he made only one major exception to this general tendency toward economic liberalism in the course of his career. This exception had to do with the technological and commercial development of Arabia's holy land.[46]

The Ḥijazi Exception: Christian Technocrats in the Cradle of Islam

A key provision of the Ottoman Empire's initiative to build a railroad to the Ḥijāz stimulated a man from Tinogasta, Argentina, to ask Riḍā for an "enlightening" fatwa about the nature of the holiest of Muslim lands. The fatwa seeker, Ilyās Laṭifullāh Abū Sulaymān, wanted to understand why non-Muslims were excluded from the Ḥijāz. He had read in an Egyptian newspaper, *al-Muʾayyad*, that Ottoman Muslim engineers had worked independently, without assistance from European Christians, on one segment of the Ḥijāz railroad track: the 330 kilometer stretch between al-ʿUlā and Medina. Why did a prohibition on the presence of non-Muslims in this part of the world arise? Was it based on a "religious commandment" or customary law?

In true Salafist form, Riḍā began his 1909 fatwa with a string of quotations from the prophetic tradition. The first of these showed that God's Messenger had wished—as he lay dying—for the disbelievers' expulsion from Arabia. Arguably, that deathbed wish referred to polytheists and the entire Arabian Peninsula. But Riḍā cited other traditions that specified a reason for expelling "the Jews and the Christians" from the Ḥijāz, the peninsula's midwestern zone: the aim was to eliminate religious competition in a territory meant solely for Islam. Most Islamic authorities, clarified Riḍā, agreed that the ban applied only to the Ḥijāz, not to Arabia as a whole, since the Yemen region could harbor non-Muslims.[47]

The prophetic order to take action in the Ḥijāz stemmed, in Riḍā's view, from this territory's resemblance to mosques: sacred spaces made solely for Muslim believers and their rites of worship. He justified this exclusive policy as well by linking it in a vague apologetic manner to Islamic politics, tolerance for transgressors, and the prevention of mishaps and disasters. What is fascinating about his fatwa is his reinterpretation of ancient proscriptions in light of the economic imperatives of Europe's imperial expansion. "There is nothing in the Ḥijāz," he asserted "that is suitable for worldly profit and the enjoyment of ornaments." The place offers "absolutely no fortune for the non-Muslim."[48] Hence, the scriptural exclusion did not affect the European quest for overseas resources and profit.

In Riḍā's religious geography, Mecca was the Muslims' inalienable endowment, their indivisible communal property. Even hunting animals was prohibited in this sacred preserve. For all of these reasons, residence to non-Muslims was strictly forbidden there. Entering the Ḥijāz for a temporary stay was another matter. Medieval jurists had typically granted non-Muslim merchants the grace of a three-day sojourn for the purposes of trade in each of Arabia's cites and ports.[49] Instead of delving into these rulings, which accommodated cross-cultural trade to a certain extent, Riḍā decided to relate only "the soundest" ruling, which he attributed to al-Shāfiʿī. Relying on this authority, he held that non-Muslims could enter "the tabooed territory" only if they received the Imam's permission—and that permission had to be granted only if their entry was advantageous to the Islamic community.

The railway to Medina, a technological project that had everything to do with Ottoman ambitions for an imperial Islamic modernity, inspired this fatwa about the right way to develop the Ḥijāz. The imperial dream collapsed in 1916, when the Ḥijāz declared itself an independent kingdom. But the first Hashemite king of the Ḥijāz, al-Ḥusayn ibn ʿAlī, continued the restrictive policy of barring or limiting non-Muslims from participating in technological projects in the region. He forbade strictly the free transfer of technology to the sacred city of Mecca. During World War I, he authorized the British to run a telegraph wire from Jeddah to his palace in Mecca. He insisted, however, on the employment of Muslim rather than Christian engineers for this installation.[50] St. John Philby, a British explorer and intelligence officer who described this telegraph line as "the first sign of modern civilization" on the caravan route, experienced the bias first-hand. In the winter of 1917 he encountered a telegraph master who objected to his intent to send a message "over the wires of the Holy Land."[51]

To Riḍā's dismay, the second and last Hashemite king of the Ḥijāz, sharif ʿAlī ibn al-Ḥusayn, loosened the restrictions. With Saudi-Wahhabi forces conquering swathes of his territory, he worried more about staying in power than about the sanctity of his kingdom. Newspapers published his telegrams, revealing his pleas for foreign intervention. In exchange for weapons and loans, he offered European powers desperate concessions for the exploitation of the Ḥijāz's mineral resources. In a 1925 article titled "The English and the Ḥijāz," Riḍā bitterly denounced him for "making lawful the sale of sacred lands to non-Muslims." Siding with the sultan of Najd, Ibn Saʿūd, Riḍā fulminated against the rumored Hashemite overture. Among other things, he recalled the Prophet Muḥammad's deathbed decree, which had urged the expulsion of "the pagans, the Jews, and the Christians" from Arabia. Only one religion must remain, he asserted, in this sacred land.[52]

Riḍā returned to this religiously exclusive doctrine following the Saudi-Wahhabi conquest. Upon assuming power in the Ḥijāz, the Saudi monarch started to draw plans for modernizing his dual realm. Among other things, he wanted to expand the existing telecommunications system. Riḍā played a key role in stirring up a critical and intense debate about these plans, whose realization depended on hiring European experts.

Several of the most famous and influential clerics discussed the Saudi modernization plans during the Islamic World Congress that Ibn Saʿūd convoked in Mecca in the summer of 1926. At this congress, Riḍā tried to rally delegates from Egypt, the Ḥijāz, Turkey, Mandatory Palestine, the Soviet Union, the British Raj, and the Dutch East Indies to support a motion barring Christian technocrats from Arabia's sacred territory. In theory, the topic was off limits. The Saudi monarch had instructed delegates not to debate foreign affairs. Disregarding his host's wishes, Riḍā allied himself with a senior delegate from Najd, the Wahhabi cleric ʿAbdallāh bin Bulayhid (d. 1940), to raise the issue. They wanted the pan-Islamic congress as well as the new king of the Ḥijāz to support their goal of "purging" Arabia of foreign influences. Ibn Saʿūd's cosmopolitan adviser, the Egyptian diplomat Ḥāfiẓ Wahba, recounted what it took to defeat their proposal behind the scenes. He forced Riḍā and his Wahhabi ally to acknowledge their lack of agreement about the precise boundaries of the zone of exclusion.[53]

Like so many other debates in this period, this territorial debate had both religious and technological dimensions. By the end of 1926 Ibn Saʿūd reached a working agreement with the Eastern Telegraph Company's representative and the governor-general of the Sudan that specified parameters for wireless and cable communications. The memorandum stipulated that, "to avoid any arrangement which might be construed as foreign interference or intervention in Hejaz local affairs," the Jeddah terminal would be staffed by "two persons of the Mahometan faith."[54]

In 1927, under considerable pressure from the Saudi monarchy, a group of scholars from Najd issued a collective edict known as "the famous fatwa." They realized that Ibn Saᶜūd wanted to develop telecommunications in his dual kingdom but faced serious internal dissent from the Bedouin militias that brought him to power. So the ad hoc council of Wahhabi clerics made the following pronouncement about the technological innovation on trial: "It is a novel thing from the end of this time, and we know not its true nature. Nor have we seen about it any discussion by a religious scholar. Therefore, we have reached a standstill in connection with this issue. Without knowledge, we cannot declare an opinion in accordance with God and his Messenger. A resolution to establish [the instrument as] lawful or prohibited would require cognizance of its true nature."[55] Historians have referred to this fatwa as an edict about "the telegraph."[56] It is worth noting, however, that telegraph wires, posts, and stations were no longer novel things in the late twenties. The focus was on radio transmissions.

The wireless telegraph relayed messages in a mysterious and suspicious way. According to Wahba, who loved to mock Wahhabi clerics, ᶜAbdallāh bin Ḥasan (d. 1959), one of Najd's eminent jurists, was all but convinced that telegraph operators had to hire jinn as messengers and offer satanic sacrifices in order to send and receive coded messages electromagnetically. Perhaps he exaggerated Wahhabi superstitions or failed to get the clerics' sense of humor. But according to another source, it took a scientific demonstration of the instrument's ability to transmit Qurʾanic verses from Mecca to Riyadh for the Saudi monarchy to persuade the Wahhabis that the devil had not really enchanted the medium.[57]

The participation of a British Christian agent in the Saudi enterprise catalyzed clerical resistance. St. John Philby, the British adventurer, worked in the kingdom as a cross-cultural broker for Marconi's Wireless Telegraph Company as well as, incidentally, for the Ford Motor Company and Standard Oil of California. He also served as a critical member of Ibn Saᶜūd's circle of unofficial foreign advisers and informants.[58] ᶜAbdallāh bin Ḥasan recoiled violently when he met Philby in 1928, at a confluence of wells near Medina, during a trip with Wahba that involved an unexpected, demystifying detour to a wireless station. Within two years Philby would convert to Islam. But at the time, Wahhabi clerics tirelessly appealed to Ibn Saᶜūd not to proceed with his plans to introduce radiotelegraphy. They argued, among other things, that Philby would import only calamities and "deliver our country to the English."[59]

Historians of the transfer of technologies from Europe to its colonies have long assigned a key role to men like Philby, salesmen and engineers specializing in the "geographic relocation" of artifacts and machines into countries that lacked "native experts."[60] A further complication in the Ḥijāz was the sacred status of the territory in Muslim eyes, which made the presence of a British Christian agent there all the more problematic.

Wahhabi Salafism or Enlightened Salafism?

The suspicious Wahhabi response to wireless telegraphy must seem a world apart from the scientifically inclined and economically open attitude toward novel technologies cultivated by Riḍā and his network of reformers before World War I. This division roughly maps onto the historical understanding of Salafism as split into two currents: the "enlightened" or "modernist" philosophy of the disciples of ʿAbduh versus the "purist" or "fundamentalist" ideology of the disciples of Ibn ʿAbd al-Wahhāb.[61] Historians have generally placed Riḍā in both currents, arguing that he drifted from the first to the second one in the late twenties when he became an apologist for Wahhabi Salafism.

This theoretical and reductive bifurcation of Salafism into two currents misses many of the nuances of Islamic legal thought. There is no need to exaggerate Riḍā's "enlightened" appreciation of technology or mock "Wahhabi" attitudes. Yes, Riḍā wrote in praise of electricity, the telegraph, and the telephone, and he marveled at "amazing" machines such as military aircraft.[62] But he had serious qualms about the gramophone's frivolous uses in mixed company. Collectively, his fatwas supported the adoption of many technologies that he considered advantageous. But they did not make a broad, indiscriminate case for technology. Clerics from Najd similarly approached technologies on a case-by-case basis. They did not treat gramophones in the same way that they treated wireless telegraphs. Actually, they developed a policy for the gradual elimination of the musical instruments. In his secret "Jeddah Report" of July 1928, British Consul Hugh Stonehewer-Bird wrote about the Ḥijāzī government's legislative initiative to restrict the import of these machines: "At present Christians who own gramophones may play them, but may not replace them when worn out. Moslems may neither import nor play."[63] Wahhabi conquerors despised gramophones, but they respected Christian foreigners' property rights, and for a while tolerated their musical tastes. They never issued a blanket ban to cover all things technological.

It is important to recognize, furthermore, the territorial dimension of Islamic judgments. Like other experts on the sacred law, Riḍā always had to ask himself a series of questions when he considered the transfer of technologies into Muslim societies. Among other factors, he had to consider the destination, for his rulings were not universally applicable. He permitted buying lottery tickets in Thailand, investing in hotels to lodge European tourists in Mandatory Beirut, or relying on French telegraph operators in Algeria. He did not authorize these entanglements in the Ḥijāz. Quite the contrary, when it came to the question of non-Muslims entering this sacred Muslim land, Riḍā saw eye to eye with Ibn Bulayhid, a notoriously conservative scholar from Najd. This pair of scholars collaborated, as we have seen, to propose to the Islamic World Congress the liberation of Arabia from Christian technocrats.

Their alliance does not mean that Riḍā came to espouse a "Wahhabi" view of things in the interwar period. As early as 1909, in his response to the fatwa seeker from Argentina, he had defended—with an abundance of scriptural citations—the Ottoman Empire's commitment to an exclusively Islamic railroad project. The political and technological circumstances were very different in 1926. But Riḍā did nothing more than to take up in a different context the old ideal of an infidel-free Ḥijāz.[64]

Thus, Riḍā made the case for maintaining the Ḥijāz as an independent Islamic preserve: a religious refuge from the global quest for profit. Writing before the discovery of oil in Saudi Arabia, he described the region as a poor country that lacked natural resources and offered nothing of value to European prospectors. Its poverty served to justify morally the exclusive Islamic doctrine: the barring of non-Muslims from Ḥijāz, if not from the wider region that comprised all of the Arabs' ancestral lands. Much of the rest of the world appeared, by contrast, as an extension of the London Bourse: a set of markets where merchants could trade with one another as equals, regardless of their religious distinctions.

Égalité for Muslim Men: An Enlightened Islamic View of Economic Exchanges

Riḍā had an unshakable belief in the principle that men of religion had the right to enjoy whatever economic opportunities existed in their countries. By his interpretation of the sacred law, Muslims residing in nations or empires under non-Muslim rule were entitled to participate fully, like others, in the financial and commercial systems in place. To deprive them of that right would be to handicap them economically. "I mean, do they believe," he asked about the pious merchants of the Dutch East Indies who had insisted on observing the ban on usury, "that God would enjoin a Muslim to suffer a loss where there exists for the other a profit? Or that God would make it a Muslim's duty to be oppressed and defrauded?" By God, a Muslim ought to have the same economic opportunities as his non-Muslim countryman.[65]

Underlying this formulation was the very modern principle that, in economic transactions, Muslims should exchange with non-Muslims as equals. Voltaire's *Letters on the English* famously expressed this Enlightenment principle when it praised the London Stock Exchange as the singular place where Jews, Christians, and Muslims traded together as equals, despite their manifestations of religious distinctions elsewhere in town. Riḍā favored extending the secular conventions of the London Bourse to nearly every marketplace, apart from the all-Muslim territory of the Ḥijāz. As the "enlightened" editor of an Islamic magazine, he repeatedly urged Muslims to refrain from burdening themselves and others with legal inequalities in the world of trade.

To appreciate the radicalism of this insistence on equality before the law, it is essential to recognize that the Qurʾan enshrined a system of inequalities. The rules that applied to men did not necessarily apply to women, and the rules that applied to women did not necessarily apply to slaves. One Qurʾanic verse, relating to inheritance, gave male offspring exactly twice the share given to female offspring (4:11). Another verse, relating to marriage and adultery, established that married female slaves deserved precisely half the physical chastisement imparted to their free counterparts for the same sexual crime (4:25). Yes, it was better in this singular case to be a convicted slave than a convicted freeman. In addition, the Qurʾan referred to a special tax, the *jizya*, levied on People of the Book who failed to obey God's prohibitions and heed the religion of truth (9:29). Social inequalities were part and parcel of the Qurʾanic approach to justice.

The ideal of equality before the law, especially for Christian and Muslim men, began to spread throughout the Ottoman Empire a generation before Riḍā's birth. An imperial edict, the Gülhane decree of 1839, established the principle of equality in taxation and conscription for Muslim and non-Muslim subjects alike. An 1856 rescript affirmed and extended these reforms. It vowed to erase from "administrative protocol" every designation of inferiority based on distinctions of religion, language, or race. Signaling a readiness "to profit by the science, the art, and the funds of Europe," it also promised to abolish "everything that can impede commerce and agriculture."[66] The constitution of 1876 built on this egalitarian legislation by identifying all imperial subjects, regardless of their religious confession, as first of all "Ottoman."[67] Not all Muslims appreciated these initiatives. Some resented the unequal privileges granted to Europeans; others begrudged the special favors enjoyed by local Christians.[68] But the intellectuals who spearheaded an Arabic literary revival in Syria and Egypt embraced the campaign for religious equality.

Voltaire's great admirer, the Egyptian reformer Rifāʿa al-Ṭahṭāwī (d. 1873), effectively disseminated in Arabic the principle legal equality. Following his mission to Paris, he wrote that "the greatest freedom in the civilized kingdom is the freedom of agriculture, trade and industry."[69] Riḍā's friend ʿAbd al-Raḥmān al-Kawākibī also cultivated the ideals of the "Islamic Enlightenment." In a work of fiction that he published in *al-Manār*, he counted the lack of "religious freedom" and the absence of "justice and equality" as causes of the decline of Islamic civilization.[70] The idea that "enlightened" traders transacted "as tho' they all profess'd the same religion" captured the imagination of Muslim intellectuals long before Voltaire's *Letters on the English* appeared in an Arabic translation more than two decades after Riḍā's death.[71]

Riḍā built on this legacy in several ways. He abided by the principle of legal equality in secular affairs even when doing so meant espousing rules of inheritance that did not favor Muslims. In 1904 he suggested—in the name of justice—that converts to Islam should not inherit property from their Christian fathers. The Islamic legal tradition had allowed this while precluding the reverse.[72] As an advocate of legal equality in the field of social and commercial transactions, Riḍā rejected this tradition. But he did not want to rule that it was lawful for converts to Christianity to inherit property from their Muslim fathers too. This constraint left him with one alternative, which he took: to rule in general against cross-religious inheritance.[73] When asked by a Montenegrin, also in 1904, about the permissibility of selling commodity futures to Muslims or non-Muslims, he answered that there was nothing wrong with this scheme. Islam's sacred law guaranteed "equality between the people in their rights, even if they differed in race and religion." Whereas other legal systems affirmed racial and confessional biases or protected colonial privileges, Islamic law placed Muslims before others only in matters that pertained to "the religion."[74]

The related topic of equal opportunity received attention in a 1930 fatwa. Could Muslims hire non-Muslim teachers? Yes, reasoned Riḍā, if they would instruct "Muslim children in the secular sciences that are beneficial, such as mathematics and economics," which caused no harm to the students' religious formation. If two equally suitable candidates presented themselves for the job, then the Muslim instructor would be preferable. Nevertheless, when comparing candidates, employers were enjoined to consider their moral character too: a virtuous infidel might make a better educator than a perverse believer.[75]

The conceptual distinction that Riḍā made between religious and secular pursuits underpinned the argument that all men, Muslim or otherwise, should enjoy access to a level playing field. His opinion that Muslims under non-Muslim rule should be able to borrow money with interest, profit indirectly from wine sales, and play the lottery depended on this distinction. His reflections against a blanket ban on usury stemmed in part from his commitment to equal opportunity. He never minimized Muslims' obligation to follow the shariʿa in many respects throughout the world. Even in China, they were expected to oppose the cult of ancestors, pray five times a day, refrain from pork, and so on. There were many global duties. So why did the ban on usury not apply to Chinese Muslims as well? First, because it had nothing to do with the work of devotion, which embodied in his view the essence of religion; and, second, because it would place Muslims at a disadvantage vis-à-vis non-Muslims. From his perspective, the ban had suited the socioeconomic circumstances of a particular time and place; it was not a universal religious commandment.[76]

The view that religious and secular acts belonged to different spheres was a modern one. It was certainly very different from the premodern Islamic perspective that established a categorical division between "devotional acts" (*ʿibādāt*) and "socioeconomic transactions" (*muʿāmalāt*) since all cases—regardless of their position within this system of classification—remained subject in theory to the sacred law. Acts of worship formed Islam's religious core in Riḍā's theology. Modern financial and commercial exchanges struck him as religiously peripheral, if not religiously irrelevant, despite the fact that the shariʿa had covered analogous exchanges. Ironically, he spent much of his career as a religious authority responding to questions about these exchanges.

Riḍā's dilemma was that some Muslims took a broader view of the scope of religion, and they pushed back against economically liberal fatwas that suggested otherwise. In a world where most Muslims lived under European rule and where foreign banks symbolized the new era of imperialism, his argument that usury was permissible in the House of War provoked strong reactions. Readers of *al-Manār* who had made a powerful commitment to making money in an "Islamic" way, such as Ibn Saʿīd Bāsalāma of the colonial Dutch town of Banjarnegara, felt that Riḍā had in effect given Muslims the license to commit the sin of usury.

Why did Riḍā dedicate himself to the cause of religious equality and freer trade? The first and most important reason was his deep and unshakable conviction that a liberal economic attitude would propel Muslims forward religiously and politically. This was not his own individual dream. It was the collective dream of Muslim reformers in Riḍā's age, and they expressed it in various ways at different times. Ismail Gasprinski gave voice to it after the 1907 crisis in Cairo, when he envisioned Islam's salvation by the grace of Muslim millionaires: devout philanthropists such as Baku's oil magnate who would spend their fortunes on madrasas and mosques. Riḍā shared his vision of prosperity in multiple rulings, including the 1930 fatwa where he explained to Ma Ruitu that trade without religious restrictions would allow Chinese Muslims to flourish and in time convert China into an Islamic nation.

In addition to enlightened Islamic values, the dominant political culture in Egypt also reinforced Riḍā's commitment to free trade outside of the Ḥijāz. It was no secret that British free traders despised "Islamic" resistance to capitalism. Lord Cromer repeatedly proclaimed that Qurʾanic principles led strict Muslims to reject modern finance and suspect interfaith commerce, and he mocked the legal contortions that Muslim regimes had to resort to in order to deal with foreign and native Christians as equals. Moreover, he justified Egypt's continued occupation with the argument that Egyptian Muslims were not yet ready to guarantee the interests of the Empire of Free Trade.[77] Aware of this position, Riḍā kept British commercial interests in mind whenever he communicated with British administrators about the possibility of political independence for the Arabs. In 1915, when he drafted for British administrators a secret constitution for the Arab Empire, he defended freedom in "religious beliefs, personal rights, and financial operations."[78] Whatever assurances British officials gave him in private about their lack of designs on colonizing the region, British censors made him realize that the one thing the empire would guarantee in public, via *al-Manār*, was "free trade to the Arabs."[79]

What affirmed, in the third place, Riḍā's economic liberalism was a pragmatic inclination to adjust religious values and norms to fit the legal and financial systems in place. The statutes, codes, and courts that determined the legality of buying and selling insurance contracts in Aden, depositing money in Java's Dutch banks, playing the lottery in Thailand, or establishing hotels in Lebanon had no connection to the rules of the shariʿa. Riḍā sanctioned these activities as a mufti dedicated to the idea of Islam as a laissez-faire religion. His fatwas, however controversial, were but an attempt at reconciliation with reality. They did nothing more radical than to legalize transactions that were already legal.

Riḍā represented the shariʿa as supporting the principle of legal equality, but he applied this idealization of the sacred law mainly to relations between men. Equality for women was an altogether different question. In his 1922 book on reviving the caliphate, Riḍā argued that Islam preceded other religions in granting women and men equality in marital affairs but that it also gave husbands a degree of authority over wives. This hierarchical order was directly linked to his belief in a patriarchal economy. Men had to toil and earn money; women had to take care of home and children under "the government" of their husbands.[80] When he considered the feminist problem that a daughter inherited fewer shares than a son, the reformer explained that, were it not so, women would be richer than men. The daughter would become a wife, and as a wife she would receive a dowry from her husband, who would eventually bear sole responsibility for the children's maintenance. Unequal inheritance shares were divinely designed, in his view, to help women and men achieve greater equality.[81] In his 1930 lecture "Renovation, Renovating, and Renovators," Riḍā denounced as heretical the idea, which a Coptic doctor had defended at the American University of Cairo, that women be granted equality before the law in matters of inheritance.[82]

This denunciation came a decade after a momentous debate in the Syrian parliament. On April 25, 1920, delegates pondered the question of giving women full citizenship in the new nation. Several politicians made passionate speeches in favor of women's suffrage. But the president of the conference, Rashīd Riḍā, persuaded his male colleagues "to table the issue of the woman's right to vote and not include it within the law." He began, reasonably enough, by disclosing that "a precedent" could be found in the shariʿa, if necessary, to justify the unprecedented initiative. Then he stated his reservation. He argued that the sacred law granted the husband, as the wife's guardian, the right to prohibit her from voting. A feminist delegate who anticipated the contention came to the debate with a prepared text. He read an argument for women's equality that Riḍā himself had made in a Qurʾanic exegesis. Riḍā replied that the statement had been quoted out of context. For the sake of unity, he urged candidates to close the door to fanatics. They debated for another minute or two the sacred law's relevance before adjourning. Thanks to Riḍā, the proposal for universal suffrage failed. Just as in France, it took several decades in Lebanon and Syria to extend the principle of *égalité* to women.[83]

What, then, was *The Lighthouse*'s light? It was the idea that Muslims could enjoy quite freely the world of goods. Everywhere in the House of War and nearly everywhere in the House of Islam, although not in the Arabian Peninsula's sacred preserve, Muslims could exchange with non-Muslims as equals. In European colonies, where most Muslims lived in Riḍā's age, and in predominantly non-Muslim countries such as China, they could justifiably act in their own self-interest and even indulge in usury. Regardless of the status of their state, they had the right to take advantage of modern technologies and commodities. Nevertheless, as followers of the sacred law, they had good reasons to contemplate and criticize the rush to consume things that either signified European cultural hegemony or modified rites of worship. This was the *nār* of *al-Manār*.

Conclusions

Devoted to fatwas about technological innovations, consumer goods made in overseas factories, and commercial interactions between Muslims and others in aging empires and fledgling nations, this book has tried to convey something of the spirit of Islam's global and material reformation in the late nineteenth and early twentieth centuries. Riḍā, the entrepreneurial mufti who founded "The Lighthouse Press," participated in this reformation alongside the international readers of his enlightened Islamic magazine. They never suffered from "technological somnambulism," the term that Langdon Winner used to criticize a philosophical lack of attention to mechanical objects and the politics of artifacts.[1] They lived in a world where strange new things gave rise to a religious awakening.

This awakening happened in the period of globalization that roughly coincided with Riḍā's lifetime. Arguably, the most significant changes took place during his formative years. Tripoli of Syria, where he grew up, was transformed in the late nineteenth century by the expansion of Ottoman trade with France and other European nations. Steamships brought to the harbor massive cargoes, resulting in a hundredfold increase in the volume of trade. Newly installed telegraph and railway systems multiplied and accelerated Tripoli's interconnections with the wider world. Ideas flowed more freely too. The patriotic madrasa that was founded in Riḍā's adolescence offered both a religious and a scientific education, and it trained students to reconcile European and Islamic concepts. Meanwhile Cairo, where he would end up, became in the late nineteenth century one of the world's most globalized cities, its character deeply marked by the completion of the Suez Canal, the establishment of Mixed Courts, the influx of foreign capital, and all of the changes that came with the British occupation.

But the main focus of this history has been on the years of *al-Manār*, 1898 to 1935. Riḍā's career as a global mufti took off—not coincidentally—in a period when goods, persons, and texts circulated with greater ease than ever before within the Empire of Free Trade and beyond it, thanks to merchants, pilgrims, and smugglers, not to mention printing presses and postal services. He launched his journal in Cairo at the beginning of an incredible boom in the city's history: a decade of migration, construction, and speculation that would end with the crash of 1907. Sensing a window of opportunity, he took a tremendous risk—as a Syrian emigrant who was equipped with little more than a diploma from an Ottoman madrasa—to create and sustain a new publishing venture dedicated to the production of an enlightened Islamic periodical. Printing at first an eight-page weekly with the expectation of attracting fifteen hundred customers, he was quickly forced by the realities of the business to reduce the print run and adapt to a monthly format. Disappointed but still hopeful, he continued to struggle as an entrepreneur in this time of prosperity. Then he began to flourish beyond every expectation by at least one measure: in 1903, the year that he launched the section on fatwas as a regular feature, he received and published letters seeking his legal advice from Montenegro, Singapore, and Russia. Even before he inherited ʿAbduh's mantle, these early signs of international recognition suggested that he might well become one of the most famous reformers in the history of Islam.

Made for a highly educated and relatively affluent readership, Riḍā's *al-Manār* was a niche product designed for readers who had already embraced the agenda to reform Islam. It circulated in many cities around the world where Muslims read Arabic, but quite unevenly. An analysis of the dates and locations of subscribers' fatwa requests reveals a few surprising trends and patterns that call into question historians' attachment to the construct of "the Middle East" as a standard unit of analysis for understanding Islam's history in the early twentieth century.

Between 1903 and 1918, for example, Riḍā's legal communications were relatively frequent with Singapore but relatively infrequent with Beirut. When Riḍā received his very first fatwa request from Beirut in 1909, he had already replied to thirty-four legal questions sent to him by at least seventeen fatwa seekers from Singapore. The disparity is astonishing when we consider that Singapore, an island located 5,365 nautical miles from the Suez Canal, hosted but a few hundred Arab merchants and their families, the members of the Ḥaḍramī diaspora, whereas Beirut, no more than 365 nautical miles from the Egyptian waterway, was one of the major centers of Arab culture in the world. Moreover, from the inauguration of the section on fatwas until the end of World War I, the total number of fatwa seekers from Singapore was slightly higher than the total number of fatwa seekers from the Ottoman Empire's Arab provinces in the Mediterranean: the set of vilayets that eventually became the French or British mandates for Lebanon, Syria, and Palestine. Several factors help to explain the discrepancy, beginning with the particular reasons for Arab Singaporean appeals to an extraterritorial legal authority. Any comprehensive explanation would need to consider, too, the effectiveness of the Ottoman ban on expatriate Arabic journals before the restoration of the constitution as well as the extent to which *al-Manār* seemed dispensable in cities such as Damascus, where Muslims had easy access to highly regarded muftis who offered advice that was similar to Riḍā's.

But there is one obvious structural reason for the disparity: communications between Cairo and Beirut happened across an imperial boundary, whereas communications between Cairo and Singapore took place within the British Empire. Until the end of World War I, *al-Manār* principally served as an Egyptian and, by extension, an imperial British legal forum. It definitely also circulated beyond Britain's sphere of influence, reaching fatwa seekers from the Dutch East Indies, the French colonies in North Africa, and the Russian Empire. But Riḍā's success as a global mufti partly depended on the extent to which empires facilitated or restricted inter-imperial communications between Muslim subjects.

As a business, the Lighthouse Press capitalized on what economists have labeled "the first globalization." This period, lasting from the 1870s to the First World War, may be characterized by neoimperialist ambitions, the investment of European capital in vast sums, and the diffusion of grand European technologies.[2] But small trans-imperial enterprises such as Riḍā's flourished in this environment, too. His publishing house's signature magazine, *al-Manār*, was created by an Arab Muslim for Arabic-reading Muslims throughout the world. Its financial viability depended on expanding by hundreds, not thousands, the initial roster of slightly more than three hundred members, who were invited pay for an annual subscription in piastres, francs, rupees, shillings, or rubles and thus to join the elite club of privileged readers.

Despite political upheavals, economic crises, and the Great Depression, Riḍā's enterprise survived in the interwar period, and this durability makes it an invaluable source for understanding changes and continuities in Islam's modern history. Too many histories have adopted World War I as a watershed and focused on the "period" either before or after this crisis, deepening our impressions of discontinuity.[3] Riḍā's political and religious horizons were greatly affected by the breakup of the Ottoman Empire, the abolition of the caliphate, the creation of mandates by the League of Nations, the declaration of Egypt's independence, and the Saudi conquest of the Ḥijāz. An imperialistic framework, fully apparent in the organic law for "the Arab Empire" that he presented to British authorities in 1915, had dominated his conception of present and future polities until World War I. Circumstances and opportunities in the war's aftermath, beginning with the chance to represent Tripoli in the General Syrian Congress, spurred him to adjust his ambitions to a national scale. In the era of the League of Nations he became, notably, one of the most prominent Syrian political activists in exile as well as the most famous scholar to defend "Wahhabi" doctrines and the new Saudi kingdom.

His publishing business also changed in certain respects after the world war. A precipitous drop in the number of subscribers requesting fatwas from Egypt, the Sudan, Syria, the Ḥijāz, Algeria, Tunisia, Singapore, and Russia suggests a major business contraction. Lebanese fatwa seekers wrote to him far more often in the interwar period than beforehand, but this was an exception to the general trend, and it reflects his rising political prominence in Syro-Lebanese affairs.

Meanwhile, with the imprimatur of al-Manār Press, he published many more books in the interwar period than in earlier years. A list gathered in the late twenties featured fifty titles. In addition to a bestseller, a reprinted edition of ʿAbduh's *Theology of Unity*, it included his own monographs, famous works such as *The Wahhabis and the Ḥijāz* and unfamiliar titles such as *Fatwas on the Reform of Women*. With Saudi financing, he collected, edited, and printed—for the first time in history, in a heavy set of tomes—the fatwas of the clerics of Najd. This publishing venture may suggest that financial and political considerations pulled him into a Saudi orbit, with implications for the transmission of Salafist doctrines. But as a matter of fact, diverse interests pulled him in different directions at the same time. In addition to publishing Wahhabi texts, he published the first Arabic translation of a work by Gandhi, *The Guide to Health*, accompanied by his admiring remarks in footnoted glosses. His business was definitely a doctrinal one. But it was also, in the ancient Greek sense of the word, ecumenical.

His approach to economic development changed little over the course of his career. He tirelessly advocated the view that Islam at its origins was an easy religion and that modern Muslims would flourish economically if they returned to this ancestral worldview, openly adopted technological and financial innovations, and freely traded with non-Muslims. Defending this prosperity gospel was not always easy. Opposition to banking with interest, concerns about the impact of new media, anticolonial consumer boycotts, and the rise of economic nationalism were among the forces that made it difficult to remain an "enlightened" reformer all of the time. He faced direct and indirect challenges from Muslims committed to imposing restrictions upon themselves, and he grappled with his own reservations about usurious loans, capitulation treaties, the frivolity of gramophone users, and the disloyalty of fedora wearers. It would have been easier at times simply to ban a class of modern objects in an unequivocal manner. But he rarely indulged in blanket prohibitions, reserving this style of judgment for archaic instruments such as prayer gongs that he thought were useless in modern times and harmful to Islam.

Why was he committed to justifying Muslim entanglements with modern objects? Principally because he believed in the need to adjust religious ideals to current realities. He was convinced that Islam's survival depended on its adaptability to the times, for Muslims would join what he saw as the inexorable march of modernity with or without their religion. He witnessed, first in Tripoli and then in Cairo, technological projects—from the installation of horse-drawn trams to the process of electrification—that made him see modernization as advantageous and inevitable. Furthermore, he came of age in a period when nearly everyone in a position of power preached the virtues of technological progress and international trade. He concentrated throughout his career as a religious reformer on bringing Islamic law into line with this developmentalist ethos.

Islam's modernist movement of reform in the late nineteenth and early twentieth centuries has long been represented as a historical aberration: a rare moment in history when a confederacy of jurists, led by ʿAbduh and Riḍā in succession, developed a "religious utilitarianism" that allowed them to sanction artificially—on the basis of European theories and values—capitalism, the innovations of the West, and the seductions of modernity. They accomplished this feat either through imaginative interpretations of the Qurʾan, the Ḥadīth, and the acts of the Salaf or by resorting to the relativistic, "pseudo-religious" notion that the Muslim community's worldly interests demanded legalization. Supposedly, the result was a veiled Eurocentric approach to modernity that was Islamic only in external appearance.[4]

Yet the modern "Salafist" tendency to condone European goods was not really so exceptional. An openness to products made by non-Muslims was one of the characteristics of Islamic legal thought in premodern times. The Qurʾan allowed Muslims to enjoy "the goods things" of Jews and Christians; the early Islamic tradition offered an abundance of accommodating precedents; and medieval jurists devised creative if convoluted ways to sanction whatever they wanted to sanction, including papers with watermarks of the cross. Salafi reformers argued that the tradition of adhering to a school of law constrained moderns' freedom of action. They caricatured their rivals' scholastic discipline and exaggerated the threat that their mode of legal reasoning presented to religion, warning that it would drive laypersons to choose modernity over Islam. But contemporary jurists who insisted on following a legal tradition nevertheless frequently ruled in favor of various technological and financial innovations.[5] On one occasion, Riḍā criticized the ruling of one his rivals, a Ḥanafi judge affiliated with al-Azhar, for its reflexive permissiveness.[6] Indeed, the history of Islamic law offers countless examples of flexible, accommodating, pragmatic rulings. Riḍā distinguished himself from others not by legalizing modern things now and then for the benefit of Muslim societies but by elaborating—based on Islamic theories and values—a utilitarian hermeneutics that allowed him to justify quite consistently nondevotional interests.

The perception that ʿAbduh and his disciples articulated "pseudo-Islamic" ideas has a long history. It can be traced to the construction of Islam's modern predicament by one of the defenders of free-trade imperialism. Holding that "Moslem law . . . discourages the outlay of capital," Lord Cromer argued that Muslim jurists needed to commit "subterfuges" in order to sanction trading with "the Christian usurer" on "the basis of equality." He knew that under Great Britain's "civilizing" influence, "agnostic" reformers could invent "legal fictions" to allow such exchanges.[7] But he saw their rulings as fundamentally non-Islamic. Such an essentialist view of Islam is historically untenable. But historians of Islamic law as well as historians of currents of religious reform from the eighteenth century onward have upheld Cromer's view by exaggerating the extent to which Muslim reformers under British rule diverged from the Islamic tradition. ʿAbduh and Riḍā worked to construct an Islam for their time. Their religious doctrines, postures, and stances were no less "Islamic" than those of the Salaf.

The conventional narrative about Riḍā's fateful role in the history of Salafism emphasizes the notion that he turned his back on the liberal, cosmopolitan, Europeanized philosophy of his mentor ʿAbduh in the aftermath of World War I. In this period, Riḍā allegedly fell prey to a "kind of literalism" that made him perceive "modernity as a threat." Losing his utilitarian convictions, he began to peddle instead, or so the story goes, Wahhabi ideology and Ḥanbali theology. Inspired by the strict, austere, purist ideals of the clerics of Najd, he convinced his followers to reject the materialism of the West and contributed to the "disenchantment and alienation" that supposedly afflicted the Islamic world after his death.[8]

This storyline underestimates continuities in Salafist thought, assigns to Riḍā powers of persuasion that no mufti has ever possessed, and fails to realize the extent to which his turn to "radical" politics simply reflected broader anticolonial trends. He embraced some revolutionary strategies rather late. He did not rush, for example, to support the Egyptian boycotts of British goods in 1922. Once he became familiar with Gandhi's philosophy of anti-imperial resistance and grew more involved in the struggles to establish nation-states in the Arabian Peninsula and the Levant, he did embrace aspects of economic nationalism.

Accordingly, he expressed a preference for patriotic "Arab" substitutes to "Frankish" imports and he criticized Muslims who rushed to wear fashionable foreign clothes. This change in his political views of consumption did not signal, however, an overall shift in his attitudes toward modernity, industrial development, or capitalism.

The radicalization thesis is not new; it dates to political conflicts between Egypt and the new Saudi state in the 1920s. These conflicts stemmed from Saudi assertions of sovereignty over the Ḥijāz and Egyptian efforts to maintain the annual tradition of pilgrims' parading into the holy land with guns and silk drapes for the Kaᶜba.[9] In this contentious climate, Egyptian scholars mocked Najd's Wahhabi clerics for their opposition to wireless telegraphy and their suspicion of technological innovation. When rumors began to circulate in Cairo that Riḍā had received an astronomical sum from Ibn Saᶜūd to publish Wahhabi tracts and promote Saudi interests, the opportunity to insinuate that Riḍā had become through and through a Wahhabi—for money—proved irresistible.[10]

To defend himself, Riḍā contended that he had been steadfast in his commitments to monotheism, the school of the Salaf, the "techniques of the age," and "the laws of creation."[11] His legal philosophy did not, in fact, change in a fundamental way as a result of his engagements with the Saudi monarchy and Wahhabi dogmas. His rulings on financial and commercial initiatives remained permissive. Strikingly, he refused to ban the import of technologies even when he developed socially conservative misgivings about their "irreligious" uses by Muslim women and men. Furthermore, he began the bold effort to reconcile his diverse commitments long before World War I. Not only did he try—whenever possible—to justify the adoption of modern things by evoking scripture and the example of the Salaf; he also experimented with an entrepreneurial interpretation of the first Muslims in light of industrial capitalistic values. This book has called his use of early Islamic acts and canons to defend economically liberal principles "laissez-faire Salafism."

But no institution, society, or code forced him to adhere ideologically or programmatically to a uniform Salafist way of reasoning legally. In 1927 Riḍā freely departed from scriptural and ancestral models to rule in favor of Muslims investing in hotels for wine-drinking European tourists in Lebanon under French rule; similarly, he ruled in 1930 that usury was licit for Muslims in China. In both cases, he resorted to a territorial rationale—developed by Ottoman jurists, who adhered to Abū Ḥanīfa's school of law—for trading in "the House of War" without observing the restrictions of "the House of Islam." Najd's Ḥanbali clerics, who insisted on the strict and universal applicability of the sacred law, scoffed at such "subjective" juridical opinions. By contrast, Riḍā identified Abū Ḥanīfa as a pious Muslim ancestor whose rulings latter-day Salafis could adopt selectively, and he had no objections to modern Muslims following the teachings of any Sunni school of law if the consequences were liberating or empowering in his eyes. Even in the late twenties and early thirties, the Salaf remained a flexible tool in his legal toolkit.

A significant exception to his enlightened approach to the diffusion of technology from Europe came into view in 1926 at the Islamic World Congress in Mecca. Riḍā then aligned himself with a Najdi cleric, Bin Bulayhid, to propose that at the very least the Ḥijāz, if not Arabia as a whole, should be liberated from the presence of non-Muslim experts. This piece of evidence seems to support the radicalization thesis. A historical investigation of the legal issue showed, however, that Riḍā had defended that exclusivist, protectionist position already in 1909, when he published a fatwa on the Ḥijāz railway project. Armed with scriptural citations, he explained why the Ottoman Empire had barred Christian engineers from working on the stretch of railroad leading toward Medina. The opinion certainly reflects both his reservations about European hegemony and his protective impulses toward sacred Muslim space. Diverging in tone and substance from his normal approach to development, it shows that he placed a significant limit on the spread of technology. This was a formidable and religiously meaningful restriction. Indeed, calls by rebellious Salafists for the expulsion of infidels from the Arabian Peninsula would eventually shake the Saudi monarchy's claims to legitimacy. But such calls came well after Riḍā's 1909 fatwa, which was rather inspired by the Ottoman Empire's religiously exclusive approach to the modernization of an exalted Islamic zone.

It is tempting to take a set of judgments on goods such as toilet paper, Qurʾanic discs, Ramaḍān telegrams, cargo insurance, lottery tickets, tourist hotels, and so on, as embodiments of the abstraction known as "modernity." Riḍā and his correspondents at times described these goods as "novel" or "modern." They thought of them as representative objects of "this age." In this vein, they tried to convey their attitude, as Muslims, toward modernity.

But it is critical to recognize, in order to understand better the relationship between legal cultures and modern things in the history of Islam, that the periodization scheme is extralegal. Toilet paper and lottery tickets posed specific technical problems whose resolution required referring to separate branches of the legal tradition. To offer legal advice about the first of these paper products, the mufti needed to think about scriptural rules concerning anal cleaning. To offer advice about the second product, he needed to think about medieval rules concerning financial dealings "in the House of War." These rules had nothing to do with each other except for the fact that they belonged to the enormous corpus of prophetic representations and juridical interpretations of God's law. If modernity was the elephant in the room, it was nevertheless possible to ignore it while judging this and that "modern" thing.

A similar point has to be made about a geopolitical construct that historians in the Cold War era projected back in time. Riḍā rarely used the term "the West." He and his correspondents referred to "Frankish" perfumes and "European" hats: qualifications that had some significance because they immediately suggested a foreign origin. For this reason, arguments for adoption or rejection had to consider the foreignness of the products. Most of the time, however, when they deliberated the legality of imports and the transfer of technologies, Muslims made no mention of the country of origin. Nor did they evoke a geopolitical barrier. They asked questions about telegraphs and gramophones, not about "British" telegraphs and "American" gramophones. The origin of these technologies either was deliberately elided in order to facilitate incorporation into Muslim societies or was simply not so culturally significant.

Moreover, the adoption and appropriation of these technologies is what provoked religious controversies. In the early twentieth century, Muslims did not have to ponder telegraphy or phonography in the abstract—as remote examples of "Western" innovation. Physical embodiments of these technologies had already made the passage into their polities; they no longer seemed entirely foreign. Actually, Muslim trendsetters' embrace of technologies that had Islamic applications gave rise to riveting debates. Experts on the sacred law were not asked to make a general case for or against "European" technology; they were asked to rule, instead, about the reliability of telegrams that announced the timing of Ramaḍān or about the permissibility of worshipping with the mediation of records of the Qurʾan. These were technical religious and legal questions that had only an incidental connection to broader, vaguer preoccupations about the rise of Europe.

However much attention this book has devoted to Riḍā's legal reflections, it has given historical priority—in terms of agency and causality—to material entanglements that catalyzed social and religious conflicts in a globalized world. By paying close attention to circumstances that gave rise to requests for fatwas, this book has diverged in one significant respect from scholarship that has addressed Riḍā's roles as a reformer. Scholars have cast him as an effective, though not especially original, propagator of nineteenth-century Islamic modernism who gradually turned, after the world war, into a crucial defender of

Islamic fundamentalism. Many of the religious and political transformations that Riḍā and his allies hoped for never took place, and no academic has argued that they set in motion a Salafist Reformation comparable in significance to the Protestant Reformation.[12] Nevertheless, historians have generally represented his doctrines and judgments as influential and impactful. They have argued, for instance, that his fatwas were an inspiring force behind a divisive movement of religious reform and revival in Southeast Asia. A hierarchical approach to the generation and dissemination of Islamic legal ideas underpins this impression that Riḍā motivated religious actors in remote climes. It is not evident that he was such an effective reformer; it is clear, however, that he was a responsive reformer.

Many of his fatwas were responses to local debates about new objects and practices. Fatwa seekers, who typically embraced a reformist agenda and financed the production of *al-Manār*, pressed Riḍā to support their side in these debates. More often than not, he gave them exactly what they paid for: a predictably accommodating ruling that justified, with multiple references to scripture, their position. Riḍā was not a neutral arbitrator. His fatwas reflected his commitments and predilections. It is difficult to imagine that they effectively resolved disputes, given the presence of social strife and ideological divisions. Still, partisans of reform sought his fatwas because they perceived them as authoritative, affirmative statements that would ideally show friends and foes that an expert on the sacred law had ruled in their favor.

The authors of fatwa requests set the agenda. They prompted the mufti to adopt stances on the issues that mattered to them. They also stimulated him to flesh out the skeleton of reform: to research and reflect on the relevance or irrelevance of the shariʿa in modern contexts. And they challenged him to define the line between heterodoxy and orthodoxy. In 1901, long before he rose to the public defense of Wahhabi clerics, Riḍā heard from an Egyptian shaykh who dared him to explain how he distinguished himself theologically from "the school of the Wahhabis."[13] Fatwa seekers did not create his scripturalist approach to legal questions, but they certainly elicited it. To respond to the accusation that he had committed a religious transgression by using toilet paper, a Sudanese correspondent asked Riḍā for a ruling based on a definitive scriptural text.[14] Conservative dressers in West Borneo started to invoke "the Book of God" to outlaw a new transcultural fashion, wearing a kaffiyeh under a hat, before an anonymous correspondent appealed to Riḍā for a fatwa.[15] In these cases, *al-Manār*'s mufti did not have to convince his readers to return to the Qurʾan. He merely had to make scriptural interventions in local debates that already pivoted on scriptural interpretations.

Lay and clerical elites—men such as Shaykh Muqbil of Bahrain, Ḥāfiẓ Ḥilmī of Kazan, Muḥammad Belkhōja of Tunis, Nūr al-Dīn of Punjab, Muḥammad ibn ʿAqīl ibn Yaḥyā of Singapore, and Ma Ruitu of Guangzhou—drafted plans about what needed to be done in their cities and states. They strove to establish and implement programs of reform. To this end, they procured fatwas from external authorities such as Riḍā and thereby participated in elaborating an ideology of reform that had both local and global resonance.

Yet Islam's material and global reformation unfolded without much direction from renowned Muslim intellectuals. Perhaps Riḍā fantasized about leading a Reformation. In his article "Of Men and Money," he celebrated, as we have seen, the influence and efficacy of reformers such as Martin Luther who were moved to act for the sake of society by spiritual rather than materialistic values.[16] No mastermind orchestrated it, but an Islamic reformation did take place in the late nineteenth and early twentieth centuries. Material forces that intellectuals had no power to control drove the process. Global technologies, commodities, and instruments of exchange in effect reformed Islamic practices on the local level. They spurred Muslims with and without a clerical education to rethink the rules of the sacred law and to distinguish religious from secular pursuits in new ways.

In local battles over the future of Islam, it is worth highlighting the agency of two social types: early adopters and conservative critics, those who enthusiastically espoused innovations and those who zealously denounced new trends and tastes. Taking it upon themselves to command the right and forbid the wrong, outspoken critics initiated round after round of debate. They were the ones who created a scandal when they noticed toilet paper in a shoe; they were the ones who denounced the interfaith commerce in Qurʾanic records. *Al-Manār*'s fatwa seekers generally conveyed their criticism indirectly, and surely they misrepresented it on occasion. But it is important to recognize that both the Muslims who rushed to adopt new technologies and the Muslims who felt compelled to speak out against them played key roles in the making of Islam's reformation. Furthermore, their conflicts and debates preceded historically the turn to muftis for fatwas. As for the products that provoked these conflicts, they came even earlier.

Inanimate objects such as banknotes did not compel Muslims to change their religious beliefs or practices in particular ways. Nevertheless, they inspired sparkling and heated communal discussions about the "right" way for Muslims to act in concert with things. Paper money was, in fact, a material cause behind local debates about the need to overhaul usury laws and alms-tax provisions. In Bahrain, where British Indian banknotes circulated, a pearl merchant and government advisor remarked that it was impossible to observe these laws and provisions literally. The medieval lawmakers who had designed them had understood the intrinsic value of silver and gold possessions but ignored the future value of paper assets. There was a pressing need, he reasoned, to revise this legal tradition. Such reflections led to the development of projects of reform. These projects arose not from readings of utilitarian philosophy in translation but from the recognition that the laws of the past did not adequately explain how to deal with new things in circulation.

Islam's reformation was not an ideational movement rooted in modern concepts; it was a materialist movement rooted in modern objects. Odeon Records, the German company that specialized in marketing "Arabian" celebrities, reformed Islamic practices more effectively than did any intellectual. It produced the shellac discs that enabled Muslim circles in Kazan, Cairo, and Singapore to listen to God's words through a new medium. The casual, indiscriminate handling of these discs in the marketplace confounded normative expectations regarding the treatment of sacred and profane objects. As Muslim consumers purchased Qurʾanic records from non-Muslim shopkeepers, perceptions changed of what it meant to exchange in a free market—where nobody in power interfered in the secular trade in religious goods. When gramophones played these records of recitation, replacing live reciters, audiences had to decide whether to suspend or modify traditional rites of prostration, which they had customarily performed at key verses. The early adopters of gramophones and their conservative critics debated these reforms intensely, setting in motion the discursive process that culminated in the publication of fatwas. Muftis who self-identified as reformers reluctantly condoned or guardedly approved each of these developments, altering religious constructs to suit consumer trends. Odeon Records and Muslim consumers were, however, the principal engines of religious change.

Just how much agency did material objects have in the process of Islamic reform? Most imports that Muslims encountered in imperial dependencies—French oil presses, American maize, Swedish timber, Russian petrol, English ironmongery, German razors, and so on—generated no religious questions. Very few foreign products stimulated thoughts about the sacred law, and these products tended to provoke not one but multiple extended debates in many parts of the world. The reason for this is obvious in some cases: novel technologies that had the capacity to affect ritual practices became controversial as states and companies developed specific Islamic applications.

Telegraphs were, like gramophones, media that could be used to communicate all sorts of information, most of it uncontroversial. Much changed when state actors decided to use this technology to convey and control the timing of the fast of Ramaḍān. Local communities encountered a new mechanism for determining events in the ritual calendar. They had to figure out whether to heed a remote political authority rather than the muezzins and imams in their neighborhoods. The decision to trust or distrust state directives was especially contentious in places like Tunisia, where a European power had established a monopoly over the telegraph network and where telegraph operators symbolized colonialism as well as Christianity. Political conditions were one key reason, then, for prolonged religious and legal debates among Muslims about uses of new media.

A diverse mix of goods, from toilet paper to alcoholic medicines to brimmed hats, that generated fatwas had one thing in common: they possessed some function that made them highly relatable to canonical proscriptions and recommendations. Muḥammad and the first Muslims did not lavish equal attention on every topic. They placed an emphasis on certain actions, values, and objects. They developed legal guidelines to curb usurious exchanges and the consumption of inebriating drinks; they commemorated the founders' styles of dress in exquisite detail; and they related multiple anecdotes, which were eventually incorporated into the canon of oral traditions, about the Prophet's preferred methods for cleaning the body after defecation.

The shariʿa, in other words, primed Islamic legal cultures to respond readily to certain kinds of objects: not to innovations in general but specifically to new technologies and commodities that seemed analogous in function to the artifacts and tools represented by scripture. Toilet paper, for instance, provoked a religious debate that may at first appear exceptional: a historical aberration that must have occurred only once in history, as a result of particular circumstances in the Sudan in 1909. But several fatwas have actually addressed, in a variety of states in the twentieth and twenty-first centuries, the permissibility of this product and the relative merits of water and stones. These fatwas could easily have emerged independently of one another as a consequence of the commodity's spread and individual Muslims' inclination to proclaim or ridicule the devout desire to follow each and every custom of the Prophet.

This does not mean that clashes were bound to happen between new products and an old cultural system. Debates about the applicability of the sacred law to unfamiliar objects were episodic, not continuous. Sparked by extrinsic contingencies such as political turns or consumer trends, they bubbled up and fizzled out. Although the shariʿa had a profound effect on the classes of objects that Muslim moderns decided to place on trial, supplying the semantic structure used to evaluate these objects' religious significance, it had surprisingly little influence on the outcome of those trials. The battle of fatwas over the permissibility of alcoholic products demonstrates how the Islamic legal tradition, with its multiplicity of precedents and principles, could be used to support diametrically opposed judgments.[17] It is critical to recognize, too, that Muslims under European hegemony did not turn to the shariʿa in order to assess every significant invention; most industrial machines and industrial products seemed religiously irrelevant to them. Even dangerous, menacing things that reflected the rising power of empire did not necessarily spark religious debates and legal trials. Muslims under colonial rule generated fatwas against toothbrushes; they did not generate fatwas against hot air balloons.

Technologies that barely penetrated Muslim societies caused little or no religious debate. It is easy to imagine an alternative world where Muslims would travel mainly by *montgolfière* and where, as a result of this, questions would arise about the right way to pray in the air. Performing prostrations would be physically challenging, what with the size of the basket, and potentially dangerous depending on the conditions of flight. Moreover, the pilot's maneuvers could make it difficult for passengers to face in the direction of Mecca. It is easy to imagine, in this vein too, fatwas that would cite oral traditions recounting Muḥammad's concessions toward locomotion by camel. According to these traditions, the Prophet prayed in the direction of travel without worrying in these circumstances about the location of Mecca. Jurists could apply the same degree of flexibility, by straightforward analogical reasoning, to the dilemma of prayer in hot air balloons. But these vehicles hovered overhead on rare occasions—notably, during the 1798 and 1911 invasions of Egypt and Libya—and they formed part of the arsenal of the enemy. They did not become entangled in Muslim societies. There was simply no practical reason for Muslims to deliberate how to behave religiously in the company of these things.

Key patterns emerge from the comprehensive analysis of particular cases, and these patterns reveal a great deal about the general preoccupations of the time. In addition to worrying about the effect of modern machines on ritual traditions, Muslim societies in the early twentieth century were especially concerned about moneymaking instruments, the purity of Muslim bodies and Muslim spaces, and the transformation of male habits of dress. Since they embodied externally the communal identity of Muslims and the cultural appeal of Europe, clothes became controversial for obvious reasons. Once modernizers decided to impose hats on all men, as a symbolic measure to signal their political commitment to breaking with the past, the reaction was of course explosive.

The imperialism of free trade resulted in an unprecedented influx of foreign persons and foreign goods into predominantly Muslim societies. Perhaps this historic passage of people and things across cultural borders gave rise to an amorphous anxiety over the best way to protect the purity of Islam from the impurities of strangers. But responses to foreign persons and objects in relation to the Islamic system of purity were complicated legally. On the face of it, the fatwas about the application of paint to mosques and the employment of Muslims to lay down the railway within the Ḥijāz seem completely unrelated. A casuistic perspective on Islamic legal debates would separate the two cases: one revolved around the use of a new foreign product that contained alcohol, a substance associated with ritual pollution, to decorate a mosque; the other one revolved around the introduction of non-Muslim persons, whose bodies were not considered technically impure by Sunni jurists, into territory that was in theory off limits to Christian persons. Both fatwas nevertheless concerned the protection of sacred space from symbolic, if not material, impurities that were linked to the expansion of Europe.

Islamic laws about ritual impurity concerned Muslim bodies as well as Muslim spaces. An interest in protecting the human body from impure substances was one of the reasons for wariness over toilet paper and tincture of iodine. The fatwas that tried to allay this concern by arguing that toilet paper was a hygienic article and that alcohol was an effective disinfectant turned this logic on its head, contending that nothing cleaned and purified the body as well as these agents of modernity.

Fatwas about banknotes, lottery tickets, cargo insurance, tourist hotels, and the sale of wine reflect a broader interest in defining the moral limits to the pursuit of profit under non-Muslim dominance. The expansion of European empires created all sorts of new economic opportunities, facilitating extensive interactions across cultural and religious boundaries. In Muslim societies, the most intense debates centered on the canonical prohibitions against usury, gambling, and trading in forbidden goods, which seemed theoretically applicable to these distinct opportunities. Perennial questions about the right way to make money were inevitably tied to a poignant concern over the effect of religious restrictions on economic development.

Whenever he responded to these questions, the mufti of Cairo's Lighthouse Press tried to dispel the shadows that darkened his readers' spirits. His fatwas offered a globally dispersed Arabic readership the liberating message that the sacred law allowed Muslims to thrive individually and collectively no matter where they lived—even under French, British, or Chinese rule in Beirut, the Punjab, or Guangzhou. He reassured these readers that the tension that they felt between being Muslim and being modern would recede if they pursued profit with pride in Islam and disregarded contemporary clerics who insisted on maintaining a regime of medieval taboos. God, he often preached, did not reveal the divine law to Muḥammad in order to make Muslims languish in poverty. Islam was fundamentally a religion of prosperity. If Muslims worldwide would free themselves from the hardships that divided them, they would achieve political power and enjoy a religious resurgence as a united community. This was the dream that inspired Riḍā's laissez-faire vision for Islam. It gave wings to the strangely modern idea that the spirit if not the letter of the sacred law would accommodate in the future what it had accommodated in the ancestral past: all the marvelous goods and wonderful inventions of this world.

NOTES

Prologue: The Parable of the *Montgolfière* and the Translation of Haleby's Corpse

1. ʿAbd al-Raḥmān al-Jabartī, *Tārīkh muddat al-Faransīs bi-Miṣr: Muḥarram-Rajab 1213 H., 15 Yūniyū-Dīsimbir 1798 M.*, ed. and trans. S. Moreh (Leiden: Brill, 1975), 23a, 24a.
2. Al-Jabartī, *Tārīkh*, 20b. According to the official French version, twenty jealous, subaltern shaykhs sparked the sedition of Cairo; see the *Courier de l'Égypte* 18 (Frimaire 7, year 7), 2–4. For a fuller account, see Henry Laurens, *L'expédition d'Égypte, 1798–1801* (Paris: Armand Colin, 1989), 148–52.
3. Al-Jabartī, *Tārīkh*, 24a–24b. Al-Jabartī's disappointment in hot air balloons did not extend to all European inventions. Elsewhere, he described European clocks and astronomical instruments admiringly as wonderful, unprecedented, extraordinary machines. See al-Jabartī, *Tārīkh*, 25a–25b.
4. On Conté's innovations, see the detailed article on "Aerostation" in *Encyclopaedia Britannica: Or, A Dictionary of Arts, Sciences, and Miscellaneous Literature*, 6th ed. (Edinburgh: Archibald Constable and Company, 1823), 1:220–22. Also see the apologetic history of G. de Gaugler, *Les compagnies d'aérostiers militaires sous la République de l'an II à l'an X* (Paris: Librairie Militaire, Maritime et Polytechnique de J. Corréard, 1857), 16–17.
5. For an account that places the *aérostiers'* expedition to Egypt in the broader context of the history of early military flights, see Jules Duhem, *Histoire de l'arme aérienne avant le moteur*, illus. (Paris: Nouvelled Editions Latines, 1964), chap. 8.
6. *Courier de l'Égypte* 20 (Frimaire 18, year 7), 2. This account dates the flight to the twentieth of Frimaire—clearly a typo given the publication date. In an earlier issue, the *Courier de l'Égypte* had announced that the event would take place on the tenth of Frimaire at Esbequier square, at a place and time that corresponds exactly to the coordinates given by al-Jabartī. Originally the flight had been scheduled on the thirtieth of Brumaire (November 20, 1798), but it was postponed; see *Courier de l'Égypte* 17 (Brumaire 30, year 7), 4.
7. *Courier de l'Égypte* 25 (Pluviôse 3, year 7), 2–3, editorializing on the flight of Nivôse 25 (January 14, 1799).

8. G. Béthuys [pseud.] (Georges-Frédéric Espitalier), *Les aérostiers militaires*, illus. by Gil Baer (Paris: H. Lecène et H. Oudin, 1889), 91–92; and F. Charles-Roux, *Bonaparte: Gouverneur d'Égypte* (Paris: Librarie Plon, 1935), 184.
9. Napoléon, *Guerre d'Orient: Campagnes de Égypte et de Syrie, 1798–1799: Mémoires pour servir à l'histoire de Napoléon, dictés par lui-même à Sainte-Hélène, et publiés par le général Bertrand* (Paris, 1847), 1:226–27. Like Napoleon, a lieutenant of artillery, Jean-Pierre Doguereau, mentioned the launching of a balloon that "greatly astonished the Egyptians" on the first of Vendémiaire, year 7 (September 22, 1798). His journal's editor rightly contends that the event, though advertised then, did not in fact take place until November 30, 1798 (Frimaire 10, year 7). See Jean-Pierre Doguereau, *Journal de l'expédition d'Égypte*, ed. C. de La Jonquière (La Vouivre: 1997), 33. On "material difficulties" causing the postponement, see C. de La Jonquière, *L'expédition d'Égypte, 1798–1801*, 2nd ed. (Paris: Henri Charles-Lavauzelle, 1899–1907), 3:382–85. Charles-Roux (*Bonaparte*, 184) confirms that Conté had built a large *montgolfière*, twelve feet in diameter, for the festival of the Republic, but it was not ready until the tenth of Frimaire. Tellingly, *Courier de l'Égypte* 8 (Vendémiaire 6, year 7), 2–4, describes the festival at length yet says nothing about a balloon.
10. On Baron Larrey's handwritten account of the event, see Gaston Tissandier, *Histoire des ballons et des aéronautes célèbres* (Paris: H. Launette & Cie, 1887), 142, and Dominique-Jean Larrey, *Relation historique et chirurgicale de l'expédition de l'armée d'Orient, en Égypte et en Syrie* (Paris, 1803), 133 and 413.
11. Edme-François Jomard, *Conté* (Paris: E. Thunot, 1849), 29–31.
12. In addition to Jomard, cited above, see Pierre-Dominique Martin, *Histoire de l'expédition française en Égypte* (J. M. Eberhart, 1815), 1:273.
13. Cf. Seymour Stanton Block, *Benjamin Franklin, Genius of Kites, Flights, and Voting Rights* (Jefferson, N.C.: McFarland, 2004), 77; and Nelly Fouchet, "La mode 'au ballon,' la ballomanie," in *Le temps des ballons: Art et histoire*, ed. Alain Dégardin et al. (Paris: Éd. de La Martinière, 1995), 41–62.
14. Ernest Renan, "L'Islamisme et la science," *Journal des débats*, March 30, 1883.
15. On the Enlightenment fascination with strange things, see Lorraine Daston and Katharine Park, *Wonders and the Order of Nature, 1150–1750* (New York: Zone Books, 2001).
16. Rifāʿa Rāfiʿ al-Ṭahṭāwī, *Takhlīṣ al-ibrīz fī talkhīṣ Bārīz* (Cairo: al-Hayʾa al-Miṣriyya al-ʿĀmma li-l-Kitāb, 1993), 248, 255–56. Al-Ṭahṭāwī did contend that Parisian philosophers' books were infected with heretical ideas.
17. Al-Ṭahṭāwī, *Takhlīṣ*, 262–64; *Galeries historiques des contemporains, ou Nouvelle biographie* (Brussels: Aug. Wahlen et Compagnie, 1819), 7:311; Louis Rousseau and Céran Lemonnier, *Promenades au Jardin des Plantes* (Paris: J. B. Baillière, 1837), 85–86; Alexandre Dumas, *Quinze jours au Sinaï* (Brussels: Meline, Cans et Compagnie, 1839), 145; John Murray, *A Handbook for Visitors to Paris; Containing a Description of the Most Remarkable Objects, with General Advice and Information for English Travellers in That Metropolis, and on the Way to It*, 4th ed., rev. (London: John Murray, 1870), 148; and Shaden M. Tageldin, *Empire and the Seductions of Translation in Egypt* (Berkeley: University of California Press, 2011), 54. "This specter of French violation," remarks Tageldin, "haunts al-Ṭahṭāwī's otherwise positive reception of French scholarship and institutions."

Introduction: Good Things Made Lawful: Euro-Muslim Objects and Laissez-Faire Fatwas

1. Muḥammad Khālid Masʿūd, "Trends in the Interpretation of Islamic Law as Reflected in the Fatāwá Literature of Deoband School: A Study of the Attitudes of the ʿUlamāʾ of Deoband to

Certain Social Problems and Inventions" (M.A. thesis, McGill University, Institute of Islamic Studies, Montreal, 1969), 39; and Muḥammad Shafīʿ, *Fatāwā-i Dārul ʿUlūm Dār Diyoband, yaʿnī Imdādul Muftin* (Karashi: Dārulishaʿat, 2001), 232–33. I am grateful to Khālid Masʿūd for sending me a copy of this recent edition of the collection of fatwas. Though undated, the fatwa clearly derives from the 1930s or early 1940s, when Muḥammad Shafīʿ headed Dār al-ʿUlūm Deoband's Fatwa Department.

2. Internet searches for the terms "global Islamic/Muslim market" yield few results before the year 2000. A business-oriented academic interest in the topic emerged in the 1970s. For two early examples, see Jack G. Kaikati, "Marketing Practices in Iran vis-à-vis Saudi Arabia," *Management International Review* 19, no. 4 (1979), 31–37; and Mushtaq Luqmani, Zahir A. Quraeshi, and Linda Delene, "Marketing in Islamic Countries: A Viewpoint," *MSU Business Topics*, Summer 1980, 17–25. For subsequent usage, see Masaaki Kotabe and Kristiaan Helsen, *Global Marketing Management* (New York: Wiley, 1998), 93–94. On the export of synthetic toothbrushes to India, see Par Kerry Segrave, *America Brushes Up: The Use and Marketing of Toothpaste and Toothbrushes in the Twentieth Century* (Jefferson, N.C.: McFarland, 2010), 27.
3. George Forrest, ed., *Selections from the Letters, Despatches and other State Papers preserved in the Military Department of the Government of India, 1857-58* (Calcutta: Military Department Press, 1893), 3, 7. Cf. Syed Ahmed Khan, *The Causes of the Indian Revolt*, with an intro. by Francis Robinson (Karachi: Oxford University Press, 2000), 10, 50–51.
4. Barbara Daly Metcalf, *Islamic Revival in British India: Deoband, 1860–1900* (Princeton, N.J.: Princeton University Press, 1982), 179–91. This orientation did not remain fixed and uniform. On internal "Deobandi discontent" in the twentieth century, see Muhammad Qasim Zaman, *Modern Islamic Thought in a Radical Age: Religious Authority and Internal Criticism* (Cambridge: Cambridge University Press, 2012), 167.
5. The term "Islamic economics" entered into scholarly discourse in the 1940s in South Asia, on the verge of the independence of India and Pakistan, as a translation of the Urdu term "*Islāmī maʿāshiyāt*." The earliest reference to it on Google Books comes from 1944, when the *Indian Journal of Economics* cited an article on the topic by a professor of theology, Manāẓir Aḥsan Gīlānī. Within five years, an Indian writer from Madras would declare: "Islamic economics has no place for the dominance of industrialists or the leadership of capitalists." He would portray it as "the only panacea" for the "clash of thoughts and ideologies" confronting the world. See Abul Amal, "Islam to the Rescue," *Ramadan Annual* (July 1949): 91–94. On the "genesis of Islamic economics," also see Timur Kuran, *Islam and Mammon: The Economic Predicaments of Islamism* (Princeton. N.J.: Princeton University Press, 2004), chap. 4; and Zaman, *Modern Islamic Thought*, 248–49. Elsewhere, Kuran has asserted that before the 1940s, "Muslim reformers who talked about defending, reforming or revitalizing Islam showed no interest in economic thought per se. Those concerned with economic issues did not promote reforms grounded in Islamic scripture or even develop a discourse that was explicitly Islamic." This assertion requires revision: Riḍā showed an interest in economic thought decades earlier, as the present book will show, and he certainly developed an Islamic discourse to deal with economic issues. Cf. Timur Kuran, "Modern Islam and the Economy," in *The New Cambridge History of Islam*, vol. 6, *Muslims and Modernity: Culture and Society since 1800*, ed. Robert W. Hefner (Cambridge: Cambridge University Press, 2010), 484.
6. For an early and influential critique of such an approach to belief as a mental state, rather than a "constituting activity in the world," see Talal Asad, *Genealogies of Religion: Discipline and Reasons of Power in Christianity and Islam* (Baltimore: Johns Hopkins University Press, 1993),

47–48. For a study of a nineteenth-century Protestant understandings of individual belief as "interiorized experience of unconditional certainty" in relation to conceptions of Islam as well as Judaism, see Reinhard Schulze, "Islam und Judentum im Angesicht der Protestantisierung der Religionen im 19. Jahrhundert," in *Judaism, Christianity, and Islam in the Course of History: Exchange and Conflicts*, ed. Lothar Gall and Dietmar Willoweit, 139–166 (Berlin: De Gruyter Oldenbourg, 2016). On fetishism and materialism in Victorian Religionswissenschaft, see Tomoko Masuzawa, "Troubles with Materiality: The Ghost of Fetishism in the Nineteenth Century," *Comparative Studies in Society and History* 42, no. 2 (2000): 242–67.

7. For a sampling of works in this emerging subfield, see Gregory Starrett, "The Political Economy of Religious Commodities in Cairo," *American Anthropologist* 97, no. 1 (1995): 51–68; Leor Halevi, *Muhammad's Grave: Death Rites and the Making of Islamic Society* (New York: Columbia University Press, 2007); Finbarr B. Flood, *Objects of Translation: Material Culture and Medieval 'Hindu-Muslim' Encounter* (Princeton, N.J.: Princeton University Press, 2009); Jamal J. Elias, *Aisha's Cushion: Religious Art, Perception, and Practice in Islam* (Cambridge, Mass.: Harvard University Press, 2012); Richard McGregor, "Dressing the Kaʿba from Cairo: The Aesthetics of Pilgrimage to Mecca" in *Religion and Material Culture: The Matter of Belief*, ed. David Morgan, 247–61 (New York: Routledge, 2009); and Travis Zadeh, "Touching and Ingesting: Early Debates over the Material Qurʾan," *Journal of the American Oriental Society* 129, no. 3 (2009): 443–66.

8. Birgit Meyer, David Morgan, Crispin Paine, and S. Brent Plate, "The Origin and Mission of Material Religion," *Religion* 40 (2010): 210.

9. Articles in the field's flagship journal, *Islamic Law and Society*, have paid relatively little attention to "material culture" or "material objects." For two notable exceptions, see Ruba Kana'an, "The *de Jure* 'Artist' of the Bobrinski Bucket: Production and Patronage of Metalwork in pre-Mongol Khurasan and Transoxiana," *Islamic Law and Society* 16, no. 2 (2009): 175–201; and Irfana Hashmi, "The Development of a Locker System at al-Azhar," *Islamic Law and Society* 25 (2018): 11–36.

10. For an example, see Hiroyuki Yanagihashi, *A History of the Early Islamic Law of Property: Reconstructing the Legal Development, 7th–9th Centuries* (Leiden: Brill, 2004).

11. On the role of material evidence, ranging from written documents to DNA tests, in Islamic legal procedures, see Lawrence Rosen, "Equity and Discretion in a Modern Islamic Legal System," *Law and Society Review* 15, no. 2 (1980–1981): 217–46; Baber Johansen, "La découverte des choses qui parlent: La légalisation de la torture judiciaire en droit musulman (xiiie-xive siècles)," *Enquête* 7 (1999): 175–202; Baber Johansen, "Signs as Evidence: The Doctrine of Ibn Taymiyya (1263–1328) and Ibn Qayyim al-Jawziyya (d. 1351) on Proof," *Islamic Law and Society* 9, no. 2 (2002): 168–93; and Ron Shaham, *The Expert Witness in Islamic Courts: Medicine and Crafts in the Service of Law* (Chicago: University of Chicago Press, 2010).

12. Khaled Fahmy, "The Anatomy of Justice: Forensic Medicine and Criminal Law in Nineteenth-Century Egypt," *Islamic Law and Society* 6, no. 2 (1999): 231.

13. For an example of the revived application of shariʿa rules of evidence in a modern context, see Tahir Wasti, *The Application of Islamic Criminal Law in Pakistan: Sharia in Practice* (Leiden: Brill, 2009), 126–27, 188–93. Formal rules can of course be applied flexibly, and Islamic judges do find ways to consider circumstantial material evidence. See, for instance, Frank E. Vogel, *Islamic Law and Legal System: Studies of Saudi Arabia* (Leiden: Brill, 2000), 144–62.

14. Gabriel García Márquez, *Cien años de soledad*, centésima edición (Buenos Aires: Editorial Sudamericana, 1995), 7.

15. John Stuart Mill, *Principles of Political Economy with Some of Their Applications to Social Philosophy* (New York: D. Appleton, 1891), 2:134–36.
16. Originally published as a pamphlet by A Manchester Manufacturer under the title "Russia" (Edinburgh: William Tait, 1836), 4. Reprinted in Richard Cobden, *The Political Writings* (London, 1867), 1:173–74.
17. Maxime Rodinson's *Islam et capitalisme* (Paris: Editions du Seuil, 1966) is the classic, corrective exploration of this Eurocentric argument. Rodinson based his characterization of this argument on academic and popular writings from the postwar period; he did not trace the European discourse back to the imperial ideology of free trade, as I have done above. He knew that Muslim reformers, in particular ʿAbduh and Riḍā, wanted to show that their religious tradition did not oppose modern economic methods, but he did not explain what they were responding to materially or ideologically. Indeed, there is an anachronistic disjunction in his presentation of the problem.
18. The Earl of Cromer, *Modern Egypt* (London: Macmillan, 1908), 2:301–4, 440–42; and *The Spectator*, November 23, 1907, pp. 6–7. On "internationalism" as an obstacle to British reforms, also see pp. 461–62, 528, 547, 557. On Cromer's transition from free-trade internationalist to free-trade imperialist, see the superb biography by Roger Owen, *Lord Cromer: Victorian Imperialist, Edwardian Proconsul* (Oxford: Oxford University Press, 2004), especially viii, 142, 147, 216–17, 233, 313, 401. For the broader British context, see Peter Cain, "Free Trade, Social Reform and Imperialism: J. A. Hobson and the Dilemmas of Liberalism, 1890–1914," in *Free Trade and Its Reception 1815–1960*, ed. Andrew Marrison, 207–223 (London: Routledge, 1998).
19. Cromer, *Modern Egypt*, 2:119.
20. On the "inclusionary pretensions of liberal theory and the exclusionary effects of liberal practices," see Uday S. Mehta, "Liberal Strategies of Exclusion," *Politics & Society* 18 (1990), 427–54.
21. Voltaire, *Letters Concerning the English Nation, A New Edition* (London: L. Davis and C. Reymers, 1760), 36; see also Voltaire, *Lettres philosophiques* (Rouen: Jore, 1734), 27.
22. Cromer, *Modern Egypt*, 2:162.
23. Cromer, *Modern Egypt*, 2:134–40.
24. Julius Wellhausen, "Mohammedanism," in *The Encyclopaedia Britannica: A Dictionary of Arts, Sciences, and General Literature*, 9th ed. (Philadelphia: Maxwell Sommerville, 1891), 16:569, 570n8.
25. Stanley Lane-Poole, *The Speeches & Table-Talk of the Prophet Mohammad* (London: Macmillan, 1882), xix, xxvi. Cromer quotes Lane-Poole's *Studies in a Mosque* (London: W. H. Allen, 1883), which happens to include the same material under a different title, on pp. 27 and 36.
26. Anon., "Istoria de Mahomet," ed. Kenneth B. Wolf, "The Earliest Lives of Muḥammad," in *Conversion and Continuity: Indigenous Christian Communities in Islamic Lands, Eighth to Eighteenth Centuries*, ed. Michael Gervers and Ramzi Jibran Bikhazi (Toronto: Pontifical Institute of Mediaeval Studies, 1990), 96; and Petrus Alfonsi, "Dialogi contra Iudaeos," ed. Klaus-Peter Mieth, *Der Dialog des Petrus Alfonsi: Seine Überlieferung im Druck und in den Handschriften: Textedition* (Berlin: Kopierservice, 1982), 65, 67. For an analysis of the latter, see Leor Halevi, "*Lex Mahomethi*: Carnal and Spiritual Representations of Islamic Law and Ritual in a Twelfth-Century Dialogue by a Jewish Convert to Christianity," in *The Islamic Scholarly Tradition: Studies in History, Law, and Thought in Honor of Professor Michael Allan Cook*, ed. Asad Q. Ahmed, Behnam Sadeghi and Michael Bonner, 315–42 (Leiden: Brill, 2011), 326.
27. It is intriguing that capitalism hardly figures in Edward Said's *Orientalism*. It does not appear in the index as a technical term, and references to it throughout the book are casual. The most significant discussion appears in the chapter titled "Orientalism Now," where Said relies

on Rodinson's *Islam and Capitalism* to criticize the cliché, incorrectly imputed to Max Weber, about the "Oriental's fundamental incapacity for trade, commerce, and economic rationality." Cobden is nowhere mentioned, and there is no discussion of the imperialism of free trade. Although he paid attention to Cromer's view that "the commercial spirit" of Egyptians, Shilluks, Indians, or Zulus, needed to be "under some control," Said did not see free-trade ideology as an essential component of "Orientalist Structures." See Edward W. Said, *Orientalism* (New York: Vintage Books, 1994), 37 and 259.

28. A. Sprenger, *The Life of Mohammad, from Original Sources*, part 1 (Allahabad: Presbyterian Mission Press, 1851), 4, 44, 45, and 182. Qurʾan 2:198 (cited by Sprenger as 2:194) simply reveals that it is not sinful "to seek bounty (*faḍl*) from your Lord." It is commonly interpreted as authorizing trade during the *ḥajj*. When Sprenger discusses the failure of Arab merchants to establish enterprises to accumulate capital from one generation to another, he makes an implicit comparison to joint-stock companies.
29. Bernard Lewis, *The Muslim Discovery of Europe* (New York: Norton, 1982), 193–94, 224–25. Also see Bernard Lewis, *The Emergence of Modern Turkey*, 2nd ed. (London: Oxford University Press, 1968), 41; and Bernard Lewis, *What Went Wrong? Western Impact and Middle Eastern Response* (London: Phoenix, 2002), 141.
30. Jalal Al-i Ahmad, *Occidentosis: A Plague from the West*, trans. Robert Campbell, intro. Hamid Algar (Berkeley, Calif.: Mizan Press, 1984), 30, 33, 55, 70, 79–81; and Jalāl Āl-e Aḥmad, *Plagued by the West (Gharbzadegi)*, trans. Paul Sprachman (Delmar, N.Y.: Caravan Books, 1982), 7, 38–39, 70–71.
31. For an effective challenge to the thesis, see Cemal Kafadar, "The Question of Ottoman Decline," *Harvard Middle Eastern and Islamic Review* 4 (1997–1998): 1–2, 30–75.
32. Nicholas Thomas, *Entangled Objects: Exchange, Material Culture, and Colonialism in the Pacific* (Cambridge, Mass.: Harvard University Press, 1991), chap. 3; and Marshall Sahlins, "'Sentimental Pessimism' and Ethnographic Experience; or, Why Culture Is Not a Disappearing 'Object,'" in *Biographies of Scientific Objects*, ed. Lorraine Daston (Chicago: University of Chicago Press, 2000), 158–202. Also see David Howes, ed., *Cross-Cultural Consumption: Global Markets, Local Realities* (London: Routledge, 1996).
33. Richard White, *The Middle Ground: Indians, Empires, and Republics in the Great Lakes Region, 1650–1815* (Cambridge: Cambridge University Press, 2011), 50; and Clifford Geertz, "Suq: The Bazaar Economy in Sefrou," in *Meaning and Order in Moroccan Society: Three Essays in Cultural Analysis*, with a photographic essay by Paul Hyman, ed. Clifford Geertz, Hildred Geertz, and Lawrence Rosen (Cambridge: Cambridge University Press, 1979), 141. For a historiographical analysis of these and other approaches to economic interactions across religious boundaries, see Leor Halevi, "Religion and Cross-Cultural Trade: A Framework for Interdisciplinary Inquiry," chap. 1 in *Religion and Trade: Cross-Cultural Exchanges in World History, 1000–1900*, ed. Francesca Trivellato, Leor Halevi, and Cátia Antunes (Oxford: Oxford University Press).
34. In a non-European context, see, in particular, Flood's *Objects of Translation*. For two outstanding examples of the appropriation of "Western" media, see Christopher Pinney, *"Photos of the Gods": The Printed Image and Political Struggle in India* (London: Reaktion Books, 2004); and Charles Hirschkind, *The Ethical Soundscape: Cassette Sermons and Islamic Counterpublics* (New York: Columbia University Press, 2006).
35. Ulf Hannerz, "The Global Ecumene as a Landscape of Modernity," in *Transnational Connections: Culture, People, Places* (London: Routledge, 1996), 44–55; and Homi K. Bhabha, *The Location of Culture* (New York: Routledge, 1994), 56.

36. Marshall Sahlins, "Cosmologies of Capitalism: The Trans-Pacific Sector of 'The World System,'" in *Culture/Power/History: A Reader in Contemporary Social Theory*, ed. Nicholas B. Dirks, Geoff Eley, Sherry B. Ortner, 412–56 (Princeton, N.J.: Princeton University Press, 1994), 413.
37. Rudolf Mrázek, *Engineers of Happy Land: Technology and Nationalism in a Colony* (Princeton, N.J.: Princeton University Press, 2002).
38. James L. Gelvin and Nile Green, eds., *Global Muslims in the Age of Stream and Print* (Berkeley: University of California Press, 2014); see also Liat Kozma, Cyrus Schayegh, and Avner Wishnitzer, eds., *A Global Middle East: Mobility, Materiality and Culture in the Modern Age, 1880–1940* (London: I. B. Tauris, 2015).
39. On Barak, *On Time: Technology and Temporality in Modern Egypt* (Berkeley: University of California Press, 2013).
40. Daniel R. Headrick, *The Tools of Empire: Technology and European Imperialism in the Nineteenth Century* (New York: Oxford University Press, 1981); and Michael Adas, *Machines as the Measure of Men: Science, Technology, and Ideologies of Western Dominance* (Ithaca, N.Y.: Cornell University Press, 1989). For a critique of the diffusionist model that calls for nuanced histories of the diverse cultural uses, effects, and meanings of technologies, see David Arnold, "Europe, Technology, and Colonialism in the 20th Century," *History and Technology* 21, no. 1 (2005): 85–106.
41. Sustained efforts to elaborate a Salafist methodology arose after Riḍā's death. References to "the method of the Salaf" began to appear in book titles in the 1970s. One recent contribution highlighted Riḍā's role in the "return" to such a method: al-Sayyid Yūsuf, *Rashīd Riḍā wa-l-ʿawda ilā manhaj al-salaf* (Cairo: Mīrīt li-l-Nashr wa-l-Maʿlūmāt, 2000).
42. Scholarship on the thought of eighteenth-century Muslims reformers has highlighted their freedom from European dominance and often characterized the work of their nineteenth- and twentieth-century counterparts as derivative or subordinate. Notable contributions to this field include Peter Gran, *Islamic Roots of Capitalism: Egypt, 1760–1840* (Austin: University of Texas Press, 1979); Nehemia Levtzion and John O. Voll, eds., *Eighteenth-Century Renewal and Reform in Islam* (Syracuse, N.Y.: Syracuse University Press, 1987); Reinhard Schulze, "Das islamische achtzehnte Jahrhundert: Versuch einer historiographischen Kritik," *Die Welt des Islams*, New Series, 30, 1/4 (1990): 140–59; Reinhard Schulze, "Was ist die islamische Aufklärung?," *Die Welt des Islams* 36, no. 3 (1996): 276–325; Bernard Haykel, *Revival and Reform in Early Modern Islam: The Legacy of Muhammad Al-Shawkānī* (Cambridge: Cambridge University Press, 2003); and Ahmad S. Dallal, *Islam Without Europe: Traditions of Reform in Eighteenth-Century Islamic Thought* (Chapel Hill: University of North Carolina Press, 2018).
43. ʿAbduh's philosophy has been described as "Salafist" due to later developments in the history of modern Islam.
44. For a nuanced analysis of change and continuity in his political conceptions, see Mahmoud Haddad, "Arab Religious Nationalism in the Colonial Era: Rereading Rashīd Riḍā's Ideas on the Caliphate," *Journal of the American Oriental Society* 117, no. 2 (1997): 253–77.
45. Rashīd Riḍā, ed., *Majmūʿat al-rasāʾil wa-l-masāʾil al-najdiyya* (Cairo: al-Manār, 1926); see, in particular, the editor's afterword to vol. 3, titled "Kalima."
46. Nabil Mouline, *Les clercs de l'Islam: Autorité religieuse et pouvoir politique en Arabie Saoudite (XVIIIe-XXIe siècles)* (Paris: Presses Universitaires de France, 2009), 19, 144–46; and David Commins, *The Wahhabi Mission and Saudi Arabia* (New York: I. B. Tauris, 2006), 137–40.
47. Martin S. Kramer, *Islam Assembled: The Advent of the Muslim Congresses* (New York: Columbia University Press, 1986), chap. 10.

48. ʿAbduh has typically been described as a "Muslim modernist," but that may not be the best description for him since he died before the term was coined and he was not principally devoted to defending "modernism." For this contention, see Marwa Elshakry, *Reading Darwin in Arabic, 1860–1950*. (Chicago: University of Chicago Press, 2013), 164–65.
49. Ana Belén Soage, "Rashīd Ridā's Legacy," *Muslim World* 98, no. 1 (2008): 3.
50. For multiple studies of Riḍā's transnational and transimperial impact, see Stéphane A. Dudoignon, Komatsu Hisao, and Kosugi Yasushi, eds., *Intellectuals in the Modern Islamic World: Transmission, Transformation, Communication* (London: Routledge 2009). The contributors offer differing assessments of the spread of "reformist" or "Manarist" ideas. One author represents Islamic reform as a "hot tide" that washed over "the whole of the Islamic world" (133). Another author argues that the elitist intellectuals who formed the "Manarist" camp failed to sway "popular religious attitudes" (50). An exaggerated view of the significance of reformist currents has stimulated a new generation of historians of modern Islam to emphasize different, local perspectives. In *Bombay Islam*, for instance, Nile Green argued that "in industrializing oceanic India, Reformist Islam was only a marginal player" in the late nineteenth and early twentieth centuries (19). Green accordingly deals with reformists as competing with others in a wider religious market. Similarly, in her history of social and religious changes in Zanzibar and along the East African coast, *Sufis and Scholars of the Sea*, Anne Bang has shown that rich, mobile, and networked merchant-scholars in East Africa changed their "tone" but not necessarily their "doctrine" as a consequence of their encounter with reformist ideas. Both Green and Bang show how, in different places in different ways, local elites appropriated reformism to their own ends. See Nile Green, *Bombay Islam: The Religious Economy of the West Indian Ocean, 1840–1915* (Cambridge: Cambridge University Press, 2011), 19; and Anne K. Bang, *Sufis and Scholars of the Sea: Family Networks in East Africa, 1860–1925* (London: RoutledgeCurzon, 2003), 135–42, 184–85.
51. Malcolm Kerr, "Rashīd Riḍā and Islamic Legal Reform: An Ideological Analysis," part 1, "Methodology," *Muslim World* 50, no. 2 (1960): 99–108, 100–101. Also see Nadav Safran, *Egypt in Search of Political Community: An Analysis of the Intellectual and Political Evolution of Egypt, 1804–1952* (Cambridge, Mass.: Harvard University Press, 1961), 83. For critiques of these perspectives, see Charles D. Smith, "The 'Crisis of Orientation': The Shift of Egyptian Intellectuals to Islamic Subjects in the 1930s," *International Journal of Middle East Studies* 4, no. 4 (1973): 382–410; and Ahmad Dallal, "Appropriating the Past: Twentieth-Century Reconstruction of Pre-Modern Islamic Thought," *Islamic Law and Society* 7, no. 3 (2000): 325–58, especially nn22, 28, and 56.
52. Wael B. Hallaq, *A History of Islamic Legal Theories: An Introduction to Sunnī* Uṣūl Al-Fiqh (Cambridge: Cambridge University Press, 1997), 214, 231, 254.
53. Reinhard Schulze, *A Modern History of the Islamic World* (New York: New York University Press, 2000), 4, 17–18.
54. Thus, for example, the article "Iṣlāḥ" by A. Merad in *The Encylcopaedia of Islam*, 2nd ed., emphasizes the "historical continuity" of the reformist ideal and it represents al-Afghānī and ʿAbduh as modern reformers who adhered to the Salafiyya. For another example of this standard genealogical approach, which overemphasizes continuities in what is without justification called the "Salafiyyah school," see Zaki Badawi, *The Reformers of Egypt* (London: Croom Helm, 1978).
55. Compare to scholarship on Riḍā's views of Christianity or "the West," which has rather highlighted how he responded to these externalities. This body of scholarship has emphasized how Riḍā defended Islam against Christian polemicists or how he approached Western ideas

with a mixture of admiration or respect. See, for example, Umar Ryad, *Islamic Reformism and Christianity: A Critical Reading of the Works of Muḥammad Rashīd Riḍā and His Associates (1898–1935)* (Leiden: Brill, 2009); Emad Eldin Shahin, *Through Muslim Eyes: M. Rashīd Riḍā and the West* (Herndon, Va.: International Institute of Islamic Thought, 1993); and Simon A. Wood. *Christian Criticisms, Islamic Proofs: Rashīd Riḍā's Modernist Defense of Islam* (Oxford: Oneworld, 2008).

56. Nancy Y. Reynolds, *A City Consumed: Urban Commerce, the Cairo Fire, and the Politics of Decolonization in Egypt* (Stanford, Calif.: Stanford University Press, 2012); Eric Davis, *Challenging Colonialism: Bank Miṣr and Egyptian Industrialization, 1920–1941* (Princeton, N.J.: Princeton Univ. Press, 1983); and Relli Shechter, *Smoking, Culture and Economy in the Middle East: The Egyptian Tobacco Market 1850–2000* (London: I. B. Tauris, 2006).

57. Ziad Fahmy, *Ordinary Egyptians: Creating the Modern Nation Through Popular Culture, 1870–1919* (Stanford, Calif.: Stanford University Press, 2011); Ali Jihad Racy, "Record Industry and Egyptian Traditional Music: 1904–1932," *Ethnomusicology* 20, no. 1 (1976): 23–48; Uri M. Kupferschmidt, "The Social History of the Sewing Machine in the Middle East," *Die Welt Des Islams*, 44, no. 2 (2004): 195–213; and Stephen Sheehi, *The Arab Imago A Social History of Portrait Photography, 1860–1910* (Princeton, N.J.: Princeton University Press, 2016).

58. Compare to the synthetic effort to identify Salafism's perennial appeal made by Bernard Haykel in "On the Nature of Salafi Thought and Action," chap. 1 in *Global Salafism: Islam's New Religious Movement*, ed. Roel Meijer (New York: Columbia University Press, 2009). Compare, as well, to the defense of the use of the term "Salafism" to describe "the most influential pattern" of Islamic reform in the late nineteenth century by Frank Griffel in "What do We Mean By 'Salafi?' Connecting Muḥammad ʿAbduh with Egypt's Nūr Party in Islam's Contemporary Intellectual History," *Die Welt des Islams* 55 (2015): 186–220.

59. Henri Lauzière, "The Construction of *Salafiyya*: Reconsidering Salafism from the Perspective of Conceptual History," *International Journal of Middle Eastern Studies* 42, no. 3 (2010): 369–89; and Henri Lauzière, *The Making of Salafism: Islamic Reform in the Twentieth Century* (New York: Columbia University Press, 2016).

60. Scholarship on fatwas has long disregarded or dismissed the agency of fatwa seekers. Relatively little has changed in this regard since one of the earliest European discussions of the topic. In 1920, Ignaz Goldziher argued without a shred of evidence that Riḍā responded to "anonymous" inquiries from all over the Islamic world that were probably "fictitious." Three generations later, Jakob Skovgaard-Petersen speculated that Goldziher was likely right, although Goldziher had made no effort to prove his charge, an accusation of dishonesty. In the 1990s, when systematic research on fatwas began, Wael Hallaq paid some attention to the ancillary role of fatwa seekers in the development of Islamic law, for they were the actors who asked muftis for practical advice in the face of new circumstances. In general, however, Hallaq was interested in demonstrating that Islamic legal doctrines "evolved" with the times; he wanted to underscore muftis' flexibility and creativity. Among other things, his article emphasized the care that premodern muftis took to reformulate and redraft fatwa seekers' questions, making them "highly legalistic" and eliminating details "deemed irrelevant as legal facts." Around this time, too, Muhammad Khalid Masud, Brinkley Messick, and David Powers recognized that the fatwa seeker's "question not only initiates the mufti's interpretive activity but also constrains it." Yet systematic investigations of fatwa seekers' contributions to Islamic law did not immediately ensue. Finally, in 2009, Masʿūd published an article that highlighted the significance of fatwa seekers' questions for the history of law and society. By and large, he focused on theoretical manuals that tried to establish normative

rules—routinely ignored, in my experience—for exchanges between fatwa seekers and muftis. Yet he also analyzed several actual exchanges and on this basis suggested that fatwa seekers played on muftis' sympathies and influenced their opinions. Ignaz Goldziher, *Die Richtungen der islamischen Koranauslegung: An der Universität Upsala gehaltene Olaus-Petri-Vorlesungen* (Leiden: Brill, 1920), 332; Jakob Skovgaard-Petersen, *Defining Islam for the Egyptian State: Muftis and Fatwas of the Dār Al-Iftā* (Leiden: Brill, 1997), 20–21; Wael B. Hallaq, "From *Fatwās* to *Furūʿ*: Growth and Change in Islamic Substantive Law." *Islamic Law and Society* 1 (1994): 29–65; Muhammad Khalid Masud, Brinkley Messick, David S. Powers, eds., *Islamic Legal Interpretation: Muftis and Their Fatwas* (Cambridge, Mass: Harvard University Press, 1996), chap. 1, (quote at 21–22); Muhammad Khalid Masud, "The Significance of *Istiftāʾ* in the *Fatwā* Discourse," *Islamic Studies* 48 (2009): 341–66.

Why have experts on fatwas taken little or no notice of fatwa seekers? Replicating the perspective of Muslim jurists who exaggerated their own authority and independence as the shariʿa's privileged interpreters, Western specialists on Islamic law have placed famous muftis on high pedestals, towering over the crowds of nameless, passive followers. Thus, the first in a series of articles on fatwa in *The Oxford Encyclopedia of the Modern Islamic World*, ed. John L. Esposito (New York: Oxford University Press, 1995), 2:8–17, explains that fatwas' "ideological authority" comes from the impression that the mufti is "the deputy and successor to the Prophet, the lawgiver." Other articles in the same encyclopedia refer to muftis as "powerful figures" who issued at times politically "effective" fatwas. Predominant in Islamic legal studies, this top-down approach to fatwas ultimately derives from muftis' own self-aggrandizing claims to knowledge and power.

Specialists in the field often refer to the impact of fatwas, but it is actually very difficult to prove historically any given fatwa's efficacy. In cases where judges, rulers, individual petitioners, or communities appear to follow a mufti's directive, there is still a need to examine those actors' diverse interests. Fatwas urging consumer boycotts, which historians of Islamic law have cited as an example of muftis' political effectiveness, emerged from below—as a result of pressure by Muslim activists on muftis. For a historical analysis of this dynamic, see Leor Halevi, "The Consumer Jihad: Boycott Fatwas and Nonviolent Resistance on the World Wide Web," *International Journal of Middle East Studies* 44 (2012): 45–70.

A hierarchical approach to Islamic law has had profound consequences upon historical understandings of the origin and spread of Salafist ideas from Cairo to the rest of the Islamic world. Historians have argued, for instance, that Riḍā's fatwas served as a mechanism for the dissemination of a disruptive "Middle Eastern" ideology to Southeast Asia, where "modernists" who found this ideology inspiring clashed with "traditionalists." Riḍā's fatwas arguably deepened the cleavage between the "New Generation" and the "Old Generation" of Muslim scholars, but they did not create the divide. Fatwa requests penned by Southeast Asian *mustaftis* reveal that the social and religious divisions preceded chronologically Riḍā's fatwas. In addition, they reveal that fatwa seekers formulated ideas about what they wanted to reform locally before they heard from any foreign reformer. Cf. Jajat Burhanudin, "Aspiring for Islamic Reform: Southeast Asian Requests for *Fatwās* in *Al-Manār*," *Islamic Law and Society* 12, no. 1 (2005): 9–26; Nico J. G. Kaptein, *Islam, Colonialism and the Modern Age in the Netherlands East Indies: A Biography of Sayyid Uthman (1822–1914)* (Leiden: Brill, 2014), 177–78; and Nico J. G. Kaptein, "Southeast Asian Debates and Middle Eastern Inspiration: European Dress in Minangkabau at the Beginning of the 20th Century," in Eric Tagliacozzo, ed., *Southeast Asia and the*

Middle East: Islam, Movement, and the Longue Durée (Stanford, California: Stanford University Press, 2009), 176–95.

61. See a translation of Khomeini's edict, together with a selection of early defenses by senior Iranian clerics, in Lisa Appignanesi and Sara Maitland, *The Rushdie File* (Syracuse, N.Y.: Syracuse University Press, 1990), 68–76. Mehdi Mozaffari, *Fatwa: Violence and Discourtesy* (Aarhus, Den.: Aarhus University Press, 1998), 39ff, analyzes the edict, which does not conform to the standard fatwa format.
62. See, for example, Muṣṭafā al-Zarqā, *Fatāwā*, ed. Majd Aḥmad Makkī, with an introduction by Yūsuf al-Qaraḍāwī (Damascus: Dār al-Qalam, 1999), 563–64; ʿAlī Jumʿa, *al-Bayān li-mā yashghalu al-adhhān: 100 Fatwā li-radd ahamm shubah al-khārij wa-lamm shaml al-dākhil* (Cairo: al-Muqaṭṭam li-l-Nashr wa-l-Tawzīʿ, 2005), 99–104; and Muḥammad ʿAlī Jumʿa, *al-Kalim al-Ṭayyib: Fatāwā ʿAṣriyya* (Cairo: Dār al-Salām, 2007), 205–10.
63. Riḍā's influence is very clear on a treatise about paper money written by ʿAbd al-Razzāq ʿAfīfī's advisee, who became an influential Saudi mufti in his own right. I am referring to ʿAbdallāh b. Sulaymān b. Maniʿ, *al-Waraq al-naqdī: tārikhuhu, ḥaqīqatuhu, qīmatuhu, ḥukmuhu* (Riyadh: Maṭābiʿ al-Riyāḍ, 1971). For two relatively lenient fatwas (by Salafi standards) on the uses of musical instruments and the radio, see Muḥammad Nāṣir al-Dīn al-Albānī, *Fatāwā al-ʿallāma Nāṣir al-Dīn al-Albānī*, ed. ʿĀdil ibn Saʿ (Beirūt: Dār al-Kutub al-ʿIlmiyya, 2011), 385–88. Al-Albānī did not explicitly cite Riḍā in these fatwas. But his application of the notion of Islam as a religion of ease (*yusr*) to a modern technology must owe something to Riḍā.
64. On the connection between Riḍā and al-Fiqī, see Richard Gauvain, *Salafi Ritual Purity: In the Presence of God* (London: Routledge, 2013), 33, 38, 284–85.
65. Leor Halevi, "Christian Impurity versus Economic Necessity: A Fifteenth-Century Fatwa on European Paper," *Speculum* 83, no. 4 (2008): 917–45. Also see Michael Cook, "Magian Cheese: An Archaic Problem in Islamic Law," *Bulletin of the School of Oriental and African Studies* 47 (1984): 449–67; and Elias, *Aisha's Cushion.*
66. On pragmatic reasoning in Islamic law before modernity, see Abraham L. Udovitch, *Partnership and Profit in Medieval Islam* (Princeton, N.J.: Princeton University Press, 1970); and Ahmed Fekry Ibrahim, *Pragmatism in Islamic Law: A Social and Intellectual History* (Syracuse, N.Y.: Syracuse University Press, 2015).
67. Although popularized by early twentieth-century reformers, methods to overcome rigid affiliation to the doctrines of one school of law have a longer history. On this topic, see Birgit Krawietz, "Cut and Paste in Legal Rules: Designing Islamic Norms with *Talfiq*," *Die Welt Des Islams* 42, no. 1 (2002): 3–40.
68. Ami Ayalon, *The Press in the Arab Middle East: A History* (New York: Oxford University Press, 1995), 170, 197–98.
69. For a succinct description, see Roger Owen and Şevket Pamuk, *A History of Middle East Economies in the Twentieth Century* (Cambridge, Mass.: Harvard University Press, 1998), 33; and E. R. J. Owen, "Lord Cromer and the Development of Egyptian Industry, 1883–1907," *Middle Eastern Studies* 2, no. 4 (1966): 282–301.
70. In certain contexts, Muslim theorists of law nevertheless represented fatwas as binding on fatwa seekers. See, for example, Masud, "The Significance of Istiftāʾ," 357.
71. Against the secular view that fatwa seekers would either search for easy, advantageous solutions to their difficulties or disregard nonbinding religious advice, Hussein Ali Agrama has analyzed several intriguing examples of the will to submit to the mufti's ethical guidance.

See his fascinating article, "Ethics, Tradition, Authority: Toward an Anthropology of the Fatwa," *American Ethnologist* 37 (2010): 4–5.

72. See my reservations above (note 60) about exaggerated claims concerning fatwas' efficacy.
73. Richard Swedberg, *Max Weber and the Idea of Economic Sociology* (Princeton, N.J.: Princeton University Press, 1998), chap. 5.
74. Cf. Douglas C. North, "Institutions," *Journal of Economic Perspectives* 5, no. 1 (1991): 97–112; and Timur Kuran, *The Long Divergence: How Islamic Law Held Back the Middle East* (Princeton, N.J.: Princeton University Press, 2011).
75. God turned Muḥammad into a prophet because he wanted him to work as a gatherer of souls, not as a collector of taxes. This, at least, is what the ʿAbbasid jurist Abū Yūsuf told Hārūn al-Rashīd when he clarified for him the precise rules for collecting taxes from non-Muslim subjects. Among other things he explained to the caliph how to raise a lawful revenue from the pigs and wines of others. See Abū Yūsuf, *Kitāb al-Kharāj* (Cairo: al-Maṭbaʿa al-Salafiyya wa-Maktabatuhā, 1927), 157.
76. This comes from a *ḥadīth* narrated by Jābir ibn ʿAbdallāh, who dates the prohibition to the conquest of Mecca. The second part of the narrative, dealing with the uses of forbidden animal fat, forms part of a polemic against the permissive attitude of the Jews. It was transmitted by several collections of *ḥadīth*. See, for one, *Sunan al-Nasāʾī*, in *Jamʿ jawāmiʿ al-aḥādīth wa-l-asānīd wa-maknaz al-ṣiḥāḥ wa-l-sunan wa-l-masānīd* (Vaduz, Liechtenstein: Thesaurus Islamicus Foundation, 2000), 2:758, no. 4686.
77. *Al-Manār* 23 (1922): 676, 678, and passim.
78. *Al-Manār* 23 (1922): 672–73.

1 The Toilet Paper Fatwa: Hygienic Innovation and the Sacred Law in the Late Imperial Era

1. Muḥammad Rashīd Riḍā, *Fatāwā al-Imām*, eds. Ṣalāḥ al-Dīn al-Munajjid and Yūsuf Q. Khūrī (Dār al-Kitab al-Jadīd: Beirut, 1970–), 2:768–69, no. 287. Originally the fatwa appeared in *al-Manār* 12 (1909): 337–38. I use the word "danger" here advisedly. For a critique of its application to Muslim purity rites, see A. Kevin Reinhart, "Impurity / No Danger," *History of Religions* 30 (1990): 1–24. As the men in the fatwa seekers' company were officers (*ḍubbāṭ*), they were presumably part of the military or police forces.
2. *Sunan al-Nasāʾī*, in *Jamʿ jawāmiʿ al-aḥādīth wa-l-asānīd wa-maknaz al-ṣiḥāḥ wa-l-sunan wa-l-masānīd* (Vaduz, Liechtenstein: Thesaurus Islamicus Foundation, 2000), 1:7–8, nos. 40–44.
3. *Sunan Ibn Mājah*, in *Jamʿ jawāmiʿ al-aḥādīth*, 1:56, no. 382.
4. *Sunan al-Nasāʾī*, in *Jamʿ jawāmiʿ al-aḥādīth*, 1:8, no. 45. Compare to Marion Holmes Katz, *Body of Text: The Emergence of the Sunni Law of Ritual Purity* (Albany: State University of New York Press, 2002), 211. Katz excludes *istinjāʾ* regulations from her revealing analysis of purity rites because she considers these mere hygienic practices. Prohibitions on facing the *qibla* while defecating in the open evince a deliberate attempt to differentiate these practices from rites of worship. But they do not mean a lack of ritual since they distinguish correct from incorrect orientations of the body. The norms of toilet etiquette (from the use of the left hand to the preference for three stones) furthermore suggest a degree of ritualization.
5. The fatwa request does not specify that the ship flew the British flag. A significant number of Italian, German, French, and Dutch vessels also made stops at ports of the Sudan, which was

then an Anglo-Egyptian condominium. But most of the steamships that docked at the old port of Suakin on the Red Sea coast, in the newly built Port Sudan, and along the Nile's main tributaries, were British. In 1908, for example, 2,233 British, 584 German, 246 Dutch, and 242 French ships traversed the canal. See Arnold Wright, chief editor, and H. A. Cartwright, assistant editor, *Twentieth Century Impressions of Egypt: Its History, People, Commerce, Industries, and Resources* (London: Lloyd's Greater Britain, 1909), 154, for a handy table detailing these ships' passages, and pp. 508–9 for notes on ways for European tourists to travel to the Sudan. I thank Roger Owen for recommending this indispensable volume to me.

6. The name and location of the Sudanese town where the toilet paper debate took place is unclear. *Al-Manār* identifies it as Karmūs or Karamūs in the Sudan. But the second edition of the *Gazetteer of Sudan*, published by the United States Board on Geographic Names (Washington, D.C., 1989), does not identify any town by that name. Perhaps it was Korgus, Kerman, Kareima, Khartum, Kurmuk, Ku`Namusa, or Karmah an-Nuzul, and an Egyptian familiar with Karmūs, Alexandria, made a mistake in transcription. I thank Larry Yarak for posting my question about this location to the H-NET List for African History and Culture, and several subscribers to that list for replying.
7. What evidence of the impact and reception of Riḍā's fatwas does exist? In addition to impressionist comments and anecdotes by contemporaries, some of his fatwas were discussed in the press—both in Arabic and in translation. My point, however, is that the vast majority of his fatwas did not produce discernible effects.
8. The Wellcome Library has a copy of the Diamond Mills Paper Company's leaflet advertising "Bromo Paper, A Perfectly Pure Article for the Water Closet," printed in New York City around 1880.
9. A. H. Scott, "Machine for Tightening Rolls of Paper," US 806847, filed April 17, 1905, patented December 12, 1905; and Bradford B. Babbitt, "Coin-Operated Machine for Furnishing Toilet Paper," US 456788 A, filed December 4, 1890, patented July 28, 1891.
10. *U.S. Supreme Court, Morgan Envelope Co. v. Albany Paper Co.*, 152 U.S. 425 (1894). See Christina Bohannan and Herbert Hovenkamp, *Creation Without Restraint: Promoting Liberty and Rivalry in Innovation* (New York: Oxford University Press, 2012), 372n21; and Mineko Mohri, "Repair and Recycle as Direct Patent Infringement," in *Spares, Repairs and Intellectual Property Rights: IEEM International Intellectual Property Programmes*, ed. Christopher Heath and Anselm Kamperman Sanders (Alphen aan den Rijn: Kluwer Law International, 2009), 62, 64.
11. *Pharmaceutical Era* 11, no. 8 (April 15, 1894): 384.
12. *Saturday Post* 173, no. 2 (1901): 31; and Bloomingdale's *Round-About New York* (Bloomingdale Brothers: New York, 1902), 423.
13. Edward L. Munson, *The Theory and Practice of Military Hygiene* (New York: William Wood and Co., 1901), 384, 569.
14. Wright and Cartwright, *Impressions of Egypt*, 362 and 371–72.
15. Army & Navy Co-Operative Society, *Yesterday's Shopping: The Army and Navy Stores Catalogue, 1907: A Facsimile of the Army & Navy Co-operative Society's 1907 Issue of Rules of the Society and Price List of Articles Sold at the Stores* (Newton Abbot, Devon, England: David & Charles Reprints, 1969), 340; U.S. Department of Commerce, *Paper and Stationery Trade of the World*, Special Consular Reports, no. 73, compiled by Grosvenor Dawe (Washington, D.C.: Government Printing Office, 1915), 7, 27, 43, 46, 405–407; U.S. Department of Commerce, *Foreign Commerce and Navigation of the United States for the Year Ending June 30, 1918* (Washington, D.C.: Government Printing Office, 1919), table no. 5, pp. 725–26; and Yves Lamontagne, "Foreign Trade of Egypt, 1935," *Commercial Intelligence Journal* 55, no. 1692 (July 4, 1936), 29.

16. M. W. Daly, *Empire on the Nile: The Anglo-Egyptian Sudan, 1898–1934* (Cambridge: Cambridge University Press, 1986), 114, 116.
17. On sanitary breakthroughs in Britain, see Barbara Penner, *Bathroom* (London: Reaktion Books, 2013), 70–81. On British sanitary policy in the Sudan, see Heather Bell, *Frontiers of Medicine in the Anglo-Egyptian Sudan, 1899–1940* (Oxford: Oxford University Press, 1999), 27, 41, 95–97, and elsewhere; and Heather J. Sharkey, *Living with Colonialism: Nationalism and Culture in the Anglo-Egyptian Sudan* (Berkeley: University of California Press, 2003), 115–16.
18. J. Lane Notter and R. H. Firth, *The Theory and Practice of Hygiene* (Notter and Firth), 3rd ed., rev. (London: J. & A. Churchill, 1908), 7, 948, 955. The original edition came out in 1896.
19. Notter and Firth, *Theory and Practice*, 954–55.
20. H. C. Squires, *The Sudan Medical Service: An Experiment in Social Medicine* (London: Heinemann, 1958), 4. Incidentally, a "floating laboratory" was charged with eradicating epidemics in the country (38).
21. William Byam, *The Road to Harley Street* (London: Geoffrey Bles, 1963), 63–66, 112–17.
22. "Sanitation in the Tropics," *Sanitary Record and Journal of Sanitary and Municipal Engineering* 46 (September 22, 1910): 297–98.
23. See Timothy Mitchell, *Colonising Egypt* (Cambridge: Cambridge University Press, 1988), 65, 99, 118; and Ghislaine Alleaume, "Hygiène publique et travaux publics: Les ingénieurs et l'assainissement du Caire (1882–1907)," *Annales islamologiques* 20 (1984): 151–82.
24. At the Qaṣr al-ʿAynī School of Medicine, hygiene counted for 75 of 475 points of the medical part of the final exam. On this component of the medical education, see Cooper Perry, *Report upon the Hospital and Medical School of Cairo* (Cairo: National Printing Department, 1908), 21, 23; and the Ministry of Education's *School of Medicine Curriculum* (Cairo: National Printing Department, 1906), 10. On the medical school and its connection to British rule, see Amira el Azhary Sonbol, *The Creation of a Medical Profession in Egypt, 1800–1922* (Syracuse, N.Y.: Syracuse University Press, 1991), 105ff. On the British emphasis on sanitation and epidemic disease, see Serge Jagailloux, *La médicalisation de l'Égypte au XIXe siècle (1798–1918)* (Paris: Éd. Recherche sur les civilisations, 1986), 130–43; and Sylvia Chiffoleau, *Médecines et médecins en Égypte: Construction d'une identité professionnelle et projet medical* (Paris: L'Harmattan, 1997), 46–47. Also see Hibba Abugideiri, "The Scientisation of Culture: Colonial Medicine's Construction of Egyptian Womanhood, 1893–1929," *Gender & History* 16, no. 1 (2004): 83–98.
25. "Sanitation Work in Egypt," *Sanitary Record, A Weekly Journal of Public Health and the Progress of Sanitary Science at Home and Abroad* 15 (April 28, 1894): 668–69. This is a paraphrase rather than a quotation of Cromer's report. Later on, the journal changed its title, as will be noticed below.
26. "Rain Drainage in Cairo," *Sanitary Record and Journal of Sanitary and Municipal Engineering* 32 (August 20, 1903): 197–99. The article remarks on the difficulties of using baskets to remove debris from narrow, busy streets.
27. Wright and Cartwright, *Impressions of Egypt*, 362, 366, 371.
28. "The Cholera in Egypt," *Sanitary Record* 30 (October 16, 1902), 378. Cf. "Military Hygiene on Active Service," *Sanitary Record* 37 (January 25, 1906), 73. On the imperial surveillance of pilgrims, see Valeska Huber, *Channelling Mobilities: Migration and Globalisation in the Suez Canal Region and Beyond, 1869–1914* (Cambridge: Cambridge University Press, 2013), chap. 6.
29. Wright and Cartwright, *Impressions of Egypt*, 415–17. Also see Huber, *Channelling Mobilities*, chaps. 6 and 7.

30. J. B. Tavernier, *Recueil de plusieurs Relations et Traitez singuliers & curieux... Avec la relation de l'interieur du Serrail du Grand Seigneur* (Paris, 1679), 459–60. There is a slightly different formulation in the 1692 Paris edition, p. 508.
31. John G. Bourke, *Scatologic Rites of All Nations: A Dissertation upon the Employment of Excrementitious Remedial Agents in Religion, Therapeutics, Divination, Witchcraft, Love-Philters, etc., in all Parts of the Globe* (Washington, D.C., W. H. Lowdermilk, 1891), 2, 142–44.
32. On anal cleansing with stones, see, for example, Ibn Abī Shayba, *Muṣannaf fī al-aḥādīth wa al-āthār*, ed. Saʿīd al-Laḥḥām (Dār al-Fikr: Beirut, 1989), 1:180–81.
33. *Sunan al-Nasāʾī*, in *Jamʿ jawāmiʿ al-aḥādīth*, 1:7, no. 40; and *Ṣaḥīḥ al-Bukhārī*, in *Jamʿ jawāmiʿ al-aḥādīth*, 1:39, nos. 155–56.
34. Aḥmad Raẓā (Riḍā) Khān, *Fatāwā-i Riẓviyya: al-ʿaṭāyā al-nabawiyya fī al-fatāwā al-Riẓviyya* (Karachi: Dār al-ʿulūm Amjadiyya, 1994), 2:153; and Arun Shourie, *The World of Fatwas or the Sharia in Action* (New Delhi: ASA Publications, 1995), 93–94. Shourie presents this as a distinct Barelvi position, which he contrasts to the Ahl-i Ḥadīth stance.
35. Riḍā, *Fatāwā*, 2:768–69, no. 287; *al-Manār* 12 (1909): 337–38.
36. Mary Douglas, *Purity and Danger: An Analysis of Concepts of Pollution and Taboo* (London: Routledge, 2001), 35, 128, 141.
37. Firth and Notter, *Theory and Practice*, 7 and 954.
38. R. W. Coppinger, "Tropical Naval Hygiene," in *Hygiene & Diseases of Warm Climates*, ed. Andrew Davidson (Edinburgh: Young J. Pentland, 1893), chap. 3.
39. Thomas Edward Scrutton, ed., *The Merchant Shipping Act, 1894* 2nd ed. (London: Wm. Clowes and Sons, 1895), eleventh schedule, articles 14 and 15, p. 574.
40. Douglas, *Purity and Danger*, 36, 41, 70.
41. On colonial endeavors to "modernize" local spaces and native bodies through new hygienic practices, see Dipesh Chakrabarty, "Open Space / Public Space: Garbage, Modernity and India," *South Asia* 14, no. 1 (1991): 15–31; Warwick Anderson, "Excremental Colonialism: Public Health and the Poetics of Pollution," *Critical Inquiry* 21 (1995): 640–69; Ruth Rogaski, *Hygienic Modernity: Meanings of Health and Disease in Treaty-Port China* (Berkeley: University of California Press, 2004); and Alison Bashford, *Imperial Hygiene: A Critical History of Colonialism, Nationalism and Public Health* (New York: Palgrave Macmillan, 2004).
42. In a different context, see, Ze'ev Maghen, *After Hardship Cometh Ease: The Jews as Backdrop for Muslim Moderation* (Berlin: Walter de Gruyter, 2006).
43. Muḥammad Rashīd Riḍā, *Yusr al-Islām wa-uṣūl al-tashrīʿ al-ʿāmm*, 2nd ed. (Cairo: Maṭbaʿat Nahḍat Miṣr, 1956), 25–26, 76–78. The book's introduction was first published in *al-Manār* 29 (1928), 63ff.
44. Wael B. Hallaq, *A History of Islamic Legal Theories: An Introduction to Sunnī* Uṣūl Al-Fiqh (Cambridge: Cambridge University Press, 1997), 215, 218–19.
45. Thus Ahmad Dallal has argued that Muslim reformers tried to reconcile traditional Islamic and modern European institutions, and in the process expanded "the functional domain of religion into areas that had not previously been covered by it." See Ahmad Dallal, "Appropriating the Past: Twentieth-Century Reconstruction of Pre-Modern Islamic Thought," *Islamic Law and Society* 7, no. 3 (2000): 337. Along these lines, also see Daniel A. Stolz, "'By Virtue of Your Knowledge': Scientific Materialism and the *Fatwās* of Rashīd Riḍā," *Bulletin of the School of Oriental and African Studies, University of London* 75, no. 2 (2012): 223–47. In the conclusion, Stolz describes Riḍā's fatwas "on a particularly empirical, atheistic brand of materialism... [as]

nothing if not an expansive effort to make Islamic tradition speak authoritatively to modern challenge." He adds, however, that the obligation to respond to questions that lay beyond his field of expertise exposed the precariousness of the mufti's authority.

46. Compare to the view that Riḍā "secularized the sharīʿa," formulated by Aziz al-Azmeh, *Islams and Modernities*, 3rd ed. (London: Verso, 2009), 129. Along these lines, too, a recent analysis of keywords of Islamic reform has argued that Riḍā and other contributors to his journal used multiple terms to distinguish "religion" conceptually from a "secular" sociopolitical sphere. See Florian Zemmin, *Modernity in Islamic Tradition: The Concept of 'Society' in the Journal* al-Manar *(Cairo, 1898–1940)* (Berlin: De Gruyter, 2018), 164–76. However, it is not entirely clear, as Talal Asad observed, what Arabic terms corresponded to the words "secular" and "secularism" in Egypt at this time. See Talal Asad, *Formations of the Secular: Christianity, Islam, Modernity* (Stanford, Calif.: Stanford University Press, 2003), chap. 7. In his fatwas, Riḍā tried systematically to distinguish what mattered religiously from what did not. His fatwas were not simply "religious" but texts that presented an eclectic mix of facts and arguments to make such distinctions.

2 Fatwas for the Partners' Club: A Global Mufti's Enterprise

1. *Al-Manār* 1 (1898): 24–25. All citations to the 1898 volume come from the 1909 edition.
2. *Al-Manār* 1 (1898): 734–35.
3. Here and elsewhere in this chapter, annual subscription costs are taken from *al-Manār*'s front covers. The reference in this instance is to the second edition of the first volume, published in 1909.
4. My main auxiliary source for the data analyzed in this chapter is the index of *mustaftis'* names and locations in the six-volume edition of Riḍā's fatwas: Muḥammad Rashīd Riḍā, *Fatāwā al-Imām*, eds. Ṣalāḥ al-Dīn al-Munajjid and Yūsuf Q. Khūrī (Dār al-Kitab al-Jadīd: Beirut, 1970–), 6:2745–59. I regularly referred to the fatwas directly as well, since they often contain additional information about *mustaftis'* background or specific location. The fatwa request from Tinogasta, Argentina, is no. 269.
5. For the last two examples, see Mouez Khalfaoui, *L'islam indien: Pluralité ou pluralisme: Le cas d'al-Fatāwā al-Hindiyya* (Frankfurt am Main: P. Lang, 2008); and Nico Kaptein, ed., *The Muhimmât al-nafâ'is: A Bilingual Meccan Fatwa Collection for Indonesian Muslims from the End of the Nineteenth Century* (Jakarta: INIS, 1997). On the rising number of Indian Ocean pilgrims, see Michael Christopher Low, "Empire and the Hajj: Pilgrims, Plagues, and Pan-Islam under British Surveillance, 1865–1908," *International Journal of Middle East Studies* 40, no. 2 (2008): 269–90; and Eric Tagliacozzo, *The Longest Journey: Southeast Asians and the Pilgrimage to Mecca* (New York: Oxford University Press, 2013), 64.
6. See in particular Nico J. G. Kaptein, *Islam, Colonialism and the Modern Age in the Netherlands East Indies: A Biography of Sayyid Uthman (1822–1914)* (Leiden: Brill, 2014), 158–59.
7. On the Transvaal fatwa, long-distance communications, and newspaper reactions, see Jakob Skovgaard-Petersen, *Defining Islam for the Egyptian State: Muftis and Fatwas of the Dār Al-Iftā* (Leiden: Brill, 1997), 126. Although addressed to ʿAbduh, the *istiftā*ʾ from the Punjab was actually answered by Riḍā. I analyze this fatwa in chap. 6.
8. *Al-Manār* 6 (1903): 274ff. Incidentally, these three questions from the Transvaal are different from the three questions from the Transvaal that ʿAbduh received around the same time.

9. *Al-Manār* 7 (1904): 258, 537.
10. *Al-Manār* 5 (1902): 51–55; and *al-Manār* 6 (1903): 862. The latter appears also in Riḍā, *Fatāwā*, 1:67–68, no. 25. This example illustrates how the distinction between responsa (*ajwiba*) and fatwas was rather arbitrary and artificial. Unfortunately, the 1970 edition of fatwas excluded the former type.
11. Riḍā, *Fatāwa*, 1:34, 60, 65, 118, and 161. Also refer to Ahmad Zaki, *L'Univers à Paris, un lettré égyptien à l'Exposition universelle de 1900*, ed. Mercedes Volait (Paris: Norma Éditions, 2015).
12. Cf. Bettina Gräf and Jakob Skovgaard-Petersen, *Global Mufti: The Phenomenon of Yūsuf Al-Qaraḍāwī* (New York: Columbia University Press, 2009).
13. Muḥammad Bakhīt rose steadily in the hierarchy of the shariʿa courts until he received the ultimate promotion, in 1915, to the office of Grand Mufti. On this figure and on Riḍā's polemics against him, see Skovgaard-Petersen, *Defining Islam*, 134–40.
14. In the 1909 edition of the first volume, he identified himself as *munshīʾ al-Manār*, the "founder of *The Lighthouse*." In an unpublished dissertation, Dyala Hamzah has argued that Riḍā should be seen mainly as a journalist and that he began to issue journalistic fatwas hesitantly, timidly, over the course of a few years. She speculates that he did not want to assume the title of mufti out of deference to his mentor, ʿAbduh, the Grand Mufti. I am not convinced that this speculative claim is right, since Riḍā issued fatwas concurrently with ʿAbduh, and ʿAbduh himself asked Riḍā to respond to several fatwa requests. Hamzah is right, however, to underscore the significance of Riḍā's journalistic enterprise to his identity. It is not just that he called himself a "journalist," the term that Hamzah uses to translate *ṣāhib jarīda*. He represented himself as the owner and editor of *al-Manār*, the Arabic Enlightenment's Press. Cf. Dyala Hamzah, "L'intérêt général (*maslaha 'âmma*) ou le triomphe de l'opinion: Fondation délibératoire (et esquisses délibératives) dans les écrits du publiciste syro-égyptien Muhammad Rashîd Ridâ (1865–1935)" (PhD thesis, L'École des hautes études en sciences sociales and Freie Universität Berlin, 2008), 107, 142–44, 265, and 267. I am grateful to Gudrun Krämer for lending me her copy of this thesis.
15. Skovgaard-Petersen, *Defining Islam*, 56, gives credit to various Azhari journals founded in the late nineteenth century for the "major novelty" of introducing "fatwa columns." But he does not specify which journals or in what year. Subsequently, on p. 73, he gives *al-Manār* credit for this "major novelty." Regardless of whether *al-Manār* was the first or one of the first journals to do this, Skovgaard-Petersen's research on the reception of the Transvaal fatwa makes clear that by December of 1903 the Egyptian media had grasped the appeal of fatwas. Somewhat earlier, in 1901, the vernacular Egyptian press began to target ʿAbduh's fatwa on banking with interest. On this development, see Indira Falk Gesink, *Islamic Reform and Conservatism: Al-Azhar and the Evolution of Modern Sunni Islam*, rev. ed. (New York: I. B. Tauris, 2010), 176–77, 188. Perhaps, as a result of the controversies, Riḍā realized that "fatwas," as opposed to merely "responsa" could sell magazines.
16. For a foundational collection of studies on the *al-Manār* as a forum for global Islamic communications, see Stéphane A. Dudoignon, Komatsu Hisao, and Kosugi Yasushi, eds., *Intellectuals in the Modern Islamic World: Transmission, Transformation, Communication* (London: Routledge 2009).
17. I have not succeeded in locating fatwa requests to *al-Manār* from women. On the circle of veiled women who read *al-Manār* in Beirut, see Amira K. Bennison, "Muslim Internationalism Between Empire and Nation-State," chap. 7 in *Religious Internationals in the Modern World: Globalization and Faith Communities Since 1750*, ed. Abigail Green and Vincent Viaene (Basingstoke,

U.K.: Palgrave Macmillan, 2012), 179–80. On the exchanges with the Lutheran *mustafti* from Denmark, see Umar Ryad, *Islamic Reformism and Christianity: A Critical Reading of the Works of Muḥammad Rashīd Riḍā and His Associates (1898–1935)* (Leiden: Brill, 2009), 286–93.

18. This was fatwa request no. 329, dating from 1910 and posed by a student from the college of law in al-Āsitānah, an Ottoman name for Istanbul.
19. These fatwa requests (nos. 370–73, 570) are listed by the index under Linja. A gazetteer describes the town as composed of 12,000 inhabitants: 5,000 Arabs, 5,000 Persians, 1,500 Africans, 56, Khōjas, 26 Hindus, and 3 Europeans (a British, a Belgian, and a German). "The majority of the inhabitants are Sunnis or Wahhābis," it claims, with not even one-fourth professing Shiʿism. J. G. Lorimer, *Gazetteer of the Persian Gulf, Oman and Central Arabia*, vol. 2, *Geographical and Statistical* (Calcutta: Superintendent Government Printing, 1908), 1097. On disputed claims to sovereignty over Linja, see Pirouz Mojtahed-Zadeh, *Security and Territoriality in the Persian Gulf: A Maritime Political Geography* (Surrey, U.K.: Curzon Press, 1999), 169–74, 180–86.
20. Giora Eliraz, *Islam in Indonesia: Modernism, Radicalism and the Middle East Dimension* (Brighton: Sussex Academic, 2004), 53; Jutta Bluhm-Warn, "Al-Manār and Ahmad Soorkattie: Links in the Chain of Transmission of Muḥammad ʿAbduh's Ideas to the Malay-Speaking World," in *Islam: Essays on Scripture, Thought, and Society: A Festschrift in Honour of Anthony H. Johns*, ed. Peter G. Riddell and Tony Street, 295–308 (Leiden: Brill, 1997), 297, 303; and Azyumardi Azra, "The Transmission of *al-Manār*'s Reformism to the Malay-Indonesian World: The Case of *al-Imām* and *al-Munīr*," in *Intellectuals in the Modern Islamic World: Transmission, Transformation, Communication*, ed. Stéphane A. Dudoignon, Komatsu Hisao, and Kosugi Yasushi (London: Routledge, 2009), 144–45.
21. Umar Ryad, "A Printed Muslim 'Lighthouse' in Cairo *al-Manār*'s Early Years, Religious Aspiration and Reception (1898–1903)," *Arabica* 56 (2009): 45; Donald J. Cioeta, "Ottoman Censorship in Lebanon and Syria, 1876–1908," *International Journal of Middle East Studies* 10, no. 2 (1979): 176–77, 185; David D. Commins, "*Al-Manār* and Popular Religion in Syria, 1898–1920," in *Intellectuals in the Modern Islamic World: Transmission, Transformation, Communication*, ed. Stéphane A. Dudoignon, Komatsu Hisao, and Kosugi Yasushi (London: Routledge, 2009), 40–54 (London: Routledge, 2006), 40; and Eliezer Tauber, "Rashīd Riḍā as a Pan-Arabist Before World War I," *Muslim World* 79 (1989): 103.
22. The earliest fatwa requests from Beirut and Damascus are nos. 276 and 321, dating from 1909 and 1910. The index lists fatwa no. 9 under the entry for Beirut as well, but that is an error since that *istiftāʾ* originated in Qara Dağh (Montenegro). In "*Al-Manār* and Popular Religion in Syria," David Commins has argued that the network of scholars affiliated with *al-Manār* had an elitist educational approach to nationalism that did not resonate with the popular nationalist camp in Syria. "The Manarists' failure to reshape popular religious attitudes in Syria in the journal's first twenty years," he concludes, "cannot be blamed on censorship" (50). The evidence presented here suggests, however, that *al-Manār* did not serve as an effective forum for Syro-Egyptian communications before 1909.
23. For his counterfatwa on transliterating the Qurʾan into "English" letters, see *al-Manār* 6 (1903): 274–77; and Hamzah, "L'intérêt général," 272–74. This was Riḍā's unsolicited response to one of three juridical questions raised by Muslims from the Transvaal, which was sent to an Egyptian newspaper that referred in turn to Muḥammad Bakhīt. For his fatwa on the impossibility of translating the Qurʾan, see *al-Manār* 11 (1908): 268–74; and Mohamed Ali Mohamed Abou Sheishaa, "A Study of the Fatwa by Rashid Rida on the Translation of the Qurʾān," a paper that has circulated through multiple websites and that was allegedly published by the

Journal of the Society for Qur'anic Studies 1, no. 1 (October 2001). My diligent librarian was unable to locate this publication in its original form. For reference, I archived a copy at http://www.webcitation.org/6hEQIAtBW, on May 3, 2016.

24. On the revival of Arabic as "the language of Islam" in India, see *al-Manār* 32 (1931): 345. Also see Albert Hourani, *Arabic Thought in the Liberal Age, 1798–1939* (Cambridge: Cambridge University Press, 1983), 299–300; Muhammad Qasim Zaman, "The Role of Arabic and the Arab Middle East in the Definition of Muslim Identity in Twentieth Century India," *Muslim World* 87, no. 3–4 (1997): 282; Jacques Waardenburg, "Muslim Enlightenment and Revitalization: Movements of Modernization and Reform in Tsarist Russia (ca. 1850–1917) and the Dutch East Indies (ca. 1900–1942)," *Die Welt des Islams* 28 (1988): 579–81; Adeeb Khalid, *The Politics of Muslim Cultural Reform: Jadidism in Central Asia* (Berkeley: University of California Press, 1998), 160–62; and Fauzan Saleh, *Modern Trends in Islamic Theological Discourse in Twentieth Century Indonesia: A Critical Survey* (Leiden: Brill, 2001), 83–84.
25. Roger Owen and Şevket Pamuk, *A History of Middle East Economies* (Cambridge, Mass.: Harvard University Press, 1998), 30, 47; Beth Baron, *The Women's Awakening in Egypt: Culture, Society, and the Press* (Chelsea, Mich.: Yale University Press, 1994), 81–84; and Ziad Fahmy, *Ordinary Egyptians: Creating the Modern Nation Through Popular Culture* (Stanford, Calif.: Stanford University Press, 2011), 32–33, 90–91, 178.
26. On *Shūrā*, which ran from 1908 to 1918, see Stéphane A. Dudoignon, "Echoes to *al-Manār* Among the Muslims of the Russian Empire: A Preliminary Research Note on Riza al-Din b. Fakhr al-Din and the *Šūrā* (1908–1918)," in *Intellectuals in the Modern Islamic World: Transmission, Transformation, Communication*, ed. Stéphane A. Dudoignon, Komatsu Hisao, and Kosugi Yasushi (London: Routledge, 2009), 85–116. Published between 1912 and 1914, Abul Kalam Azad's *al-Hilāl* was the product of various influences. On this weekly and its relation to *al-Manār*, see Gail Minault, *The Khilafat Movement: Religious Symbolism and Political Mobilization in India* (New York: Columbia University Press, 1982), 38–42. On *al-Manār*'s influence on *Tarjuman*, another one of Azad's periodicals, see Ian Henderson Douglas, *Abul Kalam Azad: An Intellectual and Religious Biography*, ed. Gail Minault and Christian W. Troll (Delhi: Oxford University Press, 1988), 47, 216–18. On *al-Munīr*, published between 1911 and 1916, see Deliar Noer, *The Modernist Muslim Movement in Indonesia, 1900–1942* (Singapore: Oxford University Press, 1973), 39–40. *Tianfang Xueli Yuekan* appeared between 1928 and 1936. On this journal's connections to *al-Manār*, see Leor Halevi, "Is China a House of Islam? Chinese Questions, Arabic Answers, and the Translation of Salafism from Cairo to Canton, 1930–1932," *Die Welt des Islams* 59, no. 1 (2019): 33–69.
27. On Riḍā's travels by steamships and railways, see Bennison, "Muslim Internationalism," 180.
28. On these connections, see Zaid Abdulagatov, "Wahhabism and Jadidism in Islamic Consciousness in Daghestan: Parallels and Contradictions," *Central Asia and the Caucasus* 6, no. 42 (2006): 92–102; Minault, *Khilafat Movement*, 39–40; Douglas, *Abul Kalam Azad*, 108; Michael Francis Laffan, *Islamic Nationhood and Colonial Indonesia: The Umma Below the Winds* (London: Routledge, 2003), 143; Zaman, "Role of Arabic," 282; Naṣr Abu Zayd, *Reformation of Islamic Thought: A Critical Historical Analysis* (Amsterdam: Amsterdam University Press, 2006), 43; and Alfian, *Muhammadiyah: The Political Behavior of a Muslim Modernist Organization Under Dutch Colonialism* (Yogyakarta, Indonesia: Gadjah Mada University Press, 1989), 104–5, 148–52.
29. Laffan, *Islamic Nationhood*, 138; and Jajat Burhanudin, "Aspiring for Islamic Reform: Southeast Asian Requests for *Fatwās* in *Al-Manār*." *Islamic Law and Society* 12, no. 1 (2005), 15.
30. Ami Ayalon, *The Press in the Arab Middle East: A History* (New York: Oxford University Press, 1995), 192.

31. Two years later, in 1907, the National Odeon Store advertised the sale of an "excellent American-made phonograph" as well as five double-sided records, guaranteed for three years, for three hundred piastres. See Ali Jihad Racy, "Musical Change and Commercial Recording in Egypt, 1904–1932" (PhD thesis, University of Illinois, 1977), 82–83. By 1930 gramophone records would cost twenty-seven to thirty-five piastres each, depending on their size, the artist, and the company. Subscriptions to *al-Manār* had by then risen to one pound. So, instead of the journal, an Egyptian could buy three records. See Frédéric Lagrange, "Musiciens et poètes en Égypte au temps de la Nahda" (PhD thesis, Université de Paris VIII, à Saint-Denis, 1994), 774–75.
32. Alfred Cunningham, *To-Day in Cairo: Its Administration, People and Politics* (London: Hurst & Blackett, 1912), 19.
33. On the wages of construction workers during the building boom, see Roger Owen, "The Cairo Building Industry and the Building Boom of 1897 to 1907," in *Colloque international sur l'histoire du Caire*, 27 Mars–5 Avril, 1969 ([Cairo]: [Ministry of Culture of the Arab Republic of Egypt], 1972), 342. On newspapermen's salaries at the turn of the century, see Ayalon, *The Press*, 201. On the salaries of muezzins and imams in 1904 and on the salaries of teachers and clerics at al-Azhar around 1911, see the tables in A. Chris Eccel, *Egypt, Islam, and Social Change: Al-Azhar in Conflict and Accommodation* (Berlin: K. Schwarz, 1984), 249, 261. On the earnings and duties of Cairo district doctors, see Cunningham, *To-Day in Cairo*, 109. On the salaries of police officers, see Arnold Wright, chief editor, and H. A. Cartwright, assistant editor, *Twentieth Century Impressions of Egypt: Its History, People, Commerce, Industries, and Resources* (London: Lloyd's Greater Britain, 1909), 409.
34. Shaykh Muqbil al-Dhakīr from Bahrain received fatwa no. 25 as well as a reply to an earlier question, which he asked before the inauguration of the fatwa section. ʿUmar Bey al-Dāʿūq's fatwa request is analyzed in the last chapter of this book.
35. In the 1909 preface to the first volume, Riḍā estimated that he had secured only a "third of a thousand" subscribers by the third or fourth year of operations. Around this time, in 1901, he boasted about the low cost of production to highlight his managerial thrift. His annual income at this point might indeed have been around 115 pounds. Editors' monthly salaries varied considerably during the first decade of the century; they ranged from 6 to 50 pounds monthly, as specified by Ayalon, *The Press*, 198, 201. There were, of course, significant expenses to set off against gross sales: the investment in a printing press, purchasing imported paper and ink, postage dues, a typesetter's salary, freelance translators' fees, and so on. Late or delinquent payments were part and parcel of this business, too; Riḍā himself complained about them. See Ryad, "A Printed Muslim 'Lighthouse' in Cairo," 35–37, 47, 52. In this article, Ryad introduces new evidence on the early financing of the enterprise. He demonstrates that Riḍā reached an agreement with an investor and business partner before he migrated to Cairo. Running the press required a fair number of employees. A 1926 photograph that Ryad published in this article (55) shows Riḍā as the owner of the press surrounded by sixteen staff members. This company included one man who wore suspenders, a tie, and a tarbush; several men in white *djellabas*; and at least one boy.

   Roughly estimating one of Riḍā's main expenses, shipping the magazine to foreign destinations, is possible. Around the turn of the century, after a succession of reductions in postage rates, the charge for mailing newspapers abroad was fixed at two *millièmes* per fifty grams. If the eighty or so pages of the monthly weighed around three hundred grams, it normally cost, at this rate, one piastre and two *millièmes* in postage per issue. Over the course of a year, mailing dues alone therefore amounted to more than fourteen piastres per foreign subscription. On Egypt's paper imports, see U.S. Department of Commerce, *Paper and Stationery Trade of the World*, Special Consular Reports, no. 73, compiled by Grosvenor Dawe (Washington, D.C.: Government Printing Office, 1915), 405–7. The American consul in Alexandria, Arthur Garrels, compiled the report, titled "Egypt." On postage rates, see Wright, *Twentieth Century Impressions*, 191.

36. Zaki Badawi, *The Reformers of Egypt* (London: Croom Helm, 1978), 99; and Charles C. Adams, *Islam and Modernism in Egypt: A Study of the Modern Reform Movement Inaugurated by Muḥammad ʿAbduh* (New York: Russell and Russell, 1933), 180.
37. Ayalon, *The Press*, 198.
38. All of this is based on the preface to the second edition of the first volume of *al-Manār*, written in Ramaḍān of AH 1327, around September of 1909. The title is "Muqaddimat al-ṭabʿa al-thāniyya li-l-mujallad al-awwal," *al-Manār*, 2nd ed. (1909): 1:1–8. Both Kosugi Yasushi and Mahmoud Haddad specify that the journal reached nearly three thousand subscribers, but it is not clear to me where they found this figure. Riḍā estimated that the number of subscribers around 1901 was *thulth al-alf*, "a third of a thousand." Cf. Kosugi Yasushi, "*Al-Manār* Revisited: The 'Lighthouse' of the Islamic Revival," in *Intellectuals in the Modern Islamic World: Transmission, Transformation, Communication*, ed. Stéphane A. Dudoignon, Komatsu Hisao, and Kosugi Yasushi (London: Routledge, 2009), 10; and Mahmoud O. Haddad, "Muḥammad Rashīd Riḍā (D. 1935)," in *Islamic Legal Thought: A Compendium of Muslim Jurists*, Studies in Islamic Law and Society, ed. David Powers, Oussama Arabi, and Susan Spectorsky (Leiden: Brill, 2013), 466–67.
39. Riḍā changed the price of an annual subscription for Egyptians from fifty piastres in 1906 to sixty in 1908, seventy in 1910, and eighty in 1913. This last price remained fixed during World War I; and it changed little in the prosperous 1920s. Between 1913 and 1929, the cost of an annual subscription rose by only twenty piastres, reaching one Egyptian pound. Despite the impact of the Great Depression, which reduced the purchasing power of money, the nominal value of subscriptions remained the same until 1933, perhaps because it was difficult to retain customers during the slump.
40. Umar Ryad, "A Prelude to *Fiqh al-Aqalliyyât*: Rashîd Ridâ's *Fatwâs* to Muslims under non-Muslim Rule," in *In-Between Spaces: Christian and Muslim Minorities in Transition in Europe and the Middle East*, ed. Christiane Timmerman, Johan Leman, Hannelore Roos, and Barbara Segaert, 239–70 (Bruxelles: P.I.E. Peter Lang, 2009), 252, no. 11.
41. Far too definitely, the World Bank's researchers have argued that the "first globalization wave" ended in 1914. See Paul Collier and David Dollar, *Globalization, Growth, and Poverty: Building an Inclusive World Economy* (Washington, D.C.: World Bank, 2002), 26. For large-scale comparisons of world trade before and after 1913, see Angus Maddison, *The World Economy: A Millennial Perspective* (Paris: OECD Development Centre Studies, 2001), 94, 102, and tables 3-2a and F-4 on pp. 127 and 362.
42. On this mortgage, see Ayalon, *The Press*, 222.
43. Martin S. Kramer, *Islam Assembled: The Advent of the Muslim Congresses* (New York: Columbia University Press, 1986), 110; and Nabil Mouline, *Les clercs de l'Islam: Autorité religieuse et pouvoir politique en Arabie Saoudite (XVIIIe–XXIe siècles)* (Paris: Presses Universitaires de France, 2011), 143, 145–46. Cf. *al-Manār* 28 (1927): 465–73.

44. Hamzah, "L'intérêt général," annexes A.1 and A.3. Hamzah's lists are more suggestive than exhaustive, but still useful. They do not include Gandhi's book, nor many of the titles listed in Gandhi's book.
45. Mahātmā Ghāndī, *Kitāb al-Ṣiḥḥa*, trans. ʿAbd al-Razzāq al-Malīḥ al-Ābādī (Cairo: Maṭbaʿat al-Manār, 1927), back cover.
46. *Al-Manār* 7 (1904): 258 and 537; see also *al-Manār* 8 (1905): 254; and *al-Manār* 14 (1911): 250. The parenthetical explanation that work, *ʿamal*, refers to position or profession (*waẓīfa*) is in the original Arabic text. For a different translation of the passage and a note about the recurring notice, see Hamzah, "L'intérêt général," 204, 272. Hamzah's translation, which cites the 1911 notice, omitted the sentence on nonsubscribers.
47. Ayalon, *The Press*, 158, Fahmy, *Ordinary Egyptians*, 74–75, and elsewhere.
48. See Bennison, "Muslim Internationalism," 180–81. Philanthropy aside, Riḍā advertised in Gandhi's *Kitāb al-Ṣiḥḥa* the sale of a new volume of his *Tafsīr* for twenty-five piastres, when printed on higher-quality pages, plus twenty piastres in shipping and handling costs.
49. *Al-Manār* 11 (1908): 144; and Hamzah, "L'intérêt général," 204.
50. Counting fatwas and *mustaftis* is not an exact science. A few scholars have referred to Riḍā's publication of "2,592" fatwas, but this is an error based on the fact that the last fatwa, no. 1061, in the six-volume edition appears on page 2,592. Arriving at an exact count of the fatwas is impossible, however. Some *mustaftis* asked multiple questions (related or unrelated) in a single letter, and the indexers made subjective, inconsistent decisions in counting series of responses as comprising either single or multiple fatwas. Puzzling, too, is the technical question about what exactly should count as a fatwa. The first fatwa listed in the 1970 collection of Riḍā's fatwas dates from 1903, but Riḍā wrote legal responsa (*ajwiba*) in earlier years that resemble what he eventually labeled "fatwas" in form. Arguably, these responsa form part of the same literary genre.

My principal reservations concern the location of *mustaftis*. The index normally lists *mustaftis* under the place from which they purportedly wrote to *al-Manār*, regardless of their ethnic origin or city of residence. Thus, for instance, a Javanese scholar sojourning in Mecca, Aḥmad Jāwī, is categorized together with other *mustaftis* from the Ḥijāz. (His request for a fatwa, no. 376 dating from 1911, happens to be the earliest one from Mecca.) This is fine and appropriate. High mobility was one the characteristics of the early twentieth century, and *al-Manār*'s correspondents were an especially mobile group. When Riḍā received letters in Arabic from Brazil or Singapore, he did not hear from indigenous Brazilians or Singaporeans; he heard from first- or second-generation Arab migrants to these places. The indexers were not consistent, however, in their practice. They did not list Aḥmad Zakī's "Parisian Questions" under France; they listed them alongside other requests from Cairo. It is possible, furthermore, that a number of *mustaftis* that Riḍā linked to destinations abroad asked for fatwas while visiting or residing in Cairo. Riḍā did not invent his *mustaftis*; many of them are known historical actors. But he might have emphasized foreign addresses—whenever possible—in order to enhance his international aura.

At least twenty-three *mustaftis* are named without being identified with any place, and this introduces a measure of indeterminacy into the statistical analysis. Not only is the data set imperfect, it is impossible as well to estimate the margin of error for calculations made with it. Nevertheless, the historical value of this collection of data should be recognized. Given that it contains a significant number of fatwas, as well as information about *mustaftis*, it offers evidence for trends and patterns.

51. By my count, this was 159 out of 430 *mustaftis*, or 37 percent.

52. The gap occurred between fatwa no. 549 (published in December 1918) and fatwa no. 550 (published in September 1920). A few of the trends analyzed in the main text can be illustrated for convenience with this table:

Mustaftis from regions with a higher concentration	1903–1918	1920–1935
Egypt	110	49
Sudan	16	3
Syria	15	4
Lebanon	5	20
Palestine	3	5
French North Africa (Tunis, Algeria)	13	6
The Hijaz	11	4
Persian Gulf (Bahrain, Kuwait, Muscat, Linja, Dubai)	6	8
Russia	12	—
The Balkans (Bosnia, Montenegro, Yugoslavia)	5	1
India (Punjab included)	6	7
Dutch East Indies (Java, Sumatra, Indonesia)	20	19
Singapore	26	—
Mustaftis from unspecified or lower concentration regions	30	26
Total number of *mustaftis* in the index	278	152

53. Riḍā became a member of the Syrian National Congress as a representative of Tripoli. On his activities in this polity around 1919, see Eyal Zisser, "Rashid Rida: On the Way to Syrian Nationalism in the Shade of Islam and Arabism," in *The Origins of Syrian Nationhood: Histories, Pioneers and Identity*, ed. Adel Beshara (London: Routledge, 2011), 135.

54. Only three *mustaftis* wrote to *al-Manār* from Iraq between 1903 and 1918.

55. This metaphor serves in my mind to qualify the present history's use of the terms "global" and "globalization." My interest is identifying long-distance and cross-cultural connections as well as some of the limits of interconnectedness in the period under analysis. For an essential critique of "the globalization fad" in historiography, see Frederick Cooper, "What Is the Concept of Globalization Good For? An African Historian's Perspective," *African Affairs* 100, no. 399 (2001): 189–213.

56. The total number of Singaporean Arabs was therefore 1,226 in 1911. It is worth noting, for comparison, that the censuses of 1900 and 1920 counted 27,399 and 44,902 Arabs, respectively, in the Dutch East Indies. Hayes Marriott, "The Peoples of Singapore: Inhabitants and Population," in Walter Makepeace et al., eds., *One Hundred Years of Singapore: Being Some Account of the Capital of the Straits Settlements from its foundation by Sir Stamford Raffles on the 6th February 1819 to the 6th February 1919* (London: John Murray, 1921), 1:360; and Natalie Mobini-Kesheh, *The Hadrami Awakening: Community and Identity in the Netherlands East Indies, 1900–1942* (Ithaca, N.Y.: Cornell South East Asia Program Publications, 1999), 21.

57. Based on the above numbers, it seems that 3.7 percent of Arab Singaporean men wrote to *al-Manār* for fatwas between 1903 and 1928. On the assertion of an Arab identity in relation to "indigenous" Muslims, see Mobini-Kesheh, *The Hadrami Awakening*, 30–31.

58. On various mechanisms for the introduction of *al-Manār* into Indonesia, see Azra, "The Transmission," 144–45.

59. See Caesar Farah, "Censorship and Freedom of Expression in Ottoman Syria and Egypt," in *Nationalism in a Non-National State: The Dissolution of the Ottoman Empire*, ed. William W. Haddad and William Ochsenwald, 151–94 (Columbus: Ohio University Press, 1977); Mahmoud Haddad, "Arab Religious Nationalist in the Colonial Era: Rereading Rashīd Riḍā's Ideas on the Caliphate," *Journal of the American Oriental Society* 117, no. 2 (1997): 267; Eliezer Tauber, "The Political Life of Rašīd Riḍā," *Arabist: Budapest Studies in Arabic*, 19–20 (1998): 265; and Ryad, "A Printed Muslim 'Lighthouse' in Cairo," 31–32. At one point during the World War, British authorities arrested Riḍā and nearly exiled him to Malta. He complained about British censorship in 1915, when the protectorate's chief censor blocked him from publishing a translation of a letter that Lord Cromer had published in *The Times*.
60. In 1908 alone, the Egyptian Post Foreign Service's Office received more than 6.5 million letters, both ordinary and registered, and it sent abroad more than 3 million newspapers, commercial papers, and samples. See Wright, *Twentieth Century Impressions*, 191.
61. Before World War I, Riḍā's British network stretched from Alexandria to Kuala Lumpur. Egypt, Singapore, the Sudan, India, and Bahrain were especially significant nodes. But the colony of Aden, in southwestern Arabia; the Transvaal, in Southeast Africa; Kuwait, at one end of the Gulf; Muscat, across the Strait of Hormuz; and Ceylon, the South Asian island in the Laccadive Sea, also generated at least one fatwa each.
62. Riḍā had heard from 278 *mustaftis* between 1903 and 1918, but from only 152 *mustaftis* between 1920 and 1935.
63. The total number or Egyptian *mustaftis* dropped by more than half from one to the next period.
64. The last fatwa request from Russia seems to be no. 428, dating from 1912. On the Russian response to "pan-Islamic" activities in 1911–1912, see Jacob M. Landau, *Pan-Islam: History and Politics* (London: Routledge, 2016), 165–67 and appendix J.
65. Best conveyed by a few numbers, the slide was truly dramatic. Riḍā had received twenty-three fatwa requests from fifteen Sudanese *mustaftis* before 1919—only three afterward; thirty-seven fatwa requests from twenty-six Singaporean *mustaftis* before 1919—zero afterward; and twenty-six fatwa requests from twelve Russian *mustaftis* between 1903 and 1912—zero afterward.
66. The difference, to be precise, was a shift from 5–20 *mustaftis*, who asked first for 10 and then for more than 150 fatwas.
67. Riḍā received only one request for a fatwa from Switzerland—and it was authored, not coincidentally, by a Syrian, the Druze exile Shakib Arslan. Similarly, a Syrian expatriate penned the request for a fatwa sent to Riḍā from Brazil. See Riḍā, *Fatāwā*, 5:2064, no. 747; *al-Manār* 29 (1928): 507; Riḍā, *Fatāwā*, 6:2410, no. 938; *al-Manār* 32 (1931): 586–87.
68. Although they relate legal theories to social realities to some extent, Wael Hallaq's intellectual histories are a good example of this approach to Islamic law. The central focus is on continuity and change in juridical hermeneutics. For my broader historiographical argument, see note 60 of the present book's introduction.
69. On the incipient reform movement in Singapore and its connection to *al-Manār*, see Abu Ibrahim Abu Shouk, "Islamic Resurgence in Indonesia: The Case of the Islah and Irshad Movement (1914–43)," in *Challenges to Religions and Islam: A Study of Muslim Movements, Personalities, Issues and Trends*, ed. Hamid Naseem Rafiabadi, vol. 2 (New Delhi, 1997), 508.
70. Riḍā, *Fatāwā*, 1:352, no. 154; *al-Manār* 8 (1905): 254–56. In this fatwa, Riḍā drew on al-Ṭabarī's exegesis of the relevant Qurʾanic verse (Q. 5:5), which named the Salafi imam and identified

the church. See Abū Ja^cfar Muḥammad al-Ṭabarī, *Tafsīr al-Ṭabarī al-musammā jāmi^c al-bayān fī tā^ɔwīl al-Qur^ɔān* (Beirut: Dār al-Kutub al-^cIlmiyya, 1992), 4:443, no. 11258.

71. Riḍā, *Fatāwā*, 1:352, no. 154; and *al-Manār* 8 (1905): 254–56. Riḍā had treated the topic at length earlier, in a responsum (*jawāb*); see *al-Manār* 3 (1900): 333–36. He wrote extensively, too, about the prohibition on pork, but in a later fatwa, where he responded to a question from Brazil; see Riḍā, *Fatāwā*, 6:2410–17, no. 938; *al-Manār* 32 (1931): 582–87. For the commentary on this verse, see Muḥammad ʿAbduh and Muḥammad Rashīd Riḍā, *Tafsīr al-Qur^ɔān al-Ḥakīm al-mushtahar bi-ism Tafsīr al-Manār*, 2nd ed. (Cairo: Dār al-Manār, 1947), 6:169–72.

3 In a Material World: European Expansion from Tripoli to Cairo

1. U.S. House of Representatives, *The Executive Documents* 81 (39th Congress, 2nd Session), *Report on the Commercial Relations of the United States with Foreign Nations for the Year Ended September 30, 1866* (Washington, D.C.: Government Printing Office, 1867), 420–23.
2. On the communal and religious conflicts in a broader historical framework, see Ussama Makdisi, *The Culture of Sectarianism: Community, History and Violence in Nineteenth-Century Ottoman Lebanon* (Berkeley: University of California Press, 2000). For a brief history of Tripoli's development in late Ottoman times, see John Gulick, *Tripoli: A Modern Arab City* (Cambridge, Mass.: Harvard University Press, 1967), 19–30.
3. Lamia Rustum Shehadeh, "The Name of Syria in Ancient and Modern Usage," in *The Origins of Syrian Nationhood: Histories, Pioneers and Identity*, ed. Adel Beshara (New York: Routledge, 2011), 22–23; and Carol Hakim, *The Origins of the Lebanese National Idea, 1840–1920* (Berkeley: University of California Press, 2013), 174, 192–93, 256.
4. U.S. House of Representatives, *Report on the Commercial Relations*, 422.
5. Caesar E. Farah, *Politics of Interventionism in Ottoman Lebanon, 1830–1861* (New York: I. B. Tauris; and Oxford: Center for Lebanese Studies, 2000), 96, 115, 222, 477–79.
6. Alfred C. Wood, *A History of the Levant Company* (Oxford: Oxford University Press, 1935), 76–77, 123–24, 163; and Noël Verney, *Les puissances étrangères dans le Levant en Syrie et en Palestine* (Paris: Librairie Guillaumin, 1900), 367–70.
7. John Bowring, *Commercial Statistics of Syria* (London: William Clowes and Sons, 1840), 17, 74, and 120. During the year 1836, according to Bowring, thirty-six ships reached Tripoli: ten French, eight Palestinian, seven Greek, six Anatolian, three Tuscan, one Sardinian, and one Austrian. Collectively they arrived with 4,629 tons and left with only 2,084 tons of merchandise. J. W. Jenks, "The Commerce of Syria," in *The Merchants' Magazine and Commercial Review*, ed. Freeman Hunt, vol. 6 (June 1842): 508, serves to confirm these figures. Over a three-year period, between 1835 and 1837, fifty-three Arab (presumably Egyptian, Palestinian, or Anatolian), twenty-seven French, twelve Greek, five Tuscan, and two Sardinian (but zero British vessels) reached Tripoli. For the broader economic and political context, see Roger Owen, *The Middle East in the World Economy, 1800–1914* (London: I. B. Tauris, 2002), 79–80.
8. The U.S. House of Representatives, *The Executive Documents* (42nd Congress, 2nd Session, 1871–1872), vol. 18, no. 220, *Annual Report on the Commercial Relations Between the United States and Foreign Nations* (Washington, D.C.: Government Printing Office, 1872), 1129–31. There were 198 steamers (66 French, 61 Egyptian, 53 Russian, and 18 British) and 1,133 sailing-vessels (all from Anatolia except for 1 American and 2 Greek boats).

9. "Renseignements économiques: Turquie d'Asie," *Questions Diplomatiques et Coloniales* 4 (May 15, 1898): 122. This journal lists 392 steamers bearing 463,345 tons and 1,532 sailboats bearing 20,959 tons. Most steamers now came from Britain (104) and Egypt under British administration (94), but France (59), Austria (59), and Russia (56) sent many vessels too. The French and Egyptian ships bore the highest tonnage.
10. U.S. Department of State, *Annual Report on the Commercial Relations Between the United States and Foreign Nations Made by the Secretary of State for the Year Ending September 30, 1870* (Washington, D.C.: Government Printing Office, 1871), 407–12. The table at the end indicates that the total value of merchandise imported to Tripoli was 1.12 million piastres, compared to 5.89 million piastres in exports. The same source, on p. 409, reveals that some merchants were primarily devoted to lending money at an interest rate of 12 to 15 percent if not much more.
11. Albert Hourani, *Arabic Thought in the Liberal Age, 1798–1939* (Cambridge: Cambridge University Press, 1983), 235.
12. On the educational development, see Jean Riffier, *Les oeuvres françaises en Syrie (1860–1923)* (Paris: L'Harmattan, 2000), 82–83. On the railroad to Homs, see Verney, *Puissances étrangères*, 313–15.
13. L. Lortet, *La Syrie d'aujourd'hui: Voyages dans la Phénicie, le Liban et la Judée: 1875–1880* (Paris: Librairie Hachette, 1884), 56–57.
14. On Ḥusayn al-Jisr, the Ottoman school that he founded, and his new theological arguments against scientific materialism, see Marwa Elshakry, *Reading Darwin in Arabic, 1860–1950* (Chicago: University of Chicago Press, 2013), chap. 4; Johannes Ebert, *Religion und Reform in der arabischen Provinz: Ḥusayn al-Ǧisr aṭ-Ṭarābulusī (1845–1909)—Ein islamischer Gelehrter zwischen Tradition und Reform* (Frankfurt am Main: P. Lang, 1991), 79–83; Eyal Zisser, "Rashid Rida: On the Way to Syrian Nationalism in the Shade of Islam and Arabism," in *Origins of Syrian Nationhood: Histories, Pioneers and Identity*, ed. Adel Beshara (New York: Routledge, 2011), 125–26; Adel A. Ziadat, *Western Science in the Arab World: The Impact of Darwinism, 1860–1930* (London: Macmillan, 1986), 16, 91–95; Rudolph Peters, "Resurrection, Revelation and Reason: Husayn al-Jisr (d. 1909) and Islamic Eschatology," in *Hidden Futures: Death and Immortality in Ancient Egypt, Anatolia, the Classical, Biblical, and Arabic-Islamic World*, ed. Jan Maarten Brenner, Van Den Hout, and R. Peters (Amsterdam: Amsterdam University Press, 1994), 221–31; and Abdulrazzak Patel, *The Arab Nahḍah: The Making of the Intellectual and Humanist Movement* (Edinburgh: Edinburgh University Press, 2013), 186–90.
15. Patel, *Arab Nahḍah*, 187.
16. Muḥammad ʿAbduh and Muḥammad Rashīd Riḍā, *Tafsīr al-Qurʾān al-Ḥakīm al-mushtahar bi-ism Tafsīr al-Manār*, 2nd ed. (Cairo: Dār al-Manār, 1947), 1:11. For a translation of the passage, see Kosugi Yasushi, "*Al-Manār* Revisited: The 'Lighthouse' of the Islamic Revival," in *Intellectuals in the Modern Islamic World: Transmission, Transformation, Communication*, ed. Stéphane A. Dugoignon, Komatsu Hisao, and Kosugi Yasushi, eds. (London: Routledge, 2009), 9.
17. On the nineteenth-century upheaval in architectural style, see Janet L. Abu-Lughod, *Cairo: 1001 Years of the City Victorious* (Princeton, N.J.: Princeton University Press, 1971), 94; and Nihal S. Tamraz, *Nineteenth-Century Cairene Houses and Palaces* (Cairo: American University in Cairo Press, 1998), 24–25.
18. Stanley Lane-Poole, *The Story of Cairo* (London: J. M. Dent & Sons, 1924), 1–3, 31. For critiques of the two-cities model, see the studies in Nezar AlSayyad, Irene A. Bierman, and Nasser Rabbat, eds., *Making Cairo Medieval* (Lanham, Md.: Lexington Books, 2005). For a watercolor of Darb al-Jamāmīz street, see David Samuel Margoliouth, *Cairo, Jerusalem, & Damascus: Three Chief Cities*

of the Egyptian Sultans, with illus. in colour by W.S.S. Tyrwhitt, and additional plates by Reginald Barratt (London: Chatto and Windus, 1907), 164.

19. Karl Baedeker, *Egypt: Handbook for Travellers*, 4th ed. (Leipzig: K. Baedeker, 1898), 56–58; and Timothy Mitchell, *Colonising Egypt* (Cambridge: Cambridge University Press, 1988), 64–65.
20. Doris Behrens-Abouseif, *Islamic Architecture in Cairo: An Introduction* (Leiden: Brill, 1989), 52–55; and Richard Yeomans, *The Art and Architecture of Islamic Cairo* (Reading, U.K.: Garnet, 2006), 32–34.
21. Tamraz, *Nineteenth-Century Cairene Houses*, 32.
22. Khaled Fahmy, "An Olfactory Tale of Two Cities: Cairo in the Nineteenth Century," in *Historians of Cairo: Essays in Honor of George Scanlon*, ed. Jill Edwards, 155–87 (Cairo: American University in Cairo Press, 2002).
23. André Raymond, *Cairo*, trans. W. Wood (Cambridge, Mass.: Harvard University Press, 2000), 324; and Abu-Lughod, *Cairo*, 133–35. On the Empain group, see Robert Vitalis, *When Capitalists Collide: Business Conflict and the End of Empire in Egypt* (Berkeley: University of California Press, 1995), 35–36; Robert L. Tignor, *State, Private Enterprise, and Economic Change in Egypt, 1918–1952* (Princeton, N.J.: Princeton University Press, 1984), 182–83; and William J. Hausman, Peter Hertner, and Mira Wilkins, *Global Electrification: Multinational Enterprise and International Finance in the History of Light and Power, 1878–2007* (Cambridge: Cambridge University Press, 2008), 102–4.
24. Donald Malcolm Reid, *Whose Pharaohs? Archaeology, Museums, and Egyptian National Identity from Napoleon to World War I* (Berkeley: University of California Press, 2002), 237–40. On the Islamic Museum and more generally on the architecture of the "Islamic revival," see Tarek Mohamed Refaat Sakr, *Early Twentieth-Century Islamic Architecture in Cairo* (Cairo: American University in Cairo Press, 1993), 18–19, 22–24. In *Nineteenth-Century Cairene Houses*, 33–34, Tamraz describes a comparable structure from this era, the Manyal Palace, as representing a "Pseudo-Islamic style." She argues that it embodies the nationalistic Islamic revival spearheaded by Muḥammad ʿAbduh. Cf. Paula Sanders, *Creating Medieval Cairo: Empire, Religion, and Architectural Preservation in Nineteenth-Century Egypt* (Cairo: American University in Cairo Press, 2008). Sanders shows that ʿAbduh actually criticized the restoration of mosques by the Comité de Conservation de Monuments de l'Art Arabe for its conversion of mosques into tourist sites (61–64). She discusses the rise of "medieval" Egypt and "medieval" Islam as European categories of analysis and preservation (46–57 and 86–87).
25. István Ormos, *Max Herz Pasha (1856–1919), His Life and Career* (Cairo: Institut Français d'Archéologie Orientale, 2009), 1:70–75 (on preservation and restoration); 2:313–31 (on the Arab Museum); and 2:372–90 (on the "Neo-Mamluk" or "Islamic Revival" style).
26. Abu-Lughod, *Cairo*, 121–25.
27. Figures based on Tignor, *State, Private Enterprise*, tables A.1–A.4.
28. Roger Owen, "Cairo Building Industry and the Building Boom of 1897 to 1907," in *Colloque international sur l'histoire du Caire*, 27 Mars–5 Avril, 1969 (Cairo: Ministry of Culture of the Arab Republic of Egypt, 1972), 342.
29. Valeska Huber, *Channeling Mobilities: Migration and Globalisation in the Suez Canal Region and Beyond, 1869–1914* (Cambridge: Cambridge University Press, 2013), 43–44.
30. Reid mentions 5,166 visitors to the museum in 1913. Reid, *Whose Pharaohs?*, 239.
31. Umar Ryad, "Islamic Reformism and Great Britain: Rashid Rida's Image as Reflected in the Journal *Al-Manār* in Cairo," *Islam and Christian-Muslim Relations* 21, no. 3 (2010): 263–85.
32. Except for an interlude in Siam in the late 1890s, Alfred Innes served in Egypt between 1891 and 1908. He has only recently come to the attention of historians of economic thought;

see L. Randall Wray, ed., *Credit and State Theories of Money: The Contributions of A. Mitchell Innes* (Cheltenham, U.K.: Edward Elgar, 2004).

33. A. Mitchell Innes, "What Is Money?," *Banking Law Journal*, May 1913, 386; and A. Mitchell Innes, "The Credit Theory of Money," *The Banking Law Journal*, January 1914, 151, 155. The quotations are from the 1914 article.
34. What we know from Riḍā is that they talked about his and ʿAbduh's views of *maṣlaḥa*; see Muhammad Qasim Zaman, *Modern Islamic Thought in a Radical Age: Religious Authority and Internal Criticism* (Cambridge: Cambridge University Press, 2012), 113.
35. For a history of this French financial enterprise in Egypt, see Samir Saul, *La France et l'Égypte de 1882 à 1914: Intérêts économiques et implications politiques* (Paris: Comité pour l'histoire économique et financière de la France, 1997), chap. 9.
36. Data drawn from the useful tables in A. E. Crouchley, *The Investment of Foreign Capital in Egyptian Companies and Public Debt* (Cairo: Government Press, Bulaq, 1936), 104–18. For his own analysis of this "rush of capital to Egypt," see 52–54.
37. Arnold Wright, chief editor, and H. A. Cartwright, assistant editor, *Twentieth Century Impressions of Egypt: Its History, People, Commerce, Industries, and Resources* (London: Lloyd's Greater Britain, 1909), 153–54, 161.
38. For a chart detailing Egypt's foreign trade year by year, see Crouchley, *Investment of Foreign Capital*, 83, 173. Also see Owen, *The Middle East in the World Economy*, 219, 241. On the growth of imports in the late 1890s, also see Robert L. Tignor, "The Introduction of Modern Banking into Egypt, 1855–1920," *Asian and African Studies* 15 (1981): 103–22.
39. For a brief, balanced, and informative overview, see Roger Owen and Şevket Pamuk, *A History of Middle East Economies* (Cambridge, Mass.: Harvard University Press, 1998), 30–35.
40. Wright, *Twentieth Century Impressions*, 158, lists the total value of cotton, cottonseed, and oil cake exports in 1907 as 23.6 million, 2.5 million, and 0.2 million Egyptian pounds (E£), respectively. All in all, these exports added up to roughly E£26.3 million—out of a grand total of E£28 million. If customs officials undervalued all exports except tobacco by 10 percent before 1911, as Roger Owen has argued, then the sum of total exports should be adjusted to E£30.7 million. By contrast, total imports that year were valued at E£26.1 million. For a sense of the American-Egyptian competition over cottonseed oilcake production, see *Manufacturers' Record: A Weekly Southern Industrial, Railroad and Financial Newspaper* 48, no. 19 (November 23, 1905): 484–86; Secretary of Agriculture (Bureau of Statistics), *The Crop Reporter* 7 (November 1905): 58–60; and U.S. Department of Commerce and Labor (Bureau of the Census, Bulletin 91), *Transportation by Water: 1906* (Washington, D.C.: Government Printing Office, 1908), 58. On the production of oil cakes in the broader context of industrial development, see Roger Owen, *Cotton and the Egyptian Economy, 1820–1914: A Study in Trade and Development* (Oxford: Clarendon, 1969), 294–95; on the undervaluation of exports, see 376–77.
41. I have based this on Owen, *The Middle East in the World Economy*, chap. 9.
42. Wright, *Twentieth Century Impressions*, 156–58. Listed by decreasing cost, there were miscellaneous unclassified articles (E£8,926,672), cotton textiles (E£3,168,088), iron and steel (E£1,969,361), coal (E£1,389,861), wood (E£1,316,871), noncotton textiles (E£1,263,169), maize and wheat flour (E£1,227,086), machinery (E£1,069,537), animals (E£719,063), tobacco and cigars (E£716,207), fresh and dried fruit (E£529,256), ironmongery and haberdashery (E£434,410), underclothing (E£430,078), clothing (E£423,650), rice (E£385,569), butter and cheese (E£289,699), petrol (E£297,000), rough and refined sugar (E£278,352), cotton thread (E£277,731), leather (E£270,764), coffee (E£261,739), sacks (E£252,836), and smoked fish and preserved foods

(E£223,784). I've slightly expanded this bare list and glossed it with the more informative treatment of imports from 1900 to 1905 by H. W. Mardon, *A Geography of Egypt and the Anglo-Egyptian Sudan* (London: Blackie & Son, 1906), 104–13.

43. Wright, *Twentieth Century Impressions*, 453–55.
44. Wright, *Twentieth Century Impressions*, 458–59.
45. Wright, *Twentieth Century Impressions*, 369, and, for a photograph of the bookstore, 372.
46. Wright, *Twentieth Century Impressions*, 370–76.
47. Wright, *Twentieth Century Impressions*, 369–77. Wright does not identify Raff's religion. But his last name, together with the fact that he married Stein's sister, indicates a Jewish affiliation. Gudrun Krämer, *The Jews in Modern Egypt, 1914–1952* (London: I. B. Tauris, 1989), 51, identifies most owners of department stores as Jewish.
48. For a critique of the relevant historiography, see Will Hanley, "Grieving Cosmopolitanism in Middle East Studies," *History Compass* 6, no. 5 (2008): 1346–67.
49. Books in Wright's prewar *Twentieth Century Impressions* series featured several states, from Argentina to Western Australia, that were not under British rule. Yet the original plan, as Wright explained in the preface to the volume on Egypt, was to cover "the outlying parts of the British Empire." In a book that he published as a "true Imperialist" following World War I, Wright wrote a "true Imperialist" history that was basically a triumphalist narrative of the British Empire's free-trade policies. See Arnold Wright, *The Romance of Colonisation: Being the Story of the Economic Development of the British Empire* (London: A. Melrose, 1923), vii, 285–94, 371.
50. Wright, *Twentieth Century Impressions*, 333.
51. Wright, *Twentieth Century Impressions*, 332–36.
52. Wright, *Twentieth Century Impressions*, 192, 216, 472.
53. "A Notable Hull Business," *Magazine of Commerce: An Illustrated Monthly for Men of Affairs* 5 (July–December 1904): 312–17.
54. Wright, *Twentieth Century Impressions*, 342–43, 365–66.
55. Peter van der Veer, "Colonial Cosmopolitanism," in *Conceiving Cosmopolitanism: Theory, Context, and Practice*, ed. Steven Vertovec and Robin Cohen (Oxford: Oxford University Press, 2002), chap. 10.
56. Wright, *Twentieth Century Impressions*, 370–71; and Harry Alis, *Promenade en Égypte* (Paris: Librairie Hachette, 1895), 205–8. For images of two of Mr. Parvis's celebrated designs, see Adam Matthew, *The Illustrated Catalogue of the Paris International Exhibition, 1878* (London: Virtue, 1878), 8.
57. Alfred Milner, *England in Egypt*, 13th ed. (New York: Howard Fertig, 1970), 24–35.
58. Afaf Lufti Sayyid-Marsot, *Egypt's Liberal Experiment, 1922–1936* (Berkeley: University of California Press, 1977), 264. On the broader significance of the 1922 proclamation for the emergence of Egypt as a nation-state, see Israel Gershoni and James P. Jankowski, *Egypt, Islam, and the Arabs: The Search for Egyptian Nationhood, 1900–1930* (Oxford: Oxford University Press, 1987), 54. On the economic policy constraints, see Owen and Pamuk, *History of Middle East Economies* 35–36.
59. William H. Wynne, *State Insolvency and Foreign Bondholders*, vol. 2, *Selected Case Histories of Governmental Foreign Bond Defaults and Debt Readjustments* (New Haven, Conn.: Yale University Press, 1951), 577–632; and Robert T. Harrison, *Gladstone's Imperialism in Egypt: Techniques of Domination* (Westport, Conn.: Greenwood, 1995), 51–56.
60. John Gallagher and Ronald Robinson, "The Imperialism of Free Trade," *Economic History Review* 6, no. 1 (1953): 1–15. There is a great deal of scholarship criticizing this classic article. For a

recent example, see Lisa Pollard, *Nurturing the Nation: The Family Politics of Modernizing, Colonizing and Liberating Egypt, 1805–1923* (Berkeley: University of California Press, 2005), 83–85.

61. For two notably different attempts to revise this imperial narrative, see AbdelAziz EzzelArab, *European Control and Egypt's Traditional Elites—A Case Study in Elite Economic Nationalism* (Lewiston, N.Y.: Edwin Mellen Press, 2002); and Pollard, *Nurturing the Nation*, 83, 90–93, and passim. Whereas Pollard's cultural and political history pays close attention to British cultural assumptions and unresolved ambiguities, EzzelArab's economic and political history aims to show how, long before the foundation of Banque Miṣr, Egyptians themselves came up with sophisticated programs to develop Egypt's economy.
62. Milner, *England in Egypt*, 13, 16, 81, 252.
63. Milner, *England in Egypt*, 33, 82–83, 314.
64. Milner, *England in Egypt*, 217, 220, 387. Given the reference to the agreement for construction of the Aswan Dam, this statement was obviously not part of the book's first edition.
65. Milner, *England in Egypt*, 214–15.
66. Earl of Cromer (Evelyn Baring), *Modern Egypt* (London: Macmillan, 1908), 2:435–37, 447–48, 455.
67. Cromer, *Modern Egypt*, 2:304–10, 453.
68. Cromer, *Modern Egypt*, 1:326–27; 2:58–59, 196. Cromer devoted an entire chapter (2:420–25) to the canker of corruption.
69. Cromer, *Modern Egypt*, 2:426.
70. Cromer, *Modern Egypt*, 2:114, 440, 461–62, 547.
71. Cromer, *Modern Egypt*, 2:161, 322, 538.
72. Cromer, *Modern Egypt*, 2:162.
73. Cromer, *Modern Egypt*, 2:179–81; and [Earl of Cromer], *Reports by His Majesty's Agent and Consul-General on the Finances, Administration, and Condition of Egypt and the Soudan in 1906* (London: Harrison and Sons, Printed for His Majesty's Stationery Office, 1907), 8.
74. On the diverse origins of Cape Muslims, see Frank R. Bradlow and Margaret Cairns, *The Early Cape Muslims: A Study of Their Mosques, Genealogy and Origins* (Cape Town, S.A.: A. A. Balkema, 1978), 80ff.
75. On Indians and Muslims in the Transvaal, see Surendra Bhana and Joy B. Brain, *Setting Down Roots: Indian Migrants in South Africa, 1860–1911* (Johannesburg: Witwatersrand University Press, 1990), 77–97; Abdulkader Tayob, *Islam in South Africa: Mosques, Imams, and Sermons* (Gainesville, Fla.: University Press of Florida, 1999), chap. 4; and Bala Pillay, *British Indians in the Transvaal: Trade, Politics and Imperial Relations, 1885–1906* (London: Longman, 1976), 137–94.
76. Mohandas K. Gandhi, *An Autobiography: The Story of My Experiments with Truth*, trans. M. Desai (Boston: Beacon Press, 1993), 147.
77. For an illustration of a hat from the Boer War, see Hilda Amphlett, *Hats: A History of Fashion in Headwear* (Buckinghamshire: R. Sadler, 1974), 174–75. See the variety of headgear in the photograph collected in Bhana and Brain, *Setting Down Roots*, between pages 120 and 121. In his analysis of the Transvaal fatwa, Éric Germain, *L'Afique du Sud musulmane: Histoire des relations entre Indiens et Malais du Cap* (Paris: Karthala, 2007), 131, cites a source from 1903 suggesting how, by disguising himself in a European hat, a Muslim would be treated as a European; the illustrations between pages 193 and 193 also show a multiplicity of hats.
78. *The Encyclopaedia Britannica: A Dictionary of Arts, Sciences, Literature and General Information*, 11th ed. (London: Encyclopaedia Britannica Company, 1910), 9:31. The article comes from the section on "Modern Egypt."

79. Wright, *Twentieth Century Impressions*, 96, 98.
80. Roughly forty years before ʿAbduh issued his fatwa, a Tunisian scholar in Paris had discussed the same problem and reached a similar conclusion. On his ruling, see Sjoerd van Koningsveld, "Between Communalism and Secularism: Modern Sunnite Discussions on Male Head-Gear and Coiffure," in *Pluralism and Identity: Studies in Ritual Behavior*, ed. Jan Platvoet and Karel van der Toorn, 327–45 (Leiden: Brill, 1995), 330–31.
81. On "slave milieu" practices by Cape Muslims, see Achmat Davids, *The Mosques of Bo-Kaap: A Social History of Islam at the Cape* (Athlone, Cape: South African Institute of Arabic and Islamic Research, 1980), 33–34. This book makes clear that doctrinal tensions arose between Cape and Indian Muslims, partly because they generally belonged to different schools of law: the Shafiʿite and Ḥanafi *madhhabs*, respectively (see 51ff, 185). The third question presented to ʿAbduh, not analyzed here, concerns a point of divergence (*khilāf*) between Shafiʿites and Ḥanafis in South Africa. Interestingly, under the influence of Abū Bakr Effendi, an orthodox-minded Turk invited by the British government to the Cape in order to introduce Ḥanafi legislation, Cape Muslims would change their headgear from a "conical straw hat" to a fez (see 7 and 23). Bradlow and Cairns, *Early Cape Muslims*, 16–17, refer to Madagascar slaves in the Cape as following a "debased," heterodox form of Islam; they also cite a description of the first mosque, which apparently resembled in style local Christian churches. Germain, *L'Afrique du Sud musulmane*, 122–23 and 173, shows how first the effendi and then the Indian immigrants placed an emphasis on the need to consume *ḥalāl* food.
82. Editions of the famous fatwa differ slightly on a few details. For an easily accessible version, see Muḥammad ʿAbduh, *al-Aʿmāl al-kāmila*, ed. Muḥammad ʿImāra (Beirut: al-Muʾassasa al-ʿArabiyya li-l-Dirāsāt wa-l-Nashr, 1972–74), 6:255–6, no. 7. The phrase in quotation marks is *dafʿan li-l-ḥaraj fī muʿāsharatihim wa-muʿāmalatihim*. I analyze the fatwa and its reception only briefly here because it has already received extensive scholarly study. See in particular Charles C. Adams, "Muḥammad ʿAbduh and the Transvaal Fatwā," in *The Macdonald Presentation Volume: A Tribute to Duncan Black Macdonald: Consisting of Articles by Former Students, Presented to Him on His Seventieth Birthday, April 9, 1933* (Freeport, N.Y.: Books for Libraries, 1968), 13–29; John O. Voll, "ʿAbduh and the Transvaal Fatwa: The Neglected Question," in *Islam and the Question of Minorities*, ed. Tamara Sonn, ed., 27–39 (Atlanta: Scholars Press, 1996); Jakob Skovgaard-Petersen, *Defining Islam for the Egyptian State: Muftis and Fatwas of the Dār al-Iftā* (Leiden: Brill, 1997), 123–33; and Indira Falk Gesink, *Islamic Reform and Conservatism: Al-Azhar and the Evolution of Modern Sunni Islam*, rev. ed. (New York: I. B. Tauris, 2010), 188–95.
83. Anthropologists have related "cosmopolitan sociability" to an ability "to find aspects of the shared human experience including aspirations for a better world within or despite what would seem to be divides of culture and belief." ʿAbduh's Transvaal fatwa seems to be an excellent example of such an approach to interreligious interactions. See Nina Glick Schiller, Darieva Tsypylma, and Sandra Gruner-Domic, "Defining Cosmopolitan Sociability in a Transnational Age: An Introduction," *Ethnic and Racial Studies* 34, no. 3 (2011): 403.
84. Muḥammad Rashīd Riḍā, "al-Tashabbuh w-l-iqtidāʾ," *al-Manār* 1 (1898): 551–57. Emad Eldin Shahin, "Muḥammad Rashīd Riḍā's Perspectives on the West as Reflected in *Al-Manār*," *Muslim World* 79, no. 2 (1989): 113–32, briefly cites this article (122) to argue more generally that Riḍā distinguished between modernization and Westernization. In the article in question, Riḍā refers to his book, *al-Ḥikma al-sharʿiyya fī muḥākamat al-Qādiriyya wa-l-Rifāʿiyya*, where he had discussed the topic earlier. On that book, see Elizabeth Sirriyeh, "Rashīd Riḍā's Autobiography of the Syrian Years, 1865–1897," *Arabic and Middle Eastern Literatures* 3, no. 2 (2000): 187. For one

version of the *ḥadīth* glossed by Riḍā, see *Ṣaḥīḥ Muslim*, in *Jamᶜ jawāmiᶜ al-aḥādīth wa-l-asānīd wa-maknaz al-ṣiḥāḥ wa-l-sunan wa-l-masānīd* (Vaduz, Liechtenstein: Thesaurus Islamicus Foundation, 2000), 2:907, no. 5534. On the *ṭayālisa kisrawiyya*, associated with Magian attire, see Norman A. Stillman, *Arab Dress: From the Dawn of Islam to Modern Times* (Leiden: Brill, 2000), 18. In Muḥammad Rashīd Riḍā, *Fatāwā al-Imām*, eds. Ṣalāḥ al-Dīn al-Munajjid and Yūsuf Q. Khūrī (Dār al-Kitab al-Jadīd: Beirut, 1970–), 3:866, no. 317.

85. *Al-Manār* 31 (1930): 280; *Al-Manār* 35 (1935): 134–35; and Umar Ryad, *Islamic Reformism and Christianity: A Critical Reading of the Works of Muḥammad Rashīd Riḍā and His Associates (1898–1935)* (Leiden: Brill, 2009), 303–4.
86. Riḍā, *Fatāwā*, 1:81–83, no. 31; *al-Manār* 7 (1904): 26. For the broader geopolitical context, see Isa Blumi, "Contesting the Edges of the Ottoman Empire: Rethinking Ethnic and Sectarian Boundaries in the Malësore, 1878–1912," *International Journal of Middle East Studies* 35 (2003): 237–56.
87. Riḍā, *Fatāwā*, 1:128–29, no. 50; *al-Manār* 7 (1904): 239.
88. Riḍā, *Fatāwā*, 2:684–85, no. 258; *al-Manār* 11 (1908): 519–20.
89. Riḍā, *Fatāwā*, 2:565–66, no. 218; *al-Manār* 10 (1907): 117–18. On this fatwa, see Andrew F. March, *Islam and Liberal Citizenship: The Search for an Overlapping Consensus* (Oxford: Oxford University Press, 2009), 192–94.
90. Riḍā, *Fatāwā*, 1:81–83, no. 31; 1:128–29, no. 50; and 2:684–85, no. 258.
91. Rudolph Peters, "Administrators and Magistrates: The Development of a Secular Judiciary in Egypt, 1842–1871," *Die Welt des Islams* 39 (1999): 378–97. Peters discusses the expansion of the system into a "five-tiered judiciary" (379). However distinct they were from the shariᶜa courts, the so-called secular councils included Islamic legal authorities, and they "were not regarded as an encroachment on the sharīᶜa" (391). On the subject of legal change in this period, also see Khaled Fahmy, "The Anatomy of Justice: Medicine and Criminal Law in Nineteenth-Century Egypt," *Islamic Law and Society* 6, no. 2 (1999): 224–71. Fahmy's article shows how in the early nineteenth century, instead of following the evidentiary standards established by the shariᶜa, Egyptian courts accepted forensic and material evidence under the imperatives of *siyāsa*. According to him, this was an internal process of legal reform that did not depend on European dominance. Defenders of novel forensic methods argued that these did not conflict with the sacred law.
92. Consular courts continued to hold jurisdiction in civil and commercial cases after the inauguration of the Mixed Courts, but only when all parties involved in a conflict belonged to the same foreign nation represented by the consulate. Scholarship on the institution of the Mixed Courts is extensive. For a history of the origins, jurisdiction, and evolution of this institution, see Mark S. W. Hoyle, *Mixed Courts of Egypt* (London: Graham & Trotman, 1991). For a narrative that examines the interplay of legal and economic factors, see Byron Cannon, *Politics of Law and the Courts in Nineteenth-Century Egypt* (Salt Lake City: University of Utah Press, 1988). On the construction and evolution of this new legal system, see Nathan J. Brown, *The Rule of Law in the Arab World: Courts in Egypt and the Gulf* (Cambridge: Cambridge University Press, 1997), chap. 2.
93. For a succinct presentation of these courts' jurisdictions, see Richard A. Debs, *Islamic Law and Civil Code: The Law of Property in Egypt* (New York: Columbia University Press, 2010), 61–71. See p. 70 for the quotation.
94. See Daniel Crecelius, "The Course of Secularization in Modern Egypt," chap. 4 in *Religion and Political Modernization*, ed. Donald Eugene Smith (New Haven, Conn.: Yale University Press, 1974), esp. pp. 77–85. Secularization, Crecelius argues on p. 85, appeared by the late

nineteenth century "to be a unilinear force heading toward" the "predictable goal" of Westernization.

4 Paper Money and Consummate Men: Capitalism and the Rise of Laissez-Faire Salafism

1. "The intention was that it should be a truly Egyptian National Bank," wrote the bank's own historian on the occasion of the institution's fiftieth anniversary. See *National Bank of Egypt, 1898–1948* (Cairo: N.B.E. Printing Press, ca. 1949), 14.
2. *National Bank of Egypt, 1898–1948*, 23, 118; Arthur Edwin Crouchley, *The Economic Development of Modern Egypt* (London: Longmans, Green, 1938), 176, 270–71; and A. E. Crouchley, *Investment of Foreign Capital in Egyptian Companies and Public Debt* (Cairo: Government Press, Bulaq, 1936), 128–29.
3. *Al-Manār* 9 (1906): 421–27, 497–504, 673–78; *al-Manār* 17 (1914): 661–66, 783–92.
4. "Al-Rijāl am al-māl," *al-Manār* 3 (1900): 505–9.
5. Qāsim Amīn, *al-Marʾa al-jadīda* (Cairo: Maṭbaʿat al-Shaʿb, 1911), 188–90.
6. ʿAbd al-Raḥmān al-Kawākibī, *al-Aʿmāl al-kāmila li-l-Kawākibī*, 3rd ed. (Beirut: Markaz Dirāsāt al-Waḥda al-ʿArabiyya, 2007), 359–60. Also see *al-Manār* 5 (1902): 899.
7. *Al-Manār* 4 (1901): 114. Also see Umar Ryad, "Islamic Reformism and Great Britain: Rashid Rida's Image as Reflected in the Journal *Al-Manār* in Cairo." *Islam and Christian-Muslim Relations* 21, no. 3 (2010): 267; Walter Walsh, *The Religious Life and Influence of Queen Victoria* (London: Swan Sonnenschein, 1902), 54–55; and Nigel Rigby and Howard J. Booth, eds., *Modernism and Empire: Writing and British Coloniality, 1890–1940* (Manchester, U.K.: Manchester University Press, 2000), 190.
8. Earl of Cromer (Evelyn Baring), *Modern Egypt* (London: Macmillan, 1908), 2:162n3.
9. U.S. National Monetary Commission, *Notes on the Postal Savings-Bank Systems of the Leading Countries* (Washington, D.C.: Government Printing Office, 1910), 23–24. This publication was prepared for the Senate's 61st Congress, 3rd session, as document no. 658. For the number of depositors, broken down according to nationality, I relied on the table of the Ministry of Finance, *Comparative Statistics of the Postal Traffic in Egypt for the Years 1880–1906* (Cairo: National Printing Department, 1906), 23. But it is interesting to note how quickly manufacturers, students, and servants adopted banking. The number of manufacturers with an account grew from 81 in 1901 to 8,619 by 1906, outranking in the process all but government employees.
10. Chibli Mallat, "The Debate on Riba and Interest in Twentieth Century Jurisprudence," in *Islamic Law and Finance*, ed. Chibli Mallat (London: Graham & Trotman, 1988), 71–74; and Indira Falk Gesink, *Islamic Reform and Conservatism: Al-Azhar and the Evolution of Modern Sunni Islam*, rev. ed. (New York: I. B. Tauris, 2010), 175–76.
11. Muḥammad ʿAbduh, *al-Aʿmāl al-kāmila*, ed. Muḥammad ʿImāra (Beirut: al-Muʾassasa al-ʿArabiyya li-l-Dirāsāt wa-l-Nashr, 1972–74), 6:251, no. 3
12. Th. Lebsohn et al., *Bulletin de legislation et de jurisprudence égyptiennes*, Year 15, *1902–1903* (Alexandria, Egypt: V. Penasson, 1903), 340.
13. *The Insurance Year Book for 1903: Life & Miscellaneous* (New York: Spectator, 1903), 126; and *The Insurance Year Book for 1907: Life, Casualty & Miscellaneous* (New York: Spectator, 1907), 143.
14. ʿAbduh, *al-Aʿmāl al-kāmila*, 6:251, no. 3. Compare to the legal definition of a life insurance contract in Egyptian legislation: Th. Lebsohn et al., *Bulletin de legislation et de jurisprudence*

égyptiennes, Year 12, *1899–1900* (Alexandria, Egypt: V Penasson, 1900), 111. On ʿAbduh's fatwas regarding insurance, also see Abdul Azim Islahi, *Economic Thinking of Arab Muslims Writers During the Nineteenth Century* (New York: Palgrave Macmillan, 2015), 73–74.

15. ʿAbduh, *al-Aʿmāl al-kāmila*, 6:265, no. 19.
16. [Earl of Cromer], *Reports by His Majesty's Agent and Consul-General on the Finances, Administration, and Condition of Egypt and the Soudan in 1901* (London: Harrison and Sons, Printed for His Majesty's Stationery Office, 1902), 27; and William Garstin, *Report upon the Administration of the Public Works Department in Egypt for 1902* (Cairo: National Printing Department, 1903), 55–56.
17. For the argument that "Egyptian surroundings" influenced interpretations of the French codes, see Mark S. W. Hoyle, *Mixed Courts of Egypt* (London: Graham & Trotman, 1991), 18–19. Evidently, however, as the case under consideration makes clear, there was a limit to this process of local adaptation.
18. H.-J.-B. Dard, ed., *Code civil avec des notes indicatives des lois romaines, coutumes, ordonnances, édits et déclarations qui ont rapport à chaque article, ou, Conférence du Code civil avec les lois anciennes*, 3rd ed. (Paris: B. Warée fils aîné, 1827), livre 3, pp. 331, 333, and 360, articles 1421, 1426, and 1531.
19. This is a major theme of Judith E. Tucker's *Women, Family, and Gender in Islamic Law* (Cambridge: Cambridge University Press, 2008), 25–26, and elsewhere.
20. Cromer, *Modern Egypt*, 2:134, 154.
21. It is instructive to compare Lady Nafīsa's case to Dame Marie Grois' case against the Compagnie du canal de Suez, also dating from 1903, yet having no connection to Islamic law. For the summary of this case, see Lebsohn et al., *Bulletin de legislation*, Year 15, *1902–1903*, 233–34.
22. ʿAbduh, *al-Aʿmāl al-kāmila*, 6:265, no. 19.
23. On the lack of Islamic legal sanction for joint-stock companies, see Timur Kuran, "The Absence of the Corporation in Islamic Law: Origins and Persistence," *American Journal of Comparative Law* 53, no, 4 (2005): 785–834.
24. On how Islamic law nevertheless accommodates some forms of speculation, see Frank E. Vogel and Samuel L. Hayes III, *Islamic Law and Finance: Religion, Risk, and Return* (The Hague: Kluwer Law International, 1998), 252.
25. Islahi, *Economic Thinking*, 60–62.
26. *Al-Manār* 9 (1906): 348–49. Cf. Mallat, "Debate on Riba," 73. Mallat's loose translation makes an unjustified interpolation, and it omits the reference to Tolstoy even though his book *What Is to Be Done?* inspired the entire passage.
27. Léon Tolstoi, *Que Faire?*, trans. Marina Polonsky et Debarre (Paris: Albert Savine, 1887), 234. Cf. Léon Tolstoï, *Ce qu'il faut faire*, trans. B. Tseytline et E. Jaubert (Paris: Albert Savine, 1888), 119–20.
28. Lyof N. Tolstoy, *What Is to Be Done? Life* (New York: Crowell, 1899), 86–87.
29. Tolstoy, *What Is to Be Done?*, 216.
30. Tolstoy, *What Is to Be Done?*, 91–92, 126–27. Cf. Tolstoï, *Ce qu'il faut faire*, 117–18, 127–28, 210.
31. Tolstoy, *What Is to Be Done?*, 94–102. This historical allegory is missing from the 1887 and 1888 French editions, so ʿAbduh must not have read it. Nevertheless, I include it because it helps to grasp the contrast between Tolstoy's and Cromer's views of capitalism and imperialism. For Commander Boutwell's memorandum detailing Consul Williams' original claims, see U.S. Department of State, *Memorandum on the Fiji Land Claims, September 1902* (Washington, D.C.: Government Printing Office, 1902), 65. Cf. David F. Long, *Gold Braid and Foreign Relations:*

Diplomatic Activities of U.S. Naval Officers, 1798–1883 (Annapolis, Md.: Naval Institute Press, 1988), 302. On the famous story of the Methodist missionary, William Moore, see James Calvert, *Fiji and the Fijians: Mission History*, ed. George S. Rowe (London: Alexander Heylin, 1858), 2:188–89. In 1867, 252 out of 323 male and 45 out of 47 female settlers were British, according to F. J. Moss, *A Planter's Experience in Egypt: Being a Concise Account of the Country, Its Present Condition, and Its Prospects as s Field for Emigration* (Auckland: Jones and Tomes, 1870), 3. After addressing the planting of cotton, Moss discusses the prospect of sugar (47).

32. A. Kudelin, "Muḥammad ʿAbdū's Letter to Leo Tolstoĭ (History of Russian-Arabic Cultural Dialogue in the Beginning of the 20th Century)," *Manuscripta Orientalia* 15, no. 1 (2009): 41–49.
33. Also see Abdullah Saeed, *Islamic Banking and Interest: A Study of the Prohibition of Riba and Its Contemporary Interpretation*, 2nd ed. (Leiden: Brill, 1999), 51–52.
34. *Al-Manār* 5 (1902): 51–55.
35. On Shaykh Muqbil's background, see Nelida Fuccaro, *Histories of City and State in the Persian Gulf: Manama Since 1800* (Cambridge: Cambridge University Press, 2009), 93, 95, 96–97, 138.
36. The problem of paper money in Islamic law has received scant attention. See, however, Nicholas A. Siegfried, "Paper Money in Islamic Legal Thought," *Arab Law Quarterly* 16, no. 4 (2001): 319–32. In addition, John Hunwick devoted a tantalizing paragraph to it in his article "Islamic Financial Institutions: Theoretical Structures and Aspects of Their Application in Sub-Saharan Africa," in *Credit, Currencies, and Culture: African Financial Institutions in Historical Perspective*, ed. Endre Stiansen and Jane I. Guyer, 72–96 (Uppsala, Sweden: Nordiska Afrikainstitutet, 1999), 92. He analyzed there a pamphlet written in Medina by a scholar from the state of Segu, in West Africa, dating from 1929. Siegfried's article treats paper money far more extensively, but it pays no attention to Riḍā's fatwas and contemporary debates on banknotes. Principally it relies principally on a Saudi monograph by Bin Maniʿ that surveyed previous discussions and acknowledged Riḍā's contributions. See ʿAbdallāh b. Sulaymān b. Maniʿ, *al-Waraq al-naqdī: tārikhuhu, ḥaqīqatuhu, qīmatuhu, ḥukmuhu* (Riyadh: Maṭābiʿ al-Riyāḍ, 1971), 149–50, 176.
37. *Ṣaḥīḥ Muslim*, in *Jamʿ jawāmiʿ al-aḥādīth wa-l-asānīd wa-maknaz al-ṣiḥāḥ wa-l-sunan wa-l-masānīd* (Vaduz, Liechtenstein: Thesaurus Islamicus Foundation, 2000), 2:676, no. 4147.
38. ʿAbd al-Razzāq b. Hammām al-Ṣanʿānī, *al-Muṣannaf*, ed. Ḥabīb al-Raḥmān al-Aʿẓamī, 2nd ed. (Beirut: al-Maktab al-Islāmī, 1983), 8:125, no. 14575.
39. Hiroyuki Yanagihashi, *A History of the Early Islamic Law of Property: Reconstructing the Legal Development, 7th–9th Centuries* (Leiden: Brill, 2004), 214–49.
40. Siegfried, "Paper Money," 323.
41. On coinages from the Umayyad period, see Clive Foss, "A Syrian Coinage of Mu`awiya?," *Revue Numismatique* 158 (2002): 353–65; Stuart D. Sears, "Before Caliphal Coins: Transitional Drahms of the Umayyad North," *American Journal of Numismatics* 15 (2003): 77–110; Luke Treadwell, "The Copper Coinage of Umayyad Iran," *Numismatic Chronicle* 168 (2008): 331–81; and Gene W. Heck, "First Century Islamic Currency: Mastering the Message from the Money," chap. 5 in *Money, Power and Politics in Early Islamic Syria: A Review of Current Debates*, ed. John Haldon (Surrey, England: Ashgate, 2010), 108–9.
42. James Onley, "The Raj Reconsidered: British India's Informal Empire and Spheres of Influence in Asia and Africa," *Asian Affairs* 40, no. 1 (2009): 54.
43. James Onley, *The Arabian Frontier of the British Raj: Merchants, Rulers and the British in the Nineteenth-Century Gulf* (New York: Oxford University Press, 2007).

44. Matthew S. Hopper, "The Globalization of Dried Fruit: Transformations in the Eastern Arabian Economy, 1860s–1920s," chap. 8 in *Global Muslims in the Age of Stream and Print*, ed. James L. Gelvin and Nile Green (Berkeley: University of California Press, 2014).
45. John Maynard Keynes, *The Collected Writings*, vol. 1, *Indian Currency and Finance* (Macmillan: St. Martin's Press for the Royal Economic Society, 1971), 29, 32. The first edition dates from 1913. See also Bazil Shaikh and Sandhya Srinivasan, *The Paper & The Promise: A Brief History of Currency & Banknotes in India* (Department of Currency Management, Museum Cell, Reserve Bank of India, 2001), 21–25.
46. *Al-Manār* 5 (1902): 51–55.
47. Abraham L. Udovitch, *Partnership and Profit in Medieval Islam* (Princeton, N.J.: Princeton University Press, 1970), 52–55, 177–79.
48. Robert Brunschvig, "Conceptions monétaires chez les juristes musulmans (viii[e]–xiii[e] siècles)," *Arabica* 14, no. 2 (1967): 118.
49. Mainly based on the monograph by Bin Mani[c], *al-Waraq al-naqdī*, Nicholas Siegfried suggests five juridical approaches, including the analogies to *suftaja* and *fulūs*; see his article "Paper Money," 327–30.
50. *Al-Manār* 5 (1902): 51–55. All quotations from this paragraph to the end of the section come from this source.
51. *Ṣaḥīḥ al-Bukhārī*, 2:750, no. 3862.
52. *Al-Manār* 10 (1907), 359–65. Riḍā's critique of Ḥanafi strictures concluded with a reference to Ibn Taymiyya's more liberal approach. It followed Ottoman precedents, discussed in depth in Oussama Arabi, "Contract Stipulations (*Shurūṭ*) in Islamic Law: The Ottoman Majalla and Ibn Taymiyya," *IJMES* 30 (1998): 29–50.
53. J. M. Keynes, "Recent Economic Events in India," *Economic Journal* 19 (1909): 51–67.
54. "India's Present Monetary Condition," *Economic Journal* 17 (1907): 47–56. On the fragility of the imperial British financial system, the purpose of council bills, and exchange crises that related to the gold standard and paper currency reserves, see David Sunderland, *Financing the Raj: The City of London and Colonial India, 1858–1940* (Woodbridge, Suffolk, U.K.: Boydell, 2003).
55. Janet L. Abu-Lughod, *Cairo: 1001 Years of the City Victorious* (Princeton, N.J.: Princeton University Press, 1971), 153; and Yunan Labib Rizq, "The Banking Revolution," *Al-Ahram Weekly* 439 (July 22–28, 1999).
56. Remarks by Lord Rathmore and George Biddulph's at the general meeting of the Bank of Egypt, published by *The Statist* on March 7, 1908, 468–70.
57. See, for example, Michael O'Malley, *Face Value: The Entwined Histories of Money & Race in America* (Chicago: University of Chicago Press, 2012), 173–74; and Mary Tone Rodgers and James E. Payne, "How the Bank of France Changed U.S. Equity Expectations and Ended the Panic of 1907," *Journal of Economic History* 74 (2014): 420–48. An early analyst of this crisis, Alexander D. Noyes, argued that Egypt's "hoarding panic" was broken only by the "instantaneous shipment" of vast quantities of gold from London. See his article "A Year After the Panic of 1907," *Quarterly Journal of Economics* 23 (1909): 202. Also see Alexander Dana Noyes, *Forty Years of American Finance: A Short Financial History of the Government and People of the United States since the Civil War, 1865–1907* (New York: G. P. Putnam's Sons, 1909), 325, 361.
58. In its apologetic history, the National Bank of Egypt maintained: "On the appearance of a crisis, gold could at that time be obtained from London, against the sale of securities in the 'fiduciary' half of the cover, in less than a week's time, or if advantage could be taken of the gold market in Paris or Milan, more quickly still." Yet, in 1904, the bank's branch in Alexandria

already faced difficulties converting paper notes to precious metal, which led the board to restrict the obligation to maintain gold coverage to Cairo. See *National Bank of Egypt, 1898–1948*, 19, 24.

59. Maurice L. Muhleman, "Egypt's Economic Position and Gold Hoarding," *North American Review* 186, no. 625 (1907): 593–601.
60. "The Business Situation: Egypt," *Economist*, November 17, 1907, 756.
61. *Al-Ahrām*, May 22, 1907, quoted in Rizq, "Banking Revolution."
62. Martin Kramer, *Islam Assembled: The Advent of the Muslim Congresses* (New York: Columbia University Press, 1986), 37.
63. A. Vambéry, "A Mahomedan Congress in Cairo," *Times* (London), October 22, 1907, 15.
64. "Khuṭbat Ismāʿīl Bey Gaṣbrinkī," trans. ʿAbd al-Wahhāb al-Najjār, *al-Manār* 10 (1907): 658–73; the quotation comes from p. 670. On p. 672, Gasprinski once more tried to reassure Europeans who feared "pan-Islamism" that the conference would deal with social and economic rather than political issues.
65. *Al-Manār* 10 (1907): 664.
66. *Al-Manār* 10 (1907): 662–63. On Zeyn al-ʿĀbdīn Taghiyev, see Xiaobing Li and Michael Molina, eds., *Oil: A Cultural and Geographic Encyclopedia of Black Gold*, vol. 1 (Santa Barbara, Calif.: ABC-CLIO, 2014), 383; Tadeusz Swietochowski, *Russian Azerbaijan, 1905–1920: The Shaping of National Identity in a Muslim Community* (Cambridge: Cambridge University Press, 1985), 23, 27, 76; Tadeusz Swietochowski, *Russia and Azerbaijan: A Borderland in Transition* (New York: Columbia University Press, 1995), 23; and A. Holly Shissler, *Between Two Empires: Ahmet Ağaoğlu and the New Turkey* (London: I. B. Tauris, 2003), 108, 130–31. According to Audrey L. Altstadt, *The Azerbaijani Turks: Power and Identity Under Russian Rule* (Stanford, Calif.: Hoover Institution Press, 1992), Taghiyev's factory in Baku employed around 1,500 persons.
67. Eric Davis, *Challenging Colonialism: Bank Miṣr and Egyptian Industrialization, 1920–1941* (Princeton, N.J.: Princeton University Press, 1983), 50, 54, 92–93, 105. On the importance of 1907, also see Robert Vitalis, *When Capitalists Collide: Business Conflict and the End of Empire in Egypt* (Berkeley: University of California Press, 1995), 40. Arguably, Ṭalʿat Ḥarb and his allies carried forward an earlier program; see AbdelAziz EzzelArab, *European Control and Egypt's Traditional Elites—A Case Study in Elite Economic Nationalism* (Lewiston, N.Y.: Edwin Pellen Press, 2002).
68. Amy J. Johnson, *Reconstructing Rural Egypt: Ahmed Hussein and the History of Egyptian Development* (Syracuse, N.Y.: Syracuse University Press, 2004), 23–24; and Davis, *Challenging Colonialism*, 88, 99.
69. Kramer, *Islam Assembled*, 52. Apparently unaware of the 1907 crisis, Kramer argued that "the commercial theme did not interest Egyptian political factions" (40). The evidence provided here shows that there was, in fact, great interest in the theme of economic revival—in large part as a result of the 1907 crisis.
70. *Al-Manār*, "al-Aṣr al-māliyy wa-l-ribā wa-l-bunūk," 10 (1907): 430–34.
71. Kramer, *Islam Assembled*, chap. 4; Riḍā covered the initiative in *al-Manār* 10 (1907): 673ff.
72. Kramer, *Islam Assembled*, 41.
73. *Al-Manār* 10 (1907): 676–77.
74. *Al-Manār* 10 (1907): 677–78. Davis, *Challenging Colonialism*, 51–53, cites a couple of proposals for establishing banks in 1907 and 1908.
75. *Al-Manār* 10 (1907): 680.
76. As a precedent to this textbook, one may cite Khalīl Ghānim's introduction to political economy and household economics, titled *Kitāb al-iqtiṣād al-siyāsī, aw, Fann tadbīr al-manzil* (Cairo:

Maṭbaʿat Jarīdat Miṣr, 1879); see Michael Ezekiel Gasper, *The Power of Representation: Publics, Peasants, and Islam in Egypt* (Stanford, Calif.: Stanford University Press, 2009), 41. One may also cite the socioeconomic reflections in Rifāʿa al-Ṭahṭāwī's *Kitāb manāhij al-albāb al-Miṣrī fī mabāhij al-ādāb al-ʿaṣriyya* (Būlāq: al-Maṭbaʿa al-Miṣriya, 1869); see Islahi, *Economic Thinking*, 43–44. Al-Ṭahṭāwī also published a translation of French commercial laws, *Qānūn al-tijāra* (Bulāq: Muḥammad ʿAlwān, 1868), but Islahi did "not find any work of political economy in his translations."

77. For an exposition of Cromer's views, see E. R. J. Owen, "Lord Cromer and the Development of Egyptian Industry, 1883–1907," *Middle Eastern Studies* 2, no. 4 (1966): 282–301.
78. Riḍā, "Mabādiʾ al-Iqtiṣād al-Siyāsī" and "al-ʿAmal," *al-Manār* 11 (1908): 617–18 and 673–80. The two-volume textbook is Muḥammad Fahmī Ḥusayn's *Mabādiʾ al-iqtiṣād al-siyāsī* (Cairo: Maṭbaʿat al-Saʿāda, 1908); the chapter excerpted by Riḍā appears in vol. 1, pp. 64–73. For early use of the expression "laissez-faire" in connection with foreign traders, see François Quesnay, *Physiocratie, ou Constitution naturelle du gouvernement le plus avantageux au genre humain*, vol. 5, *Discussions et développemens sur quelques-unes des notions de l'économie politique* (Yverdon, 1769), 105–6.
79. See Adam Smith, *Tharwat al-umam* (Cairo: Dār al-Qāhira li-l-Ṭibāʿa, 1959). John Stuart Mill's "On Liberty" was translated by Ṭahā al-Sibāʿī during Riḍā's lifetime, under the title *al-Ḥurriyya* (Cairo: Maktabat al-Maṭbaʿat al-Shaʿb, 1922). The only mention of Karl Marx that I located in *al-Manār* is an article by Muḥammad al-Ghazālī, "Fī muḥīt al-daʿwāt," *al-Manār* 35 (1940): 531. The earliest translation of Karl Marx's *Das Kapital* seems to be a 1947 edition titled *Raʾs al-māl*, published in Cairo by Maktabat al-Naḥḍa al-Miṣriyya.
80. ʿAbduh cited Voltaire, Diderot, Rousseau, and Renan in *al-Manār* 5 (1902): 401.
81. Thus, for instance, see the quotations of Montesquieu in Muḥammad Rūḥī al-Khālidī, "Inqilāb al-ʿuthmānī wa-Turkiyyā al-fatāt: Ikhtilāl al-māliyya wa-irhāq al-falāḥ" *al-Manār* 11 (1908): 844. Also see Rafīq Bey al-ʿAẓm, "Asbāb suqūṭ al-dawla al-umawiyya," *al-Manār* 12 (1910): 945–46. The first article is replete with English and French keywords, such as pan-Islamism, théocratique, décentralisation, and féodalité. Yūsuf Āṣāf had translated Montesquieu's *De l'esprit des lois* under the title *Uṣūl al-nawāmis wa-l-sharāʾiʾ* (Cairo: al-Maṭbaʿa al-ʿUmūmiyya, 1891).
82. Muḥammad Rashīd Riḍā, "Iḥtifāl li-takrīm Aḥmad Fatḥī Zaghlūl," *al-Manār* 16 (1913): 550. Referenced here are the translations of Gustave Le Bon's *Lois psychologiques de l'évolution des peuples* (Sirr taṭawwūr al-umam) and Edmond Demolins's *À quoi tient la supériorité des Anglo-Saxons?* (Sirr taqaddum al-inklīz al-saksūniyyin), in addition to several other works. On the impact of Demolins and Le Bon on Egyptian intellectuals, see Timothy Mitchell, *Colonising Egypt* (Cambridge: Cambridge University Press, 1988), 110–11 and 122–25.
83. Louis de Jaucourt, "Monnoie," in *Encyclopédie, ou dictionnaire raisonné des sciences, des arts et des métiers, etc.*, ed. Denis Diderot and Jean le Rond d'Alembert (Chicago: University of Chicago, ARTFL Encyclopédie Project, Spring 2016), eds. Robert Morrissey and Glenn Roe, http://encyclopedie.uchicago.edu/, vol. 10, 644–63; and Rebecca L. Spang, *Stuff and Money in the Time of the French Revolution* (Cambridge, Mass.: Harvard University Press, 2015), 42–43.
84. Riḍā, "al-Intiqād ʿalā Muḥammad Farīd Wajdī," *al-Manār* 10 (1907): 470–71.
85. Al-Manār, "al-ʿAmal," *al-Manār* 11 (1908): 673–80.
86. Leor Halevi, "Is China a House of War? Chinese Questions, Arabic Answers, and the Translation of Salafism from Cairo to Canton, 1930–1932," *Die Welt des Islams* 59, no. 1 (2019): 33–69.
87. Riḍā, *al-Manār* 1 (1898): 9–13.

88. Riḍā, *al-Manār* 1 (1898): 77–79.
89. Riḍā, *al-Manār* 4 (1901): 732–36, 776–78; and Riḍā, *al-Manār* 5 (1902): 172–75 and passim. The main title of the series was "al-Umarāʾ wa-l-ḥukkām wa-nawʿ ḥukūmat al-islāmiyya."
90. Already in the first installment, Riḍā announced that the "the Salaf and the Khalaf" would figure as a topic; see "al-Muḥāwārāt bayna al-muṣliḥ wa-l-muqallid," *al-Manār* 3 (1900): 665–66. Albert Hourani, *Arabic Thought in the Liberal Age, 1798–1939* (Cambridge: Cambridge University Press, 1983), 230, drew on this dialogue to show that Riḍā's conception of the Salaf was far more rigid than ʿAbduh's. On the dialogue generally, see Jakob Skovgaard-Petersen, "Portrait of the Intellectual as a Young Man: Rashīd Riḍā's *Muḥāwārāt al-muṣliḥ wa-al-muqallid* (1906)," *Islam and Christian-Muslim Relations* 12, no. 1 (2001): 93–104. In the article "al-Salaf wa'l-Khalaf," *Encyclopaedia of Islam*, 2nd ed., ed. P. Bearman et al. (Leiden: Brill, 1954–), 8:900, E. Chaumont discusses several late medieval uses of this binary concept. Remarkably, he says, "there does not exist any special monograph on the theme," which remains neglected to this day. In quite a different context, see Joan DeJean, *Ancients Against Moderns: Culture Wars and the Making of a Fin de Siècle* (Chicago: University of Chicago Press, 1997), 6–15; and David A. Boruchoff, "The Three Greatest Inventions of Modern Times: An Idea and Its Public," chap. 6 in *Entangled Knowledge: Scientific Discourses and Cultural Difference*, ed. Klaus Hock (Münster: Waxmann, 2012).
91. *Al-Manār* 4 (1901): 462–66. In addition, Aḥmad Muḥammad al-Alfī requested an evaluation of an Indo-Islamic eschatological exegesis, *The Miracles of the Messiah*, written by the founder of the Aḥmadiyya Muslim Community. On "madhhab al-salaf," also see *al-Manār* 8 (1905): 614–20.
92. Itzchak Weismann, *Taste of Modernity: Sufism, Salafiyya, and Arabism in Late Ottoman Damascus* (Leiden: Brill, 2001), 280, 300–301.
93. Louis Massignon, "Les vraies origines dogmatiques du Wahhabisme," *Revue du monde musulman* 36 (1918–1919): 324–25. Cf. Henri Lauzière, "The Construction of *Salafiyya*: Reconsidering Salafism from the Perspective of Conceptual History," *International Journal of Middle East Studies* 42, no. 3 (2010): 369–89. On the effect that Ṣiddīq Ḥasan Khān had on a key reformer from Baghdad, Khayr al-Dīn al-Alūsī, see David Dean Commins, *Islamic Reform: Politics and Social Change in Late Ottoman Syria* (New York: Oxford University Press, 1990), 24–25.
94. See, for example, the entry on "Salafi" in *The Oxford Dictionary of Islam*, ed. John L. Esposito (Oxford: Oxford University Press, 2003), 275.
95. Originally published in 1884–1885, the journal did include an article with a promising title, "The Muslim Community's Past and Present; and a Treatment for its Maladies" (*Māḍī al-umma wa-ḥāḍiruhā wa-ʿilāj ʿilalihā*). But it did not represent the Salaf as a panacea. See Jamāl al-Dīn al-Afghānī and Muḥammad ʿAbduh, *al-ʿUrwa al-Wuthqa, wa-l-thawra al-taḥrīriyya al-kubra* (Cairo: Dār al-ʿArab, 1957), 13ff. On this topic, also see Lauzière, "The Construction of *Salafiyya*," 374.
96. Ernest Renan, "L'Islamisme et la science," *Journal des débats*, March 30, 1883.
97. Gemmal Eddine Afghan, [Lettre au Directeur], *Journal des débats*, May 18, 1883.
98. For a balanced reassessment, see Mark Sedgwick, *Muhammad Abduh* (London: Oneworld, 2010), 35, 66, 126.
99. Muḥammad ʿAbduh, *Risālat al-tawḥīd* (Cairo: al-Maṭbaʿa al-ʿĀmira al-Khayriyya, 1906), 8, 10.
100. ʿAbduh, *Risālat al-tawḥīd*, 11–13.
101. For a translation and discussion of ʿAbduh's autobiographical text, see Frank Griffel, "What Do We Mean by 'Salafi?' Connecting Muḥammad ʿAbduh with Egypt's Nūr Party in Islam's

Contemporary Intellectual History." *Die Welt des Islams* 55 (2015): 198–99. Griffel argues that ʿAbduh combined "an almost Kantian definition of Enlightenment with the notion of Salafism."

102. Muḥammad ʿAbduh, "al-Iḍṭihād fī al-Naṣrāniyya wa-l-Islām," *al-Manār* 5 (1902): 401ff; and Muḥammad ʿAbduh, *al-Islām wa-l-Naṣrāniyya maʿ al-ʿilm wa-l-madaniyya*, ed. Muḥammad Rashīd Riḍā, 2nd ed. (Cairo: al-Manār, 1905), 167–68. I have emphasized the date of these publications by ʿAbduh as well as the fact that they appeared under the auspices of *al-Manār* because scholars have uniformly represented Riḍā as building upon ʿAbduh's formulations. A chronological account of references to "the Salaf" by them shows, however, that ʿAbduh made some of his most significant appeals to "the ancestors" after Riḍā began his acclamations and that their references differed in substance and style.
103. See Peter Bernholz, *Monetary Regimes and Inflation: History, Economic and Political Relationships* (Cheltenham, U.K.: E. Elgar, 2003), 3, 14–15.
104. *Al-Manār* 22 (1921): 747–51. Typically, it is impossible to determine how long it took for Riḍā to respond to fatwa requests. In this instance, it is clear, however, that a question raised in July 1921 received a reply three months later, in October 1921.
105. Muḥammad Rashīd Riḍā, *Fatāwā al-Imām*, eds. Ṣalāḥ al-Dīn al-Munajjid and Yūsuf Q. Khūrī (Dār al-Kitab al-Jadīd: Beirut, 1970–), 5:1974–78, no. 717; and *al-Manār* 28 (1927): 575–78.
106. I have evoked here the title to Timur Kuran's book, *The Long Divergence: How Islamic Law Held Back the Middle East* (Princeton, N.J.: Princeton University Press, 2011), to suggest the similarity between Riḍā's thesis and Kuran's more developed, institutional-economic argument. Kuran does not cite Riḍā in the book, although Riḍā is perhaps the best example of a Muslim jurist who endeavored, albeit rather late, to reform Islamic law to encourage banking with interest, joint-stock corporations, and other capitalist institutions.
107. Muḥammad Rashīd Riḍā, *al-Khilāfa aw al-imāma al-ʿuẓmā: Mabāḥith sharʿiyya, siyāsiya, ijtimāʿiyya, iṣlāhiyya* (Cairo: Maṭbaʿat al-Manār, 1922), 97–102. The passage quoted was also analyzed in Hourani, *Arabic Thought*, 238.
108. Riḍā, *al-Khilāfa*, 97–102.
109. Davis, *Challenging Colonialism*; and Robert L. Tignor, "Bank Miṣr and Foreign Capitalism," *International Journal of Middle East Studies* 8 (1977): 161–81.
110. Israel Gershoni and James P. Jankowski, *Egypt, Islam, and the Arabs: The Search for Egyptian Nationhood, 1900–1930* (Oxford: Oxford University Press, 1987), 233.
111. As an "Islamic" banker, Riḍā would have had no problem sanctioning mutually advantageous interest-bearing loans, which did not fall (from his perspective) under the Qurʾanic ban on usury. He published and generally agreed with a fatwa written by a jurist from Hyderabad that made an extended case for the legality of such loans. See Muḥammad Rashīd Riḍā, *al-Ribā wa-l-muʿāmalāt fī al-Islām* (Port Said, al-Ẓāhir, Egypt: Maktabat al-thaqāfa al-dīniyya, 2001), 57–58, 63–66. On p. 7, Riḍā says that the fatwa was originally printed by al-Ḥukūma al-Āṣafiyya. The first installment, "al-Istiftāʾ fī ḥaqīqat al-ribā," appeared in *al-Manār* 30 (1929): 273–91. Subsequent installments were published under different titles, such as "Ḥaqīqat Ribā al-Qurʾān," in vol. 30 (1929–1930): 419–39, 501–3, 585–92, 665–72, 771–76; and vol. 31 (1930): 37–45. See the fine discussion of this fatwa in Muhammad Qasim Zaman, *Modern Islamic Thought in a Radical Age: Religious Authority and Internal Criticism* (Cambridge: Cambridge University Press, 2012), 120ff. Of course, the first "Islamic" banks that represented themselves as usury-free institutions emerged much later in Egyptian history; see Samer Soliman, "The Rise and Decline of the Islamic Banking Model in Egypt,"

in *The Politics of Islamic Finance*, ed. Clement M. Henry and Rodney Wilson, 265–85 (Edinburgh: Edinburgh University Press, 2004), 271.

5 The Qurʾan in the Gramophone: Sounds of Islamic Modernity from Cairo to Kazan

1. Muḥammad Rashīd Riḍā, *Fatāwā al-Imām*, eds. Ṣalāḥ al-Dīn al-Munajjid and Yūsuf Q. Khūrī (Dār al-Kitab al-Jadīd: Beirut, 1970–), 3:955–56, no. 354; and *al-Manār* 13 (1910): 906–8. Allen Koenigsberg's *The Patent History of the Phonograph, 1877-1912: A Source Book Containing 2,118 U.S. Sound Recording Patents & 1,013 Inventors Arranged Numerically, Chronologically and Alphabetically* (Brooklyn, N.Y.: AMP Press, 1990) profiles the period's many models. It showcases the Victrola and its predecessors on pp. lxi–lxv. See also Kyle S. Barnett, "Furniture Music: The Phonograph as Furniture, 1900–1930," *Journal of Popular Music Studies* 18, no. 3 (2006): 305, 312. For an authoritative though dated history of the phonograph, see Oliver Read and Walter L. Welch, *From Tin Foil to Stereo: Evolution of the Phonograph*, 2nd ed. (Indianapolis: H. W. Sams, 1976).
2. Andre Millard, *America on Record: A History of Recorded Sound*, 2nd ed. (Cambridge: Cambridge University Press, 2005), 41–2, 45–46, 62.
3. Muḥammad Kāmil al-Khulaʿī, *Kitāb al-mūsiqā al-Sharqī* (Maktabat al-Dār al-ʿArabiyya li-l-Kitāb: Cairo, 1993), 24. Also cited by A. J. Racy, *Making Music in the Arab World: The Culture and Artistry of* Ṭarab (Cambridge: Cambridge University Press, 2003), 71.
4. John Philip Sousa, "The Menace of Mechanical Music," *Appleton's Magazine* 8 (1906): 278–84. For Sousa's congressional statement, also see U.S. Congress, *Arguments Before the Committees on Patents of the Senate and House of Representatives, Conjointly, on the Bills S. 6330 and H.R. 19853, to Amend and Consolidate the Acts Respecting Copyright. June 6-9, 1906* (Washington, D.C.: Government Printing Office, 1906), 23–25.
5. Franz Kafka, *Letters to Felice*, ed. Erich Heller and Jürgen Born; trans. James Stern and Elizabeth Duckworth (New York: Schocken, 1973), 69–70 (November 27, 1912); and Friedrich A. Kittler, *Gramophone, Film, Typewriter*, trans. G. Winthrop-Young and M. Wutz (Stanford, Calif.: Stanford University Press, 1999), 225–26.
6. Walter Benjamin, "The Work of Art in the Age of Mechanical Reproduction," in *Illuminations*, ed. Hannah Arendt, trans. Harry Zohn, 217–51 (New York: Schocken, 1968), 220–21.
7. Benjamin, "Work of Art," 221–24.
8. Walter Benjamin, "Capitalism as Religion," trans. Chad Kautzer, chap. 15 in *The Frankfurt School on Religion: Key Writings by the Major Thinkers*, ed. Eduardo Mendieta (New York: Routledge, 2005); see also Michael Löwy, "Capitalism as Religion: Walter Benjamin and Max Weber," *Historical Materialism* 15 (2009): 60–73.
9. See Jonathan Sterne, *The Audible Past: Cultural Origins of Sound Reproduction* (Durham, N.C.: Duke University Press, 2003), 204–5, where Berliner's speech is quoted more fully and analyzed. Also see Peter Tschmuck, *Creativity and Innovation in the Music Industry*, 2nd ed. (Berlin: Spring-Verlag, 2012), 19–22.
10. Roland Gelatt, *The Fabulous Phonograph, 1877-1977*, 2nd rev. ed. (New York: Collier, 1977), 112.
11. Gelatt, *The Fabulous Phonograph*, 112.
12. Tschmuck, *Creativity and Innovation*, 27–30; and Anna Fishzon, *Fandom, Authenticity, and Opera: Mad Acts and Letter Scenes in Fin-de-Siècle Russia* (New York: Palgrave Macmillan, 2013), 117–18.

13. On the importance of the imperial Russian market and on Tatar recordings, see Pekka Gronow, "The Record Industry Comes to the Orient," *Ethnomusicology* 25 (1981): 255–56.
14. Michael S. Kinnear, *The Gramophone Company's Persian Recordings, 1899 to 1934: A Complete Numerical Catalogue* (Heidelberg, Aust.: Bajakhana, 2000); and Michael S. Kinnear, *The Gramophone Company's First Indian Recordings, 1899–1908* (Bombay: Popular Prakashan, 1994).
15. Arnold Wright, chief editor, and H. A. Cartwright, assistant editor, *Twentieth Century Impressions of Egypt: Its History, People, Commerce, Industries, and Resources* (London: Lloyd's Greater Britain, 1909), 472.
16. I have placed the terms "global market segmentation" and "the Islamic consumer" in quotation marks to highlight the anachronism in play. These terms entered into academic discourse in the 1970s and 1980s.
17. Antonio Gramsci, *Prison Notebooks*, vol. 2, ed. and trans. Joseph Buttigieg (New York: Columbia University Press, 2011), 215–20. Cf. Ronald Kline and Trevor Pinch, "Users as Agents of Technological Change: The Social Construction of the Automobile in the Rural United States," *Technology and Culture* 37, no. 4 (1996): 763–95.
18. Michael J. Piore and Charles F. Sabel, *The Second Industrial Divide: Possibilities for Prosperity* (New York: Basic, 1984), 258–82; David Harvey, *The Condition of Postmodernity* (Oxford: Basil Blackwell, 1989), chaps. 8–9; and Fredric Jameson, *Postmodernism, or, The Cultural Logic of Late Capitalism* (London: Verso, 1991). Also see David Gartman, "Postmodernism; or, The Cultural Logic of Post-Fordism?," *Sociological Quarterly* 39, no. 1 (1998): 119–37; Krishan Kumar, *From Post-Industrial to Post-Modern Society*, 2nd ed. (Malden, Mass.: Blackwell, 2005), chap. 4; and Ash Amin, "Post-Fordism: Models, Fantasies and Phantoms of Transition," in *Post-Fordism: A Reader*, ed. Ash Amin (Oxford, U.K.: Blackwell, 1994), 1–40.
19. Ziad Fahmy, *Ordinary Egyptians: Creating the Modern Nation Through Popular Culture* (Stanford, Calif.: Stanford University Press, 2011), 73.
20. Identical advertisements for the rival gramophone shops ran repeatedly in 1907 issues of *al-Mu᾽ayyad*. The National Odeon Store column reproduced here appeared in the November 28, 1907, issue, a day after the Francis Shop published one of its advertisements. On these and other advertisements, see Ali Jihad Racy, "Record Industry and Egyptian Traditional Music: 1904–1932," *Ethnomusicology* 20 (1976): 23–48.
21. On the emergence of Arab disc records and on Salāma Ḥijāzī, see Racy, *Making Music in the Arab World*, 25, 69. On the history of recording in Egypt, on Odeon, and on Salāma Ḥijāzī, see Ali Jihad Racy, "Musical Change and Commercial Recording in Egypt, 1904–1932" (Ph.D. thesis: University of Illinois, 1977), 79–123, as well as the article cited above. On Salāma Ḥijāzī's background in Qur᾽anic recitation, see Maḥmūd Aḥmad al-Ḥifnī, *Al-Shaykh Salāma Ḥijāzī, rā᾽id al-masraḥ al-ʿArabī* (Cairo: Dār al-Kātib al-ʿArabī, 1968) 27. For a list of Ḥijāzī's records that includes several religious titles, see Dār al-Kutub al-Qawmīya (Egypt), *Fihris al-mūsīqā wa-l-ghinā᾽ al-ʿArabī al-qadīm: al-Musajjala ʿalā usṭuwānāt*, vol. 1 (Cairo: Maṭbaʿat Dār al-Kutub al-Miṣriyya, 1998), 126–32. On the Gramophone Company's recordings, see Gronow, "Record Industry Comes to the Orient," 255. I thank A. J. Racy for corresponding with me about Salāma Ḥijāzī.
22. H. et J. Blumenthal Frères, "Odéon: Chants arabes sur disques double face" (1913/1914). The Blumenthal brothers, Julius and Hermann Blumenthal, eventually opened their own record-pressing factory. I am extremely grateful to Frédéric Lagrange for sharing a copy of this catalog with me.
23. Alternatively, it was a British company's record. The disc by "Abū Salāma al-Ḥijāzī" was surely a German-Egyptian product. But Odeon was not the only company that made Qur᾽anic discs.

A 1907 Zonophone/Gramophone catalog featured samples of Qurʾanic recitation by Muḥammad Salīm (al-Shaykh). For his discography, see Frédéric Lagrange, "Musiciens et poètes en Égypte au temps de la Nahda" (PhD thesis, Université de Paris VIII, à Saint-Denis, 1994), 843–48.

24. I have borrowed this term from Finbarr B. Flood's *Objects of Translation: Material Culture and Medieval "Hindu-Muslim" Encounter* (Princeton, N.J.: Princeton University Press, 2009), a book dedicated to the concept of "transcultural" artifacts.
25. See Stéphane A. Dudoignon, "Status, Strategies and Discourses of a Muslim 'Clergy' under a Christian Law: Polemics about the Collection of the *Zakāt* in Late Imperial Russia," in *Islam in Politics in Russia and Central Asia: Early Eighteenth to Late Twentieth Centuries*, ed. Stéphane A. Dudoignon and Komatsu Hisao, 43–73 (London: Routledge, 2001). On p. 71, he warns against exaggerating the *jadidi-qadimi* divide. Similarly, Adeeb Khalid, *Politics of Muslim Cultural Reform: Jadidism in Central Asia* (Berkeley: University of California Press, 1998), 99, argues for the porousness of the boundary.
26. For a brief, useful account of *jadidism*, see Galina M. Yemelianova, *Russia and Islam: A Historical Survey* (New York: Palgrave, 2002), 74–92. For greater nuance, see Khalid, *Politics of Muslim Cultural Reform*; and Ingeborg Baldauf, "Jadidism in Central Asia Within Reformism and Modernism in the Muslim World," *Die Welt des Islams* 41, no. 1 (2001): 72–88. On the *jadidi-qadimi* cleavage in relation to Russian policy, see Robert Geraci, "Russian Orientalism at an Impasse: Tsarist Education Policy and the 1910 Conference on Islam," in *Russia's Orient: Imperial Borderlands and Peoples, 1700–1917*, ed. Daniel R. Brower and Edward J. Lazzerini, 138–61 (Bloomington: Indiana University Press, 1997). On the *jadidi* embrace of new media (newspapers in particular) after the 1905 revolution, see James H. Meyer, *Turks Across Empires: Marketing Muslim Identity in the Russian-Ottoman Borderlands, 1856–1914* (Oxford: Oxford University Press, 2014), 88–90. Although interested in the "marketing" of an ethnic-religious identity, Meyer pays no attention to gramophone records and external, capitalistic efforts to profit from this identity.
27. Azade-Ayşe Rorlich, *The Volga Tatars: A Profile in National Resilience* (Stanford, Calif.: Hoover Institution Press, 1986), 93. Cf. Galina M. Yemelianova, "The National Identity of the Volga Tatars at the Turn of the 19th Century: Tatarism, Turkism and Islam," *Central Asian Survey* 16, no. 4 (1997): 558. Writing against studies that have "assumed the *Jadidist* triumph in the first two decades of the 20th century," Yemelianova points out that *qadimi mektebs* predominated in rural areas.
28. Yemelianova, "National Identity of the Volga Tatars," 558.
29. Riḍā, *Fatāwā*, 3:955–56, no. 354.
30. Azade-Ayşe Rorlich, "'The Temptation of the West:' Two Tatar Travellers' Encounter with Europe at the End of the Nineteenth Century," in *Passé Turco-Tatar, Présent Soviétique: Études offertes à Alexandre Bennigsen*, ed. Ch. Lemercier-Quelquejay, G. Veinstein and S. E. Wimbush, 389–410 (Paris: Éditions de l'École des hautes études en sciences sociales, 1986). On the eventual change from a pro-European to an anti-European position, see Khalid, *Politics of Muslim Cultural Reform*, 138, 294.
31. Zavdat S. Minnullin, "Fraternal and Benevolent Associations of Tatar Students in Muslim Countries at the Beginning of the Twentieth Century," in *Muslim Culture in Russia and Central Asia from the 18th to the Early 20th Centuries*, vol. 2, *Inter-Regional and Inter-Ethnic Relations*, ed. Anke von Kügelgen, Michael Kemper, and Allen J. Frank, 271–280 (Berlin: Schwarz, 1998), 274, 280.
32. Riḍā, *Fatāwā*, 3:942–94, no. 352; and *al-Manār* 13 (1910): 830–32.
33. Quotes in the rest of this section are from Riḍā, *Fatāwā*, 3:955–56, no. 354.
34. Millard, *America on Record*, 60, 62; and Gelatt, *Fabulous Phonograph*, 112–13, 135, 141.

35. For an exemplary article on the topic, see Frédéric Lagrange, "'Mettre en musique': La sélection et l'interprétation de la *qaṣīda* dans le répertoire égyptien savant enregistré sur disques 78 tours (1903–1925)," *Quaderni di Studi Arabi* 7 (2012): 169–206.
36. I am grateful to Ali Jihad Racy and Frédéric Lagrange for pointing out to me that, despite his training as a reciter, Salāma Ḥijāzī probably did not record recitations.
37. Fadlou Shehadi, *Philosophies of Music in Medieval Islam* (Leiden: Brill, 1995): 99–100; Kristina Nelson, *The Art of Reciting the Qurʾan* (Austin: University of Texas Press, 1985), 41; and Michael Cook, *Commanding Right and Forbidding Wrong in Islamic Thought* (Cambridge: Cambridge University Press, 2000), 413–14. On Islam and music, see Nelson, *Art of Reciting*, 32–35; Amnon Shiloah, *Music in the World of Islam: A Socio-cultural Study* (Detroit: Wayne State University Press, 1995), 31–44; and Habib Hassan Touma, *The Music of the Arabs*, trans. Laurie Schwarts, new ed. (Portland: Amadeus Press, 2003), 152–67.
38. I have slightly modified here the translation in Nelson, *Art of Reciting*, 41–42.
39. Cook, *Commanding Right*, 90–91, 98, 100, 172; see other instances under the indexed term, "Destruction of offending objects: musical instruments."
40. Cook, *Commanding Right*, 186.
41. Khalid, *Politics of Muslim Cultural Reform*, 150, 153. On a humorous controversy over a singing mullah, see Robert D. Crews, *For Prophet and Tsar: Islam and Empire in Russia and Central Asia* (Cambridge, Mass.: Harvard University Press, 2006), 130–31. In a different Central Asian context, see Hiromi Lorraine Sakata, *Music in the Mind: The Concepts of Music and Musician in Afghanistan* (Kent, Ohio: Kent State University Press, 1983), 38 and 76.
42. See N. Hanif, *Biographical Encyclopaedia of Sufis: Central Asia and Middle East* (New Delhi: Sarup & Sons, 2002), 283; and N. Hanif, *Biographical Encyclopaedia of Sufis: Africa and Europe* (New Delhi: Sarup & Sons, 2002), 115, 126. Hanif notes *jadids*' affiliation with the Naqshabandi order.
43. Khalid, *Politics of Muslim Cultural Reform*, 128–29, 152–54.
44. William A. Graham, "Qurʾan as Spoken Word: An Islamic Contribution to the Understanding of Scripture," *Approaches to Islam in Religious Studies*, ed. Richard Martin (Tucson: University of Arizona Press, 1985), 23–40; and Angelika Neuwirth, "Vom Rezitationstext über die Liturgie zum Kanon. Zu Entstehung und Wiederauflösung der Surenkomposition im Verlauf der Entwicklung eines islamischen Kultus," in *The Qur'ān as Text*, ed. Stefan Wild, 69–107 (Leiden: Brill, 1996).
45. Nelson, *Art of Reciting*, 32, 152, 177.
46. Nelson, *Art of Reciting*, 144–45, 151–52.
47. Frédéric Lagrange, "Réflexions sur quelques enregistrements de cantillation coranique en Égypte (de l'ère du disque 78 tours à l'époque moderne)," *Revue des Traditions Musicales des Mondes Arabe et Méditerranéen* 2 (2008): 31–32; and Virginia Danielson, *The Voice of Egypt: Umm Kulthūm, Arabic Song, and Egyptian Society in the Twentieth Century* (Chicago: University of Chicago Press, 1997), 23–26.
48. Lagrange, "Mettre en musique," 184–85.
49. These prostrations are known as *sujūd al-tilāwa*. See al-Shīrazī al-Firūzabādhī, *Kitāb al-Tanbīh*, trans. G.-H. Bousquet (Algiers: La Maison des Livres, 1949), part 1, p. 43; and Muḥammad al-Ghazālī, *Iḥyāʾ ʿulūm al-dīn*, 5 vols. (Beirut: Dār al-kutub al-ʿilmiyya, n.d.), vol. 1, book 8, sec. 7, p. 327.
50. Lagrange, "Réflexions," lists the relevant discography on pp. 52–54. He does *not* raise the ritual issue, which comes up in fatwas, concerning the performance of *sujūd al-tilāwa*. Another frequently recorded Qurʾanic chapter, al-Isrāʾ, also had a verse of prostration (17:109).

51. Compare to Robin Bernstein's account of a "scriptive thing," which in her analysis prompts and structures a course of behavior, in her book *Racial Innocence: Performing American Childhood from Slavery to Civil Rights* (New York: New York University Press, 2011), 70–71.
52. Riḍā, *Fatāwā*, 2:690, no. 261; and *al-Manār* 11 (1908): 582. The fatwa seeker in this instance was Muḥammad Najīb al-Tūntārī. Fatwa requests from Dongola, Sudan, and Singapore, cited below, also deal in part with the issue.
53. Crews, *For Prophet and Tsar*, 97.
54. On gramophone prices in this period, see Catriona Kelly, "'Better Halves?' Representations of Women in Russian Urban Popular Entertainments, 1870–1910," in *Women and Society in Russia and the Soviet Union*, ed. Linda Edmondson (Cambridge: Cambridge University Press, 1992), 25–26n21.
55. Lagrange, "Réflexions," 41–42. Lagrange's observation applies to commercial disc records. However, a partial inventory of ethnographic recordings of the Qur᾿an in wax cylinders suggests a concentration, in that medium, on short suras.
56. Riḍā, *Fatāwā*, 3:955–56, no. 354. Riḍā refers explicitly in this fatwa to the juridical presumption that "the foundation of things is permissibility" (*al-aṣl fī al-ashyā᾿ al-ibāḥa*). In the late 1920s, in the course of making a broader argument against judicial activism, Riḍā would return to this principle. See his *Yusr al-Islām wa-uṣūl al-tashrīᶜ al-ᶜāmm*, 2nd ed. (Cairo: Maṭbaᶜat Nahḍat Miṣr, 1956), 25–26.
57. Riḍā, *Fatāwā*, 3:955–56, no. 354.
58. On the early fatwas about the phonograph and on the subsequent rivalry with Riḍā, see Nico J. G. Kaptein, *Islam, Colonialism and the Modern Age in the Netherlands East Indies: A Biography of Sayyid Uthman (1822–1914)* (Leiden: Brill, 2014), 168–85, 195–97. See as well Jan Just Witkam, "Fatwa's over de fonografie van de koran," *ZemZem* 2 (2007): 82–95, 139–40. Witkam gives a good sense of the international dimension of these discussions, highlighting treatises by Sayyid ᶜUthmān (Batavia, 1899), Muḥammad Bakhīt al-Muṭīᶜī (Cairo, 1906–1907), and ᶜAbdallāh al-Zawāwī (Malakka, 1908). NB: Bakhīt is misidentified in the article as Najib.
59. For a paraphrase of Muḥammad Bakhīt's letter (*risāla*) on the phonograph, see the scientific review *al-Muqtaṭaf* 31 (1906) 353; and the analysis by Racy, "Record Industry," 34. For Riḍā's critique, see his article "Risālatān fī al-qirā᾿a al-fūnūghrāf wa-l-sikurtā" in *al-Manār* 9 (1906): 153. The debate between the muftis concerned not only phonographs and insurance but also juridical methods; see Jakob Skovgaard-Petersen, *Defining Islam for the Egyptian State: Muftis and Fatwas of the Dār Al-Iftā* (Leiden: Brill, 1997), 139–40.
60. Riḍā, *Fatāwā*, 2:609–12, no. 235; and *al-Manār* 10 (1907): 439–42.
61. Riḍā, *Fatāwā*, 2:609–12, no. 235; and *al-Manār* 10 (1907): 439–42. On Ḥasan ibn ᶜAlawī ibn Shihāb and another earlier controversy that embroiled him, see Ulrike Freitag, *Indian Ocean Migrants and State Formation in Hadhramaut: Reforming the Homeland* (Brill: Leiden, 2003), 246–47.
62. Riḍā, *Fatāwā*, 2:609–12, no. 235; and *al-Manār* 10 (1907): 439–42.
63. Riḍā, *Fatāwā*, 2:609–12, no. 235; and *al-Manār* 10 (1907): 439–42.
64. Riḍā, *Fatāwā*, 2:609–12, no. 235; and *al-Manār* 10 (1907): 439–42.
65. U.S. Congress, *Arguments Before the Committees on Patents*, 26–27; the statement for Victor was made by Horace Pettit. More generally, on the early American legislative debate over the ownership of sound, see Stuart Banner, *American Property: A History of How, Why, and What We Own* (Cambridge, Mass.: Harvard University Press, 2011), 109–20; and Alex Sayf Cummings, *Democracy of Sound: Music Piracy and the Remaking of American Copyright in the Twentieth Century* (Oxford: Oxford University Press, 2013), 21–29.

66. Michael Cook, *The Koran: A Very Short Introduction* (Oxford: Oxford University Press, 2000), 59–60.
67. Leor Halevi, "Religion and Cross-Cultural Trade: A Framework for Interdisciplinary Inquiry," in *Religion and Trade: Cross-Cultural Exchanges in World History, 1000–1900*, ed. Francesca Trivellato, Leor Halevi, and Cátia Antunes. Oxford: Oxford University Press), 55.
68. Tan Sooi Beng, "The 78 RPM Record Industry in Malaya Prior to World War II," *Asian Music* 28, no. 1 (1996–1997): 1–41; and Andreas Zangger, *The Swiss in Singapore* (Singapore: Didier Millet, 2013), 98.
69. See Piney Kesting, "A Doorway in Time," *Saudi Aramco World* 44, no. 5 (1993): 32–39. and Göran Larsson, *Muslims and the New Media Historical and Contemporary Debates* (Surrey, U.K.: Ashgate, 2011), 176–78. Also see Witkam, "Fatwa's over de fonografie"; and Kaptein, *Islam, Colonialism and the Modern Age*, 195–97.
70. Riḍā, *Fatāwā*, 3:1058, 1062, no. 397; and *al-Manār* 14 (1911): 671–73.
71. Riḍā, *Fatāwā*, 3:1035–40, no. 386; and *al-Manār* 14 (1911): 502–6.
72. Irfan Shahīd, *Byzantium and the Arabs in the Sixth Century*, vol. 2, part 1, *Toponymy, Monuments, Historical Geography, and Frontier Studies* (Washington, D.C.: Dumbarton Oaks), 204; and Jonathan Bloom, *Minaret: Symbol of Islam* (Oxford: Oxford University Press, 1989), 23.
73. See Touraj Atabaki, "Time, Labour-Discipline and Modernization in Turkey and Iran: Some Comparative Remarks," in *The State and the Subaltern: Modernization, Society and the State in Turkey and Iran*, ed. Touraj Atabaki, 1–16 (London: I. B. Tauris, 2007), 2.
74. David S. Landes, *Revolution in Time: Clocks and the Making of the Modern World* (Cambridge, Mass.: Harvard University Press, 1983), 57, 68, 77.
75. See Finbarr B. Flood, "The Medieval Trophy as an Art Historical Trope: Coptic and Byzantine 'Altars' in Islamic Contexts," *Muqarnas* 18 (2001): 62–63, 72, for an interesting distinction between the use of bells and *semantrons* in cross-cultural polemics. Compare to Atabaki, "Time, Labour-Discipline and Modernization," who argues that public clocks were opposed because they were associated with church bells.
76. On the close association between mechanical clocks and monasteries or churches, see Landes, *Revolution in Time*, 59, 68–69.
77. Remark by Anthony Reid, from a transcript of an interview with Margaret Coffey, on ABC Radio National, April 17, 2005. On the Dutch reconstruction of what was then known as Mesjid Raya, see Holly S. Smith, *Aceh: Art and Culture* (Singapore: Oxford University Press, 1997), 46. Smith says that the rulers of Aceh "actually banned the people from using the place, considering it inappropriate for public prayer service."
78. In an article titled "L'usage de la cloche chez les musulmans de Java" the *Revue du monde musulman* 15, no. 9 (1911): 386–87, published Hurgronje's letter as a newsworthy gloss to the fatwas on the *nāqūs* that had appeared earlier in *al-Manār*. For additional information on the *beḍug/bĕdoug*, see Eric Robert Taylor, *Musical Instruments of South-East Asia* (Singapore: Oxford University Press, 1989), 43 and 79. Also see Nico J. G. Kaptein, "The Voice of the 'Ulamâ': Fatwas and Religious Authority in Indonesia," *Archives de sciences sociales des religions* 125, no. 1 (2004): 118–19.
79. The quotation of al-Shabrāmallisī's text in the first of the Javanese fatwas printed in *al-Manār* 14 (1911), 502–3, is only an excerpt. For the extended discussion on the *nāqūs*, see *Ḥāshiyat Abī al-Ḍiyā᾿ Nūr al-Dīn ʿAlī ibn ʿAlī al-Shabrāmallisī*, printed alongside Muḥammad ibn Aḥmad al-Ramlī, *Nihāyat al-muḥtāj ilā sharḥ al-Minhāj fī al-fiqh ʿalā madhhab al-Imām al-Shāfiʿī*, 2nd ed., vol. 1 (Cairo: Muṣṭafā al-Bābī al-Ḥalabī, 1967), 399–400.

80. On personal links between Indonesian scholars and *al-Manār*, see Michael Francis Laffan, *Islamic Nationhood and Colonial Indonesia: The Umma Below the Winds* (London: Routledge, 2003), 137–39, 148–49; and Jajat Burhanudin, "Aspiring for Islamic Reform: Southeast Asian Requests for *Fatwās* in *Al-Manār*," *Islamic Law and Society* 12, no. 1 (2005): 12–17.
81. Riḍā, *Fatāwā*, 3:1035–40, no. 386; and *al-Manār* 14 (1911): 502–6.
82. See Danielson, *Voice of Egypt*, 27–28, 85–86. On the industry's decline in the 1930s, see Gronow, "Record Industry Comes to the Orient," 268, 275.
83. Riḍā, *Fatāwā*, 5:1915–16, no. 699; and *al-Manār* 28 (1927): 120.
84. Riḍā had dealt with the question about prostrations and phonographic recitations already in the 1908 fatwa issued to a Russian subscriber, *Fatāwā*, 2:690, no. 261.
85. Riḍā, *Fatāwā*, 6:2456–57, no. 960; and *al-Manār* 33 (1933): 429.
86. Riḍā, *Fatāwā*, 5:2145, no. 794; and *al-Manār* 30 (1929): 188.
87. Burnet Hershey, "Jazz Latitude," *New York Times Book Review & Magazine*, June 25, 1922; and *The Spectator*, "Wintering in Egypt," November 30, 1934, 38.
88. Frédéric Lagrange, "Women in the Singing Business, Women in Songs," *History Compass* 7, no. 1 (2009): 226–50; and Fahmy, *Ordinary Egyptians*, 73, 112–14.
89. Kittler, *Gramophone, Film, Typewriter*, 7–8, 16, 50, 69–70.

6 Telegraphs, Photographs, Railways, Law Codes: Tools of Empire, Tools of Islam

1. On the categorization of Hindus and others in South Asian Islamic legal thought, see Yohanan Friedmann, "Islamic Thought in Relation to the Indian Context," in *Islam et société en Asie du Sud*, ed. Marc Gaborieau, 79–91 (Paris: Editions de l'École des hautes études en sciences sociales, 1986).
2. *Al-Manār* 7 (1904): 575–76; and Muḥammad Rashīd Riḍā, *Fatāwa al-Imām*, eds. Ṣalāḥ al-Dīn al-Munajjid and Yūsuf Q. Khūrī (Dār al-Kitab al-Jadīd: Beirut, 1970–), 1:228–29, no. 98. Nūr al-Dīn inquired about the permissibility of "*al-shahāda bi-l-tilighrāf wa-ʿalayhi 'l-majūs wa-l-naṣārā*."
3. *Al-Manār* 7 (1904): 577–80; and Riḍā, *Fatāwa*, 1:231–36, no. 101. The fatwa seeker is identified by the titles *al-ṭabīb al-mawlawī* and *al-mufti fī Banjāb*. On the Aḥmadiyya leader Nūr al-Dīn and on this movement's loyalty to British rule, see Yohanan Friedmann, *Prophecy Continuous: Aspects of Aḥmadī Religious Thought and Its Medieval Background* (New Delhi: Oxford University Press, 2003), 13–14, 19, 35–36.
4. On the court cases of 1903 and 1904, see Maulana Muhammad Ali, *The Founder of the Ahmadiyya Movement: A Short Study of the Life of Hazrat Mirza Ghulam Ahmad*, new ed., ed. Zahid Aziz (Wembley, U.K.: Ahmadiyya Anjuman Lahore Publications, 2008), 51–52. On Khwaja Kamāl al-Dīn (d. 1932), Mirza Ghulam Ahmad's lawyer in the defamation case tried in Gurdaspur, see Ron Geaves, *Islam and Britain: Muslim Mission in an Age of Empire* (London: Bloomsbury Academic, 2018), 96–97.
5. *Al-Manār* 7 (1904): 577.
6. Shyamala Bhatia, *Social Change and Politics in Punjab, 1898–1910* (New Delhi: Enkay, 1987), 189.
7. On the Anglo-Indian legal system in the Punjab, with references to British efforts to codify customary "tribal" law and the eventual movement for restoring the shariʿa, see David Gilmartin, *Empire and Islam: Punjab and the Making of Pakistan* (Berkeley: University of California Press, 1988), 13–14, 63, 86, 92.

8. Broadly speaking, this chapter therefore contributes to scholarship on Islam and empire in the late nineteenth and early twentieth centuries, which has paid attention to the religious effects of technological and legal innovations. See, for example, the references to legal systems and transportation mechanisms in a recent collection of essays by David Motadel, ed., *Islam and the European Empires* (Oxford: Oxford University Press, 2014).
9. For an exemplary article that served to establish continuities in Riḍā's political thought, see Mahmoud Haddad's "Arab Religious Nationalist in the Colonial Era: Rereading Rashīd Riḍā's Ideas on the Caliphate," *Journal of the American Oriental Society* 117, no. 2 (1997): 255, 257.
10. Eliezer Tauber, "Rashīd Riḍā as a Pan-Arabist Before World War I," *Muslim World* 79 (1989), 102, 106–108.
11. Cf. Ahmad Dallal, "Appropriating the Past: Twentieth-Century Reconstruction of Pre-Modern Islamic Thought," *Islamic Law and Society* 7, no. 3 (2000): 337, 358; and Katharina A. Ivanyi, "Who's in Charge? The *Tafsir Al-Manar* on Questions of Religious and Political Authority," *Maghreb Review* 32, nos. 2–3 (2007): 175–95. I respond to Dallal's key argument at the end of this chapter. Ivanyi's article laments Riḍā's "vague and noncommittal" proposals for the constitution of religious and political authority in an Islamic nation-state. These proposals are almost identical, however, to the proposals that he made in the 1915 "General Organic Law of the Arab Empire" (to be analyzed at the end of this chapter), where he clearly envisioned an empire, not a nation-state.
12. On "imperial repertories," see Jane Burbank and Frederick Cooper, *Empires in World History: Power and the Politics of Difference* (Princeton, N.J.: Princeton University Press, 2010), 2–3, 287ff.
13. Eyal Zisser, "Rashid Rida: On the Way to Syrian Nationalism in the Shade of Islam and Arabism," in *The Origins of Syrian Nationhood: Histories, Pioneers and Identity*, ed. Adel Beshara, 123–40 (London: Routledge, 2011); and Elizabeth F. Thompson, "Rashid Rida and the 1920 Syrian-Arab Constitution: How the French Mandate Undermined Islamic Liberalism," chap. 15 in *The Routledge Handbook of the History of the Middle East Mandates*, ed. Cyrus Schayegh and Andrew Arsan, (London: Routledge, 2015).
14. Ami Ayalon, *The Press in the Arab Middle East: A History* (New York: Oxford University Press, 1995), 19, 56, 61–62.
15. *Al-Manār* 3 (1900): 361–64. On voluntary donations from Egypt, India, and other places, see William Ochsenwald, *The Hijaz Railroad* (Charlottesville: University Press of Virginia, 1980), 69–76.
16. Ochsenwald, *Hijaz Railway*, 30–34, 53.
17. Ochsenwald, *Hijaz Railway*, 34, 120–26.
18. Achille Sékaly, *Le Congrès du khalifat (Le Caire, 13–19 mai 1926) et le Congrès du monde musulman (La Mekke, 7 juin–5 juillet 1926)* (Paris: E. Leroux, 1926), 155–62; Uri M. Kupferschmidt, *The Supreme Muslim Council: Islam Under the British Mandate for Palestine* (Leiden: Brill, 1987), 191. Like Riḍā in 1900, one of the Indian eminences in the 1926 congress, Maulana Shawkat ʿAlī (d. 1939), described the railway project as a jihad. He also thanked the delegates who promoted the project for conforming to the prophetic imperative to expel the Christians and the Jews from Arabia.
19. Ochsenwald, *Hijaz Railway*, 11, 74–76. Lord Cromer, Ochsenwald reveals, prohibited Egyptian officials from complying with the collection of the special Ottoman tax on Muslim households.
20. Riḍā, *Fatāwa*, 3:1119–21, no. 430; and *al-Manār* 15 (1912): 30–31.
21. On this topic, see Feroz Ahmad, "Ottoman Perceptions of the Capitulations 1800–1914," *Journal of Islamic Studies* 11, no. 1 (2000): 1–20.

22. Edward Mead Earle, *Turkey, the Great Powers, and the Bagdad Railway: A Study in Imperialism* (New York: Macmillan, 1924), 81. Also see V. Necla Geyikdaği, *Foreign Investment in the Ottoman Empire International Trade and Relations 1854–1914* (London: Tauris Academic Studies, 2011), 49, 74, and passim. On the connection between the Ottoman foreign debt and railway projects in this period, also see Murat Birdal, *The Political Economy of Ottoman Public Debt: Insolvency and European Financial Control in the Late Nineteenth Century* (London: Tauris Academic Studies, 2010), 88–89, 171.
23. "Baghdad Railroad Convention," in *The Middle East and North Africa in World Politics: A Documentary Record*, vol. 1, *European Expansion, 1535–1914*, ed. and trans. Jacob C. Hurewitz, 495–506 (New Haven, Conn.: Yale Univ. Press, 1975), art. 1, 6, 10, 12.
24. Geyikdaği, *Foreign Investment*, 117. For details on the 1903 concession, see E. Pech, *Manuel des sociétés anonymes fonctionnant en Turquie*, 5th ed. (Constantinople: Gérard Frères, 1911), 238–39. For the broader historical context, see Jacques Tobie, "L'électrification dans l'aire syro-libanaise des origines à la fin du mandat français," *Outre-mers* 89, nos. 334–35 (2002): 527–54.
25. Ross Burns, *Damascus: A History* (London: Routledge, 2005), 258.
26. Concerning the Société anonyme impériale de Tramways et Eclairage électriques de Damas, see the "Rapport de M. I. Misson, Consul à Damas," in Royaume de Belgique, *Recueil consulaire contenant les rapports commerciaux des agents belges à l'étranger*, tome 156 (Bruxelles: Vromant & Co., 1912), 485–87, consulted through the HathiTrust archive.
27. Except where indicated, this paragraph is based on Ochsenwald, *Hijaz Railroad*, 107, 109, 118, 139–42.
28. The enterprise was the Société Ottomane du Chemin de fer Damas–Hamah et Prolongements.
29. Jean Riffier, *Les œuvres françaises en Syrie, 1860–1923* (Paris: L'Harmattan, 2000), 308–9. On the "new wave" of French developments in the Ottoman railway projects between 1905 and 1914, see Jacques Thobie, *Intérêts et impérialisme français dans l'empire ottoman (1895–1914)* (Paris: Publications de la Sorbonne, 1977), 317–73. On competition between French and German interests around 1910 to 1912, see L. Bruce Fulton, "France and the End of the Ottoman Empire," chap. 6 in *The Great Powers and the End of the Ottoman Empire*, ed. Marian Kent (London: George Allen & Unwin, 1984), 158–59.
30. Ironically, manufacturing difficulties forced the Ottomans to commission steel rails and traverses from Belgian and German factories. On this topic, see Murat Özyüksel, *The Hejaz Railway and the Ottoman Empire: Modernity, Industrialisation and Ottoman Decline* (London: I. B. Tauris, 2014), 109.
31. Riḍā, *Fatāwa*, 3:1119–21, no. 430; and *al-Manār* 15 (1912): 30–31.
32. This remained for a long time the official position of mainstream agitators for national independence. As late as 1919, the Egyptian delegation promised to perpetuate the capitulations as part of its strategic campaign for self-determination. See the documents in A. L. P. Burdett, *Arab Dissident Movements, 1905–1955*, vol. 1, *1905–1920* (Chippenham, Wiltshire, UK: Archive Editions, 1996), 93, 414. See p. 93 for Muḥammad Farīd's remarks, which I translated from French into English.
33. Roland Wenzlhuemer, *Connecting the Nineteenth-Century World: The Telegraph and Globalization* (Cambridge: Cambridge University Press, 2013), 211.
34. See Ilham Khuri-Makdisi, "Fin-de-Siècle Egypt: A Nexus for Mediterranean and Global Radical Networks," chap. 4 in *Global Muslims in the Age of Stream and Print*, ed. James L. Gelvin and Nile Green (Berkeley: University of California Press, 2014), 79.
35. Soli Shahvar, "Concession Hunting in the Age of Reform: British Companies and the Search for Government Guarantees; Telegraph Concessions through Ottoman Territories, 1855–58,"

Middle Eastern Studies 38, no. 4 (2002): 169–93; and Yakup Bektas, "The Sultan's Messenger: Cultural Constructions of Ottoman Telegraphy, 1848–1880," *Technology and Culture* 41, no. 4 (2000): 669–96.

36. "Convention Between Great Britain and Turkey, for the Establishment of Telegraphic Communications," ratified October 31, 1864, printed in *British and Foreign State Papers*, vol. 54, *1863–1864* (London: William Ridgway, 1869), 20–29. For a similar convention between Britain and Persia, ratified May 1, 1866, see, Hurewitz, *The Middle East and North Africa in World Politics*, 1:360–63. The latter convention was wonderfully detailed in its material specifications. It established, for example, that the British Government would for "a reasonable price" procure wire insulators, Morse instruments, and "two hundred iron posts for the marshy tracts of Bushire."
37. On the importance of inter-imperial collaboration as well as the globalization of capitalism to explain the control and organization of telecommunications in this period, see Dwayne Roy Winseck and Robert M. Pike, *Communication and Empire: Media, Markets and Globalization, 1860–1930* (Durham, N.C.: Duke University Press, 2007).
38. Christina Phelps Harris, "The Persian Gulf Submarine Telegraph of 1864," *Geographical Journal* 135 (1969): 169–90; and Daniel R. Headrick, *The Invisible Weapon Telecommunications and International Politics 1851–1945* (New York: Oxford University Press, 1991), 20–24. After a few years, the British had to find alternatives to telegraph island, but progress in the Gulf happened in fits and starts, and efforts to establish stations at times ended with violence. See, for example, Shaul Yanai, *The Political Transformation of Gulf Tribal States: Elitism and the Social Contract in Kuwait, Bahrain and Dubai, 1918–1970s* (Brighton, U.K.: Sussex Academic Press, 2014), 27.
39. Şerif Mardin, *Religion, Society, and Modernity in Turkey* (Syracuse, N.Y.: Syracuse University Press, 2006), 106.
40. On the wired road from Tripoli to Beirut via Qalamūn, see Karl Baedeker (Firm), *Palestine and Syria: Handbook for Travellers* (Leipzig: Karl Baedeker, 1876), 512. Also see Eugene Rogan, "Instant Communication: The Impact of the Telegraph in Ottoman Syria," in *The Syrian Land: Processes of Integration and Fragmentation: Bilād Al-Shām from the 18th to the 20th Century*, ed. Thomas Philipp and Birgit Schäbler (Stuttgart: F. Steiner, 1998), 117; and Eugene L. Rogan, *Frontiers of the State in the Late Ottoman Empire: Transjordan, 1850–1921* (Cambridge: Cambridge University Press, 1999), 63–65.
41. Clive Leatherdale, *Britain and Saudi Arabia, 1925–1939: The Imperial Oasis* (London: F. Cass, 1983), 79. On Bedouin tribes cutting telegraph lines, see Valeska Huber, *Channelling Mobilities: Migration and Globalisation in the Suez Canal Region and Beyond, 1869–1914* (Cambridge: Cambridge University Press, 2013), 161.
42. Yakup Bektaş, "Crossing Communal Boundaries: Technology and Cultural Diversity in the 19th Century Ottoman Empire," in *Multicultural Science in the Ottoman Empire*, ed. Ekmeleddin Ihsanoglu,, Kostas Chatzis, and Efthymios Nikolaidis, 139–47 (Turnhout, Belg.: Brepols, 2003). The quotation appears on p. l45.
43. Roderic H. Davison, *Essays in Ottoman and Turkish History, 1774–1923: The Impact of the West* (Austin: University of Texas Press, 1990), 150.
44. *Cook's Handbook for Palestine and Syria*, new ed. (London: Thomas Cook & Son, 1907), 5. Incidentally, the cost for an internal Ottoman telegram to a nonremote province was half a piastre per word. The corresponding rate for an international telegram to Egypt was a single franc.
45. Arnold Wright, chief editor, and H. A. Cartwright, assistant editor, *Twentieth Century Impressions of Egypt: Its History, People, Commerce, Industries, and Resources* (London: Lloyd's Greater Britain, 1909), 191; Karl Baedeker, *Egypt and the Sudân: Handbook for Travellers*, 6th ed. (Leipzig:

Karl Baedeker, 1908), xviii–xix. Incidentally, the tariff was twenty *millièmes* (2 piastres) for eight words. Egyptians could send a four-hundred-word telegram for E£1.

46. Even in the relatively independent telegraph of the Ottoman Empire, the number and the status of foreign experts employed (French speakers in particular) was not insignificant. See Davison, *Essays*, 155.
47. R. Michael Feener, "New Networks and New Knowledge: Migrations, Communications and the Refiguration of the Muslim Community in the Nineteenth and Early Twentieth Centuries," chap. 2 in *The New Cambridge History of Islam*, vol. 6: *Muslims and Modernity: Culture and Society Since 1800*, ed. Robert W. Hefner, (Cambridge, UK: Cambridge University Press, 2010), 42–43.
48. Rudolph Peters, "Religious Attitudes Towards Modernization in the Ottoman Empire: A Nineteenth-Century Pious Text on Steamships, Factories, and the Telegraph," *Die Welt des Islams* 26 (1986): 88, 93.
49. This section builds on earlier treatments of fatwas about telegraphy. Jakob Skovgaard-Petersen's *Defining Islam for the Egyptian State: Muftis and Fatwas of the Dār Al-Iftā* (Leiden: Brill, 1997), 80–99, analyzed 1910 and 1911 treatises on the subject written by Jamāl al-Dīn al-Qāsimī and Muḥammad Bakhīt al-Muṭīʿī. Among other things, he dealt with the distinction between *shahāda* and *khabar* and the debate over the new moon. In "Islamic Calendar Times," chap. 6 of *The Global Transformation of Time, 1870–1950* (Cambridge, Mass.: Harvard University Press, 2015), Vanessa Ogle turned to fatwas about telegraphy as part of a broader exploration of scientific and religious debates about time and its instruments.
50. In addition to the scholarship concerning material evidence cited in the introduction, see Jeanette A. Wakin, *The Function of Documents in Islamic Law: The Chapters on Sales from Ṭaḥāwī's* Kitāb al-shurūṭ al-kabīr (Albany: State University of New York Press, 1972), 1–10; and Baber Johansen, "Formes de langage et fonctions publiques: stéréotypes, témoins et offices dans la preuve par l'écrit en droit musulman," *Arabica* 44 (1997): 333–76.
51. On questions of equality/inequality, see Anver M. Emon, *Religious Pluralism and Islamic Law: "Dhimmīs" and Others in the Empire of Law* (Oxford: Oxford University Press, 2012), 138. For a progressive interpretation by one of Riḍā successors in Egypt, see Kate Zebiri, *Mahmūd Shaltūt and Islamic Modernism* (Oxford: Clarendon, 1993), 102.
52. Alan M. Guenther, "Syed Mahmood and the Transformation of Muslim Law in British India" (PhD diss., McGill University, 2004), 205.
53. Warren Hastings, *Mufassal Regulations* (1780), as quoted by Scott Alan Kugle, "Framed, Blamed and Renamed: The Recasting of Islamic Jurisprudence in Colonial South Asia," *Modern Asian Studies* 35 (2001): 262n16.
54. Whitley Stokes, *The Anglo-Indian Codes: Adjective Law* (Oxford: Clarendon, 1888), 812, as cited by Elizabeth Kolsky, *Colonial Justice in British India* (Cambridge: Cambridge University Press, 2010), 117.
55. James Fitzjames Stephen, ed., *The Indian Evidence Act (I. of 1872), with an Introduction on the Principles of Judicial Evidence* (London: Macmillan, 1872), chap. 4, art. 59, p. 178; and chap. 6, art. 92, pp. 189–91.
56. On the internal debates behind these legal reforms, see Kolsky, *Colonial Justice*, 110–22. Kolsky shows that British codifiers maintained the admissibility oaths and oral testimonials, despite their doubts about their truthfulness, because they did not want to risk excluding any method for what one commissioner called "the admission of truth." For a brief treatment of the colonial insistence on documentary evidence, see Michael R. Anderson, "Islamic Law and the Colonial Encounter in British India," in *Institutions and Ideologies: A SOAS South Asia Reader*, ed. David Arnold and Peter Robb, 165–85 (Surrey, U.K.: Curzon Press, 1993), 178–79.

57. Christopher Pinney, *Camera Indica: The Social Life of Indian Photographs* (Chicago: University of Chicago Press, 1997), 69–70. I am grateful to Barry Flood for this reference.
58. Stephen, *Indian Evidence Act*, chap. 5, art, 88, p. 187.
59. Deep Kanta Lahiri Choudhury, *Telegraphic Imperialism: Crisis and Panic in the Indian Empire, c.1830–1920* (Basingstoke, U.K.: Palgrave Macmillan, 2010), 68–75.
60. *The Emperor vs. Janan*, Criminal Appeal No. 605 of 1902, reported by Alweyne Turner, ed., *The Punjab Record or Reference Book for Civil Officers*, vol. 38 (Lahore: Civil and Military Gazette Press, 1904), 39–41.
61. Stephen, *Indian Evidence Act*, chap. 5, art. 63, pp. 179–80.
62. Charles F. Williams, ed., *The American and English Encyclopaedia of Law* (Long Island, N.Y.: Edward Thompson, 1894), 25:876–81. It is a measure of late nineteenth-century legal interest in new media that this publication devoted approximately 150 pages to "telegraphs and telephones." On the distinction between the original and the wired telegram, I have also consulted Tarapada Banerji, *The Indian Evidence Act, No. 1 of 1872* (Calcutta: Mukhurji & Co., 1896), 271. His brief comment on article 88 reads: "In England the original message is the best evidence, and in the absence of proof that the original has been destroyed, no copy is admissible in evidence."
63. Guenther, "Syed Mahmood," 159, 243. On p. 247, Guenther translates the verb "*mansūkh hōnā*" as referring to "abolishment" of previous rules of evidence. The original English text, at article 2, refers to the "repeal" of "all rules of evidence" that had not been incorporated into statutes, acts, or regulations, in force. The Islamic term "*mansūkh*" has the connotation of a lawful abrogation.
64. For the historical background, see Uma Yaduvansh, "Decline of the Role of the Qāḍīs in India, 1793–1876," *Studies in Islam* 6 (1969): 155–71; Tahir Mahmood, *Muslim Personal Law: Role of the State in the Indian Subcontinent*, 2nd ed. (Nagpur: All India Reporter, 1983), 54–59; and Robert Ivermee, "*Shari'at* and Muslim Community in Colonial Punjab, 1865–1885," *Modern Asian Studies* 48 (2014): 1068–95.
65. Riḍā, *Fatāwa*, 1:228–29, no. 98; and *al-Manār* 7 (1904): 575–76.
66. See David A. King, "On the Role of the Muezzin and the *Muwaqqit* in Medieval Islamic Society," in *Tradition, Transmission, Transformation: Proceedings of Two Conferences on Pre-Modern Science Held at the University of Oklahoma*, ed. F. Jamil Ragep, Sally P. Ragep, Steven Livesey, 285–346 (Leiden: Brill, 1996), 289–95; and David A. King, *Astronomy in the Service of Islam* (Aldershot, U.K.: Variorum, 1993), art. 1, p. 252.
67. Rogan, "Instant Communication," 119.
68. Riḍā, *Fatāwa*, 1:67–68, no. 25; and *al-Manār* 6 (1904): 862. Due to internal references to places, dates, and past issues of *al-Manār*, this exchange gives a sense of the speed of Islamic legal communications in the era. The Bahraini shaykh penned his question at some point after reading an article in the November 20, 1903, issue of *al-Manār*; Riḍā published his fatwa in response in the February 3, 1904 issue. The entire exchange transpired in ten weeks.
69. Ogle, *Global Transformation of Time*, 164; On Barak, *On Time: Technology and Temporality in Modern Egypt* (Berkeley: University of California Press, 2013), 123–24; and Daniel A. Stolz, *The Lighthouse and the Observatory: Islam, Science, and Empire in Late Ottoman Egypt* (Cambridge: Cambridge University Press, 2018), 259–62. Barak argues that what "virtually conditioned" Riḍā's response was the telegraphic dissemination of "Cairo time" to Egypt's provinces. He contends that Riḍā "accepted the centralizing logic of his day" and that he "succumbed to the authority of the central government of the nation-state, thus ensuring temporal harmony." The problem

for Muslim communities overseas, he speculates, was the speed by which Egyptian newspapers travelled on steamships and trains. Stolz's book reached my desk when the present book was already in press. His nuanced discussion of Riḍā's fatwas on the subject confirms and extends Ogle's and Barak's analyses.

70. Kmar Bendana, "M'hamed Belkhûja (Tunis, 1869–1943): Un historien en situation colonial," *Revue d'histoire des sciences humaines* 24, no. 1 (2011): 17–34.
71. Riḍā, *Fatāwa*, 3:875–78, no. 323; and *al-Manār* 13 (1910): 187–91. (An apparent misprint in *al-Manār* indicates pp. 161, 188–91.) For the historical context, see Kenneth J. Perkins, *Tunisia: Crossroads of the Islamic and European Worlds* (London: Helm, 1986), 92–95; Arnold H. Green, *The Tunisian Ulama, 1873–1915: Social Structure and Response to Ideological Currents* (Leiden: Brill, 1978), 208–9; Carmel Sammut, *L'impérialisme capitaliste français et le nationalisme tunisien (1881–1914)* (Paris: Publisud, 1983), 121–37, 263–70; and Taoufik Ayadi, *Mouvement réformiste et mouvements populaires à Tunis (1906–1912)* (Tunis: Imprimerie officielle de la République tunisienne, 1986), 49–68.
72. On France's telegraph monopoly, see Donald Vernon McCay, "The French in Tunisia," *Geographical Review* 35 (1945): 376, 383; Marcel Emerit, "La Pénétration industrielle et commerciale en Tunisie et les origines du Protectorat," *Revue Africaine* 96 (1952): 199–202; and Perkins, *Tunisia*, 75. On telegraph lines reaching remote places in Tunisia, see Frank Edward Johnson, "The Mole Men: An Account of the Troglodytes of Southern Tunisia," *National Geographic Magazine* 22 (1911): 821. Nomads frequently cut telegraph lines; see Nancy Elizabeth Gallagher, *Medicine and Power in Tunisia, 1780–1900* (Cambridge: Cambridge University Press, 2002), 73. For a broader perspective on the French telegraphic network, see Daniel R. Headrick, *The Tentacles of Progress: Technology Transfer in the Age of Imperialism, 1850–1940* (Oxford: Oxford University Press, 1988), 110–13.
73. On favorable attitudes by the *ʿulamāʾ* toward the telegraph, see Green, *Tunisian Ulama*, 105, 121.
74. M. W. Daly, *Empire on the Nile: The Anglo-Egyptian Sudan, 1898–1934* (Cambridge: Cambridge University Press, 1986), 208–9; Haim Shaked, *The Life of the Sudanese Mahdi*, foreword by P. M. Holt (New Brunswick, N.J.: Transaction, 1978), 5, 133, 155; and Richard Leslie Hill, *Egypt in the Sudan, 1820–1881* (London: Oxford University Press, 1959), 100–101, 130–31, 157–58.
75. Riḍā, *Fatāwa*, 3:875–78, no. 323; and *al-Manār* 13 (1910): 187–91.
76. Riḍā, *Fatāwa*, 1:65–66, no. 23; and *al-Manār* 6 (1903): 860.
77. For context, see Allen J. Frank, *Muslim Religious Institutions in Imperial Russia: The Islamic World of Novouzensk District and the Kazakh Inner Horde, 1780–1910* (Leiden: Brill, 2001), 105–6, 120–33; and Robert D. Crews, *For Prophet and Tsar: Islam and Empire in Russia and Central Asia* (Cambridge, Mass.: Harvard University Press, 2006), 49–60.
78. Riḍā, *Fatāwa*, 3:1061, no. 396.
79. See Jamal J. Elias, *Aisha's Cushion: Religious Art, Perception, and Practice in Islam* (Cambridge, Mass.: Harvard University Press, 2012), 9–12; and Leor Halevi, "Christian Impurity vs. Economic Necessity: A Fifteenth-Century Fatwa on European Paper." *Speculum* 83, no. 4 (2008): 940–41.
80. Riḍā, *Fatāwa*, 1:65–66, no. 23; and *al-Manār* 6 (1903): 860.
81. For the correspondence with Ḥājjī ʿAbdallāh Aḥmad, see Riḍā, *Fatāwa* 3:1060–62, no. 396; and *al-Manār* 14 (1911): 671–73. In response to a Meccan query, see Riḍā, *Fatāwa* 3:1141–44, no. 439; and *al-Manār* 15 (1912): 903–6. In response to a Singaporean question about sculpture, engraving and photography, see Riḍā, *Fatāwa* 4:1392–1418, no. 547; and *al-Manār* 20 (1917): 220–35, 270–76. On Ḥājjī ʿAbdallāh Aḥmad, see Azyumardi Azra, "Transmission of al-Manār's Reformism

to the Malay-Indonesian World: The Case of *al-Imām* and *al-Munīr*," in *Intellectuals in Modern Islamic World: Transmission, Transformation, Communication*, ed. Stéphane A. Dudoignon, Komatsu Hisao, and Kosugi Yasushi (London: Routledge, 2009), 153–56. On the 1916 controversy involving Ḥājjī ʿAbdallāh Aḥmad's use of photos, see Deliar Noer, *The Modernist Muslim Movement in Indonesia, 1900–1942* (Singapore: Oxford University Press, 1973), 39, 96. In a subsequent chapter, we'll turn to Ḥājjī ʿAbdallāh Aḥmad's 1911 questions about dress.

82. Indira Falk Gesink, *Islamic Reform and Conservatism: Al-Azhar and the Evolution of Modern Sunni Islam*, rev. ed. (New York: I. B. Tauris, 2010), 183–86, 194–95.
83. Gérard de Nerval, "Les femmes du Caire: Scènes de la vie égyptienne," *Revue des deux mondes* 14 (1846): 413. De Nerval wrote: "Elles se décident sans difficulté à laisser étudier les formes des principales races de l'Égypte, mais la plupart tiennent à conserver leur figure voilée; c'est là le dernier refuge de la pudeur orientale."
84. Alexander A. Boddy, *From the Egyptian Ramleh: Sketches of Delta Life and Scenes in Lower Egypt* (London: Gay & Bird, 1900), 30.
85. Percy R. Salmon, *A Photographic Expedition in Egypt, Palestine, Turkey & Greece* (London: Strangeways & Sons, 1903), 16. Along these lines, publications emerged with titles such as *On the Nile with the Camera* by Anthony Wilkin (New York: 1897).
86. W. M. Flinders Petrie, *A Season in Egypt: 1887* (London: Field & Tuer, 1888), 4.
87. Charles S. Myers, "Contributions to Egyptian Anthropology: Tatuing," *Journal of the Anthropological Institute of Great Britain and Ireland* 33 (January–June 1903): 82–89, at 83. Also see Charles S. Myers, "Contributions to Egyptian Anthropometry. II.—The Comparative Anthropometry of the Most Ancient and Modern Inhabitants," *Journal of the Anthropological Institute of Great Britain and Ireland* 35 (January–June 1905): 80–91.
88. Charles S. Myers, "Contributions to Egyptian Anthropology: V. General Conclusions," *Journal of the Anthropological Institute of Great Britain and Ireland* 38 (1908): 99–147, at 102–3. In this article, Myers revealed that he left his archive of anthropometric measurements, together with the photographs, at the Royal Anthropological Institute. Also see Omnia El Shakry, *The Great Social Laboratory: Subjects of Knowledge in Colonial and Postcolonial Egypt* (Stanford, Calif.: Stanford University Press, 2007), 18.
89. Stephen Sheehi, *Arab Imago: A Social History of Portrait Photography, 1860–1910* (Princeton, N.J.: Princeton University Press, 2016), xxi, 11, 61–64, 184–85.
90. For the broader context of police photography in the late nineteenth century, see Peter Hamilton, "Policing the Face," chap. 3 in *The Beautiful and the Damned: The Creation of Identity in Nineteenth Century Photography*, ed. Peter Hamilton and Roger Hargreaves (Aldershot, U.K.: Lund Humphries, 2001); and Pinney, *Camera Indica*, 21–25. To my regret, I have not succeeded in locating any treatment of the topic by historians of photography in Egypt, who have largely been interested in Orientalism. See, for example, see Ali Behdad and Luke Gartlan, eds., *Photography's Orientalism: New Essays on Colonial Representation* (Los Angeles: Getty Research Institute, 2013).
91. Mario M. Ruiz, "Intimate Disputes, Illicit Violence Gender, Law, and the State in Colonial Egypt, 1849–1923" (PhD thesis: University of Michigan, 2004), 131.
92. Sheehi, *Arab Imago*, 172.
93. Harold Tollefson, *Policing Islam: The British Occupation of Egypt and the Anglo-Egyptian Struggle over Control of the Police, 1882–1914* (Westport, Conn.: Greenwood Press, 1999), 88.
94. Tollefson, *Policing Islam*, 116, remarks that in 1901 the Anthropometric Bureau began "to rely only on fingerprints." Tollefson's book generally disregards photography, however, and I

doubt that this was the case. Photographs of crime scenes were probably taken during the collection of fingerprints. Furthermore, it is clear that Cairo's Anthropometric Bureau collected cephalic measurements because Harvey Pasha gave a biometrician access to a random sample of a "series of 10,000 measurements of modern Egyptian criminals." This exchange is recorded in J. I. Craig, "The Anthropometry of Modern Egyptians," *Biometrika* 8 (1911): 66–78. On ways to make and use "judiciary portraits," the classic work is Alphonse Bertillon's *La photographie judiciaire, avec un appendice sur la classification et l'identification anthropométriques* (Paris: Gauthier-Villars, 1890). On the relationship between photography and anthropometry, see James R. Ryan, *Picturing the Empire: Photography and the Visualization of the British Empire* (London: Reaktion, 1997), chap. 5.

95. Swift Macneill, Comment in the Debate on the Consolidated Fund, (Appropriation) Bill, August 19, 1907, in *The Parliamentary Debates* (authorised ed.), 4th series, 2nd sess. of the 28th Parliament of the United Kingdom of Great Britain and Ireland, 7 Edward VII, vol. 181, no. 13 (London: Wyman and Sons, 1907), col. 294–97. In an earlier parliamentary debate on the Denshawi Sentences, held on July 19, 1906, the same member of parliament brought up the issue and pointedly asked whether military or civilian photographers had captured the executions.
96. Riḍā, *Fatāwa*, 1:231–36, no. 101; *al-Manār* 7 (1904): 577–80.
97. Riḍā, *Fatāwa*, 1:231–36, no. 101; *al-Manār* 7 (1904): 577–80. On Riḍā's fatwas concerning non-Muslim judiciary systems, also see Umar Ryad, "A Prelude to *Fiqh al-Aqalliyyât*: Rashîd Ridâ's Fatwâs to Muslims Under Non-Muslim Rule." In *In-Between Spaces: Christian and Muslim Minorities in Transition in Europe and the Middle East*, ed. Christiane Timmerman, Johan Leman, Hannelore Roos, and Barbara Segaert, 239–70 (Bruxelles: P.I.E. Peter Lang, 2009), 251–52.
98. Leonard Wood, *Islamic Legal Revival: Reception of European Law and Transformations in Islamic Legal Thought in Egypt, 1875–1952* (Oxford: Oxford University Press, 2016), 57–62, 79–80. Wood writes that Riḍā consistently argued against man-made European law, upheld the "supremacy" of the shariʿa, and "rejected the notion of a separation between religion and state in Muslim societies, calling this concept a Christian innovation." Perhaps in some respects, but the 1904 fatwa for Punjab shows a different aspect of his thought.
99. Riḍā, *al-Manār* 12 (1909): 239–240. Cf. Zaki Badawi, *The Reformers of Egypt* (London: Croom Helm, 1978), 103, which elides the Ottoman context.
100. Eliezer Tauber, *The Emergence of Arab Movements* (London: Routledge, 1993), 64–65; and Tauber, "Rashīd Riḍā as a Pan-Arabist," 105.
101. Sayid Mohamed Rashid Rida, "General Organic Law of the Arab Empire," Wingate Papers, held by Durham University Library, Archives and Special Collections, SAD. 135/7/102-104 (December 1–31, 1915).
102. Tauber, "Riḍā as a Pan-Arabist," 106–8, 111.
103. Rida, "General Organic Law," 1, art. 1.
104. Rida, "General Organic Law," 1-2, art. 5.
105. Rida, "General Organic Law," 2, art. 7, 9, and 10.
106. Rida, "General Organic Law," 3, art. 12 and 13.
107. Rida, "General Organic Law," 2, art. 10.
108. Dallal, "Appropriating the Past," 337, 358. Written to affirm "the role of Islamic discursive culture and ideology in society," the article criticized economic historians for positing "a problematic dichotomy between the 'unreal' ideas and the 'real' material forces at work in society."

7 Arabian Slippers: The Turn to Nationalistic Consumption

1. On the earlier, form-fitting style of the turn of the century, see Brent Shannon, *The Cut of His Coat: Men, Dress, and Consumer Culture in Britain, 1860–1914* (Athens: Ohio State University Press, 2006), 82–83. On the Roaring Twenties' baggy trousers, see Maria Costantino, *Men's Fashion in the Twentieth Century: From Frock Coats to Intelligent Fibers* (New York: Costume & Fashion Press, 1997), 36–38.
2. Muḥammad Rashīd Riḍā, *Fatāwā al-Imām*, ed. Ṣalāḥ al-Dīn al-Munajjid and Yūsuf Q. Khūrī (Dār al-Kitab al-Jadīd: Beirut, 1970–), 5:2055, no. 740; and *al-Manār* 29 (1928): 108–9. The relevant, oft-cited *ḥadīth* was recorded by Aḥmad ibn al-Ḥusayn al-Bayhaqī, *al-Sunan al-kubrā*, ed. Muḥammad ʿAbd al-Qādir ʿAṭā (Beirut: Manshūrāt Muḥammad ʿAlī Bayḍūn and Dār al-Kutub al-ʿIlmiyya, 2003), 2:235 (as marked on the margins), no. 3263. Incidentally, there were unisex Coptic clothes in the early Islamic period, but the concern over their revealing the body's shape was directed at female usage. For a relevant set of traditions by Ibn Abī Shayba and Ibn Ḥanbal, see Aḥmad b. Abī Bakr b. Ismāʿīl al-Būṣīrī, *Itḥāf al-khiyara al-mahara bi-zawāʾid al-masānīd al-ʿashara* (Riyadh: Dār al-Waṭan li-l-Nashr, 1999), 4:502, nos. 4021–23. (I consulted this work only in an online edition). These sartorial traditions relate that the Prophet gave a Coptic garment (originally given to him by Diḥya al-Kalbī) to Usāma ibn Zayd, who in turn gave it to his wife. When Muḥammad found out about this, he suggested that she should wear under it a fine cape (*ghilāla*). He feared that it would reveal "the shape of her bones" (*ḥajm al-ʿiẓāmiha*). ʿUmar I's order against men dressing their women in form-fitting Coptic clothes was part of a caliphal sermon against avaricious consumption in a time of war; see M. J. de Goeje and E. Prym, eds., *Annales quos scripsit Abu Djafar Mohammed Ibn Djarir At-Tabari* (Leiden: Brill, 1893), ser. 1, vol. 5, p. 2759.
3. Riḍā, *Fatāwā*, 6:2351, no. 887; and *al-Manār* 31 (1930): 737–38. The question was from ʿAyḍa b. Aḥmad al-Baḥrī al-Sadafī from Ṣōlō (apparently Surakarta in Central Java).
4. In 1907 imported textiles goods were valued at over E£7 million, when no other class of imports reached E£4 million. In 1920 the value of imported yarns and textiles surpassed E£34 million; the second most valuable import category that year was not even half that much. In 1921, as a result of the cotton crisis, the value of imported yarns and textiles dropped very sharply, by more than 50 percent. Still, it remained the leading class of imports. Arnold Wright, chief editor, and H. A. Cartwright, assistant editor, *Twentieth Century Impressions of Egypt: Its History, People, Commerce, Industries, and Resources* (London: Lloyd's Greater Britain, 1909), 157–58, tables; and E. Homan Mulock, Department of Overseas Trade, *Report on the Economic and Financial Situation of Egypt, dated April, 1922* (London: His Majesty's Stationery Office, 1922), app. 5.
5. Muḥammad Rashīd Riḍā, "Kalimat fī al-ḥijāb," *al-Manār* 2 (1899): 369–73; and Muḥammad Rashīd Riḍā, *Ḥuqūq al-nisāʾ fī al-Islām: wa-ḥaẓẓihinna min al-iṣlāḥ al-Muḥammadī al-ʿāmm: Nidāʾ li-l-jins al-laṭīf*, ed. Muḥammad Nāṣir al-Dīn al-Albānī (Beirut: al-Maktab al-Islāmī, 1984), 182–84. Also see Juan Ricardo Cole, "Feminism, Class, and Islam in Turn -of-the-Century Egypt," *International Journal of Middle East Studies* 13, no. 4 (1981): 392–93, 403; Valerie J. Hoffman-Ladd, "Polemics on the Modesty and Segregation of Women in Contemporary Egypt," *International Journal of Middle East Studies* 19, no. 1 (1987): 26–27; and Kenneth M. Cuno, *Modernizing Marriage: Family, Ideology, and Law in Nineteenth and Early Twentieth Century Egypt* (New York: Syracuse University Press, 2015): 108–9.
6. Margot Badran, *Feminists, Islam, and Nation: Gender and the Making of Modern Egypt* (Princeton, N.J.: Princeton University Press, 1995); Beth Baron, *Egypt as a Woman: Nationalism, Gender, and*

Politics (Berkeley: University of California Press, 2005); Mona L. Russell, *Creating the New Egyptian Woman: Consumerism, Education, and National Identity, 1863–1922* (New York: Palgrave Macmillan, 2004); Lisa Pollard, *Nurturing the Nation: The Family Politics of Modernizing, Colonizing and Liberating Egypt, 1805–1923* (Berkeley: University of California Press, 2005), 43, 149–52, 183; and Nancy Y. Reynolds, *A City Consumed: Urban Commerce, the Cairo Fire, and the Politics of Decolonization in Egypt* (Stanford, Calif.: Stanford University Press, 2012), 73–81, 86–93.

7. Riḍā, *Fatāwā*, 1:127, no. 49; and *al-Manār* 7 (1904): 238–39.
8. The historiography on Egyptian culture from nominal independence to decolonization is vast, and I cite it here selectively. For a helpful overview that focuses on the expansion of new media and the question of periodization, read Walter Armbrust, "The Formation of National Culture in Egypt in the Interwar Period: Cultural Trajectories," *History Compass* 7, no. 1 (2009): 155–80.
9. For a reproduction of this photograph, see Umar Ryad, "A Printed Muslim 'Lighthouse' in Cairo: *Al-Manār*'s Early Years, Religious Aspiration and Reception (1898–1903)." *Arabica* 56 (2009): 53.
10. Note the discussion of Riḍā's use of these early Islamic narratives in chapter 3 of the present book, in the section titled "Beneficial or Harmful Imitation?"
11. Riḍā, *Fatāwā*, 3:1057–60, no. 395; and *al-Manār* 14 (1911): 669–71.
12. Riḍā, *Fatāwā*, 1:267–68, no. 118; and *al-Manār* 7 (1904): 737.
13. Riḍā, *Fatāwā*, 1:267–68, no. 118; and *al-Manār* 7 (1904): 737. On the *burnous rouge* as a controversial symbol of accommodation, see Benjamin Claude Brower, *A Desert Named Peace: The Violence of France's Empire in the Algerian Sahara, 1844–1902* (New York: Columbia University Press, 2009), 134.
14. Riḍā, *Fatāwā*, 3:865–66, no. 317; and *al-Manār* 13 (1910): 111–12.
15. Many historians have contributed to this field. In addition to the studies by Azyumardi Azra, Jutta Bluhm-Warn, Jajat Burhanudin, and Nico Kaptein, cited earlier, see Mona Abaza, "Southeast Asia and the Middle East: *Al-Manar* and Islamic Modernity," in *From the Mediterranean to the China Sea: Miscellaneous Notes*, ed. Claude Guillot, Denys Lombard, and Roderich Ptak, 93–111 (Wiesbaden: Harrassowitz, 1998); and Ahmed Ibrahim Abushouk, "*Al-Manār* and the Ḥadhramī Elite in the Malay-Indonesian World: Challenge and Response," *Journal of the Royal Asiatic Society* 17, no. 3 (2007): 301–22.
16. Riḍā, *Fatāwā*, 3:867–88, no. 318; and *al-Manār* 13 (1910): 113–14. The *istiftā*ʾ refers to "*al-burnayṭa fawq al-kūfiyya*." For the Pact of ʿUmar, see Muḥammad b. al-Walīd al-Ṭurṭūshī, *Sirāj al-mulūk*, ed. Muḥammad Fatḥī Abū Bakr (Cairo: al-Dār al-Miṣriyya al-Lubnāniyya, 1994), 2:543; and Albrecht Noth, "Problems of Differentiation Between Muslims and Non-Muslims: Re-Reading the 'Ordinances of ʿUmar' (*Al-Shurūṭ al-ʿUmariyya*)," chap. 5 in *Muslims and Others in Early Islamic Society*, ed. Robert Hoyland (Burlington, Vt.: Ashgate, 2004).
17. See questions 1 and 2 of fatwa no. 395 (Riḍā, *Fatāwā*, 3:1057–60). This exchange was also analyzed in Nico J. Kaptein, "Southeast Asian Debates and Middle Eastern Inspiration: European Dress in Minangkabau at the Beginning of the 20th Century," in *Southeast Asia and the Middle East: Islam, Movement, and the Longue Durée*, ed. Eric Tagliacozzo, 176–95 (Stanford, Calif.: Stanford University Press, 2009), 185–86. *Al-Manār* identifies the questions as coming from Pōndoq Fādagh, Java. Abaza, "Southeast Asia and the Middle East," 108, identifies this place as "Pondok (Fadagh in Arabic)," located in Bogor, West Java, but this seems to be a mistake. The *mustafti*, Ḥājjī ʿAbdallāh Aḥmad (1878–1933), was from Padang Pandjang, a town in the highlands of West Sumatra, who moved to the coastal city of Padang in 1906. On this figure, see Deliar

Noer, *Modernist Muslim Movement in Indonesia, 1900–1942* (Singapore: Oxford University Press, 1973), 38–39. On internal Muslim conflicts within Padang, described as a pluralistic colonial city, see Freek Colombijn, *Patches of Padang: The History of An Indonesian Town in the Twentieth Century and the Use of Urban Space* (Leiden: Research School for Asian, African, and American Studies, 1994), 68–69.

18. Like Hurgronje, K. F. Holle, an honorary adviser on native affairs, argued against strict government restrictions on *ḥājjī* dress. See Sartono Kartodirdjo, *The Peasants' Revolt of Banten in 1888: Its Conditions, Course and Sequel. A Case Study of Social Movements in Indonesia* ('S-Gravenhage: Martinus Nijhoff, 1966), 304–6; Noer, *Modernist Muslim Movement*, 27, 164–65; and Kaptein, "Southeast Asian Debates," 179–80.
19. Kees van Dijk, "Sarong, Jubbah, and Trousers: Appearance as a Means of Distinction and Discrimination," in *Outward Appearances: Dressing State and Society in Indonesia*, ed. Henk Schulte Nordholt, 39–83 (Leiden: KITLV Press, 1997); and Rudolf Mrázek, *Engineers of Happy Land: Technology and Nationalism in a Colony* (Princeton, N.J.: Princeton University Press, 2002), 132–39. As late as 1905, Arabs were charged a fine for violating the sumptuary law, notes Nico J. Kaptein in "Southeast Asian Debates and Middle Eastern Inspiration: European Dress in Minangkabau at the Beginning of the 20th Century," in *Southeast Asia and the Middle East: Islam, Movement, and the Longue Durée*, ed. Eric Tagliacozzo, 176–95 (Stanford, Calif.: Stanford University Press, 2009), 177.
20. Kaptein, "Southeast Asian Debates," 183, 193n26, cites sources claiming that Muslims in European clothes enjoyed *lower* fares on trains and ships.
21. For a dated but still effective description of these dynamics, see Clifford Geertz, *Islam Observed: Religious Development in Morocco and Indonesia* (Chicago: University of Chicago Press, 1971), 9–13, 65–70. On the creation of provincial-customary law by the Dutch, and on its relation to a universalizing Islamic law, see John R. Bowen, *Islam, Law and Equality in Indonesia: An Anthropology of Public Reasoning* (Cambridge: Cambridge University Press, 2003) 46–52, 67–68.
22. Noer, *Modernist Muslim Movement*, 8 and 21, specifies that Muslims with more specialized knowledge of Islam (known as *kijahi* in Java, *sjech* in Sumatra) opposed, in particular, the wearing of Dutch clothes by Indonesians. Following Kaptein, "Southeast Asian Debates," 182–83, I have used the social labels Kaum Muda and Kaum Tua, but I am not convinced that the actors in this drama identified themselves according to these terms around 1910.
23. Cf. Kaptein, "Southeast Asian Debates," 186, who represents the editor of *al-Munīr* as a naïve recipient of legal wisdom from Cairo.
24. On Mālik ibn Anas's ruling about the consumption of clothes manufactured by Christians, see Leor Halevi, "Christian Impurity versus Economic Necessity: A Fifteenth-Century Fatwa on European Paper," *Speculum* 83, no. 4 (2008): 931.
25. Riḍā, *Fatāwā*, 3:1057–60, no. 395.
26. Riḍā, *Fatāwā*, 3:867–88, no. 318.
27. *Al-Manār* 14 (1911): 907–11; and Riḍā, *Fatāwā*, 3:1097–102, no. 421. On the connection between Meccan ʿAlawīs and the Ḥaḍramī diaspora, see Anne K. Bang, *Sufis and Scholars of the Sea: Family Networks in East Africa, 1860–1925* (London: RoutledgeCurzon, 2003), 31–32.
28. *Al-Manār* 14 (1911): 907–11; and Riḍā, *Fatāwā*, 3:1097–102, no. 421.
29. Angelo Lodi, *Storia delle origini dell'aeronautica militare, 1884–1915: Aerostieri, dirigibilisti, aviatori dell'Esercito e della Marina in Italia nel periodo pionieristico*, vol. 1 (Roma: Edizioni Bizzarri, 1976), chap. 4, esp. pp. 170–72.

30. In their enthusiasm for bombers, military historians have forgotten this fact, but it was commemorated at the time. See the section "Palloni e Dirigibili" in Vicenzo Lioy, *L'Italia in Africa*, Serie Storico-Militare, vol. 3: *L'Opera dell'Aeronautica*, tome 1: *Eritrea-Libia (1888–1932)* (Roma: Istituto poligrafico dello Stato, 1964), chap. 1. This publication includes a picture of a hot air balloon directed by an unusual horse-drawn carriage, titled "Pallone in osservazione verso le linee nemiche."
31. Lodi, *Storia delle origini dell'aeronautica militare*, 142; and W. H. Beehler, *The History of the Italian-Turkish War, September 29, 1911 to October 18, 1912* (Annapolis, Md.: Advertiser-Republican, 1913), 31, 34, 54.
32. For a brief account of this war, see Mesut Uyar and Edward J. Erickson, *A Military History of the Ottomans: From Osman to Atatürk* (Santa Barbara, Calif.: ABC-CLIO, 2009), 222–25.
33. René North, *Military Uniforms, 1686–1918*, illus. by John Berry (New York: Grosset & Dunlap, 1970), 120–21.
34. Riḍā, *Fatāwā*, 3:1098–101, no. 421; Roderic H. Davison, *Reform in the Ottoman Empire, 1856–1876* (Princeton, N.J.: Princeton University Press, 1963), 30–31; and Donald Quataert, "Clothing Laws, State, and Society in the Ottoman Empire, 1720–1829," *International Journal of Middle East Studies* 29, no. 3 (1997): 403–25.
35. Riḍā, *Fatāwā*, 3:865–66, no. 317.
36. Riḍā, *Fatāwā*, 3:1101–2, no. 421.
37. A. L. P. Burdett, *Arab Dissident Movements, 1905–1955*, vol. 1, *1905–1920* (Chippenham, U.K.: Archive Editions, 1996), 142.
38. For the quotation and an analysis of the Wafdist Women's Central Committee, see Badran, *Feminists, Islam, and Nation*, 83–84.
39. On the boycotts, also see Reynolds, *A City Consumed*, chap. 3; Baron, *Egypt as a Woman*, 168–69; and Russell, *Creating the New Egyptian Woman*, 89–92.
40. Reynolds, *A City Consumed*, 89. Similarly, in *Creating the New Egyptian Woman*, Russell concludes that "targeted stores and items had an elite and limited audience" (91). This conclusion may well be valid for Cairo, but it does not suit the situation in the provincial towns. British diplomatic reports, cited below, indicate considerable participation by fellaheen, who boycotted the Egyptian Markets Company.
41. I have based this analysis on figures given by Robert L. Tignor, *State, Private Enterprise, and Economic Change in Egypt, 1918–1952* (Princeton, N.J.: Princeton University Press, 1984), tables A.13 and 2.2.
42. "Report on General Situation in Egypt for Period from January 12 to 18, 1922," E 1039/61/16, printed in Peter Woodward, ed., *British Documents on Foreign Affairs: Reports and Papers from the Foreign Office Confidential Print*, part 2, *From the First to the Second World War*, series G, *Africa, 1914–1939*, vol. 4: *Egypt and the Soudan, December 1921–December 1922* (Frederick, Md.: University Publications of America, 1994), 37.
43. Reynolds, *City Consumed*, 89. Also see Eric Davis, *Challenging Colonialism: Bank Miṣr and Egyptian Industrialization, 1920–1941* (Princeton, N.J.: Princeton University Press, 1983), 116–17, 122–23. Davis claims that a split developed between "political" and "economic" approaches to nationalism, but political and economic agendas were inextricably bound in this period.
44. Mulock, *Report on the Economic and Financial Situation of Egypt*, 12, 14–16.
45. Ḥusayn Waṣfī Riḍā, *al-Manār* 11 (1908): 798–800. Hesitancy about the use of the term "*muqāṭaʿa*" to designate the new concept of "boycotting" is clear in this article.

46. On this boycott, see Palmira Johnson Brummett, *Image and Imperialism in the Ottoman Revolutionary Press, 1908–1911* (Albany: State University of New York Press, 2000), 175–76; and Michelle U. Campos, *Ottoman Brothers Muslims, Christians, and Jews in Early Twentieth-Century Palestine* (Stanford, Calif.: Stanford University Press, 2011), 100–109. Campos tells of crowds chanting the slogan "God will destroy the infidels."
47. *Al-Manār* 23 (January 28, 1922): 77.
48. *Al-Manār* 23 (March 29, 1922): 226–27.
49. "Report on the General Situation in Egypt for the Period from February 9 to 15, 1922," E 2273/61/16, and "Report on General Situation in Egypt for Period from February 16 to 22, 1922," E 2509/61/16, in Woodward, *British Documents: Egypt and the Soudan*, 74–75, 82–89. On the mob in the Egyptian Markets Company in Shandawil (Girga), see E 1039/61/16, cited above.
50. Malak Badrawi, *Political Violence in Egypt 1910–1924: Secret Societies, Plots and Assassinations* (Richmond, Surrey, U.K.: Curzon Press, 2000), 182–90; Janice J. Terry, *The Wafd, 1919–1952: Cornerstone of Egyptian Political Power* (London: Third World Centre for Research and Publishing, 1982), 131, 147–48; and "Egypt: The Bomb Conspiracy," *Near East* 21, no. 569 (April 6, 1922): 448.
51. "Field-Marshal Viscount Allenby to the Marquess Curzon of Kedleston," E 846/1/16, and "Report on the General Situation in Egypt for Period from January 19 to 25, 1922," E 1333/61/16, in Woodward, *British Documents: Egypt and the Soudan*, 32, 43–45.
52. Sayid Mohamed Rashid Rida, "Translation of a Memorandum by . . . the Head of the Arab Party in Egypt and Syria," Wingate Papers, held by Durham University Library, Archives and Special Collections, SAD. 135/7/60-99 (December 1–31, 1915).
53. Rida, "Translation of a Memorandum," reasons 13 and 14.
54. Rida, "Translation of a Memorandum," introductory section and reason 8. According to the memorandum, the speech was delivered to the "General Mohammedan Assembly," but the institution was surely Nadwat al-ʿUlamāʾ in Lucknow, which Riḍā visited in 1912.
55. Rida, "General Organic Law of the Arab Empire," Wingate Papers, held by Durham University Library, Archives and Special Collections, SAD. 135/7/102-104. December 1–31, 1915. Also see Mahmoud Haddad, "Arab Religious Nationalism in the Colonial Era: Rereading Rashīd Riḍā's Ideas on the Caliphate," *Journal of the American Oriental Society* 117, no. 2 (1997): 265, 267, 269.
56. Rida, "Translation of a Memorandum." Also see Haddad, "Arab Religious Nationalism," 265–66.
57. Eliezer Tauber, *The Emergence of the Arab Movements* (London: Routledge, 1993), 111.
58. *Al-Manār* 23 (1922): 713–14; and Haddad, "Arab Religious Nationalism," 272.
59. Erez Manela, *The Wilsonian Moment: Self-Determination and the International Origins of Anticolonial Nationalism* (Oxford: Oxford University Press, 2007), 157, 217–18; Umar Ryad, "Islamic Reformism and Great Britain: Rashid Rida's Image as Reflected in the Journal *Al-Manār* in Cairo." *Islam and Christian-Muslim Relations* 21, no. 3 (2010): 271; Haddad, "Arab Religious Nationalism," 268; and Eliezer Tauber, "The Political Life of Rašīd Riḍā," *Arabist: Budapest Studies in Arabic* 19–20 (1998): 261–72.
60. For a brief discussion of Ataturk's dress reforms in the course of Ottoman and Turkish history, see John Norton, "Faith and Fashion in Turkey," in *Languages of Dress in the Middle East*, ed. Nancy Lindisfarne-Tapper and Bruce Ingham, 149–77 (Surrey, U.K.: Curzon, 1997), 158–62. On the debate over the secular Turkish model in Egypt, see Wilson Chacko Jacob, *Working Out Egypt: Effendi Masculinity and Subject Formation in Colonial Modernity, 1870–1940* (Durham, N.C.: Duke University Press, 2010), 203–6, 338. Jacob analyzes an editorial by Fikrī Abāẓa, the editor

of *al-Muṣawwar*, that criticized Ataturk's ban as well as the unveiling of Turkey's First Lady, Latife Uşakizâde, shortly after the couple's divorce. Ironically, *al-Muṣawwar*, which Jacob describes as "perhaps the magazine par excellence of Egyptian modernity in the interwar period," was the principal publisher of notorious advertisements for new Western fashions.

61. Hunt Janin, *The Pursuit of Learning in the Islamic World, 610–2003* (Jefferson, N.C.: McFarland, 2005), 149–50; and Menter Sahinler, *Origine, influence et actualité du Kémalisme* (Paris: Publisud, 1995), 162.
62. On the change in the tone of his fatwas, see Mahmoud Haddad, "Muḥammad Rashīd Riḍā (D. 1935), in *Islamic Legal Thought: A Compendium of Muslim Jurists*. Studies in Islamic Law and Society, ed. David Powers, Oussama Arabi, and Susan Spectorsky (Leiden: Brill, 2013), 475–76.
63. In formulating this argument, I found it useful to think about S. N. Eisenstadt's "Multiple Modernities," *Daedalus* 129, no.1 (2000): 1–30. Formulating a diachronic juxtaposition, he compared a Western attempt to monopolize the concept of modernity in the postwar period with the diverse modernities of earlier and later periods. In contrast, the distinction between Riḍā's and Ataturk's visions for the future of Islam is an example of a synchronic clash of modernities in the interwar period.
64. *Al-Manār* 23 (1922): 431–35. Translated by Haddad, "Rashīd Riḍā (D. 1935)," 480–85.
65. Riḍā, *Fatāwā*, 6:1829–35, no. 665; and *al-Manār* 26 (1925–1926): 416 (nos. 3–6), 421–24, 496–98. Translated by Haddad, "Rashīd Riḍā (D. 1935)," 485–90. As a pan-Islamist who advocated Arabic as the medium for global Muslim communication, Riḍā also opposed keenly Kemalism, particularly the role in that nationalist program of translating the Qurʾān into Turkish. On this matter, see J. J. G. Jansen, *The Interpretation of the Koran in Modern Egypt* (Leiden: Brill, 1980), 10–11.
66. *Al-Muṣawwar* 100 (September 10, 1926): 7. On the significance of this advertisement in its original appearance, see Julian Sivulka, "Historical and Psychological Perspectives of the Erotic Appeal in Advertising," in chap. 3 in *Sex in Advertising: Perspectives on the Erotic Appeal*, ed. Tom Reichert and Jacqueline Lambiase (New York: Routledge, 2003), 47.
67. An English version of the same advertisement appeared in *The China Press* and *South China Morning Post* in 1927.
68. *Al-Muṣawwar* 176 (February 24, 1928): 30.
69. *Al-Muṣawwar* 174 (February 1, 1928): 10. The advertisement specified that Anzora hair cream was available in Port Saʿīd and Baghdad.
70. *Al-Muṣawwar* 165 (December 9, 1927): 8.
71. The changing styles of Queen Soraya, who visited both Paris and Cairo during her 1928 tour, caused quite a stir in Egypt, and this inspired Riḍā to make a sardonic comment. See Thomas Wide, "Astrakhan, Borqa', Chadari, Dreshi: The Economy of Dress in Early-Twentieth-Century Afghanistan," chap. 6 in *Anti-Veiling Campaigns in the Muslim World: Gender, Modernism and the Politics of Dress*, ed. Stephanie Cronin (London: Routledge, 2014), 185–86. For comparison, see Patricia L. Baker, "Politics of Dress: The Dress Reform Laws of 1920s/30s Iran," chap. 10 in *Languages of Dress in the Middle East*, ed. Nancy Lindisfarne-Tapper and Bruce Ingham (Surrey, U.K.: Curzon, 1997).
72. Riḍā, *Fatāwā*, 6:2308–9, no. 844; and *al-Manār* 31 (1930): 271, 277. For the translation of this fatwa into Chinese, see "Religious Rules for Women's Haircuts" [Funü jian fa de duan fa, 妇女剪发的断法], *Tianfang xueli yuekan* 5, nos. 3–4 (December 1932–January 1933). For a fuller treatment of the exchange, see Leor Halevi, "Is China a House of Islam? Chinese Questions, Arabic Answers, and the Translation of Salafism from Cairo to Canton, 1930–1932," *Die Welt des Islams* 59, no. 1 (2019): 33–69. I am grateful to Ms. Chin-Ting Huang for assistance with the Chinese.

73. Abdul Ali, "The Image of Mahatma Gandhi in Arabic Literature," in *New Issues: New Approaches (Essays in Literary Criticism)*, Suresh Chandra, 138–48 (New Delhi: Anmol, 2002), 140–41; and Muḥammad Khusayn Khān Shaghā, "Al-Zaʿīm Ghāndī wa al-Zuʿamāʾ al-ʿArab," *Thaqāfat al-Hind* 41, no. 2 (1990): 170–71. The last article quotes a letter about Gandhi that Riḍā sent to ʿAbd al-Razzāq al-Malīḥ 'Ābādī. It also mentions a translation published by Riḍā of a book by Gandhi titled *al-Inḍibāt al-Nafs* ("The Disciplining of the Self"). This may or may not be the book discussed below under a different title, the *Kitāb al-Ṣiḥḥa*. The authors mention that Riḍā personally met Gandhi when he visited India. But I have not been able to verify this anecdote. When Gandhi visited Lucknow and other cities in 1912, Gandhi was based in South Africa, so this sounds improbable. A more likely occasion for a meeting would be September 1931, when Gandhi's ship reached the Suez Canal and he met with local reporters.
74. Raymond F. Betts, *Uncertain Dimensions: Western Overseas Empires in the Twentieth Century* (Minneapolis: University of Minnesota Press, 1985), 151.
75. On the many meanings of cloth in this context, see C. A. Bayly, "The Origins of Swadeshi (Home Industry): Cloth and Indian Society, 1700–1930," chap. 10 in *The Social Life of Things: Commodities in Cultural Perspective*, ed. Arjun Appadurai (Cambridge: Cambridge University Press, 1986).
76. The battle of fatwas over alcohol appeared in *al-Manār* 23 (1922): 657–79 and *al-Manār* 24 (1923): 733–52. I plan to examine this fatwa in a separate article.
77. Riḍā, *Fatāwā*, 6:1829–35, no. 665; and Riḍā, *Fatāwā*, 6:2351, no. 887.
78. *Al-Manār* 24 (1923): 60; and Muḥammad Rashīd Riḍā, *al-Khilāfa aw al-imāma al-ʿuẓmā: Mabāḥith sharʿiyya, siyāsiya, ijtimāʿiyya, iṣlāhiyya* (Cairo: Maṭbaʿat al-Manār, 1922), 59–60. As the leader of India's Muslims, Riḍā mentioned Abul Kalam Azad, Muhammad ʿAli (Jauhar), and Shawkat ʿAli.
79. Antoinette M. Burton, *The Trouble with Empire: Challenges to Modern British Imperialism* (Oxford: Oxford University Press, 2015), 103.
80. *Al-Manār* 32 (1932): 112.
81. *Al-Manār* 30 (1930): 794–95.
82. Cf. Manela, *Wilsonian Moment.*
83. The first installment appeared in *al-Manār* 26 (1926): 691–98; the last, in vol. 28 (1928): 729–75. Mahātmā Ghāndī's *Kitāb al-Ṣiḥḥa*, trans. ʿAbd al-Razzāq al-Malīḥ 'Ābādī. (Cairo: Maṭbaʿat al-Manār, 1927) appeared in its entirety as a publication of Riḍā's press.
84. Romain Rolland's *Mahatma Gandhi* was translated into Arabic by ʿUmar Fākhūrī at some point between 1924 and 1928. Riḍā mentioned this publication in *al-Manār* 29 (1928): 240.
85. Ghāndī, *Kitāb al-Ṣiḥḥa*, 2. (N.B.: Here and in several instances below, the reference is to Riḍā's footnote on the page.) The earliest Arabic translation of Milton's epic poem seems to be a 1982 book titled *al-Firdaws al-mafqūd* (Cairo: al-Hayʾa al-Miṣriyya al-ʿĀmma li-l-Kitāb, 2001), by Muḥammad ʿInānī.
86. Ghāndī, *Kitāb al-Ṣiḥḥa*, 5–6, 29, 48, 50.
87. Ghāndī, *Kitāb al-Ṣiḥḥa*, 49–50. It is not clear to me whether in the original text Gandhi referred to leather *chappals*, as I would assume given Gandhi's history with them, or wooden *padukas*.
88. *Al-Manār* 31 (1930): 219ff. Among other things, what prompted Riḍā's reaction was the publication of Jules Sicard's *Le monde musulman dans les possessions françaises: Algérie, Tunisie, Maroc, Afrique occidentale française* (Paris: Librairie Coloniale et Orientaliste Émile Larose, 1928). This work of Orientalist sociology was a revision of a manual, originally written in 1919, in order to assist France militarily with its "indigenous" affairs. As for the proposal to translate Muḥammad's bones to the Louvre, it was made by D. Kimon in his self-published book *La*

pathologie de l'Islam et les moyens de le détruire: étude psychologique, 2nd ed. (Paris, 1897). On the centennial celebrations of French colonization as a turning point in Algeria's history, see Said Ali Alghailani, "Islam and the French Decolonization of Algeria: The Role of the Algerian Ulama 1919–1940" (Ph.D. thesis: Indiana University, 2002), 103–5, 303, 321–22. On Riḍā's responses in 1900 and 1930, see Haddad, "Arab Religious Nationalism," 260; and Umar Ryad, *Islamic Reformism and Christianity: A Critical Reading of the Works of Muḥammad Rashīd Riḍā and His Associates (1898–1935)* (Leiden: Brill, 2009), 45–46.

89. Kerry A. Chase, *Trading Blocs: States, Firms, and Regions in the World Economy* (Ann Arbor: University of Michigan Press, 2005), 54–59.
90. For the details, see National Institute of Economic and Social Research, *Trade Regulations & Commercial Policy of the United Kingdom* (Cambridge: Cambridge University Press, 1943), 19–20.
91. For a wonderful history of the denouement, see Frank Trentmann, *Free Trade Nation: Commerce, Consumption, and Civil Society in Modern Britain* (Oxford: Oxford University Press, 2008), chaps. 6–7. See also Anthony Howe, *Free Trade and Liberal England, 1846–1946* (Oxford: Clarendon, 1997), chap. 8.
92. *Al-Manār* 31 (1931): 770–77; and *al-Manār* 32 (1931–1932): 49–60, 226–31. There is a partial English translation of this text by Emad Eldin Shahin, titled "Renewal, Renewing, and Renewers," in *Modernist Islam, 1840–1940: A Sourcebook*, ed. Charles Kurzman, 77–85 (Oxford: Oxford University Press, 2002). Shahin placed the lecture in the Royal Institute of Geography, but the word "geography" does not appear in Riḍā's text. On the Society of the Oriental League and its clubhouse, see Yunan Labib Rizk, "The Forgotten Orient File," *Al-Ahram Weekly* 516 (January 11–17, 2001).
93. *Al-Manār* 31 (1931): 773, 774. On ties between Ḥasan al-Bannāʾ, the Muslim Brotherhood's founder, and Riḍā, see Brynjar Lia, *The Society of the Muslim Brothers in Egypt: The Rise of an Islamic Mass Movement, 1928–1942* (Reading, U.K.: Ithaca Press, 1998), 29, 56.
94. *Al-Manār* 31 (1931): 771–72.
95. *Al-Manār* 32 (1932): 230–31.
96. *Al-Manār* 32 (1932): 226–27, 230. Shahin's translation omitted this intriguing exchange with an anonymous Indian Salafist. But it is an important piece of evidence for understanding better the kinds of compromises that Salafis in the interwar period had to make in order to work effectively alongside other Islamic nationalists in various countries. On this historical development, see Henri Lauzière, *The Making of Salafism: Islamic Reform in the Twentieth Century* (New York: Columbia University Press, 2016), 103–7.
97. *Al-Manār* 32 (1931): 56–57.
98. *Al-Manār* 32 (1931): 56–57.
99. Riḍā, *Fatāwā*, 6:1829–35, no. 665.
100. *Al-Manār* 32 (1931): 56.
101. See Reynolds, *A City Consumed*, 124–28; Relli Shechter, "Press Advertising in Egypt: Business Realities and Local Meaning, 1882–1956," *Arab Studies Journal* 10/11 (2002/2003): 57; and Relli Shechter, "Reading Advertisements in a Colonial/Development Context: Cigarette Advertising and Identity Politics in Egypt, c1919–1939," *Journal of Social History* 39 (2005): 492. On related cultural and commercial developments in the early thirties, see Israel Gershoni and James P. Jankowski, *Redefining the Egyptian Nation, 1930–1945* (Cambridge: Cambridge University Press, 1995), 18–19; and Uri M. Kupferschmidt, *European Department Stores and Middle Eastern Consumers: The Orosdi-Back Saga* (Istanbul: Ottoman Bank Archives and Research Centre, 2007), 46–47.
102. Gudrun Krämer, *Hasan al-Banna* (New York: Oneworld, 2014), 33.

103. *Majallatī* 1, no. 7 (1935): 678. The advertisement was for Sharikat Dukhān wa-Sajāʾir al-Itiḥḥād; see Relli Shechter, *Smoking, Culture and Economy in the Middle East: The Egyptian Tobacco Market 1850–2000* (London: I. B. Tauris, 2006), 111–12.
104. *Majallatī* 1, no. 4 (1935): 410.
105. On the Piastre Plan and its factory, called Maṣnaʿ Ṭarbūsh al-Qirsh in the 1935 advertisement, see Reynolds, *A City Consumed*, 97–98.

8 Lottery Tickets, Luxury Hotels, and Christian Experts: Economic Liberalism Versus Islamic Exclusivism in a Territorial Framework

1. Muḥammad Rashīd Riḍā, *Fatāwā al-Imām*, ed. Ṣalāḥ al-Dīn al-Munajjid and Yūsuf Q. Khūrī (Dār al-Kitab al-Jadīd: Beirut, 1970–), 6:2300ff, no. 841; and *al-Manār* 31 (1930): 272ff. On this exceptional legal correspondence between Rashīd Riḍā of Cairo and the Yunnanese scholar Ma Ruitu of Guangzhou, see Leor Halevi, "Is China a House of Islam?" Chinese Questions, Arabic Answers, and the Translation of Salafism from Cairo to Canton, 1930–1932," *Die Welt des Islams* 59, no. 1 (2019): 33–69. On Chinese-Egyptian exchanges between Muslim scholars and journalists in the 1930s, see Zvi Ben-Dor Benite, "Taking ʿAbduh to China: Chinese-Egyptian Intellectual Contact in the Early Twentieth Century," in *Global Muslims in the Age of Steam and Print*, ed. James L. Gelvin and Nile Green, 249–67 (Berkeley: University of California Press, 2014); and Matsumoto Masumi, "Rationalizing Patriotism Among Muslim Chinese: The Impact of the Middle East on the *Yuehua* Journal," in *Intellectuals in the Modern Islamic World: Transmission, Transformation, Communication*, ed. Stéphane A. Dudoignon, Komatsu Hisao, and Kosugi Yasushi, 117–42 (London: Routledge, 2009). On the question of identity, see Jonathan N. Lipman, "Hyphenated Chinese: Sino-Muslim Identity in Modern China," in *Remapping China: Fissures in Historical Terrain*, ed. Gail Hershatter, Emily Honig, Jonathan N. Lipman, and Randall Stross, 97–112 (Stanford, Calif.: Stanford University Press, 1996). I am grateful to Jonathan Lipman and Matsumoto Masumi for helping me to understand better many aspects of Sino-Muslim history.
2. Paul W. Werth, *The Tsar's Foreign Faiths: Toleration and the Fate of Religious Freedom in Imperial Russia* (Oxford: Oxford University Press, 2014), 208–9, 232. I am grateful to Jane Burbank for lending me this book.
3. Many years later, after the October Revolution of 1917, he would write a sympathetic account of Bolshevism, describing socialists as representing the vast majority of the world's inhabitants, the workers "whose voice . . . is the voice of God." He found the revolutionary rhetoric inspiring and appreciated the revolt against capitalism and colonialism. For a translation of this fatwa, titled "Socialism, Bolshevism, and Religion," see Anouar Abdel-Maled, ed., *Contemporary Arab Political Thought*, trans. Michael Pallis (London: Zed, 1983), 155–59.
4. Riḍā, *Fatāwā*, 1:372–73, no. 158; and *al-Manār* 8 (1905): 291.
5. Robert D. Crews, *For Prophet and Tsar: Islam and Empire in Russia and Central Asia* (Cambridge, Mass.: Harvard University Press, 2006), 52.
6. Majid Khadduri, *War and Peace in the Law of Islam* (Baltimore: Johns Hopkins University Press, 1955), 293.
7. Umar Ryad, "A Prelude to *Fiqh al-Aqalliyât*: Rashîd Ridâ's *Fatwâs* to Muslims Under Non-Muslim Rule," in *In-Between Spaces: Christian and Muslim Minorities in Transition in Europe and the Middle East*, ed. Christiane Timmerman, Johan Leman, Hannelore Roos, and Barbara Segaert, 239–70 (Bruxelles: P.I.E. Peter Lang, 2009), 252–54.

8. Riḍā, *Fatāwā*, 2:508–11, no. 191; and *al-Manār* 9 (1906): 205–7.
9. Riḍā, *Fatāwā*, 2:508–11, no. 191; and *al-Manār* 9 (1906): 205–7.
10. Riḍā, *Fatāwā*, 2:508–11, no. 191; and *al-Manār* 9 (1906): 205–7.
11. Hydrographic Office, U.S. Secretary of the Navy, *Red Sea and Gulf of Aden Pilot; Comprising the Suez Canal, the Gulfs of Suez and Akaba, the Red Sea and Strait of Bab el Mandeb, the Gulf of Aden with Sokotia and Adjacent Islands, and the Southeast Coast of Arabia to Ras al Hadd* (Washington, D.C.: Government Printing Office, 1916), 384.
12. Riḍā, *Fatāwā*, 2:405–10, no. 164; and *al-Manār* 8 (1905): 588–92. For an intensive and insightful analysis of this fatwa, see Brinkley Messick, "Madhhabs and Modernities," chap. 11 in *The Islamic School of Law: Evolution, Devolution, and Progress*, ed. Peri Berman, Rudolph Peters, and Frank E. Vogel (Cambridge, Mass.: Islamic Legal Studies Program, Harvard Law School, 2005). Scott Reese's description of Aden as an "imperial community" that offered local and foreign residents multiple legal avenues captures perfectly the historical context. See Scott Steven Reese, *Imperial Muslims: Islam, Community and Authority in the Indian Ocean, 1839–1937* (Edinburgh: Edinburgh University Press, 2018), 4–6, 81–82.
13. An Italian agency, Riunione Adriatica di Sicurtà, offered maritime insurance. The French firm la Sécurité did so as well, but its instruments were typically called *assurances*.
14. Janet Ewald and William G. Clarence-Smith, "The Economic Role of the Hadhrami Diaspora in the Red Sea and Gulf of Aden, 1820s to 1930s," in *Hadhrami Traders, Scholars and Statesmen in the Indian Ocean, 1750s–1960s*, ed. Ulrike Freitag and William G. Clarence-Smith, 281–96 (Leiden: Brill, 1997).
15. Khaled Abou El Fadl, "Islamic Law and Muslim Minorities: The Juristic Discourse on Muslim Minorities from the Second/Eighth to the Eleventh/Seventeenth Centuries," *Islamic Law and Society* 1, no. 2 (1994): 159–63.
16. Riḍā, *Fatāwā*, 4:1602, no. 601; and *al-Manār* 23 (1922): 588. The question was posed by ʿAbdallāh b. Muḥammad al-Masʿūdī. For the broader context, see James A. Warren, *Gambling, the State and Society in Thailand, c. 1800–1945* (London: Routledge, 2013), 56–58.
17. Riḍā, *Fatāwā*, 4:1602, no. 601.
18. Riḍā, *Fatāwā*, 6:2300ff, no. 841.
19. Other factors contributed to their rejection of a Ḥanafi approach to trade in a House of Islam, which was designed to accommodate travelers and minorities. Muslims in Southeast Asia constituted most of the population, and they generally adhered to the Shafiʿite school of law.
20. Riḍā, *Fatāwā*, 5:1974–78, no. 717; and *al-Manār* 28 (1927): 575–78. Called *al-Wifāq*, "The Concord," in Arabic, the journal is identified by WorldCat as *Al-Wivac: soerat chabar minggoean berdasar politiek Islam berazaskan Islam*, founded in 1925 in Buitenzorg. Edited by Muḥammad b. Muḥammad Saʿīd al-Fattah, the journal played a role in Ḥaḍramī disputes; see Natalie Mobini-Kesheh, *Hadrami Awakening: Community and Identity in the Netherlands East Indies, 1900–1942* (Ithaca, N.Y.: Cornell South East Asia Program Publications, 1999), 93n12.
21. Riḍā, *Fatāwā*, 6:2582–85, no. 1054; and *al-Manār* 35 (1935): 127–29.
22. See Majid Khadduri, *The Islamic Law of Nations: Shaybānī's Siyar* (Baltimore: Johns Hopkins University Press, 1966), 173–74, where Abū Yūsuf's dissent is also recorded.
23. For criticism of the Ḥanafi ruling by ʿAlawī ibn Aḥmad al-Saqqāf and other Shafiʿites, see Messick, "Madhhabs and Modernities," 165–68; and Aḥmad ibn al-Naqīb al-Miṣrī, *ʿUmdat al-sālik wa-ʿuddat al-nāsik*, ed. and trans. by Nūḥ Ḥā Mīm Keller under the title *Reliance of the Traveller*, rev. ed. (Beltsville, Md.: Amana, 1994), 943–47.

24. On Riḍā's family's Shafiʿite background, see Mahmoud Haddad, "Muḥammad Rashīd Riḍā," in *Islamic Legal Thought: A Compendium of Muslim Jurists*. Studies in Islamic Law and Society, ed. David Powers, Oussama Arabi, and Susan Spectorsky (Leiden: Brill, 2013), 457–58.
25. Abou El Fadl, "Islamic Law and Muslim Minorities," 157, 171, 189.
26. Muḥammad Amīn Ibn ʿĀbidīn, *Ḥāshiyat radd al-muḥtār ʿalā al-Durr al-Mukhtār*, 2nd ed. (Cairo: Maktabat wa-Maṭbaʿat Muṣṭafā al-Bābī al-Ḥalabī wa-Awlādihi, 1966), 4:169. See also pp. 170–71, which deals with the insurance of goods transferred across the border between the House of Islam and the House of War.
27. A search of digital sources for the keywords "Riḍā and Ibn Taymiyya" or "Riḍā and Ḥanbalism" will confirm the prevalence of the thesis. For two influential formulations, see Albert Hourani, *Arabic Thought in the Liberal Age, 1798–1939* (Cambridge: Cambridge University Press, 1983), 163, 231; and Nabil Mouline, *Les clercs de l'Islam: Autorité religieuse et pouvoir politique en Arabie Saoudite (XVIII*[e]*-XXI*[e] *siècles)* (Paris: Presses Universitaires de France, 2009), 145–46.
28. For a partial bibliography of al-Manār Press's nonserialized publications, see Dyala Hamzah, "L'intérêt général, (*maslaha 'âmma*) ou le triomphe de l'opinion: Fondation délibératoire (et esquisses délibératives) dans les écrits du publiciste syro-égyptien Muhammad Rashîd Ridâ (1865–1935)" (PhD thesis, L'École des hautes études en sciences sociales and Freie Universität Berlin, 2008), 314–16.
29. See, for example, the reformulation of Hourani's thesis in Souad Tagelsir Ali, *Religion, Not a State: Ali ʿAbd al-Raziq's Islamic Justification of Political Secularism* (Salt Lake City: University of Utah Press, 2009), 58–59.
30. *Al-Manār* 4 (1901): 462–66, discussed in chapter 4 of the present book in the section "The Rise of Salafism."
31. In addition to the second edition of ʿAbduh's *Theology of Unity*, al-Manār Press published books by Jamāl al-Dīn al-Qāsimī (d. 1914), Muḥamamd Shiblī Nuʿmānī (d. 1914), and Muḥammad Tawfīq Sidqī (d. 1920).
32. Aḥmad ibn ʿAbd al-Ḥalīm ibn Taymiyya, *al-Ṣūfiyya wa-l-fuqarāʾ: fatwā li-shaykh al-Islām Ibn Taymiyya* (Cairo: Maṭbaʿat al-Manār, 1909); Aḥmad ibn ʿAbd al-Ḥalīm Ibn Taymiyya, *Qāʿida Jalīla fī al-Tawassul wa-l-Wasīla* (Cairo: Maṭbaʿat al-Manār, 1909); and Muḥammad ibn Abī Bakr ibn Qayyim al-Jawzyya, *Kitāb Ighāthat al-lahfān fī ḥukm ṭalāq al-ghaḍbān*, ed. Jamāl al-Dīn al-Qāsimī (1914) (Cairo: Maṭbaʿat al-Manār, 1909). Besides these books, al-Manār's list of monographs in the prewar period consisted of publications by modern reformers. In her bibliography of al-Manār's nonserial publications, Hamzah, "L'intérêt général," 314–16, lists several but not all of these books.
33. One debatable exception would be Muḥammad ibn Aḥmad Dhahabī's *Kitāb al-ʿulūw li-l-ʿAlī al-Ghaffār fī ṣaḥīḥ al-akhbār wa-saqīmihā*, ed. Rashīd Riḍā (Cairo: Maṭbaʿat al-Manār, 1913). But this book, by a prolific Shafiʿite author, was apparently written under Ibn Taymiyya's influence.
34. Aḥmad ibn ʿAbd al-Ḥalīm ibn Taymiyya, *al-Masāʾil al-mārdīniyya*, ed. Muḥammad Ḥāmid al-Fiqī, critically annotated by Khālid b. Muḥammad b. ʿUthmān al-Miṣrī (Fayyum, Egypt: Dār al-Falāḥ, 2003), 251; Aḥmad ibn ʿAbd al-Ḥalīm ibn Taymiyya, *Iqtiḍāʾ al-ṣirāṭ al-mustaqīm li-mukhālafat aṣḥāb al-jaḥīm*, ed. Nāṣir b. ʿAbd al-Karīm al-ʿAql, 2 vols. in 1 (Riyadh: Maktabat al-Rushd, n.d.), 354, 522; and Aḥmad ibn ʿAbd al-Ḥalīm ibn Taymiyya, *Majmūʿ fatāwā Shaykh al-Islām*, ed. ʿAbd al-Raḥmān b. Muḥammad b. Qāsim (Medina: Maktabat al-Malik Fahd al-Waṭaniyya, 2004), 29:275–77.

35. Sulaymān ibn ʿAbdallāh ibn al-Shaykh Muḥammad ibn ʿAbd al-Wahhāb, "Fī ḥukm al-safar ilā bilād al-shirk wa-l-iqāma fī-hā li-l-tijāra wa-iẓhār ʿalāmāt al-nifāq wa-muwālāt al-kuffār," in Rashīd Riḍā, ed., *Majmūʿat al-tawḥid al-najdiyya* (Cairo: al-Manār, 1927; reprinted in Riyadh, 1999), 266–67.
36. ʿAbd al-Raḥmān ibn Ḥasan ibn Shaykh al-Islām, "Kitāb al-imān wa-l-radd ʿalā ahl al-bidaʿ: hādhihi fawāʾid majmūʿa tasthamil ʿalā shayʾ min al-taqriyāt," in *Majmūʿat al-rasāʾil wa-l-masāʾil al-najdiyya*, ed. Rashīd Riḍā (Cairo: al-Manār, 1926–28), 2:117; and ʿAbd al-Laṭīf al-Azharī, "Masʾala bayʿ al-kuffār mā yastaʿīnūna bi-hi ʿalā al-muslimīn," in *Majmūʿat al-rasāʾil wa-l-masāʾil al-najdiyya*, ed. Rashīd Riḍā (Cairo: al-Manār, 1926–28), 3:36–37.
37. Mouline, *Clercs de l'Islam*, employs the term "*hanbalo-wahhâbisme*" to emphasize the connection. Unlike "traditional Wahhabis," some Salafis did reject loyalty to the Ḥanbali school. On this topic, see Bernard Haykel, "On the Nature of Salafi Thought and Action," in *Global Salafism: Islam's New Religious Movement*, ed. Roel Meijer (New York: Columbia University Press, 2009), 42–43. On tensions in Ottoman Syria between a Salafist and the Ḥanafi establishment, see David Dean Commins, *Islamic Reform: Politics and Social Change in Late Ottoman Syria* (New York: Oxford University Press, 1990), 22–24, 70–76.
38. Riḍā, *Fatāwā*, 6:2302, 2309, no. 845; and *al-Manār* 31 (1930): 277.
39. Riḍā, *Fatāwā*, 6:2307, no. 843; and *al-Manār* 31 (1930): 276.
40. Mahmoud Haddad, "Arab Religious Nationalism in the Colonial Era: Rereading Rashīd Riḍā's Ideas on the Caliphate," *Journal of the American Oriental Society* 117, no. 2 (1997): 260, 262.
41. On the Ottoman Decentralization Party, see A. A. Duri, *The Historical Formation of the Arab Nation: A Study in Identity and Consciousness*, trans. Lawrence I. Conrad (London: Croom Helm, 1987), 203–4, 277–80, 296–97. Also see Eliezer Tauber, "Rashīd Riḍā and Fayṣal's Kingdom in Syria," *Muslim World* 85, no. 3–4 (1995): 235–45; and Eyal Zisser, "Rashid Rida: On the Way to Syrian Nationalism in the Shade of Islam and Arabism," in *The Origins of Syrian Nationhood: Histories, Pioneers and Identity*, ed. Adel Beshara, 123–40 (London: Routledge, 2011).
42. ʿUmar al-Dāʿūq collaborated with French authorities in drafting the 1926 constitution for Lebanon. The society he represented was called Jamʿiyyat al-Maqāṣid al-Khayriyya al-Islāmiyya. On this figure, see Charles Winslow, *Lebanon: War and Politics in a Fragmented Society* (London: Routledge, 1996), 56; Eliezer Tauber, *The Formation of Modern Syria and Iraq* (Abingdon, U.K.: Routledge, 1995), 58, 59; and Kais M. Firro, *Inventing Lebanon: Nationalism and the State Under the Mandate* (London: I. B. Tauris, 2003), 78, 85, 101, 133.
43. Samir Kassir, *Beirut*, trans. M. B. DeBevoise (Berkeley: University of California Press, 2010), 305–6; and Liliane Buccianti-Barakat, "Beyrouth sous le mandat français ou la 'Nice de l'Orient,'" in *Le tourisme dans l'empire français: politiques, pratiques et imaginaires (XIXe-XXe siècles): un outil de la domination coloniale?*, ed. Colette Zytnicki and Habib Kazdaghli (Paris: Publications de la Société française d'histoire d'outre-mer, 2009), 73–78.
44. Riḍā, *Fatāwā*, 5:1917–21, no. 700; and *al-Manār* 28 (May 2, 1927): 181–85.
45. Riḍā, *Fatāwā*, 5:1917–21, no. 700; and *al-Manār* 28 (May 2, 1927): 181–85.
46. Strikingly, this response came in the wake of the French suppression of a nationalist insurgency, the Great Syrian Revolt, and a year after the promulgation of the May 1926 constitution, which established both the principle of equality under the law for all citizens of the republic and, as a "provisional" measure, the rule of equal confessional representation in branches of the government. See David D. Grafton, *The Christians of Lebanon: Political Rights in Islamic Law* (London: Tauris Academic Studies, 2003), 100–102.

47. Riḍā, *Fatāwā*, 2:713–16, no. 269; and *al-Manār* 12 (1909): 97–99
48. Riḍā, *Fatāwā*, 2:713–16, no. 269; and *al-Manār* 12 (1909): 97–99.
49. Antoine Fattal, *Le statut légal des non-musulmans en pays d'Islam* (Beirut: Imprimerie catholique, 1958), 86–87.
50. Lowell Thomas, "King Hussein and His Arabian Knights," *Asia: The American Magazine on the Orient* 20 (1920): 400–401.
51. H. St. J. B. Philby, *The Heart of Arabia: A Record of Travel & Exploration* (London: Constable, 1922), 1:219.
52. Muḥammad Rashīd Riḍā, "al-Inklīz wa-l-Ḥijāz," *al-Manār* 26 (1925): 394–400. On sharif ʿAlī's diplomacy at this time, see Martin Kramer, "Shaykh Maraghi's Mission to the Hijaz, 1925," *Asian and African Studies* (Haifa), 16 (1982): 121–36.
53. Ḥāfiẓ Wahba, *Jazīrat al-ʿArab fī al-qarn al-ʿishrīn* (Cairo: Lajnat al-Taʾlīf, 1935), 297–99.
54. Penelope Tuson and Emma Quick, eds., *Arabian Treaties, 1600–1960*, vol. 4, *Saudi Arabia* (Melksham, U.K.: Archive Editions, 1992), p. 92, article 9.
55. Wahba, *Jazīrat al-ʿArab*, 319. Here Wahba glosses the term "*barqā*" or "*barqī*" as referring to *al-tilighrāf al-lā-silkī*, the wireless telegraph.
56. See, for example, Mouline, *Clercs de l'Islam*, 137–38, 155.
57. Wahba, *Jazīrat al-ʿArab*, 307–9; and Ḥāfiẓ Wahba, *Arabian Days* (London: Ebenezer Baylis, 1964), 57–60. Wahba omitted the name of the divine from Najd in the Arabic edition, but he disclosed it in the English translation. For a similar anecdote, concerning the "wireless telephone," which is in this instance associated with "the American unbelievers," see William A. Eddy, "King Ibn Saʿūd: 'Our Faith and Your Iron,'" *Middle East Journal* 17, no. 3 (1963): 258. Cf. Michael Darlow and Barbara Bray, *Ibn Saud: The Desert Warrior Who Created the Kingdom of Saudi Arabia* (New York: Skyhorse, 2012), 385–86.
58. On Philby's cross-cultural brokering activities in the early 1930s, when he represented the Eastern Telegraph Company, see Joseph Kostiner, *The Making of Saudi Arabia, 1916–1936: From Chieftaincy to Monarchical State* (New York: Oxford University Press, 1993), 149; Peter Sluglett and Marion Farouk-Sluglett, "The Precarious Monarchy: Britain, Abd al-Aziz ibn Saud and the Establishment of the Kingdom of Hijaz, Najd and its Dependences, 1925–1932," chap. 3 in *State, Society and Economy in Saudi Arabia*, ed. Tim Niblock (New York: St. Martin's, 1982), 48; Clive Leatherdale, *Britain and Saudi Arabia, 1925–1939: The Imperial Oasis* (London: Frank Cass, 1983), 78–79; Leslie McLoughlin, *Ibn Saud: Founder of a Kingdom* (London: Palgrave Macmillan, 1993), 118–19; and Darlow and Bray, *Ibn Saud*, 368–71.
59. Wahba, *Jazīrat al-ʿArab*, 149, 308.
60. Daniel R. Headrick, *The Tentacles of Progress: Technology Transfer in the Age of Imperialism, 1850–1940* (Oxford: Oxford University Press, 1988), 10.
61. For an intriguing attempt to represent the two currents as compatible, see Sheikh Ḥāfiẓ Wahba, "Wahhabism in Arabia: Past and Present," trans. A. A. Shukry, *Islamic Review* 17, no. 8 (August 1929): 283–84, 287. The text, based on a lecture that Wahba delivered in London, argues that Muḥammad ʿAbduh and his "enlightened" Egyptian disciples followed "Modern Wahhabism" in practice. Cf. Henri Lauzière, *The Making of Salafism: Islamic Reform in the Twentieth Century* (New York: Columbia University Press, 2016), 10–11, 65, 68–69; and David Commins, "From Wahhabi to Salafi," chap. 8 in *Saudi Arabia in Transition: Insights on Social, Political, Economic and Religious Change*, ed. Bernard Haykel, Thomas Hegghammer, and Stéphane Lacroix (New York: Cambridge University Press, 2015), 157–59, 164.

62. Lauzière, *The Making of Salafism*, 69, quoting *al-Manār* 29 (1928): 146. On pp. 65–68, Lauzière argues that Riḍā admired the Saudi monarch because "he was flexible and willing to adopt the technological dimension of modernity."
63. FO 371/13010, E 4286/484/91, "Jeddah Report for the Period July 1 to July 31, 1928," by Consul F. H. W. Stonehewer-Bird to Sir Austen Chamberlain, dispatched on August 3, 1928. Also see Michael Cook, *Commanding Right and Forbidding Wrong in Islamic Thought* (Cambridge: Cambridge University Press, 2000), 186. I am indebted to Michael Cook for providing me with a copy of the source.
64. Historians have emphasized the doctrinal differences and historical resentments that drove Ottomans and Wahhabis apart. See, for instance, Commins, "From Wahhabi to Salafi," 152–55.
65. Riḍā, *Fatāwā*, 5:1974–78, no. 717; and *al-Manār* 28 (1927): 575–78.
66. J. C. Hurewitz, ed., *The Middle East and North Africa in World Politics: A Documentary Record*, vol. 1: *European Expansion, 1535–1914*, 2nd ed. (New Haven, Conn.: Yale University Press, 1975), 269–71, 315–18. On the topic, see Duri, *Historical Formation*, 143, 163, 231.
67. Roderic H. Davison, "Turkish Attitudes Concerning Christian-Muslim Equality in the Nineteenth Century," *American Historical Review* 59, no. 4 (1954): 848, 852.
68. In "Turkish Attitudes," Davison surely exaggerated when he wrote of the "general antipathy" (859) of Muslims to the promise of equality; his statement that "a strong prejudice against innovation" would have motivated Muslim theologians to oppose the legislation was mere speculation (855–56). Also see Nathan J. Brown, *Rule of Law in the Arab World: Courts in Egypt and the Gulf* (Cambridge: Cambridge University Press, 1997), 55–56. Cf. Timothy Mitchell, *Colonising Egypt* (Cambridge: Cambridge University Press, 1988), 115–16.
69. For a convenient translation, see Charles Kurzman, ed., *Modernist Islam, 1840–1940: A Sourcebook* (Oxford: Oxford University Press, 2002), 37–39. Also see the excerpts and analysis in Abdul Azim Islahi, *Economic Thinking of Arab Muslims Writers During the Nineteenth Century* (New York: Palgrave Macmillan, 2015), 48–49.
70. ʿAbd al-Raḥmān al-Kawākibī, *al-Aʿmāl al-kāmila li-l-Kawākibī*, 3rd ed. (Beirut: Markaz Dirāsāt al-Waḥda al-ʿArabiyya, 2007), 359–60.
71. In 1959, Cairo's Dār al-Maʿārif Press published ʿAdil Zuʿaytir's Arabic translation of Votaire's *Les Lettres philophiques*. But to try to trace the peregrinations of Voltaire's ideas from eighteenth-century London to twentieth-century Cairo would be a pointless exercise: a quest for the European origins of a belated Muslim Enlightenment. For an inspiring exhortation for historians to move past a Eurocentric approach to the Enlightenment, see Sebastian Conrad, "Enlightenment in Global History: A Historiographical Critique," *American Historical Review* 117 (2012): 999–1027.
72. Yohanan Friedmann, *Tolerance and Coercion in Islam: Interfaith Relations in the Muslim Tradition* (Cambridge: Cambridge University Press, 2003), 35, 113, 135.
73. Riḍā, *Fatāwā*, 1:130, no. 51; and *al-Manār* 7 (1904): 258.
74. Riḍā, *Fatāwā*, 1:223–23, no. 92; and *al-Manār* 7 (1904): 527 or 537 (the latter number was apparently a misprint). On the relation of Islamic law to commodity futures, see the fine book by Mohammad Hashim Kamali, *Islamic Commercial Law: An Analysis of Futures and Options* (Cambridge: Islamic Texts Society, 2000).
75. Riḍā, *Fatāwā*, 6:2272, no. 818; and *al-Manār* 31 (1930): 52.
76. See, for instance, Riḍā, *Fatāwā*, 5:1974–78, no. 717.

77. As discussed in the introduction and chapter 3 of the present book.
78. Muḥammad Rashīd Riḍā, "General Organic Law," Wingate Papers, held by Durham University Library, Archives and Special Collections, SAD. 135/7/102-104. December 1–31, 1915.
79. Muḥammad Rashīd Riḍā, "Translation of a Memorandum by . . . the Head of the Arab Party in Egypt and Syria," Wingate Papers, held by Durham University Library, Archives and Special Collections, SAD. 135/7/60-99. December 1–31, 1915.
80. Muḥammad Rashīd Riḍā, *al-Khilāfa aw al-imāma al-ʿuẓmā: Mabāḥith sharʿiyya, siyāsiya, ijtimāʿiyya, iṣlāhiyya* (Cairo: Maṭbaʿat al-Manār, 1922), 99.
81. Judith E. Tucker, *Women, Family, and Gender in Islamic Law* (Cambridge: Cambridge University Press, 2008), 160–61. Also see Peter R. Knauss, *The Persistence of Patriarchy: Class, Gender, and Ideology in Twentieth Century Algeria* (New York: Praeger, 1987), 55; and Margot Badran, *Feminists, Islam, and Nation: Gender and the Making of Modern Egypt* (Princeton, N.J.: Princeton University Press, 1995), 134.
82. *Al-Manār* 31 (1931): 773–74.
83. For the transcript of this parliamentary debate in translation, see Akram Fouad Khater, *Sources in the History of the Modern Middle East* (Boston: Houghton Mifflin, 2004), 211–19.

Conclusions

1. Langdon Winner, "Technologies as Forms of Life," chap. 8 in *Readings in the Philosophy of Technology*, ed. David Kaplan (Lanham, Md.: Rowman and Littlefield, 2004).
2. See, for instance, Thomas Piketty, *Capital in the Twenty-First Century*, trans. Arthur Goldhammer (Cambridge, Mass.: Harvard University Press, 2014), 28.
3. For example, a recent, authoritative volume on Islamic history in the period of European dominance adopts World War I as a watershed. Nearly every article deals with developments either before or after the war, which makes it difficult to appreciate continuities. See Francis Robinson, ed., *The Islamic World in the Age of Western Dominance*, vol. 5 of *The New Cambridge History of Islam* (Cambridge: Cambridge University Press, 2010).
4. Wael B. Hallaq, *History of Islamic Legal Theories: An Introduction to Sunnī Uṣūl Al-Fiqh* (Cambridge: Cambridge University Press, 1997), 200, 217.
5. Thus, as shown in chapter 8, ʿAlawī ibn Aḥmad al-Saqqāf found a way to condone the sale of securities in Aden even though he had to approach the question as a Shafiʿite jurist. Along these lines, Nico J. G. Kaptein, *Islam, Colonialism and the Modern Age in the Netherlands East Indies: A Biography of Sayyid Uthman (1822–1914)* (Leiden: Brill, 2014), 267, concluded that Sayyid ʿUthman, a defender of *taqlīd*, favored steamships, trains, the telegraph, street lights, printing presses, and so on, even though he had reservations about the religious uses of phonographs and telescopes.
6. Note, for example, Riḍā's criticism of Muḥammad Bakhīt al-Muṭīʿī's permissive ruling in favor of the phonograph, discussed in chapter 5.
7. Earl of Cromer (Evelyn Baring), *Modern Egypt* (London: Macmillan, 1908), 2:162, 426, as discussed in the present book's introduction and chapter 3.
8. Ana Belén Soage, "Rashīd Ridā's Legacy," *Muslim World* 98, no. 1 (2008): 1–23. The radicalization thesis is an old and persistent one, and I cite Soage's synthesis merely for convenience. See, for another example, Nadav Safran, *Egypt in Search of Political Community: An Analysis of the Intellectual and Political Evolution of Egypt, 1804–1952* (Cambridge, Mass.: Harvard University Press,

1961), 84. Safran claimed argued that the failure of Riḍā's plans for reviving the caliphate gradually drove him "away from his initial mild liberalism toward an uncompromising legal and traditional puritanism akin to the spirit of the Wahhabis of Arabia." Political scientists have accepted this thesis because it confirms their impression that Riḍā shifted from "modernizing Islam" to "Islamizing modernity." See Mehran Kamrava, "Contextualizing Innovation in Islam," in *Innovation in Islam: Traditions and Contributions*, ed. Mehran Kamrava (Berkeley: University of California Press, 2011), 9.

9. The debate over Egyptian pilgrims' right to carry guns and the drapes for the Kaʿba into the Ḥijāz under Saudi rule was one of the causes of political tension. See Martin Kramer, "Shaykh Maraghi's Mission to the Hijaz, 1925." *Asian and African Studies* (Haifa), 16 (1982): 121–36; and Rainer Brunner, "Education, Politics, and the Struggle for Intellectual Leadership: Al-Azhar Between 1927 and 1945," in *Guardians of Faith in Modern Times: ʿUlamaʾ in the Middle East*, ed. Meir Hatina, 109–40 (Leiden: Brill, 2009), 128–29. Also see *Al-Manār* 28 (1927): 465–73.
10. For historical context, see Martin S. Kramer, *Islam Assembled: The Advent of the Muslim Congresses* (New York: Columbia University Press, 1986), 110; and Nabil Mouline, *Les clercs de l'Islam: Autorité religieuse et pouvoir politique en Arabie Saoudite (XVIIIe-XXIe siècles)* (Paris: Presses Universitaires de France, 2009), 143–45.
11. *Al-Manār* 28 (1927): 3.
12. A scholar has argued, however, that ʿAbduh and Riḍā were the essential reformers behind an "Islamic legal Reformation." See Felicitas Opwis, "Changes in Modern Islamic Legal Theory: Reform or Reformation?," chap. 2 in *An Islamic Reformation?*, ed. Michaelle Browers and Charles Kurzman (Lanham, Md.: Lexington Books, 2004).
13. *Al-Manār* 4 (1901): 462–63.
14. *Al-Manār* 12 (1909): 337–38; and Riḍā, *Fatāwā*, 2:768–69, no. 287.
15. *Al-Manār* 13 (1910): 113–14; and Riḍā, *Fatāwā*, 3:867–68, no. 318.
16. "Al-Rijāl am al-māl," *al-Manār* 3 (1900): 505–9, as discussed in chapter 4 of the present book.
17. I briefly described this battle of fatwas, to which I will devote a separate article, at the end of the introduction.

SELECTED BIBLIOGRAPHY

The thirty-five volumes of *al-Manār*, 1898 to 1935, are the main primary source on which this book is based, and I normally turned to the facsimile edition of this journal printed by Dār al-Wafāʾ of al-Manṣūra. In addition, to understand better the historical context of certain legal and religious discussions, I researched a few other Arabic journals published in a targeted way. These journals include *al-Muqtaṭaf, al-Muʾayyad, al-Muṣawwar*, and *Majallatī*. Many editors and reporters wrote to *al-Manār* from different parts of the world. Riḍā's fatwas were translated and discussed in journals such as *al-Fiṭra al-Islāmiyya* (Buenos Aires, Argentina), *Shura* (Orenburg, Russia), *al-Hilāl* (Calcutta, India), *al-Munīr* (Padang, Dutch East Indies), and *Tianfang xueli yuekan* (Guangzhou, China). I hired two research assistants, native Chinese speakers, to help me assess the translations of Riḍā's fatwas in one of these journals, but I lacked the time, resources, and linguistic competence to examine the other journals as well. To understand better the historical context behind international requests for fatwas, I usually turned to local and regional historical studies in English or French. The selected bibliography that follows acknowledges my debt to these studies. It also includes a few indispensable primary and secondary sources as well as theoretical and methodological discussions that I found especially engaging. It specifies only a fraction of the texts that I consulted to write this book, and to which I refer in the notes.

Abaza, Mona. "Southeast Asia and the Middle East: Al-Manar and Islamic Modernity." In *From the Mediterranean to the China Sea: Miscellaneous Notes*, ed. Claude Guillot, Denys Lombard, and Roderich Ptak, 93–111. Wiesbaden: Harrassowitz, 1998.

ʿAbduh, Muḥammad. *Al-Aʿmāl al-kāmila*, ed. Muḥammad ʿImāra. Beirut: al-Muʾassasa al-ʿArabiyya li-l-Dirāsāt wa-l-Nashr, 1972–74.

——. *Al-Islām wa-l-Naṣrāniyya maᶜ al-ᶜilm wa-l-madaniyya*, ed. Muḥammad Rashīd Riḍā. 2nd ed. Cairo: al-Manār, 1905.

——. *Risālat al-tawḥīd*. Cairo: al-Maṭbaᶜa al-ᶜĀmira al-Khayriyya, 1906.

ᶜAbduh, Muḥammad, and Muḥammad Rashīd Riḍā. *Tafsīr al-Qurʾān al-Ḥakīm, al-mushtahar bi-ism Tafsīr al-Manār*. 2nd ed. Cairo: Dār al-Manār, 1947.

Abou El Fadl, Khaled. "Islamic Law and Muslim Minorities: The Juristic Discourse on Muslim Minorities from the Second/Eighth to the Eleventh/Seventeenth Centuries," *Islamic Law and Society* 1, no. 2 (1994): 141–87.

Abushouk, Ahmed Ibrahim. "Al-Manār and the Ḥadhramī Elite in the Malay-Indonesian World: Challenge and Response," *Journal of the Royal Asiatic Society* 17, no. 3 (2007): 301–22.

Adams, Charles C. *Islam and Modernism in Egypt: A Study of the Modern Reform Movement Inaugurated by Muḥammad ᶜAbduh*. New York: Russell and Russell, 1933.

——. "Muḥammad ᶜAbduh and the Transvaal Fatwā." In *The Macdonald Presentation Volume: A Tribute to Duncan Black Macdonald: Consisting of Articles by Former Students, Presented to Him on His Seventieth Birthday, April 9, 1933*, 13–29. Freeport, N.Y.: Books for Libraries, 1968.

Adas, Michael. *Machines as the Measure of Men: Science, Technology, and Ideologies of Western Dominance*. (Ithaca, N.Y.: Cornell University Press, 1989.

Afghan, Gemmal Eddine. [Lettre au Directeur]. *Journal des débats*, May 18, 1883.

Afghānī, Jamāl al-Dīn al-, and Muḥammad ᶜAbduh. *Al-ᶜUrwa al-Wuthqa, wa-l-thawra al-taḥrīriyya al-kubra*. Cairo: Dār al-ᶜArab, 1957.

Ahmad, Feroz. "Ottoman Perceptions of the Capitulations 1800–1914." *Journal of Islamic Studies* 11, no. 1 (2000): 1–20.

Alleaume, Ghislaine. "Hygiène publique et travaux publics: Les ingénieurs et l'assainissement du Caire (1882–1907)." *Annales islamologiques* 20 (1984): 151–82.

Amīn, Qāsim. *Al-Marʾa al-jadīda*. Cairo: Maṭbaᶜat al-Shaᶜb, 1911.

Anderson, Michael R. "Islamic Law and the Colonial Encounter in British India." In *Institutions and Ideologies: A SOAS South Asia Reader*, ed. David Arnold and Peter Robb, 165–85. Surrey, U.K.: Curzon, 1993).

Anderson, Warwick. "Excremental Colonialism: Public Health and the Poetics of Pollution." *Critical Inquiry* 21 (1995): 640–69.

Appadurai, Arjun, ed., *The Social Life of Things: Commodities in Cultural Perspective*. Cambridge: Cambridge University Press, 1986.

Armbrust, Walter. "The Formation of National Culture in Egypt in the Interwar Period: Cultural Trajectories." *History Compass* 7, no. 1 (2009): 155–80.

Arnold, David. "Europe, Technology, and Colonialism in the 20th Century." *History and Technology* 21, no. 1 (2005): 85–106.

Asad, Talal. *Formations of the Secular: Christianity, Islam, Modernity*. Stanford, Calif.: Stanford University Press, 2003.

——. *Genealogies of Religion: Discipline and Reasons of Power in Christianity and Islam*. Baltimore: Johns Hopkins University Press, 1993.

Atabaki, Touraj, ed., *The State and the Subaltern: Modernization, Society and the State in Turkey and Iran*. London: I. B. Tauris, 2007.

Ayadi, Taoufik. *Mouvement réformiste et mouvements populaires à Tunis (1906–1912)*. Tunis: Imprimerie officielle de la République tunisienne, 1986.

Ayalon, Ami. *The Press in the Arab Middle East: A History*. New York: Oxford University Press, 1995.

Badran, Margot. *Feminists, Islam, and Nation: Gender and the Making of Modern Egypt*. Princeton, N.J.: Princeton University Press, 1995.

Badrawi, Malak. *Political Violence in Egypt 1910–1924: Secret Societies, Plots and Assassinations*. Richmond, Surrey, U.K.: Curzon, 2000.

Baktaş, Yakup. "Crossing Communal Boundaries: Technology and Cultural Diversity in the 19th Century Ottoman Empire." In *Multicultural Science in the Ottoman Empire*, ed. Ekmeleddin Ihsanoglu, Kostas Chatzis, and Efthymios Nikolaidis, 139–47. Turnhout, Belgium: Brepols, 2003.

Baldauf, Ingeborg. "Jadidism in Central Asia Within Reformism and Modernism in the Muslim World." *Die Welt des Islams* 41, no. 1 (2001): 72–88.

Bang, Anne K. *Sufis and Scholars of the Sea: Family Networks in East Africa, 1860–1925*. London: Routledge-Curzon, 2003.

Barak, On. *On Time: Technology and Temporality in Modern Egypt*. Berkeley: University of California Press, 2013.

Baron, Beth. *Egypt as a Woman: Nationalism, Gender, and Politics*. Berkeley: University of California Press, 2005.

——. *The Women's Awakening in Egypt: Culture, Society, and the Press*. Chelsea, Mich.: Yale University Press, 1994.

Bektas, Yakup. "The Sultan's Messenger: Cultural Constructions of Ottoman Telegraphy, 1848–1880." *Technology and Culture* 41, no. 4 (2000): 669–96.

Benjamin, Walter. "Capitalism as Religion," trans. Chad Kautzer. Chap. 15 in *The Frankfurt School on Religion: Key Writings by the Major Thinkers*, ed. Eduardo Mendieta. New York: Routledge, 2005.

——. "The Work of Art in the Age of Mechanical Reproduction." In *Illuminations*, ed. Hannah Arendt, trans. Harry Zohn. New York: Schocken, 1968.

Bennison, Amira K. "Muslim Internationalism Between Empire and Nation-State." Chap. 7 in *Religious Internationals in the Modern World: Globalization and Faith Communities Since 1750*, ed. Abigail Green and Vincent Viaene. Basingstoke, U.K.: Palgrave Macmillan, 2012).

Beshara, Adel, ed. *The Origins of Syrian Nationhood: Histories, Pioneers and Identity*. New York: Routledge, 2011.

Betts, Raymond F. *Uncertain Dimensions: Western Overseas Empires in the Twentieth Century*. Minneapolis: University of Minnesota Press, 1985.

Birdal, Murat. *The Political Economy of Ottoman Public Debt: Insolvency and European Financial Control in the Late Nineteenth Century*. London: Tauris Academic Studies, 2010.

Bluhm-Warn, Jutta. "*Al-Manār* and Ahmad Soorkattie: Links in the Chain of Transmission of Muḥammad ʿAbduh's Ideas to the Malay-Speaking World." In *Islam: Essays on Scripture, Thought and Society: A Festschrift in Honour of Anthony H. Johns*, ed. Peter G. Riddell and Tony Street, 295–308. Leiden: Brill, 1997.

Blumenthal Frères, H. et J. "Odéon: Chants arabes sur disques double face" (1913/1914).

Bowen, John R. *Islam, Law and Equality in Indonesia: An Anthropology of Public Reasoning*. Cambridge: Cambridge University Press, 2003.

Brower, Benjamin Claude. *A Desert Named Peace: The Violence of France's Empire in the Algerian Sahara, 1844–1902*. (New York: Columbia University Press, 2009.

Browers, Michaelle, and Charles Kurzman. *An Islamic Reformation?* Lanham, Md.: Lexington Books, 2004.

Brown, Daniel W. *Rethinking Tradition in Modern Islamic Thought*. Cambridge: Cambridge University Press, 1996.

Brown, Nathan J. *The Rule of Law in the Arab World: Courts in Egypt and the Gulf.* Cambridge: Cambridge University Press, 1997.

Brummett, Palmira Johnson. *Image and Imperialism in the Ottoman Revolutionary Press, 1908–1911.* Albany: State University of New York Press, 2000.

Brunner, Rainer. "Education, Politics, and the Struggle for Intellectual Leadership: Al-Azhar Between 1927 and 1945." In *Guardians of Faith in Modern Times: 'Ulama' in the Middle East*, ed. Meir Hatina, 109–40. Leiden: Brill, 2009.

Burbank, Jane, and Frederick Cooper. *Empires in World History: Power and the Politics of Difference.* Princeton, N.J.: Princeton University Press, 2010.

Burhanudin, Jajat. "Aspiring for Islamic Reform: Southeast Asian Requests for *Fatwās* in *Al-Manār.*" *Islamic Law and Society* 12, no. 1 (2005): 9–26.

Burton, Antoinette M. *The Trouble with Empire: Challenges to Modern British Imperialism.* Oxford: Oxford University Press, 2015.

Cain, Peter. "Free Trade, Social Reform and Imperialism: J. A. Hobson and the Dilemmas of Liberalism, 1890–1914." In *Free Trade and Its Reception 1815–1960*, ed. Andrew Marrison, 207–23. London: Routledge, 1998.

Cannon, Byron. *Politics of Law and the Courts in Nineteenth-Century Egypt.* Salt Lake City: University of Utah Press, 1988.

Chakrabarty, Dipesh. "Open Space / Public Space: Garbage, Modernity and India." *South Asia* 14, no. 1 (1991): 15–31.

Choudhury, Deep Kanta Lahiri. *Telegraphic Imperialism: Crisis and Panic in the Indian Empire, c. 1830–1920.* Basingstoke, U.K.: Palgrave Macmillan, 2010.

Cole, Juan Ricardo. "Feminism, Class, and Islam in Turn -of-the-Century Egypt." *International Journal of Middle East Studies* 13, no. 4 (1981): 387–407.

Commins David Dean. "From Wahhabi to Salafi." Chap. 8 in *Saudi Arabia in Transition: Insights on Social, Political, Economic and Religious Change*, ed. Bernard Haykel, Thomas Hegghammer, and Stéphane Lacroix. New York: Cambridge University Press, 2015.

——. *Islamic Reform: Politics and Social Change in Late Ottoman Syria.* New York: Oxford University Press, 1990.

——. *The Wahhabi Mission and Saudi Arabia.* New York: I. B. Tauris, 2006.

Conrad, Sebastian. "Enlightenment in Global History: A Historiographical Critique." *The American Historical Review* 117 (2012): 999–1027.

Cook, Michael. *Commanding Right and Forbidding Wrong in Islamic Thought.* Cambridge: Cambridge University Press, 2000.

——. "Magian Cheese: An Archaic Problem in Islamic Law." *Bulletin of the School of Oriental and African Studies* 47 (1984): 449–67.

Cooper, Frederick. "What Is the Concept of Globalization Good For? An African Historian's Perspective." *African Affairs* 100, no. 399 (2001): 189–213.

Crecelius, Daniel. "The Course of Secularization in Modern Egypt." Chap. 4 in *Religion and Political Modernization*, ed. Donald Eugene Smith. New Haven, Conn.: Yale University Press, 1974.

——. "Nonideological Responses of the Egyptian Ulama to Modernization." Chap. 7 in *Scholars, Saints, and Sufis: Muslim Religious Institutions in the Middle East Since 1500*, ed. Nikki R. Keddie. Berkeley: University of California Press, 1972.

Crews, Robert D. *For Prophet and Tsar: Islam and Empire in Russia and Central Asia.* Cambridge, Mass.: Harvard University Press, 2006.

Cromer, Earl of (Evelyn Baring). *Modern Egypt.* London: Macmillan, 1908.

Crouchley, A. E. *The Investment of Foreign Capital in Egyptian Companies and Public Debt*. Cairo: Government Press, Bulaq, 1936.

Dallal, Ahmad. "Appropriating the Past: Twentieth-Century Reconstruction of Pre-Modern Islamic Thought," *Islamic Law and Society* 7, no. 3 (2000): 325–58.

Daly, M. W. *Empire on the Nile: The Anglo-Egyptian Sudan, 1898–1934*. Cambridge: Cambridge University Press, 1986.

Danielson, Virginia. *The Voice of Egypt: Umm Kulthūm, Arabic Song, and Egyptian Society in the Twentieth Century*. Chicago: University of Chicago Press, 1997.

Davids, Achmat. *The Mosques of Bo-Kaap: A Social History of Islam at the Cape*. Athlone, Cape: South African Institute of Arabic and Islamic Research, 1980.

Davis, Eric. *Challenging Colonialism: Bank Miṣr and Egyptian Industrialization, 1920–1941*. Princeton, N.J.: Princeton University Press, 1983.

Davison, Roderic H. *Essays in Ottoman and Turkish History, 1774–1923: The Impact of the West*. Austin: University of Texas Press, 1990.

——. *Reform in the Ottoman Empire, 1856–1876*. Princeton, N.J.: Princeton University Press, 1963.

——. "Turkish Attitudes Concerning Christian-Muslim Equality in the Nineteenth Century." *American Historical Review* 59, no. 4 (1954): 844–64.

Debs, Richard A. *Islamic Law and Civil Code: The Law of Property in Egypt*. New York: Columbia University Press, 2010.

Douglas, Mary. *Purity and Danger: An Analysis of Concepts of Pollution and Taboo*. London: Routledge, 2001.

Dudoignon, Stéphane A., and Komatsu Hisao, eds. *Islam in Politics in Russia and Central Asia (Early Eighteenth to Late Twentieth Centuries)*. London: Routledge, 2001.

Dudoignon, Stéphane A., Komatsu Hisao, and Kosugi Yasushi, eds. *Intellectuals in the Modern Islamic World: Transmission, Transformation, Communication*. London: Routledge, 2009.

Dūrī, ʿAbd al-ʿAzīz. *The Historical Formation of the Arab Nation: A Study in Identity and Consciousness*, trans. Lawrence I. Conrad. London: Croom Helm, 1987.

Earle, Edward Mead. *Turkey, the Great Powers, and the Bagdad Railway: A Study in Imperialism*. New York: Macmillan, 1924.

Ebert, Johannes. *Religion und Reform in der arabischen Provinz: Ḥusayn al-Ǧisr aṭ-Ṭarābulusī (1845–1909)—Ein islamischer Gelehrter zwischen Tradition und Reform*. Frankfurt am Main: P. Lang, 1991.

Eccel, A. Chris. *Egypt, Islam, and Social Change: Al-Azhar in Conflict and Accommodation*. Berlin: K. Schwarz, 1984.

Eisenstadt, S. N. "Multiple Modernities." *Daedalus* 129, no.1 (2000): 1–30.

Elias, Jamal J. *Aisha's Cushion: Religious Art, Perception, and Practice in Islam*. Cambridge, Mass.: Harvard University Press, 2012.

Elshakry, Marwa. *Reading Darwin in Arabic, 1860–1950*. Chicago: University of Chicago Press, 2013.

El Shakry, Omnia. *The Great Social Laboratory: Subjects of Knowledge in Colonial and Postcolonial Egypt*. Stanford, Calif.: Stanford University Press, 2007.

EzzelArab, AbdelAziz. *European Control and Egypt's Traditional Elites—A Case Study in Elite Economic Nationalism*. Lewiston, N.Y.: Edwin Mellen Press, 2002.

Fahmy, Khaled. "An Olfactory Tale of Two Cities: Cairo in the Nineteenth Century." In *Historians of Cairo: Essays in Honor of George Scanlon*, ed. Jill Edwards, 155–87. Cairo: American University in Cairo Press, 2002.

——. "The Anatomy of Justice: Forensic Medicine and Criminal Law in Nineteenth-Century Egypt." *Islamic Law and Society* 6, no. 2 (1999): 224–71.

Fahmy, Ziad. *Ordinary Egyptians: Creating the Modern Nation Through Popular Culture*. Stanford, Calif.: Stanford University Press, 2011.

Farah, Caesar. "Censorship and Freedom of Expression in Ottoman Syria and Egypt." In *Nationalism in a Non-National State: The Dissolution of the Ottoman Empire*, ed. William W. Haddad and William Ochsenwald, 151–94. Columbus: Ohio University Press, 1977.

Firro, Kais M. *Inventing Lebanon: Nationalism and the State Under the Mandate*. London: I. B. Tauris, 2003.

Flood, Finbarr B. *Objects of Translation: Material Culture and Medieval "Hindu-Muslim" Encounter*. Princeton, N.J.: Princeton University Press, 2009.

Frank, Allen J. *Muslim Religious Institutions in Imperial Russia: The Islamic World of Novouzensk District and the Kazakh Inner Horde, 1780–1910*. Leiden: Brill, 2001.

Freitag, Ulrike. *Indian Ocean Migrants and State Formation in Hadhramaut: Reforming the Homeland*. Brill: Leiden, 2003.

Freitag, Ulrike, and William G. Clarence-Smith, eds., *Hadhrami Traders, Scholars and Statesmen in the Indian Ocean, 1750s–1960s*. Leiden: Brill, 1997.

Friedmann, Yohanan. *Prophecy Continuous: Aspects of Aḥmadī Religious Thought and Its Medieval Background*. New Delhi: Oxford University Press, 2003.

Gallagher John, and Ronald Robinson. "The Imperialism of Free Trade." *Economic History Review* 6, no. 1 (1953): 1–15.

Gauvain, Richard. *Salafi Ritual Purity: In the Presence of God*. London: Routledge, 2013.

Geaves, Ron. *Islam and Britain: Muslim Mission in an Age of Empire*. London: Bloomsbury Academic, 2018.

Gelvin James L., and Nile Green, eds., *Global Muslims in the Age of Stream and Print*. Berkeley: University of California Press, 2014.

Geraci, Robert. "Russian Orientalism at an Impasse: Tsarist Education Policy and the 1910 Conference on Islam." In *Russia's Orient: Imperial Borderlands and Peoples, 1700–1917*, ed. Daniel R. Brower and Edward J. Lazzerini, 138–161. Bloomington: Indiana University Press, 1997.

Germain, Éric. *L'Afrique du Sud musulmane: Histoire des relations entre Indiens et Malais du Cap*. Paris: Karthala, 2007.

Gershoni, Israel, and James P. Jankowski, *Egypt, Islam, and the Arabs: The Search for Egyptian Nationhood, 1900–1930*. Oxford: Oxford University Press, 1987.

——. *Redefining the Egyptian Nation, 1930–1945*. Cambridge: Cambridge University Press, 1995.

Gesink, Indira Falk. *Islamic Reform and Conservatism: Al-Azhar and the Evolution of Modern Sunni Islam*. Rev. ed. New York: I. B. Tauris, 2010.

Geyikdaği, V. Necla. *Foreign Investment in the Ottoman Empire International Trade and Relations 1854–1914*. London: Tauris Academic Studies, 2011.

Ghāndī, Mahātmā. *Kitāb al-Ṣiḥḥa*, trans. *ʿAbd al-Razzāq al-Malīḥ al-Ābādī*. Cairo: Maṭbaʿat al-Manār, 1927.

Gilmartin, David. *Empire and Islam: Punjab and the Making of Pakistan*. Berkeley: University of California Press, 1988.

Gräf, Bettina, and Jakob Skovgaard-Petersen, *Global Mufti: The Phenomenon of Yūsuf Al-Qaraḍāwī*. New York: Columbia University Press, 2009.

Gramsci, Antonio. *Prison Notebooks*, vol. 2, ed. and trans. Joseph Buttigieg, 215–20. New York: Columbia U. Press, 2011.

Gran, Peter. *Islamic Roots of Capitalism: Egypt, 1760–1840*. Austin: University of Texas Press, 1979.

Green, Arnold H. *The Tunisian Ulama, 1873–1915: Social Structure and Response to Ideological Currents*. Leiden: Brill, 1978.

Green, Nile. *Bombay Islam: The Religious Economy of the West Indian Ocean, 1840–1915*. Cambridge: Cambridge University Press, 2011.

Griffel Frank. "What do We Mean By 'Salafi?' Connecting Muḥammad ʿAbduh with Egypt's Nūr Party in Islam's Contemporary Intellectual History." *Die Welt des Islams* 55 (2015): 186–220.

Gronow, Pekka. "The Record Industry Comes to the Orient." *Ethnomusicology* 25 (1981): 251–84.

Guenther, Alan M. "Syed Mahmood and the Transformation of Muslim Law in British India." PhD dissertation, McGill University, 2004.

Haddad, Mahmoud. "Arab Religious Nationalism in the Colonial Era: Rereading Rashīd Riḍā's Ideas on the Caliphate," *Journal of the American Oriental Society* 117, no. 2 (1997): 253–77.

——. "Muḥammad Rashīd Riḍā (D. 1935)." In *Islamic Legal Thought: A Compendium of Muslim Jurists.* Studies in Islamic Law and Society, ed. David Powers, Oussama Arabi, and Susan Spectorsky. Leiden: Brill, 2013.

Hakim, Carol. *The Origins of the Lebanese National Idea, 1840-1920.* Berkeley: University of California Press, 2013.

Halevi, Leor. "Christian Impurity versus Economic Necessity: A Fifteenth-Century Fatwa on European Paper." *Speculum* 83, no. 4 (2008): 917–45.

——. "Is China a House of Islam? Chinese Questions, Arabic Answers, and the Translation of Salafism from Cairo to Canton, 1930–1932," *Die Welt des Islams* 59, no. 1 (2019): 33–69.

——. "The Consumer Jihad: Boycott Fatwas and Nonviolent Resistance on the World Wide Web." *International Journal of Middle East Studies* 44 (2012): 45–70.

——. "Religion and Cross-Cultural Trade: A Framework for Interdisciplinary Inquiry." Chap. 1 in *Religion and Trade: Cross-Cultural Exchanges in World History, 1000–1900*, ed. Francesca Trivellato, Leor Halevi, and Cátia Antunes. Oxford: Oxford University Press.

Hallaq, Wael B. *A History of Islamic Legal Theories: An Introduction to Sunnī* Uṣūl Al-Fiqh. Cambridge: Cambridge University Press, 1997.

Hamzah, Dyala. "L'intérêt général (*maslaha 'âmma*) ou le triomphe de l'opinion: Fondation délibératoire (et esquisses délibératives) dans les écrits du publiciste syro-égyptien Muhammad Rashîd Ridâ (1865–1935)." PhD thesis, L'École des hautes études en sciences sociales and Freie Universität Berlin, 2008.

Hannerz, Ulf. "The Global Ecumene as a Landscape of Modernity." In *Transnational Connections: Culture, People, Places*. London: Routledge, 1996.

Hausman, William J., Peter Hertner, and Mira Wilkins. *Global Electrification: Multinational Enterprise and International Finance in the History of Light and Power, 1878-2007.* Cambridge: Cambridge University Press, 2008.

Haykel, Bernard. "On the Nature of Salafi Thought and Action." Chap. 1 in *Global Salafism: Islam's New Religious Movement*, ed. Roel Meijer. New York: Columbia University Press, 2009.

Headrick, Daniel R. *The Tentacles of Progress: Technology Transfer in the Age of Imperialism, 1850–1940.* Oxford: Oxford University Press, 1988.

——. *The Tools of Empire: Technology and European Imperialism in the Nineteenth Century.* New York: Oxford University Press, 1981.

Hefner, Robert W., ed. *The New Cambridge History of Islam.* Vol. 6, *Muslims and Modernity: Culture and Society Since 1800.* Cambridge, UK: Cambridge University Press, 2010.

Hirschkind, Charles. *The Ethical Soundscape: Cassette Sermons and Islamic Counterpublics.* New York: Columbia University Press, 2006.

Hoffman-Ladd, Valerie J. "Polemics on the Modesty and Segregation of Women in Contemporary Egypt." *International Journal of Middle East Studies* 19, no. 1 (1987): 23–50.

Hourani, Albert. *Arabic Thought in the Liberal Age, 1798–1939.* Cambridge: Cambridge University Press, 1983.

Howe, Anthony. *Free Trade and Liberal England, 1846–1946*. Oxford: Clarendon, 1997.

Howes, David, ed. *Cross-Cultural Consumption: Global Markets, Local Realities*. London: Routledge, 1996.

Huber, Valeska. *Channelling Mobilities: Migration and Globalisation in the Suez Canal Region and Beyond, 1869–1914*. Cambridge: Cambridge University Press, 2013.

Hurgronje, Snouck. "L'usage de la cloche chez les musulmans de Java." *Revue du monde musulman* 15, no. 9 (1911): 386–87.

Ḥusayn, Muḥammad Fahmī. *Mabādiʾ al-iqtiṣād al-siyāsī*. Cairo: Maṭbaʿat al-Saʿāda, 1908.

Ibrahim, Ahmed Fekry. *Pragmatism in Islamic Law: A Social and Intellectual History*. Syracuse, N.Y.: Syracuse University Press, 2015.

Islahi, Abdul Azim. *Economic Thinking of Arab Muslims Writers During the Nineteenth Century*. New York: Palgrave Macmillan, 2015.

Jacob, Wilson Chacko. *Working Out Egypt: Effendi Masculinity and Subject Formation in Colonial Modernity, 1870–1940*. Durham, N.C.: Duke University Press, 2010.

Jamʿ jawāmiʿ al-aḥādīth wa-l-asānīd wa-maknaz al-ṣiḥāḥ wa-l-sunan wa-l-masānīd. Vaduz, Liechtenstein: Thesaurus Islamicus Foundation, 2000.

Johansen, Baber. "La découverte des choses qui parlent: La légalisation de la torture judiciaire en droit musulman (xiiie-xive siècles)." *Enquête* 7 (1999): 175–202.

Kamrava, Mehran, ed., *Innovation in Islam: Traditions and Contributions*. Berkeley: University of California Press, 2011.

Kaptein, Nico J. G. *Islam, Colonialism and the Modern Age in the Netherlands East Indies: A Biography of Sayyid Uthman (1822–1914)*. Leiden: Brill, 2014.

——, ed. *The Muhimmât al-nafâ'is: A Bilingual Meccan Fatwa Collection for Indonesian Muslims from the End of the Nineteenth Century*. Jakarta: INIS, 1997.

——. "Southeast Asian Debates and Middle Eastern Inspiration: European Dress in Minangkabau at the Beginning of the 20th Century." In *Southeast Asia and the Middle East: Islam, Movement, and the Longue Durée*, ed. Eric Tagliacozzo, 176–95. Stanford, Calif.: Stanford University Press, 2009).

——. "The Voice of the ʿUlamāʾ: Fatwas and Religious Authority in Indonesia." *Archives de sciences sociales des religions* 125, no. 1 (2004): 115–30.

Kawākibī, ʿAbd al-Raḥmān al-. *Al-Aʿmāl al-kāmila li-l-Kawākibī*. 3rd ed. Beirut: Markaz Dirāsāt al-Waḥda al-ʿArabiyya, 2007.

Kerr, Malcolm H. *Islamic Reform: The Political and Legal Theories of Muḥammad ʿAbduh and Rashīd Riḍā*. Berkeley: University of California Press, 1966.

——. "Rashīd Riḍā and Islamic Legal Reform: An Ideological Analysis." Part I, "Methodology." *The Muslim World* 50, no. 2 (1960): 99–108.

Khalfaoui, Mouez. *L'islam indien: Pluralité ou pluralisme: Le cas d'al-Fatāwā al-Hindiyya*. Frankfurt am Main: P. Lang, 2008.

Khalid, Adeeb. *The Politics of Muslim Cultural Reform: Jadidism in Central Asia*. Berkeley: University of California Press, 1998.

Kittler, Friedrich A. *Gramophone, Film, Typewriter*, trans. G. Winthrop-Young and M. Wutz. Stanford, Calif.: Stanford University Press, 1999.

Kline, Ronald, and Trevor Pinch, "Users as Agents of Technological Change: The Social Construction of the Automobile in the Rural United States." *Technology and Culture* 37, no. 4 (1996): 763–95.

Kolsky, Elizabeth. *Colonial Justice in British India*. Cambridge: Cambridge University Press, 2010.

Koningsveld, Sjoerd van. "Between Communalism and Secularism: Modern Sunnite Discussions on Male Head-Gear and Coiffure." In *Pluralism and Identity: Studies in Ritual Behavior*, ed. Jan Platvoet and Karel van der Toorn, 327–45. Leiden: Brill, 1995.

Kostiner, Joseph. *The Making of Saudi Arabia, 1916–1936: From Chieftaincy to Monarchical State*. New York: Oxford University Press, 1993.

Kozma, Liat, Cyrus Schayegh, and Avner Wishnitzer, eds., *A Global Middle East: Mobility, Materiality and Culture in the Modern Age, 1880–1940*. London: I. B. Tauris, 2015.

Kramer, Martin S. *Islam Assembled: The Advent of the Muslim Congresses*. New York: Columbia University Press, 1986.

——. "Shaykh Maraghi's Mission to the Hijaz, 1925." *Asian and African Studies* (Haifa), 16 (1982): 121–36.

Krawietz, Birgit. "Cut and Paste in Legal Rules: Designing Islamic Norms with *Talfiq*," *Die Welt Des Islams* 42, no. 1 (2002): 3–40.

Kugle, Scott Alan. "Framed, Blamed and Renamed: The Recasting of Islamic Jurisprudence in Colonial South Asia." *Modern Asian Studies* 35 (2001): 257–313.

Kupferschmidt, Uri M. *European Department Stores and Middle Eastern Consumers: The Orosdi-Back Saga*. Istanbul: Ottoman Bank Archives and Research Centre, 2007.

——. "The Social History of the Sewing Machine in the Middle East." *Die Welt Des Islams*, 44, no. 2 (2004): 195–213.

——. *The Supreme Muslim Council: Islam Under the British Mandate for Palestine*. Leiden: Brill, 1987.

Kuran, Timur. *Islam and Mammon: The Economic Predicaments of Islamism*. Princeton, N.J.: Princeton University Press, 2004.

——. *The Long Divergence: How Islamic Law Held Back the Middle East*. Princeton, N.J.: Princeton University Press, 2011.

Laffan, Michael Francis. *Islamic Nationhood and Colonial Indonesia: The Umma Below the Winds*. London: Routledge, 2003.

Lagrange, Frédéric. "'Mettre en musique': La sélection et l'interprétation de la qaṣīda dans le répertoire égyptien savant enregistré sur disques 78 tours (1903–1925)." *Quaderni di Studi Arabi* 7 (2012): 169–206.

——. "Musiciens et poètes en Égypte au temps de la Nahda." PhD thesis, Université de Paris VIII, à Saint-Denis, 1994.

Landau, Jacob M. *Pan-Islam: History and Politics*. London: Routledge, 2016.

Laurens, Henry. *L'expédition d'Égypte, 1798–1801*. Paris: Armand Colin, 1989.

Lauzière, Henri. "The Construction of *Salafiyya*: Reconsidering Salafism from the Perspective of Conceptual History." *International Journal of Middle East Studies* 42, no. 3 (2010): 369–89.

——. *The Making of Salafism: Islamic Reform in the Twentieth Century*. New York: Columbia University Press, 2016.

Lewis, Bernard. *The Muslim Discovery of Europe*. New York: Norton, 1982.

Lia, Brynjar. *The Society of the Muslim Brothers in Egypt: The Rise of an Islamic Mass Movement, 1928–1942*. Reading, U.K.: Ithaca Press, 1998.

Lipman, Jonathan N. "Hyphenated Chinese: Sino-Muslim Identity in Modern China." In *Remapping China: Fissures in Historical Terrain*, ed. Gail Hershatter, Emily Honig, Jonathan N. Lipman, and Randall Stross, 97–112 (Stanford, Calif.: Stanford University Press, 1996).

Low, Michael Christopher. "Empire and the Hajj: Pilgrims, Plagues, and Pan-Islam under British Surveillance, 1865–1908." *International Journal of Middle East Studies* 40, no. 2 (2008): 269–90.

Löwy, Michael. "Capitalism as Religion: Walter Benjamin and Max Weber." *Historical Materialism* 15 (2009): 60–73.

Mallat, Chibli. "The Debate on Riba and Interest in Twentieth Century Jurisprudence." In *Islamic Law and Finance*, ed. Chibli Mallat, 69–88. London: Graham & Trotman, 1988.

Manela, Erez. *The Wilsonian Moment: Self-Determination and the International Origins of Anticolonial Nationalism.* Oxford: Oxford University Press, 2007.

March, Andrew F. *Islam and Liberal Citizenship: The Search for an Overlapping Consensus.* Oxford: Oxford University Press, 2009.

Massignon, Louis, "Les vraies origines dogmatiques du Wahhabisme." *Revue du monde musulman* 36 (1918–1919): 324–25.

Masʿūd, Muḥammad Khālid. "Trends in the Interpretation of Islamic Law as Reflected in the Fatāwá Literature of Deoband School: A Study of the Attitudes of the ʿUlamāʾ of Deoband to Certain Social Problems and Inventions." M.A. thesis, McGill University, Institute of Islamic Studies, Montreal, 1969.

Masud, Muhammad Khalid, Brinkley Messick, David S. Powers, eds., *Islamic Legal Interpretation: Muftis and Their Fatwas.* Cambridge, Mass: Harvard University Press, 1996).

Masuzawa, Tomoko. "Troubles with Materiality: The Ghost of Fetishism in the Nineteenth Century." *Comparative Studies in Society and History* 42, no. 2 (2000): 242–67.

Mehta, Uday S. "Liberal Strategies of Exclusion." *Politics & Society* 18 (1990): 427–54.

Messick, Brinkley. "Madhhabs and Modernities." Chap. 11 in *The Islamic School of Law: Evolution, Devolution, and Progress*, ed. Peri Berman, Rudolph Peters, and Frank E. Vogel. Cambridge, Mass.: Islamic Legal Studies Program, Harvard Law School, 2005.

Metcalf, Barbara Daly. *Islamic Revival in British India: Deoband, 1860–1900.* Princeton, N.J.: Princeton University Press, 1982.

Meyer, Birgit, David Morgan, Crispin Paine, and S. Brent Plate, "The Origin and Mission of Material Religion." *Religion* 40 (2010): 210.

Meyer, James H. *Turks Across Empires: Marketing Muslim Identity in the Russian-Ottoman Borderlands, 1856–1914.* Oxford: Oxford University Press, 2014.

Mill, John Stuart. *Principles of Political Economy with Some of Their Applications to Social Philosophy.* New York: D. Appleton, 1891.

Milner, Alfred. *England in Egypt.* 13th ed. New York: Howard Fertig, 1970.

Minault, Gail. *The Khilafat Movement: Religious Symbolism and Political Mobilization in India.* New York: Columbia University Press, 1982.

Mitchell, Timothy Franck. *Colonising Egypt.* Cambridge: Cambridge University Press, 1988.

Mobini-Kesheh, Natalie. *The Hadrami Awakening: Community and Identity in the Netherlands East Indies, 1900–1942.* Ithaca, N.Y.: Cornell South East Asia Program Publications, 1999.

Motadel, David, ed., *Islam and the European Empires.* Oxford: Oxford University Press, 2014.

Mouline, Nabil. *Les clercs de l'Islam: Autorité religieuse et pouvoir politique en Arabie Saoudite (XVIIIe-XXIe siècles).* Paris: Presses Universitaires de France, 2009.

Mozaffari, Mehdi. *Fatwa: Violence and Discourtesy.* Aarhus, Den.: Aarhus University Press, 1998.

Mrázek, Rudolf. *Engineers of Happy Land: Technology and Nationalism in a Colony.* Princeton, N.J.: Princeton University Press, 2002.

Nelson, Kristina. *The Art of Reciting the Qurʾan.* Austin: University of Texas Press, 1985.

Noer, Deliar. *The Modernist Muslim Movement in Indonesia, 1900–1942.* Singapore: Oxford University Press, 1973.

Ochsenwald, William. *The Hijaz Railroad.* Charlottesville: University Press of Virginia, 1980.

Ogle, Vanessa. *The Global Transformation of Time, 1870–1950.* Cambridge, Mass.: Harvard University Press, 2015.

Onley, James. *The Arabian Frontier of the British Raj: Merchants, Rulers and the British in the Nineteenth-Century Gulf.* New York: Oxford University Press, 2007.

Owen, E. R. J. "Lord Cromer and the Development of Egyptian Industry, 1883–1907." *Middle Eastern Studies* 2, no. 4 (1966): 282–301.

Owen, Roger. "The Cairo Building Industry and the Building Boom of 1897 to 1907." In *Colloque international sur l'histoire du Caire*, 27 Mars–5 Avril, 1969, 337–50. Le Claire: Ministry of Culture of the Arab Republic of Egypt, 1973.

——. *The Middle East in the World Economy, 1800–1914*. London: I. B. Tauris, 2002.

Owen, Roger, and Sevket Pamuk. *A History of Middle East Economies in the Twentieth Century*. Cambridge, Mass.: Harvard University Press, 1998.

Özyüksel, Murat. *The Hejaz Railway and the Ottoman Empire: Modernity, Industrialisation and Ottoman Decline*. London: I. B. Tauris, 2014.

Patel, Abdulrazzak. *The Arab Nahḍah: The Making of the Intellectual and Humanist Movement*. Edinburgh: Edinburgh University Press, 2013.

Perkins, Kenneth J. *Tunisia: Crossroads of the Islamic and European Worlds*. London: Helm, 1986.

Peters, Rudolph. "Administrators and Magistrates: The Development of a Secular Judiciary in Egypt, 1842–1871." *Die Welt des Islams* 39 (1999).

——. "Religious Attitudes Towards Modernization in the Ottoman Empire: A Nineteenth-Century Pious Text on Steamships, Factories, and the Telegraph." *Die Welt des Islams* 26 (1986): 76–105.

Pinney, Christopher. *Camera Indica: The Social Life of Indian Photographs*. Chicago: University of Chicago Press, 1997.

Pollard, Lisa. *Nurturing the Nation: The Family Politics of Modernizing, Colonizing and Liberating Egypt, 1805–1923*. Berkeley: University of California Press, 2005.

Racy, Ali Jihad. "Musical Change and Commercial Recording in Egypt, 1904–1932." PhD thesis, University of Illinois, 1977.

——. "Record Industry and Egyptian Traditional Music: 1904–1932." *Ethnomusicology* 20, no. 1 (1976): 23–48.

Reese, Scott Steven. *Imperial Muslims: Islam, Community and Authority in the Indian Ocean, 1839–1937*. Edinburgh: Edinburgh University Press, 2018.

Reid, Donald Malcolm. *Whose Pharaohs? Archaeology, Museums, and Egyptian National Identity from Napoleon to World War I*. Berkeley: University of California Press, 2002.

Reinhart, A. Kevin. "Impurity / No Danger." *History of Religions* 30 (1990): 1–24.

Reynolds, Nancy Y. *A City Consumed: Urban Commerce, the Cairo Fire, and the Politics of Decolonization in Egypt*. Stanford, Calif.: Stanford University Press, 2012.

Riḍā, Muḥammad Rashīd. *Al-Khilāfa aw al-imāma al-ʿuẓmā: Mabāḥith sharʿiyya, siyāsiya, ijtimāʿiyya, iṣlāḥiyya*. Cairo: Maṭbaʿat al-Manār, 1922.

——. *Al-Ribā wa-l-muʿāmalāt fī al-Islām*. Port Said, al-Ẓāhir, Egypt: Maktabat al-thaqāfa al-dīniyya, 2001.

——. *Fatāwā al-Imām*, ed. *Ṣalāḥ al-Dīn al-Munajjid and Yūsuf Q. Khūrī*. Dār al-Kitab al-Jadīd: Beirut, 1970–.

——. "General Organic Law of the Arab Empire." Wingate Papers, held by Durham University Library, Archives and Special Collections, SAD. 135/7/102-104. December 1–31, 1915.

——. *Ḥuqūq al-nisāʾ fī al-Islām: wa-ḥaẓẓihinna min al-iṣlāḥ al-Muḥammadī al-ʿāmm: Nidāʾ li-l-jins al-laṭif*, ed. Muḥammad Nāṣir al-Dīn al-Albānī. Beirut: al-Maktab al-Islāmī, 1984.

——, ed. *Majmūʿat al-rasāʾil wa-l-masāʾil al-najdiyya*. Cairo: al-Manār, 1926–28.

——. "Translation of a Memorandum by . . . the Head of the Arab Party in Egypt and Syria." Wingate Papers, held by Durham University Library, Archives and Special Collections, SAD. 135/7/60-99. December 1–31, 1915.

——. *Yusr al-Islām wa-uṣūl al-tashrīʿ al-ʿāmm*. 2nd ed. Cairo: al-Mu'tamar al-Islamī, 1956.

Riffier, Jean. *Les œuvres françaises en Syrie, 1860–1923*. Paris: L'Harmattan, 2000.

Rodinson, Maxime. *Islam et capitalism*. Paris: Editions du Seuil, 1966.

Rogan, Eugene L. *Frontiers of the State in the Late Ottoman Empire: Transjordan, 1850–1921*. Cambridge: Cambridge University Press, 1999.

Ruiz, Mario M. "Intimate Disputes, Illicit Violence Gender, Law, and the State in Colonial Egypt, 1849–1923." PhD thesis, University of Michigan, 2004.

Russell, Mona L. *Creating the New Egyptian Woman: Consumerism, Education, and National Identity, 1863–1922*. New York: Palgrave Macmillan, 2004.

Ryad, Umar. *Islamic Reformism and Christianity: A Critical Reading of the Works of Muḥammad Rashīd Riḍā and His Associates (1898–1935)*. Leiden: Brill, 2009.

——. "Islamic Reformism and Great Britain: Rashid Rida's Image as Reflected in the Journal *Al-Manār* in Cairo." *Islam and Christian-Muslim Relations* 21, no. 3 (2010): 263–85.

—. "A Prelude to *Fiqh al-Aqalliyyât*: Rashîd Ridâ's Fatwâs to Muslims Under Non-Muslim Rule." In *In-Between Spaces: Christian and Muslim Minorities in Transition in Europe and the Middle East*, ed. Christiane Timmerman, Johan Leman, Hannelore Roos, and Barbara Segaert, 239–70. Bruxelles: P.I.E. Peter Lang, 2009.

——. "A Printed Muslim 'Lighthouse' in Cairo: Al-Manār's Early Years, Religious Aspiration and Reception (1898–1903)." *Arabica* 56 (2009): 27–60.

Safran, Nadav. *Egypt in Search of Political Community: An Analysis of the Intellectual and Political Evolution of Egypt, 1804–1952*. Cambridge, Mass.: Harvard University Press, 1961.

Sahlins, Marshall. "Cosmologies of Capitalism: The Trans-Pacific Sector of 'The World System.'" In *Culture/Power/History: A Reader in Contemporary Social Theory*, ed. Nicholas B. Dirks, Geoff Eley, Sherry B. Ortner, 412–456. Princeton, N.J.: Princeton University Press, 1994.

—. "'Sentimental Pessimism' and Ethnographic Experience; or, Why Culture Is Not a Disappearing 'Object.'" In *Biographies of Scientific Objects*, ed. Lorraine Daston, 158–202. Chicago: University of Chicago Press, 2000.

Sammut, Carmel. *L'impérialisme capitaliste français et le nationalisme tunisien (1881–1914)*. Paris: Publisud, 1983.

Saul, Samir. *La France et l'Égypte de 1882 à 1914: Intérêts économiques et implications politiques*. Paris: Comité pour l'histoire économique et financière de la France, 1997.

Sayyid-Marsot, Afaf Lufti. *Egypt's Liberal Experiment, 1922–1936*. Berkeley: University of California Press, 1977.

Schiller Nina Glick, Darieva Tsypylma, and Sandra Gruner-Domic. "Defining Cosmopolitan Sociability in a Transnational Age: An Introduction." *Ethnic and Racial Studies* 34, no. 3 (2011): 399–418.

Schulze, Reinhard. *Islamischer Internationalismus Im 20 Jahrhundert: Untersuchungen Zur Geschichte Der Islamischen Weltliga*. Leiden: Brill, 1990.

—. *A Modern History of the Islamic World*. New York: New York University Press, 2000.

—. "Was ist die islamische Aufklärung?" *Die Welt des Islams* 36, no. 3 (1996): 276–325.

Sékaly, Achille. *Le Congrès du khalifat (Le Caire, 13–19 mai 1926) et le Congrès du monde musulman (La Mekke, 7 juin–5 juillet 1926)*. Paris: E. Leroux, 1926.

Shahin, Emad Eldin. "Muḥammad Rashīd Riḍā's Perspectives on the West as Reflected in *Al-Manār*." *Muslim World* 79, no. 2 (1989): 113–32.

Sharkey, Heather J. *Living with Colonialism: Nationalism and Culture in the Anglo-Egyptian Sudan*. Berkeley: University of California Press, 2003.

Shechter, Relli. "Press Advertising in Egypt: Business Realities and Local Meaning, 1882–1956." *Arab Studies Journal* 10/11 (2002/2003): 44–66.

—. "Reading Advertisements in a Colonial/Development Context: Cigarette Advertising and Identity Politics in Egypt, c1919–1939." *Journal of Social History* 39 (2005): 483–503.

——. *Smoking, Culture and Economy in the Middle East: The Egyptian Tobacco Market 1850–2000*. London: I. B. Tauris, 2006.

Sheehi, Stephen. *The Arab Imago: A Social History of Portrait Photography, 1860–1910*. Princeton, N.J.: Princeton University Press, 2016.

Sirriyeh, Elizabeth. "Rashīd Riḍā's Autobiography of the Syrian Years, 1865–1897." *Arabic and Middle Eastern Literatures* 3, no. 2 (2000): 179–94.

Skovgaard-Petersen, Jakob, *Defining Islam for the Egyptian State: Muftis and Fatwas of the Dār Al-Iftā*. Leiden: Brill, 1997.

——. "Portrait of the Intellectual as a Young Man: Rashīd Riḍā's *Muḥāwārāt al-muṣliḥ wa-al-muqallid* (1906)." *Islam and Christian-Muslim Relations* 12, no. 1 (2001): 93–104.

Smith Charles D. "The 'Crisis of Orientation': The Shift of Egyptian Intellectuals to Islamic Subjects in the 1930s." *International Journal of Middle East Studies* 4, no. 4 (1973): 382–410.

Soage, Ana Belén. "Rashīd Ridā's Legacy." *Muslim World* 98, no. 1 (2008): 1–23.

Soliman, Samer. "The Rise and Decline of the Islamic Banking Model in Egypt." In *The Politics of Islamic Finance*, ed. Clement M. Henry and Rodney Wilson, 265–85. Edinburgh: Edinburgh University Press, 2004.

Starrett, Gregory S. "The Political Economy of Religious Commodities in Cairo." *American Anthropologist* 97, no. 1 (1995): 51–68.

Stolz, Daniel A. *The Lighthouse and the Observatory: Islam, Science, and Empire in Late Ottoman Egypt*. Cambridge: Cambridge University Press, 2018.

Tageldin, Shaden M. *Empire and the Seductions of Translation in Egypt*. Berkeley: University of California Press, 2011.

Tauber, Eliezer. *The Emergence of Arab Movements*. London: Routledge, 1993.

——. "The Political Life of Rašīd Riḍā." *Arabist: Budapest Studies in Arabic* 19–20 (1998).

——. "Rashīd Riḍā as a Pan-Arabist Before World War I." *Muslim World* 79 (1989).

Taylor, Eric Robert. *Musical Instruments of South-East Asia* (Singapore: Oxford University Press, 1989)

Thobie, Jacques. *Intérêts et impérialisme français dans l'empire ottoman (1895–1914)*. Paris: Publications de la Sorbonne, 1977.

Thomas, Nicholas. *Entangled Objects: Exchange, Material Culture, and Colonialism in the Pacific*. Cambridge, Mass.: Harvard University Press, 1991.

Thompson, Elizabeth F. "Rashid Rida and the 1920 Syrian-Arab Constitution: How the French Mandate Undermined Islamic Liberalism." Chapter 15 in *The Routledge Handbook of the History of the Middle East Mandates*, ed. Cyrus Schayegh and Andrew Arsan. London: Routledge, 2015.

Tignor, Robert L. "Bank Miṣr and Foreign Capitalism." *International Journal of Middle East Studies* 8 (1977): 161–81.

——. *State, Private Enterprise, and Economic Change in Egypt, 1918–1952*. Princeton, N.J.: Princeton University Press, 1984.

Tobie, Jacques. "L'électrification dans l'aire syro-libanaise des origines à la fin du mandat français." *Outre-mers* 89, nos. 334–35 (2002): 527–54.

Tollefson, Harold. *Policing Islam: The British Occupation of Egypt and the Anglo-Egyptian Struggle Over Control of the Police, 1882–1914*. Westport, Conn.: Greenwood Press, 1999.

Trentmann, Frank. *Free Trade Nation: Commerce, Consumption, and Civil Society in Modern Britain*. Oxford: Oxford University Press, 2008.

Tucker, Judith E. *Women, Family, and Gender in Islamic Law*. Cambridge: Cambridge University Press, 2008.

Udovitch, Abraham L. *Partnership and Profit in Medieval Islam*. Princeton, N.J.: Princeton University Press, 1970.

Veer, Peter van der. "Colonial Cosmopolitanism." Chap. 10 in *Conceiving Cosmopolitanism: Theory, Context, and Practice*, ed. Steven Vertovec and Robin Cohen. Oxford: Oxford University Press, 2002.

Verney, Noël. *Les puissances étrangères dansi le Levant en Syrie et en Palestine*. Paris: Librairie Guillaumin, 1900.

Vitalis, Robert. *When Capitalists Collide: Business Conflict and the End of Empire in Egypt*. Berkeley: University of California Press, 1995.

Voll, John O. "ʿAbduh and the Transvaal Fatwa: The Neglected Question." In *Islam and the Question of Minorities*, ed. Tamara Sonn, 27–39. Atlanta: Scholars Press, 1996.

Waardenburg, Jacques. "Muslim Enlightenment and Revitalization: Movements of Modernization and Reform in Tsarist Russia (ca. 1850–1917) and the Dutch East Indies (ca. 1900–1942)." *Die Welt des Islams* 28 (1988): 569–84.

Wahba, Ḥāfiẓ. *Jazīrat al-ʿArab fī al-qarn al-ʿishrīn*. Cairo: Lajnat al-Taʾlīf, 1935.

——. "Wahhabism in Arabia: Past and Present," trans. A. A. Shukry. *Islamic Review* 17, no. 8 (August 1929): 279–90.

Weismann, Itzchak. *Taste of Modernity: Sufism, Salafiyya, and Arabism in Late Ottoman Damascus*. Leiden: Brill, 2001.

Wenzlhuemer, Roland. *Connecting the Nineteenth-Century World: The Telegraph and Globalization*. Cambridge: Cambridge University Press, 2013.

Werth, Paul W. *The Tsar's Foreign Faiths: Toleration and the Fate of Religious Freedom in Imperial Russia*. Oxford: Oxford University Press, 2014.

Winner, Langdon. "Technologies as Forms of Life." Chap. 8 in *Readings in the Philosophy of Technology*, David Kaplan. Lanham, Md.: Rowman and Littlefield, 2004.

Winseck, Dwayne Roy, and Robert M. Pike. *Communication and Empire: Media, Markets and Globalization, 1860–1930*. Durham, N.C.: Duke University Press, 2007.

Wood, Leonard. *Islamic Legal Revival: Reception of European Law and Transformations in Islamic Legal Thought in Egypt, 1875–1952*. Oxford: Oxford University Press, 2016.

Wright, Arnold. *The Romance of Colonisation: Being the Story of the Economic Development of the British Empire*. London: A. Melrose, 1923.

Wright, Arnold, chief editor, and H. A. Cartwright, assistant editor, *Twentieth Century Impressions of Egypt: Its History, People, Commerce, Industries, and Resources*. London: Lloyd's Greater Britain, 1909.

Yemelianova, Galina M. "The National Identity of the Volga Tatars at the Turn of the 19th Century: Tatarism, Turkism and Islam." *Central Asian Survey* 16, no. 4 (1997): 543–72.

Zaman, Muhammad Qasim. *Modern Islamic Thought in a Radical Age: Religious Authority and Internal Criticism*. Cambridge: Cambridge University Press, 2012.

——. "The Role of Arabic and the Arab Middle East in the Definition of Muslim Identity in Twentieth Century India." *Muslim World* 87, no. 3–4 (1997): 272–98.

Ziadat, Adel A. *Western Science in the Arab World: The Impact of Darwinism, 1860–1930*. London: Macmillan, 1986.

Zisser, Eyal. "Rashid Rida: On the Way to Syrian Nationalism in the Shade of Islam and Arabism." In *The Origins of Syrian Nationhood: Histories, Pioneers and Identity*, ed. Adel Beshara, 123–40. London: Routledge, 2011.

INDEX

Abājī, Muṣṭafā, 196
ʿAbbās Ḥilmī Pasha (khedive), 101–2
ʿAbduh, Muḥammad, 47, 182; on banking, 100–107; capitalism and, 101–7; fatwas and, 101–7; *Islam and Christianity Between Science and Civilization* by, 125; Muslim reform by, 18–19, 20, 54–55, 124, 256, 273n43, 274n48, 274n54; Riḍā and, 54–55, 125–26; Salafism and, 124–25; *Theology of Unity* by, 124–25; Transvaal fatwa and, 87–90, 94–95
ʿĀbidīn Palace, 73
Abū Ḥanīfa, 234–36, 257. *See also* Ḥanafī school of law
Abū Qīr Bay, 2–3
Abū Qīr mosque, 78
Abū Yūsuf, 278n75
Aceh War, 197
Aden, 229–31, 234
advertising, 38, 192; gramophone and, 135–37, *137*, 308n20; for "Made in Egypt" goods, 222–24, *223*; in *al-Muṣawwar*, 211–14; during Roaring Twenties, 210–16, *212*, *213*, *215*
ʿAfīfī, ʿAbd al-Razzāq, 25
Afghānī, Jamāl al-Dīn al-, 18–19, 124
agency, 28, 259; of early adopters and conservative critics, 261; of famous reformers, 44; of fatwa seekers, 28, 61–63, 260, 275n60; of local religious authorities, 177–78; of material objects, 262; of pious Salaf, 99
Agrama, Hussein Ali, 277n71
Ahl-i Ḥadīth, 124
Aḥmad, Ghulām, 160
Aḥmad, Ḥājjī ʿAbdallāh, 150, 180
Aḥmad, Jalāl Āl-i, 14
ʿĀʾisha's curtains, 26, 179–80
ʿAlawī, Sālim ibn Aḥmad al-ʿAṭṭās al-, 63
Albānī, Muḥammad Nāṣir al-Dīn al-, 25
Albany Perforated Wrapping Paper Company, 33
alcohol, 30, 216–17, 225, 240, 263
Alderson, George Beeton, 78
Alfī, Aḥmad Muḥammad al-, 122
Allen, Alderson & Co., 78
Allenby, Edmund, 206
Amanullah Khan, 214
Amīn, Qāsim, 99–100
animal fat, 7, 29, 278n76
animal slaughter, 63–65, 89–90
Anṣār al-Sunna al-Muḥammadiyya, 25–26
anthropology, 16–17
Anthropometric Bureau, 183, 320n94
anti-British boycotts: banking and, 204; on clothing, 203–5; free trade and, 202–9; identity and, 204; nationalist economics and, 202–5; politics and, 202–9; Riḍā on, 205–9; by women, 202–3; World War I and, 205
Arab Empire, 161, 187–88, 249, 321n11
Arabian Celebrity Odeon Records, 136, *138*
Arabian slippers, 216–19

Cairo, 63–65; British rule in, 74–75; global trade and cosmopolitan consumption in, before World War I, 75–81, 294n40, 294n42; gramophone in, 134–36; Ibn Ṭūlūn Mosque in, 73; Khedivial Library and Museum of Arab Antiquities, 73–74, *74*; map, from 1905, *71*; photography in, 180–81; population and demographics of, 74–75; Riḍā and Sycamore Lane in, 70–75; ʿĀbidīn Palace in, 73
Caliphate and the Grand Imamate, The (Riḍā), 129
Camera Indica (Pinney), 171
cameras. *See* photography
canonical legislation, 129
Cape Muslims, 297n81
capital investments, 23, 75–76; banking and, 114–15; in Egypt, 82–84; by European corporations, 164–65; in *al-Manār*, 55–57; stock shares and, 103–5
capitalism: ʿAbduh and, 101–7; banking and, 101–7; British rule and, 75–87; in Egypt, 75–81, 117; for ethno-religious markets, 133–37; factory production and, 133–34, 135; fatwas on, 101–7; free trade and, 75–81; globalization and, 17; gramophone and, 131–37; hygiene and, 33; impurity, material culture, and, 146–50, 265; Islamic law and, 11–14; Muslim reform and, 97–98; in *Orientalism*, 271n27; pan-Islamism and, 117–19; protectorate capitalism and British narrative, 82–87; religion and, 12; Riḍā on, 118, 129–30; Salafism and, 97–100; scientific innovation and technology and, 131–37; secularization and, 132–33; in Tripoli, 66–67
"Capitalism as Religion" (Benjamin), 133
carpets and rugs, 78
Cassel, Ernest Joseph, 96
censorship, 50, 53, 206–7, 290n59
China: flappers in, 214–16; as House of Islam, 225–27, 231–33, 330n1; as House of War, 232–33; Riḍā on, 225–26, 231–37
cholera, 38–39, 66, 74
Christianity: Christian festivities, 91–92; Christian technocrats, 240–44, 258; church bells in, 150–54; clothing and, 197, 199; crosses as symbols of, 91; French Catholics, 176; gramophone invention and papal communications, 131–32; at Lasallian Brothers' Christian school, 68; meat consumption in, 63–65, 89–90; missionaries, 45, 91; Muslim reform and, 43, 274n55; Protestants, 9, 269n6; religious ceremonies, 91–92
church bells, 150–54
citizenship, 70, 225, 227, 250
civil disobedience, 217–18
clothing, 26, 78–79; anti-British boycott on, 203–5; Arabian slippers, 216–19; Ataturk on, 209–10, 326n60; Christianity and, 197, 199; Coptic garments, 191–92, 193, 322n2; Dutch Empire and, 196–98, 324n22; European, 87–90, *89*, 191–202, 209–10, 216–19, 296n77; fatwas on, 194, 195–202, 210–19; in free trade, 192–94; French trousers, 191–92, 194; hats, 87–90, *89*, 209–10, 296n77; *ḥijāb*, 192; hosiery, 211; identity and, 87–88; imitation through, 191–94; *al-Manār* on, 192–93; manners and, 198; men's fashions, 192, 195–97, 211–12; neckties, 195, 197; Orientalists and, 197–98; in Ottoman Empire, 196, 199, 201, *201*; Prophet and, 91, 222, 322n7; in Roaring Twenties, 210–16; soldiers' apparel, 195–202, *201*; for women, 192, 211
Cobden, Richard, 11–12
Cohen, Joseph, 78
Cold War, 14
colonial cosmopolitanism, *80*, 81
colonialism, 27; currency and, 105–6, 109–10; in Fiji, 106; foreign commodity and, 40–41, 217–19; French, 1–6, 195–96, 238–40; hygiene and, 34–41, 280n24, 281n41; Islamic law and, 94–95; *al-Manār* and, 59–60; railway and, 162–63; scientific innovation and technology and, 159–62. *See also* British rule
commerce: Europe's civilizing, 10–16, 164–66, 271n17; interfaith, 63–64; Ottoman Empire and European corporations, 164–66; scripture and, 100; ships relating to, 67, 76, 229–30, 291n7, 292n9; in Syria, 66–67, 291n7; in Tripoli, 66–69, 291n7, 292n10. *See also* capitalism; free trade
Compagnie d'aérostiers, 2
Conté, Nicolas-Jacques, 2–5
Cook, Thomas, 168, 316n44
Cooper, Frederick, 289n55, 314n12
Coptic garments, 191–92, 193, 322n2
cosmopolitan consumption, 75–81, 294n40, 294n42
cosmopolitanism, colonial, *80*, 81
cosmopolitan sociability, 90, 297n83

Francis Shop, 136, *137*, 308n20
Franco-Prussian war, 67
Fred Phillips & Co., 78
freedom, of religion, 227–29
free trade: in Aden, 229–31, 234; anti-British boycotts and, 202–9; British rule relating to, 77–83, 295n49; capitalism and, 75–81; clothing and, 192–94; cosmopolitan consumption and, before World War I, 75–81, 294n40, 294n42; in Egypt, 12, 75–81, 126; Europe's civilizing commerce and, 11–14, 271n17; exclusion in, 12; during *ḥajj*, 272n28; in House of War, 226; imperialism of, 12–14, 264–65; industrialization and, 11–12; internationalism and, 271n18; Islamic economics and, 9; nationalist economics and, 220–24; Orientalists and Mecca, 13–14, 271n27; politics and, 227–29; Prophet and, 13; Qurʾan relating to, 85–86; religion and, 246; Riḍā on, 194, 195, 205–9, 263–66; tariffs and, 220; in Tripoli, 66–69, 76
French Catholics, 176
French colonialism, 1–6, 195–96, 238–40
French trousers, 191–92, 194
fundamentalism, 17–21, 64–65, 259–60
furniture, 81

Gallagher, John, 83
Gallery of Comparative Anatomy, 5–6
gambling, 231–32, 245
Gandhi, Mahatma, 54–55, 87, 194, 216–19, 254, 328n73, 328n87
Gasprinski, Ismail: pan-Islamism and, 115–19, 303n64; Russian reform and, 139–40
Gelvin, James L., 17
"General Organic Law of the Arab Empire, The" (Riḍā), 187–88, 321n11
German goods, 204–5, 221–22
Ghānim, Khalīl, 303n76
Gīlānī, Manāẓir Aḥsan, 269n5
global ecumene, 16
global Islamic market, 7, 269n2
globalization: capitalism and, 17, 115; cross-cultural entanglements and, 16–17; economic history and periodization of, 142, 253, 287n41; fear of cultural hegemony and, 14; first wave of, 287n41; of Islamic communications, 57–59, 253, 262–63; Islamic reform, *al-Manār* and, 49–52, 253; qualification of the concept of, 289n55; religion and, 251–52; Riḍā and, 126, 251; Salafism and, 64; warps of, 59; world trade and, 142
global market segmentation, 135, 308n16
global mufti, 27, 48, 253
Global Muslims in the Age of Steam and Print (Gelvin and Green), 17
global trade. *See* free trade
gold, 109, 114–15, 302nn57–58
Goldziher, Ignaz, 275n60
gong, in Javanese mosque, 150–54
government: in Egypt, 81–87; imperialism and government authority, 187–88
gramophone, 22, 47, 244, 286n31; advertising and, 135–37, *137*, 308n20; Berliner and, 131–32; in Cairo, 134–36; capitalism and, 131–37; Catholicism and, 131–32; conservative arguments on, 138–44; critics of, 132; fatwas on, 146–50; founding of, 131–32; *jadidis* on, 138–42, 144, 146, 156; language and, 134–35; in *al-Manār*, 143, 154–55; modernist arguments on, 138–39; National Odeon Store and, 136–37, *137*, *138*, 140–43, 308n20; *qadimis* on, 138–42; Qurʾan and, 131, 133, 136–37, 140–50, 156–58, 308n23; Riḍā on, 144–46, 147–50, 154–55; rituals and, 133; in Russia, 134, 135–36, 138–46, 156–57; in Singapore, 146–50; by Victor Talking Machines, 131, 134, 141, 148–49. *See also* phonograph
Gramophone, Film, Typewriter (Kittler), 156–57
Gramophone Company Limited, 134–36
Gramsci, Antonio, 135
Grand Mufti. *See* ʿAbduh, Muḥammad
Great Depression, 220, 222–23
Great Syrian Revolt, 333n46
Green, Nile, 17, 274n50
Guide to Health (Gandhi), 218–19, 254

Hackh, Hugo, 78
Ḥadīth, 29
Ḥāfiẓ, ʿAbd al-, 150
hairstyles, 196, 210
ḥajj, 182, 192, 272n28
Haleby's corpse, 5–6
Hallaq, Wael, 43–44, 275n60, 290n68
Ḥamdī, Nafīsa, 103–5, 300n21
Ḥamdī, Pasha Ismāʿīl, 103
Hamilton, Charles, 170–71
Hamzah, Dyala, 283n14

CPSIA information can be obtained
at www.ICGtesting.com
Printed in the USA
LVHW092221120820
662170LV00001BA/1/J

9 780231 188661